PROBLEM IDENTIFIED
AND YOU'RE PROBABLY
NOT PART OF THE
SOLUTION

Other DILBERT® books from Andrews McMeel Publishing

14 Years of Loyal Service in a Fabric-Covered Box
ISBN: 0-7407-7365-89

Freedom's Just Another Word for People Finding Out You're Useless
ISBN: 0-7407-7815-39

Dilbert 2.0: 20 Years of Dilbert
ISBN: 0-7407-7735-1

This Is the Part Where You Pretend to Add Value
ISBN: 0-7407-7227-9

Cubes and Punishment
ISBN: 0-7407-6837-9

Positive Attitude
ISBN: 0-7407-6379-2

Try Rebooting Yourself
ISBN: 0-7407-6190-0

What Would Wally Do?
ISBN: 0-7407-5769-5

Thriving on Vague Objectives
ISBN: 0-7407-5533-1

The Fluorescent Light Glistens Off Your Head
ISBN: 0-7407-5113-1

It's Not Funny If I Have to Explain It
ISBN: 0-7407-4658-8

Don't Stand Where the Comet Is Assumed to Strike Oil
ISBN: 0-7407-4539-5

Words You Don't Want to Hear During Your Annual Performance Review
ISBN: 0-7407-3805-4

When Body Language Goes Bad
ISBN: 0-7407-3298-6

What Do You Call a Sociopath in a Cubicle? Answer: A Coworker
ISBN: 0-7407-2663-3

Another Day in Cubicle Paradise
ISBN: 0-7407-2194-1

When Did Ignorance Become a Point of View?
ISBN: 0-7407-1839-8

Excuse Me While I Wag
ISBN: 0-7407-1390-6

Dilbert—A Treasury of Sunday Strips: Version 00
ISBN: 0-7407-0531-8

Random Acts of Management
ISBN: 0-7407-0453-2

Dilbert Gives You the Business
ISBN: 0-7407-0338-2 hardcover
ISBN: 0-7407-0003-0 paperback

Don't Step in the Leadership
ISBN: 0-8362-7844-5

Journey to Cubeville
ISBN: 0-8362-7175-0 hardcover
ISBN: 0-8362-6745-1 paperback

I'm Not Anti-Business, I'm Anti-Idiot
ISBN: 0-8362-5182-2

Seven Years of Highly Defective People
ISBN: 0-8362-5129-6 hardcover
ISBN: 0-8362-3668-8 paperback

Casual Day Has Gone Too Far
ISBN: 0-8362-2899-5

Fugitive from the Cubicle Police
ISBN: 0-8362-2119-2

It's Obvious You Won't Survive by Your Wits Alone
ISBN: 0-8362-0415-8

Still Pumped from Using the Mouse
ISBN: 0-8362-1026-3

Bring Me the Head of Willy the Mailboy!
ISBN: 0-8362-1779-9

Shave the Whales
ISBN: 0-8362-1740-3

Dogbert's Clues for the Clueless
ISBN: 0-8362-1737-3

Always Postpone Meetings with Time-Wasting Morons
ISBN: 0-8362-1758-6

Build a Better Life by Stealing Office Supplies
ISBN: 0-8362-1757-8

For ordering information, call 1-800-223-2336.

PROBLEM IDENTIFIED AND YOU'RE PROBABLY NOT PART OF THE SOLUTION

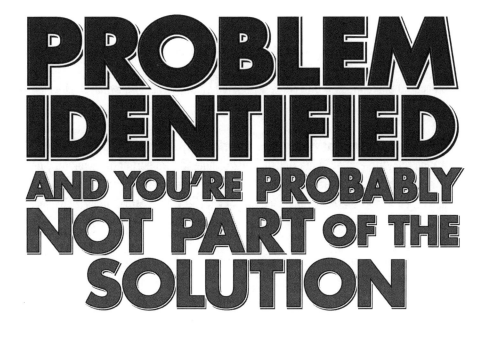

by SCOTT ADAMS

Andrews McMeel
Publishing, LLC
Kansas City • Sydney • London

10 11 12 13 14 BAM 10 9 8 7 6 5 4 3 2 1

ISBN-13: 978-0-7407-8534-4
ISBN-10: 0-7407-8534-6

Library of Congress Control Number: 2009943084

www.andrewsmcmeel.com

www.dilbert.com

───── **ATTENTION: SCHOOLS AND BUSINESSES** ─────

For Shelly

Introduction

Today I was filling out a form for my medical insurance. As I have come to expect when filling out forms, there was a box asking for a mystery code. I briefly considered making an educated guess, but that's never a good strategy on medical forms. I imagined myself on the operating table, gasping for air, with the nurses and doctors all huddled around my paperwork, debating whether or not this was the new code for doctor-assisted suicide, gender reassignment surgery, or experimental medications.

I thought about calling my health care provider to ask for help, but I have trouble getting past automated phone directories because I refuse to listen. The robotic voice is so monotonous that my mind wanders. When the voice stops, I start guessing which option I probably liked. This usually involves a false memory of what the voice was saying when I was feeling most optimistic, mingled with my general feelings of whether or not I have a lucky number. In the end I just stab at a number on my keypad and hope to eventually be transferred to the right department before they disconnect me or my cell phone drops the call.

I made the call and somehow reached a nice fellow who told me what code to put in the box. I was up against a deadline, so he advised me to fax my form to a special and secret number where the rush forms go. This is problematic because my fax machine has fantasies of being a shredder. I lose about one in four documents, and I wasn't feeling lucky. My first try resulted in a mangled original, and I had no way of knowing whether it was properly received. So I sent it again, then wondered if I had inadvertently signed up for two health care programs, which means I would later have to cancel one, and probably accidently cancel both without realizing it. I would eventually die in an ambulance en route to the Uninsured People's Hospital, which I assume is not nearby.

My point is that the world has become so complicated that there's not much difference between having a plan and acting completely randomly. Your odds of getting a good result are just about the same. On the plus side, you no longer need to fret over making the right choices; there aren't any. Just sit back and enjoy the ride.

S.Adams

Scott Adams

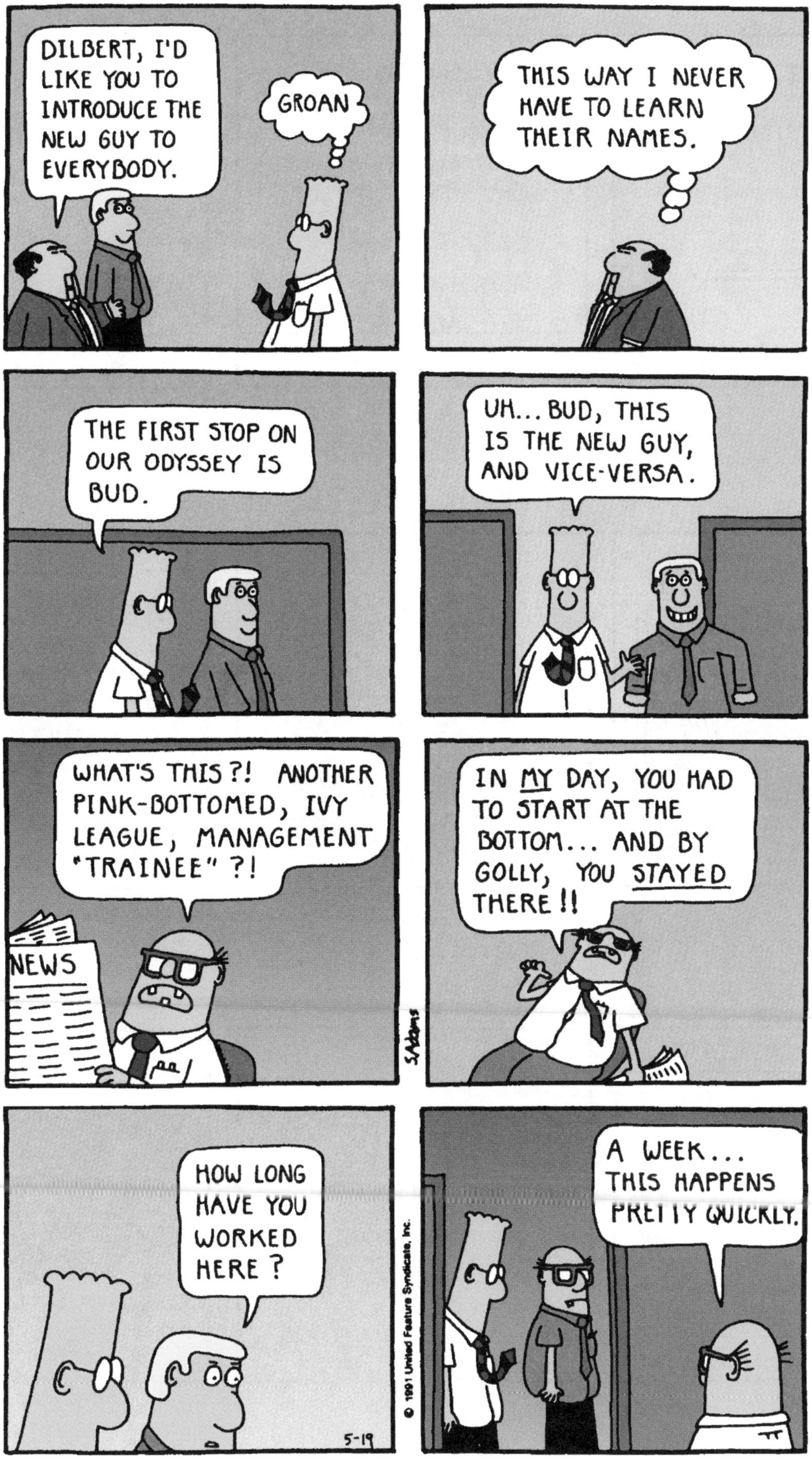

DILBERT, I'D LIKE YOU TO INTRODUCE THE NEW GUY TO EVERYBODY.
GROAN
THIS WAY I NEVER HAVE TO LEARN THEIR NAMES.
THE FIRST STOP ON OUR ODYSSEY IS BUD.
UH... BUD, THIS IS THE NEW GUY, AND VICE-VERSA.
WHAT'S THIS?! ANOTHER PINK-BOTTOMED, IVY LEAGUE, MANAGEMENT "TRAINEE"?!
NEWS
IN MY DAY, YOU HAD TO START AT THE BOTTOM... AND BY GOLLY, YOU STAYED THERE!!
S. Adams
HOW LONG HAVE YOU WORKED HERE?
5-19
© 1991 United Feature Syndicate, Inc.
A WEEK... THIS HAPPENS PRETTY QUICKLY.

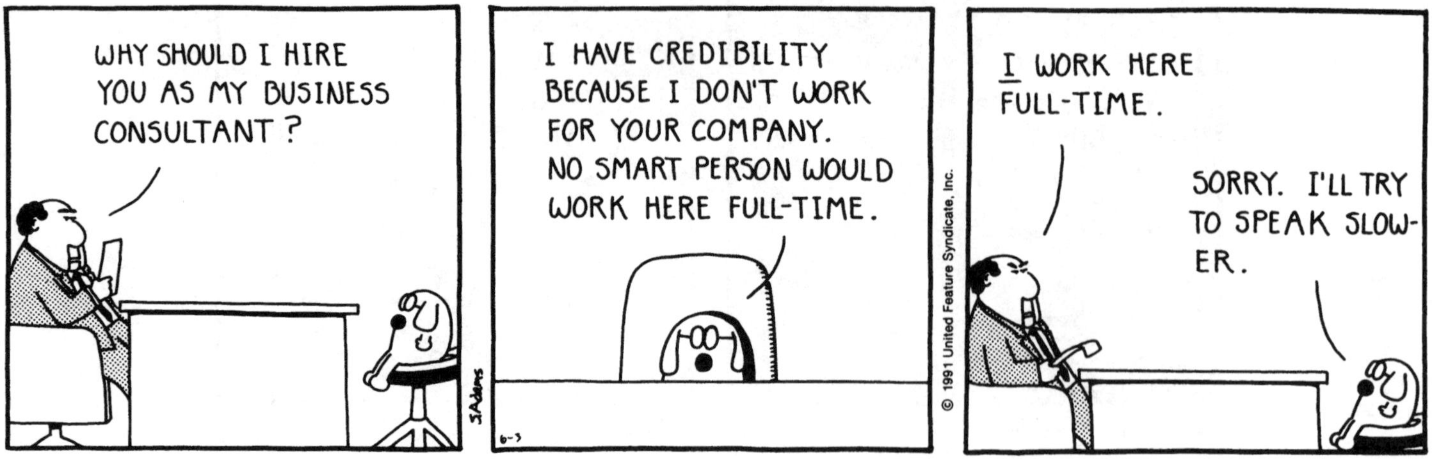
WHY SHOULD I HIRE YOU AS MY BUSINESS CONSULTANT?
I HAVE CREDIBILITY BECAUSE I DON'T WORK FOR YOUR COMPANY. NO SMART PERSON WOULD WORK HERE FULL-TIME.
I WORK HERE FULL-TIME.
SORRY. I'LL TRY TO SPEAK SLOW-ER.

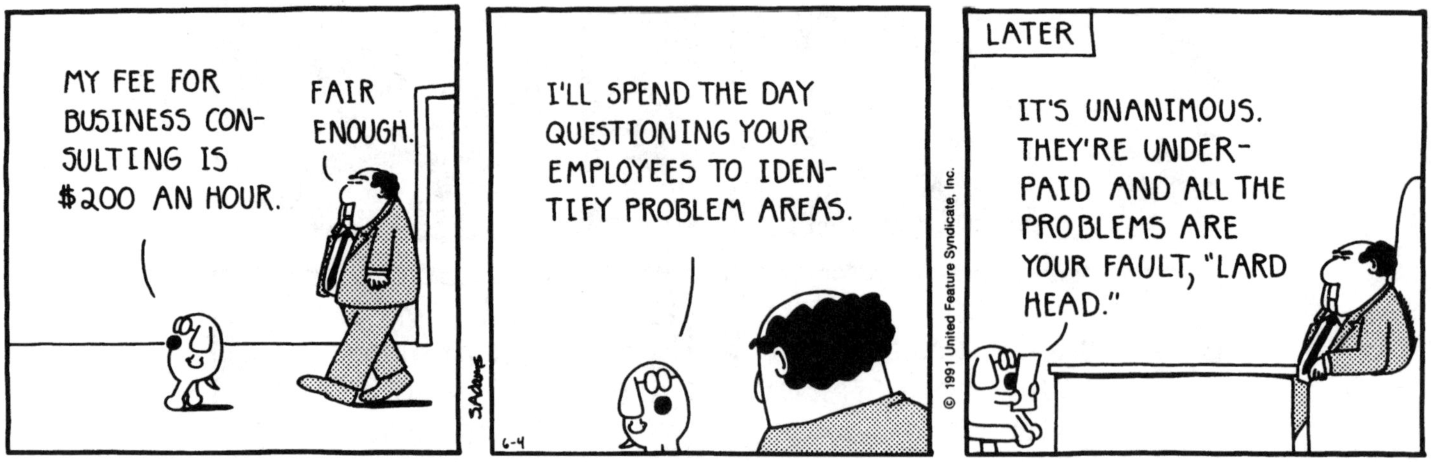
MY FEE FOR BUSINESS CON-SULTING IS $200 AN HOUR.
FAIR ENOUGH.
I'LL SPEND THE DAY QUESTIONING YOUR EMPLOYEES TO IDEN-TIFY PROBLEM AREAS.
LATER
IT'S UNANIMOUS. THEY'RE UNDER-PAID AND ALL THE PROBLEMS ARE YOUR FAULT, "LARD HEAD."

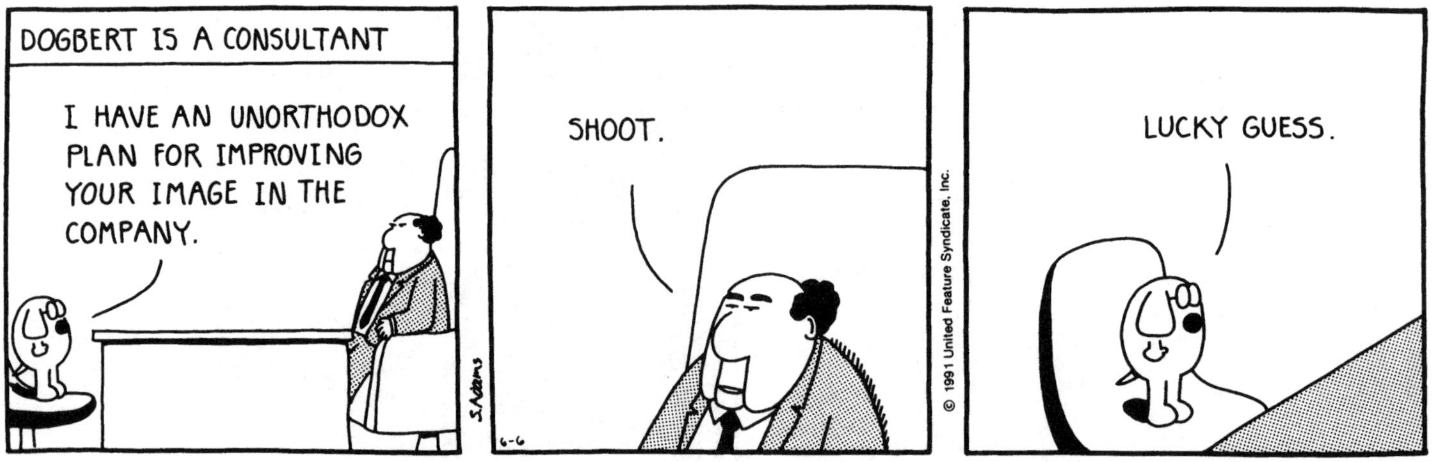
DOGBERT IS A CONSULTANT
I HAVE AN UNORTHODOX PLAN FOR IMPROVING YOUR IMAGE IN THE COMPANY.
SHOOT.
LUCKY GUESS.

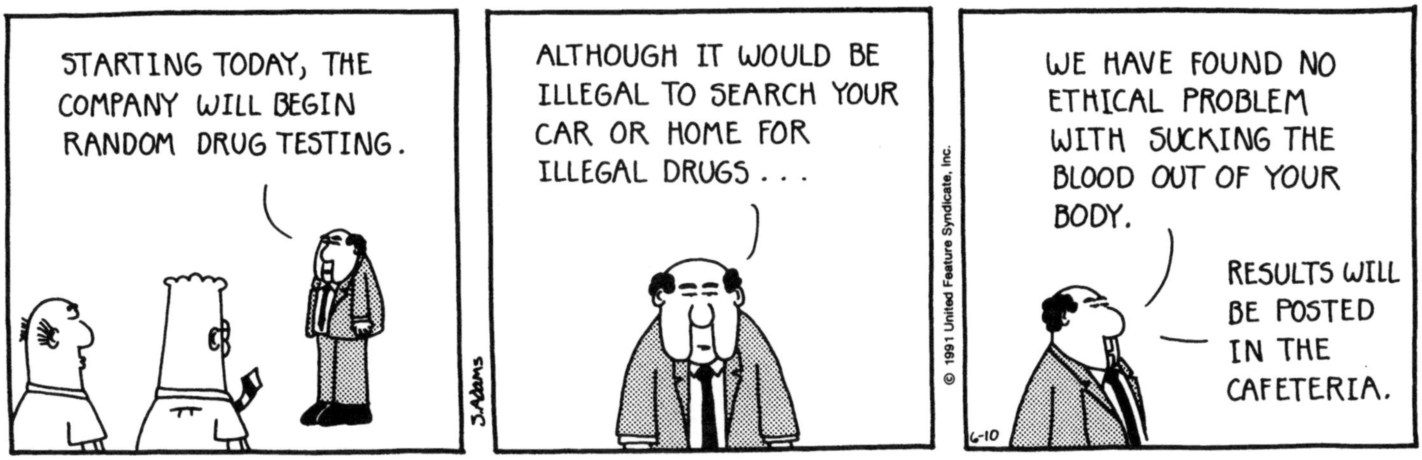
STARTING TODAY, THE COMPANY WILL BEGIN RANDOM DRUG TESTING.
ALTHOUGH IT WOULD BE ILLEGAL TO SEARCH YOUR CAR OR HOME FOR ILLEGAL DRUGS . . .
WE HAVE FOUND NO ETHICAL PROBLEM WITH SUCKING THE BLOOD OUT OF YOUR BODY.
RESULTS WILL BE POSTED IN THE CAFETERIA.
© 1991 United Feature Syndicate, Inc.

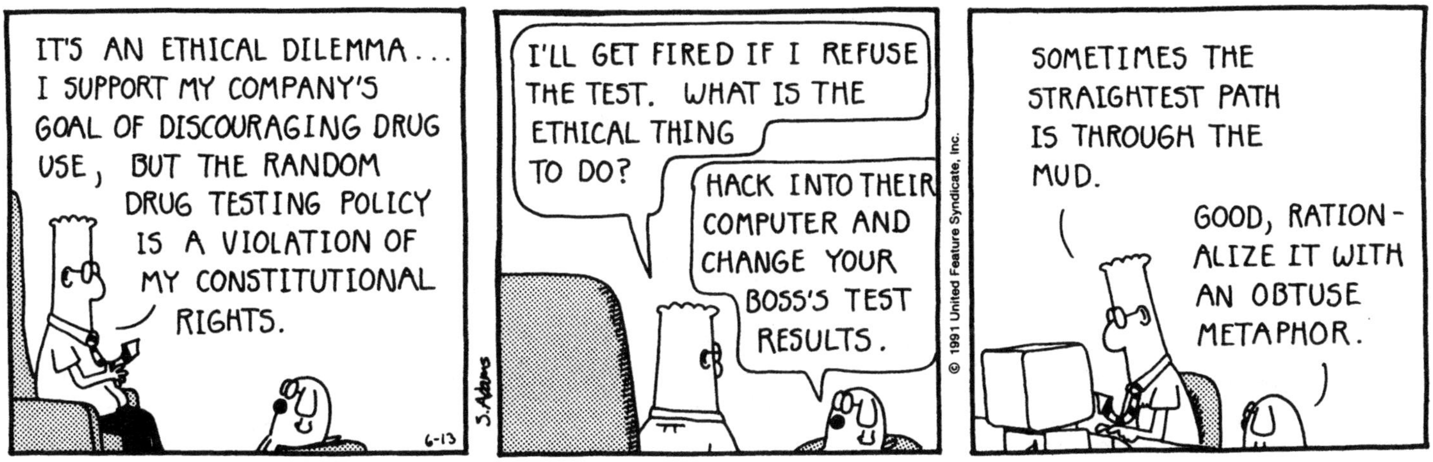
IT'S AN ETHICAL DILEMMA . . . I SUPPORT MY COMPANY'S GOAL OF DISCOURAGING DRUG USE, BUT THE RANDOM DRUG TESTING POLICY IS A VIOLATION OF MY CONSTITUTIONAL RIGHTS.
I'LL GET FIRED IF I REFUSE THE TEST. WHAT IS THE ETHICAL THING TO DO?
HACK INTO THEIR COMPUTER AND CHANGE YOUR BOSS'S TEST RESULTS.
SOMETIMES THE STRAIGHTEST PATH IS THROUGH THE MUD.
GOOD, RATION-ALIZE IT WITH AN OBTUSE METAPHOR.
© 1991 United Feature Syndicate, Inc.

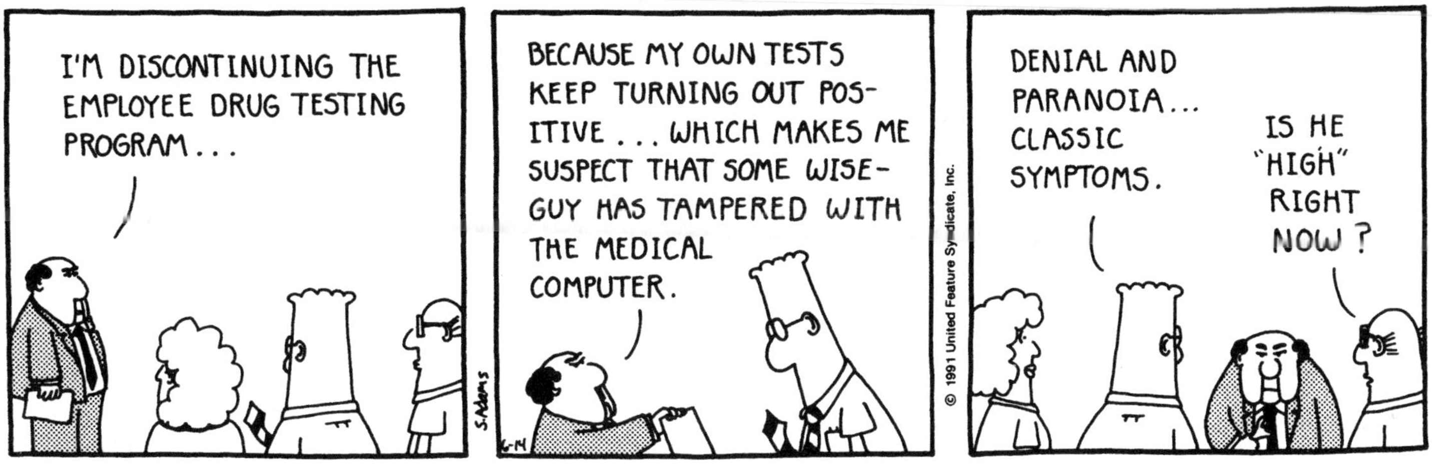
I'M DISCONTINUING THE EMPLOYEE DRUG TESTING PROGRAM . . .
BECAUSE MY OWN TESTS KEEP TURNING OUT POS-ITIVE . . . WHICH MAKES ME SUSPECT THAT SOME WISE-GUY HAS TAMPERED WITH THE MEDICAL COMPUTER.
DENIAL AND PARANOIA . . . CLASSIC SYMPTOMS.
IS HE "HIGH" RIGHT NOW ?
© 1991 United Feature Syndicate, Inc.

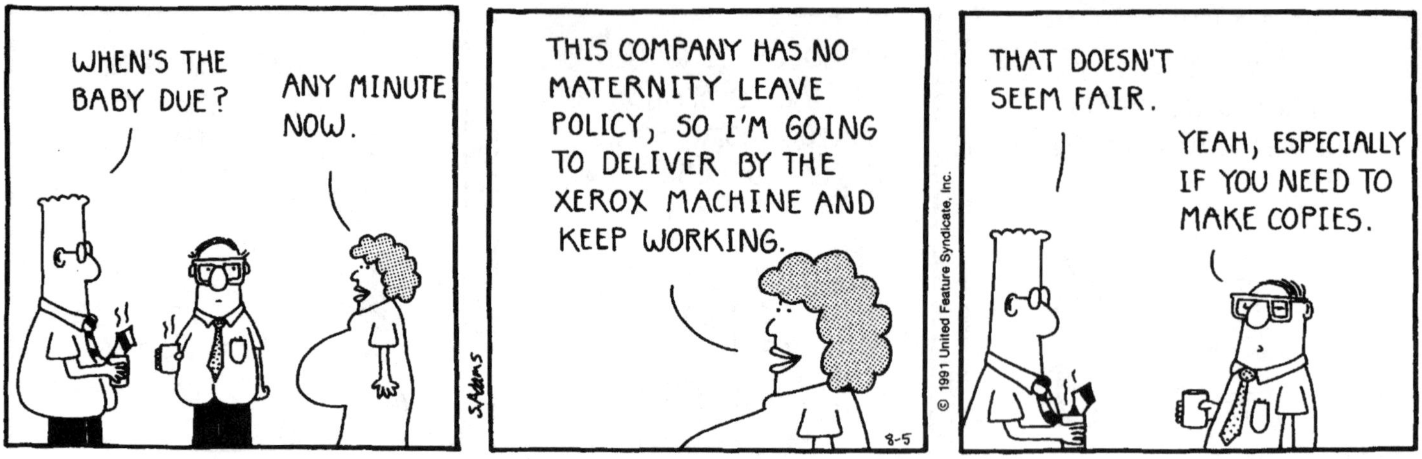
WHEN'S THE BABY DUE?
ANY MINUTE NOW.
THIS COMPANY HAS NO MATERNITY LEAVE POLICY, SO I'M GOING TO DELIVER BY THE XEROX MACHINE AND KEEP WORKING.
THAT DOESN'T SEEM FAIR.
YEAH, ESPECIALLY IF YOU NEED TO MAKE COPIES.
© 1991 United Feature Syndicate, Inc.

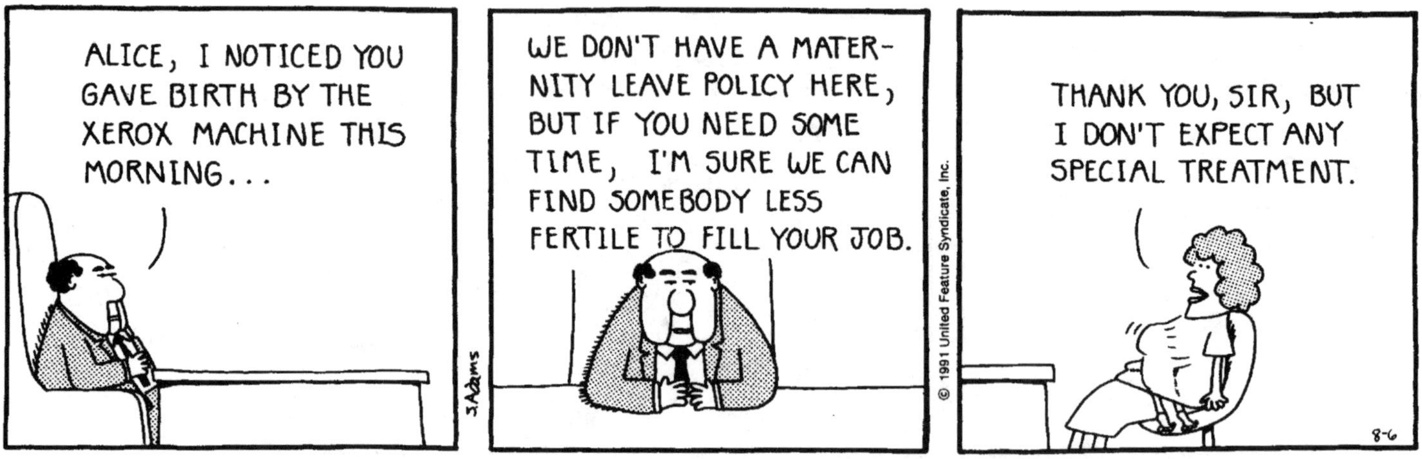
ALICE, I NOTICED YOU GAVE BIRTH BY THE XEROX MACHINE THIS MORNING...
WE DON'T HAVE A MATERNITY LEAVE POLICY HERE, BUT IF YOU NEED SOME TIME, I'M SURE WE CAN FIND SOMEBODY LESS FERTILE TO FILL YOUR JOB.
THANK YOU, SIR, BUT I DON'T EXPECT ANY SPECIAL TREATMENT.
© 1991 United Feature Syndicate, Inc.

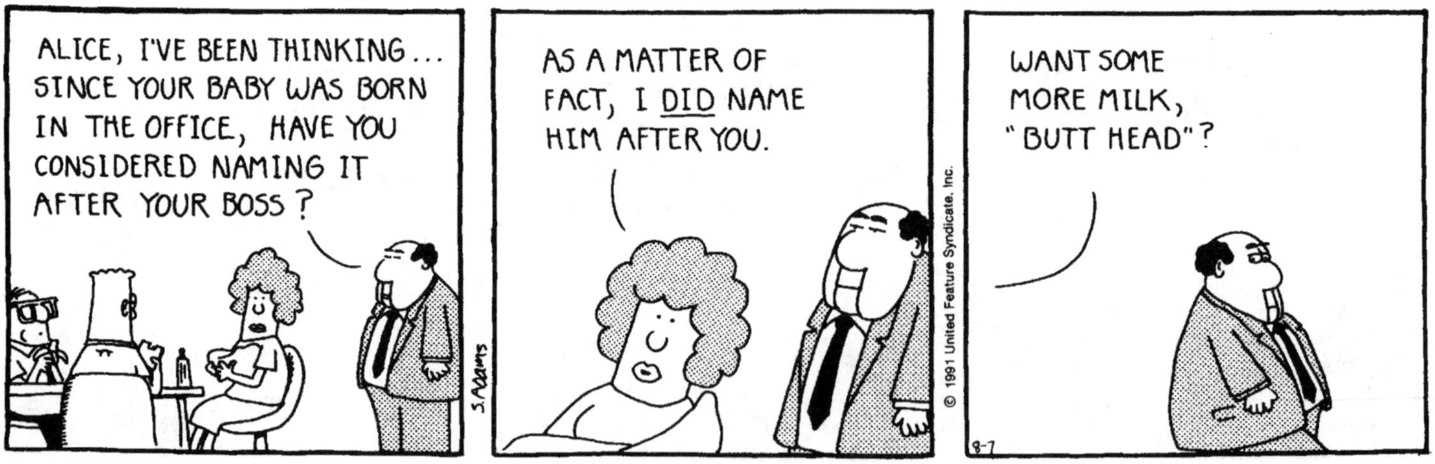
ALICE, I'VE BEEN THINKING... SINCE YOUR BABY WAS BORN IN THE OFFICE, HAVE YOU CONSIDERED NAMING IT AFTER YOUR BOSS?
AS A MATTER OF FACT, I DID NAME HIM AFTER YOU.
WANT SOME MORE MILK, "BUTT HEAD"?
© 1991 United Feature Syndicate, Inc.

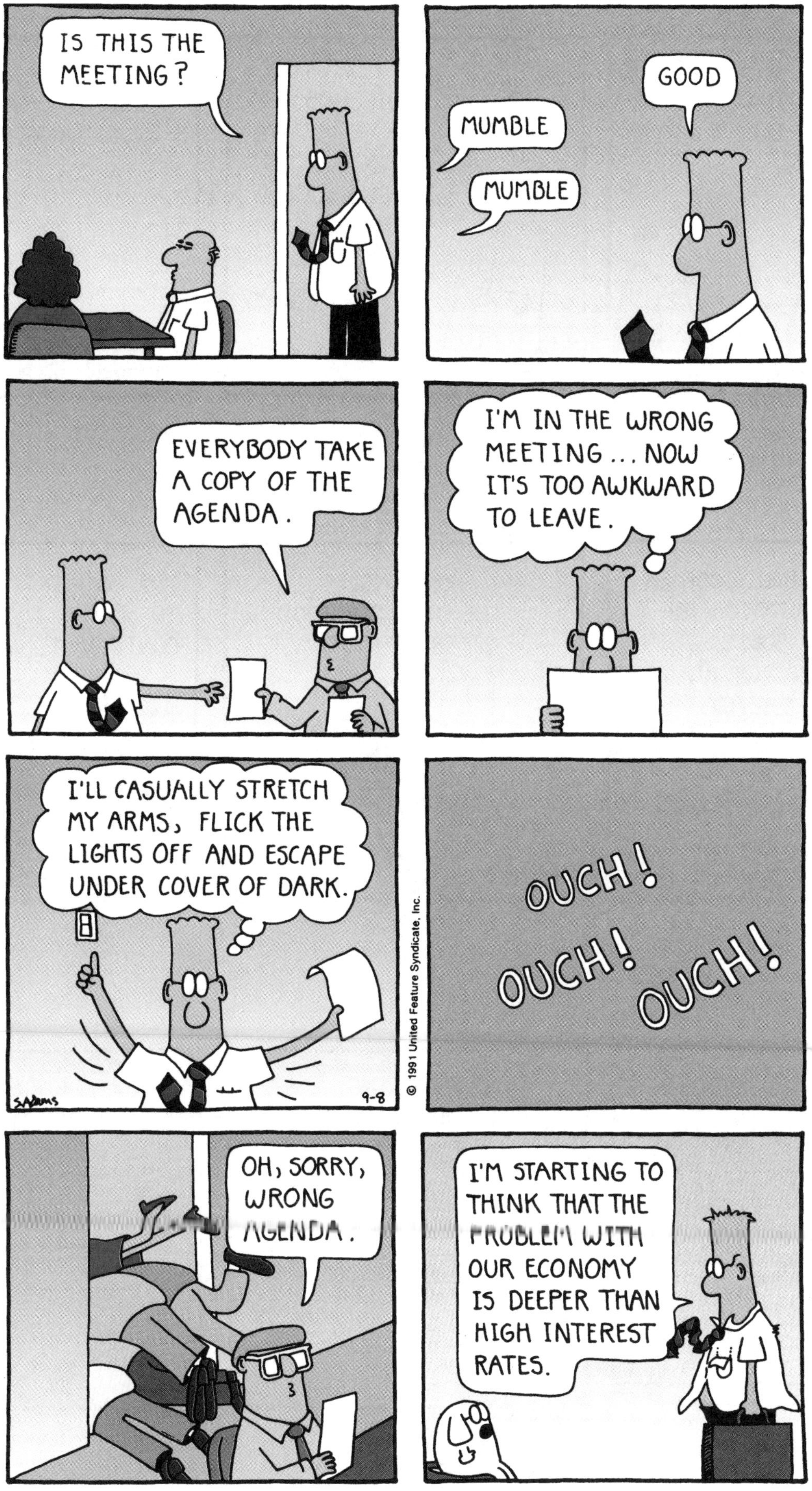
IS THIS THE MEETING?
MUMBLE
GOOD
MUMBLE
EVERYBODY TAKE A COPY OF THE AGENDA.
I'M IN THE WRONG MEETING... NOW IT'S TOO AWKWARD TO LEAVE.
I'LL CASUALLY STRETCH MY ARMS, FLICK THE LIGHTS OFF AND ESCAPE UNDER COVER OF DARK.
S.ADAMS
9-8
© 1991 United Feature Syndicate, Inc.
OUCH!
OUCH!
OUCH!
OH, SORRY, WRONG AGENDA.
I'M STARTING TO THINK THAT THE PROBLEM WITH OUR ECONOMY IS DEEPER THAN HIGH INTEREST RATES.

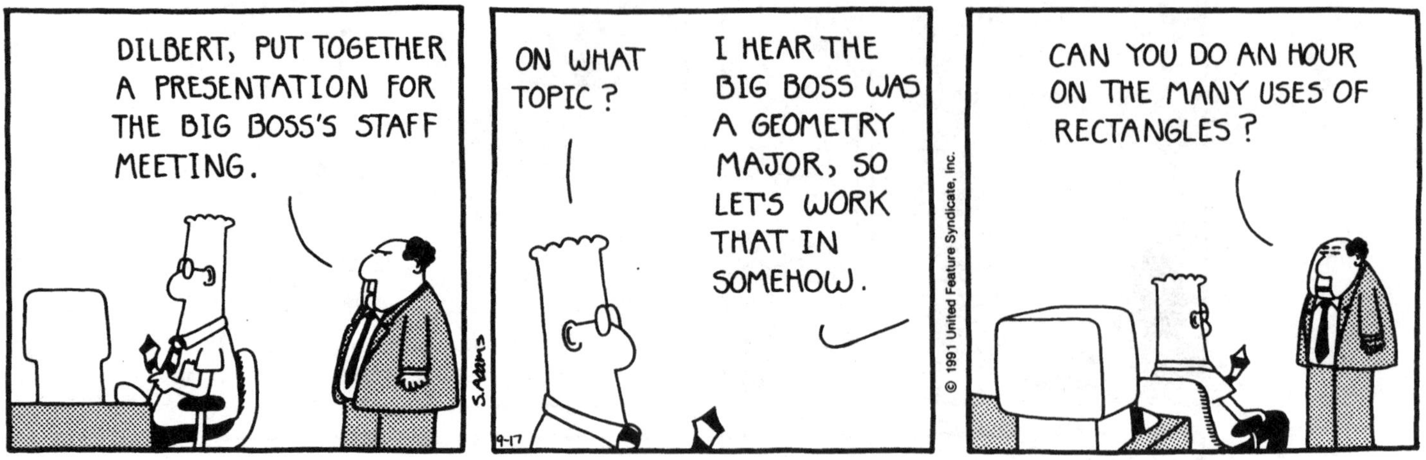
DILBERT, PUT TOGETHER A PRESENTATION FOR THE BIG BOSS'S STAFF MEETING.
ON WHAT TOPIC?
I HEAR THE BIG BOSS WAS A GEOMETRY MAJOR, SO LET'S WORK THAT IN SOMEHOW.
CAN YOU DO AN HOUR ON THE MANY USES OF RECTANGLES?
S.Adams
9-17
© 1991 United Feature Syndicate, Inc.

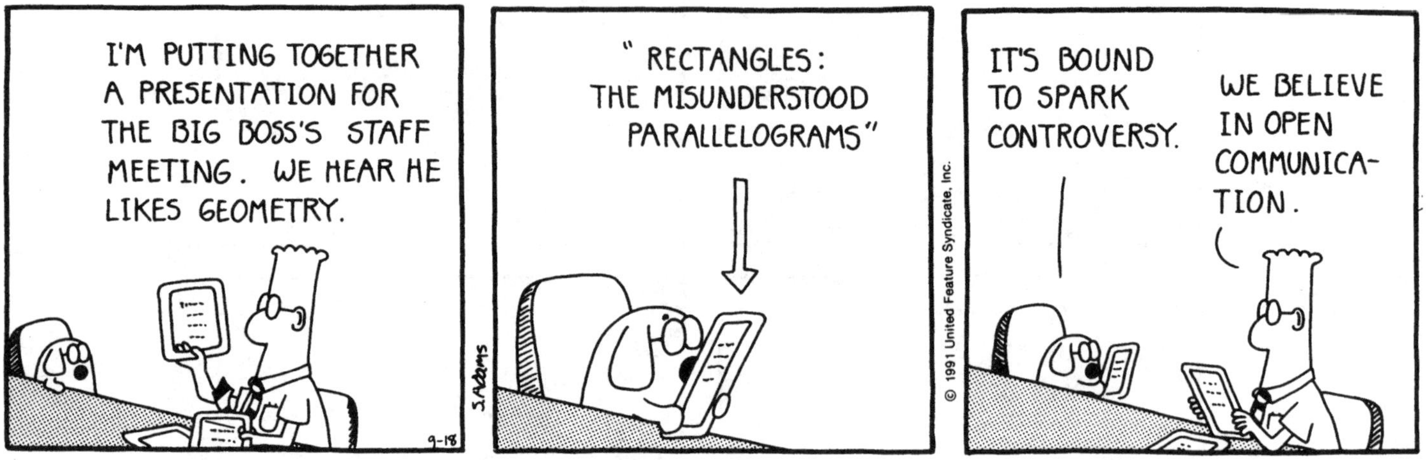
I'M PUTTING TOGETHER A PRESENTATION FOR THE BIG BOSS'S STAFF MEETING. WE HEAR HE LIKES GEOMETRY.
9-18
S.Adams
" RECTANGLES: THE MISUNDERSTOOD PARALLELOGRAMS"
IT'S BOUND TO SPARK CONTROVERSY.
WE BELIEVE IN OPEN COMMUNICATION.
© 1991 United Feature Syndicate, Inc.

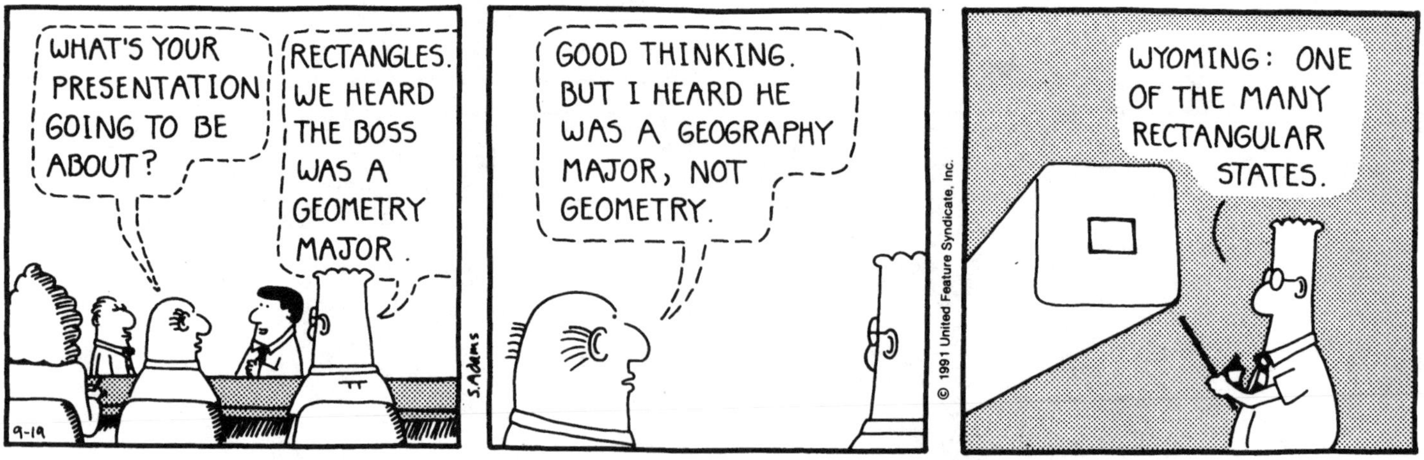
WHAT'S YOUR PRESENTATION GOING TO BE ABOUT?
RECTANGLES. WE HEARD THE BOSS WAS A GEOMETRY MAJOR.
9-19
S.Adams
GOOD THINKING. BUT I HEARD HE WAS A GEOGRAPHY MAJOR, NOT GEOMETRY.
WYOMING: ONE OF THE MANY RECTANGULAR STATES.
© 1991 United Feature Syndicate, Inc.

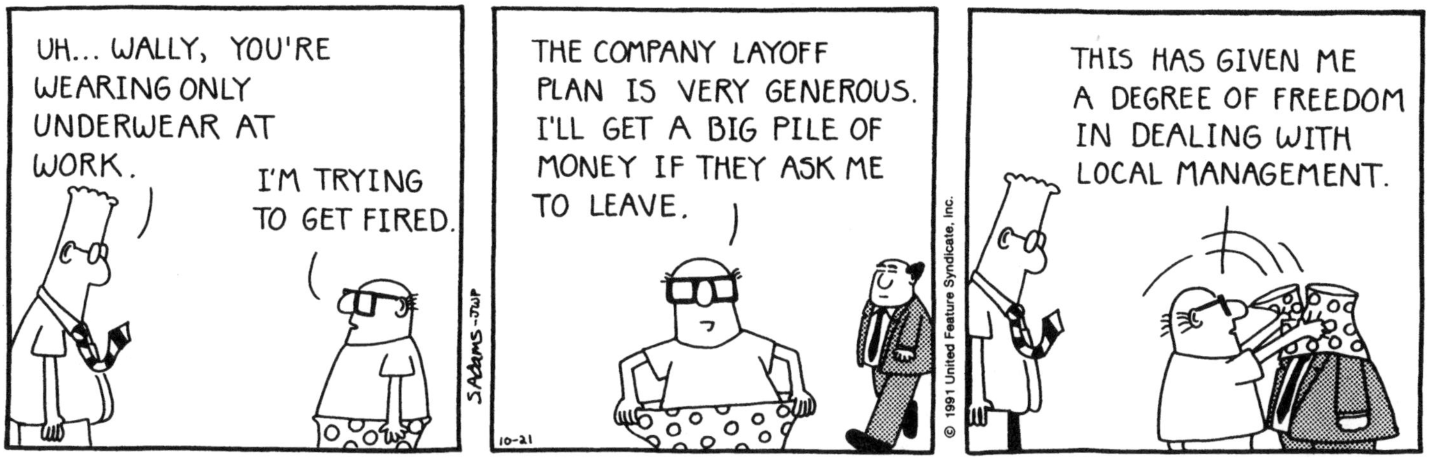
UH... WALLY, YOU'RE WEARING ONLY UNDERWEAR AT WORK.
I'M TRYING TO GET FIRED.
THE COMPANY LAYOFF PLAN IS VERY GENEROUS. I'LL GET A BIG PILE OF MONEY IF THEY ASK ME TO LEAVE.
THIS HAS GIVEN ME A DEGREE OF FREEDOM IN DEALING WITH LOCAL MANAGEMENT.
10-21
© 1991 United Feature Syndicate, Inc.

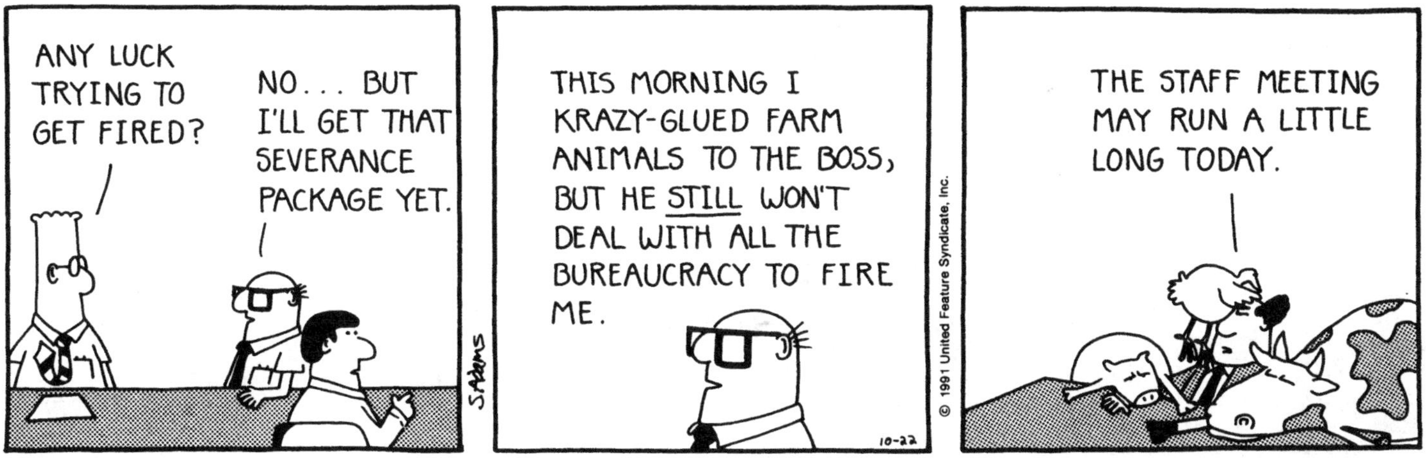
ANY LUCK TRYING TO GET FIRED?
NO... BUT I'LL GET THAT SEVERANCE PACKAGE YET.
THIS MORNING I KRAZY-GLUED FARM ANIMALS TO THE BOSS, BUT HE STILL WON'T DEAL WITH ALL THE BUREAUCRACY TO FIRE ME.
THE STAFF MEETING MAY RUN A LITTLE LONG TODAY.
10-22
© 1991 United Feature Syndicate, Inc.

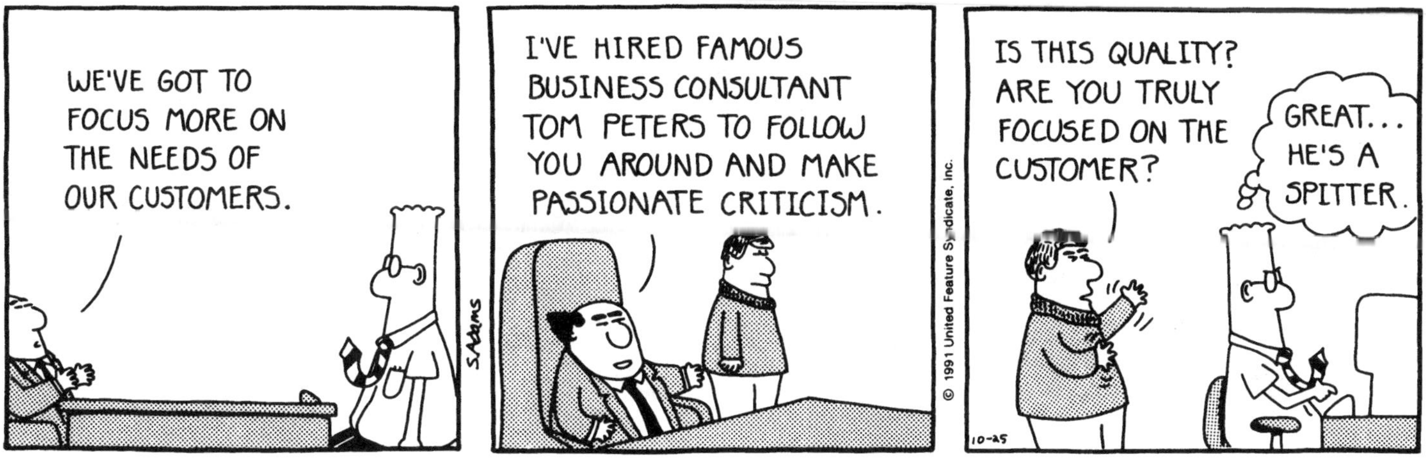
WE'VE GOT TO FOCUS MORE ON THE NEEDS OF OUR CUSTOMERS.
I'VE HIRED FAMOUS BUSINESS CONSULTANT TOM PETERS TO FOLLOW YOU AROUND AND MAKE PASSIONATE CRITICISM.
IS THIS QUALITY? ARE YOU TRULY FOCUSED ON THE CUSTOMER?
GREAT... HE'S A SPITTER.
10-25
© 1991 United Feature Syndicate, Inc.

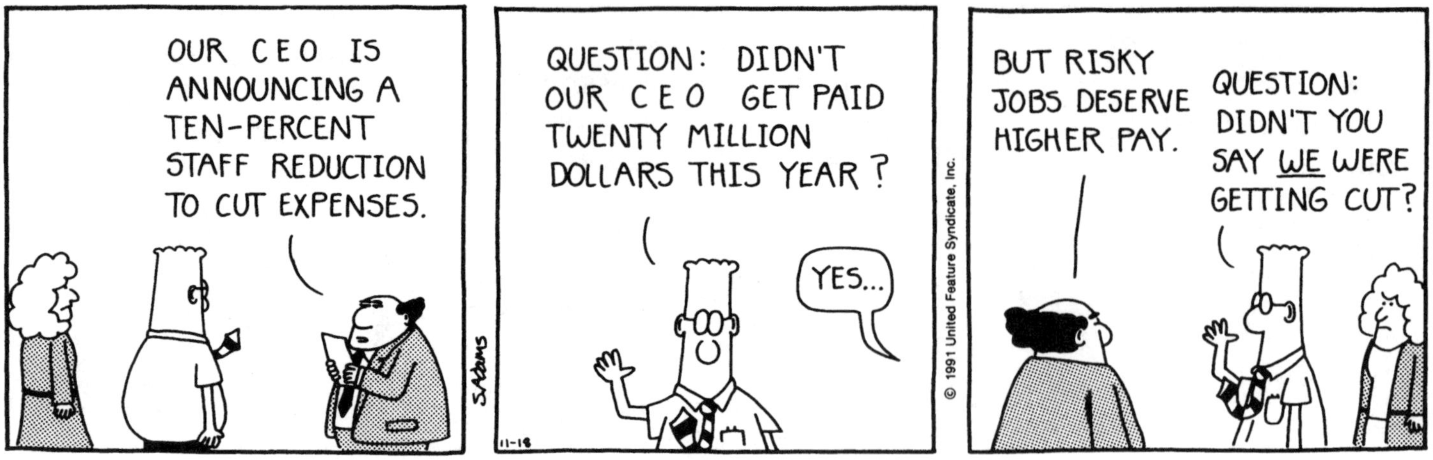
OUR CEO IS ANNOUNCING A TEN-PERCENT STAFF REDUCTION TO CUT EXPENSES.
QUESTION: DIDN'T OUR CEO GET PAID TWENTY MILLION DOLLARS THIS YEAR?
YES...
BUT RISKY JOBS DESERVE HIGHER PAY.
QUESTION: DIDN'T YOU SAY WE WERE GETTING CUT?
S.Adams
11-18
© 1991 United Feature Syndicate, Inc.

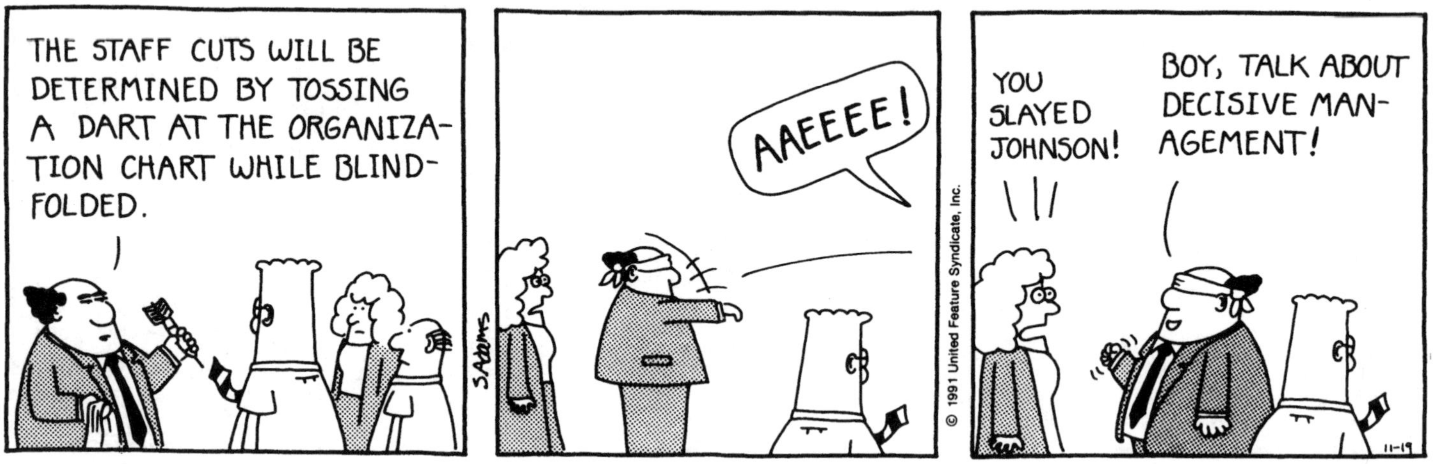
THE STAFF CUTS WILL BE DETERMINED BY TOSSING A DART AT THE ORGANIZATION CHART WHILE BLINDFOLDED.
AAEEEE!
YOU SLAYED JOHNSON!
BOY, TALK ABOUT DECISIVE MANAGEMENT!
S.Adams
11-19
© 1991 United Feature Syndicate, Inc.

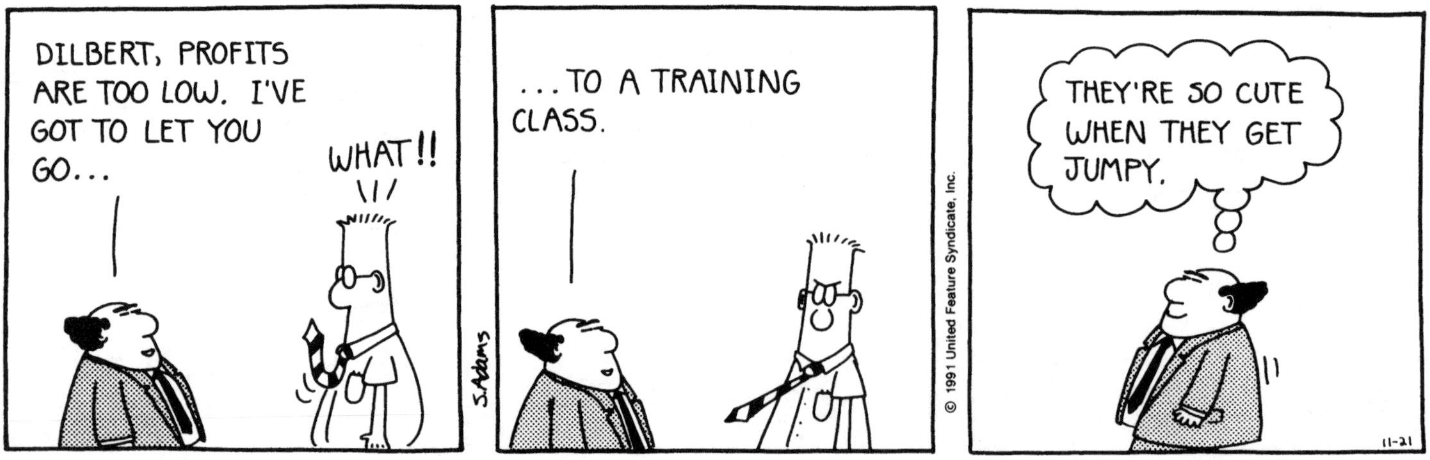
DILBERT, PROFITS ARE TOO LOW. I'VE GOT TO LET YOU GO...
WHAT!!
...TO A TRAINING CLASS.
THEY'RE SO CUTE WHEN THEY GET JUMPY.
S.Adams
11-21
© 1991 United Feature Syndicate, Inc.

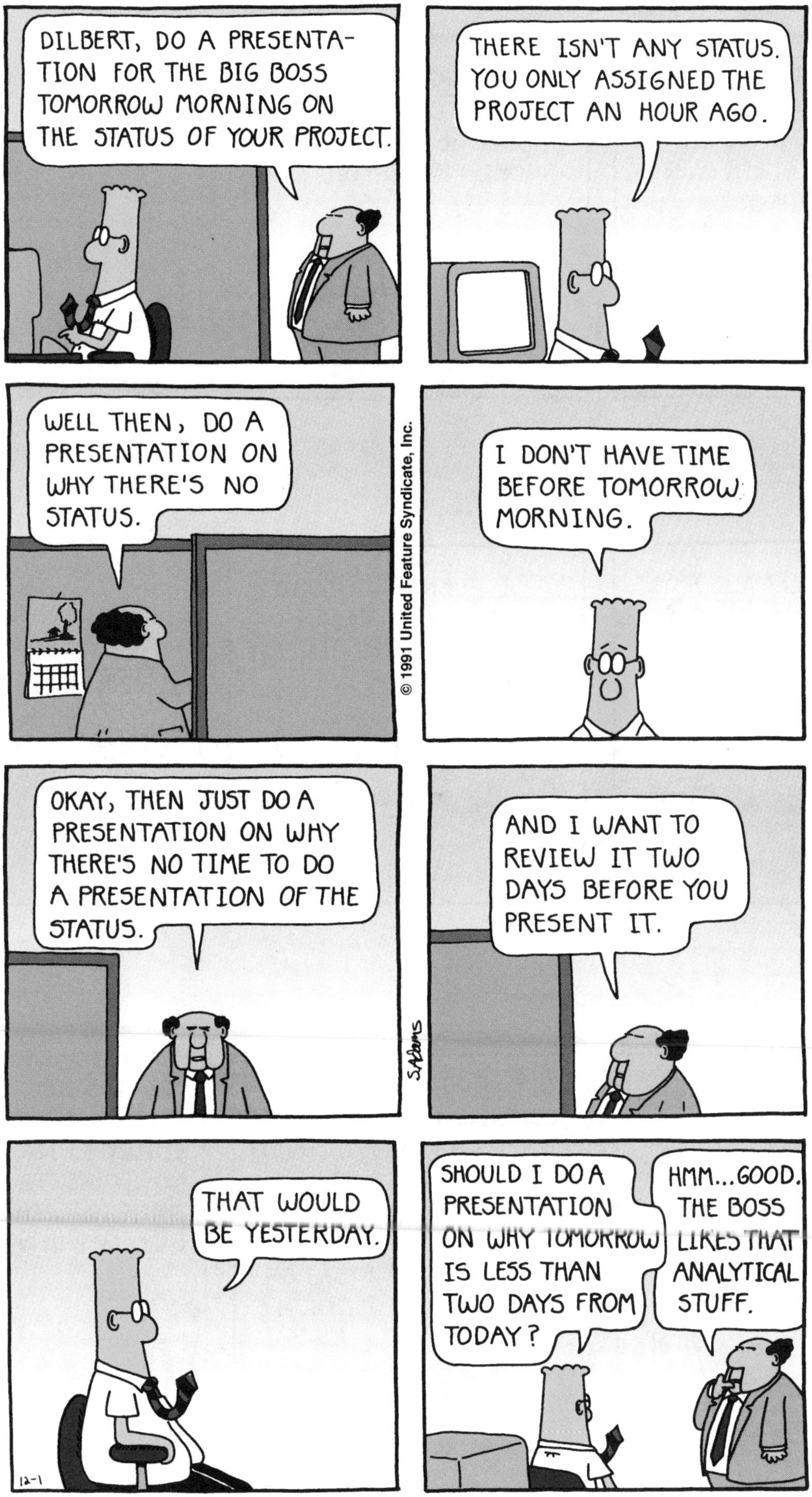
DILBERT, DO A PRESENTATION FOR THE BIG BOSS TOMORROW MORNING ON THE STATUS OF YOUR PROJECT.
THERE ISN'T ANY STATUS. YOU ONLY ASSIGNED THE PROJECT AN HOUR AGO.
WELL THEN, DO A PRESENTATION ON WHY THERE'S NO STATUS.
I DON'T HAVE TIME BEFORE TOMORROW MORNING.
© 1991 United Feature Syndicate, Inc.
OKAY, THEN JUST DO A PRESENTATION ON WHY THERE'S NO TIME TO DO A PRESENTATION OF THE STATUS.
AND I WANT TO REVIEW IT TWO DAYS BEFORE YOU PRESENT IT.
S.Adams
THAT WOULD BE YESTERDAY.
12-1
SHOULD I DO A PRESENTATION ON WHY TOMORROW IS LESS THAN TWO DAYS FROM TODAY?
HMM...GOOD. THE BOSS LIKES THAT ANALYTICAL STUFF.

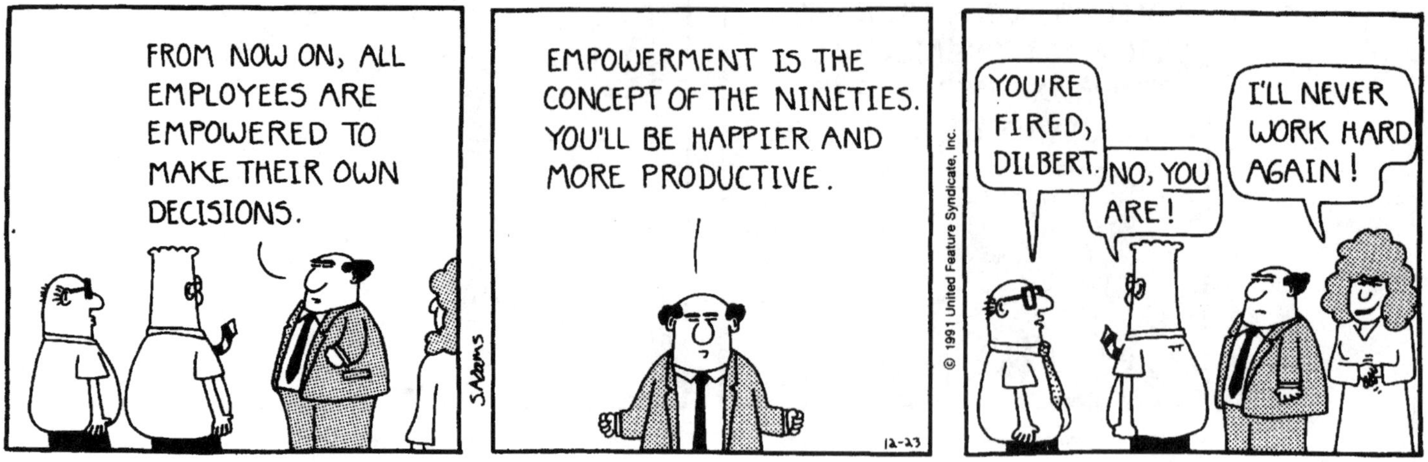

FROM NOW ON, ALL EMPLOYEES ARE EMPOWERED TO MAKE THEIR OWN DECISIONS.
S.Adams
EMPOWERMENT IS THE CONCEPT OF THE NINETIES. YOU'LL BE HAPPIER AND MORE PRODUCTIVE.
12-23
© 1991 United Feature Syndicate, Inc.
YOU'RE FIRED, DILBERT.
NO, YOU ARE!
I'LL NEVER WORK HARD AGAIN!

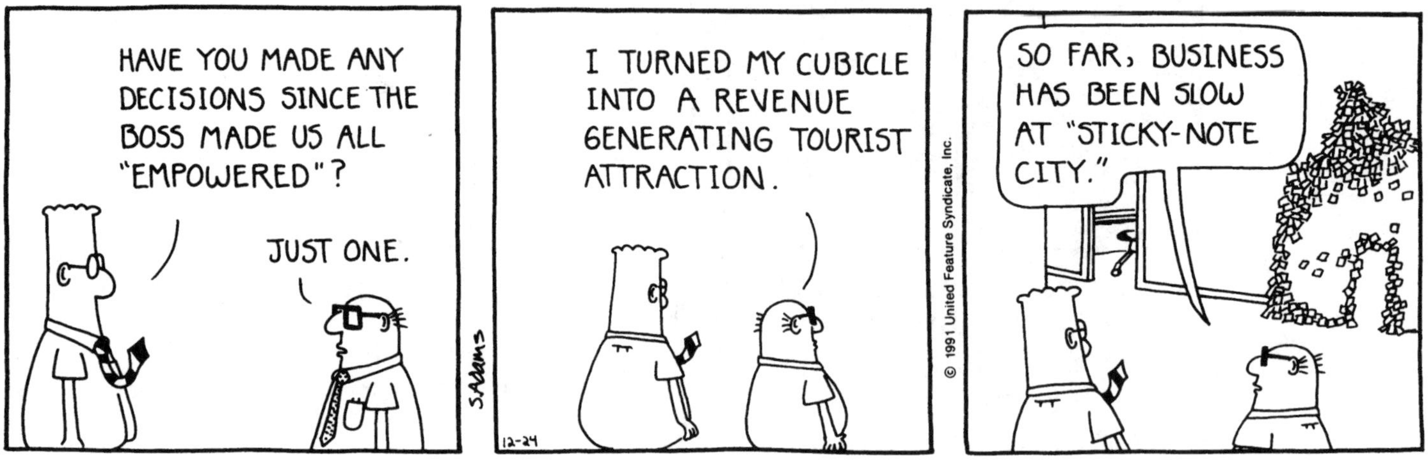

HAVE YOU MADE ANY DECISIONS SINCE THE BOSS MADE US ALL "EMPOWERED"?
JUST ONE.
S.Adams
12-24
I TURNED MY CUBICLE INTO A REVENUE GENERATING TOURIST ATTRACTION.
© 1991 United Feature Syndicate, Inc.
SO FAR, BUSINESS HAS BEEN SLOW AT "STICKY-NOTE CITY."

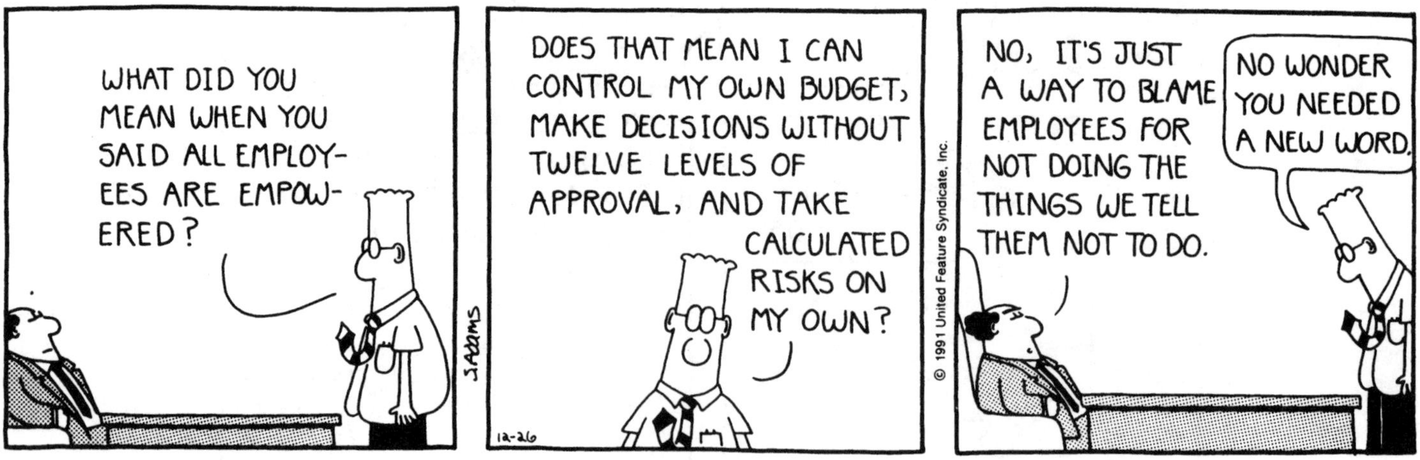

WHAT DID YOU MEAN WHEN YOU SAID ALL EMPLOYEES ARE EMPOWERED?
S.Adams
DOES THAT MEAN I CAN CONTROL MY OWN BUDGET, MAKE DECISIONS WITHOUT TWELVE LEVELS OF APPROVAL, AND TAKE CALCULATED RISKS ON MY OWN?
12-26
© 1991 United Feature Syndicate, Inc.
NO, IT'S JUST A WAY TO BLAME EMPLOYEES FOR NOT DOING THE THINGS WE TELL THEM NOT TO DO.
NO WONDER YOU NEEDED A NEW WORD.

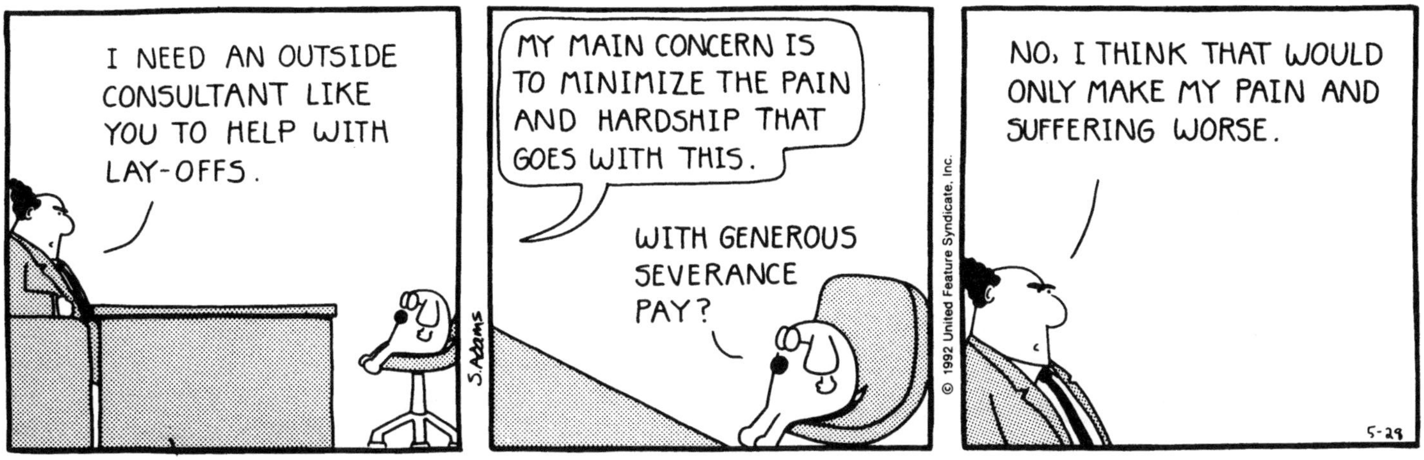
I NEED AN OUTSIDE CONSULTANT LIKE YOU TO HELP WITH LAY-OFFS.
MY MAIN CONCERN IS TO MINIMIZE THE PAIN AND HARDSHIP THAT GOES WITH THIS.
WITH GENEROUS SEVERANCE PAY?
NO, I THINK THAT WOULD ONLY MAKE MY PAIN AND SUFFERING WORSE.
© 1992 United Feature Syndicate, Inc.

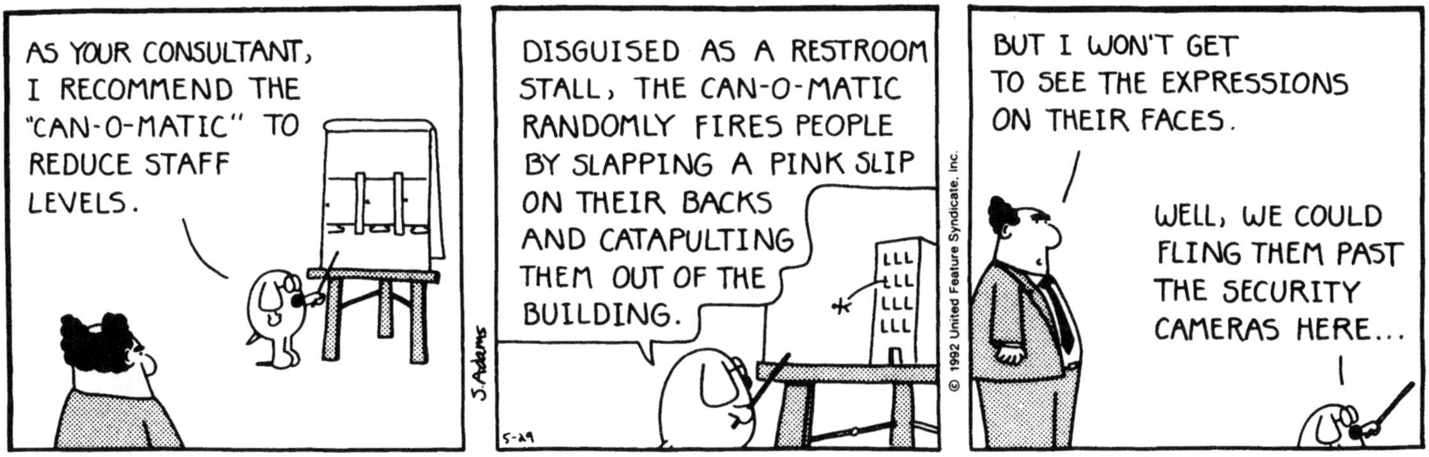
AS YOUR CONSULTANT, I RECOMMEND THE "CAN-O-MATIC" TO REDUCE STAFF LEVELS.
DISGUISED AS A RESTROOM STALL, THE CAN-O-MATIC RANDOMLY FIRES PEOPLE BY SLAPPING A PINK SLIP ON THEIR BACKS AND CATAPULTING THEM OUT OF THE BUILDING.
BUT I WON'T GET TO SEE THE EXPRESSIONS ON THEIR FACES.
WELL, WE COULD FLING THEM PAST THE SECURITY CAMERAS HERE...
© 1992 United Feature Syndicate, Inc.

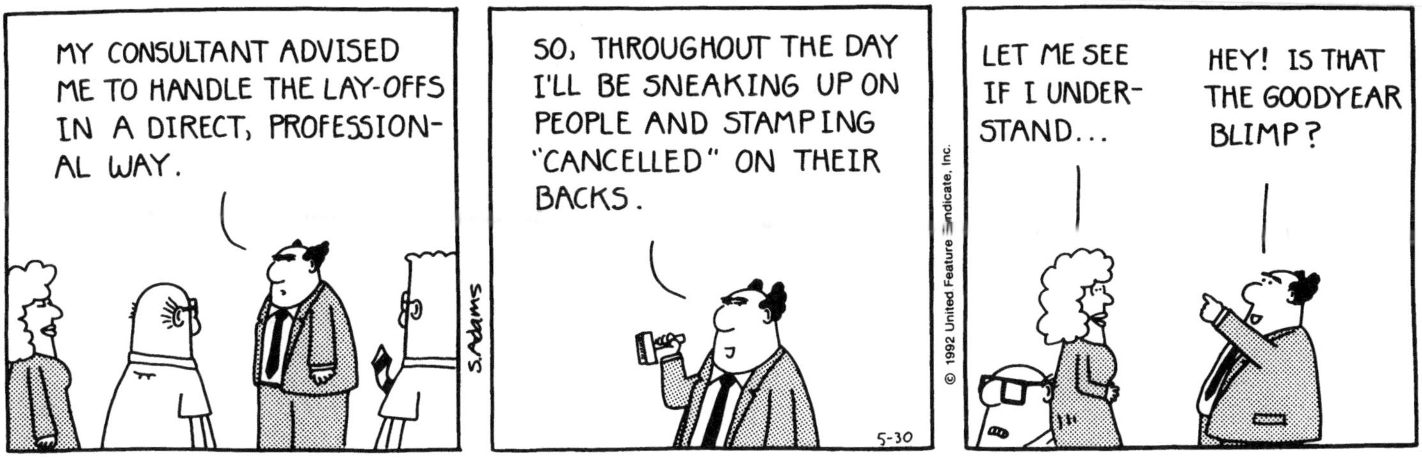
MY CONSULTANT ADVISED ME TO HANDLE THE LAY-OFFS IN A DIRECT, PROFESSION-AL WAY.
SO, THROUGHOUT THE DAY I'LL BE SNEAKING UP ON PEOPLE AND STAMPING "CANCELLED" ON THEIR BACKS.
LET ME SEE IF I UNDER-STAND...
HEY! IS THAT THE GOODYEAR BLIMP?

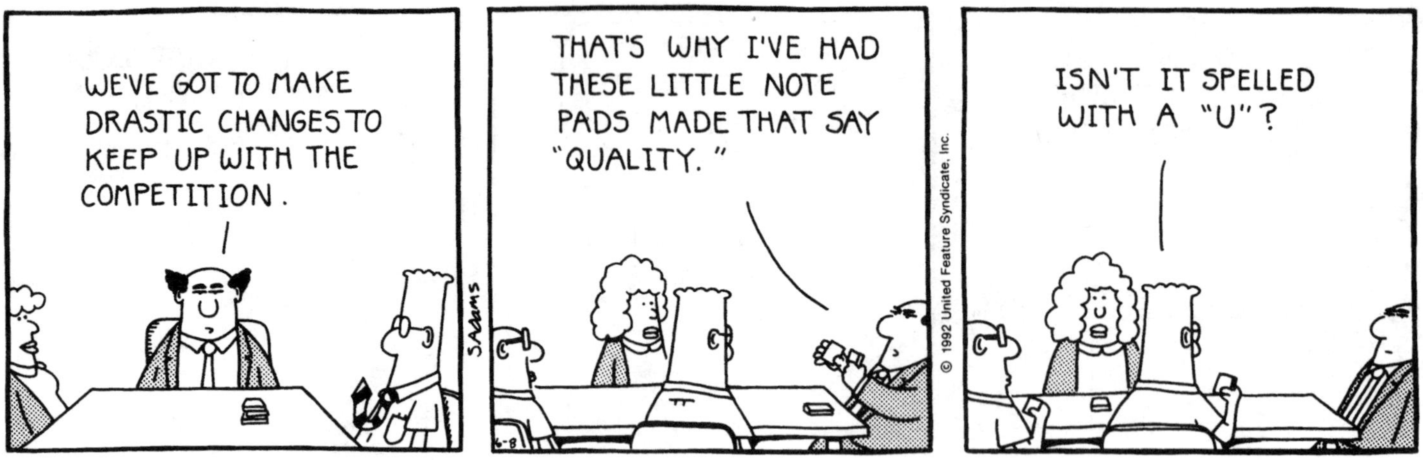
WE'VE GOT TO MAKE DRASTIC CHANGES TO KEEP UP WITH THE COMPETITION.
S.Adams
THAT'S WHY I'VE HAD THESE LITTLE NOTE PADS MADE THAT SAY "QUALITY."
6-8
© 1992 United Feature Syndicate, Inc.
ISN'T IT SPELLED WITH A "U"?

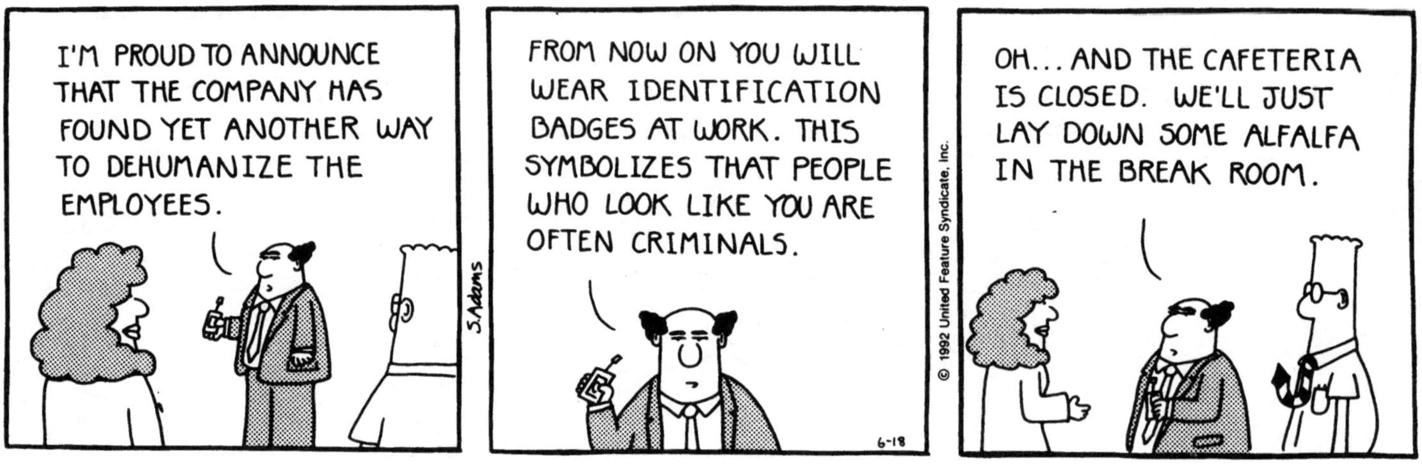
I'M PROUD TO ANNOUNCE THAT THE COMPANY HAS FOUND YET ANOTHER WAY TO DEHUMANIZE THE EMPLOYEES.
S.Adams
FROM NOW ON YOU WILL WEAR IDENTIFICATION BADGES AT WORK. THIS SYMBOLIZES THAT PEOPLE WHO LOOK LIKE YOU ARE OFTEN CRIMINALS.
6-18
© 1992 United Feature Syndicate, Inc.
OH... AND THE CAFETERIA IS CLOSED. WE'LL JUST LAY DOWN SOME ALFALFA IN THE BREAK ROOM.

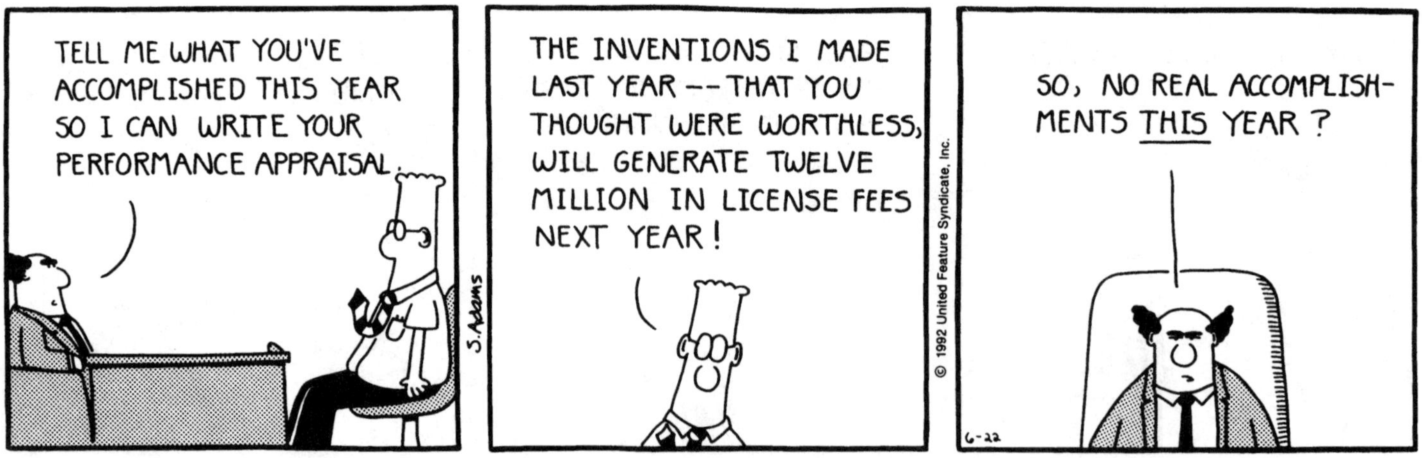
TELL ME WHAT YOU'VE ACCOMPLISHED THIS YEAR SO I CAN WRITE YOUR PERFORMANCE APPRAISAL.
S.Adams
THE INVENTIONS I MADE LAST YEAR -- THAT YOU THOUGHT WERE WORTHLESS, WILL GENERATE TWELVE MILLION IN LICENSE FEES NEXT YEAR!
© 1992 United Feature Syndicate, Inc.
SO, NO REAL ACCOMPLISHMENTS THIS YEAR?
6-22

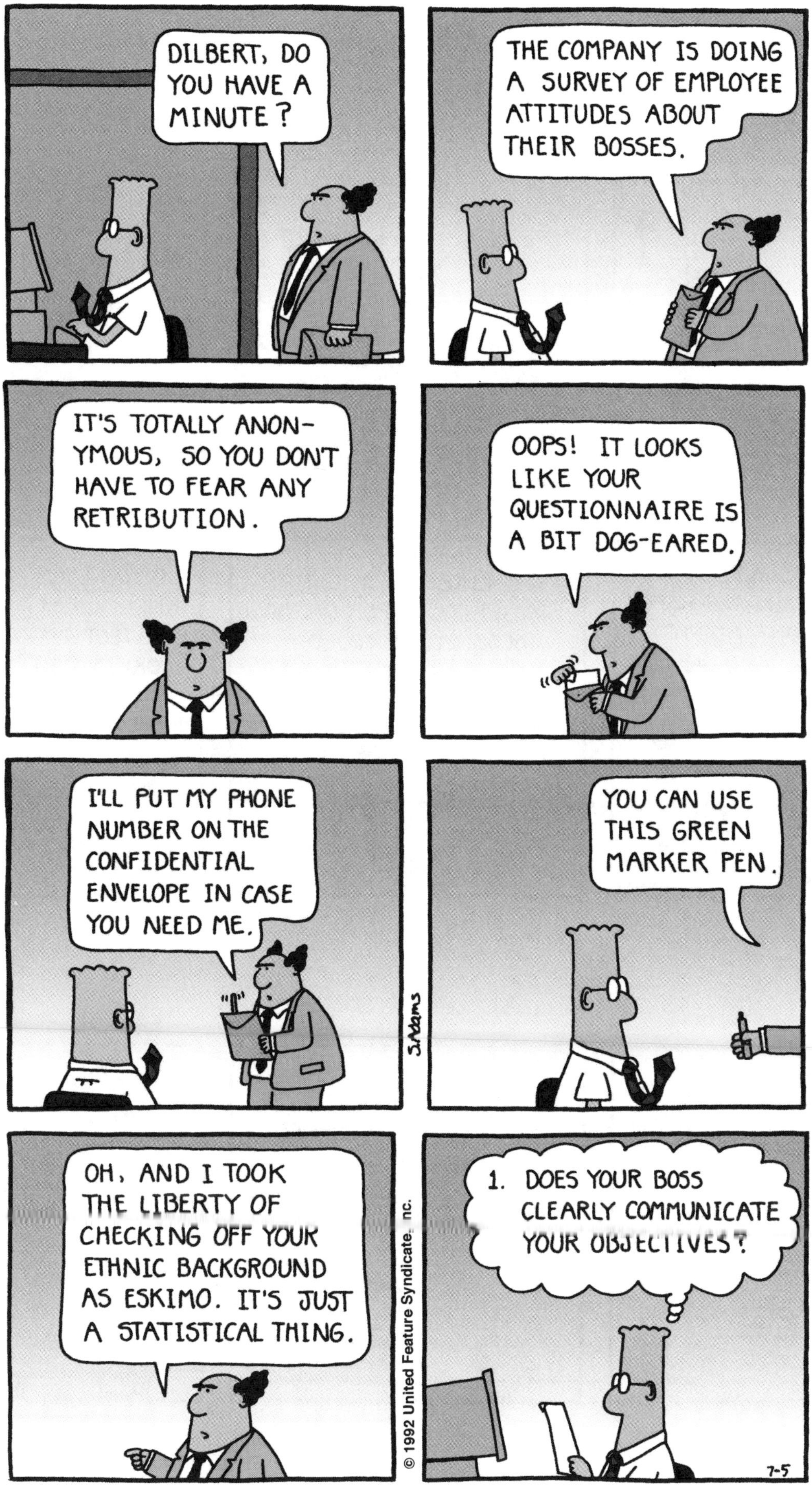
DILBERT, DO YOU HAVE A MINUTE?
THE COMPANY IS DOING A SURVEY OF EMPLOYEE ATTITUDES ABOUT THEIR BOSSES.
IT'S TOTALLY ANONYMOUS, SO YOU DON'T HAVE TO FEAR ANY RETRIBUTION.
OOPS! IT LOOKS LIKE YOUR QUESTIONNAIRE IS A BIT DOG-EARED.
I'LL PUT MY PHONE NUMBER ON THE CONFIDENTIAL ENVELOPE IN CASE YOU NEED ME.
S.Adams
YOU CAN USE THIS GREEN MARKER PEN.
OH, AND I TOOK THE LIBERTY OF CHECKING OFF YOUR ETHNIC BACKGROUND AS ESKIMO. IT'S JUST A STATISTICAL THING.
© 1992 United Feature Syndicate, Inc.
1. DOES YOUR BOSS CLEARLY COMMUNICATE YOUR OBJECTIVES?
7-5

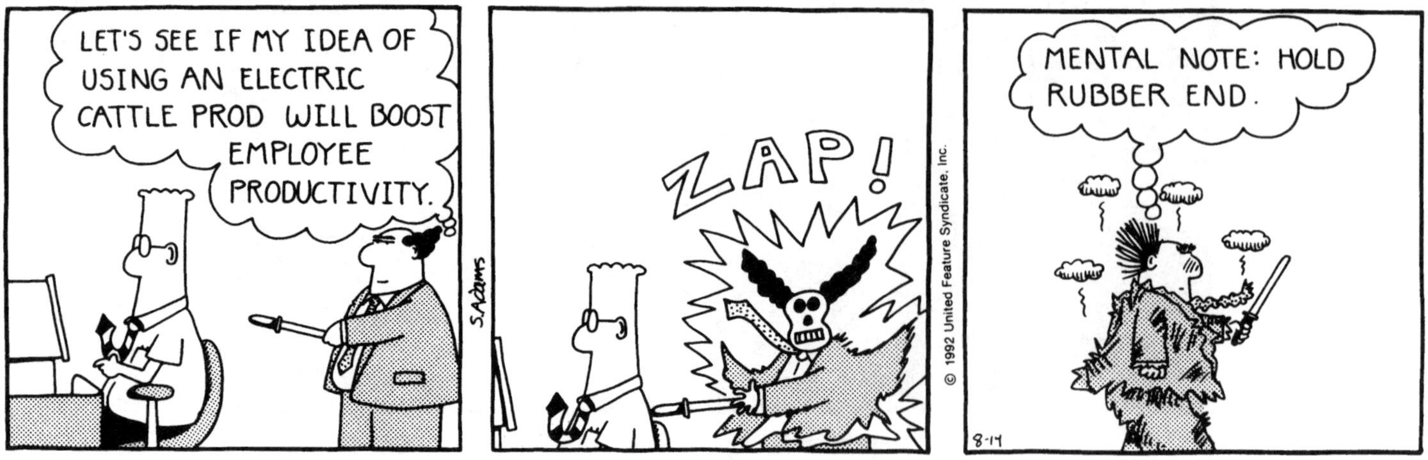
LET'S SEE IF MY IDEA OF USING AN ELECTRIC CATTLE PROD WILL BOOST EMPLOYEE PRODUCTIVITY.
S. Adams
ZAP!
© 1992 United Feature Syndicate, Inc.
MENTAL NOTE: HOLD RUBBER END.
8-14

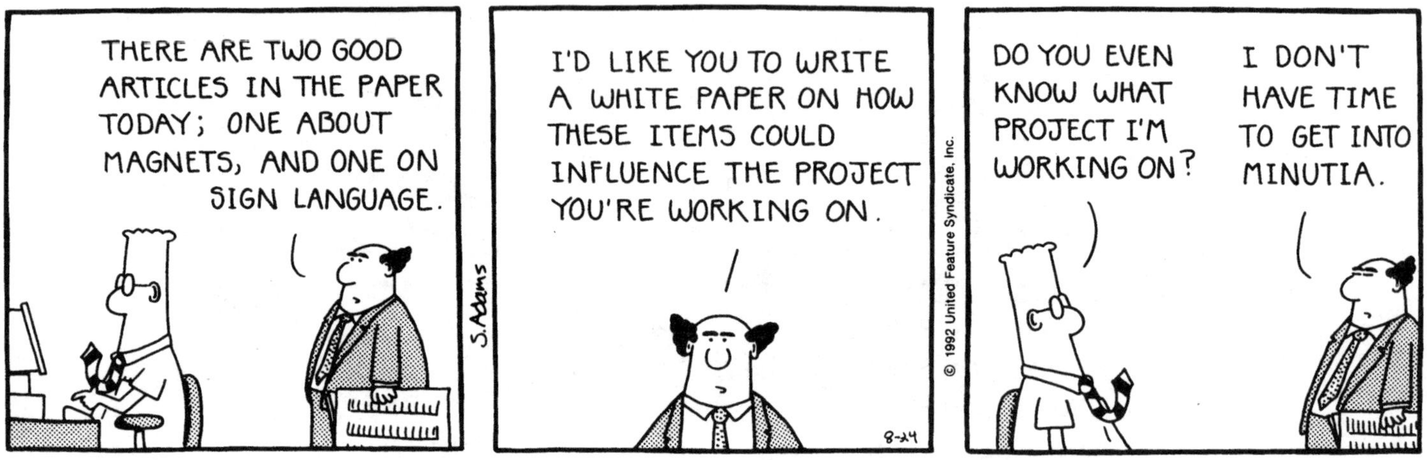
THERE ARE TWO GOOD ARTICLES IN THE PAPER TODAY; ONE ABOUT MAGNETS, AND ONE ON SIGN LANGUAGE.
S. Adams
I'D LIKE YOU TO WRITE A WHITE PAPER ON HOW THESE ITEMS COULD INFLUENCE THE PROJECT YOU'RE WORKING ON.
8-24
© 1992 United Feature Syndicate, Inc.
DO YOU EVEN KNOW WHAT PROJECT I'M WORKING ON?
I DON'T HAVE TIME TO GET INTO MINUTIA.

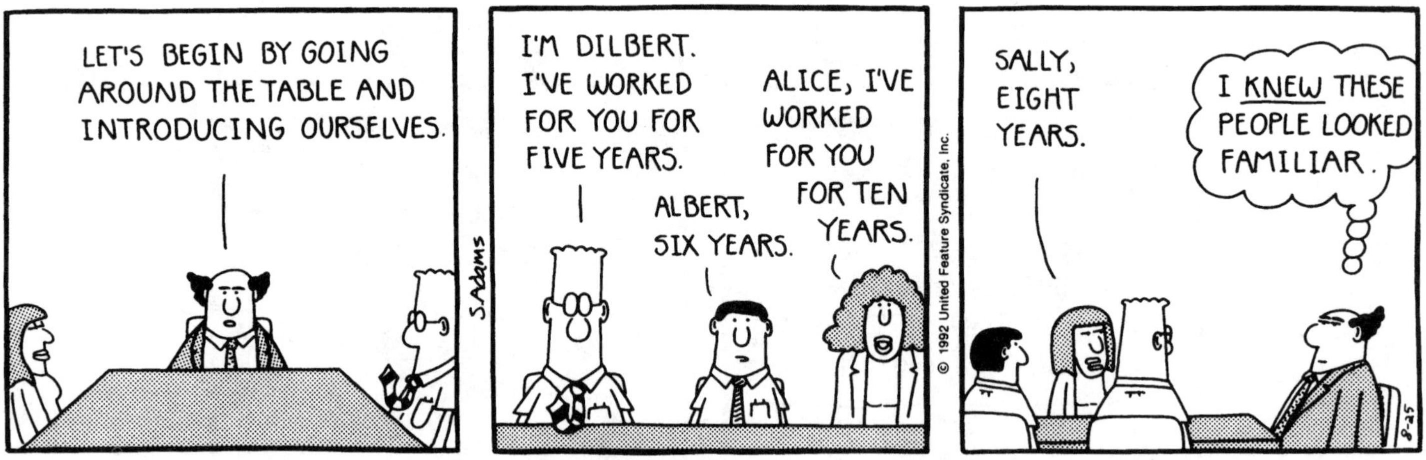
LET'S BEGIN BY GOING AROUND THE TABLE AND INTRODUCING OURSELVES.
S. Adams
I'M DILBERT. I'VE WORKED FOR YOU FOR FIVE YEARS.
ALBERT, SIX YEARS.
ALICE, I'VE WORKED FOR YOU FOR TEN YEARS.
© 1992 United Feature Syndicate, Inc.
SALLY, EIGHT YEARS.
I KNEW THESE PEOPLE LOOKED FAMILIAR.
8-25

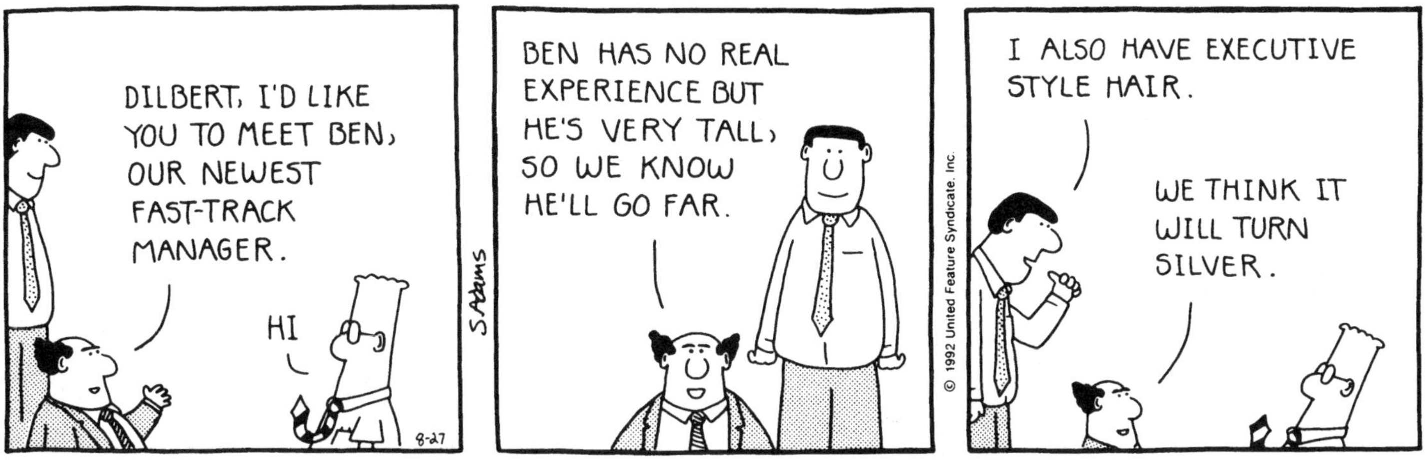
DILBERT, I'D LIKE YOU TO MEET BEN, OUR NEWEST FAST-TRACK MANAGER.
HI
S.Adams
8-27
BEN HAS NO REAL EXPERIENCE BUT HE'S VERY TALL, SO WE KNOW HE'LL GO FAR.
© 1992 United Feature Syndicate, Inc.
I ALSO HAVE EXECUTIVE STYLE HAIR.
WE THINK IT WILL TURN SILVER.

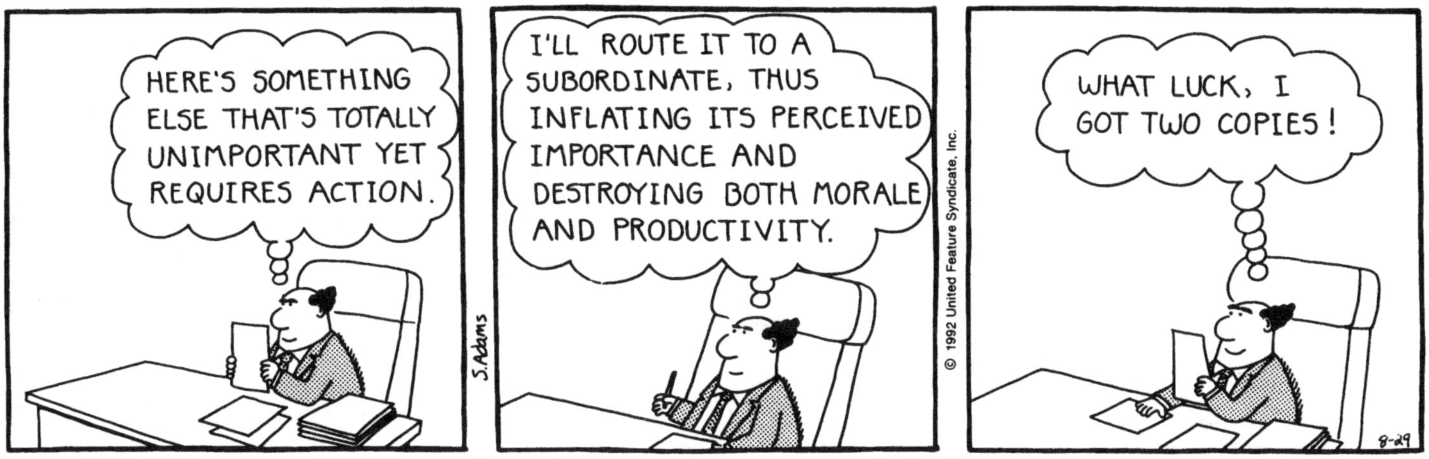
HERE'S SOMETHING ELSE THAT'S TOTALLY UNIMPORTANT YET REQUIRES ACTION.
S.Adams
I'LL ROUTE IT TO A SUBORDINATE, THUS INFLATING ITS PERCEIVED IMPORTANCE AND DESTROYING BOTH MORALE AND PRODUCTIVITY.
© 1992 United Feature Syndicate, Inc.
WHAT LUCK, I GOT TWO COPIES!
8-29

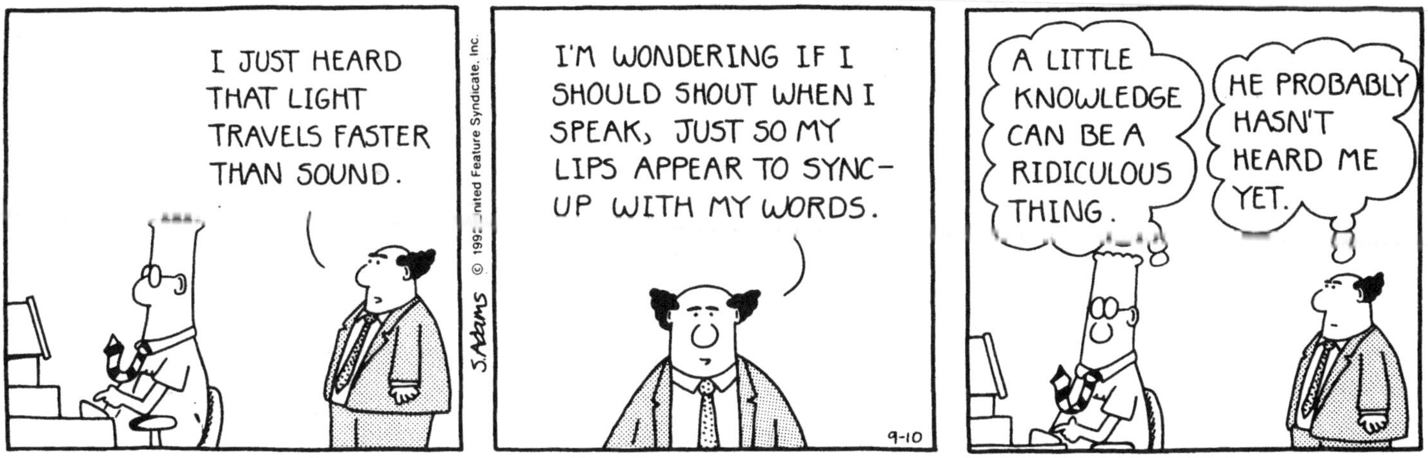
I JUST HEARD THAT LIGHT TRAVELS FASTER THAN SOUND.
S.Adams
© 1992 United Feature Syndicate, Inc.
I'M WONDERING IF I SHOULD SHOUT WHEN I SPEAK, JUST SO MY LIPS APPEAR TO SYNC-UP WITH MY WORDS.
9-10
A LITTLE KNOWLEDGE CAN BE A RIDICULOUS THING.
HE PROBABLY HASN'T HEARD ME YET.

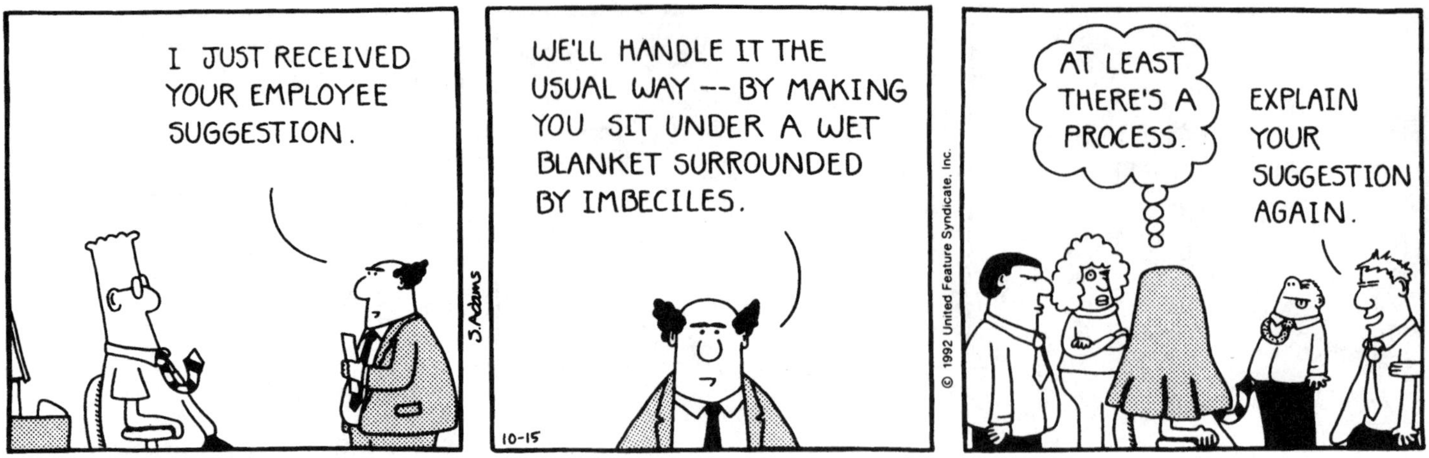
I JUST RECEIVED YOUR EMPLOYEE SUGGESTION.
S. Adams
WE'LL HANDLE IT THE USUAL WAY -- BY MAKING YOU SIT UNDER A WET BLANKET SURROUNDED BY IMBECILES.
10-15
© 1992 United Feature Syndicate, Inc.
AT LEAST THERE'S A PROCESS.
EXPLAIN YOUR SUGGESTION AGAIN.

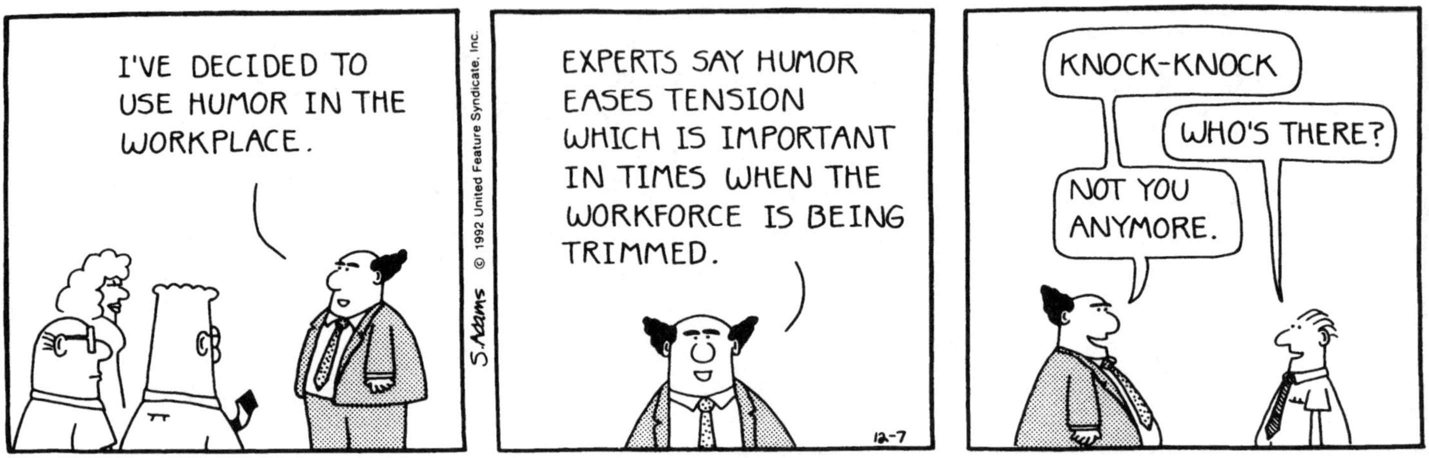
I'VE DECIDED TO USE HUMOR IN THE WORKPLACE.
S. Adams
© 1992 United Feature Syndicate, Inc.
EXPERTS SAY HUMOR EASES TENSION WHICH IS IMPORTANT IN TIMES WHEN THE WORKFORCE IS BEING TRIMMED.
12-7
KNOCK-KNOCK
WHO'S THERE?
NOT YOU ANYMORE.

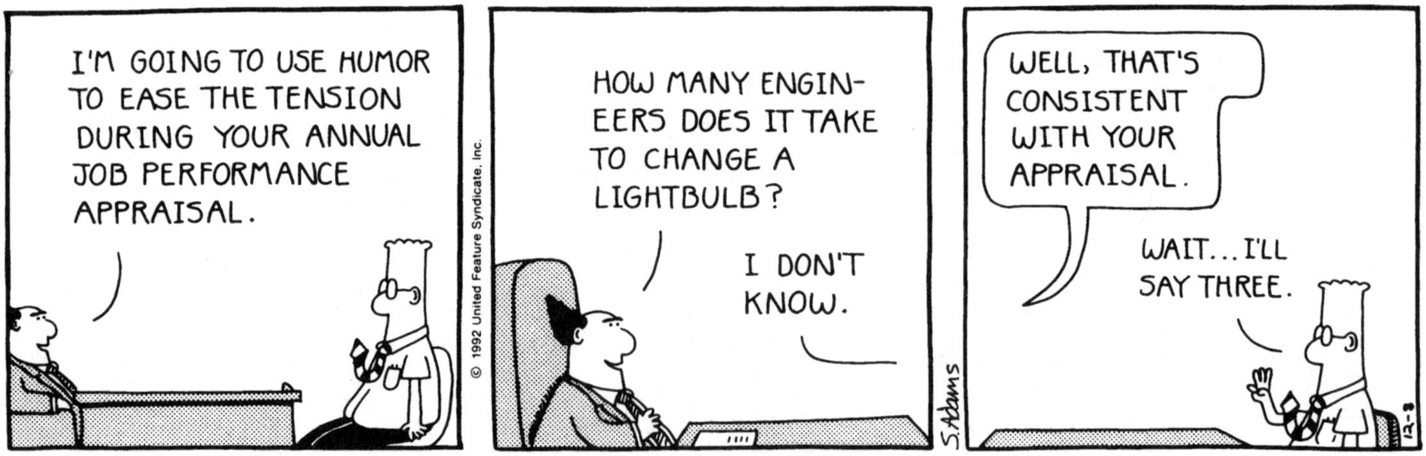
I'M GOING TO USE HUMOR TO EASE THE TENSION DURING YOUR ANNUAL JOB PERFORMANCE APPRAISAL.
© 1992 United Feature Syndicate, Inc.
HOW MANY ENGINEERS DOES IT TAKE TO CHANGE A LIGHTBULB?
I DON'T KNOW.
S. Adams
WELL, THAT'S CONSISTENT WITH YOUR APPRAISAL.
WAIT... I'LL SAY THREE.
12-8

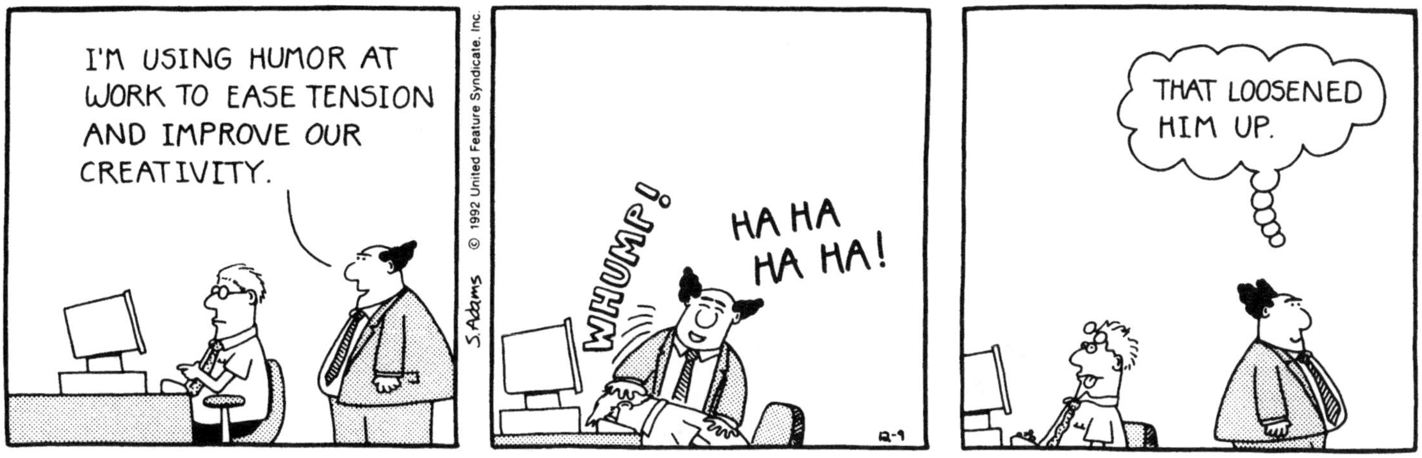
I'M USING HUMOR AT WORK TO EASE TENSION AND IMPROVE OUR CREATIVITY.
S. Adams © 1992 United Feature Syndicate, Inc.
WHUMP!
HA HA HA HA!
12-9
THAT LOOSENED HIM UP.

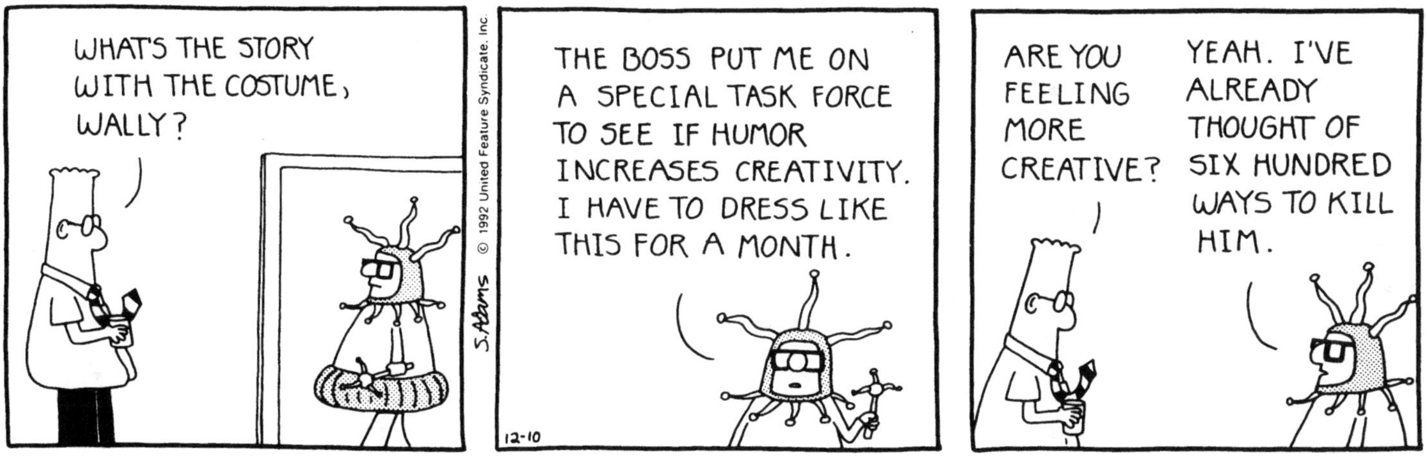
WHAT'S THE STORY WITH THE COSTUME, WALLY?
S. Adams © 1992 United Feature Syndicate, Inc.
THE BOSS PUT ME ON A SPECIAL TASK FORCE TO SEE IF HUMOR INCREASES CREATIVITY. I HAVE TO DRESS LIKE THIS FOR A MONTH.
12-10
ARE YOU FEELING MORE CREATIVE?
YEAH. I'VE ALREADY THOUGHT OF SIX HUNDRED WAYS TO KILL HIM.

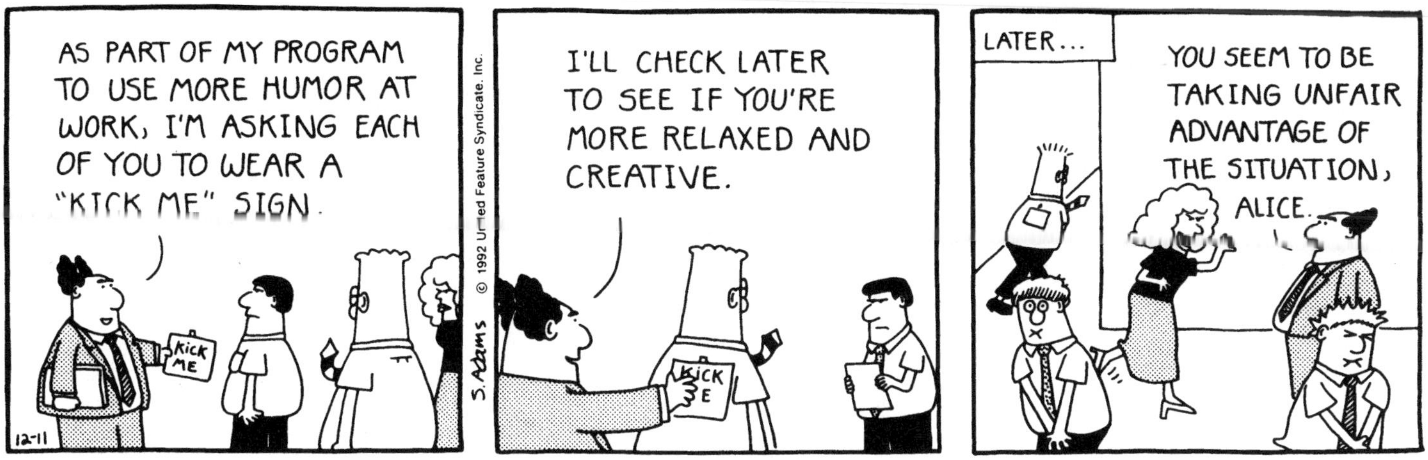
AS PART OF MY PROGRAM TO USE MORE HUMOR AT WORK, I'M ASKING EACH OF YOU TO WEAR A "KICK ME" SIGN.
KICK ME
12-11
S. Adams © 1992 United Feature Syndicate, Inc.
I'LL CHECK LATER TO SEE IF YOU'RE MORE RELAXED AND CREATIVE.
LATER...
YOU SEEM TO BE TAKING UNFAIR ADVANTAGE OF THE SITUATION, ALICE.

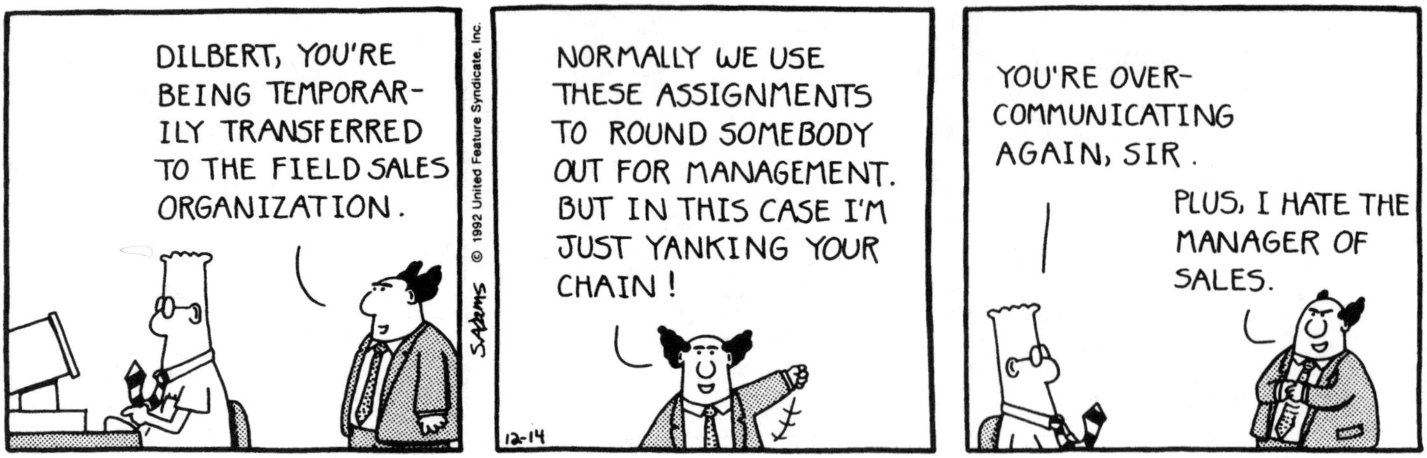

DILBERT, YOU'RE BEING TEMPORARILY TRANSFERRED TO THE FIELD SALES ORGANIZATION.
S.Adams © 1992 United Feature Syndicate, Inc.
NORMALLY WE USE THESE ASSIGNMENTS TO ROUND SOMEBODY OUT FOR MANAGEMENT. BUT IN THIS CASE I'M JUST YANKING YOUR CHAIN!
12-14
YOU'RE OVER-COMMUNICATING AGAIN, SIR.
PLUS, I HATE THE MANAGER OF SALES.

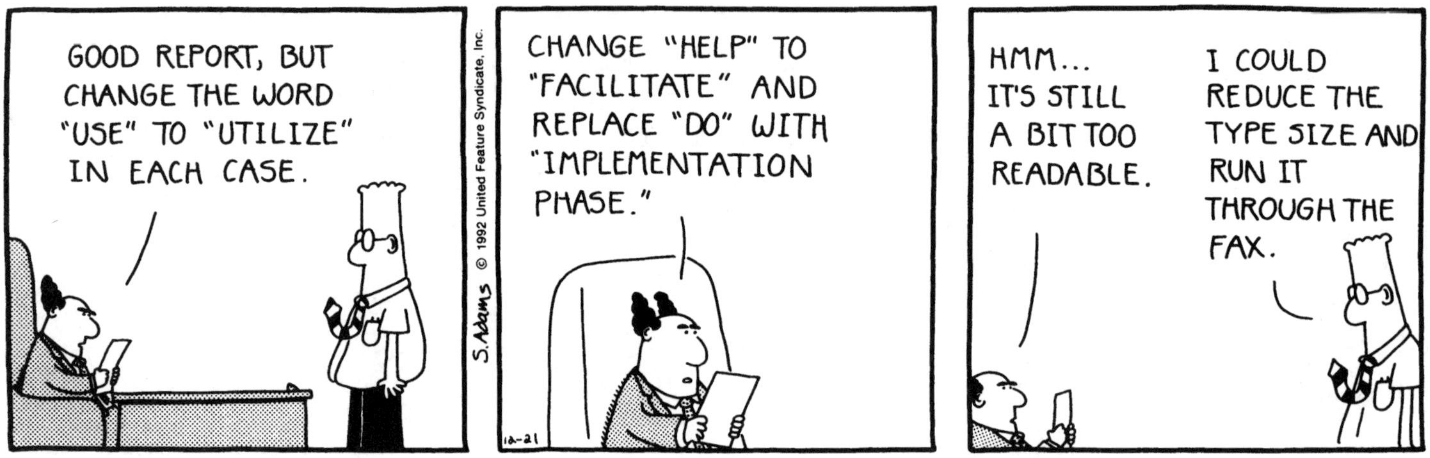

GOOD REPORT, BUT CHANGE THE WORD "USE" TO "UTILIZE" IN EACH CASE.
S.Adams © 1992 United Feature Syndicate, Inc.
CHANGE "HELP" TO "FACILITATE" AND REPLACE "DO" WITH "IMPLEMENTATION PHASE."
12-21
HMM... IT'S STILL A BIT TOO READABLE.
I COULD REDUCE THE TYPE SIZE AND RUN IT THROUGH THE FAX.

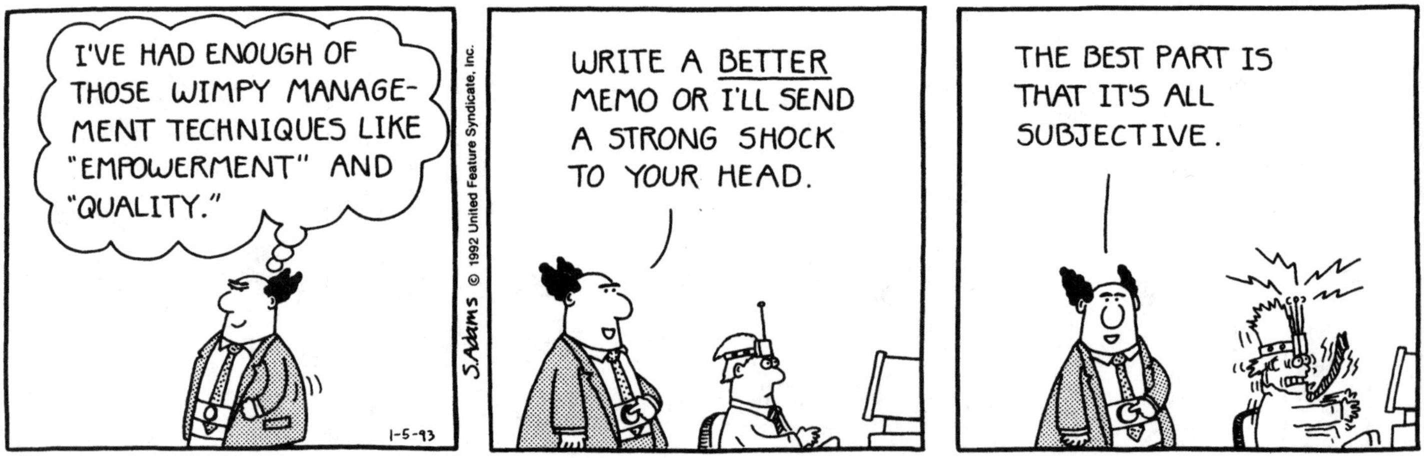

I'VE HAD ENOUGH OF THOSE WIMPY MANAGEMENT TECHNIQUES LIKE "EMPOWERMENT" AND "QUALITY."
1-5-93
S.Adams © 1992 United Feature Syndicate, Inc.
WRITE A BETTER MEMO OR I'LL SEND A STRONG SHOCK TO YOUR HEAD.
THE BEST PART IS THAT IT'S ALL SUBJECTIVE.

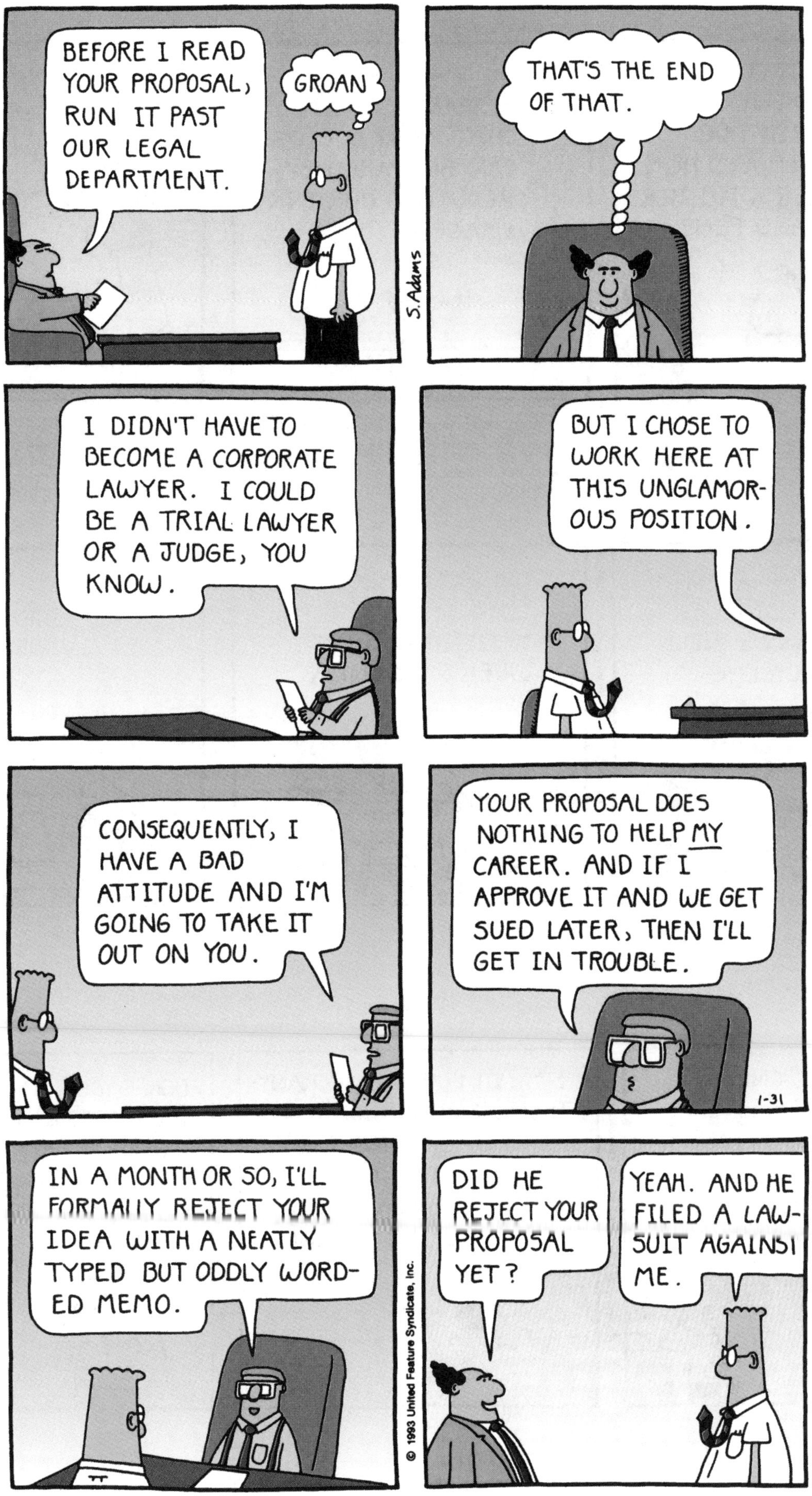

BEFORE I READ YOUR PROPOSAL, RUN IT PAST OUR LEGAL DEPARTMENT.
GROAN
S. Adams
THAT'S THE END OF THAT.
I DIDN'T HAVE TO BECOME A CORPORATE LAWYER. I COULD BE A TRIAL LAWYER OR A JUDGE, YOU KNOW.
BUT I CHOSE TO WORK HERE AT THIS UNGLAMOR-OUS POSITION.
CONSEQUENTLY, I HAVE A BAD ATTITUDE AND I'M GOING TO TAKE IT OUT ON YOU.
YOUR PROPOSAL DOES NOTHING TO HELP MY CAREER. AND IF I APPROVE IT AND WE GET SUED LATER, THEN I'LL GET IN TROUBLE.
1-31
IN A MONTH OR SO, I'LL FORMALLY REJECT YOUR IDEA WITH A NEATLY TYPED BUT ODDLY WORD-ED MEMO.
© 1993 United Feature Syndicate, Inc.
DID HE REJECT YOUR PROPOSAL YET?
YEAH. AND HE FILED A LAW-SUIT AGAINST ME.

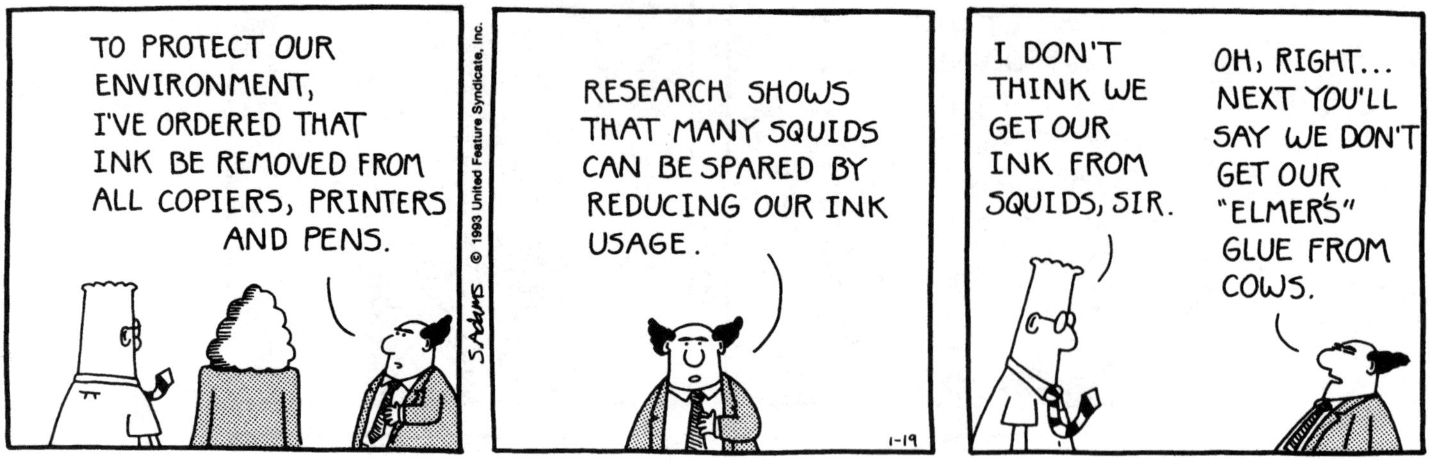
TO PROTECT OUR ENVIRONMENT, I'VE ORDERED THAT INK BE REMOVED FROM ALL COPIERS, PRINTERS AND PENS.
RESEARCH SHOWS THAT MANY SQUIDS CAN BE SPARED BY REDUCING OUR INK USAGE.
I DON'T THINK WE GET OUR INK FROM SQUIDS, SIR.
OH, RIGHT... NEXT YOU'LL SAY WE DON'T GET OUR "ELMER'S" GLUE FROM COWS.

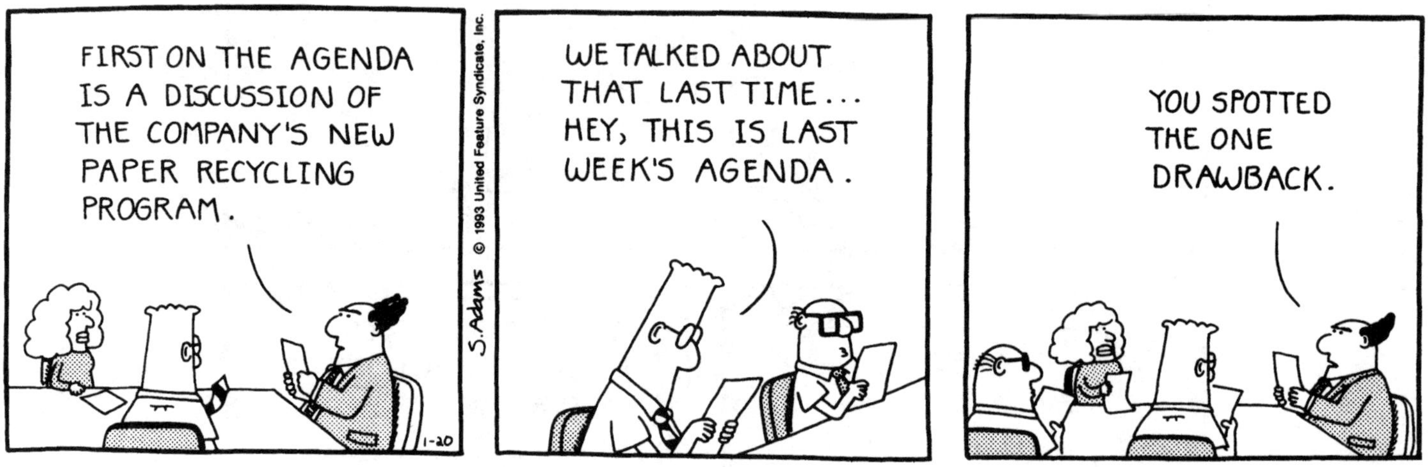
FIRST ON THE AGENDA IS A DISCUSSION OF THE COMPANY'S NEW PAPER RECYCLING PROGRAM.
WE TALKED ABOUT THAT LAST TIME... HEY, THIS IS LAST WEEK'S AGENDA.
YOU SPOTTED THE ONE DRAWBACK.

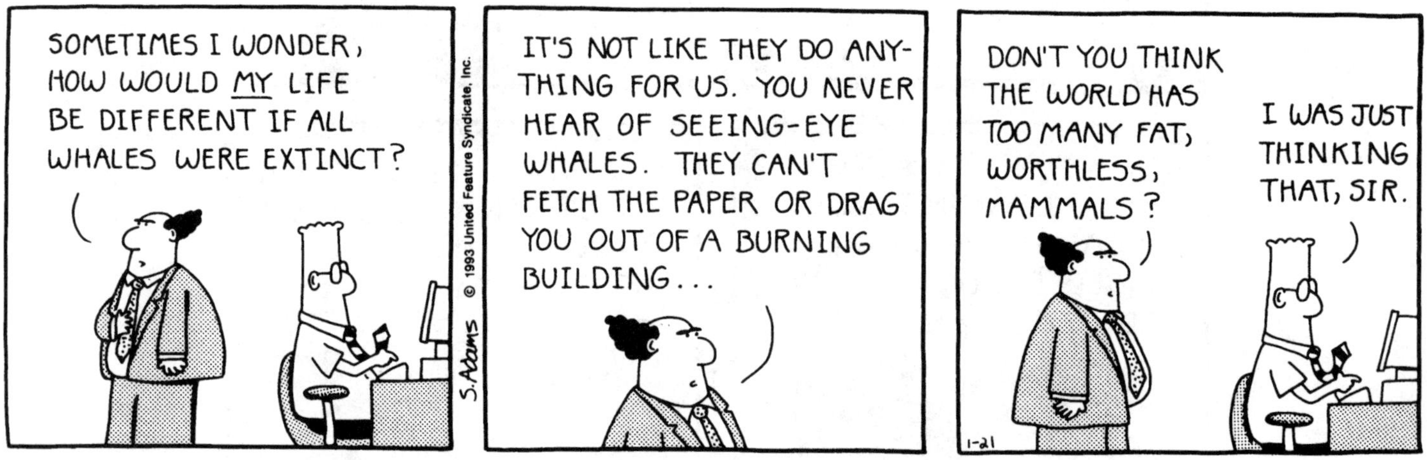
SOMETIMES I WONDER, HOW WOULD MY LIFE BE DIFFERENT IF ALL WHALES WERE EXTINCT?
IT'S NOT LIKE THEY DO ANYTHING FOR US. YOU NEVER HEAR OF SEEING-EYE WHALES. THEY CAN'T FETCH THE PAPER OR DRAG YOU OUT OF A BURNING BUILDING...
DON'T YOU THINK THE WORLD HAS TOO MANY FAT, WORTHLESS, MAMMALS?
I WAS JUST THINKING THAT, SIR.

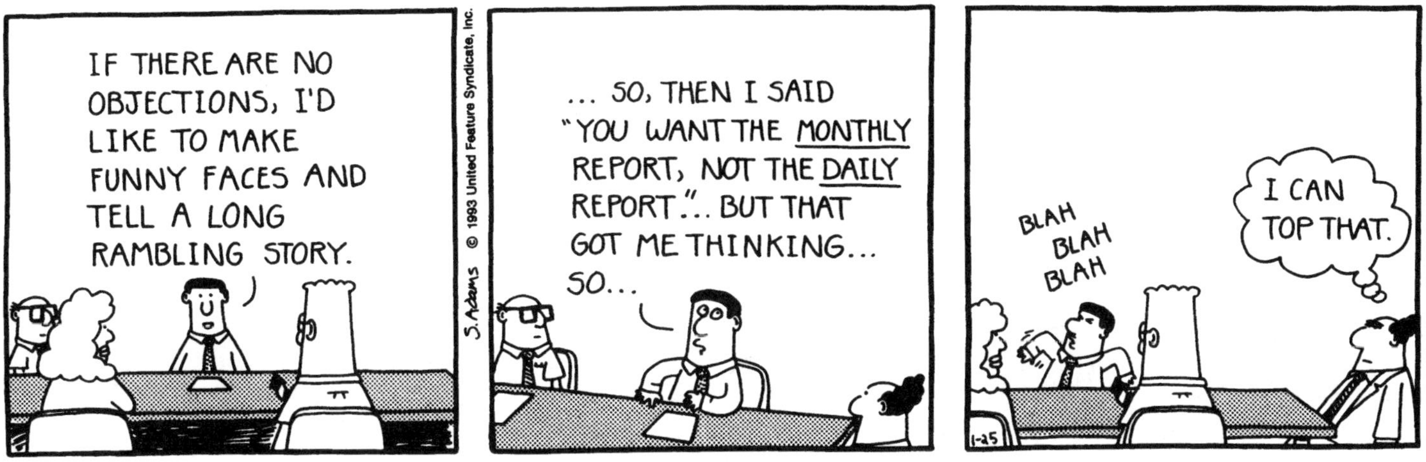

IF THERE ARE NO OBJECTIONS, I'D LIKE TO MAKE FUNNY FACES AND TELL A LONG RAMBLING STORY.
S. Adams © 1993 United Feature Syndicate, Inc.
... SO, THEN I SAID "YOU WANT THE MONTHLY REPORT, NOT THE DAILY REPORT."... BUT THAT GOT ME THINKING... SO...
BLAH BLAH BLAH
I CAN TOP THAT.
1-25

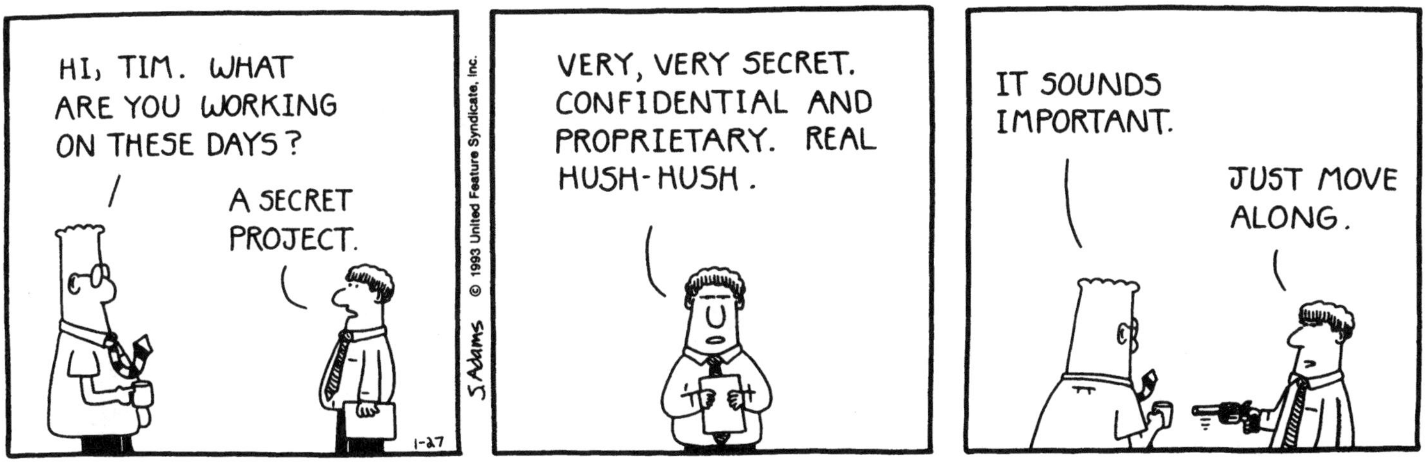

HI, TIM. WHAT ARE YOU WORKING ON THESE DAYS?
A SECRET PROJECT.
1-27
S. Adams © 1993 United Feature Syndicate, Inc.
VERY, VERY SECRET. CONFIDENTIAL AND PROPRIETARY. REAL HUSH-HUSH.
IT SOUNDS IMPORTANT.
JUST MOVE ALONG.

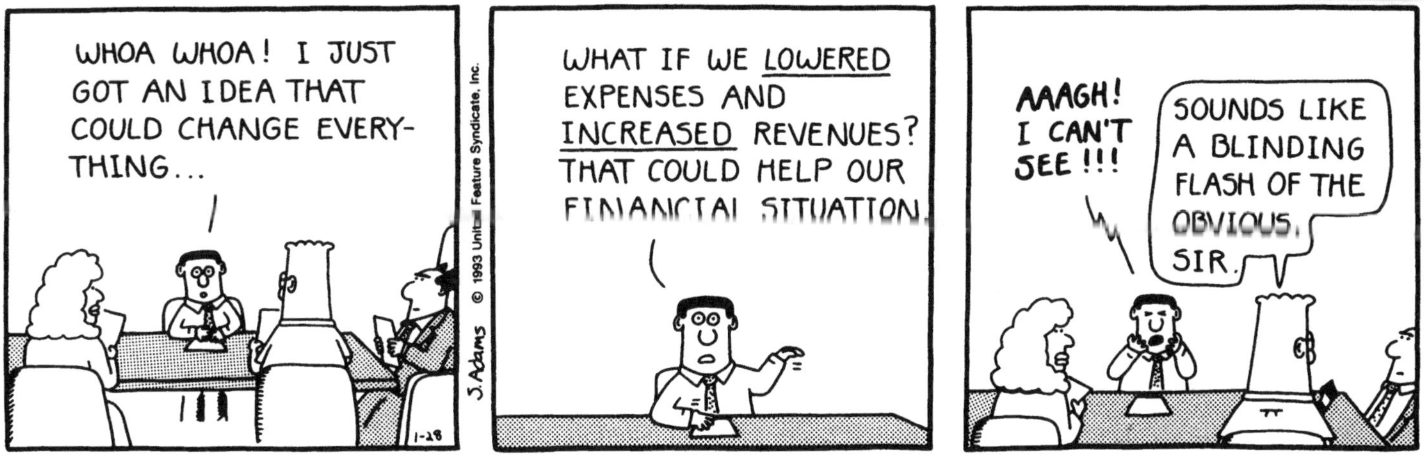

WHOA WHOA! I JUST GOT AN IDEA THAT COULD CHANGE EVERYTHING...
1-28
S. Adams © 1993 United Feature Syndicate, Inc.
WHAT IF WE LOWERED EXPENSES AND INCREASED REVENUES? THAT COULD HELP OUR FINANCIAL SITUATION.
AAAGH! I CAN'T SEE!!!
SOUNDS LIKE A BLINDING FLASH OF THE OBVIOUS, SIR.

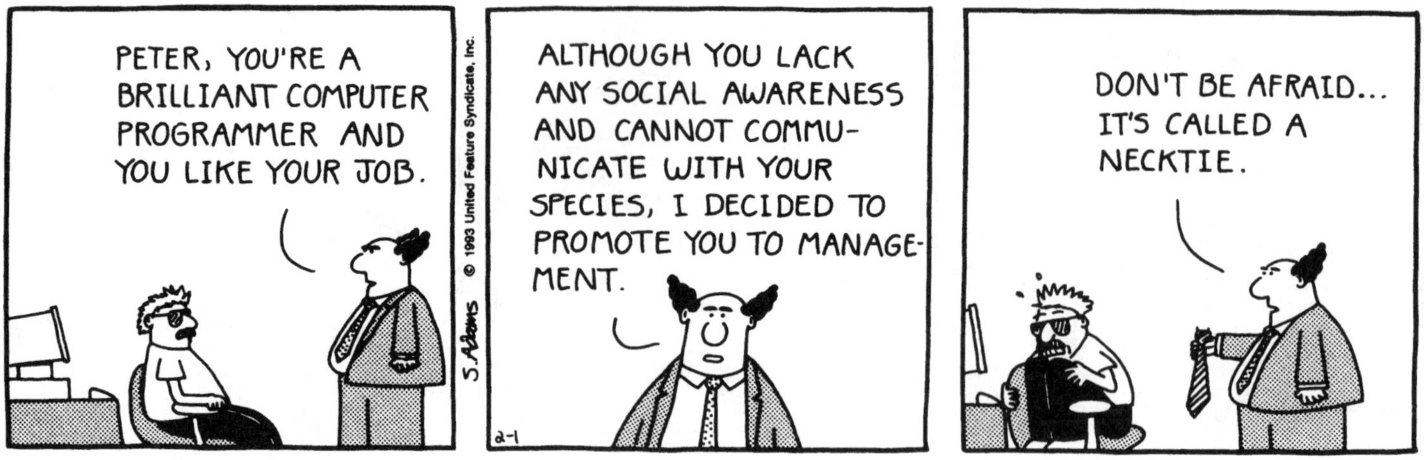
PETER, YOU'RE A BRILLIANT COMPUTER PROGRAMMER AND YOU LIKE YOUR JOB.
S. Adams © 1993 United Feature Syndicate, Inc.
ALTHOUGH YOU LACK ANY SOCIAL AWARENESS AND CANNOT COMMUNICATE WITH YOUR SPECIES, I DECIDED TO PROMOTE YOU TO MANAGEMENT.
2-1
DON'T BE AFRAID... IT'S CALLED A NECKTIE.

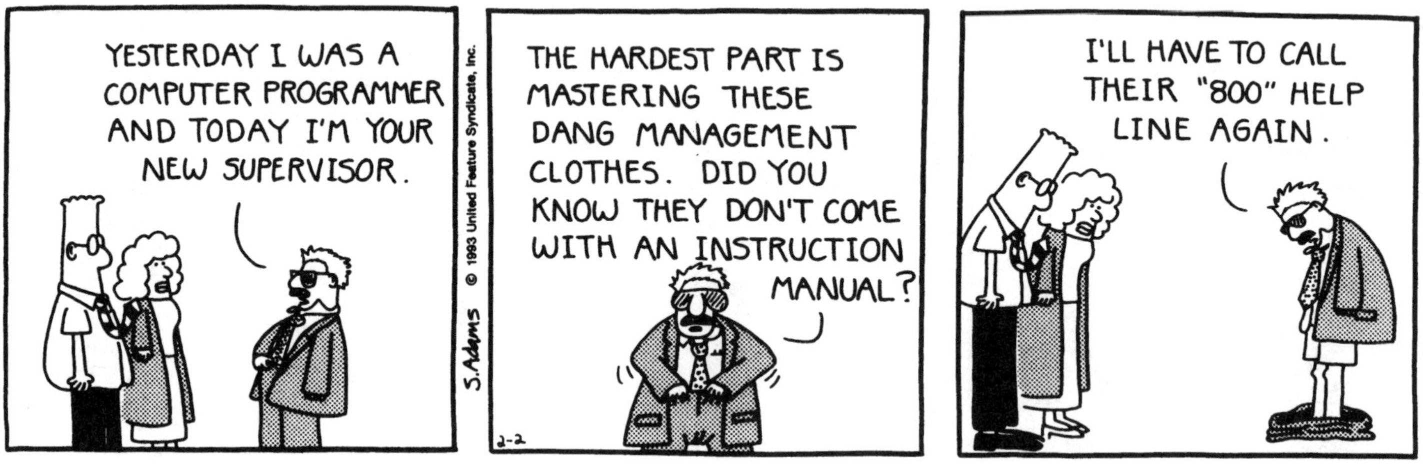
YESTERDAY I WAS A COMPUTER PROGRAMMER AND TODAY I'M YOUR NEW SUPERVISOR.
S. Adams © 1993 United Feature Syndicate, Inc.
THE HARDEST PART IS MASTERING THESE DANG MANAGEMENT CLOTHES. DID YOU KNOW THEY DON'T COME WITH AN INSTRUCTION MANUAL?
2-2
I'LL HAVE TO CALL THEIR "800" HELP LINE AGAIN.

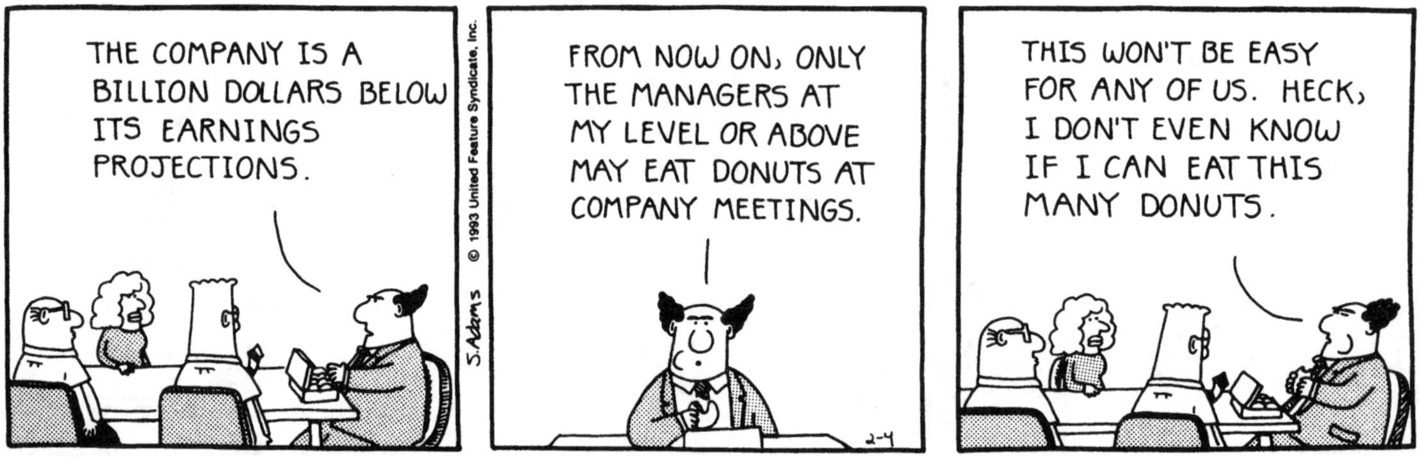
THE COMPANY IS A BILLION DOLLARS BELOW ITS EARNINGS PROJECTIONS.
S. Adams © 1993 United Feature Syndicate, Inc.
FROM NOW ON, ONLY THE MANAGERS AT MY LEVEL OR ABOVE MAY EAT DONUTS AT COMPANY MEETINGS.
2-4
THIS WON'T BE EASY FOR ANY OF US. HECK, I DON'T EVEN KNOW IF I CAN EAT THIS MANY DONUTS.

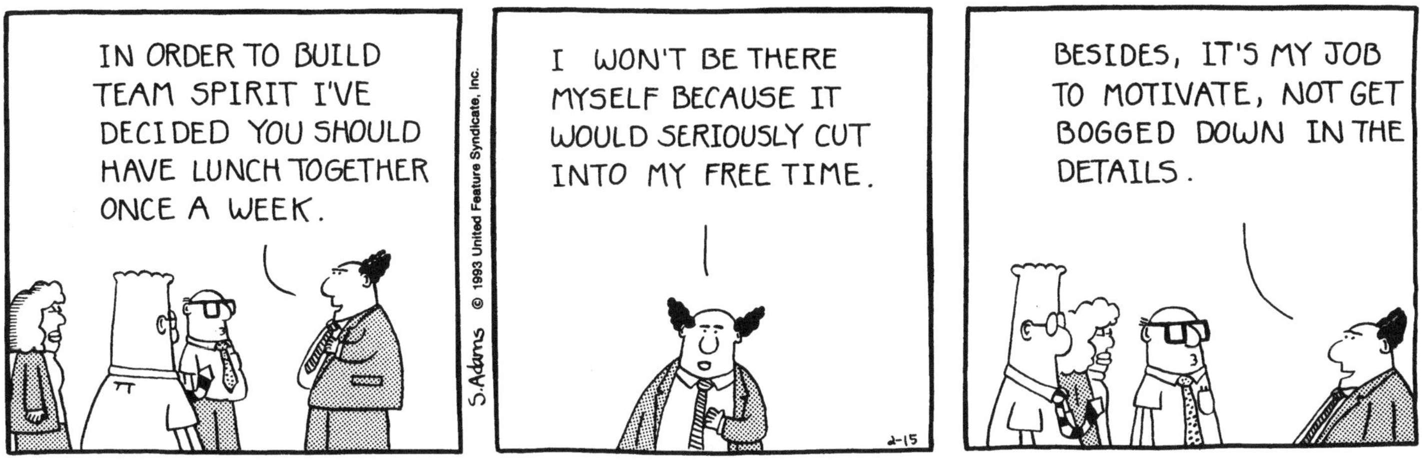
IN ORDER TO BUILD TEAM SPIRIT I'VE DECIDED YOU SHOULD HAVE LUNCH TOGETHER ONCE A WEEK.
S. Adams © 1993 United Feature Syndicate, Inc.
I WON'T BE THERE MYSELF BECAUSE IT WOULD SERIOUSLY CUT INTO MY FREE TIME.
2-15
BESIDES, IT'S MY JOB TO MOTIVATE, NOT GET BOGGED DOWN IN THE DETAILS.

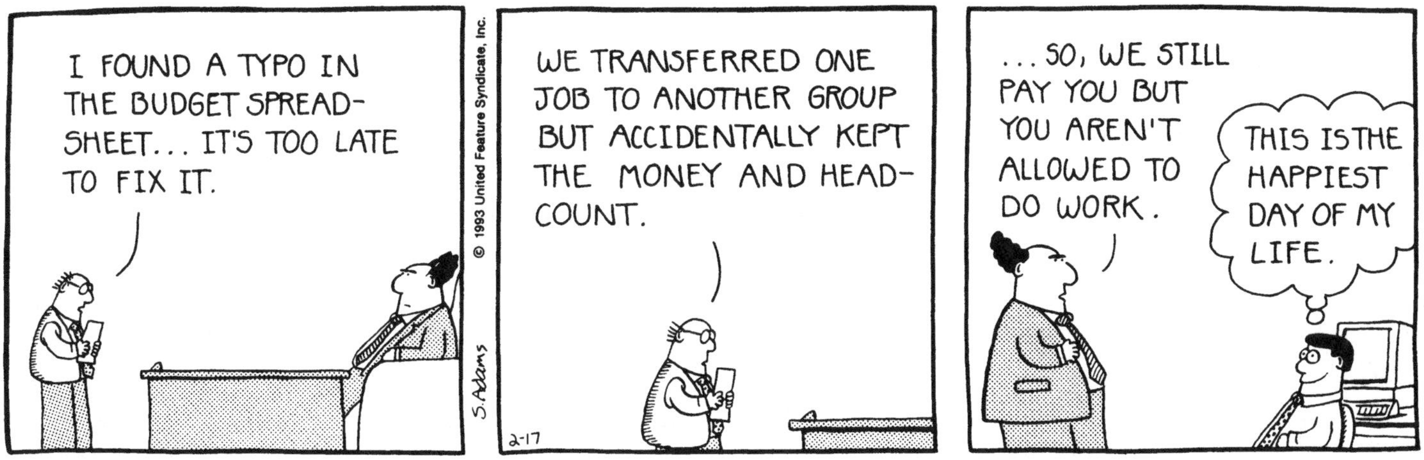
I FOUND A TYPO IN THE BUDGET SPREAD-SHEET... IT'S TOO LATE TO FIX IT.
S. Adams © 1993 United Feature Syndicate, Inc.
2-17
WE TRANSFERRED ONE JOB TO ANOTHER GROUP BUT ACCIDENTALLY KEPT THE MONEY AND HEAD-COUNT.
...SO, WE STILL PAY YOU BUT YOU AREN'T ALLOWED TO DO WORK.
THIS IS THE HAPPIEST DAY OF MY LIFE.

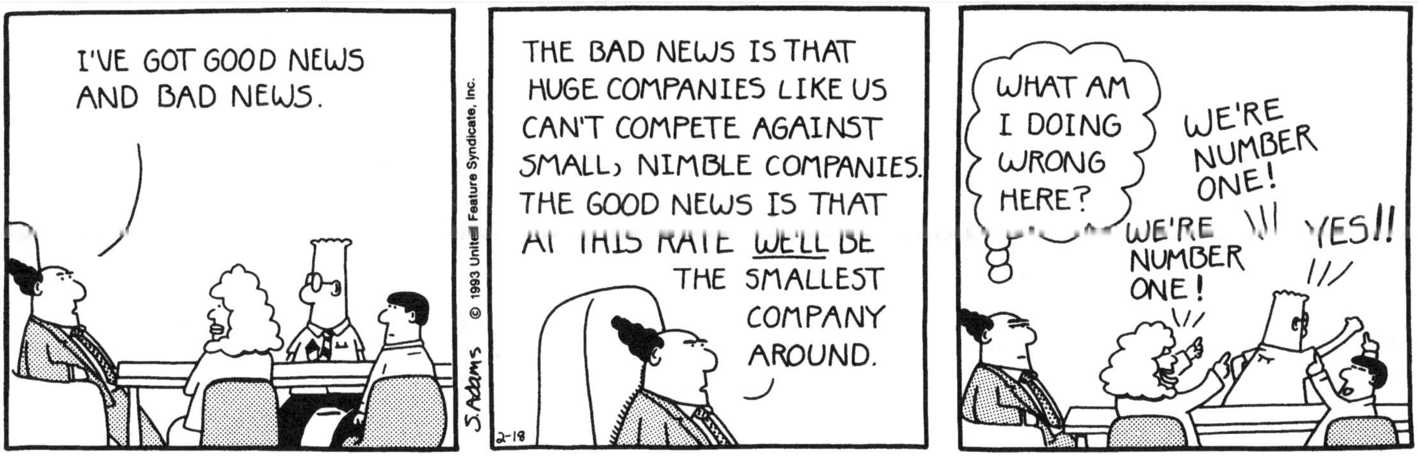
I'VE GOT GOOD NEWS AND BAD NEWS.
S. Adams © 1993 United Feature Syndicate, Inc.
2-18
THE BAD NEWS IS THAT HUGE COMPANIES LIKE US CAN'T COMPETE AGAINST SMALL, NIMBLE COMPANIES. THE GOOD NEWS IS THAT AT THIS RATE WE'LL BE THE SMALLEST COMPANY AROUND.
WHAT AM I DOING WRONG HERE?
WE'RE NUMBER ONE!
WE'RE NUMBER ONE!
YES!!

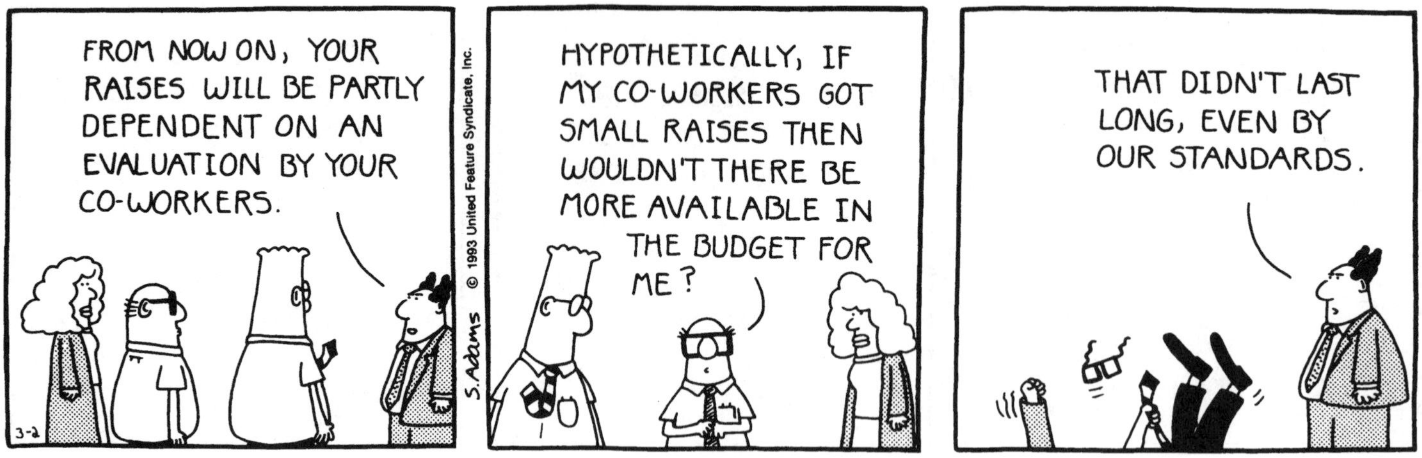
FROM NOW ON, YOUR RAISES WILL BE PARTLY DEPENDENT ON AN EVALUATION BY YOUR CO-WORKERS.
© 1993 United Feature Syndicate, Inc.
S. Adams
HYPOTHETICALLY, IF MY CO-WORKERS GOT SMALL RAISES THEN WOULDN'T THERE BE MORE AVAILABLE IN THE BUDGET FOR ME?
THAT DIDN'T LAST LONG, EVEN BY OUR STANDARDS.

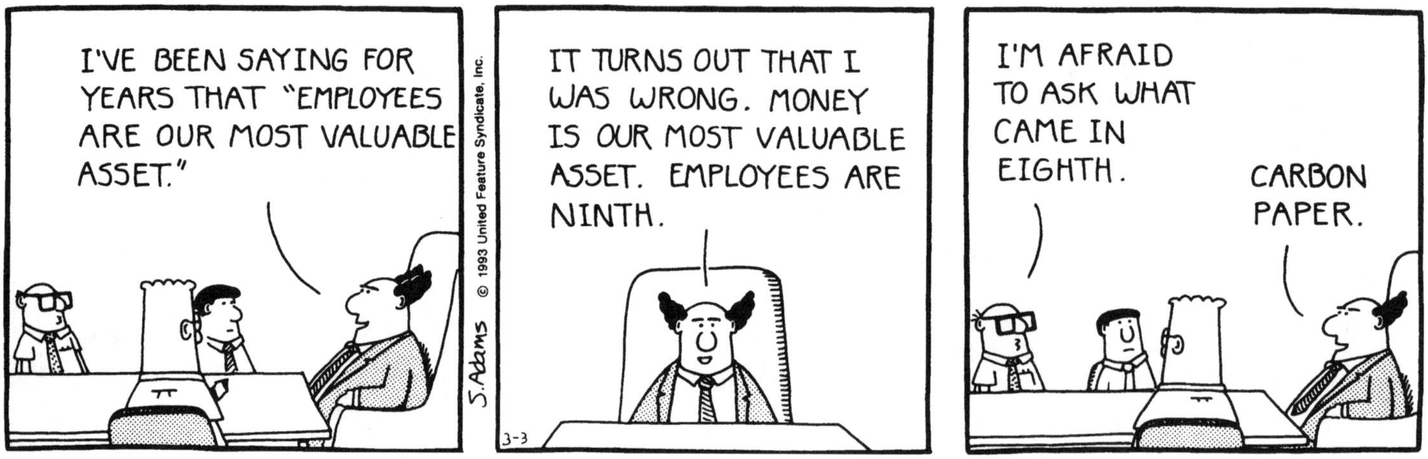
I'VE BEEN SAYING FOR YEARS THAT "EMPLOYEES ARE OUR MOST VALUABLE ASSET."
© 1993 United Feature Syndicate, Inc.
S. Adams
IT TURNS OUT THAT I WAS WRONG. MONEY IS OUR MOST VALUABLE ASSET. EMPLOYEES ARE NINTH.
I'M AFRAID TO ASK WHAT CAME IN EIGHTH.
CARBON PAPER.

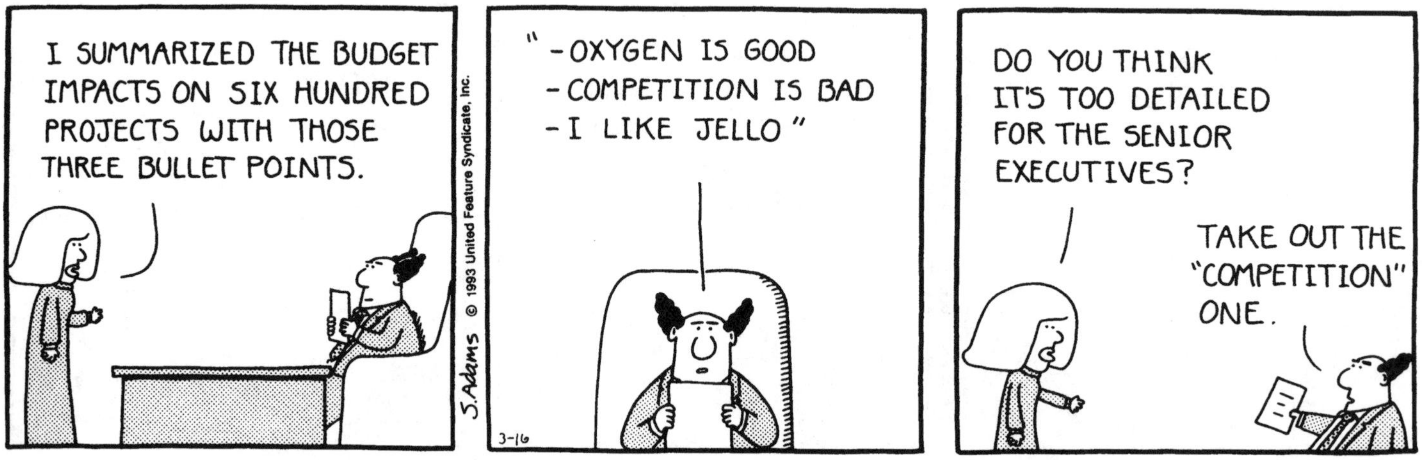
I SUMMARIZED THE BUDGET IMPACTS ON SIX HUNDRED PROJECTS WITH THOSE THREE BULLET POINTS.
© 1993 United Feature Syndicate, Inc.
S. Adams
" -OXYGEN IS GOOD
-COMPETITION IS BAD
-I LIKE JELLO "
DO YOU THINK IT'S TOO DETAILED FOR THE SENIOR EXECUTIVES?
TAKE OUT THE "COMPETITION" ONE.

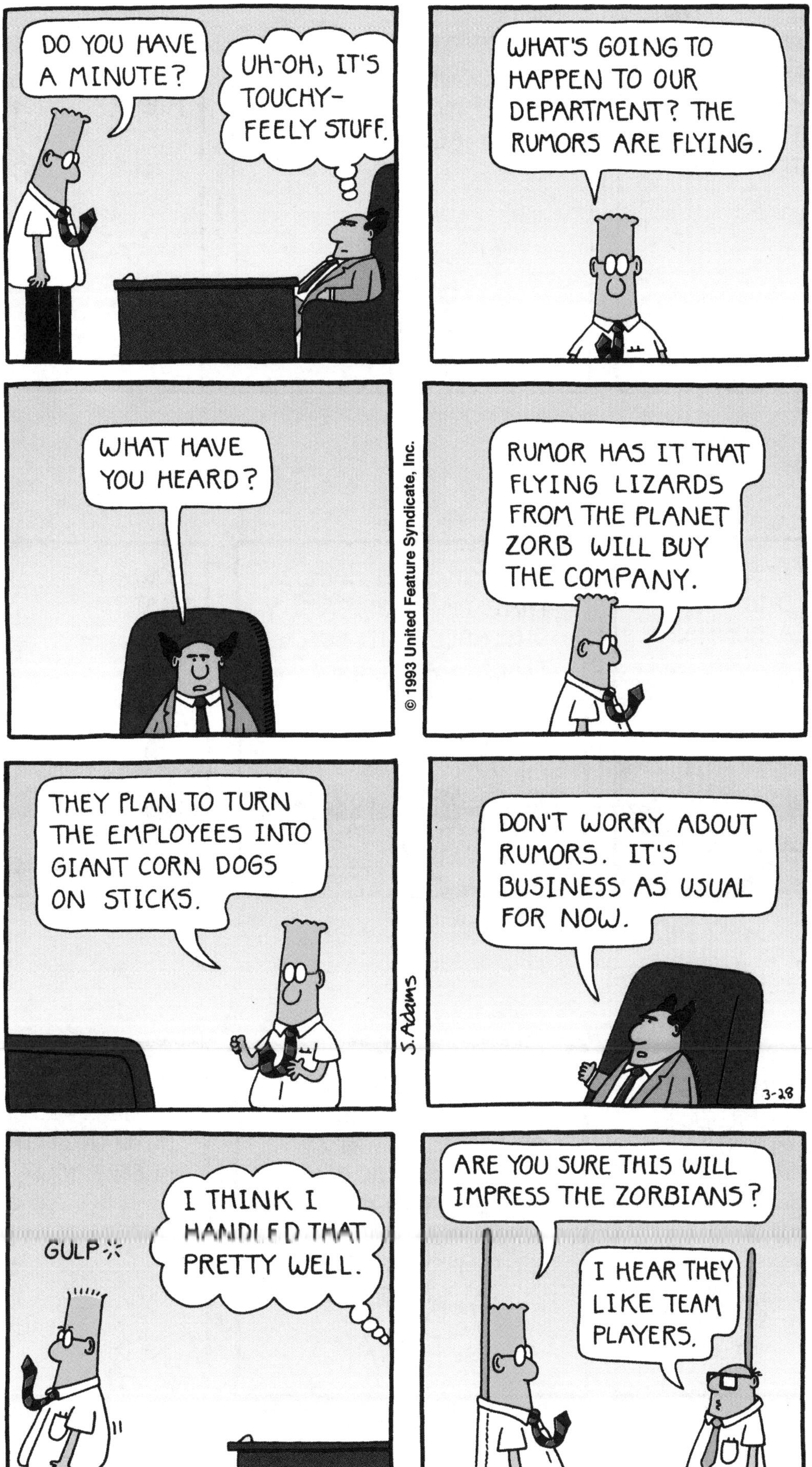
DO YOU HAVE A MINUTE?
UH-OH, IT'S TOUCHY-FEELY STUFF.
WHAT'S GOING TO HAPPEN TO OUR DEPARTMENT? THE RUMORS ARE FLYING.
WHAT HAVE YOU HEARD?
© 1993 United Feature Syndicate, Inc.
RUMOR HAS IT THAT FLYING LIZARDS FROM THE PLANET ZORB WILL BUY THE COMPANY.
THEY PLAN TO TURN THE EMPLOYEES INTO GIANT CORN DOGS ON STICKS.
S. Adams
DON'T WORRY ABOUT RUMORS. IT'S BUSINESS AS USUAL FOR NOW.
3-28
GULP
I THINK I HANDLED THAT PRETTY WELL.
ARE YOU SURE THIS WILL IMPRESS THE ZORBIANS?
I HEAR THEY LIKE TEAM PLAYERS.

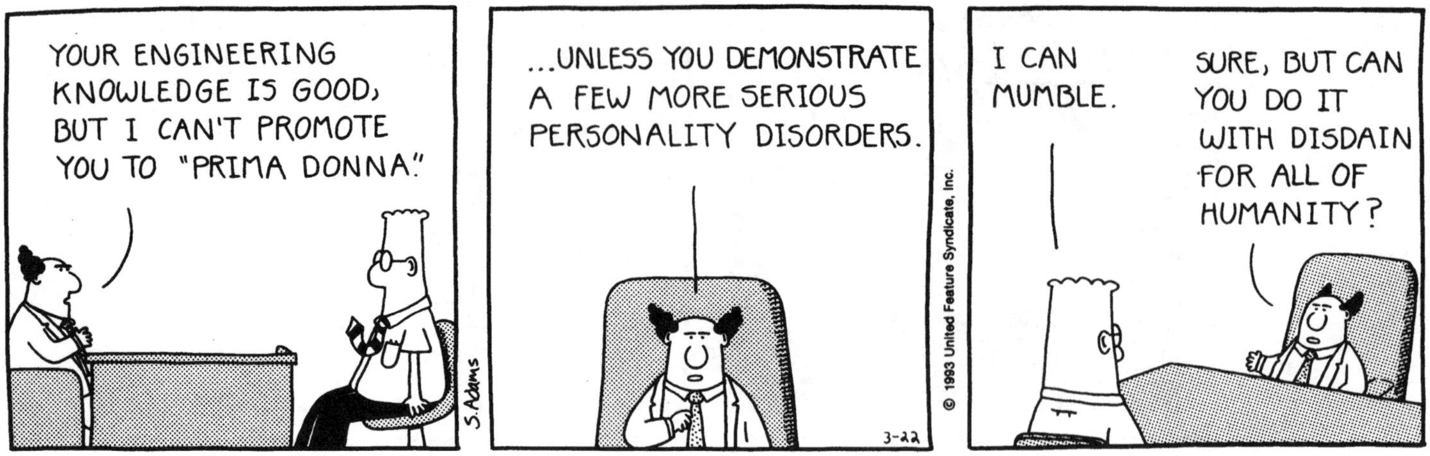
YOUR ENGINEERING KNOWLEDGE IS GOOD, BUT I CAN'T PROMOTE YOU TO "PRIMA DONNA."
S. Adams
...UNLESS YOU DEMONSTRATE A FEW MORE SERIOUS PERSONALITY DISORDERS.
3-22
© 1993 United Feature Syndicate, Inc.
I CAN MUMBLE.
SURE, BUT CAN YOU DO IT WITH DISDAIN FOR ALL OF HUMANITY?

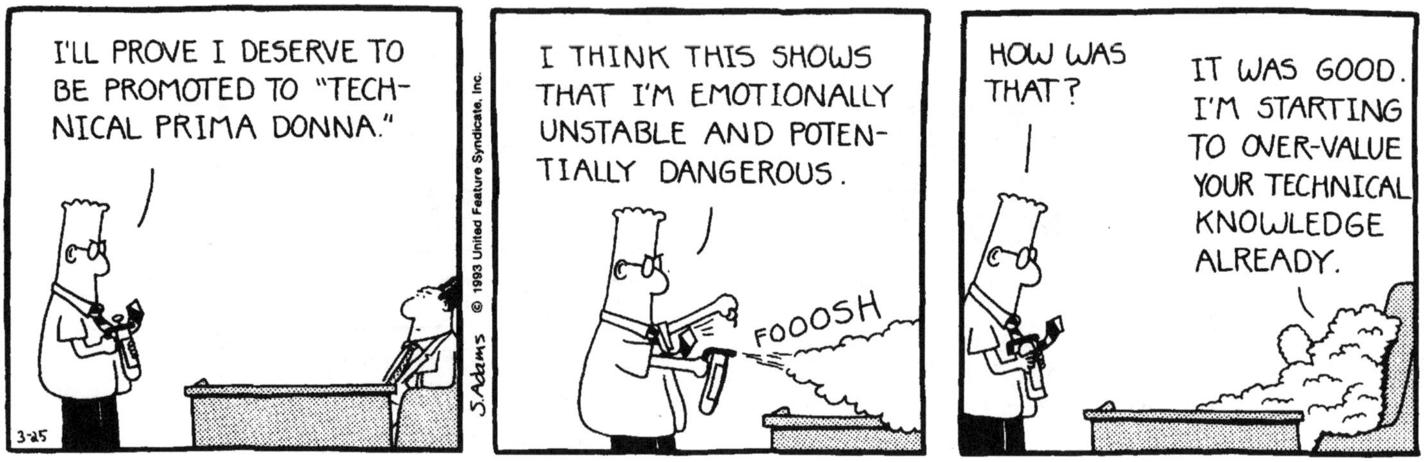
I'LL PROVE I DESERVE TO BE PROMOTED TO "TECHNICAL PRIMA DONNA."
3-25
S. Adams
© 1993 United Feature Syndicate, Inc.
I THINK THIS SHOWS THAT I'M EMOTIONALLY UNSTABLE AND POTENTIALLY DANGEROUS.
FOOOSH
HOW WAS THAT?
IT WAS GOOD. I'M STARTING TO OVER-VALUE YOUR TECHNICAL KNOWLEDGE ALREADY.

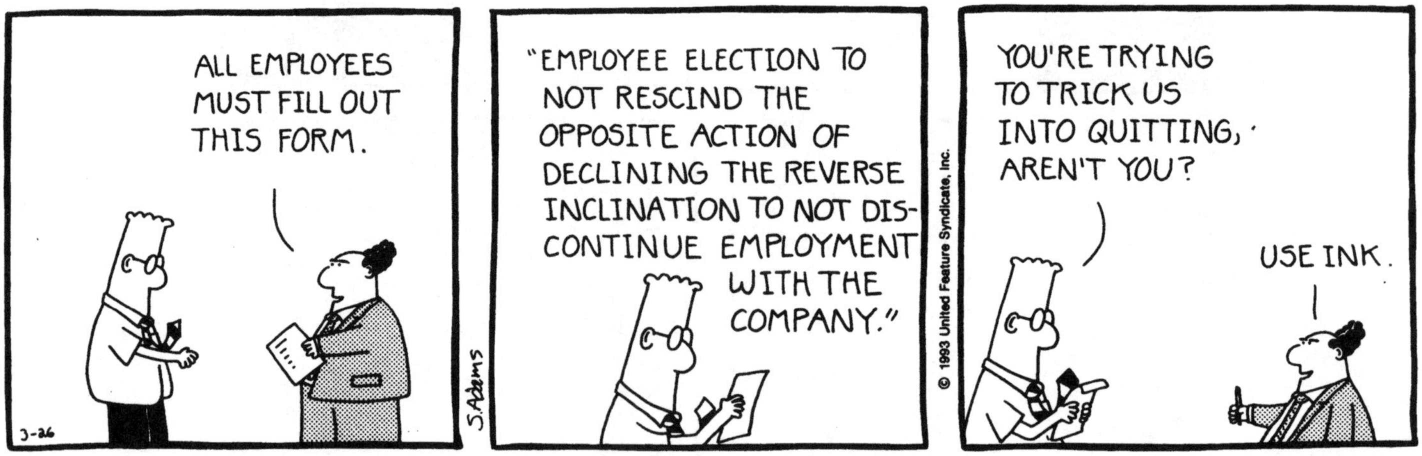
ALL EMPLOYEES MUST FILL OUT THIS FORM.
3-26
S. Adams
"EMPLOYEE ELECTION TO NOT RESCIND THE OPPOSITE ACTION OF DECLINING THE REVERSE INCLINATION TO NOT DISCONTINUE EMPLOYMENT WITH THE COMPANY."
© 1993 United Feature Syndicate, Inc.
YOU'RE TRYING TO TRICK US INTO QUITTING, AREN'T YOU?
USE INK.

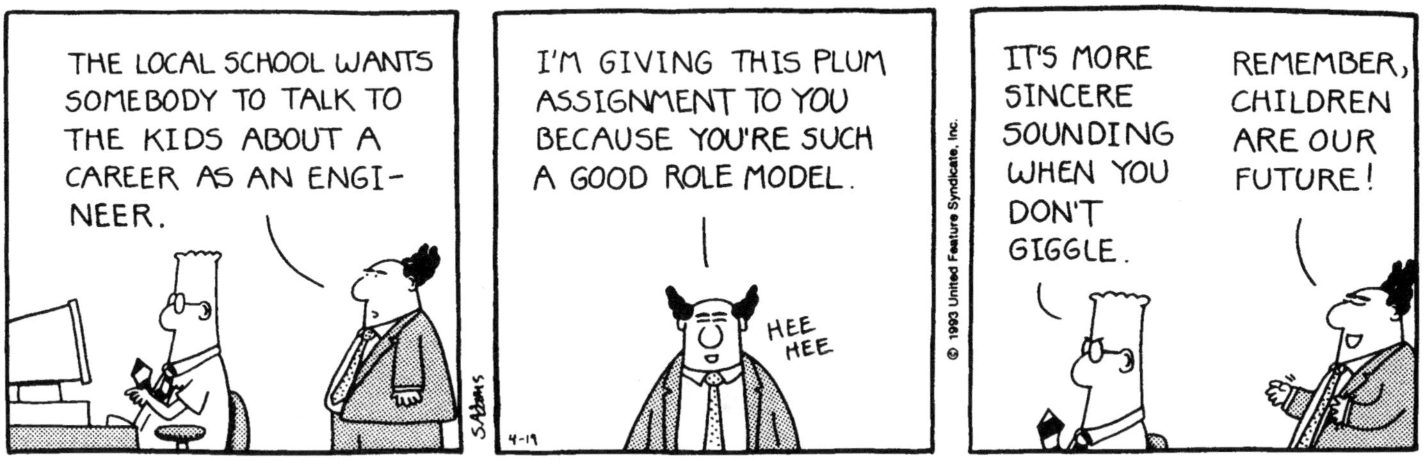
THE LOCAL SCHOOL WANTS SOMEBODY TO TALK TO THE KIDS ABOUT A CAREER AS AN ENGI-NEER.
S.Adams
4-19
I'M GIVING THIS PLUM ASSIGNMENT TO YOU BECAUSE YOU'RE SUCH A GOOD ROLE MODEL.
HEE HEE
© 1993 United Feature Syndicate, Inc.
IT'S MORE SINCERE SOUNDING WHEN YOU DON'T GIGGLE.
REMEMBER, CHILDREN ARE OUR FUTURE!

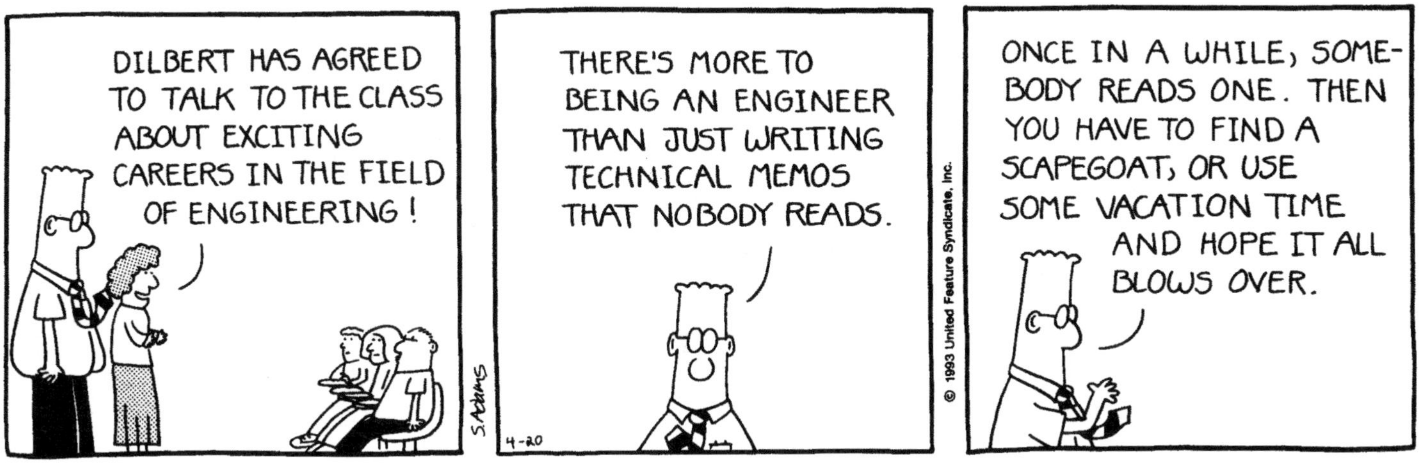
DILBERT HAS AGREED TO TALK TO THE CLASS ABOUT EXCITING CAREERS IN THE FIELD OF ENGINEERING!
S.Adams
4-20
THERE'S MORE TO BEING AN ENGINEER THAN JUST WRITING TECHNICAL MEMOS THAT NOBODY READS.
© 1993 United Feature Syndicate, Inc.
ONCE IN A WHILE, SOME-BODY READS ONE. THEN YOU HAVE TO FIND A SCAPEGOAT, OR USE SOME VACATION TIME AND HOPE IT ALL BLOWS OVER.

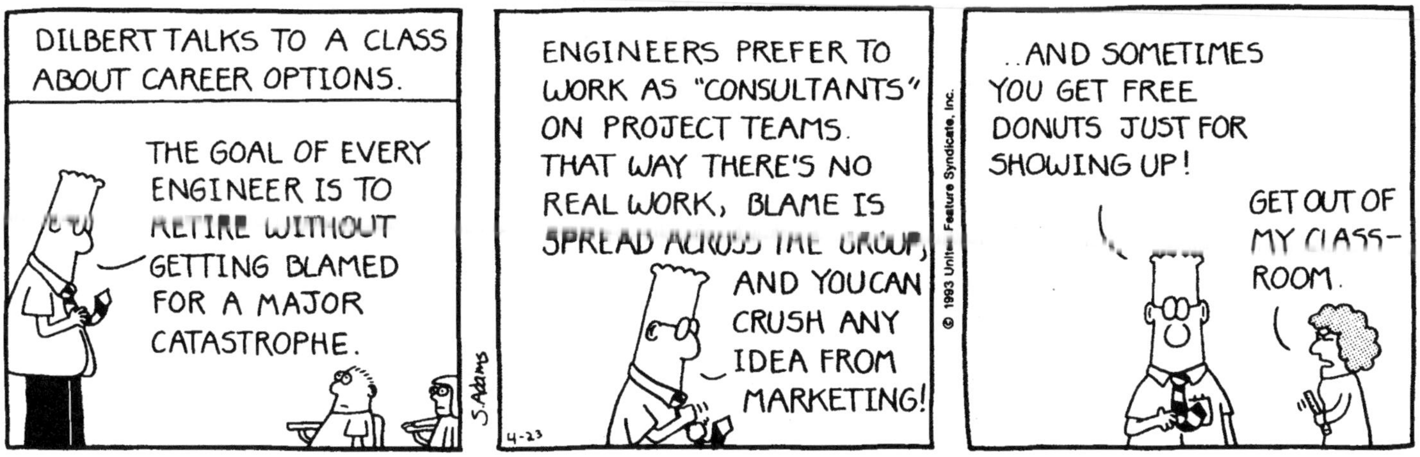
DILBERT TALKS TO A CLASS ABOUT CAREER OPTIONS.
THE GOAL OF EVERY ENGINEER IS TO RETIRE WITHOUT GETTING BLAMED FOR A MAJOR CATASTROPHE.
S.Adams
4-23
ENGINEERS PREFER TO WORK AS "CONSULTANTS" ON PROJECT TEAMS. THAT WAY THERE'S NO REAL WORK, BLAME IS SPREAD ACROSS THE GROUP, AND YOU CAN CRUSH ANY IDEA FROM MARKETING!
© 1993 United Feature Syndicate, Inc.
..AND SOMETIMES YOU GET FREE DONUTS JUST FOR SHOWING UP!
GET OUT OF MY CLASS-ROOM.

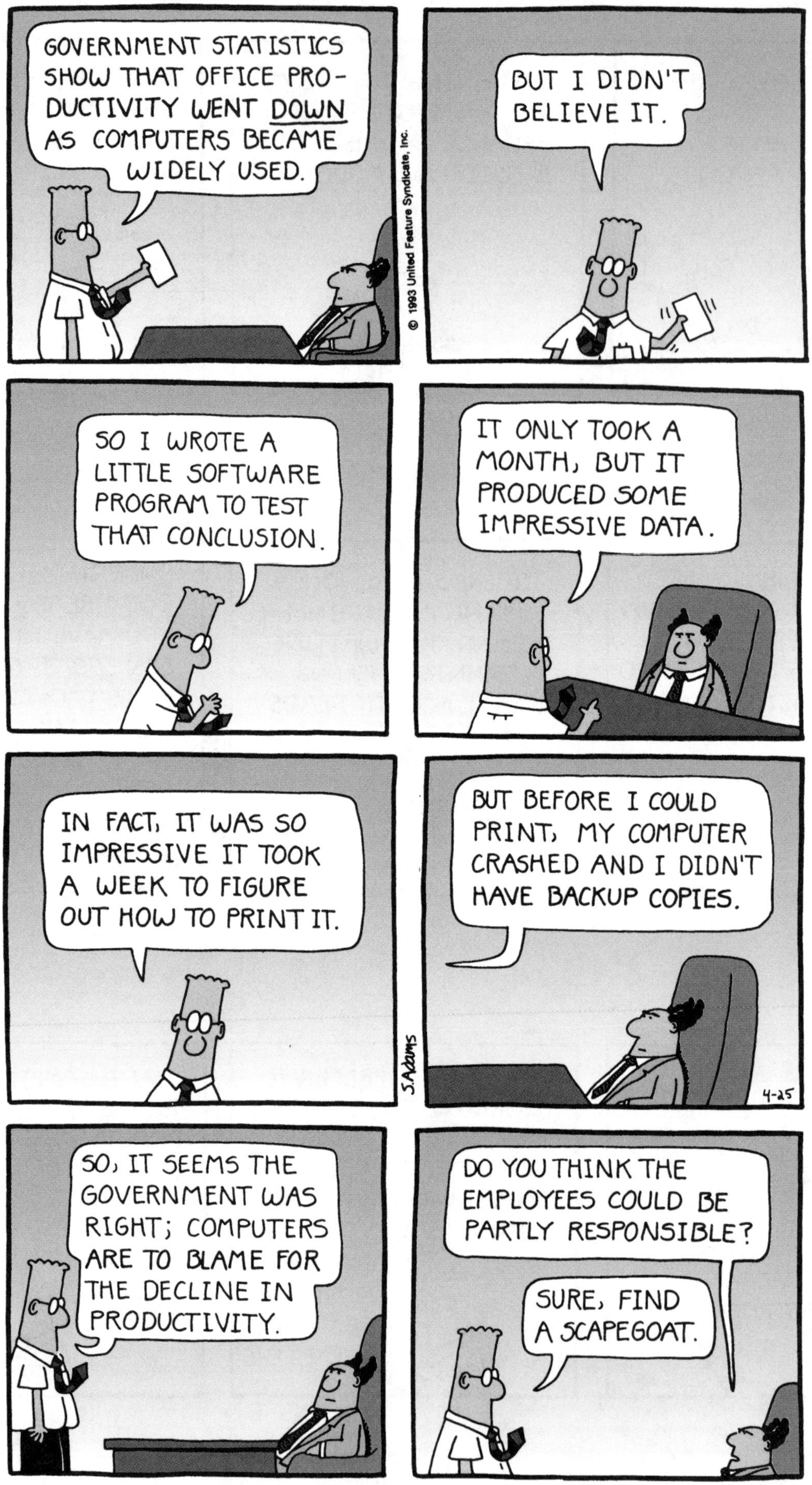
GOVERNMENT STATISTICS SHOW THAT OFFICE PRO- DUCTIVITY WENT DOWN AS COMPUTERS BECAME WIDELY USED.
© 1993 United Feature Syndicate, Inc.
BUT I DIDN'T BELIEVE IT.
SO I WROTE A LITTLE SOFTWARE PROGRAM TO TEST THAT CONCLUSION.
IT ONLY TOOK A MONTH, BUT IT PRODUCED SOME IMPRESSIVE DATA.
IN FACT, IT WAS SO IMPRESSIVE IT TOOK A WEEK TO FIGURE OUT HOW TO PRINT IT.
S. Adams
BUT BEFORE I COULD PRINT, MY COMPUTER CRASHED AND I DIDN'T HAVE BACKUP COPIES.
4-25
SO, IT SEEMS THE GOVERNMENT WAS RIGHT; COMPUTERS ARE TO BLAME FOR THE DECLINE IN PRODUCTIVITY.
DO YOU THINK THE EMPLOYEES COULD BE PARTLY RESPONSIBLE?
SURE, FIND A SCAPEGOAT.

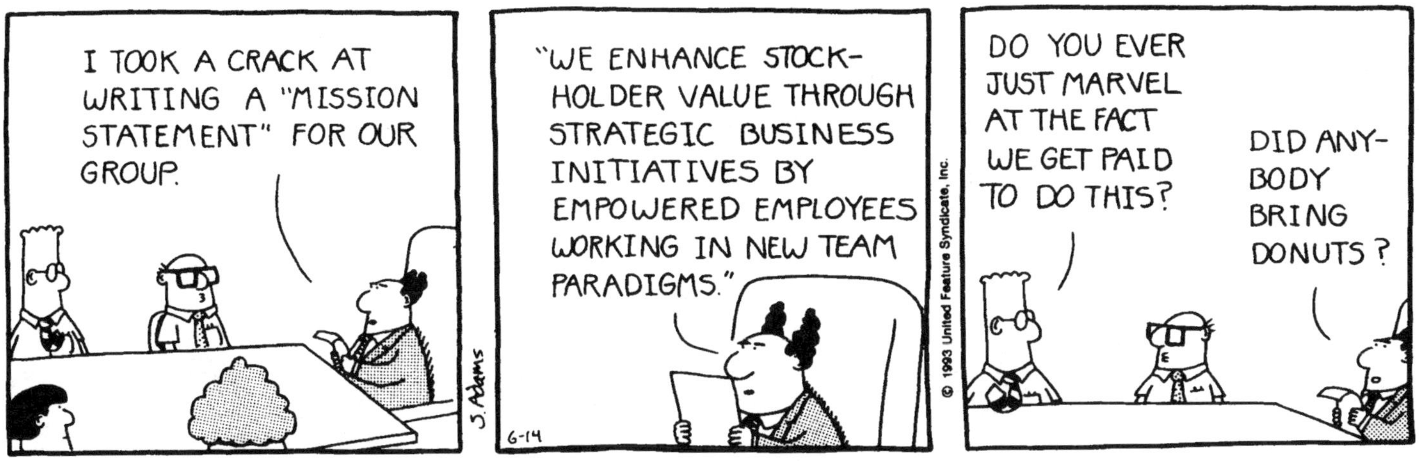
I TOOK A CRACK AT WRITING A "MISSION STATEMENT" FOR OUR GROUP.
"WE ENHANCE STOCKHOLDER VALUE THROUGH STRATEGIC BUSINESS INITIATIVES BY EMPOWERED EMPLOYEES WORKING IN NEW TEAM PARADIGMS."
DO YOU EVER JUST MARVEL AT THE FACT WE GET PAID TO DO THIS?
DID ANYBODY BRING DONUTS?
S. Adams
6-14
© 1993 United Feature Syndicate, Inc.

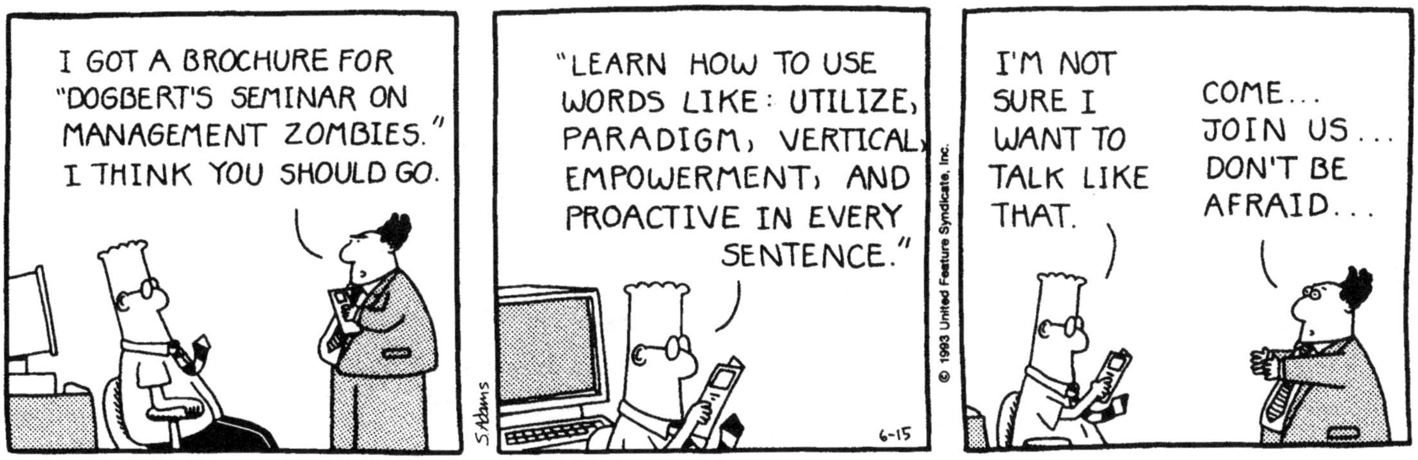
I GOT A BROCHURE FOR "DOGBERT'S SEMINAR ON MANAGEMENT ZOMBIES." I THINK YOU SHOULD GO.
"LEARN HOW TO USE WORDS LIKE: UTILIZE, PARADIGM, VERTICAL, EMPOWERMENT, AND PROACTIVE IN EVERY SENTENCE."
I'M NOT SURE I WANT TO TALK LIKE THAT.
COME... JOIN US... DON'T BE AFRAID...
S. Adams
6-15
© 1993 United Feature Syndicate, Inc.

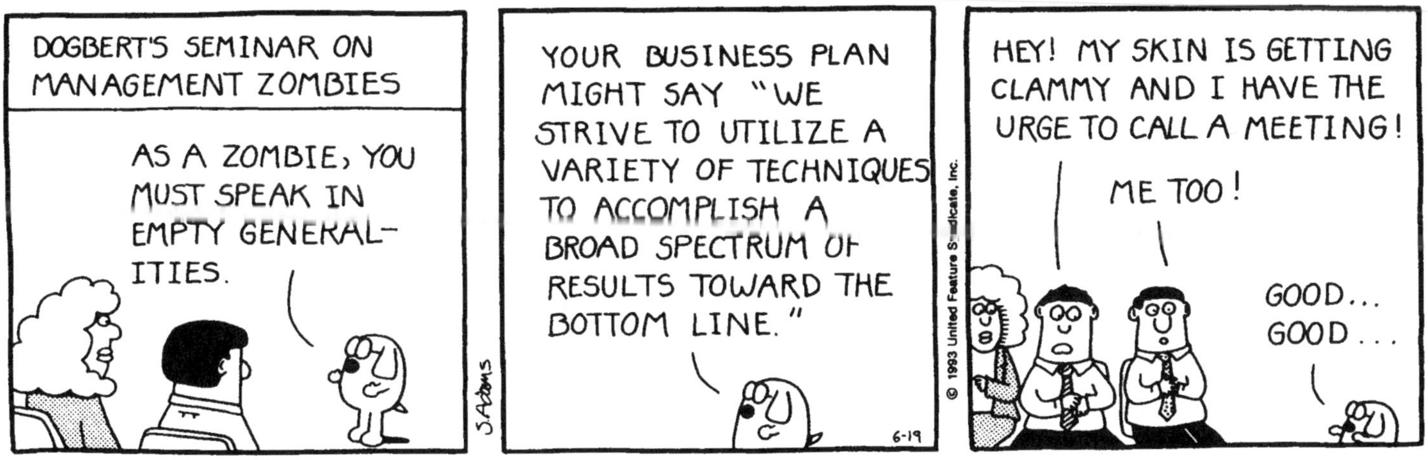
DOGBERT'S SEMINAR ON MANAGEMENT ZOMBIES
AS A ZOMBIE, YOU MUST SPEAK IN EMPTY GENERALITIES.
YOUR BUSINESS PLAN MIGHT SAY "WE STRIVE TO UTILIZE A VARIETY OF TECHNIQUES TO ACCOMPLISH A BROAD SPECTRUM OF RESULTS TOWARD THE BOTTOM LINE."
HEY! MY SKIN IS GETTING CLAMMY AND I HAVE THE URGE TO CALL A MEETING!
ME TOO!
GOOD... GOOD...
S. Adams
6-19
© 1993 United Feature Syndicate, Inc.

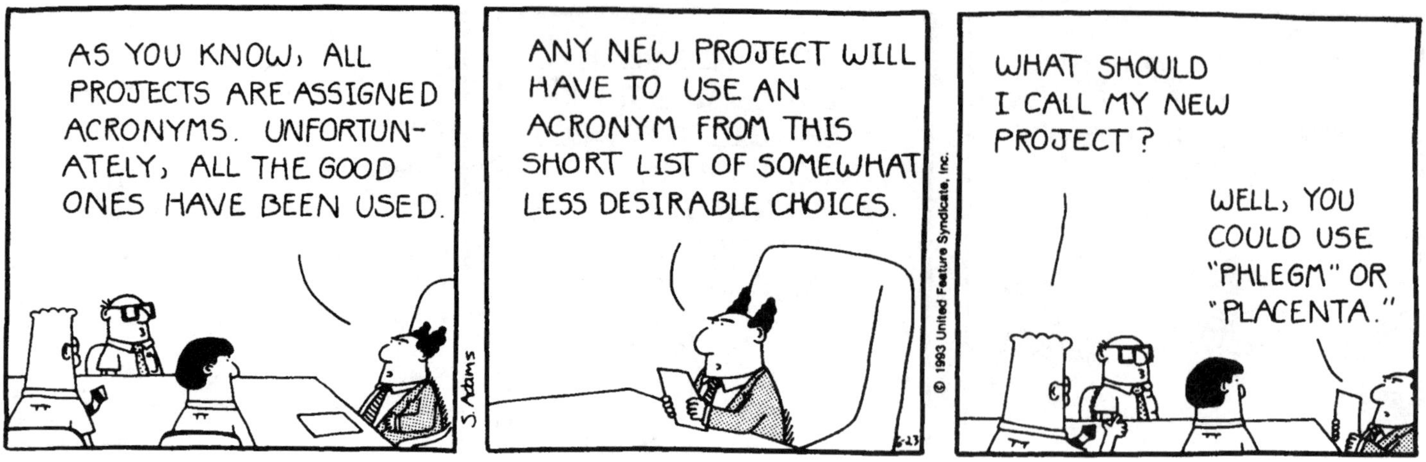
AS YOU KNOW, ALL PROJECTS ARE ASSIGNED ACRONYMS. UNFORTUNATELY, ALL THE GOOD ONES HAVE BEEN USED.
S. Adams
ANY NEW PROJECT WILL HAVE TO USE AN ACRONYM FROM THIS SHORT LIST OF SOMEWHAT LESS DESIRABLE CHOICES.
6-23
© 1993 United Feature Syndicate, Inc.
WHAT SHOULD I CALL MY NEW PROJECT?
WELL, YOU COULD USE "PHLEGM" OR "PLACENTA."

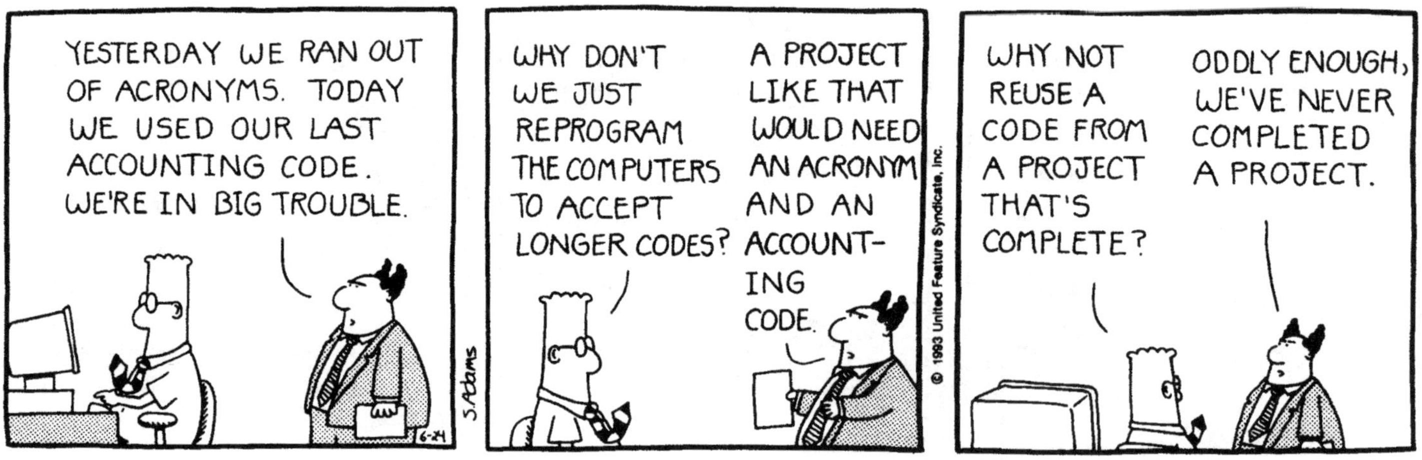
YESTERDAY WE RAN OUT OF ACRONYMS. TODAY WE USED OUR LAST ACCOUNTING CODE. WE'RE IN BIG TROUBLE.
6-24
S. Adams
WHY DON'T WE JUST REPROGRAM THE COMPUTERS TO ACCEPT LONGER CODES?
A PROJECT LIKE THAT WOULD NEED AN ACRONYM AND AN ACCOUNTING CODE.
© 1993 United Feature Syndicate, Inc.
WHY NOT REUSE A CODE FROM A PROJECT THAT'S COMPLETE?
ODDLY ENOUGH, WE'VE NEVER COMPLETED A PROJECT.

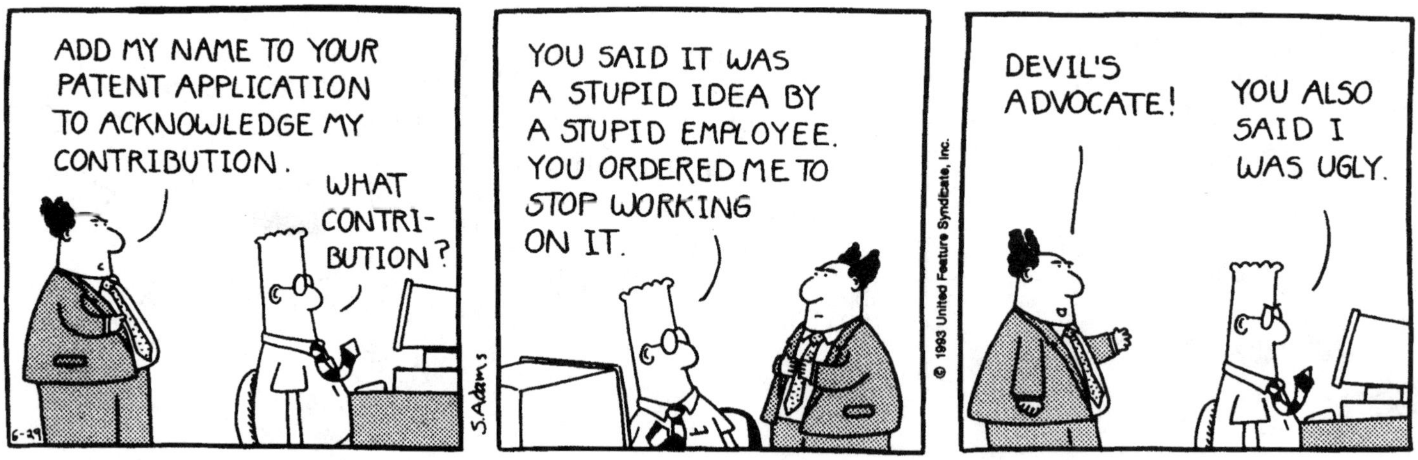
ADD MY NAME TO YOUR PATENT APPLICATION TO ACKNOWLEDGE MY CONTRIBUTION.
WHAT CONTRIBUTION?
6-29
S. Adams
YOU SAID IT WAS A STUPID IDEA BY A STUPID EMPLOYEE. YOU ORDERED ME TO STOP WORKING ON IT.
© 1993 United Feature Syndicate, Inc.
DEVIL'S ADVOCATE!
YOU ALSO SAID I WAS UGLY.

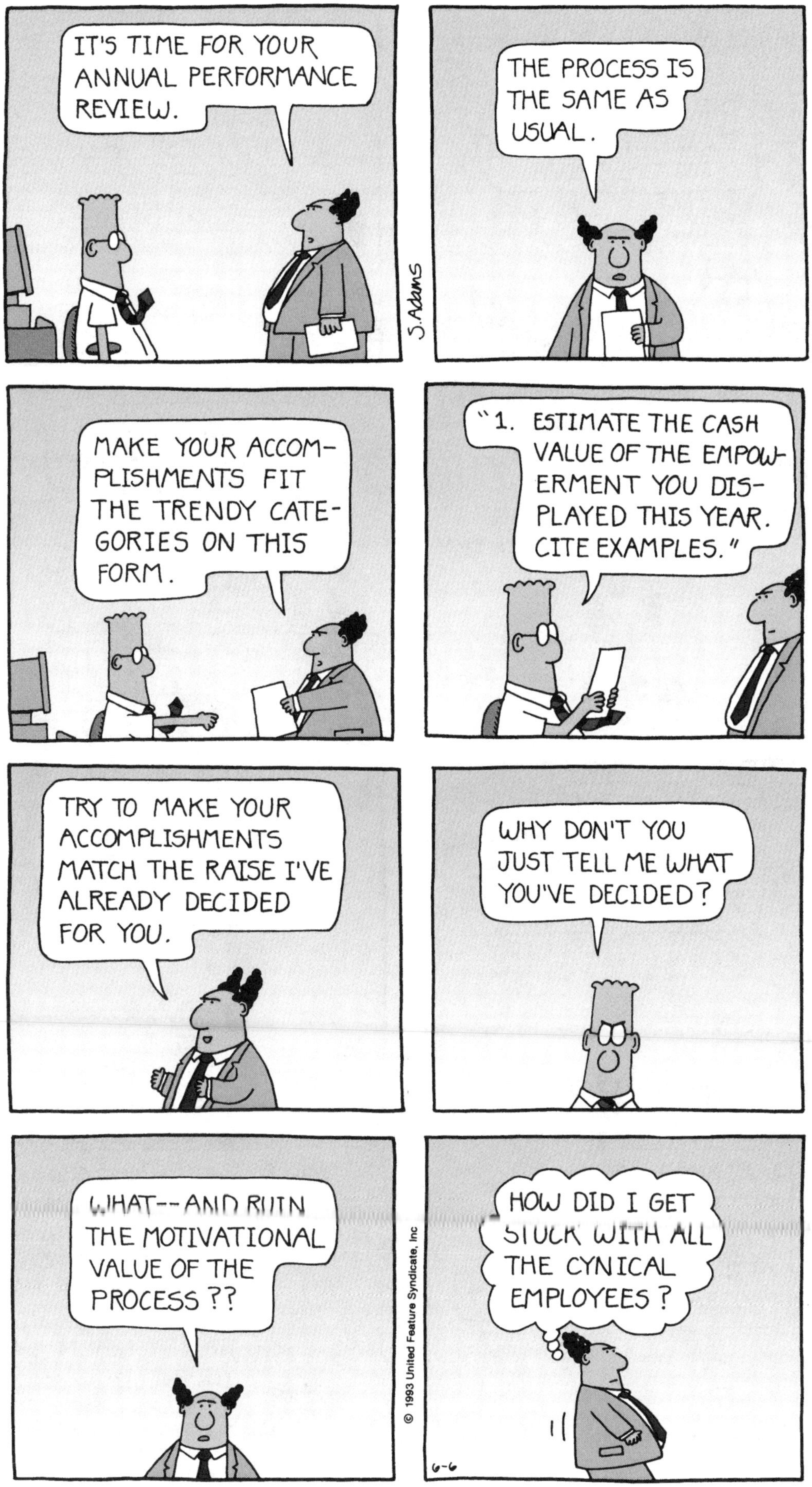
IT'S TIME FOR YOUR ANNUAL PERFORMANCE REVIEW.
S. Adams
THE PROCESS IS THE SAME AS USUAL.
MAKE YOUR ACCOMPLISHMENTS FIT THE TRENDY CATEGORIES ON THIS FORM.
"1. ESTIMATE THE CASH VALUE OF THE EMPOWERMENT YOU DISPLAYED THIS YEAR. CITE EXAMPLES."
TRY TO MAKE YOUR ACCOMPLISHMENTS MATCH THE RAISE I'VE ALREADY DECIDED FOR YOU.
WHY DON'T YOU JUST TELL ME WHAT YOU'VE DECIDED?
WHAT--AND RUIN THE MOTIVATIONAL VALUE OF THE PROCESS??
© 1993 United Feature Syndicate, Inc
HOW DID I GET STUCK WITH ALL THE CYNICAL EMPLOYEES?
6-6

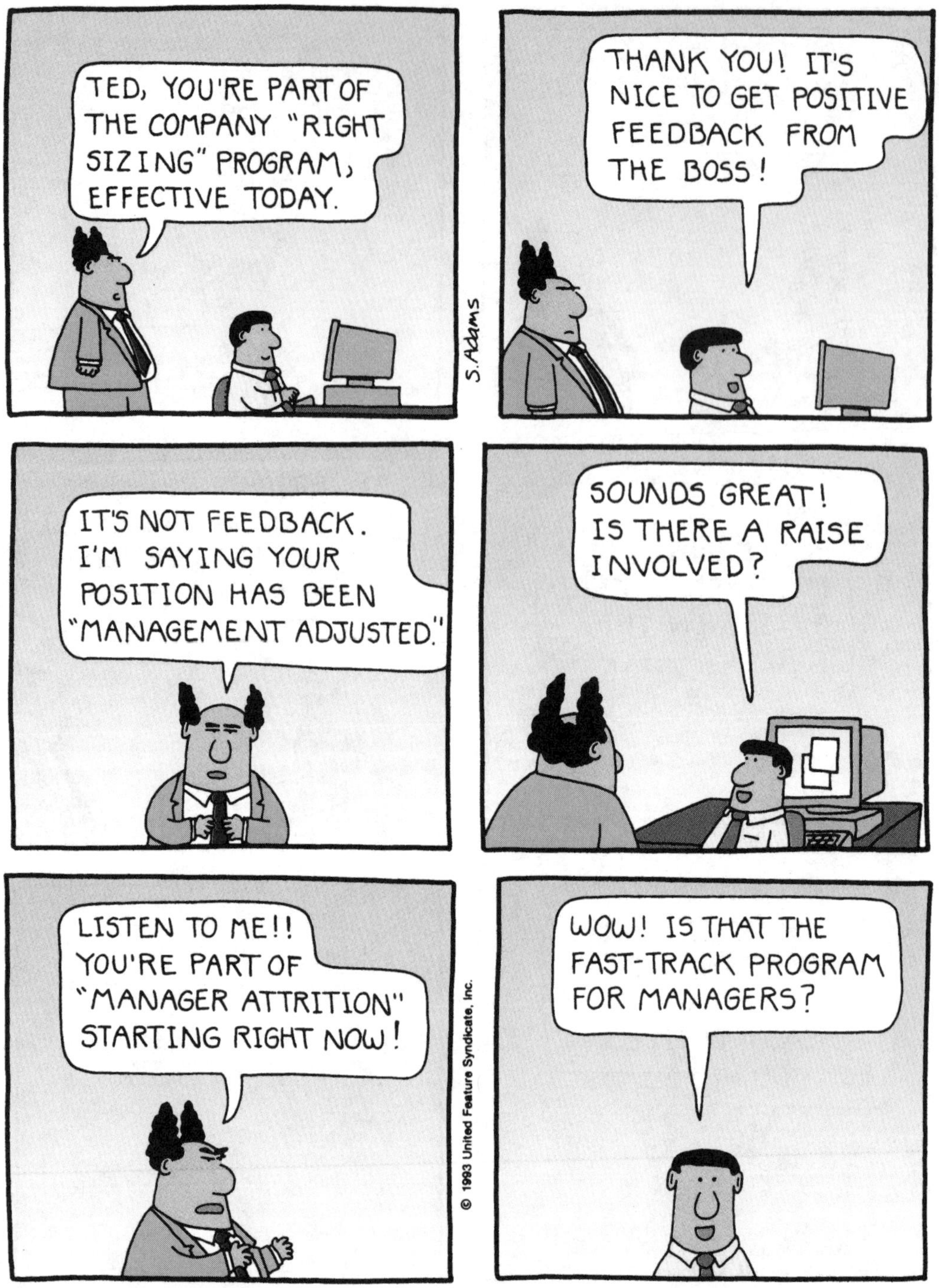
TED, YOU'RE PART OF THE COMPANY "RIGHT SIZING" PROGRAM, EFFECTIVE TODAY.
S. Adams
THANK YOU! IT'S NICE TO GET POSITIVE FEEDBACK FROM THE BOSS!
IT'S NOT FEEDBACK. I'M SAYING YOUR POSITION HAS BEEN "MANAGEMENT ADJUSTED."
SOUNDS GREAT! IS THERE A RAISE INVOLVED?
LISTEN TO ME!! YOU'RE PART OF "MANAGER ATTRITION" STARTING RIGHT NOW!
© 1993 United Feature Syndicate, Inc.
WOW! IS THAT THE FAST-TRACK PROGRAM FOR MANAGERS?

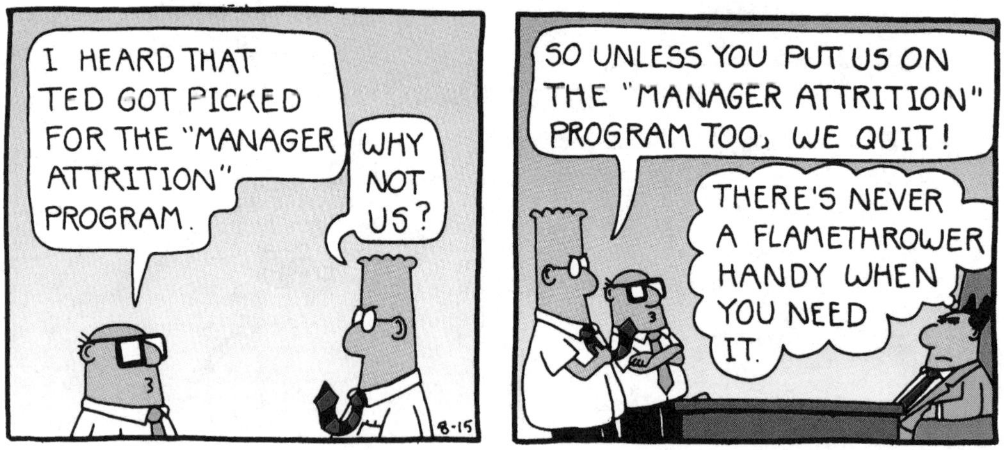
I HEARD THAT TED GOT PICKED FOR THE "MANAGER ATTRITION" PROGRAM.
WHY NOT US?
8-15
SO UNLESS YOU PUT US ON THE "MANAGER ATTRITION" PROGRAM TOO, WE QUIT!
THERE'S NEVER A FLAMETHROWER HANDY WHEN YOU NEED IT.

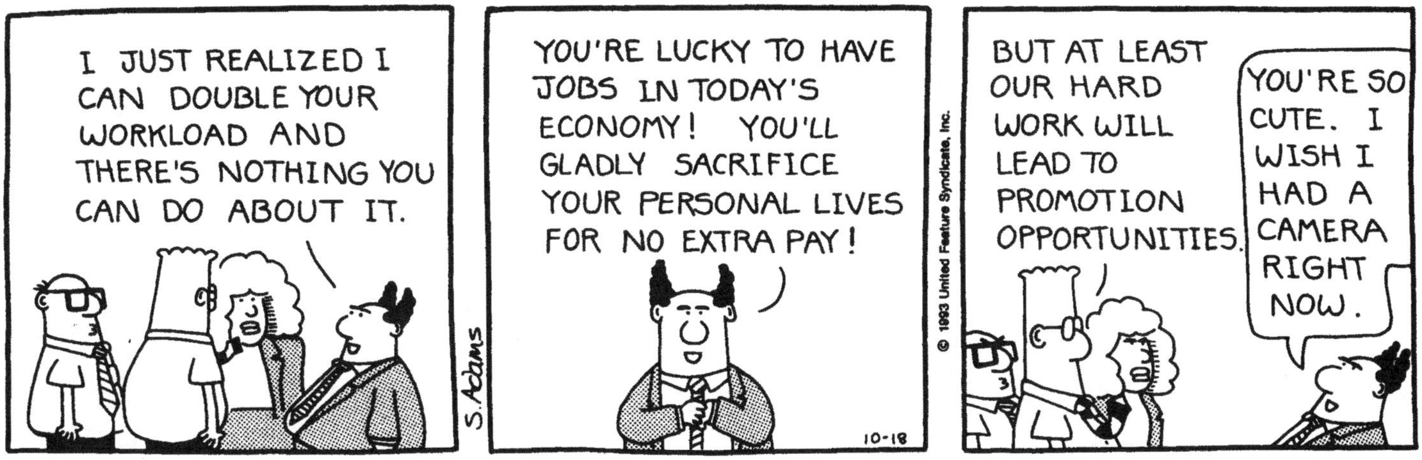
I JUST REALIZED I CAN DOUBLE YOUR WORKLOAD AND THERE'S NOTHING YOU CAN DO ABOUT IT.
S. ADAMS
YOU'RE LUCKY TO HAVE JOBS IN TODAY'S ECONOMY! YOU'LL GLADLY SACRIFICE YOUR PERSONAL LIVES FOR NO EXTRA PAY!
10-18
© 1993 United Feature Syndicate, Inc.
BUT AT LEAST OUR HARD WORK WILL LEAD TO PROMOTION OPPORTUNITIES.
YOU'RE SO CUTE. I WISH I HAD A CAMERA RIGHT NOW.

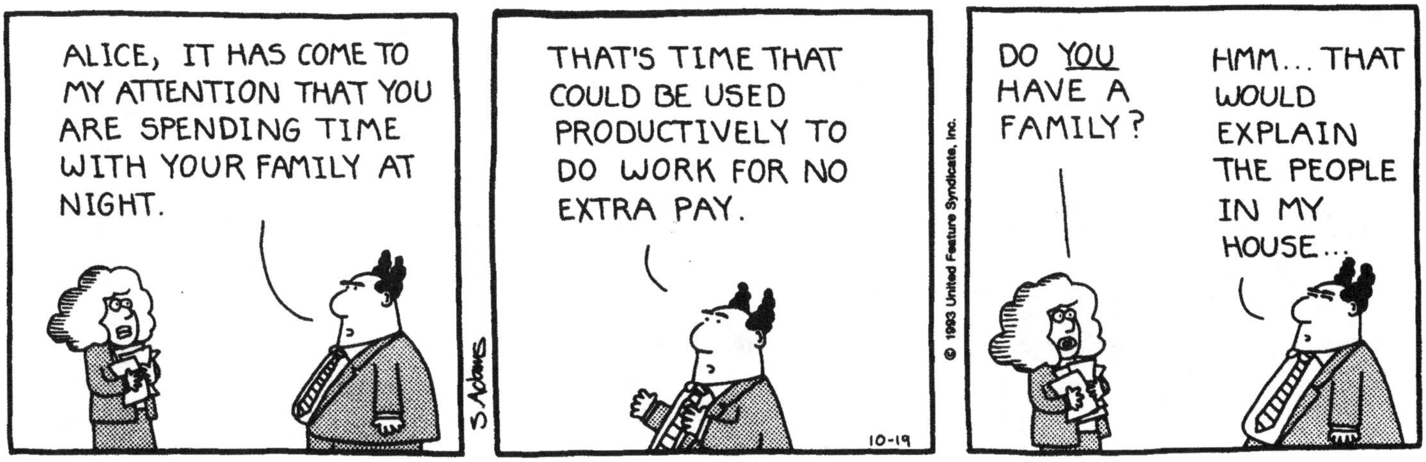
ALICE, IT HAS COME TO MY ATTENTION THAT YOU ARE SPENDING TIME WITH YOUR FAMILY AT NIGHT.
S. ADAMS
THAT'S TIME THAT COULD BE USED PRODUCTIVELY TO DO WORK FOR NO EXTRA PAY.
10-19
© 1993 United Feature Syndicate, Inc.
DO YOU HAVE A FAMILY?
HMM... THAT WOULD EXPLAIN THE PEOPLE IN MY HOUSE...

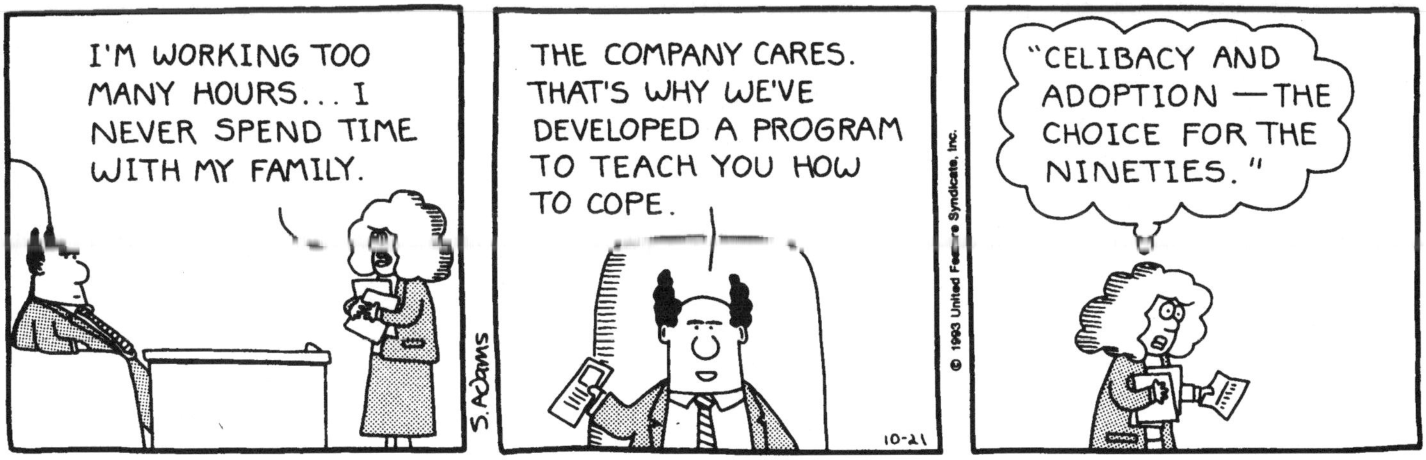
I'M WORKING TOO MANY HOURS... I NEVER SPEND TIME WITH MY FAMILY.
S. ADAMS
THE COMPANY CARES. THAT'S WHY WE'VE DEVELOPED A PROGRAM TO TEACH YOU HOW TO COPE.
10-21
© 1993 United Feature Syndicate, Inc.
"CELIBACY AND ADOPTION — THE CHOICE FOR THE NINETIES."

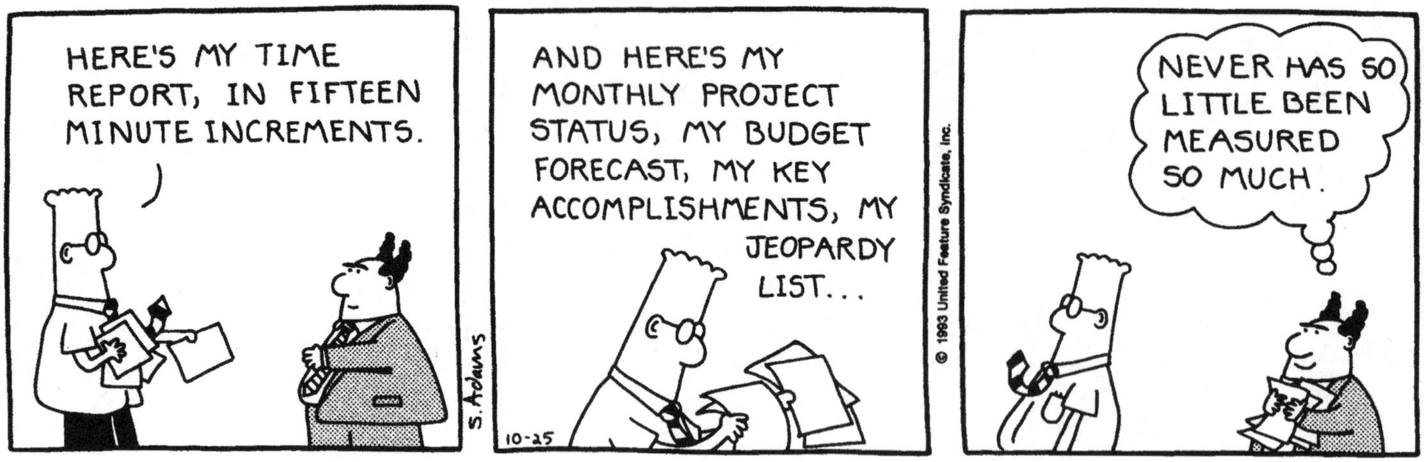
HERE'S MY TIME REPORT, IN FIFTEEN MINUTE INCREMENTS.
S. Adams
AND HERE'S MY MONTHLY PROJECT STATUS, MY BUDGET FORECAST, MY KEY ACCOMPLISHMENTS, MY JEOPARDY LIST...
10-25
© 1993 United Feature Syndicate, Inc.
NEVER HAS SO LITTLE BEEN MEASURED SO MUCH.

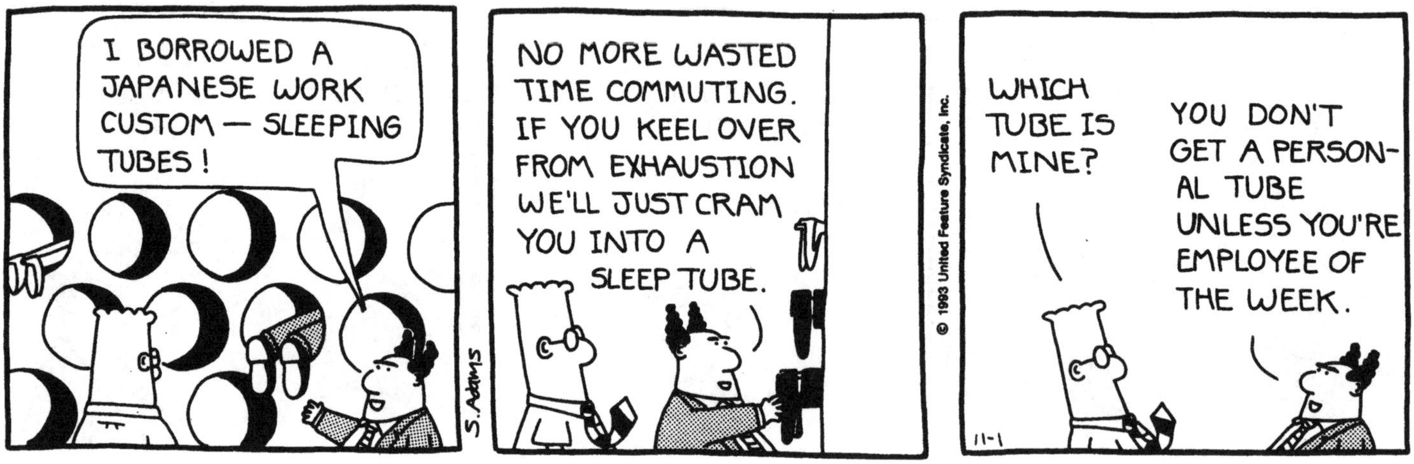
I BORROWED A JAPANESE WORK CUSTOM — SLEEPING TUBES!
S. Adams
NO MORE WASTED TIME COMMUTING. IF YOU KEEL OVER FROM EXHAUSTION WE'LL JUST CRAM YOU INTO A SLEEP TUBE.
© 1993 United Feature Syndicate, Inc.
WHICH TUBE IS MINE?
YOU DON'T GET A PERSONAL TUBE UNLESS YOU'RE EMPLOYEE OF THE WEEK.
11-1

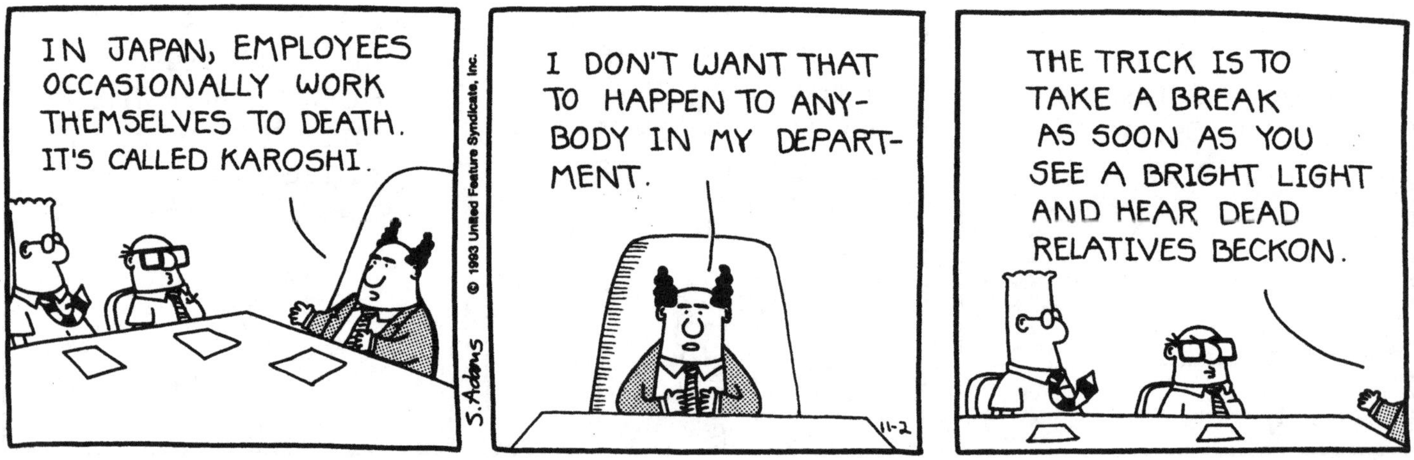
IN JAPAN, EMPLOYEES OCCASIONALLY WORK THEMSELVES TO DEATH. IT'S CALLED KAROSHI.
S. Adams
© 1993 United Feature Syndicate, Inc.
I DON'T WANT THAT TO HAPPEN TO ANYBODY IN MY DEPARTMENT.
11-2
THE TRICK IS TO TAKE A BREAK AS SOON AS YOU SEE A BRIGHT LIGHT AND HEAR DEAD RELATIVES BECKON.

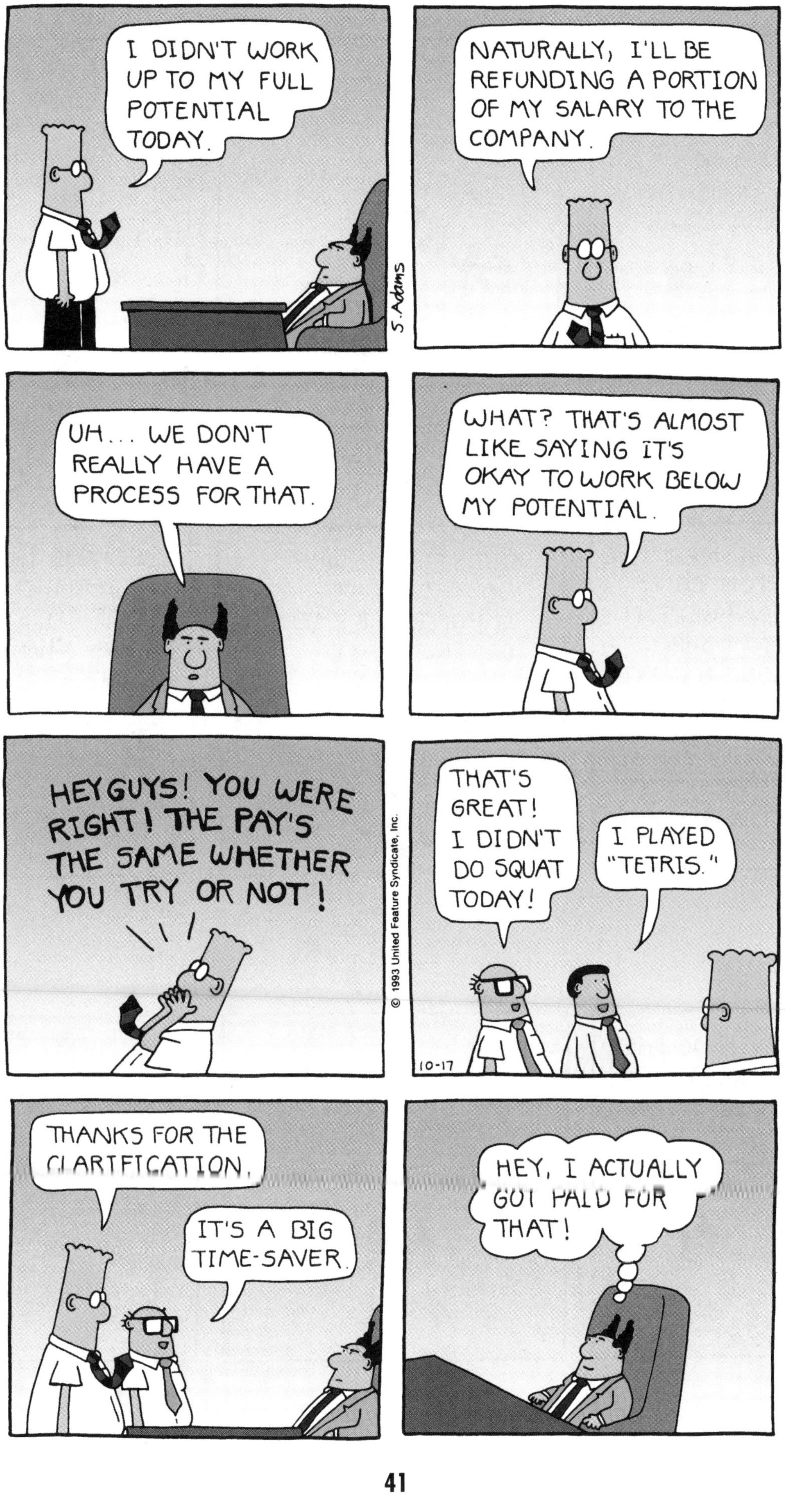
I DIDN'T WORK UP TO MY FULL POTENTIAL TODAY.
S. Adams
NATURALLY, I'LL BE REFUNDING A PORTION OF MY SALARY TO THE COMPANY.
UH... WE DON'T REALLY HAVE A PROCESS FOR THAT.
WHAT? THAT'S ALMOST LIKE SAYING IT'S OKAY TO WORK BELOW MY POTENTIAL.
HEY GUYS! YOU WERE RIGHT! THE PAY'S THE SAME WHETHER YOU TRY OR NOT!
© 1993 United Feature Syndicate, Inc.
THAT'S GREAT! I DIDN'T DO SQUAT TODAY!
I PLAYED "TETRIS."
10-17
THANKS FOR THE CLARIFICATION.
IT'S A BIG TIME-SAVER.
HEY, I ACTUALLY GOT PAID FOR THAT!

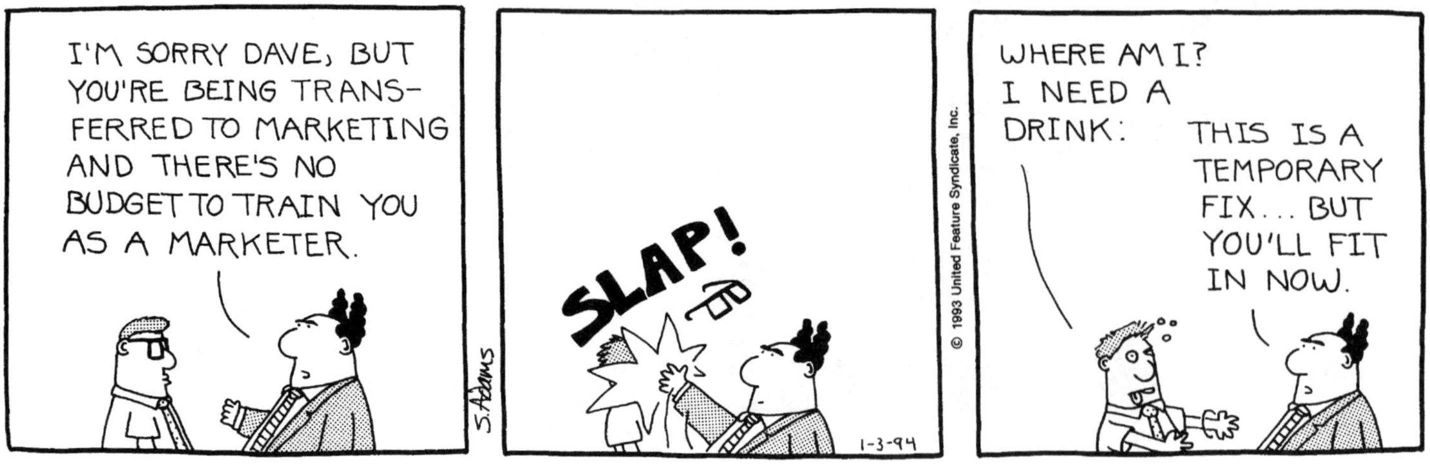
I'M SORRY DAVE, BUT YOU'RE BEING TRANSFERRED TO MARKETING AND THERE'S NO BUDGET TO TRAIN YOU AS A MARKETER.
S. Adams
SLAP!
1-3-94
© 1993 United Feature Syndicate, Inc.
WHERE AM I? I NEED A DRINK.
THIS IS A TEMPORARY FIX... BUT YOU'LL FIT IN NOW.

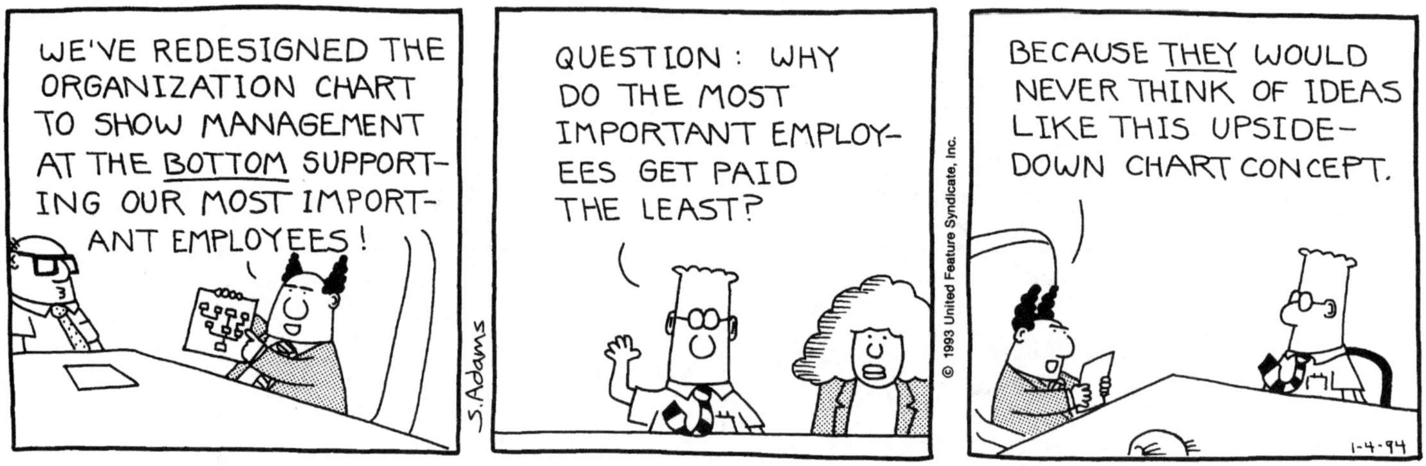
WE'VE REDESIGNED THE ORGANIZATION CHART TO SHOW MANAGEMENT AT THE BOTTOM SUPPORTING OUR MOST IMPORTANT EMPLOYEES!
S. Adams
QUESTION: WHY DO THE MOST IMPORTANT EMPLOYEES GET PAID THE LEAST?
© 1993 United Feature Syndicate, Inc.
BECAUSE THEY WOULD NEVER THINK OF IDEAS LIKE THIS UPSIDE-DOWN CHART CONCEPT.
1-4-94

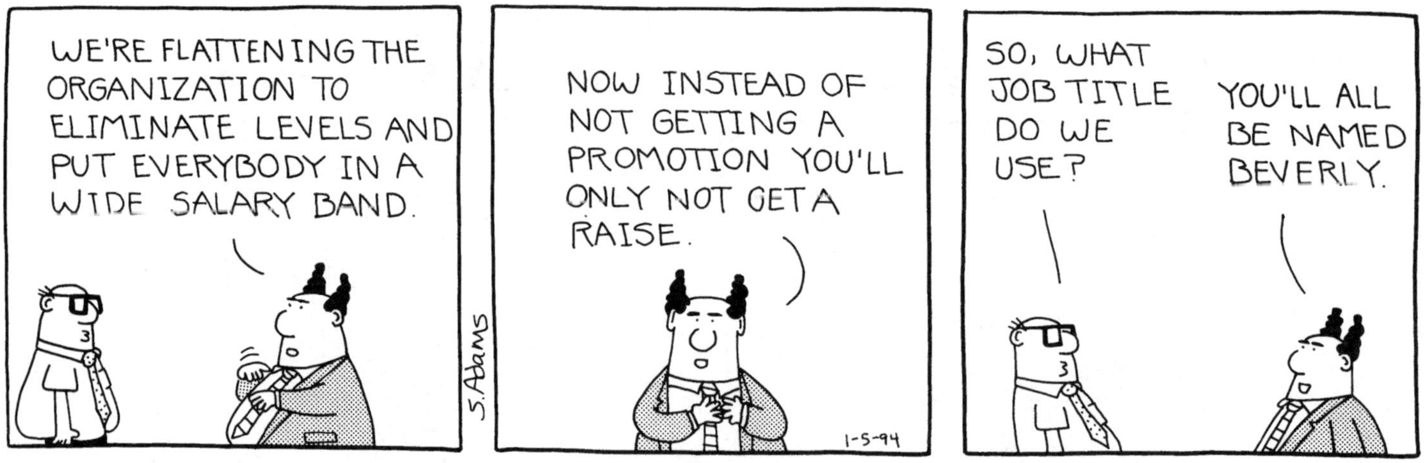
WE'RE FLATTENING THE ORGANIZATION TO ELIMINATE LEVELS AND PUT EVERYBODY IN A WIDE SALARY BAND.
S. Adams
NOW INSTEAD OF NOT GETTING A PROMOTION YOU'LL ONLY NOT GET A RAISE.
1-5-94
SO, WHAT JOB TITLE DO WE USE?
YOU'LL ALL BE NAMED BEVERLY.

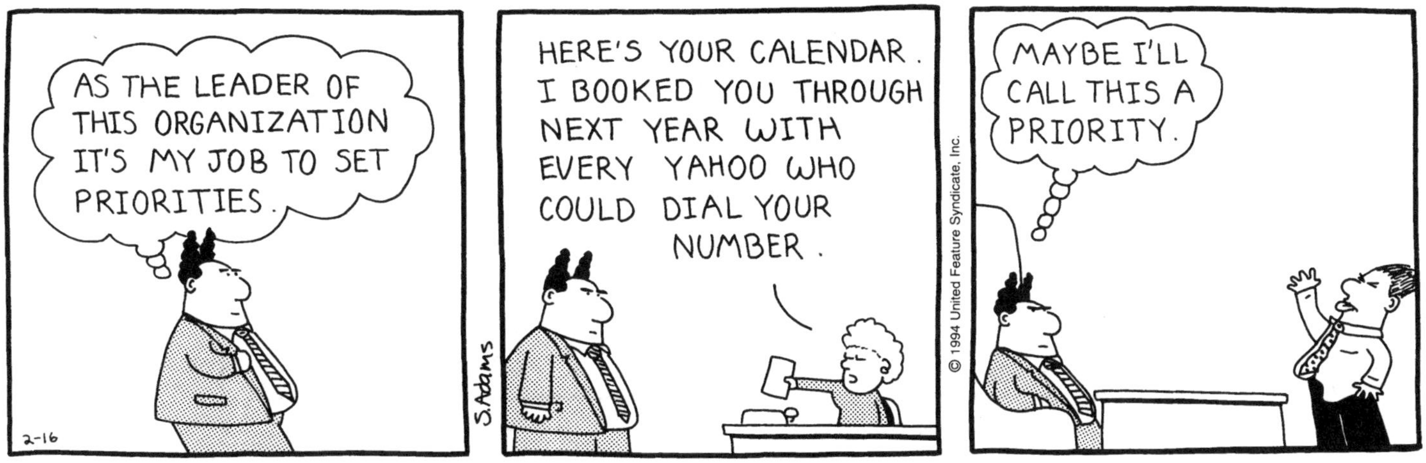
AS THE LEADER OF THIS ORGANIZATION IT'S MY JOB TO SET PRIORITIES.
2-16
S. Adams
HERE'S YOUR CALENDAR. I BOOKED YOU THROUGH NEXT YEAR WITH EVERY YAHOO WHO COULD DIAL YOUR NUMBER.
© 1994 United Feature Syndicate, Inc.
MAYBE I'LL CALL THIS A PRIORITY.

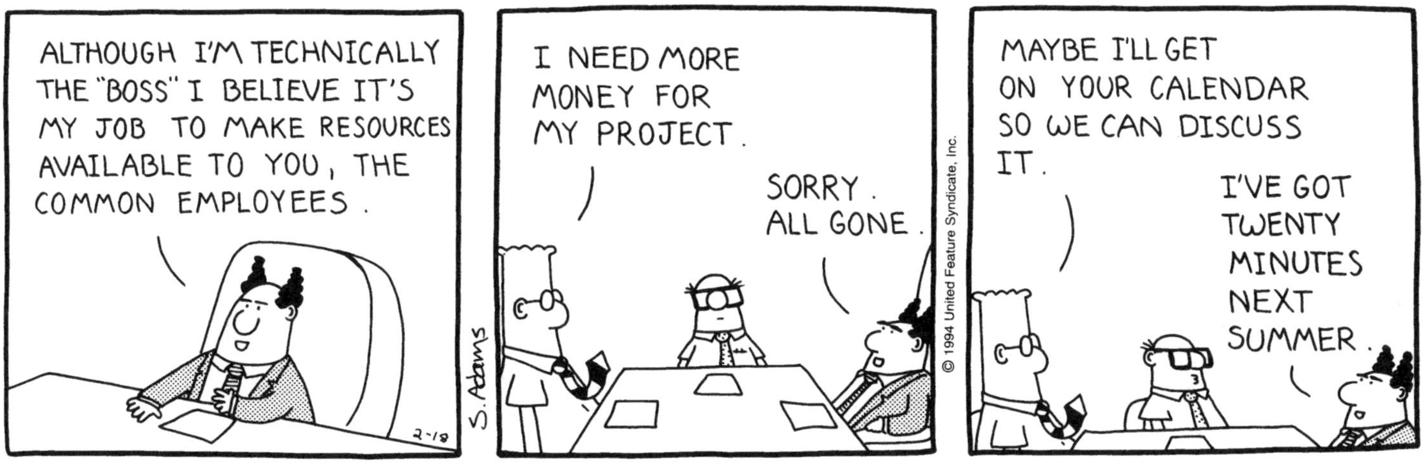
ALTHOUGH I'M TECHNICALLY THE "BOSS" I BELIEVE IT'S MY JOB TO MAKE RESOURCES AVAILABLE TO YOU, THE COMMON EMPLOYEES.
2-18
S. Adams
I NEED MORE MONEY FOR MY PROJECT.
SORRY. ALL GONE.
© 1994 United Feature Syndicate, Inc.
MAYBE I'LL GET ON YOUR CALENDAR SO WE CAN DISCUSS IT.
I'VE GOT TWENTY MINUTES NEXT SUMMER.

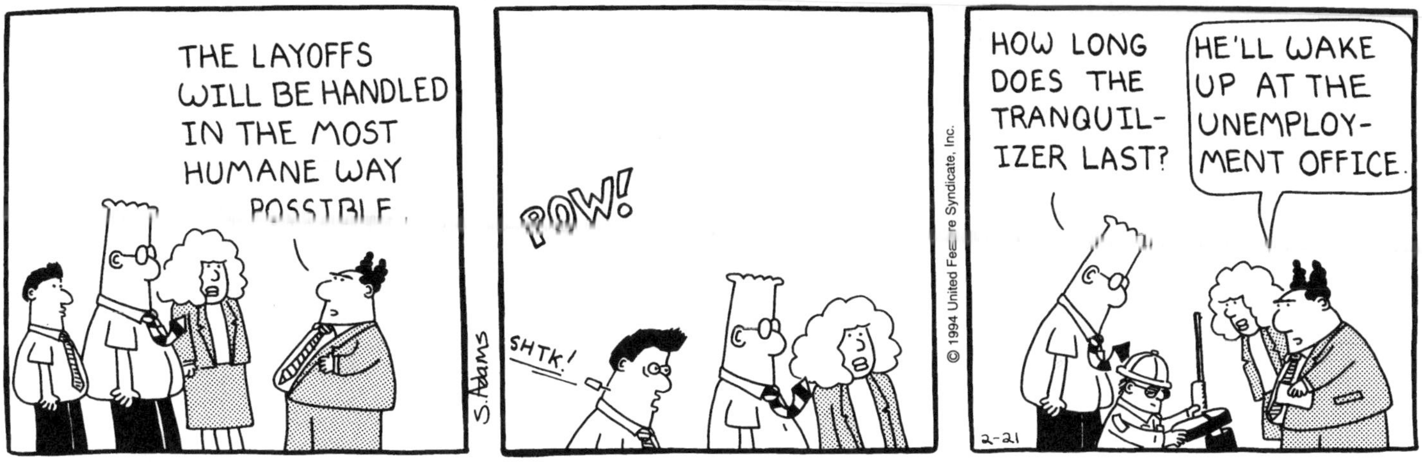
THE LAYOFFS WILL BE HANDLED IN THE MOST HUMANE WAY POSSIBLE.
S. Adams
POW!
SHTK!
© 1994 United Feature Syndicate, Inc.
HOW LONG DOES THE TRANQUIL-IZER LAST?
HE'LL WAKE UP AT THE UNEMPLOY-MENT OFFICE.
2-21

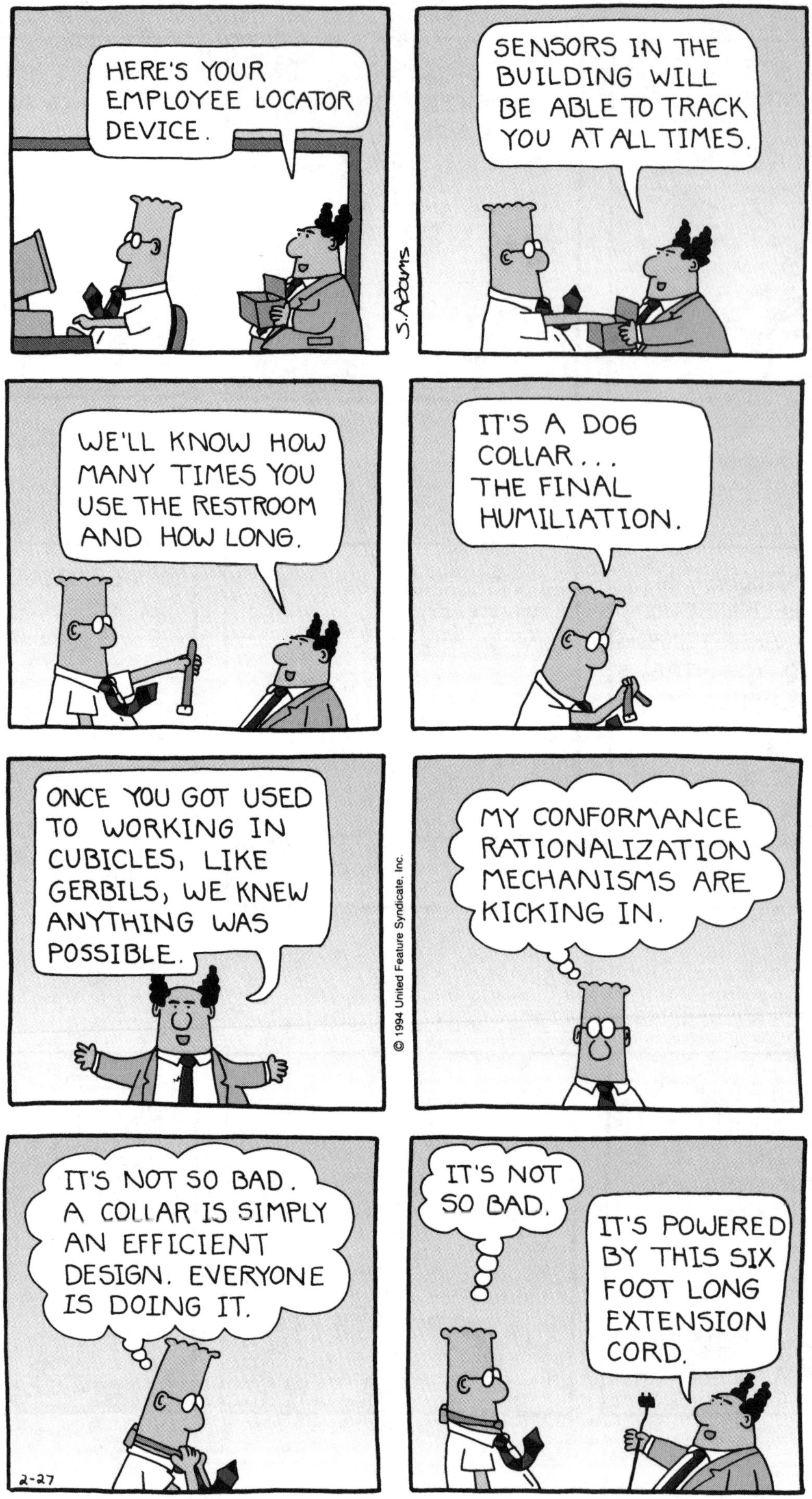
HERE'S YOUR EMPLOYEE LOCATOR DEVICE.
S. Adams
SENSORS IN THE BUILDING WILL BE ABLE TO TRACK YOU AT ALL TIMES.
WE'LL KNOW HOW MANY TIMES YOU USE THE RESTROOM AND HOW LONG.
IT'S A DOG COLLAR . . . THE FINAL HUMILIATION.
ONCE YOU GOT USED TO WORKING IN CUBICLES, LIKE GERBILS, WE KNEW ANYTHING WAS POSSIBLE.
© 1994 United Feature Syndicate, Inc.
MY CONFORMANCE RATIONALIZATION MECHANISMS ARE KICKING IN.
IT'S NOT SO BAD. A COLLAR IS SIMPLY AN EFFICIENT DESIGN. EVERYONE IS DOING IT.
2-27
IT'S NOT SO BAD.
IT'S POWERED BY THIS SIX FOOT LONG EXTENSION CORD.

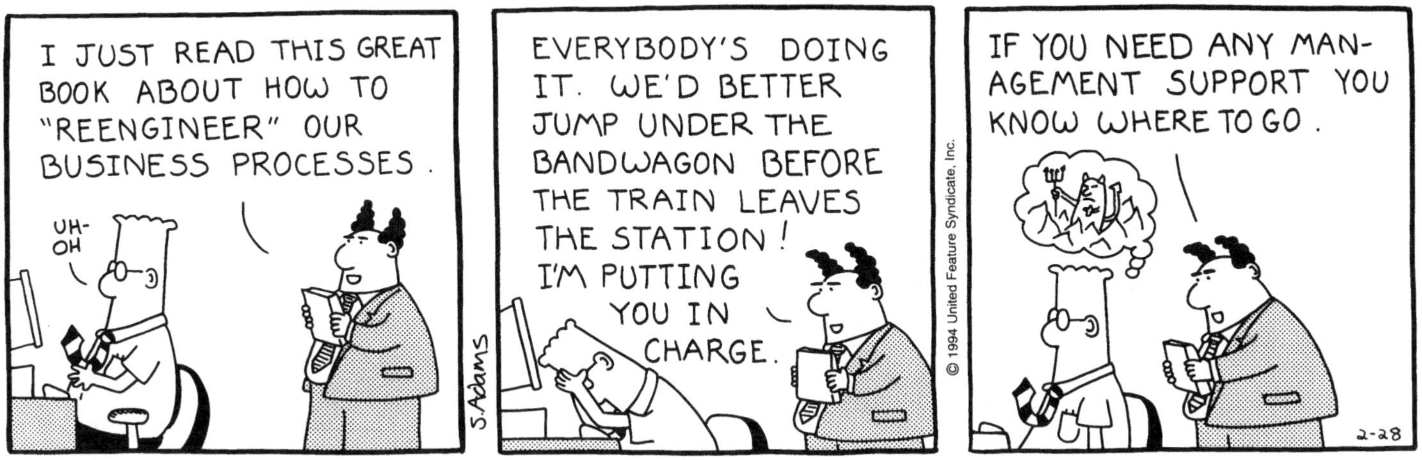
I JUST READ THIS GREAT BOOK ABOUT HOW TO "REENGINEER" OUR BUSINESS PROCESSES.
UH-OH
EVERYBODY'S DOING IT. WE'D BETTER JUMP UNDER THE BANDWAGON BEFORE THE TRAIN LEAVES THE STATION!
I'M PUTTING YOU IN CHARGE.
IF YOU NEED ANY MANAGEMENT SUPPORT YOU KNOW WHERE TO GO.
S. Adams
© 1994 United Feature Syndicate, Inc.
2-28

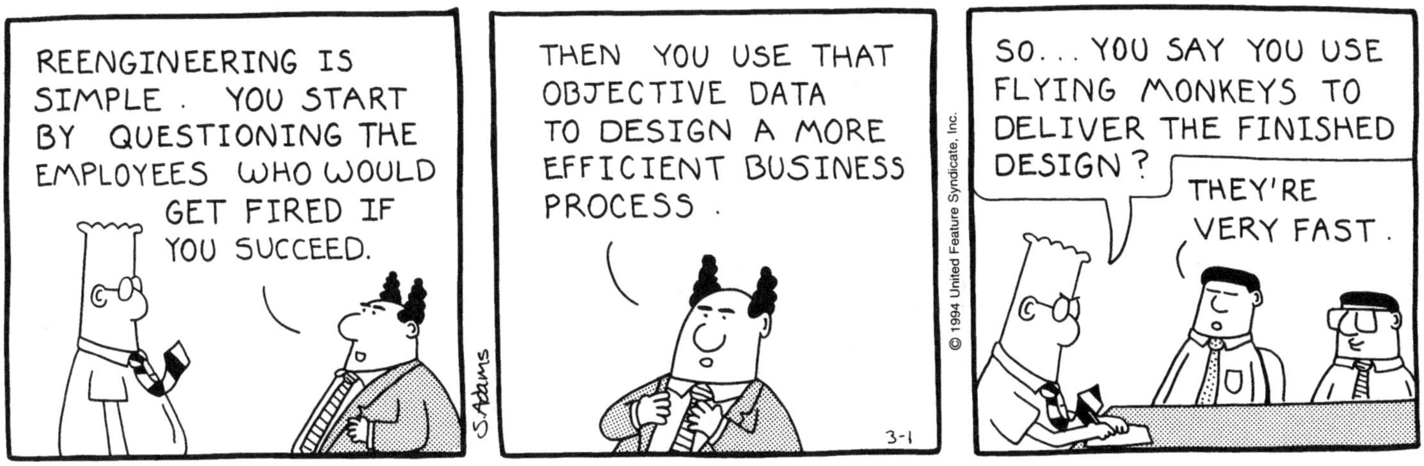
REENGINEERING IS SIMPLE. YOU START BY QUESTIONING THE EMPLOYEES WHO WOULD GET FIRED IF YOU SUCCEED.
THEN YOU USE THAT OBJECTIVE DATA TO DESIGN A MORE EFFICIENT BUSINESS PROCESS.
SO... YOU SAY YOU USE FLYING MONKEYS TO DELIVER THE FINISHED DESIGN?
THEY'RE VERY FAST.
S. Adams
© 1994 United Feature Syndicate, Inc.
3-1

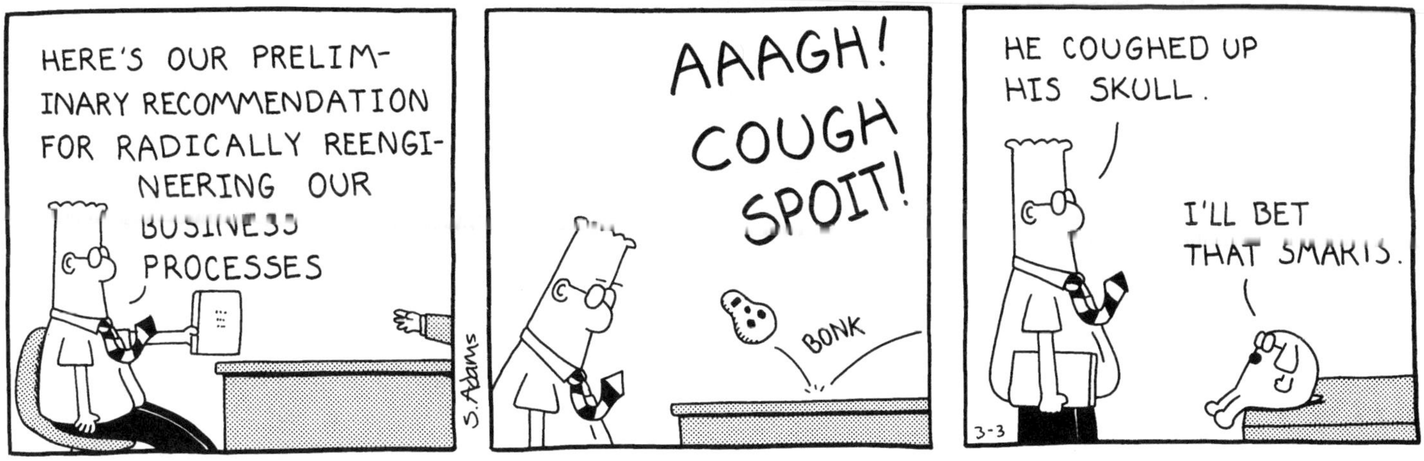
HERE'S OUR PRELIMINARY RECOMMENDATION FOR RADICALLY REENGINEERING OUR BUSINESS PROCESSES
AAAGH! COUGH SPOIT!
BONK
HE COUGHED UP HIS SKULL.
I'LL BET THAT SMARTS.
S. Adams
3-3

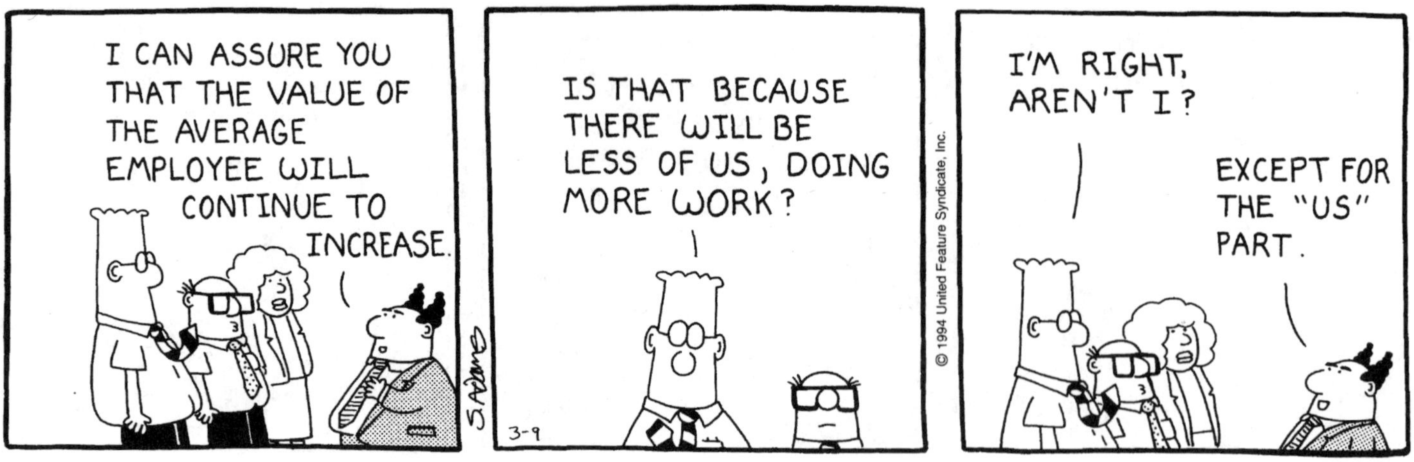
I CAN ASSURE YOU THAT THE VALUE OF THE AVERAGE EMPLOYEE WILL CONTINUE TO INCREASE.
S. Adams
3-9
IS THAT BECAUSE THERE WILL BE LESS OF US, DOING MORE WORK?
© 1994 United Feature Syndicate, Inc.
I'M RIGHT, AREN'T I?
EXCEPT FOR THE "US" PART.

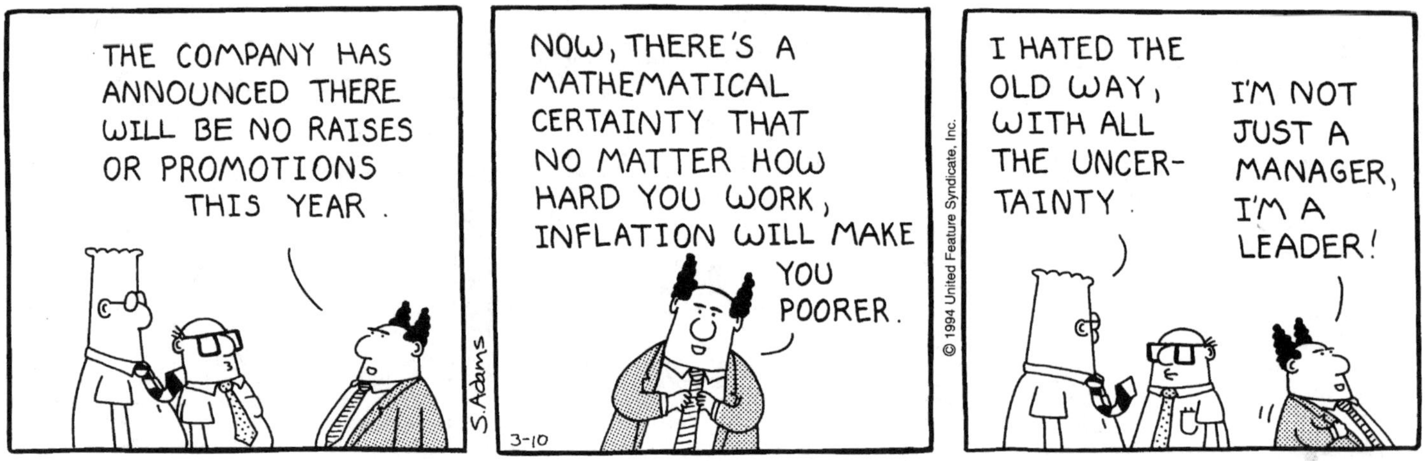
THE COMPANY HAS ANNOUNCED THERE WILL BE NO RAISES OR PROMOTIONS THIS YEAR.
S. Adams
3-10
NOW, THERE'S A MATHEMATICAL CERTAINTY THAT NO MATTER HOW HARD YOU WORK, INFLATION WILL MAKE YOU POORER.
© 1994 United Feature Syndicate, Inc.
I HATED THE OLD WAY, WITH ALL THE UNCERTAINTY.
I'M NOT JUST A MANAGER, I'M A LEADER!

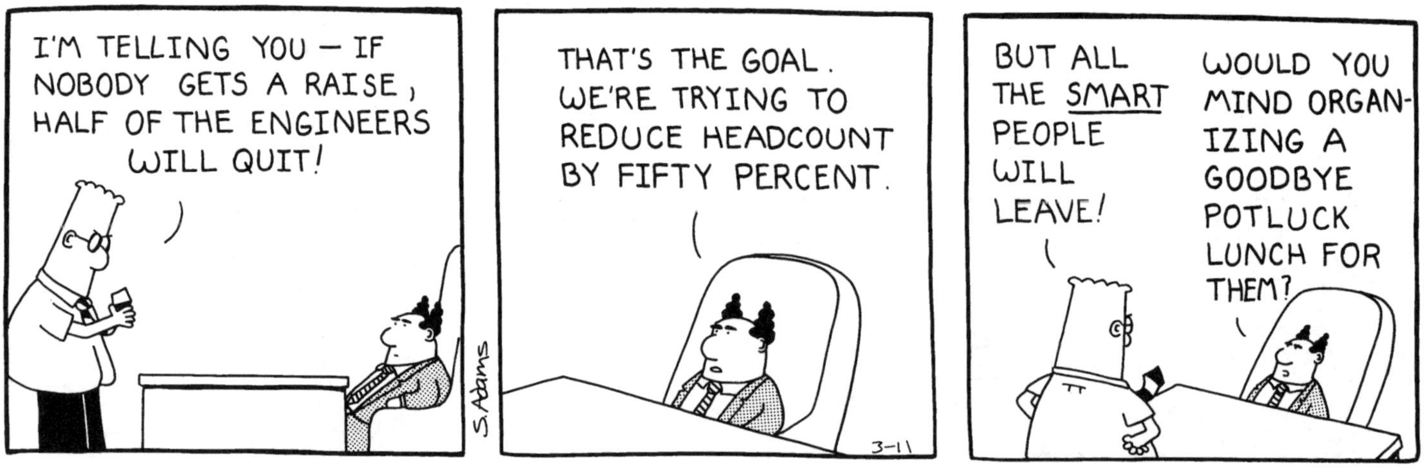
I'M TELLING YOU — IF NOBODY GETS A RAISE, HALF OF THE ENGINEERS WILL QUIT!
S. Adams
THAT'S THE GOAL. WE'RE TRYING TO REDUCE HEADCOUNT BY FIFTY PERCENT.
3-11
BUT ALL THE SMART PEOPLE WILL LEAVE!
WOULD YOU MIND ORGANIZING A GOODBYE POTLUCK LUNCH FOR THEM?

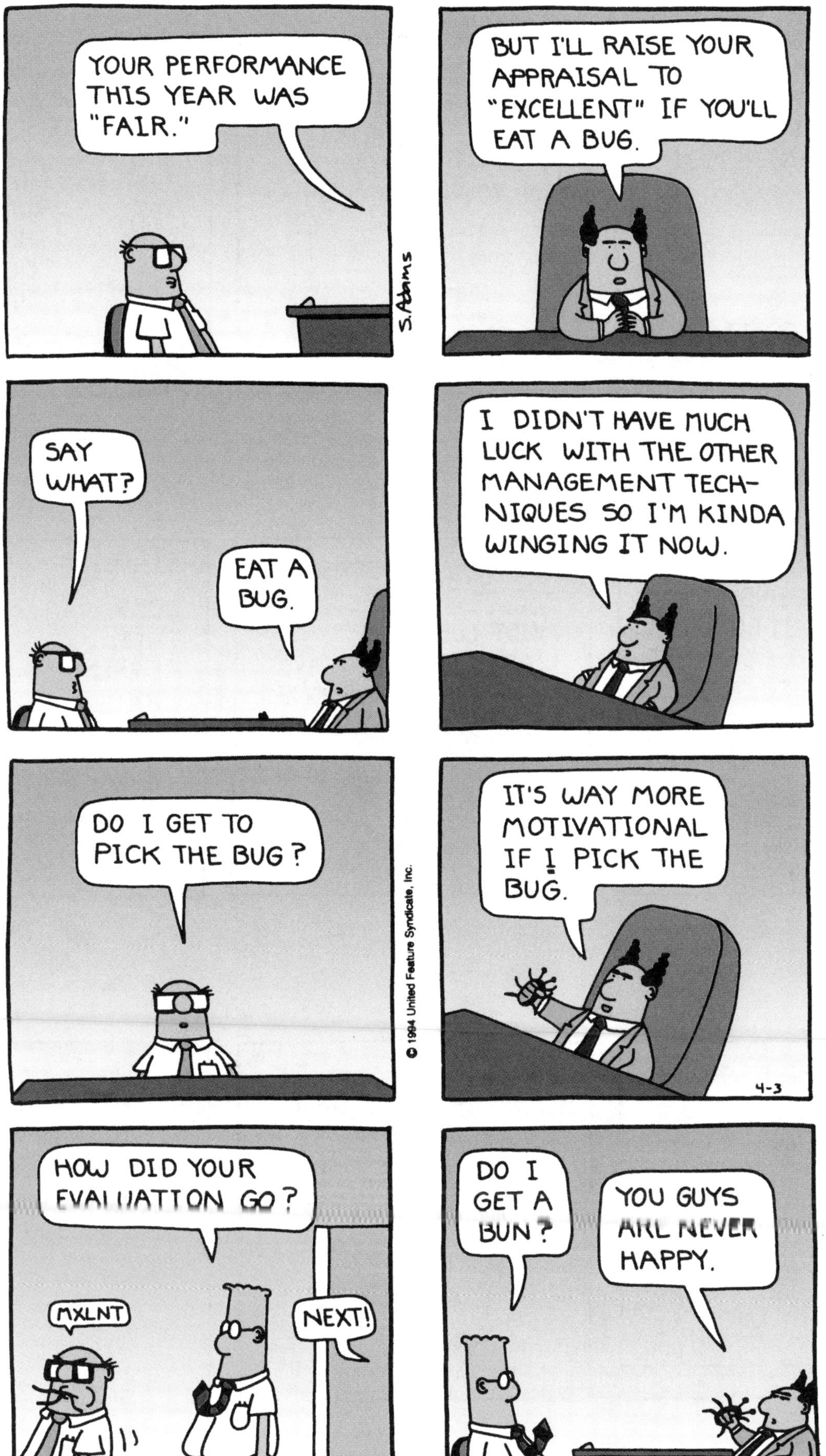
YOUR PERFORMANCE THIS YEAR WAS "FAIR."
S. Adams
BUT I'LL RAISE YOUR APPRAISAL TO "EXCELLENT" IF YOU'LL EAT A BUG.
SAY WHAT?
EAT A BUG.
I DIDN'T HAVE MUCH LUCK WITH THE OTHER MANAGEMENT TECH-NIQUES SO I'M KINDA WINGING IT NOW.
DO I GET TO PICK THE BUG?
© 1994 United Feature Syndicate, Inc.
IT'S WAY MORE MOTIVATIONAL IF I PICK THE BUG.
4-3
HOW DID YOUR EVALUATION GO?
MXLNT
NEXT!
DO I GET A BUN?
YOU GUYS ARE NEVER HAPPY.

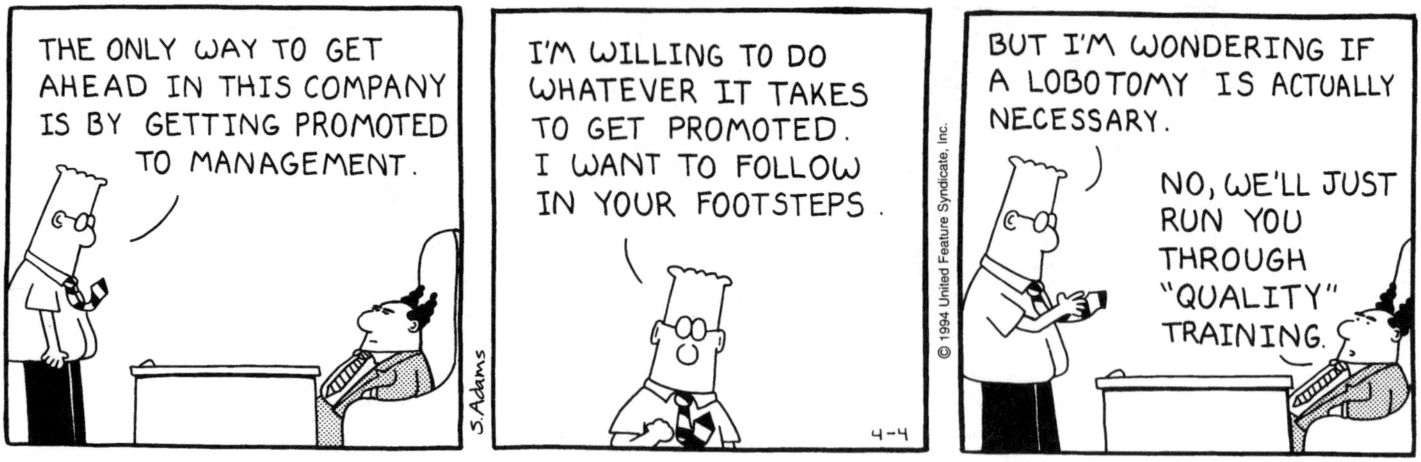
THE ONLY WAY TO GET AHEAD IN THIS COMPANY IS BY GETTING PROMOTED TO MANAGEMENT.
S. Adams
I'M WILLING TO DO WHATEVER IT TAKES TO GET PROMOTED. I WANT TO FOLLOW IN YOUR FOOTSTEPS.
4-4
© 1994 United Feature Syndicate, Inc.
BUT I'M WONDERING IF A LOBOTOMY IS ACTUALLY NECESSARY.
NO, WE'LL JUST RUN YOU THROUGH "QUALITY" TRAINING.

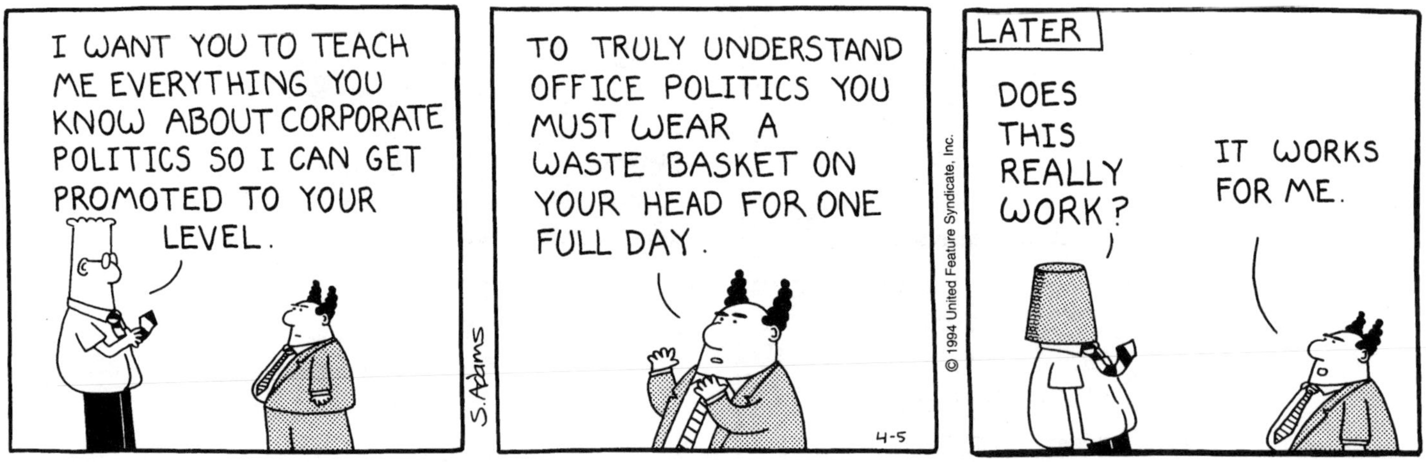
I WANT YOU TO TEACH ME EVERYTHING YOU KNOW ABOUT CORPORATE POLITICS SO I CAN GET PROMOTED TO YOUR LEVEL.
S. Adams
TO TRULY UNDERSTAND OFFICE POLITICS YOU MUST WEAR A WASTE BASKET ON YOUR HEAD FOR ONE FULL DAY.
4-5
© 1994 United Feature Syndicate, Inc.
LATER
DOES THIS REALLY WORK?
IT WORKS FOR ME.

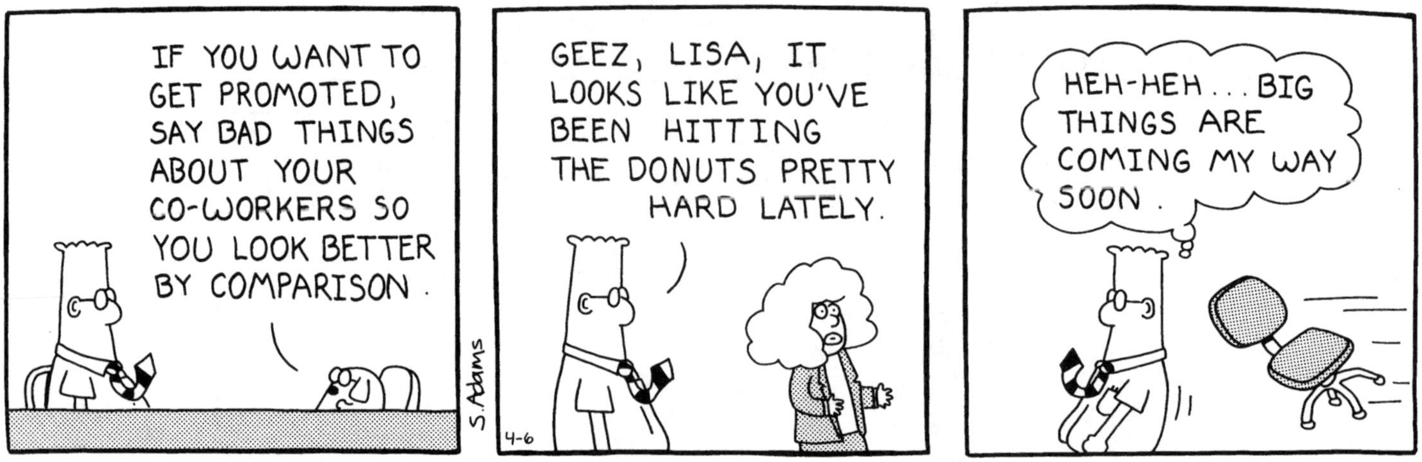
IF YOU WANT TO GET PROMOTED, SAY BAD THINGS ABOUT YOUR CO-WORKERS SO YOU LOOK BETTER BY COMPARISON.
S. Adams
4-6
GEEZ, LISA, IT LOOKS LIKE YOU'VE BEEN HITTING THE DONUTS PRETTY HARD LATELY.
HEH-HEH... BIG THINGS ARE COMING MY WAY SOON.

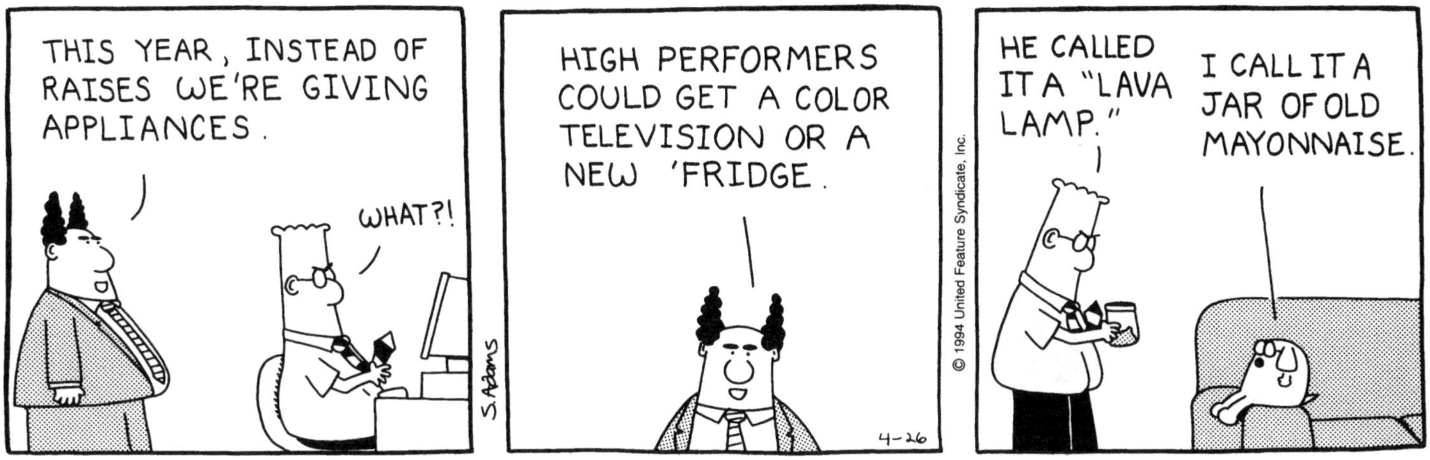
THIS YEAR, INSTEAD OF RAISES WE'RE GIVING APPLIANCES.
WHAT?!
S. Adams
HIGH PERFORMERS COULD GET A COLOR TELEVISION OR A NEW 'FRIDGE.
4-26
© 1994 United Feature Syndicate, Inc.
HE CALLED IT A "LAVA LAMP."
I CALL IT A JAR OF OLD MAYONNAISE.

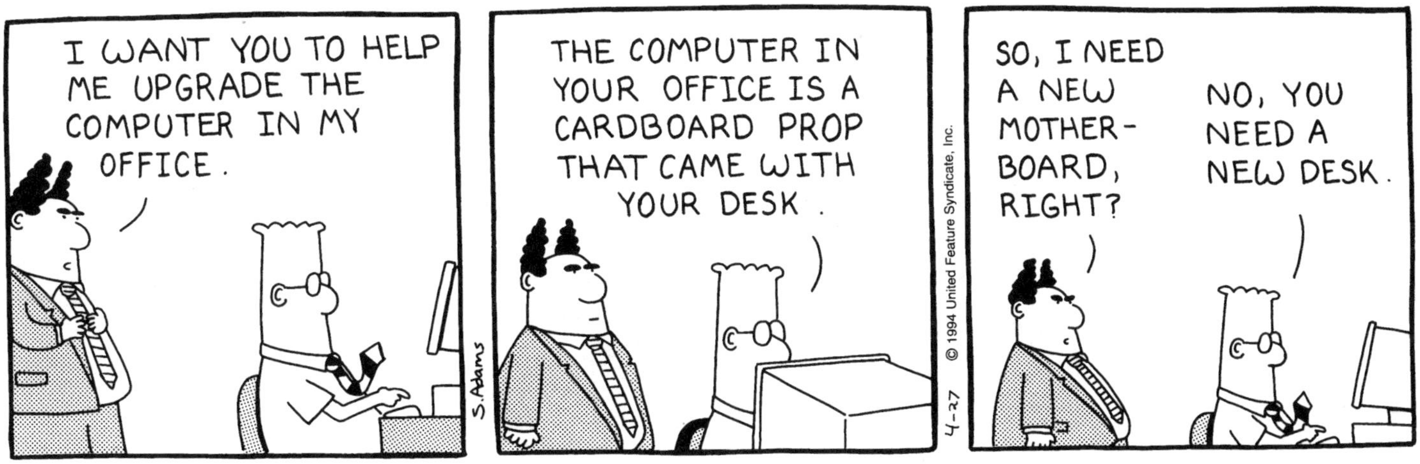
I WANT YOU TO HELP ME UPGRADE THE COMPUTER IN MY OFFICE.
S. Adams
THE COMPUTER IN YOUR OFFICE IS A CARDBOARD PROP THAT CAME WITH YOUR DESK.
4-27
© 1994 United Feature Syndicate, Inc.
SO, I NEED A NEW MOTHER-BOARD, RIGHT?
NO, YOU NEED A NEW DESK.

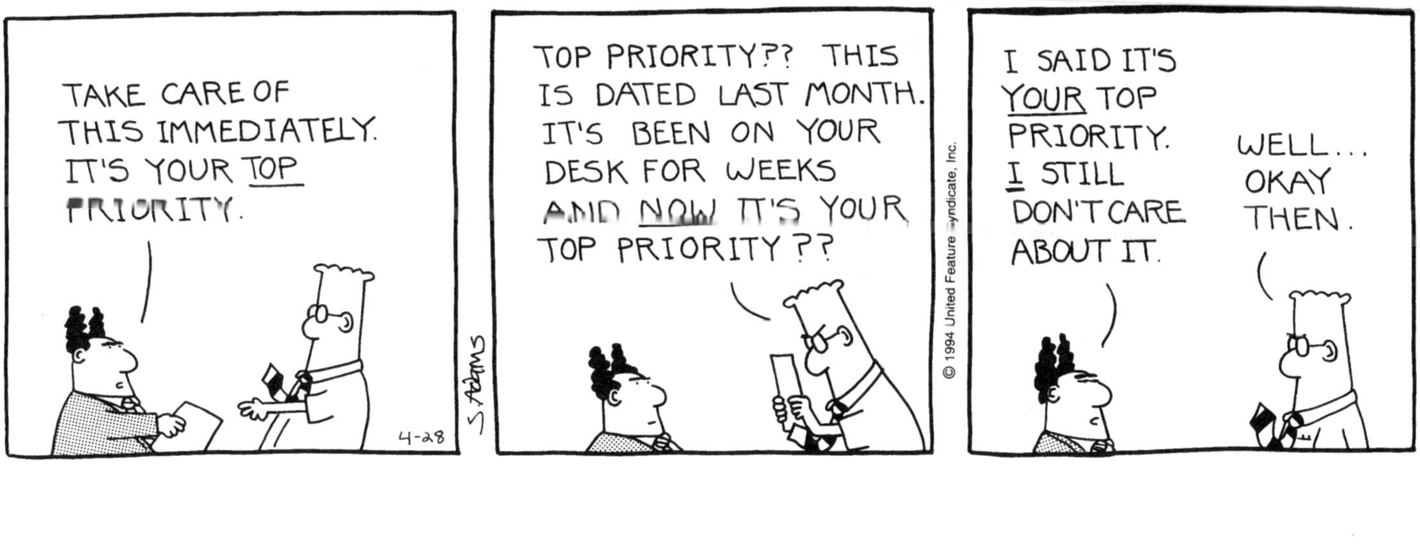
TAKE CARE OF THIS IMMEDIATELY. IT'S YOUR TOP PRIORITY.
4-28
S. Adams
TOP PRIORITY?? THIS IS DATED LAST MONTH. IT'S BEEN ON YOUR DESK FOR WEEKS AND NOW IT'S YOUR TOP PRIORITY??
© 1994 United Feature Syndicate, Inc.
I SAID IT'S YOUR TOP PRIORITY. I STILL DON'T CARE ABOUT IT.
WELL... OKAY THEN.

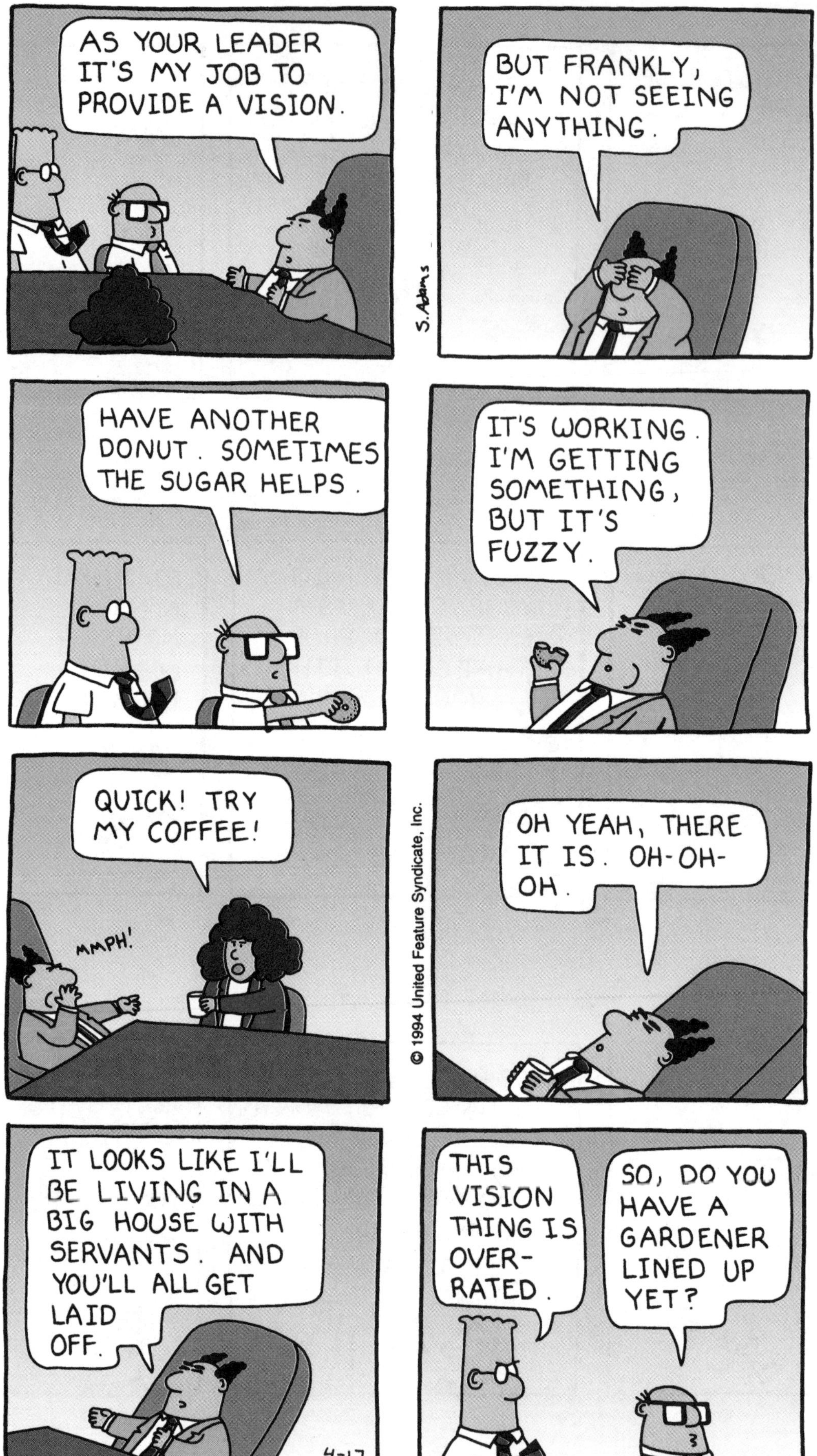
AS YOUR LEADER IT'S MY JOB TO PROVIDE A VISION.
S. Adams
BUT FRANKLY, I'M NOT SEEING ANYTHING.
HAVE ANOTHER DONUT. SOMETIMES THE SUGAR HELPS.
IT'S WORKING. I'M GETTING SOMETHING, BUT IT'S FUZZY.
QUICK! TRY MY COFFEE!
MMPH!
© 1994 United Feature Syndicate, Inc.
OH YEAH, THERE IT IS. OH-OH-OH.
IT LOOKS LIKE I'LL BE LIVING IN A BIG HOUSE WITH SERVANTS. AND YOU'LL ALL GET LAID OFF.
4-17
THIS VISION THING IS OVER-RATED.
SO, DO YOU HAVE A GARDENER LINED UP YET?

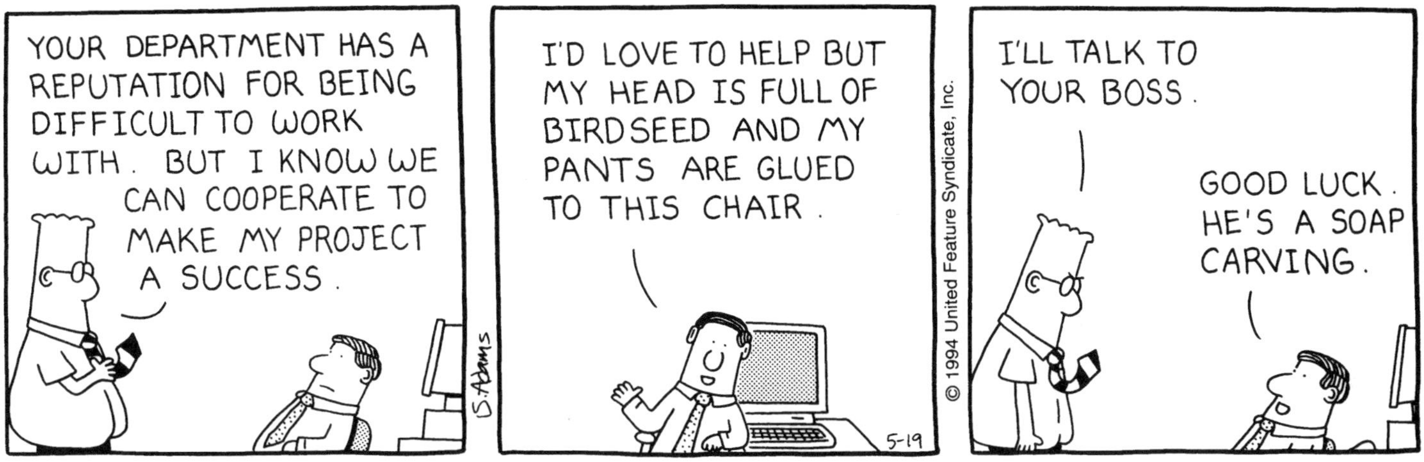
YOUR DEPARTMENT HAS A REPUTATION FOR BEING DIFFICULT TO WORK WITH. BUT I KNOW WE CAN COOPERATE TO MAKE MY PROJECT A SUCCESS.
S. Adams
I'D LOVE TO HELP BUT MY HEAD IS FULL OF BIRDSEED AND MY PANTS ARE GLUED TO THIS CHAIR.
5-19
© 1994 United Feature Syndicate, Inc.
I'LL TALK TO YOUR BOSS.
GOOD LUCK. HE'S A SOAP CARVING.

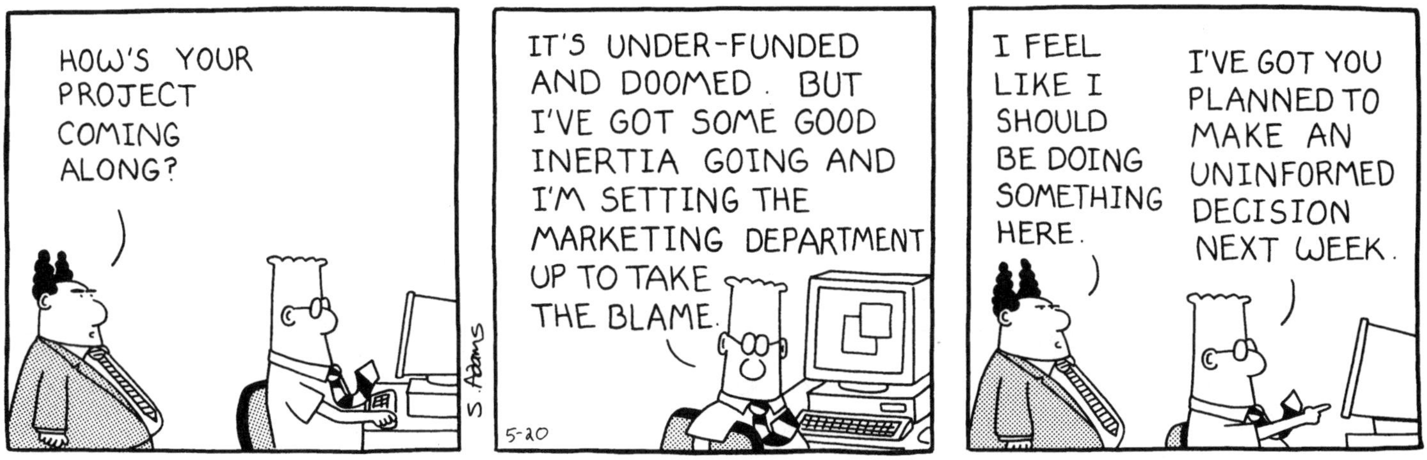
HOW'S YOUR PROJECT COMING ALONG?
S. Adams
IT'S UNDER-FUNDED AND DOOMED. BUT I'VE GOT SOME GOOD INERTIA GOING AND I'M SETTING THE MARKETING DEPARTMENT UP TO TAKE THE BLAME.
5-20
I FEEL LIKE I SHOULD BE DOING SOMETHING HERE.
I'VE GOT YOU PLANNED TO MAKE AN UNINFORMED DECISION NEXT WEEK.

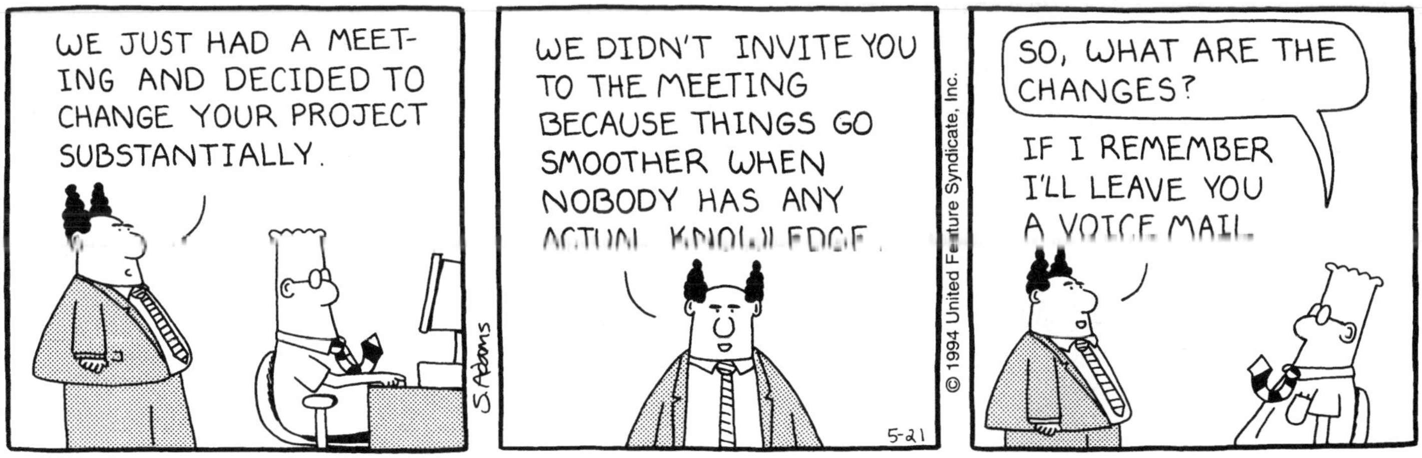
WE JUST HAD A MEETING AND DECIDED TO CHANGE YOUR PROJECT SUBSTANTIALLY.
S. Adams
WE DIDN'T INVITE YOU TO THE MEETING BECAUSE THINGS GO SMOOTHER WHEN NOBODY HAS ANY ACTUAL KNOWLEDGE.
5-21
© 1994 United Feature Syndicate, Inc.
SO, WHAT ARE THE CHANGES?
IF I REMEMBER I'LL LEAVE YOU A VOICE MAIL.

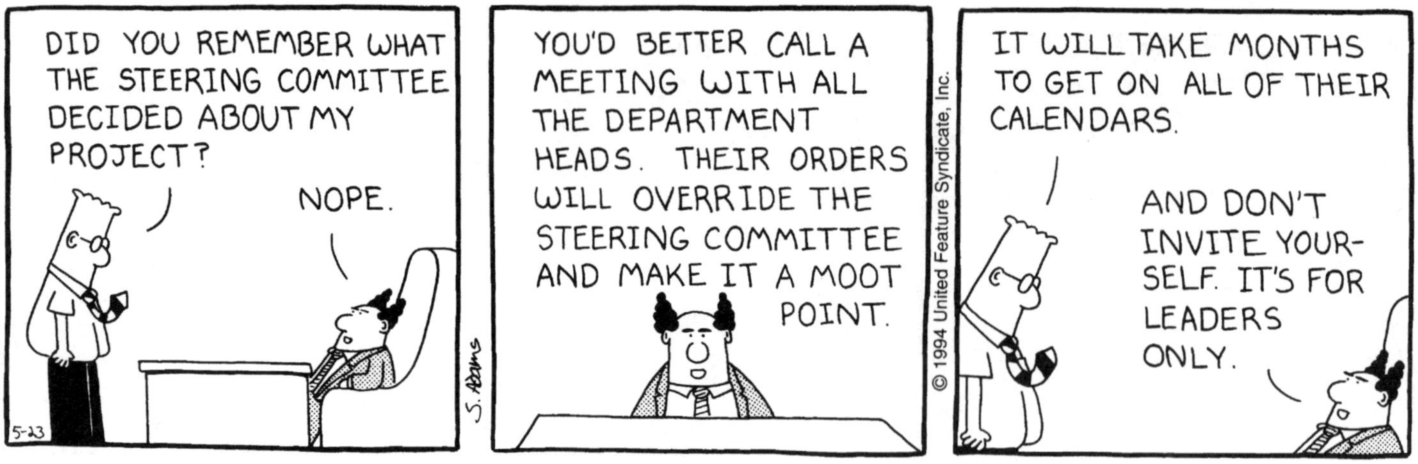
DID YOU REMEMBER WHAT THE STEERING COMMITTEE DECIDED ABOUT MY PROJECT?
NOPE.
S. Adams
5-23
YOU'D BETTER CALL A MEETING WITH ALL THE DEPARTMENT HEADS. THEIR ORDERS WILL OVERRIDE THE STEERING COMMITTEE AND MAKE IT A MOOT POINT.
© 1994 United Feature Syndicate, Inc.
IT WILL TAKE MONTHS TO GET ON ALL OF THEIR CALENDARS.
AND DON'T INVITE YOURSELF. IT'S FOR LEADERS ONLY.

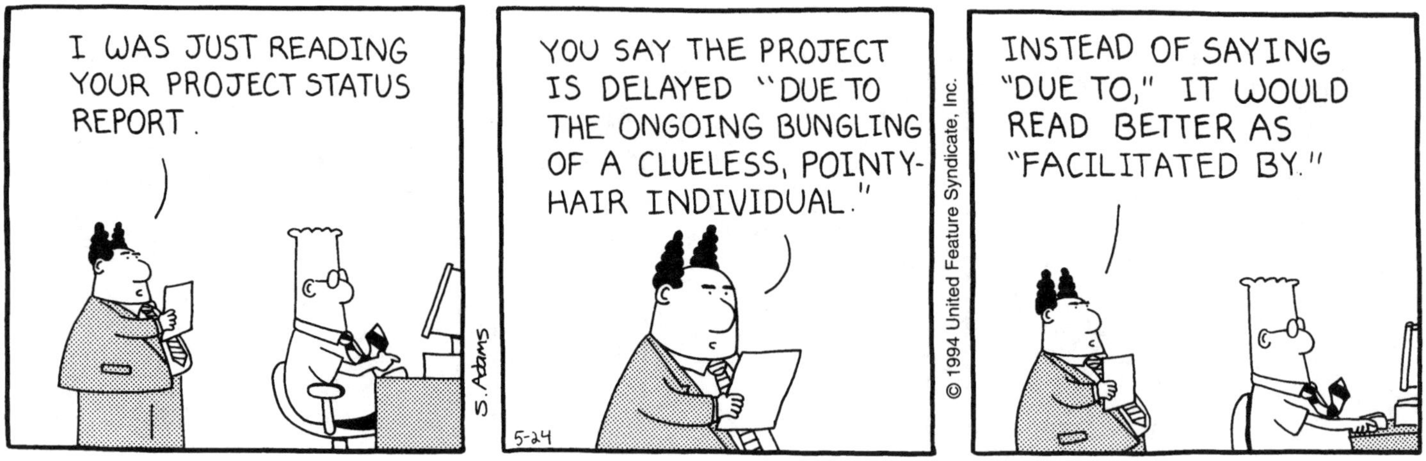
I WAS JUST READING YOUR PROJECT STATUS REPORT.
S. Adams
5-24
YOU SAY THE PROJECT IS DELAYED "DUE TO THE ONGOING BUNGLING OF A CLUELESS, POINTY-HAIR INDIVIDUAL."
© 1994 United Feature Syndicate, Inc.
INSTEAD OF SAYING "DUE TO," IT WOULD READ BETTER AS "FACILITATED BY."

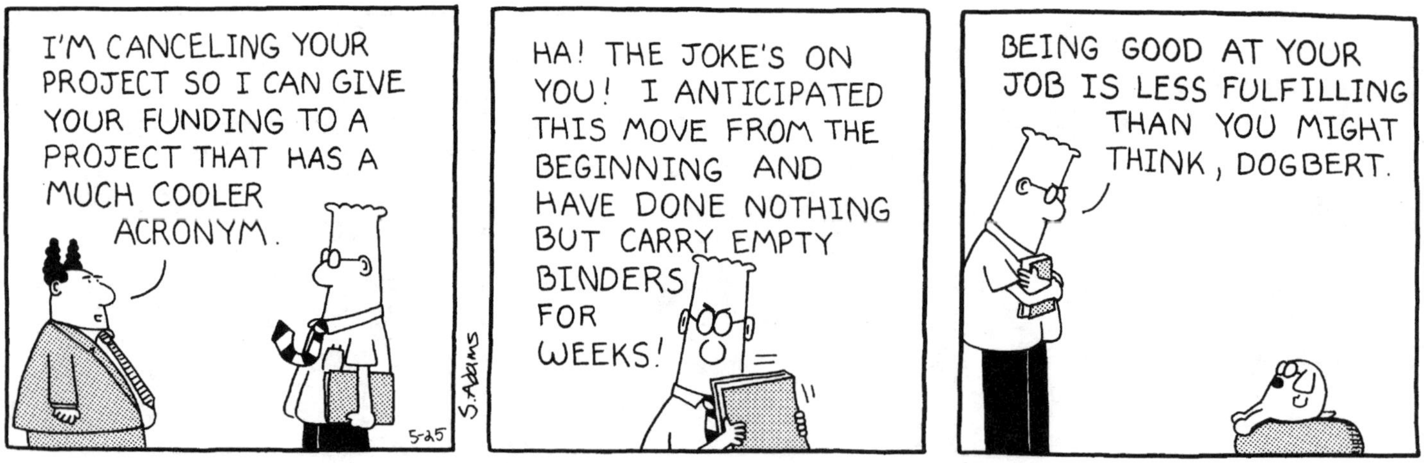
I'M CANCELING YOUR PROJECT SO I CAN GIVE YOUR FUNDING TO A PROJECT THAT HAS A MUCH COOLER ACRONYM.
S. Adams
5-25
HA! THE JOKE'S ON YOU! I ANTICIPATED THIS MOVE FROM THE BEGINNING AND HAVE DONE NOTHING BUT CARRY EMPTY BINDERS FOR WEEKS!
BEING GOOD AT YOUR JOB IS LESS FULFILLING THAN YOU MIGHT THINK, DOGBERT.

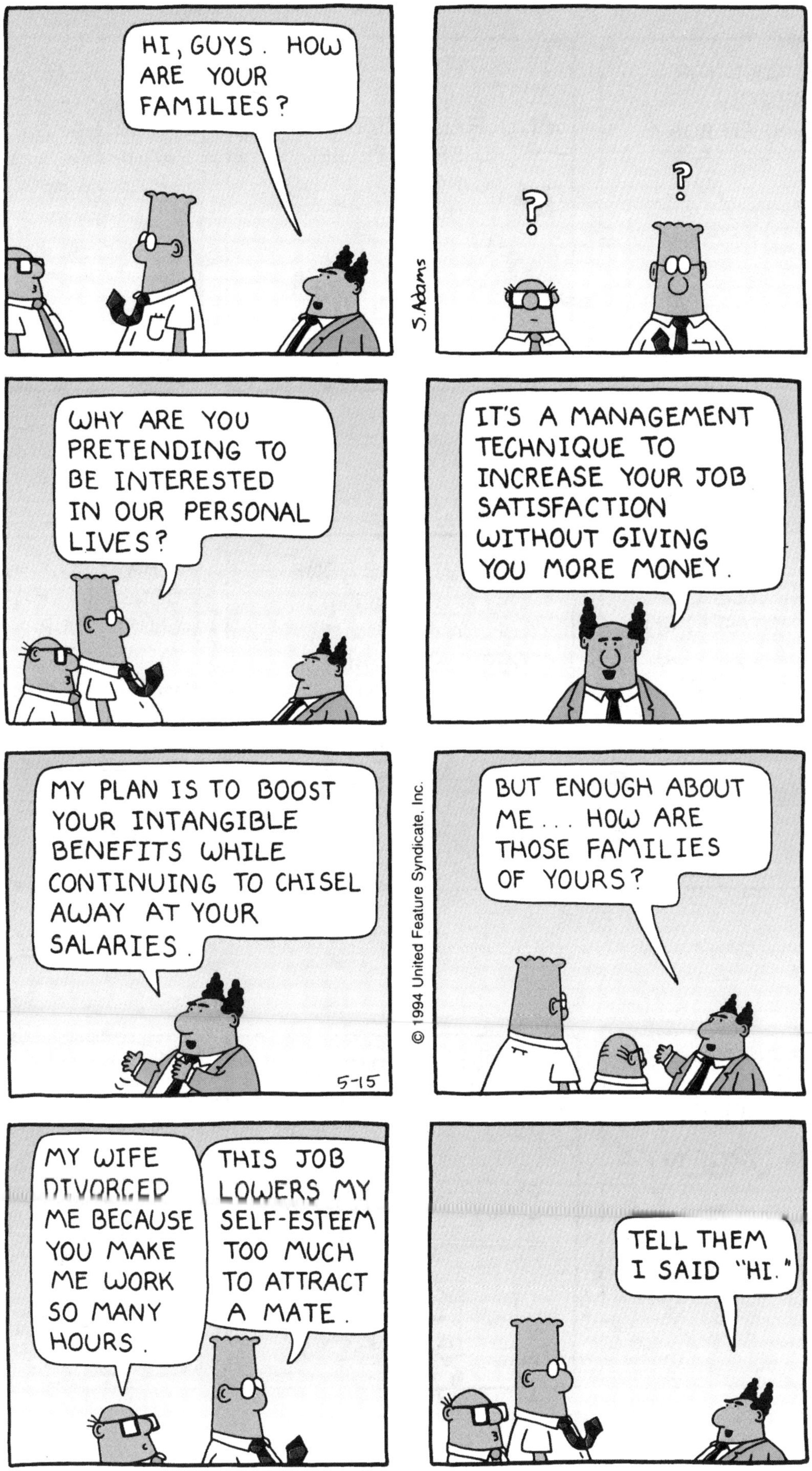
HI, GUYS. HOW ARE YOUR FAMILIES?
S. Adams
?
?
WHY ARE YOU PRETENDING TO BE INTERESTED IN OUR PERSONAL LIVES?
IT'S A MANAGEMENT TECHNIQUE TO INCREASE YOUR JOB SATISFACTION WITHOUT GIVING YOU MORE MONEY.
MY PLAN IS TO BOOST YOUR INTANGIBLE BENEFITS WHILE CONTINUING TO CHISEL AWAY AT YOUR SALARIES.
5-15
BUT ENOUGH ABOUT ME... HOW ARE THOSE FAMILIES OF YOURS?
MY WIFE DIVORCED ME BECAUSE YOU MAKE ME WORK SO MANY HOURS.
THIS JOB LOWERS MY SELF-ESTEEM TOO MUCH TO ATTRACT A MATE.
TELL THEM I SAID "HI."

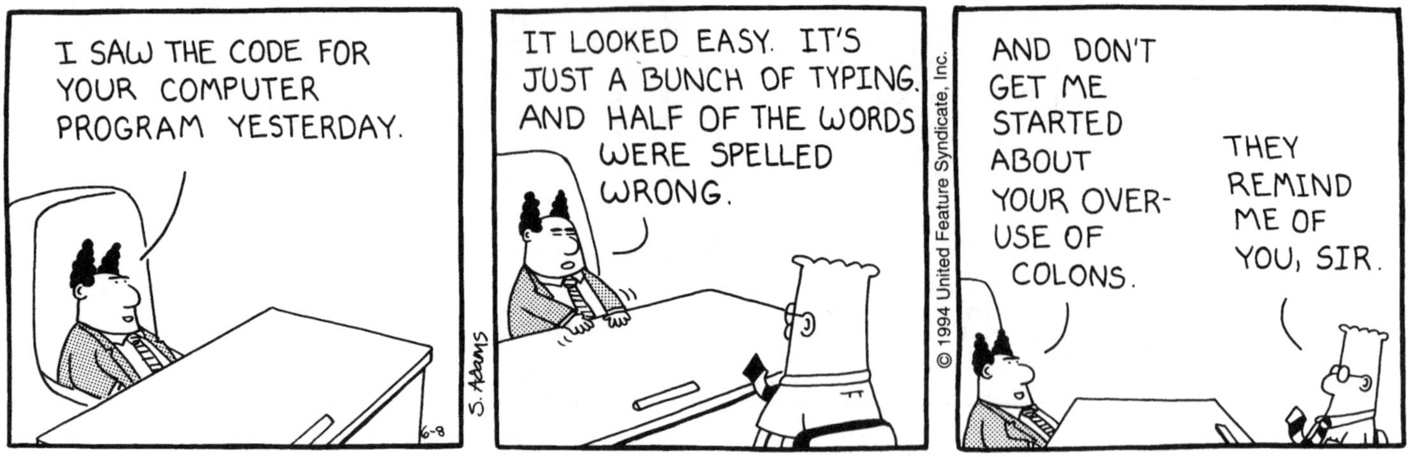
I SAW THE CODE FOR YOUR COMPUTER PROGRAM YESTERDAY.
IT LOOKED EASY. IT'S JUST A BUNCH OF TYPING. AND HALF OF THE WORDS WERE SPELLED WRONG.
AND DON'T GET ME STARTED ABOUT YOUR OVER-USE OF COLONS.
THEY REMIND ME OF YOU, SIR.
© 1994 United Feature Syndicate, Inc.

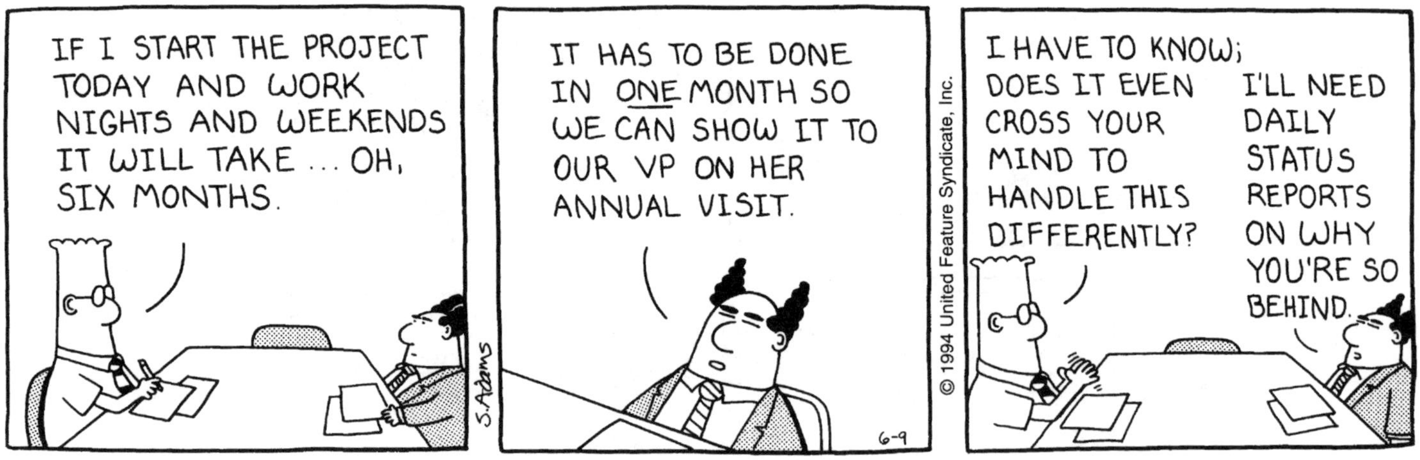
IF I START THE PROJECT TODAY AND WORK NIGHTS AND WEEKENDS IT WILL TAKE ... OH, SIX MONTHS.
IT HAS TO BE DONE IN ONE MONTH SO WE CAN SHOW IT TO OUR VP ON HER ANNUAL VISIT.
I HAVE TO KNOW; DOES IT EVEN CROSS YOUR MIND TO HANDLE THIS DIFFERENTLY?
I'LL NEED DAILY STATUS REPORTS ON WHY YOU'RE SO BEHIND.
© 1994 United Feature Syndicate, Inc.

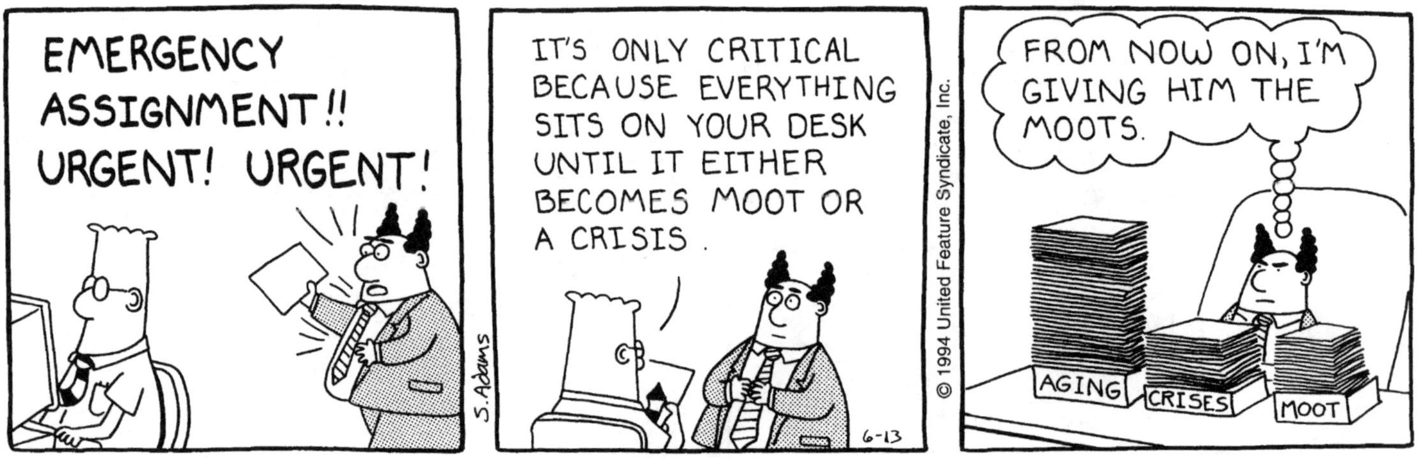
EMERGENCY ASSIGNMENT!! URGENT! URGENT!
IT'S ONLY CRITICAL BECAUSE EVERYTHING SITS ON YOUR DESK UNTIL IT EITHER BECOMES MOOT OR A CRISIS.
FROM NOW ON, I'M GIVING HIM THE MOOTS.
AGING
CRISES
MOOT
© 1994 United Feature Syndicate, Inc.

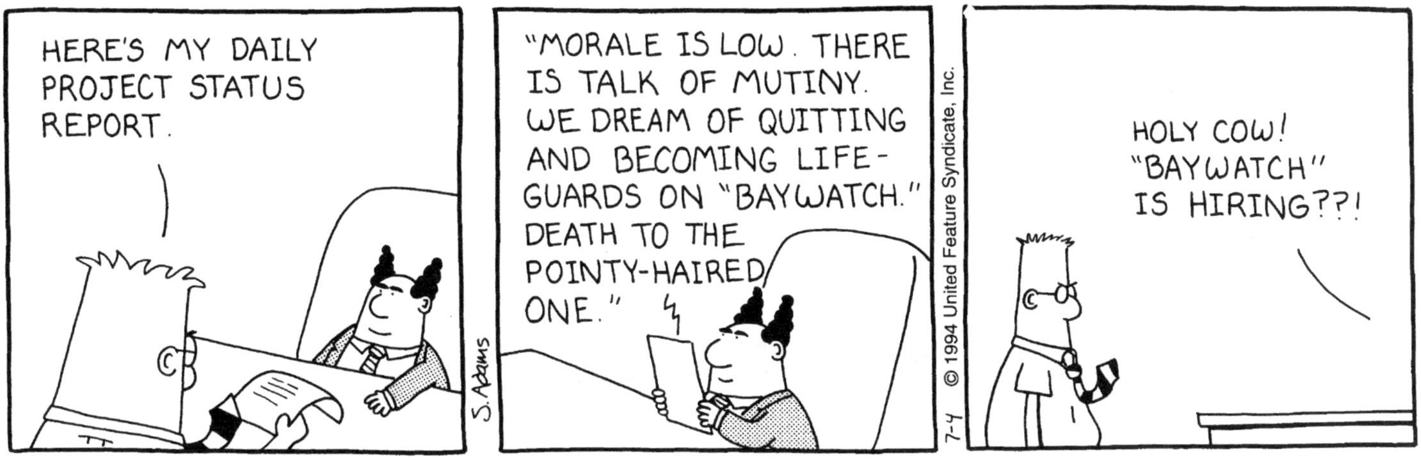
HERE'S MY DAILY PROJECT STATUS REPORT.
"MORALE IS LOW. THERE IS TALK OF MUTINY. WE DREAM OF QUITTING AND BECOMING LIFE-GUARDS ON "BAYWATCH." DEATH TO THE POINTY-HAIRED ONE."
HOLY COW! "BAYWATCH" IS HIRING??!
S. Adams
7-4 © 1994 United Feature Syndicate, Inc.

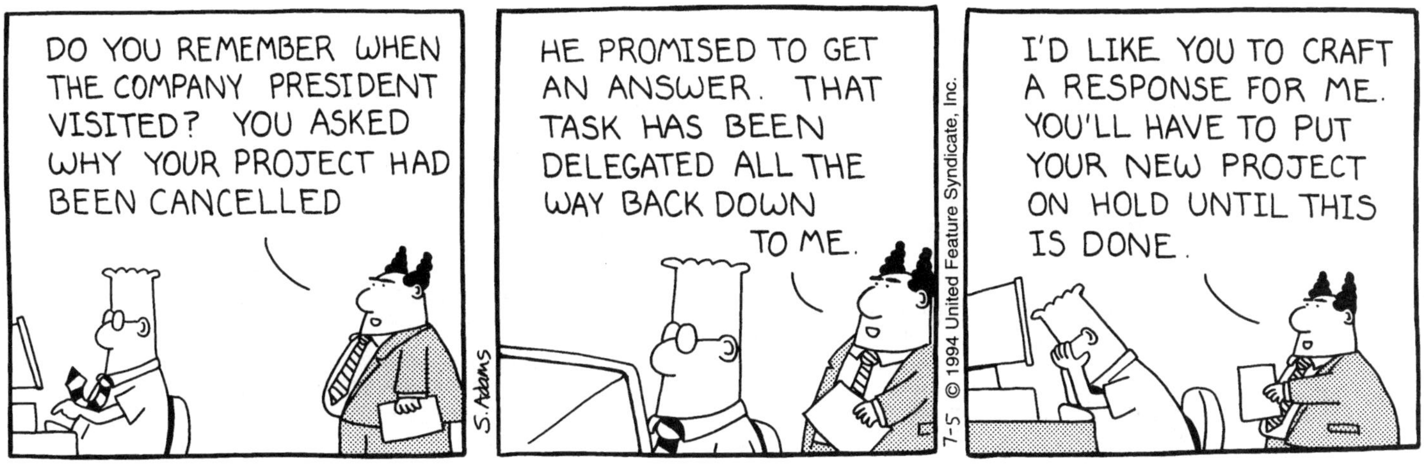
DO YOU REMEMBER WHEN THE COMPANY PRESIDENT VISITED? YOU ASKED WHY YOUR PROJECT HAD BEEN CANCELLED
HE PROMISED TO GET AN ANSWER. THAT TASK HAS BEEN DELEGATED ALL THE WAY BACK DOWN TO ME.
I'D LIKE YOU TO CRAFT A RESPONSE FOR ME. YOU'LL HAVE TO PUT YOUR NEW PROJECT ON HOLD UNTIL THIS IS DONE.
S. Adams
7-5 © 1994 United Feature Syndicate, Inc.

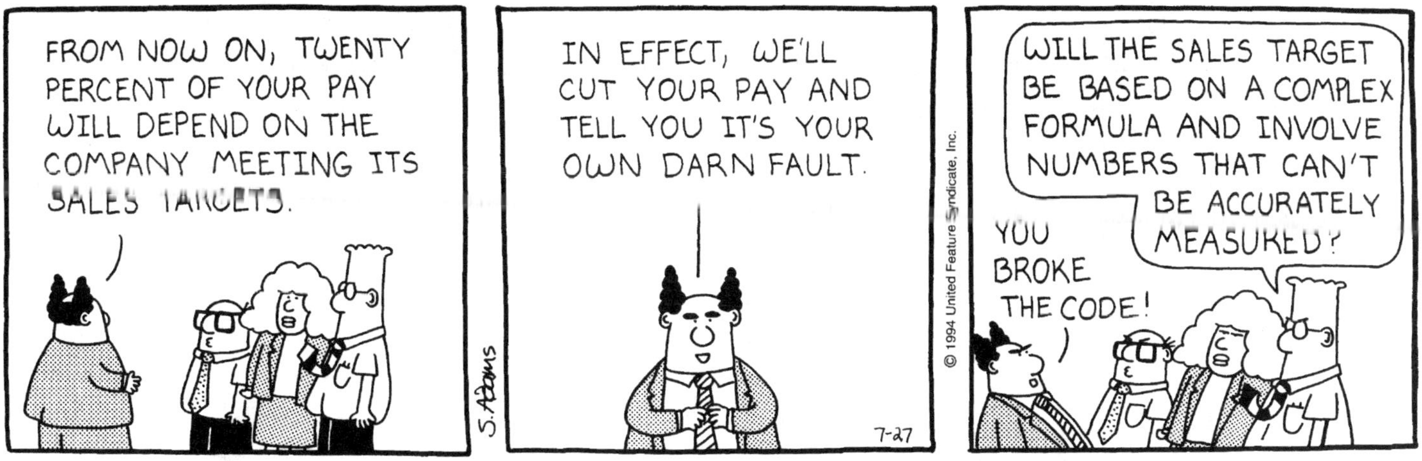
FROM NOW ON, TWENTY PERCENT OF YOUR PAY WILL DEPEND ON THE COMPANY MEETING ITS SALES TARGETS.
IN EFFECT, WE'LL CUT YOUR PAY AND TELL YOU IT'S YOUR OWN DARN FAULT.
WILL THE SALES TARGET BE BASED ON A COMPLEX FORMULA AND INVOLVE NUMBERS THAT CAN'T BE ACCURATELY MEASURED?
YOU BROKE THE CODE!
S. Adams
7-27
© 1994 United Feature Syndicate, Inc.

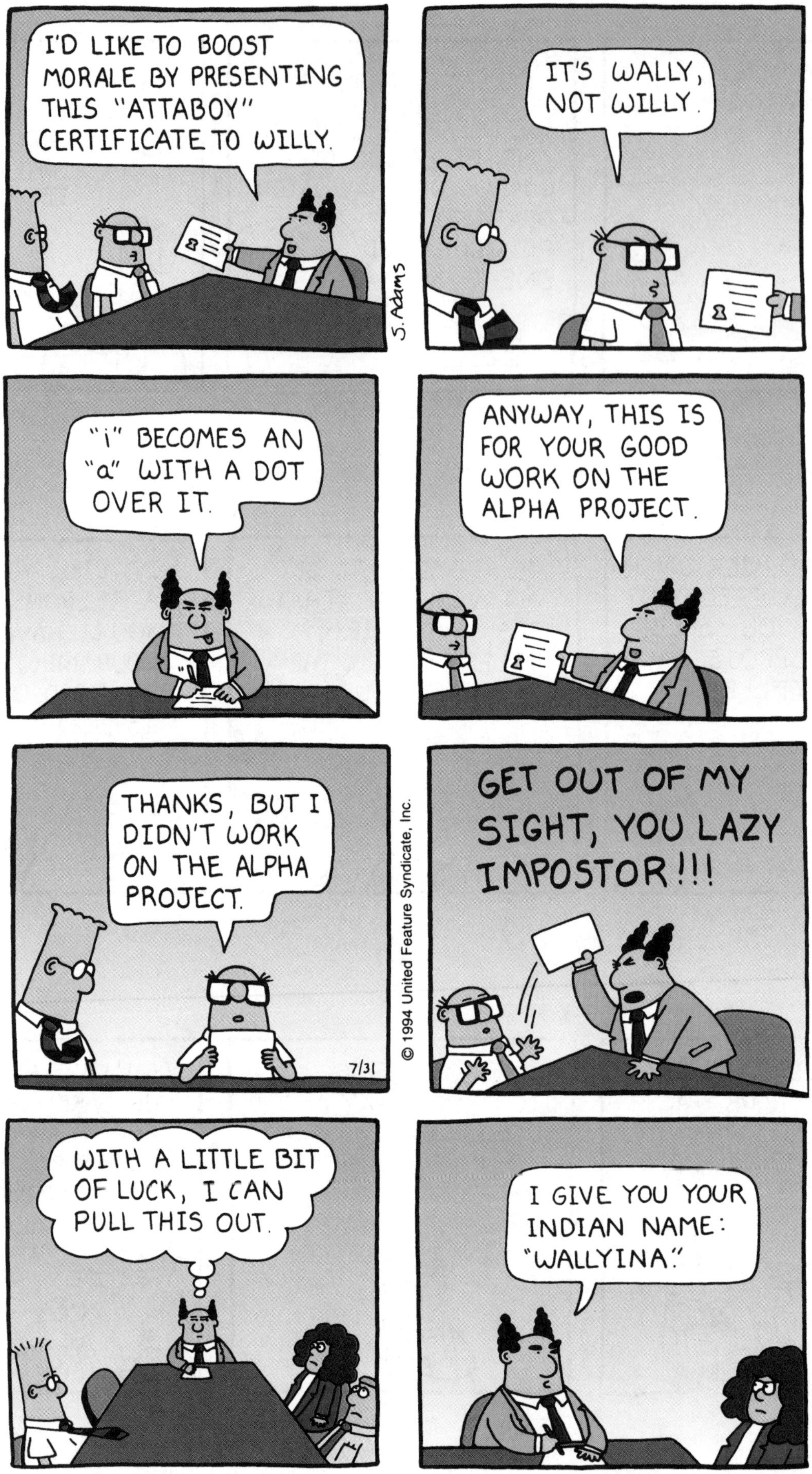
I'D LIKE TO BOOST MORALE BY PRESENTING THIS "ATTABOY" CERTIFICATE TO WILLY.
S. Adams
IT'S WALLY, NOT WILLY.
"i" BECOMES AN "a" WITH A DOT OVER IT.
ANYWAY, THIS IS FOR YOUR GOOD WORK ON THE ALPHA PROJECT.
THANKS, BUT I DIDN'T WORK ON THE ALPHA PROJECT.
7/31
© 1994 United Feature Syndicate, Inc.
GET OUT OF MY SIGHT, YOU LAZY IMPOSTOR!!!
WITH A LITTLE BIT OF LUCK, I CAN PULL THIS OUT.
I GIVE YOU YOUR INDIAN NAME: "WALLYINA."

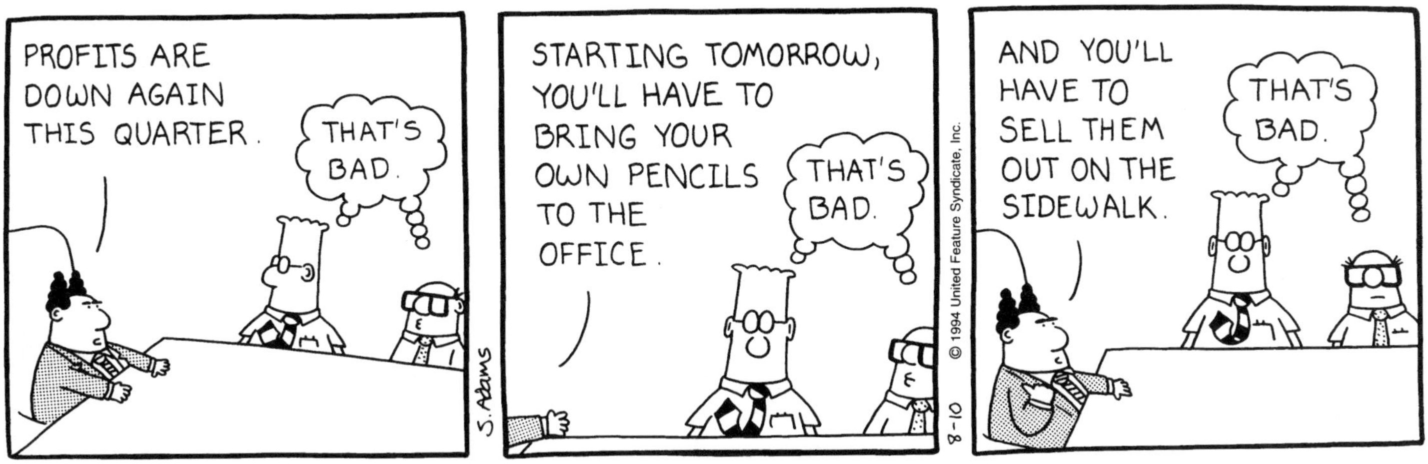
PROFITS ARE DOWN AGAIN THIS QUARTER.
THAT'S BAD.
STARTING TOMORROW, YOU'LL HAVE TO BRING YOUR OWN PENCILS TO THE OFFICE.
THAT'S BAD.
AND YOU'LL HAVE TO SELL THEM OUT ON THE SIDEWALK.
THAT'S BAD.
S. Adams
8-10
© 1994 United Feature Syndicate, Inc.

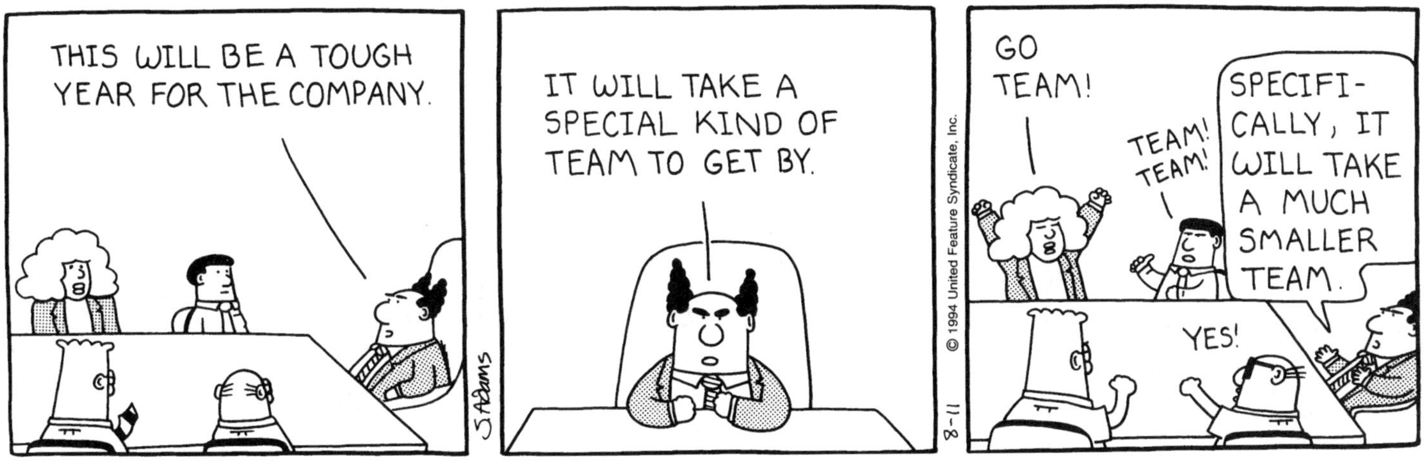
THIS WILL BE A TOUGH YEAR FOR THE COMPANY.
IT WILL TAKE A SPECIAL KIND OF TEAM TO GET BY.
GO TEAM!
TEAM! TEAM!
SPECIFI-CALLY, IT WILL TAKE A MUCH SMALLER TEAM.
YES!
S. Adams
8-11
© 1994 United Feature Syndicate, Inc.

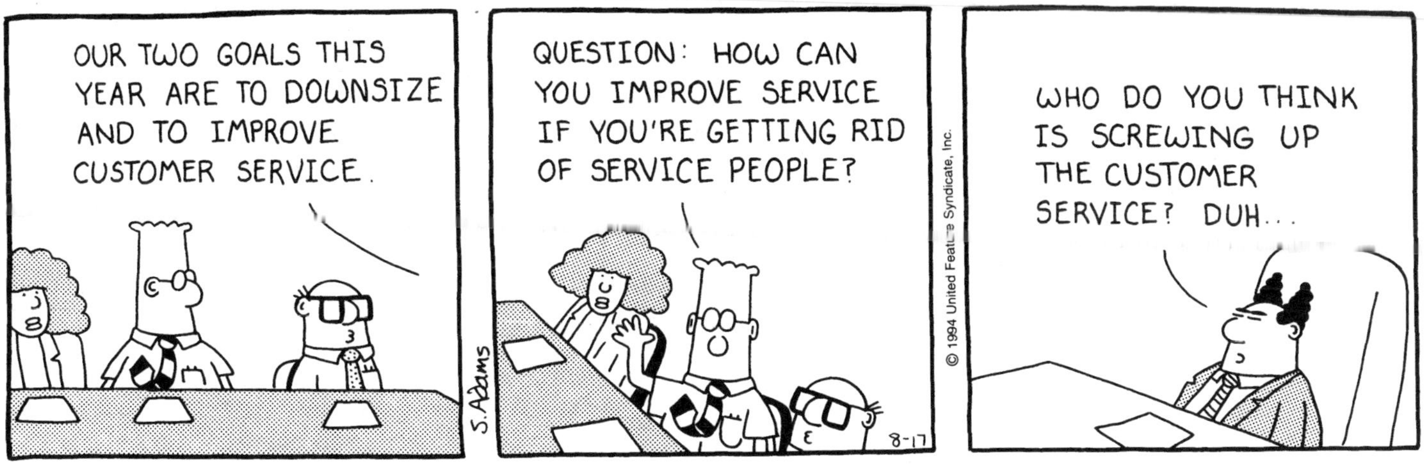
OUR TWO GOALS THIS YEAR ARE TO DOWNSIZE AND TO IMPROVE CUSTOMER SERVICE.
QUESTION: HOW CAN YOU IMPROVE SERVICE IF YOU'RE GETTING RID OF SERVICE PEOPLE?
WHO DO YOU THINK IS SCREWING UP THE CUSTOMER SERVICE? DUH...
S. Adams
8-17
© 1994 United Feature Syndicate, Inc.

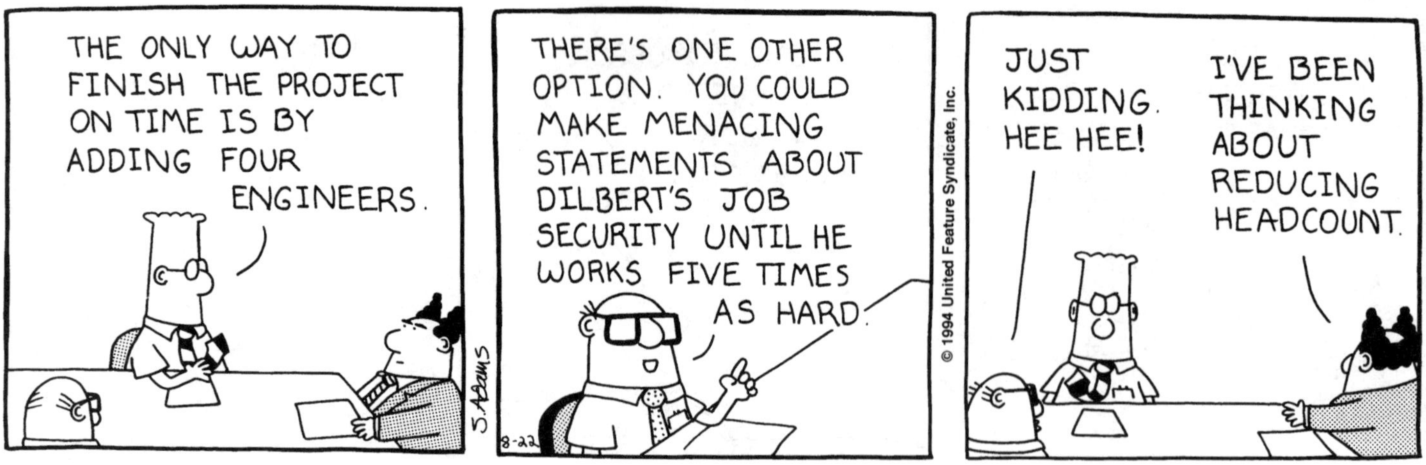
THE ONLY WAY TO FINISH THE PROJECT ON TIME IS BY ADDING FOUR ENGINEERS.
S. Adams
8-22
THERE'S ONE OTHER OPTION. YOU COULD MAKE MENACING STATEMENTS ABOUT DILBERT'S JOB SECURITY UNTIL HE WORKS FIVE TIMES AS HARD.
© 1994 United Feature Syndicate, Inc.
JUST KIDDING. HEE HEE!
I'VE BEEN THINKING ABOUT REDUCING HEADCOUNT.

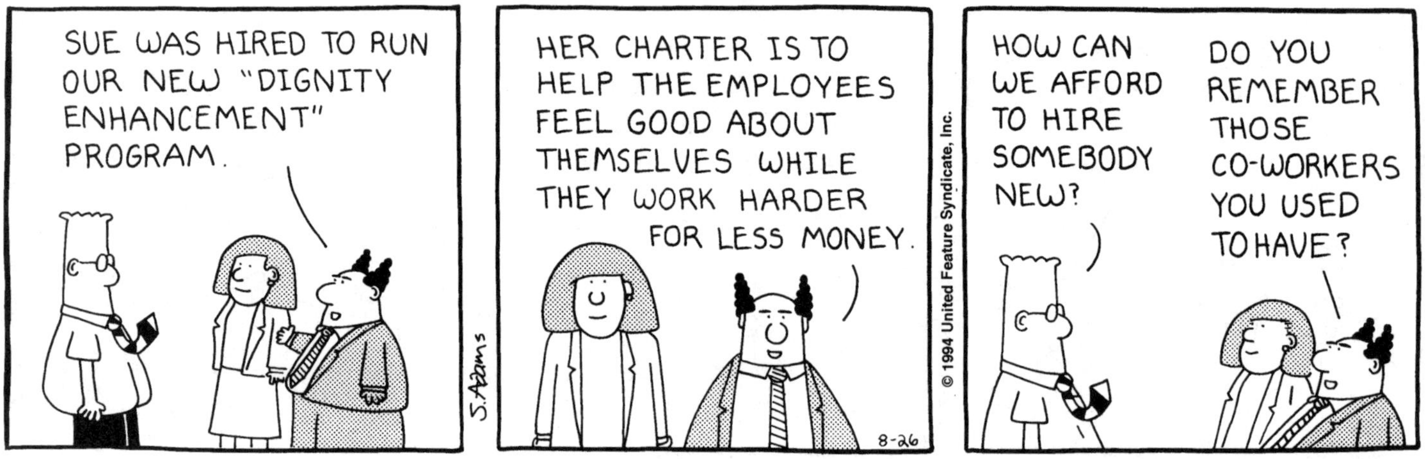
SUE WAS HIRED TO RUN OUR NEW "DIGNITY ENHANCEMENT" PROGRAM.
S. Adams
HER CHARTER IS TO HELP THE EMPLOYEES FEEL GOOD ABOUT THEMSELVES WHILE THEY WORK HARDER FOR LESS MONEY.
8-26
© 1994 United Feature Syndicate, Inc.
HOW CAN WE AFFORD TO HIRE SOMEBODY NEW?
DO YOU REMEMBER THOSE CO-WORKERS YOU USED TO HAVE?

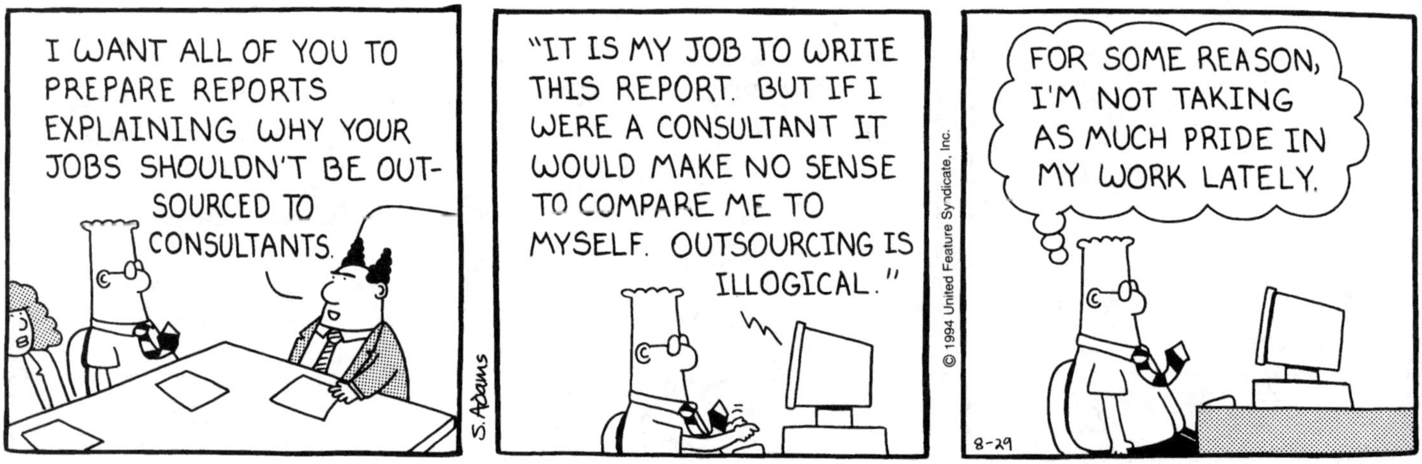
I WANT ALL OF YOU TO PREPARE REPORTS EXPLAINING WHY YOUR JOBS SHOULDN'T BE OUT-SOURCED TO CONSULTANTS.
S. Adams
"IT IS MY JOB TO WRITE THIS REPORT. BUT IF I WERE A CONSULTANT IT WOULD MAKE NO SENSE TO COMPARE ME TO MYSELF. OUTSOURCING IS ILLOGICAL."
© 1994 United Feature Syndicate, Inc.
FOR SOME REASON, I'M NOT TAKING AS MUCH PRIDE IN MY WORK LATELY.
8-29

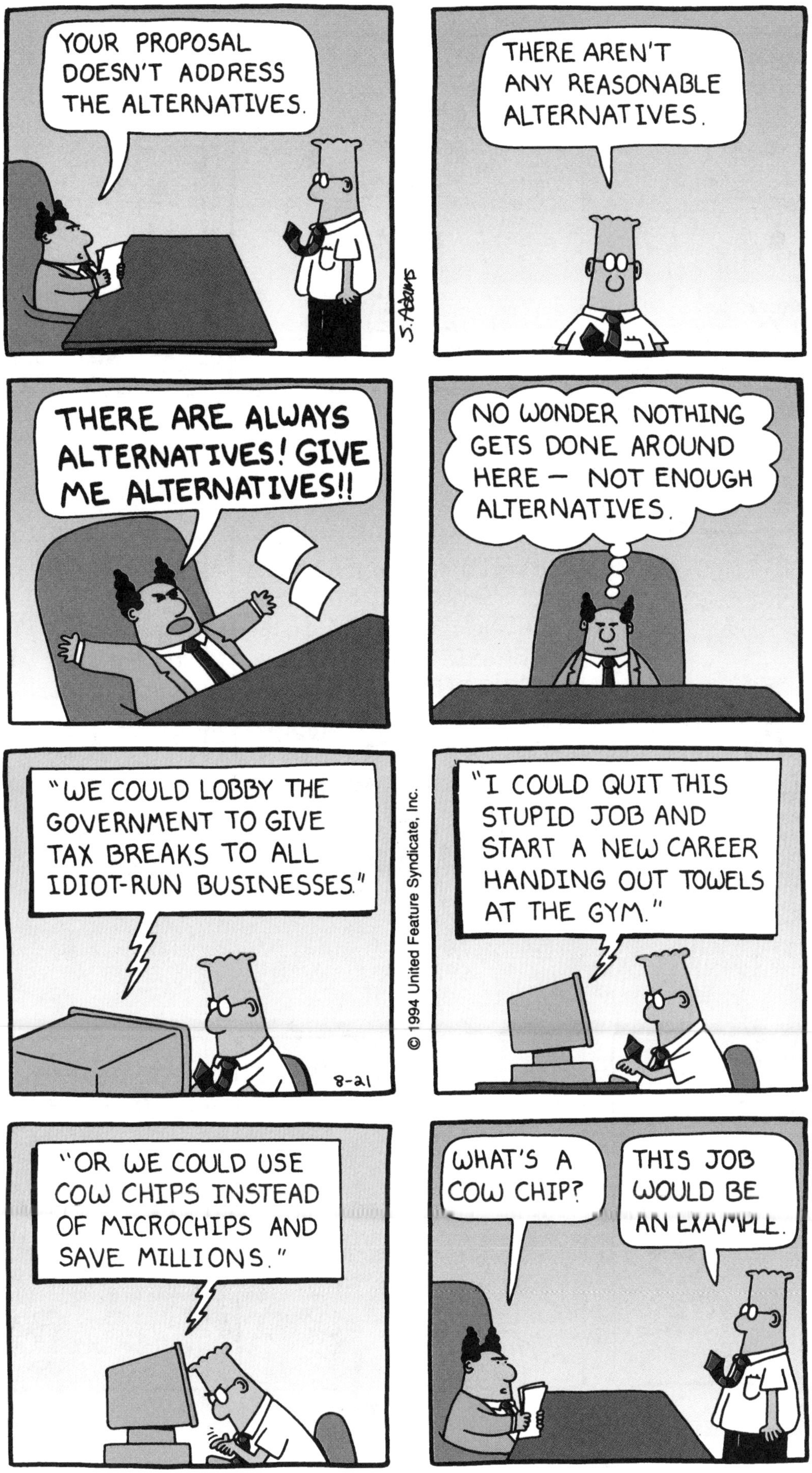
YOUR PROPOSAL DOESN'T ADDRESS THE ALTERNATIVES.
THERE AREN'T ANY REASONABLE ALTERNATIVES.
S. Adams
THERE ARE ALWAYS ALTERNATIVES! GIVE ME ALTERNATIVES!!
NO WONDER NOTHING GETS DONE AROUND HERE — NOT ENOUGH ALTERNATIVES.
"WE COULD LOBBY THE GOVERNMENT TO GIVE TAX BREAKS TO ALL IDIOT-RUN BUSINESSES."
8-21
© 1994 United Feature Syndicate, Inc.
"I COULD QUIT THIS STUPID JOB AND START A NEW CAREER HANDING OUT TOWELS AT THE GYM."
"OR WE COULD USE COW CHIPS INSTEAD OF MICROCHIPS AND SAVE MILLIONS."
WHAT'S A COW CHIP?
THIS JOB WOULD BE AN EXAMPLE.

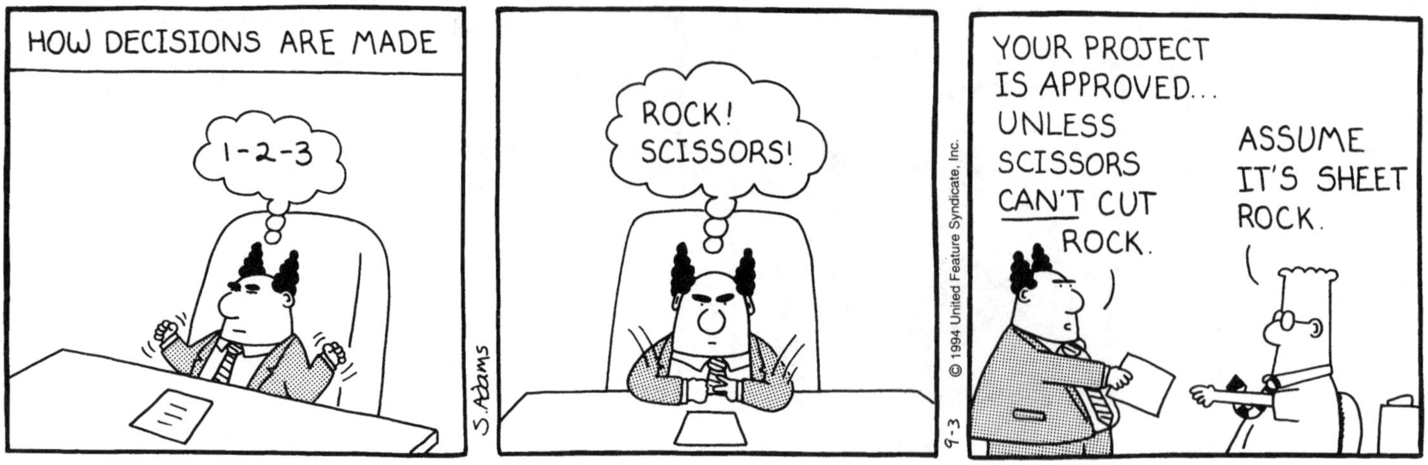
HOW DECISIONS ARE MADE
1-2-3
ROCK! SCISSORS!
YOUR PROJECT IS APPROVED... UNLESS SCISSORS CAN'T CUT ROCK.
ASSUME IT'S SHEET ROCK.
S. Adams
9-3
© 1994 United Feature Syndicate, Inc.

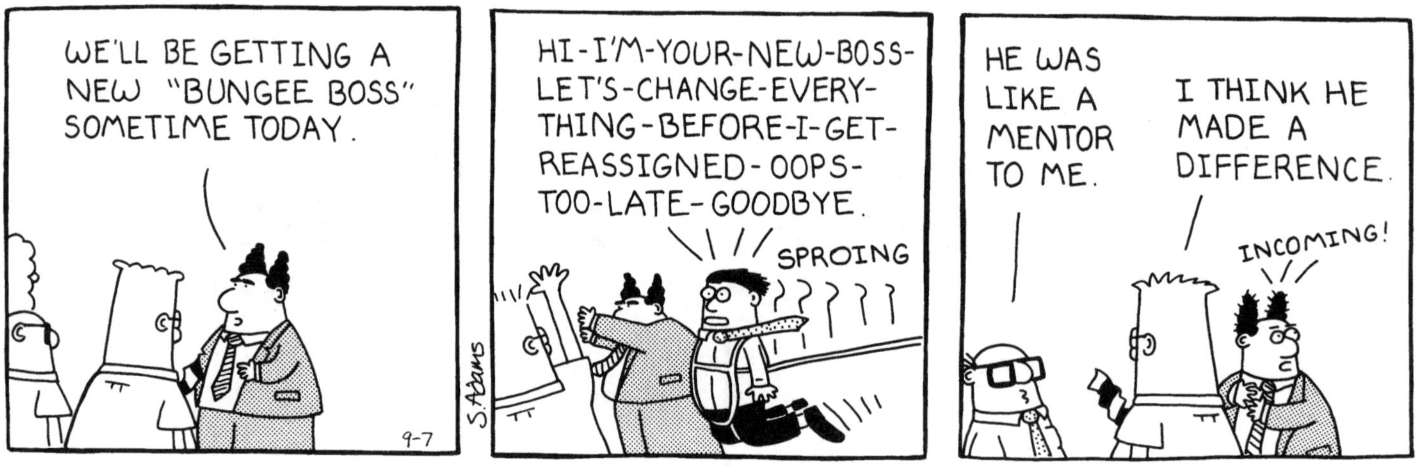
WE'LL BE GETTING A NEW "BUNGEE BOSS" SOMETIME TODAY.
9-7
HI-I'M-YOUR-NEW-BOSS-LET'S-CHANGE-EVERY-THING-BEFORE-I-GET-REASSIGNED-OOPS-TOO-LATE-GOODBYE.
SPROING
S. Adams
HE WAS LIKE A MENTOR TO ME.
I THINK HE MADE A DIFFERENCE.
INCOMING!

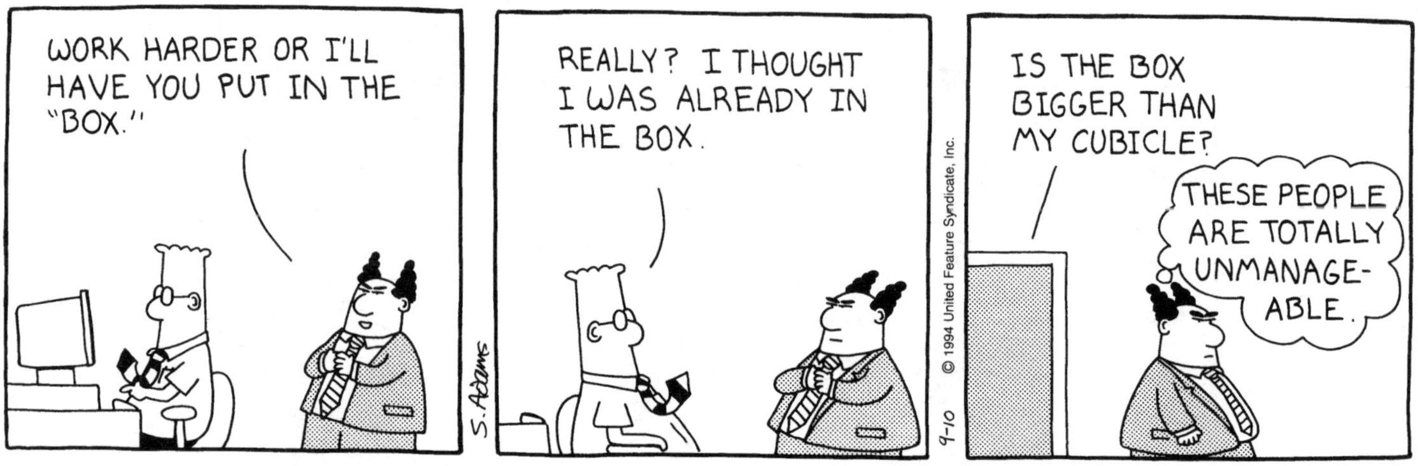
WORK HARDER OR I'LL HAVE YOU PUT IN THE "BOX."
S. Adams
REALLY? I THOUGHT I WAS ALREADY IN THE BOX.
IS THE BOX BIGGER THAN MY CUBICLE?
THESE PEOPLE ARE TOTALLY UNMANAGE-ABLE.
9-10
© 1994 United Feature Syndicate, Inc.

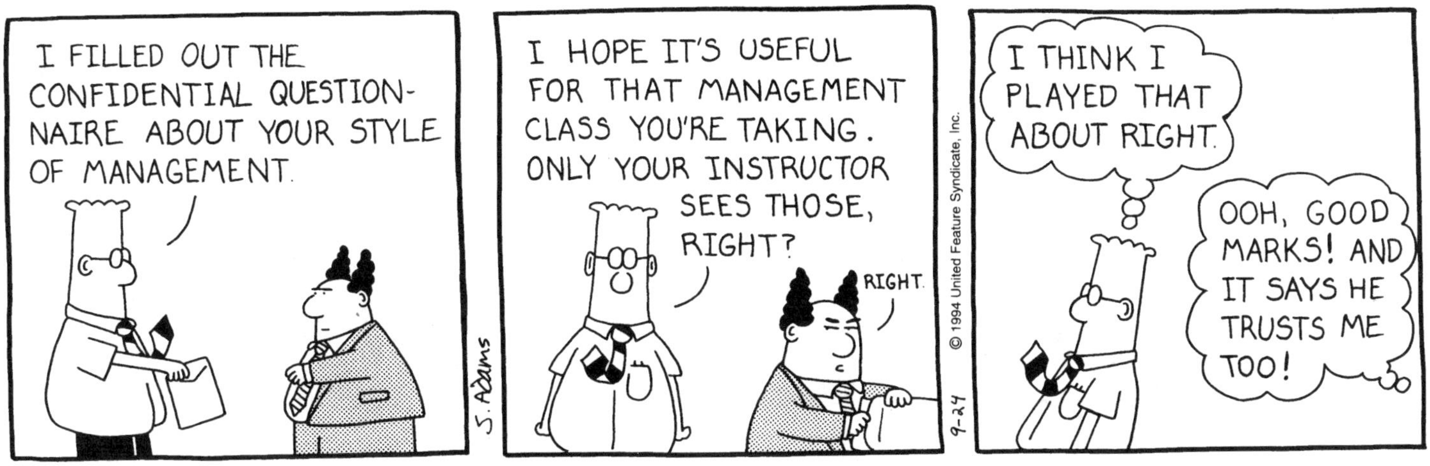
I FILLED OUT THE CONFIDENTIAL QUESTION-NAIRE ABOUT YOUR STYLE OF MANAGEMENT.
S. Adams
I HOPE IT'S USEFUL FOR THAT MANAGEMENT CLASS YOU'RE TAKING. ONLY YOUR INSTRUCTOR SEES THOSE, RIGHT?
RIGHT.
© 1994 United Feature Syndicate, Inc.
9-24
I THINK I PLAYED THAT ABOUT RIGHT.
OOH, GOOD MARKS! AND IT SAYS HE TRUSTS ME TOO!

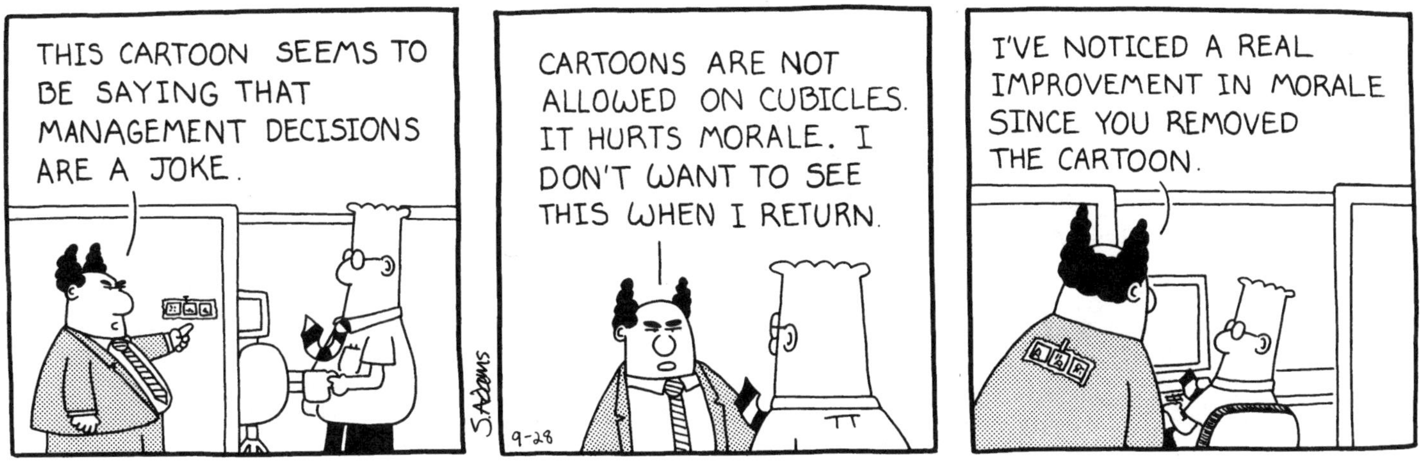
THIS CARTOON SEEMS TO BE SAYING THAT MANAGEMENT DECISIONS ARE A JOKE.
S. Adams
9-28
CARTOONS ARE NOT ALLOWED ON CUBICLES. IT HURTS MORALE. I DON'T WANT TO SEE THIS WHEN I RETURN.
I'VE NOTICED A REAL IMPROVEMENT IN MORALE SINCE YOU REMOVED THE CARTOON.

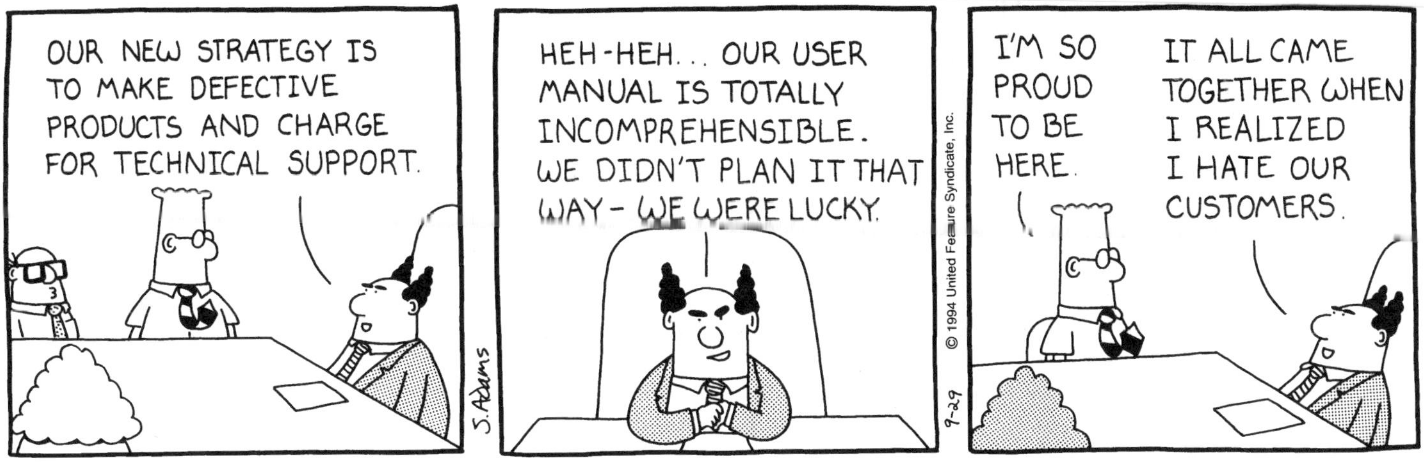
OUR NEW STRATEGY IS TO MAKE DEFECTIVE PRODUCTS AND CHARGE FOR TECHNICAL SUPPORT.
S. Adams
HEH-HEH... OUR USER MANUAL IS TOTALLY INCOMPREHENSIBLE. WE DIDN'T PLAN IT THAT WAY - WE WERE LUCKY.
© 1994 United Feature Syndicate, Inc.
9-29
I'M SO PROUD TO BE HERE.
IT ALL CAME TOGETHER WHEN I REALIZED I HATE OUR CUSTOMERS.

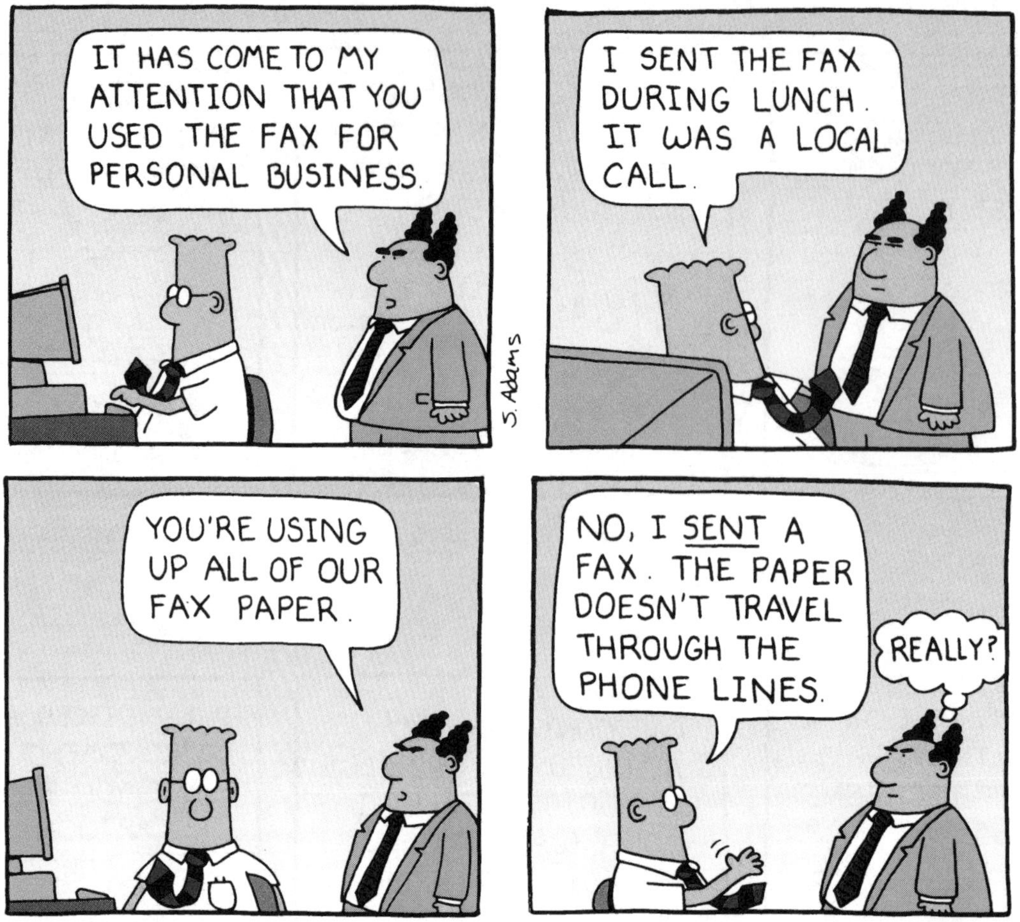
IT HAS COME TO MY ATTENTION THAT YOU USED THE FAX FOR PERSONAL BUSINESS.
S. Adams
I SENT THE FAX DURING LUNCH. IT WAS A LOCAL CALL.
YOU'RE USING UP ALL OF OUR FAX PAPER.
NO, I SENT A FAX. THE PAPER DOESN'T TRAVEL THROUGH THE PHONE LINES.
REALLY?

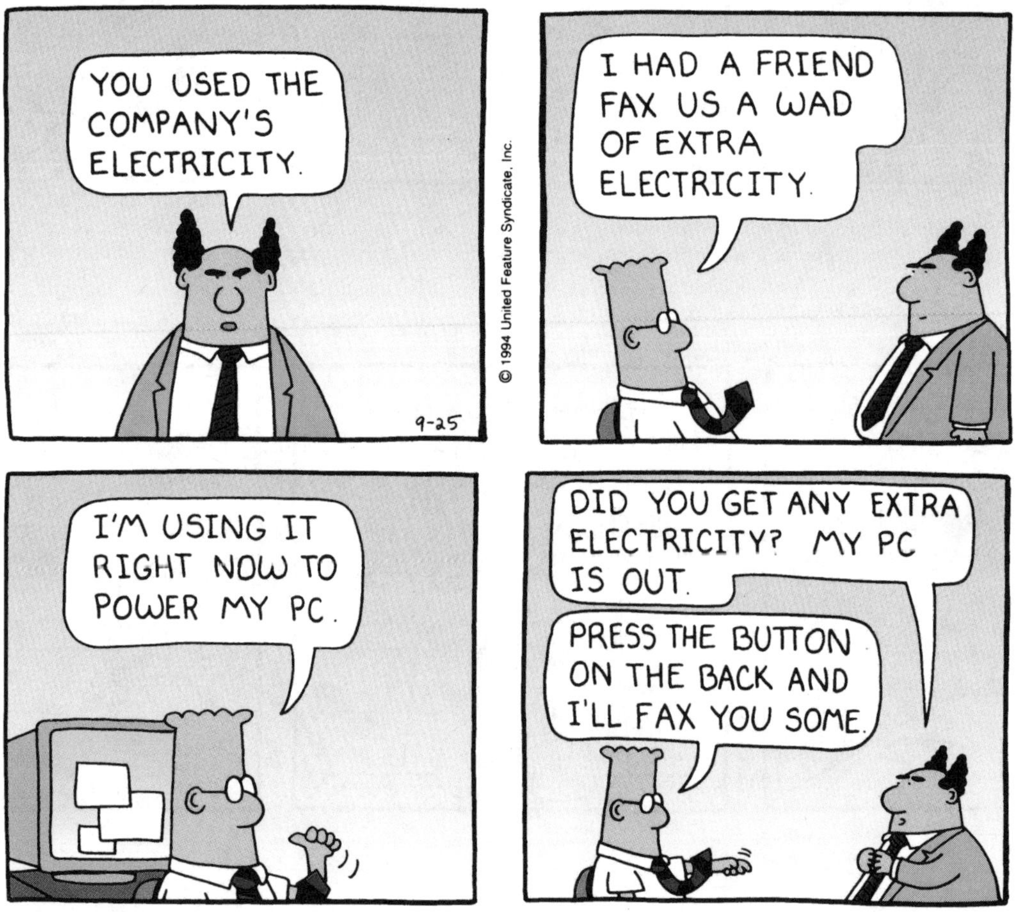
YOU USED THE COMPANY'S ELECTRICITY.
9-25
I HAD A FRIEND FAX US A WAD OF EXTRA ELECTRICITY.
I'M USING IT RIGHT NOW TO POWER MY PC.
DID YOU GET ANY EXTRA ELECTRICITY? MY PC IS OUT.
PRESS THE BUTTON ON THE BACK AND I'LL FAX YOU SOME.

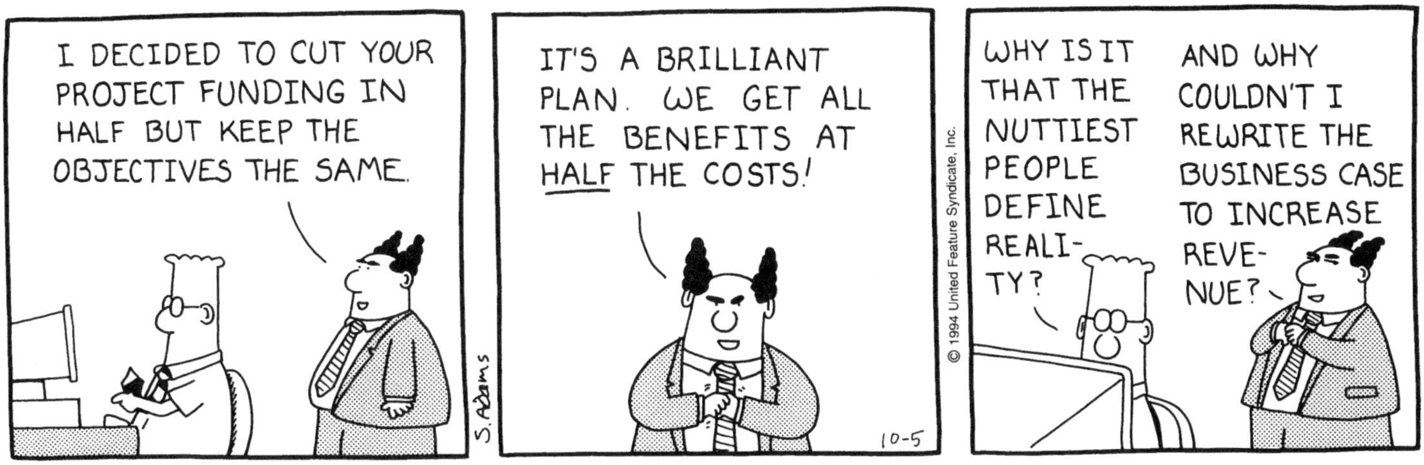
I DECIDED TO CUT YOUR PROJECT FUNDING IN HALF BUT KEEP THE OBJECTIVES THE SAME.
S. Adams
IT'S A BRILLIANT PLAN. WE GET ALL THE BENEFITS AT HALF THE COSTS!
10-5
© 1994 United Feature Syndicate, Inc.
WHY IS IT THAT THE NUTTIEST PEOPLE DEFINE REALI-TY?
AND WHY COULDN'T I REWRITE THE BUSINESS CASE TO INCREASE REVE-NUE?

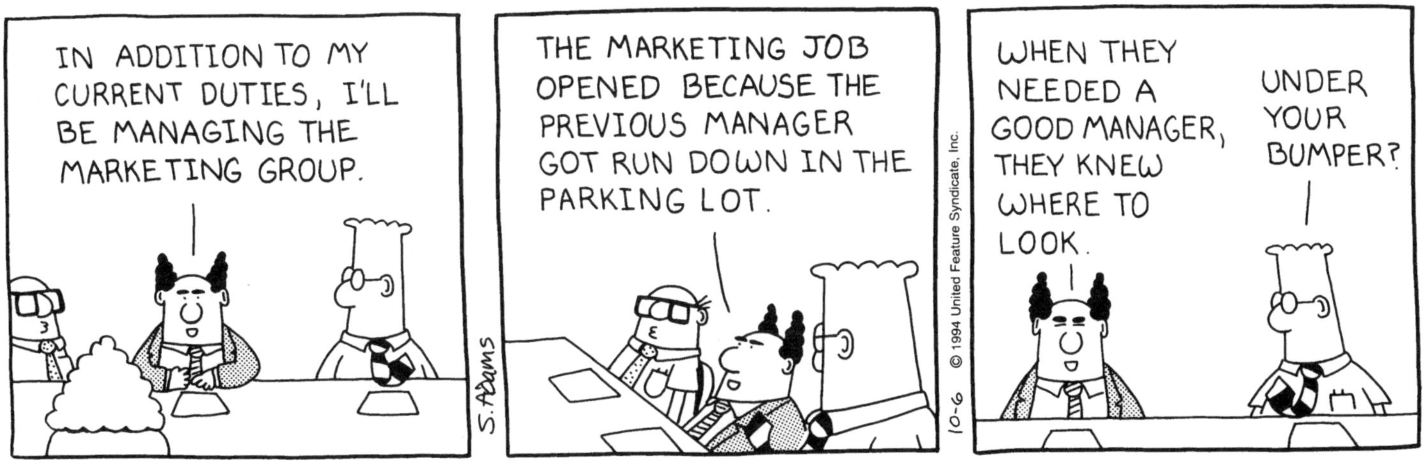
IN ADDITION TO MY CURRENT DUTIES, I'LL BE MANAGING THE MARKETING GROUP.
S. Adams
THE MARKETING JOB OPENED BECAUSE THE PREVIOUS MANAGER GOT RUN DOWN IN THE PARKING LOT.
10-6
© 1994 United Feature Syndicate, Inc.
WHEN THEY NEEDED A GOOD MANAGER, THEY KNEW WHERE TO LOOK.
UNDER YOUR BUMPER?

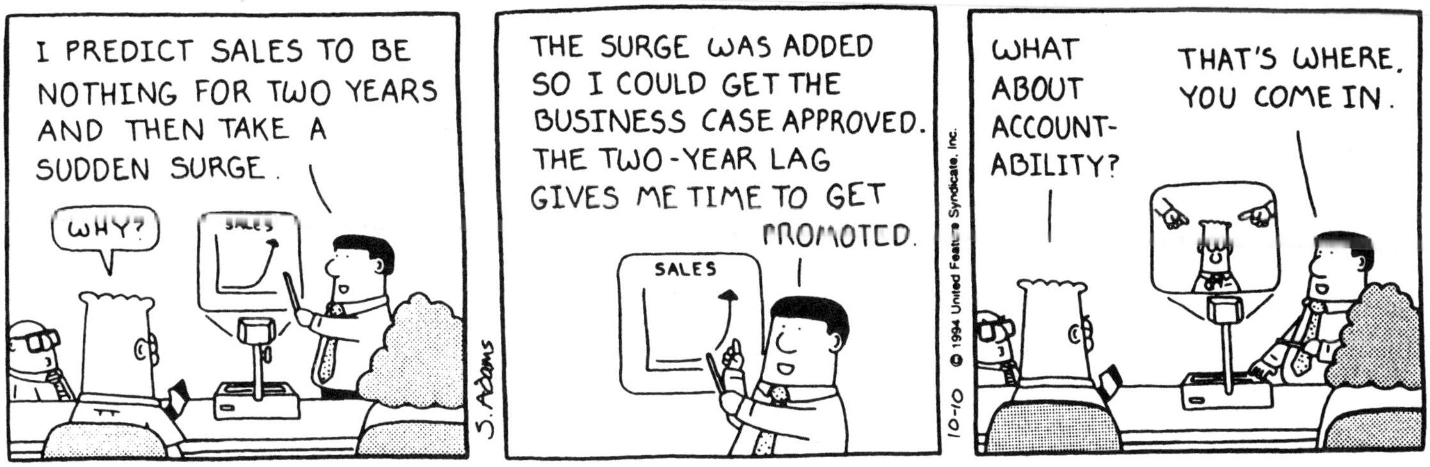
I PREDICT SALES TO BE NOTHING FOR TWO YEARS AND THEN TAKE A SUDDEN SURGE.
WHY?
S. Adams
THE SURGE WAS ADDED SO I COULD GET THE BUSINESS CASE APPROVED. THE TWO-YEAR LAG GIVES ME TIME TO GET PROMOTED.
SALES
10-10
WHAT ABOUT ACCOUNT-ABILITY?
THAT'S WHERE YOU COME IN.

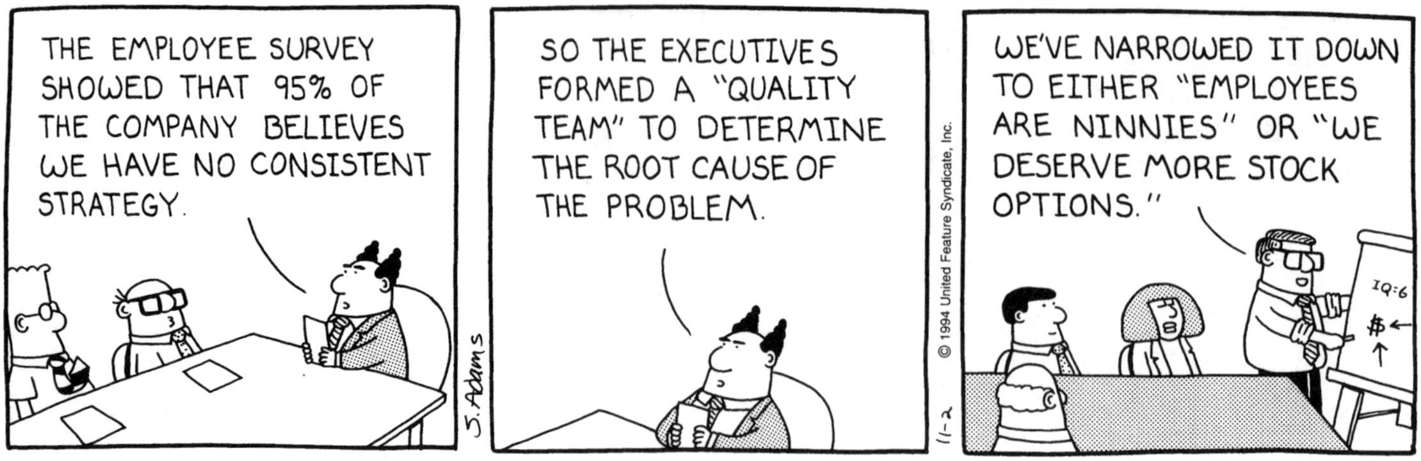
THE EMPLOYEE SURVEY SHOWED THAT 95% OF THE COMPANY BELIEVES WE HAVE NO CONSISTENT STRATEGY.
S. Adams
SO THE EXECUTIVES FORMED A "QUALITY TEAM" TO DETERMINE THE ROOT CAUSE OF THE PROBLEM.
11-2
© 1994 United Feature Syndicate, Inc.
WE'VE NARROWED IT DOWN TO EITHER "EMPLOYEES ARE NINNIES" OR "WE DESERVE MORE STOCK OPTIONS."
IQ:6
$

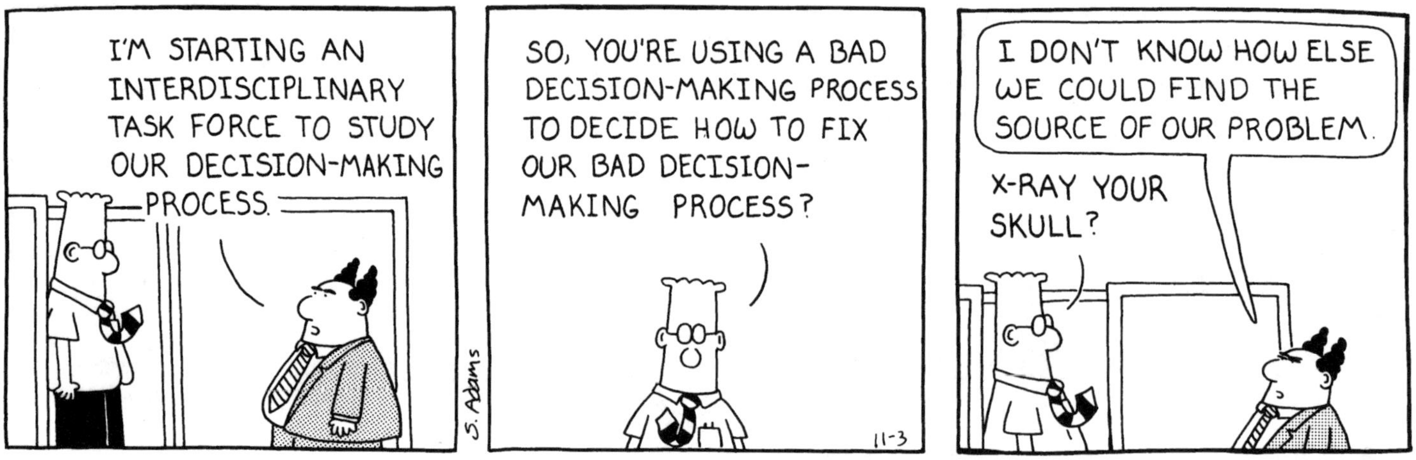
I'M STARTING AN INTERDISCIPLINARY TASK FORCE TO STUDY OUR DECISION-MAKING PROCESS.
S. Adams
SO, YOU'RE USING A BAD DECISION-MAKING PROCESS TO DECIDE HOW TO FIX OUR BAD DECISION-MAKING PROCESS?
11-3
I DON'T KNOW HOW ELSE WE COULD FIND THE SOURCE OF OUR PROBLEM.
X-RAY YOUR SKULL?

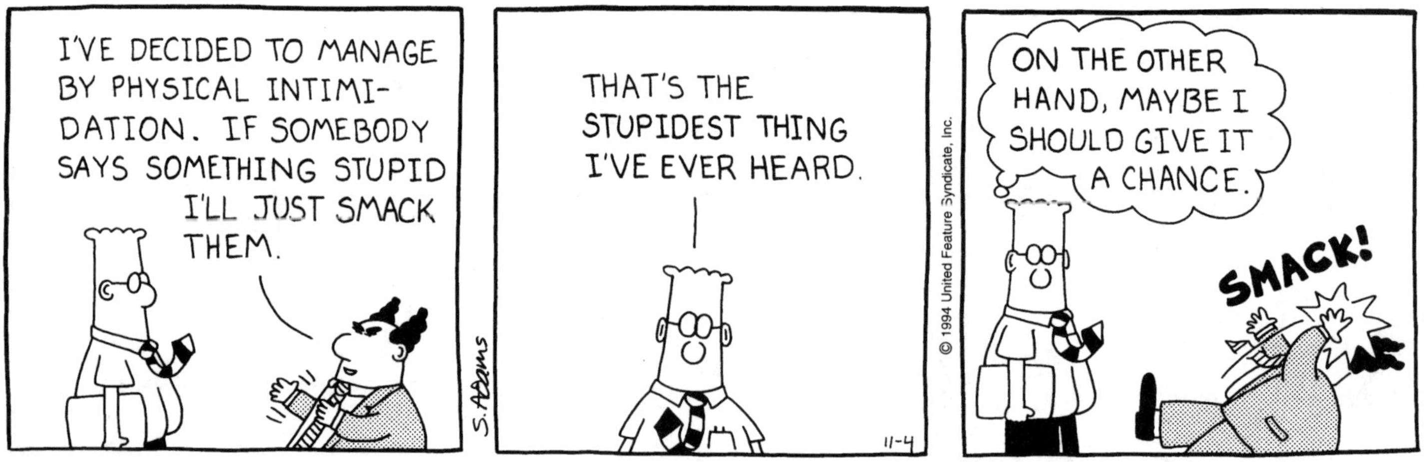
I'VE DECIDED TO MANAGE BY PHYSICAL INTIMIDATION. IF SOMEBODY SAYS SOMETHING STUPID I'LL JUST SMACK THEM.
S. Adams
THAT'S THE STUPIDEST THING I'VE EVER HEARD.
11-4
© 1994 United Feature Syndicate, Inc.
ON THE OTHER HAND, MAYBE I SHOULD GIVE IT A CHANCE.
SMACK!

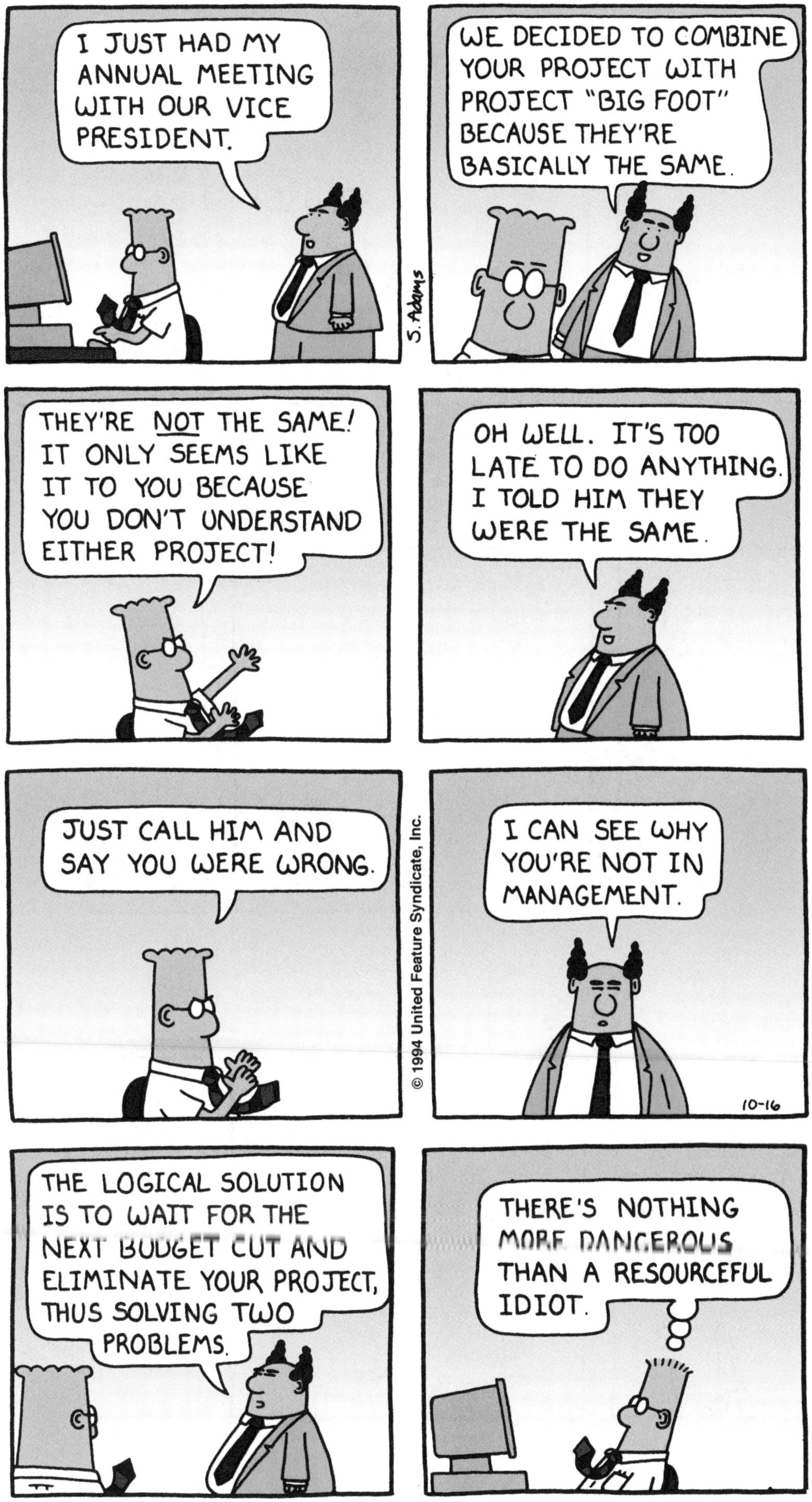
I JUST HAD MY ANNUAL MEETING WITH OUR VICE PRESIDENT.
S. Adams
WE DECIDED TO COMBINE YOUR PROJECT WITH PROJECT "BIG FOOT" BECAUSE THEY'RE BASICALLY THE SAME.
THEY'RE NOT THE SAME! IT ONLY SEEMS LIKE IT TO YOU BECAUSE YOU DON'T UNDERSTAND EITHER PROJECT!
OH WELL. IT'S TOO LATE TO DO ANYTHING. I TOLD HIM THEY WERE THE SAME.
JUST CALL HIM AND SAY YOU WERE WRONG.
© 1994 United Feature Syndicate, Inc.
I CAN SEE WHY YOU'RE NOT IN MANAGEMENT.
10-16
THE LOGICAL SOLUTION IS TO WAIT FOR THE NEXT BUDGET CUT AND ELIMINATE YOUR PROJECT, THUS SOLVING TWO PROBLEMS.
THERE'S NOTHING MORE DANGEROUS THAN A RESOURCEFUL IDIOT.

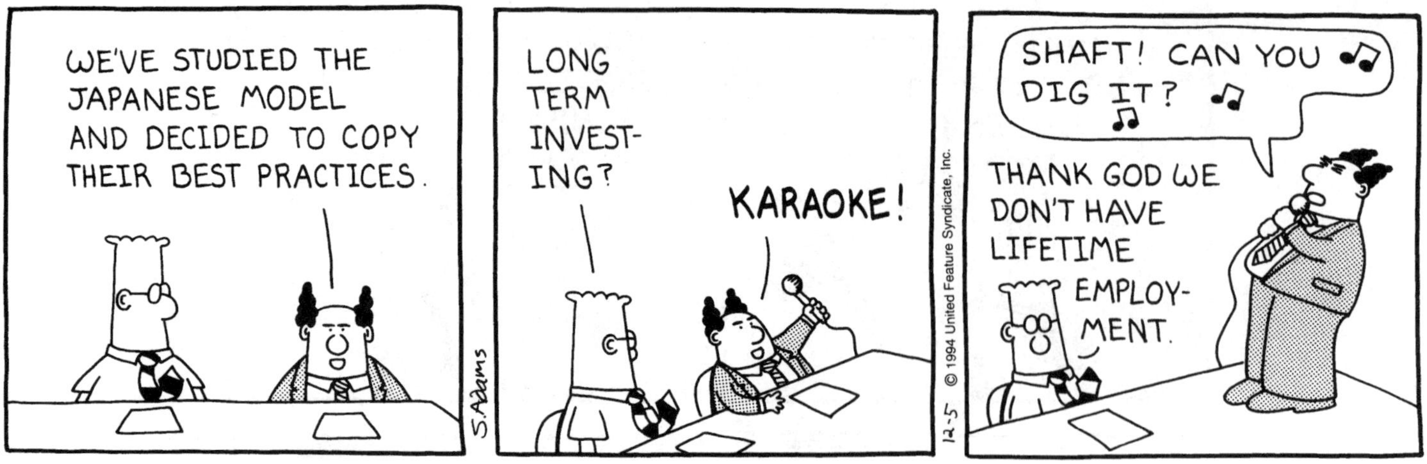
WE'VE STUDIED THE JAPANESE MODEL AND DECIDED TO COPY THEIR BEST PRACTICES.
S. Adams
LONG TERM INVEST-ING?
KARAOKE!
12-5 © 1994 United Feature Syndicate, Inc.
SHAFT! CAN YOU DIG IT?
THANK GOD WE DON'T HAVE LIFETIME EMPLOY-MENT.

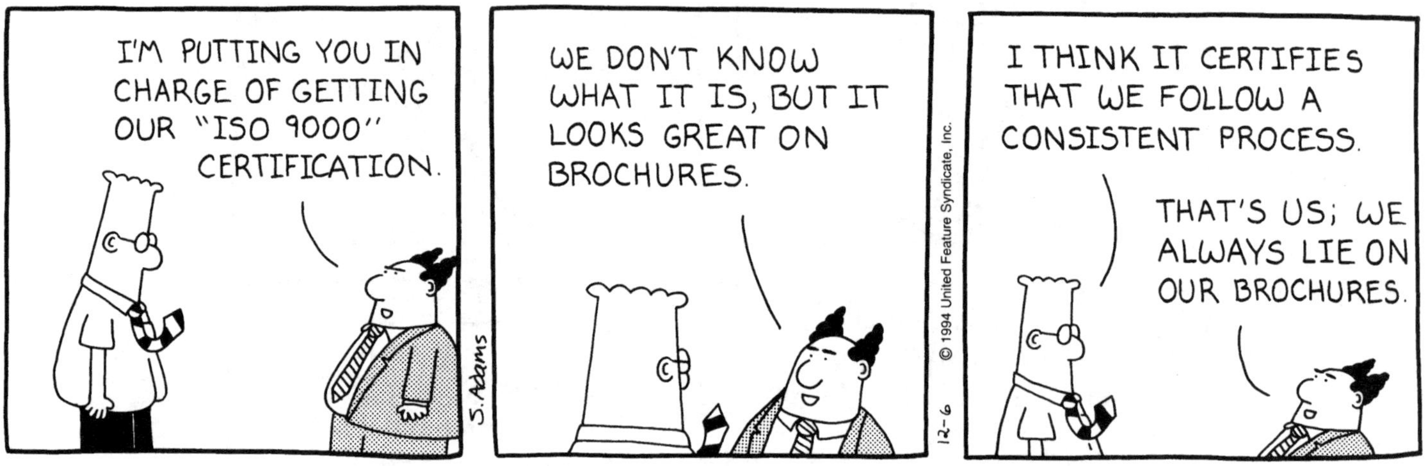
I'M PUTTING YOU IN CHARGE OF GETTING OUR "ISO 9000" CERTIFICATION.
S. Adams
WE DON'T KNOW WHAT IT IS, BUT IT LOOKS GREAT ON BROCHURES.
12-6 © 1994 United Feature Syndicate, Inc.
I THINK IT CERTIFIES THAT WE FOLLOW A CONSISTENT PROCESS.
THAT'S US; WE ALWAYS LIE ON OUR BROCHURES.

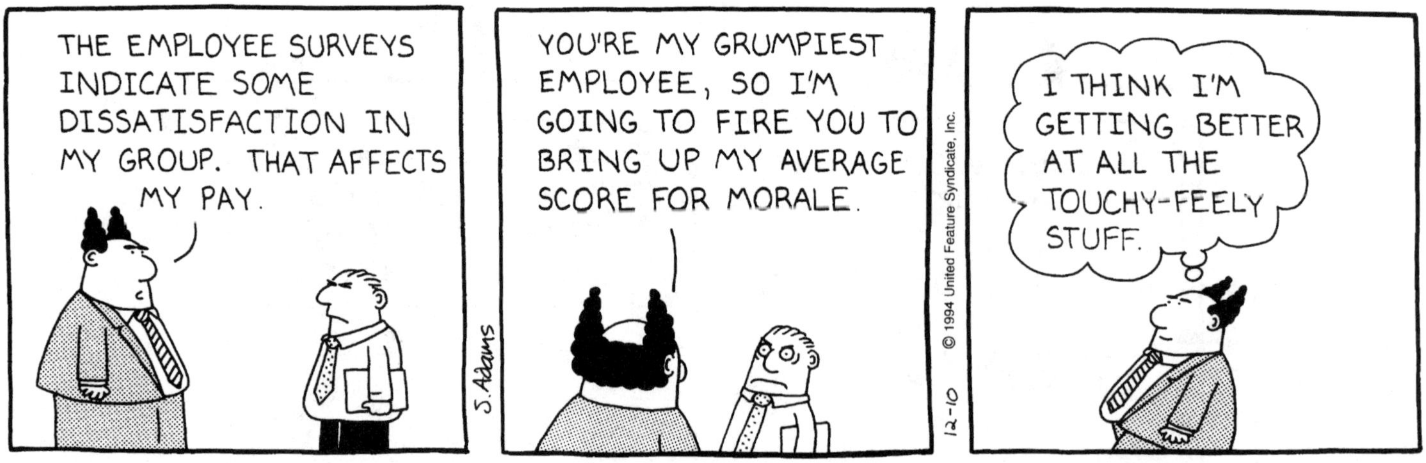
THE EMPLOYEE SURVEYS INDICATE SOME DISSATISFACTION IN MY GROUP. THAT AFFECTS MY PAY.
S. Adams
YOU'RE MY GRUMPIEST EMPLOYEE, SO I'M GOING TO FIRE YOU TO BRING UP MY AVERAGE SCORE FOR MORALE.
12-10 © 1994 United Feature Syndicate, Inc.
I THINK I'M GETTING BETTER AT ALL THE TOUCHY-FEELY STUFF.

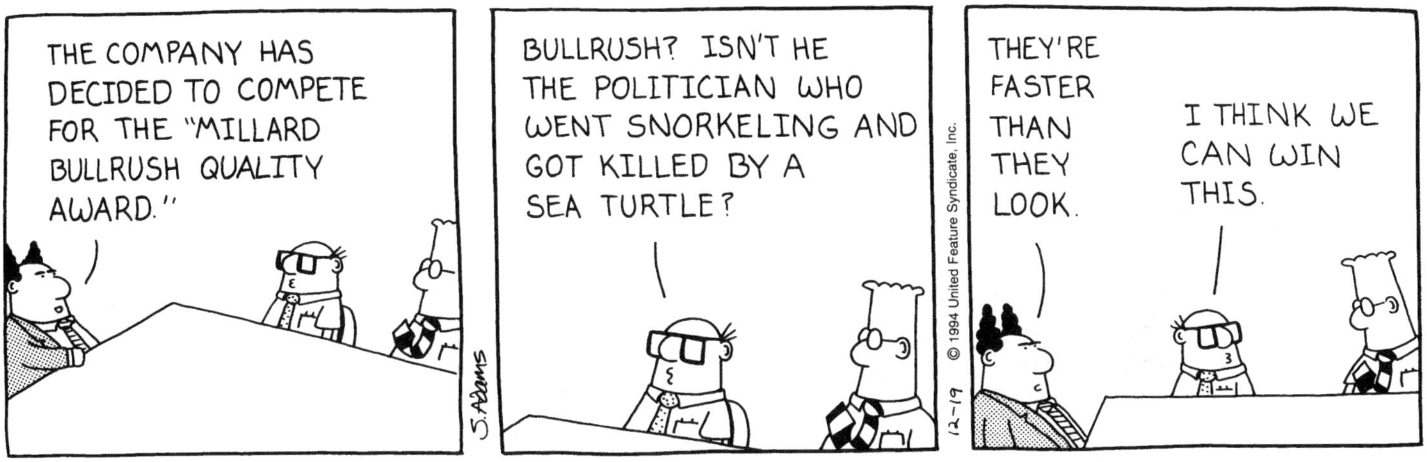
THE COMPANY HAS DECIDED TO COMPETE FOR THE "MILLARD BULLRUSH QUALITY AWARD."
BULLRUSH? ISN'T HE THE POLITICIAN WHO WENT SNORKELING AND GOT KILLED BY A SEA TURTLE?
THEY'RE FASTER THAN THEY LOOK.
I THINK WE CAN WIN THIS.
S. Adams
12-19
© 1994 United Feature Syndicate, Inc.

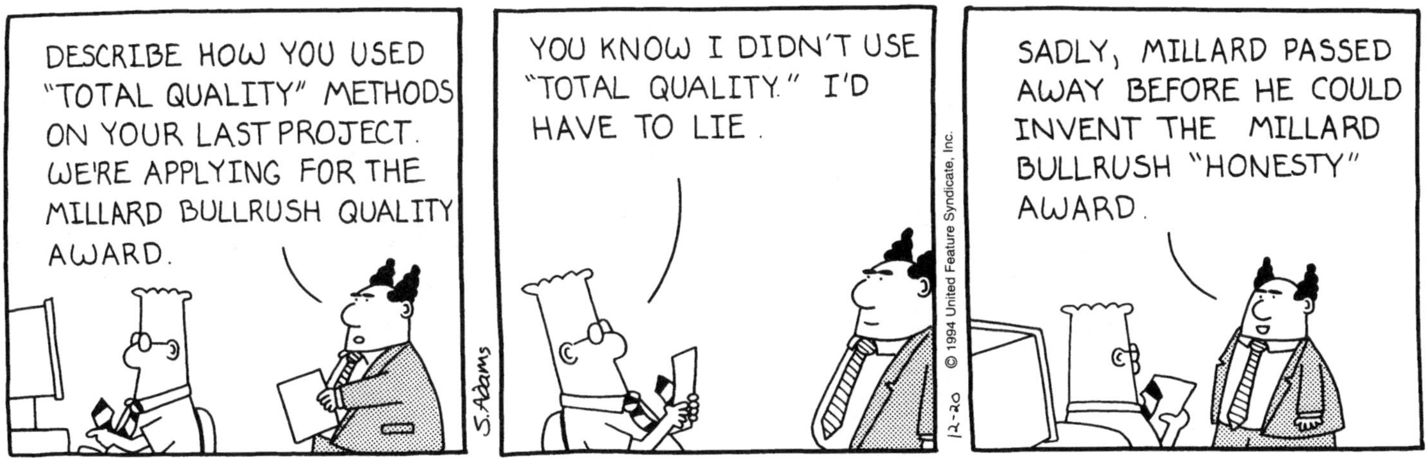
DESCRIBE HOW YOU USED "TOTAL QUALITY" METHODS ON YOUR LAST PROJECT. WE'RE APPLYING FOR THE MILLARD BULLRUSH QUALITY AWARD.
YOU KNOW I DIDN'T USE "TOTAL QUALITY." I'D HAVE TO LIE.
SADLY, MILLARD PASSED AWAY BEFORE HE COULD INVENT THE MILLARD BULLRUSH "HONESTY" AWARD.
S. Adams
12-20
© 1994 United Feature Syndicate, Inc.

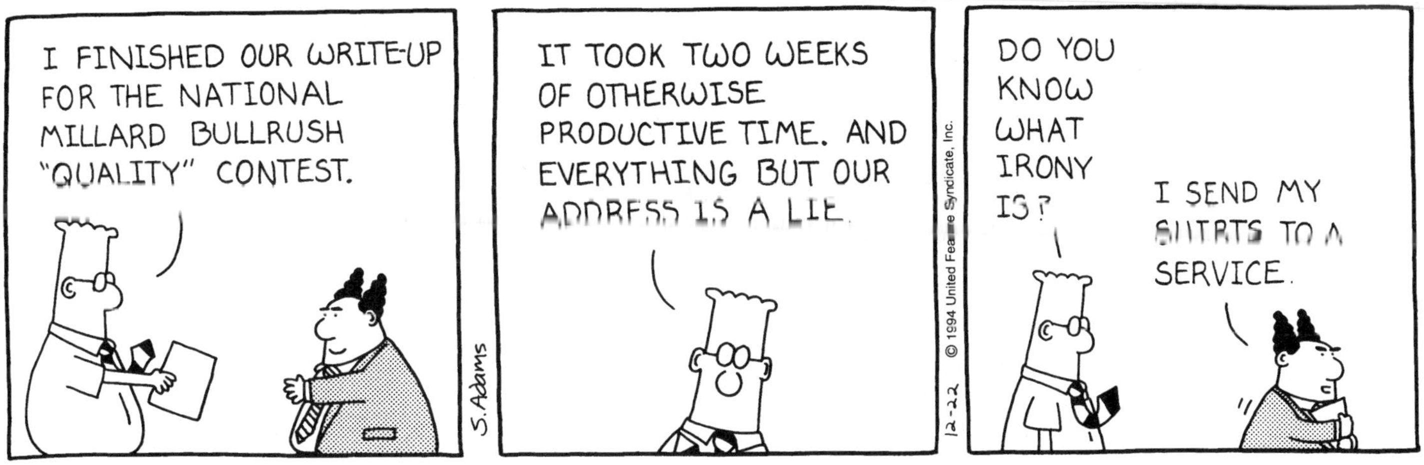
I FINISHED OUR WRITE-UP FOR THE NATIONAL MILLARD BULLRUSH "QUALITY" CONTEST.
IT TOOK TWO WEEKS OF OTHERWISE PRODUCTIVE TIME. AND EVERYTHING BUT OUR ADDRESS IS A LIE.
DO YOU KNOW WHAT IRONY IS?
I SEND MY SHIRTS TO A SERVICE.
S. Adams
12-22
© 1994 United Feature Syndicate, Inc.

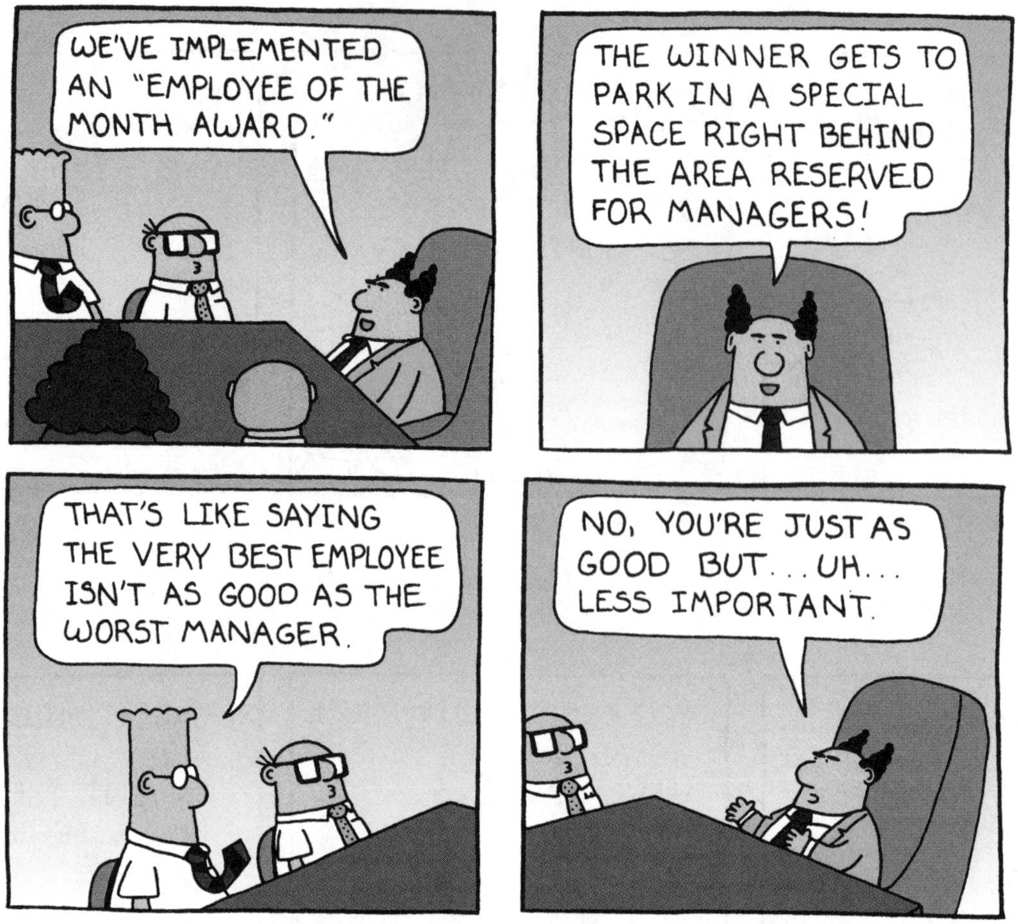
WE'VE IMPLEMENTED AN "EMPLOYEE OF THE MONTH AWARD."
THE WINNER GETS TO PARK IN A SPECIAL SPACE RIGHT BEHIND THE AREA RESERVED FOR MANAGERS!
THAT'S LIKE SAYING THE VERY BEST EMPLOYEE ISN'T AS GOOD AS THE WORST MANAGER.
NO, YOU'RE JUST AS GOOD BUT...UH... LESS IMPORTANT.

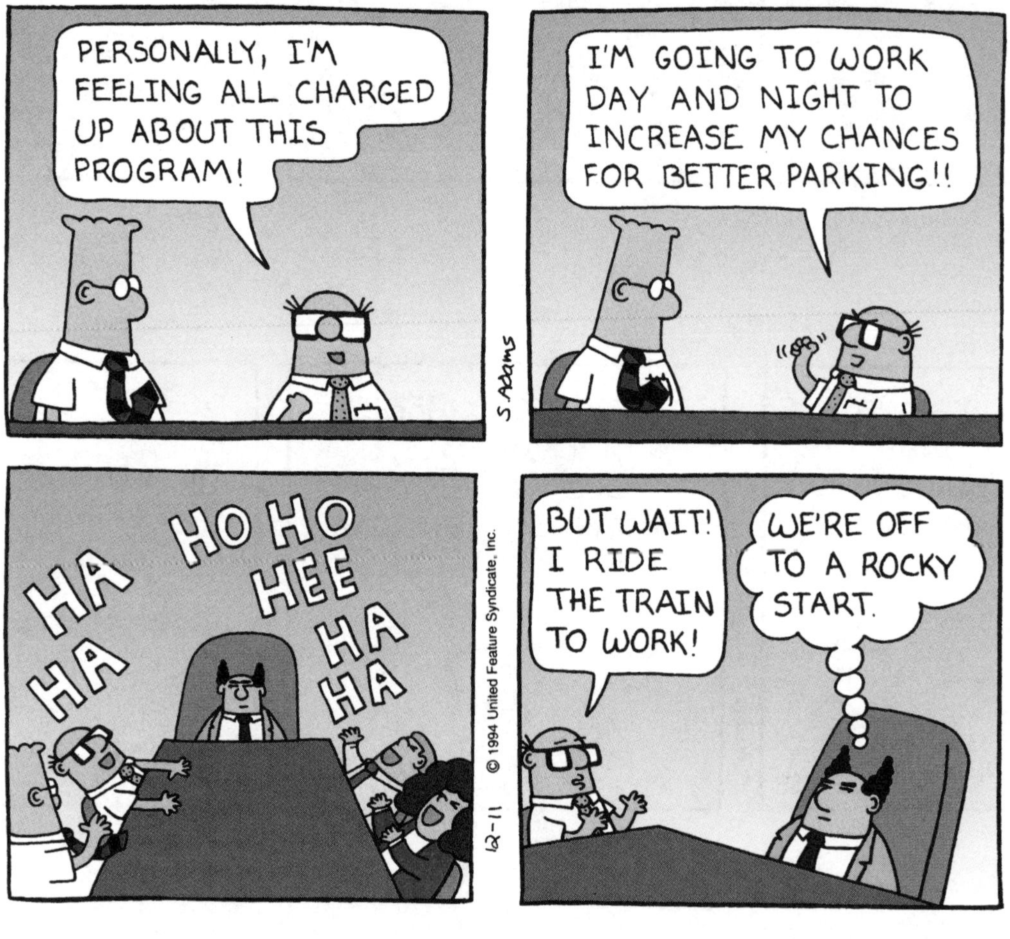
PERSONALLY, I'M FEELING ALL CHARGED UP ABOUT THIS PROGRAM!
I'M GOING TO WORK DAY AND NIGHT TO INCREASE MY CHANCES FOR BETTER PARKING!!
S. Adams
HA HA
HO HO
HEE
HA HA
© 1994 United Feature Syndicate, Inc.
12-11
BUT WAIT! I RIDE THE TRAIN TO WORK!
WE'RE OFF TO A ROCKY START.

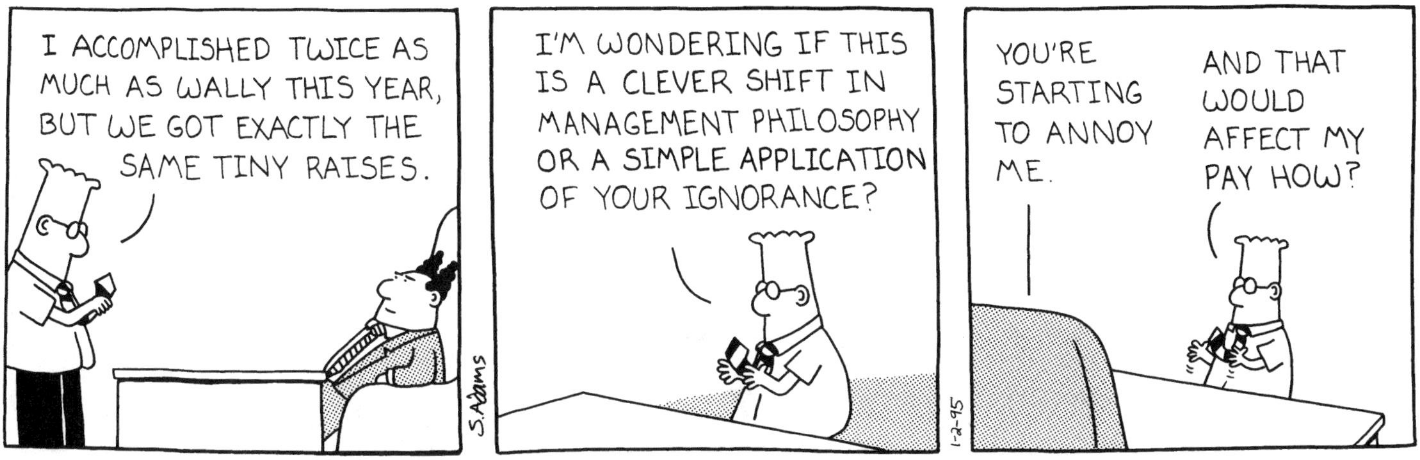
I ACCOMPLISHED TWICE AS MUCH AS WALLY THIS YEAR, BUT WE GOT EXACTLY THE SAME TINY RAISES.
S. Adams
I'M WONDERING IF THIS IS A CLEVER SHIFT IN MANAGEMENT PHILOSOPHY OR A SIMPLE APPLICATION OF YOUR IGNORANCE?
1-2-95
YOU'RE STARTING TO ANNOY ME.
AND THAT WOULD AFFECT MY PAY HOW?

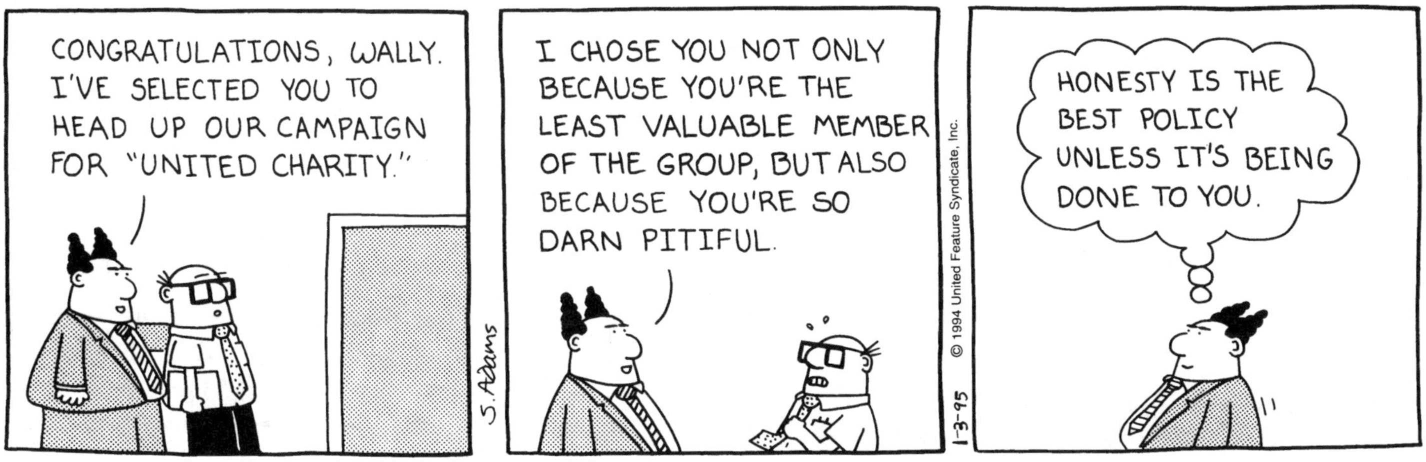
CONGRATULATIONS, WALLY. I'VE SELECTED YOU TO HEAD UP OUR CAMPAIGN FOR "UNITED CHARITY."
S. Adams
I CHOSE YOU NOT ONLY BECAUSE YOU'RE THE LEAST VALUABLE MEMBER OF THE GROUP, BUT ALSO BECAUSE YOU'RE SO DARN PITIFUL.
1-3-95
© 1994 United Feature Syndicate, Inc.
HONESTY IS THE BEST POLICY UNLESS IT'S BEING DONE TO YOU.

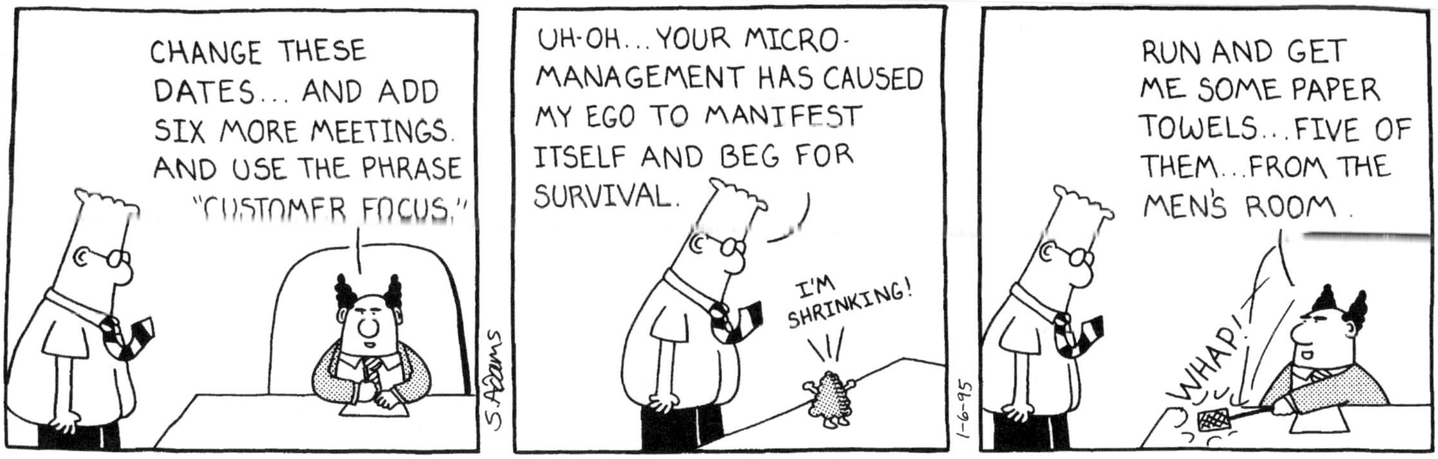
CHANGE THESE DATES... AND ADD SIX MORE MEETINGS. AND USE THE PHRASE "CUSTOMER FOCUS."
S. Adams
UH-OH... YOUR MICRO-MANAGEMENT HAS CAUSED MY EGO TO MANIFEST ITSELF AND BEG FOR SURVIVAL.
I'M SHRINKING!
1-6-95
RUN AND GET ME SOME PAPER TOWELS... FIVE OF THEM... FROM THE MEN'S ROOM.
WHAP!

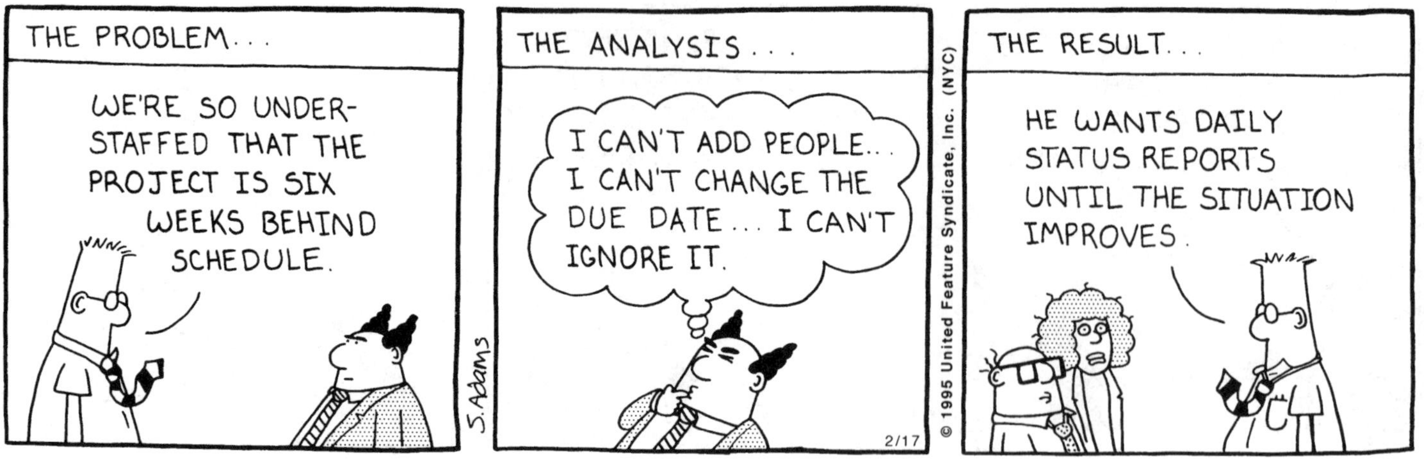
THE PROBLEM...
WE'RE SO UNDER-STAFFED THAT THE PROJECT IS SIX WEEKS BEHIND SCHEDULE.
THE ANALYSIS...
I CAN'T ADD PEOPLE... I CAN'T CHANGE THE DUE DATE... I CAN'T IGNORE IT.
THE RESULT...
HE WANTS DAILY STATUS REPORTS UNTIL THE SITUATION IMPROVES.
S. Adams
2/17
© 1995 United Feature Syndicate, Inc. (NYC)

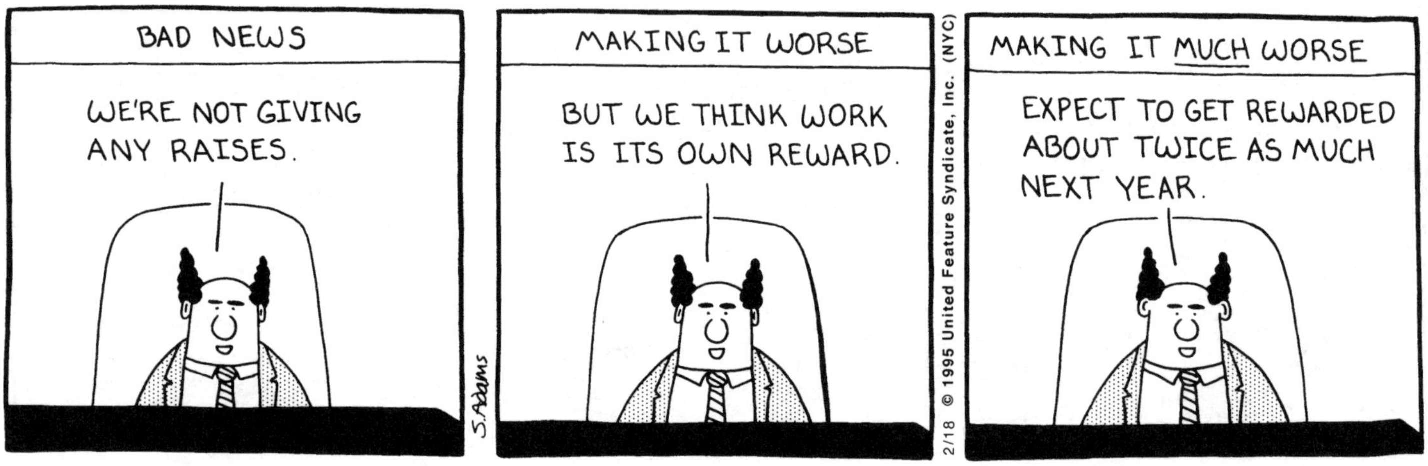
BAD NEWS
WE'RE NOT GIVING ANY RAISES.
MAKING IT WORSE
BUT WE THINK WORK IS ITS OWN REWARD.
MAKING IT MUCH WORSE
EXPECT TO GET REWARDED ABOUT TWICE AS MUCH NEXT YEAR.
S. Adams
2/18 © 1995 United Feature Syndicate, Inc. (NYC)

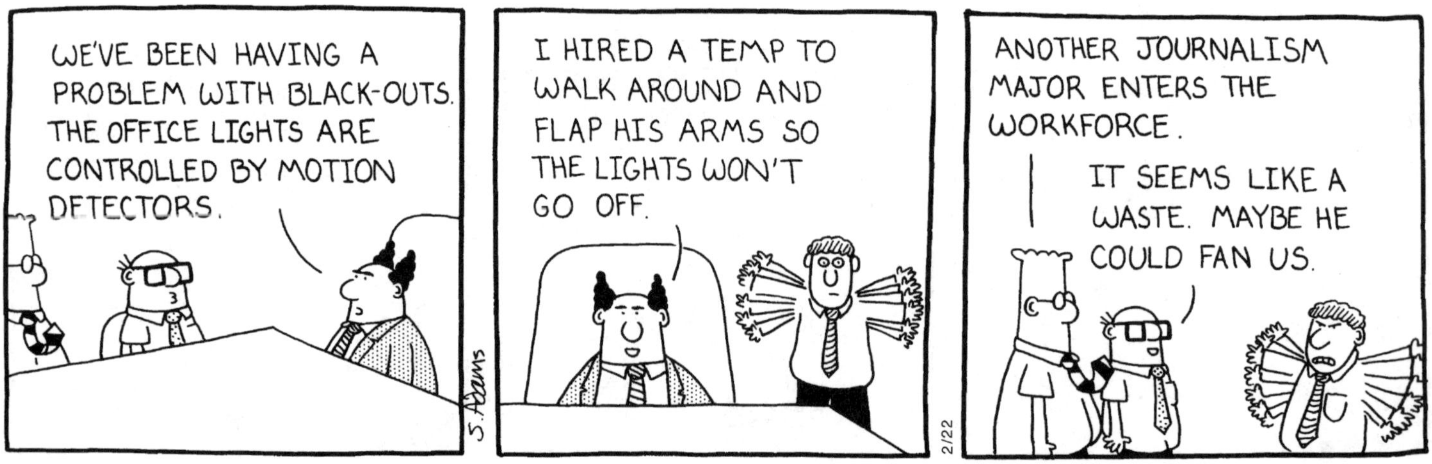
WE'VE BEEN HAVING A PROBLEM WITH BLACK-OUTS. THE OFFICE LIGHTS ARE CONTROLLED BY MOTION DETECTORS.
I HIRED A TEMP TO WALK AROUND AND FLAP HIS ARMS SO THE LIGHTS WON'T GO OFF.
ANOTHER JOURNALISM MAJOR ENTERS THE WORKFORCE.
IT SEEMS LIKE A WASTE. MAYBE HE COULD FAN US.
S. Adams
2/22

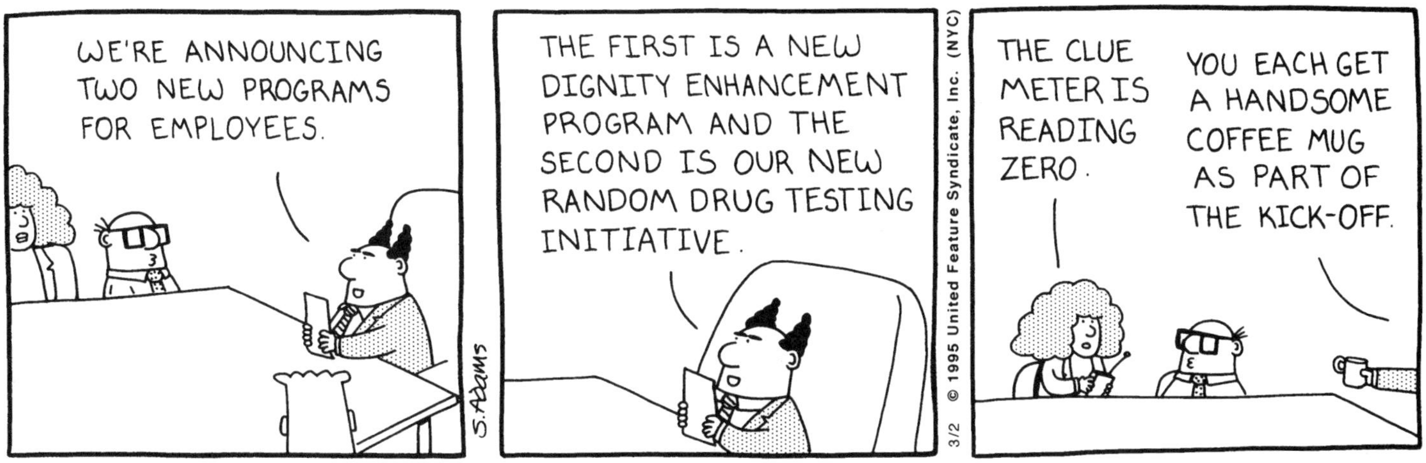
WE'RE ANNOUNCING TWO NEW PROGRAMS FOR EMPLOYEES.
S. Adams
THE FIRST IS A NEW DIGNITY ENHANCEMENT PROGRAM AND THE SECOND IS OUR NEW RANDOM DRUG TESTING INITIATIVE.
© 1995 United Feature Syndicate, Inc. (NYC)
3/2
THE CLUE METER IS READING ZERO.
YOU EACH GET A HANDSOME COFFEE MUG AS PART OF THE KICK-OFF.

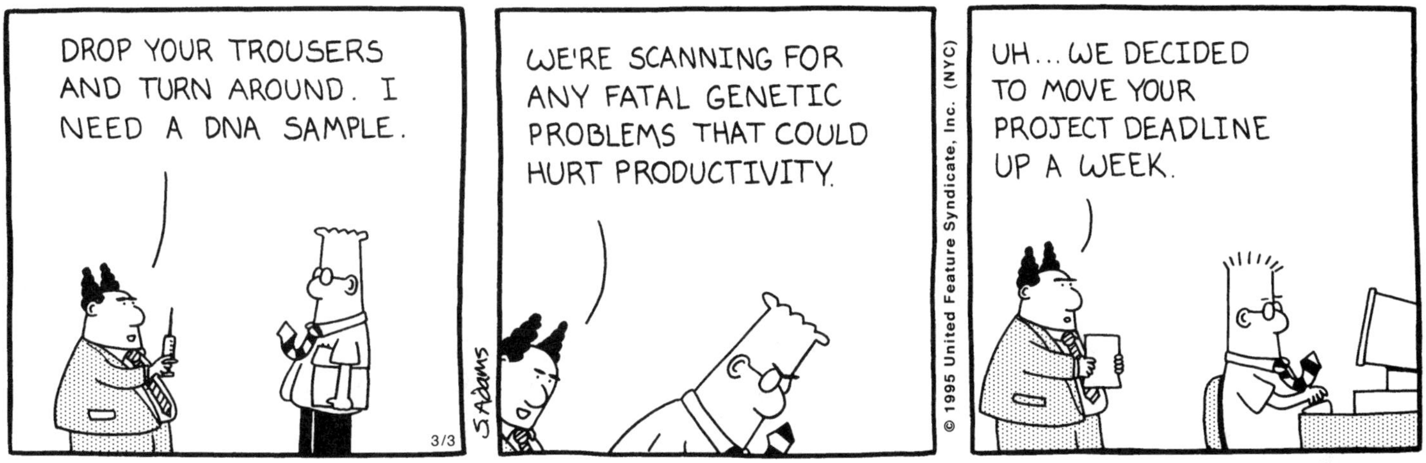
DROP YOUR TROUSERS AND TURN AROUND. I NEED A DNA SAMPLE.
3/3
S. Adams
WE'RE SCANNING FOR ANY FATAL GENETIC PROBLEMS THAT COULD HURT PRODUCTIVITY.
© 1995 United Feature Syndicate, Inc. (NYC)
UH... WE DECIDED TO MOVE YOUR PROJECT DEADLINE UP A WEEK.

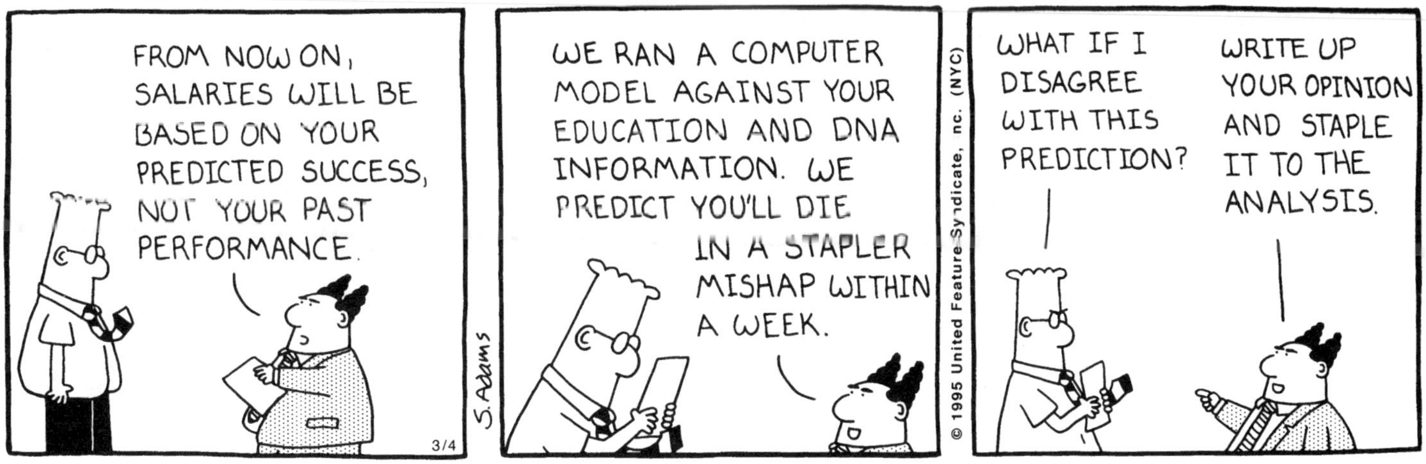
FROM NOW ON, SALARIES WILL BE BASED ON YOUR PREDICTED SUCCESS, NOT YOUR PAST PERFORMANCE.
3/4
S. Adams
WE RAN A COMPUTER MODEL AGAINST YOUR EDUCATION AND DNA INFORMATION. WE PREDICT YOU'LL DIE
IN A STAPLER MISHAP WITHIN A WEEK.
© 1995 United Feature Syndicate, Inc. (NYC)
WHAT IF I DISAGREE WITH THIS PREDICTION?
WRITE UP YOUR OPINION AND STAPLE IT TO THE ANALYSIS.

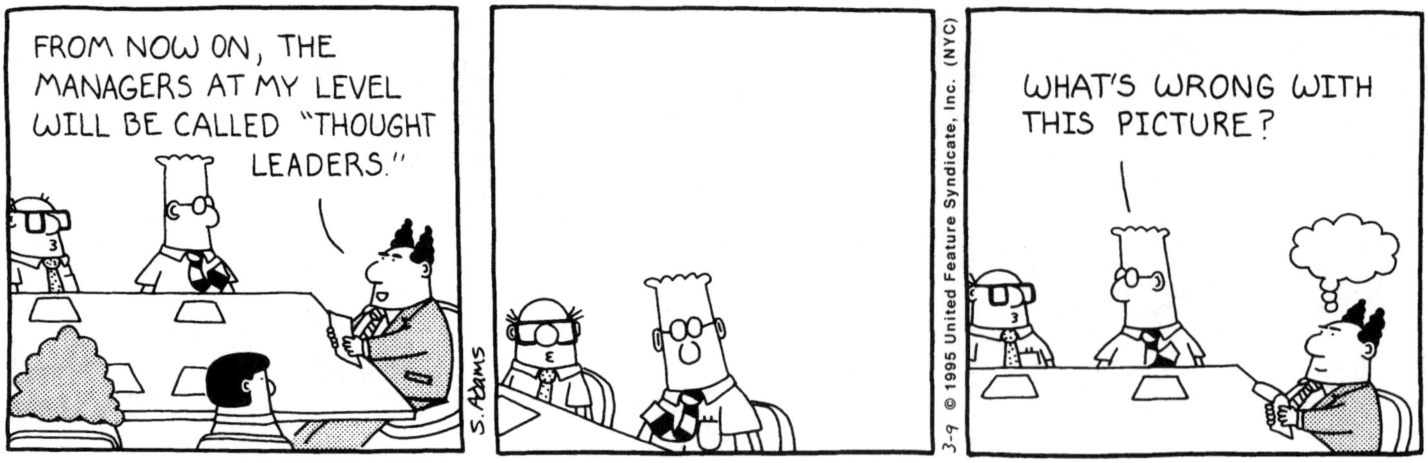
FROM NOW ON, THE MANAGERS AT MY LEVEL WILL BE CALLED "THOUGHT LEADERS."
S. Adams
3-9 © 1995 United Feature Syndicate, Inc. (NYC)
WHAT'S WRONG WITH THIS PICTURE?

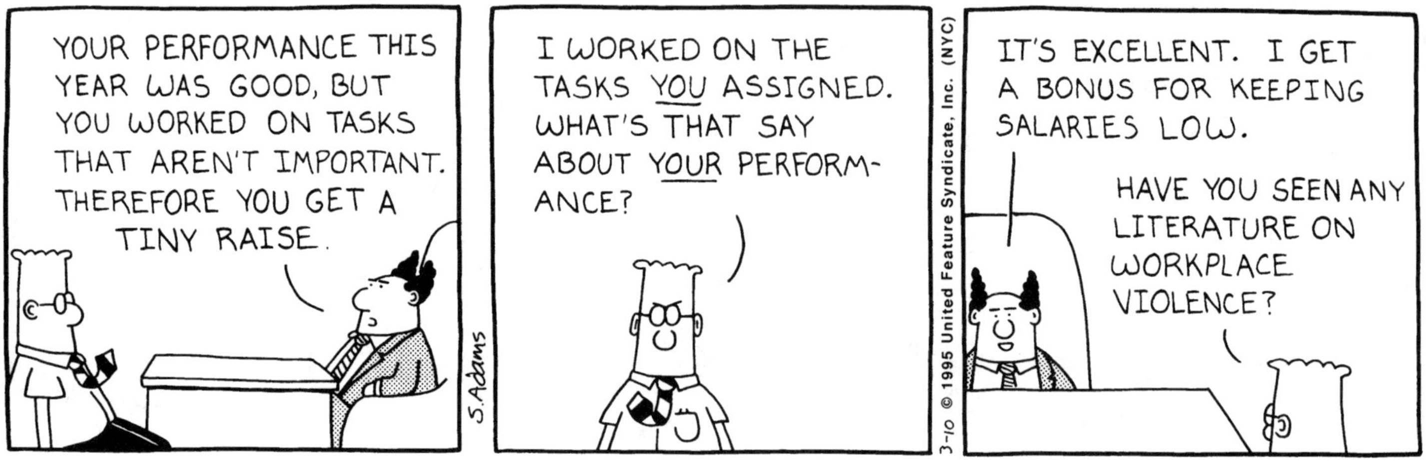
YOUR PERFORMANCE THIS YEAR WAS GOOD, BUT YOU WORKED ON TASKS THAT AREN'T IMPORTANT. THEREFORE YOU GET A TINY RAISE.
S. Adams
I WORKED ON THE TASKS YOU ASSIGNED. WHAT'S THAT SAY ABOUT YOUR PERFORMANCE?
3-10 © 1995 United Feature Syndicate, Inc. (NYC)
IT'S EXCELLENT. I GET A BONUS FOR KEEPING SALARIES LOW.
HAVE YOU SEEN ANY LITERATURE ON WORKPLACE VIOLENCE?

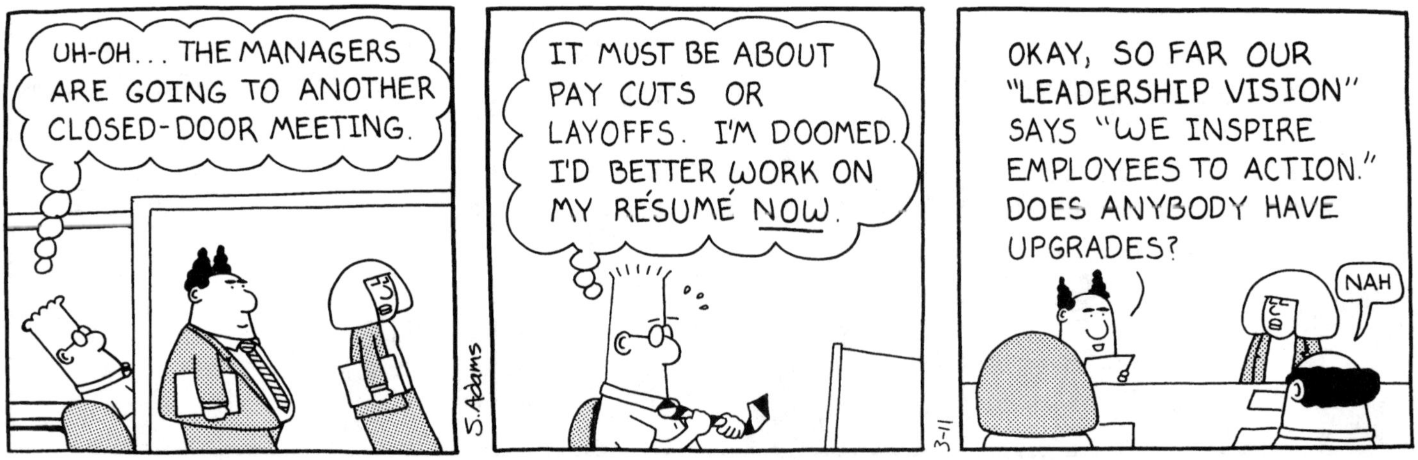
UH-OH... THE MANAGERS ARE GOING TO ANOTHER CLOSED-DOOR MEETING.
S. Adams
IT MUST BE ABOUT PAY CUTS OR LAYOFFS. I'M DOOMED. I'D BETTER WORK ON MY RÉSUMÉ NOW.
3-11
OKAY, SO FAR OUR "LEADERSHIP VISION" SAYS "WE INSPIRE EMPLOYEES TO ACTION." DOES ANYBODY HAVE UPGRADES?
NAH

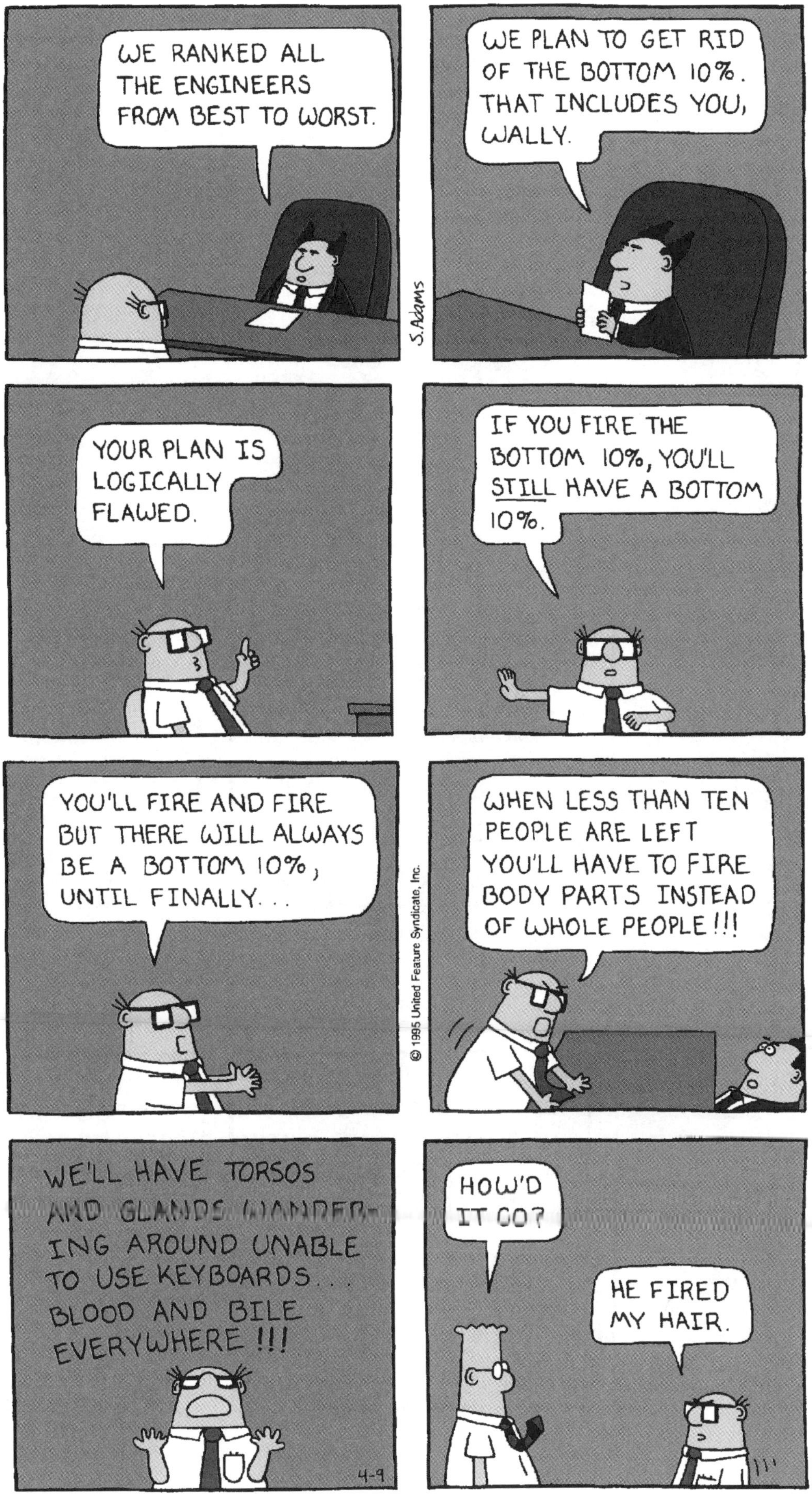
WE RANKED ALL THE ENGINEERS FROM BEST TO WORST.
WE PLAN TO GET RID OF THE BOTTOM 10%. THAT INCLUDES YOU, WALLY.
S. Adams
YOUR PLAN IS LOGICALLY FLAWED.
IF YOU FIRE THE BOTTOM 10%, YOU'LL STILL HAVE A BOTTOM 10%.
YOU'LL FIRE AND FIRE BUT THERE WILL ALWAYS BE A BOTTOM 10%, UNTIL FINALLY...
© 1995 United Feature Syndicate, Inc.
WHEN LESS THAN TEN PEOPLE ARE LEFT YOU'LL HAVE TO FIRE BODY PARTS INSTEAD OF WHOLE PEOPLE!!!
WE'LL HAVE TORSOS AND GLANDS WANDER-ING AROUND UNABLE TO USE KEYBOARDS... BLOOD AND BILE EVERYWHERE!!!
4-9
HOW'D IT GO?
HE FIRED MY HAIR.

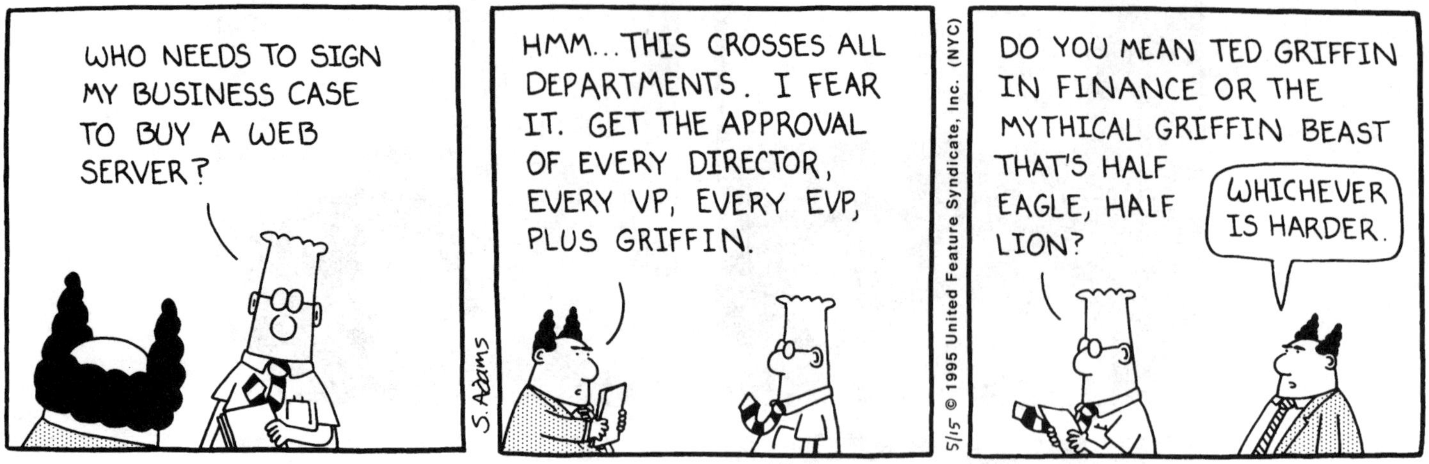
WHO NEEDS TO SIGN MY BUSINESS CASE TO BUY A WEB SERVER?
S. Adams
HMM... THIS CROSSES ALL DEPARTMENTS. I FEAR IT. GET THE APPROVAL OF EVERY DIRECTOR, EVERY VP, EVERY EVP, PLUS GRIFFIN.
5/15 © 1995 United Feature Syndicate, Inc. (NYC)
DO YOU MEAN TED GRIFFIN IN FINANCE OR THE MYTHICAL GRIFFIN BEAST THAT'S HALF EAGLE, HALF LION?
WHICHEVER IS HARDER.

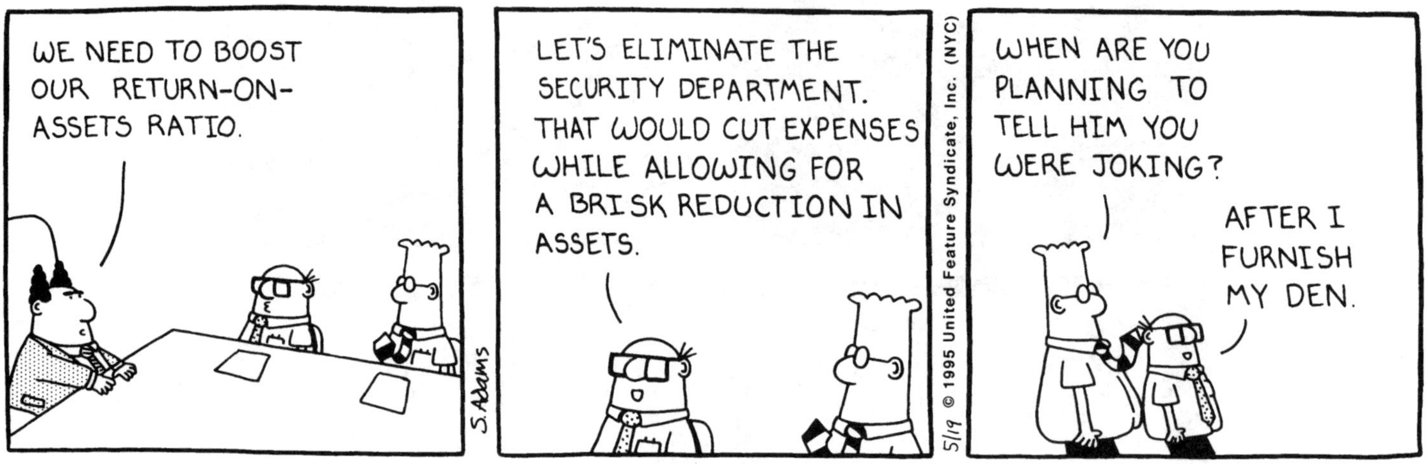
WE NEED TO BOOST OUR RETURN-ON-ASSETS RATIO.
S. Adams
LET'S ELIMINATE THE SECURITY DEPARTMENT. THAT WOULD CUT EXPENSES WHILE ALLOWING FOR A BRISK REDUCTION IN ASSETS.
5/19 © 1995 United Feature Syndicate, Inc. (NYC)
WHEN ARE YOU PLANNING TO TELL HIM YOU WERE JOKING?
AFTER I FURNISH MY DEN.

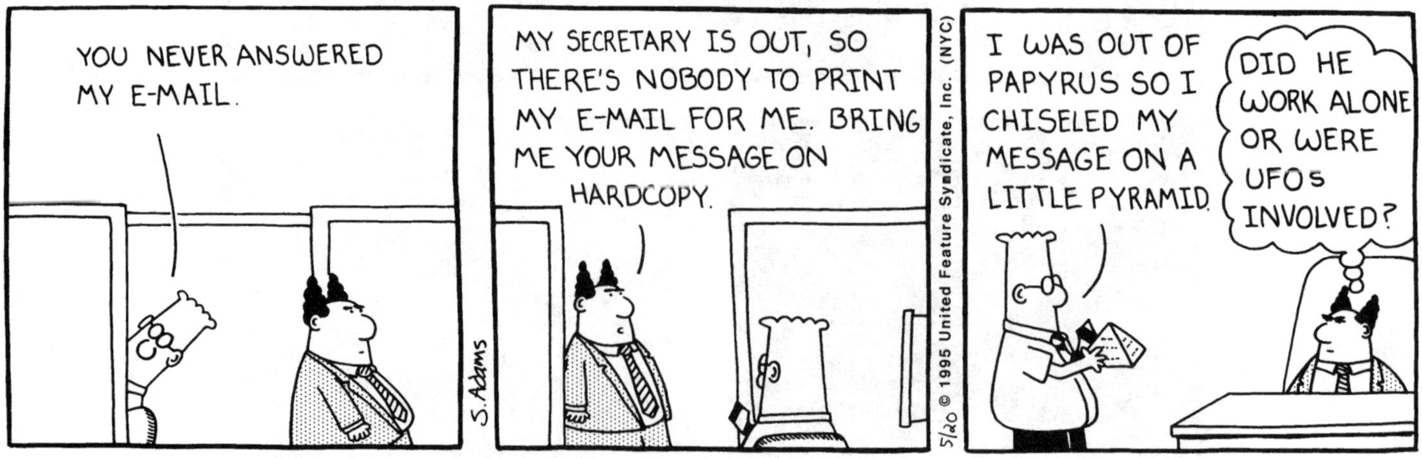
YOU NEVER ANSWERED MY E-MAIL.
S. Adams
MY SECRETARY IS OUT, SO THERE'S NOBODY TO PRINT MY E-MAIL FOR ME. BRING ME YOUR MESSAGE ON HARDCOPY.
5/20 © 1995 United Feature Syndicate, Inc. (NYC)
I WAS OUT OF PAPYRUS SO I CHISELED MY MESSAGE ON A LITTLE PYRAMID.
DID HE WORK ALONE OR WERE UFOs INVOLVED?

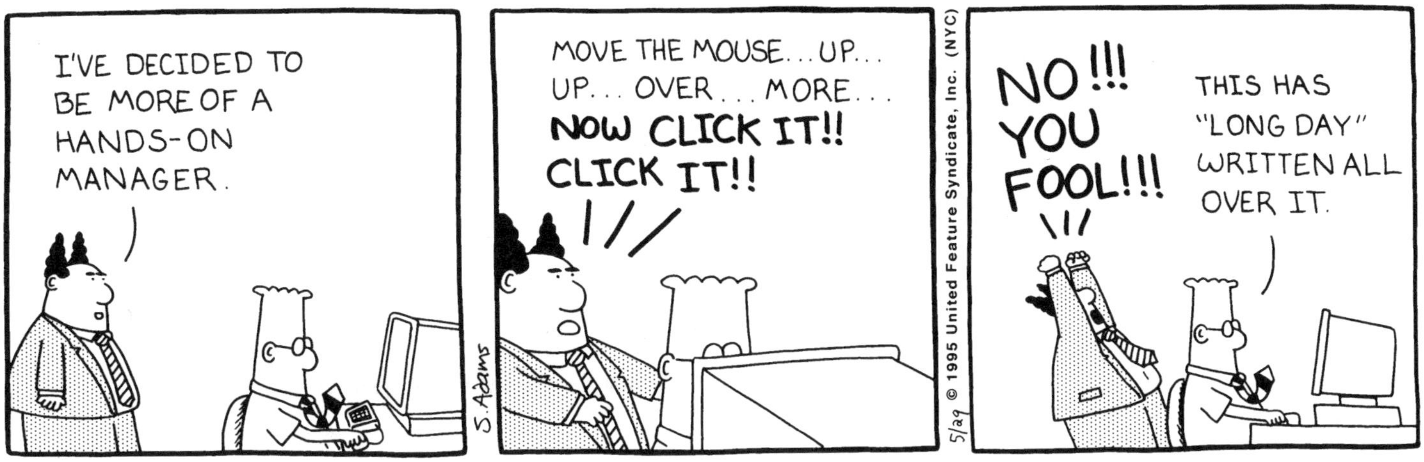
I'VE DECIDED TO BE MORE OF A HANDS-ON MANAGER.
MOVE THE MOUSE... UP... UP... OVER... MORE... NOW CLICK IT!! CLICK IT!!
S. Adams
© 1995 United Feature Syndicate, Inc. (NYC)
5/29
NO!!! YOU FOOL!!!
THIS HAS "LONG DAY" WRITTEN ALL OVER IT.

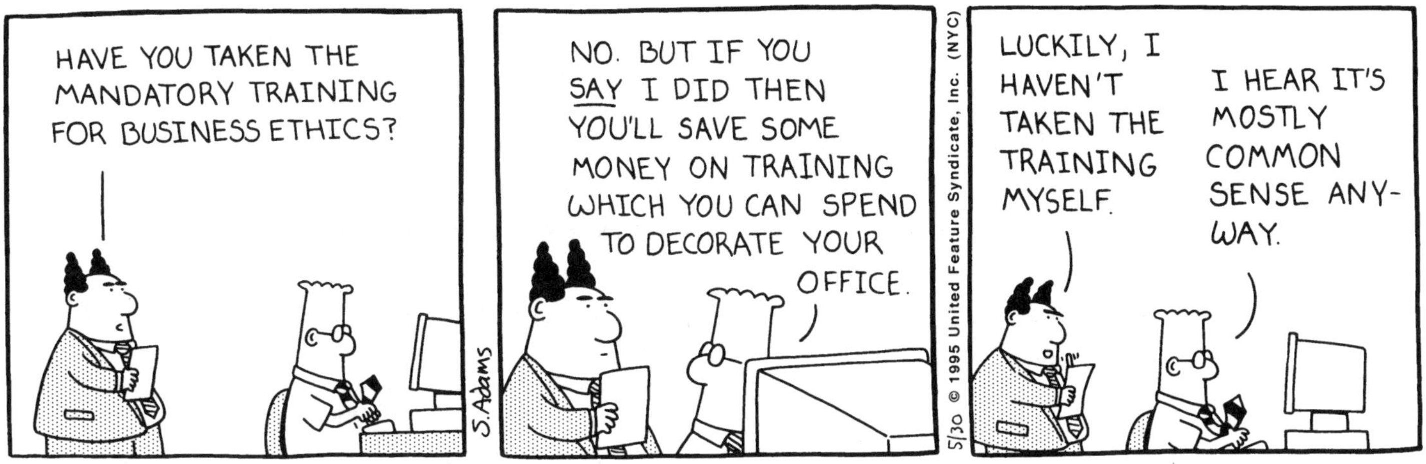
HAVE YOU TAKEN THE MANDATORY TRAINING FOR BUSINESS ETHICS?
NO. BUT IF YOU SAY I DID THEN YOU'LL SAVE SOME MONEY ON TRAINING WHICH YOU CAN SPEND TO DECORATE YOUR OFFICE.
S. Adams
© 1995 United Feature Syndicate, Inc. (NYC)
5/30
LUCKILY, I HAVEN'T TAKEN THE TRAINING MYSELF.
I HEAR IT'S MOSTLY COMMON SENSE ANYWAY.

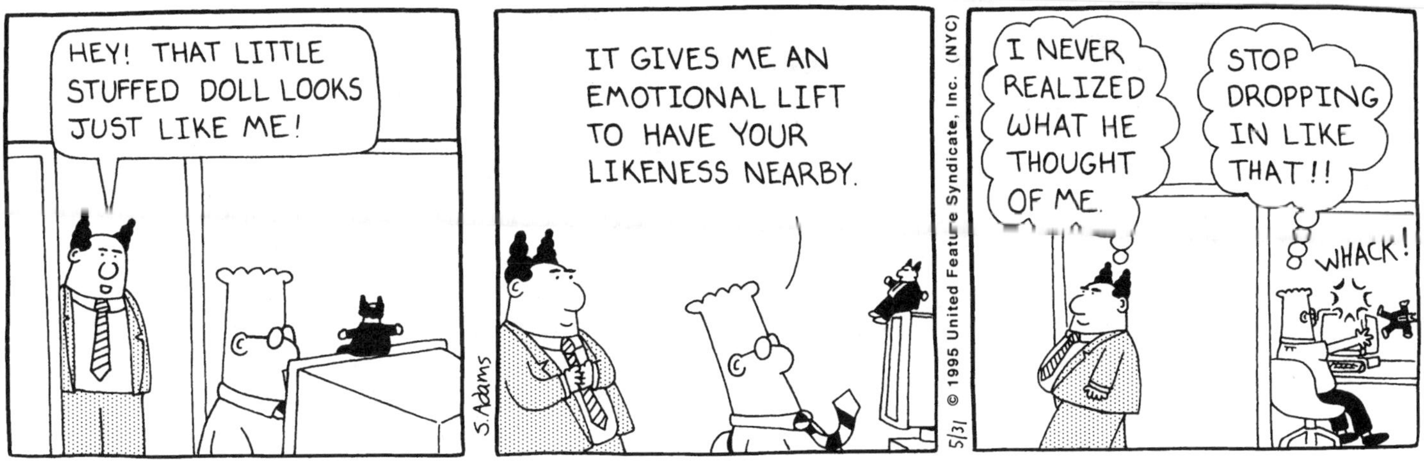
HEY! THAT LITTLE STUFFED DOLL LOOKS JUST LIKE ME!
IT GIVES ME AN EMOTIONAL LIFT TO HAVE YOUR LIKENESS NEARBY.
S. Adams
© 1995 United Feature Syndicate, Inc. (NYC)
5/31
I NEVER REALIZED WHAT HE THOUGHT OF ME.
STOP DROPPING IN LIKE THAT!!
WHACK!

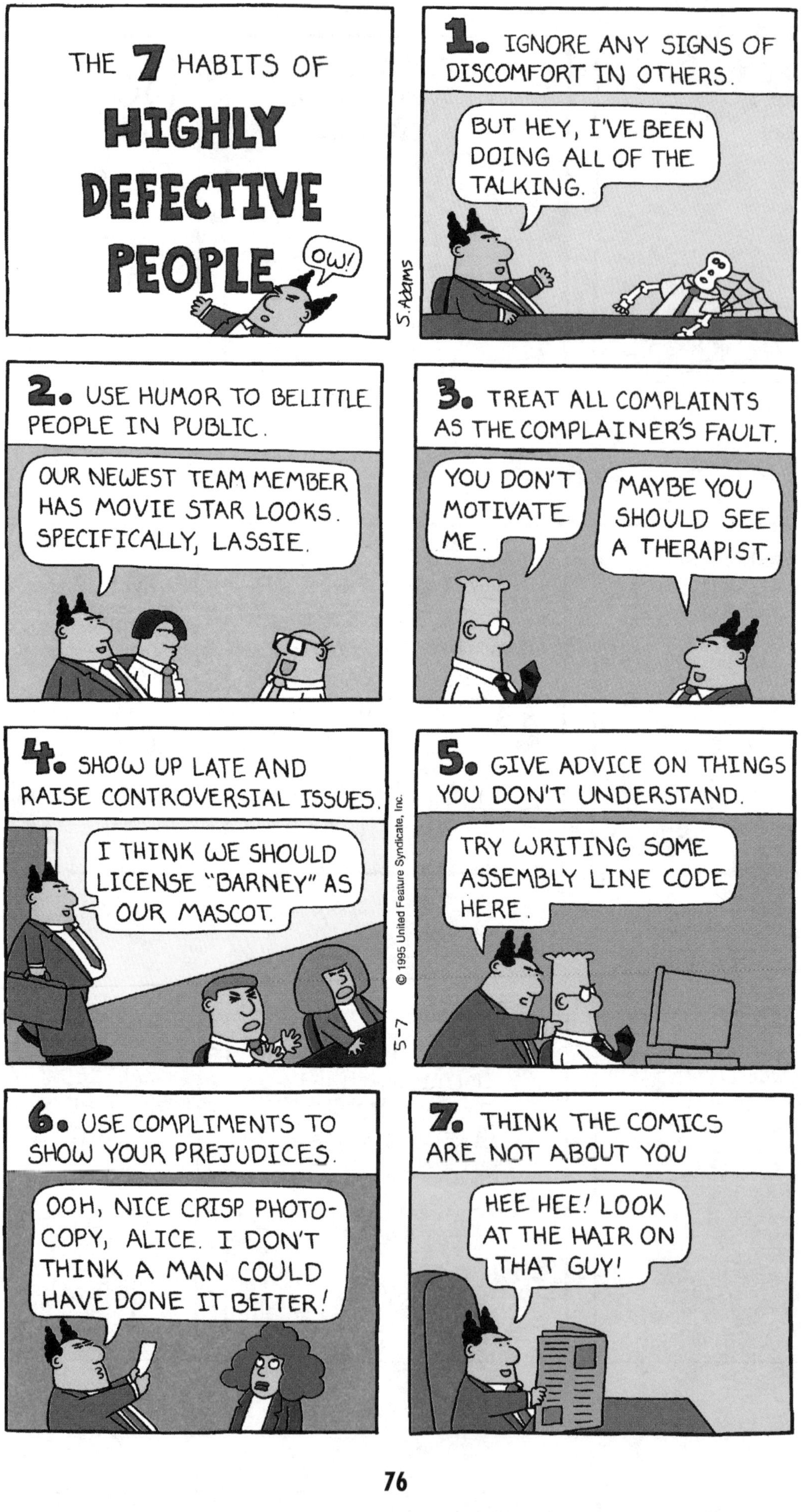
THE 7 HABITS OF HIGHLY DEFECTIVE PEOPLE
OW!
S. Adams
1. IGNORE ANY SIGNS OF DISCOMFORT IN OTHERS.
BUT HEY, I'VE BEEN DOING ALL OF THE TALKING.
2. USE HUMOR TO BELITTLE PEOPLE IN PUBLIC.
OUR NEWEST TEAM MEMBER HAS MOVIE STAR LOOKS. SPECIFICALLY, LASSIE.
3. TREAT ALL COMPLAINTS AS THE COMPLAINER'S FAULT.
YOU DON'T MOTIVATE ME.
MAYBE YOU SHOULD SEE A THERAPIST.
4. SHOW UP LATE AND RAISE CONTROVERSIAL ISSUES.
I THINK WE SHOULD LICENSE "BARNEY" AS OUR MASCOT.
© 1995 United Feature Syndicate, Inc.
5-7
5. GIVE ADVICE ON THINGS YOU DON'T UNDERSTAND.
TRY WRITING SOME ASSEMBLY LINE CODE HERE.
6. USE COMPLIMENTS TO SHOW YOUR PREJUDICES.
OOH, NICE CRISP PHOTO-COPY, ALICE. I DON'T THINK A MAN COULD HAVE DONE IT BETTER!
7. THINK THE COMICS ARE NOT ABOUT YOU
HEE HEE! LOOK AT THE HAIR ON THAT GUY!

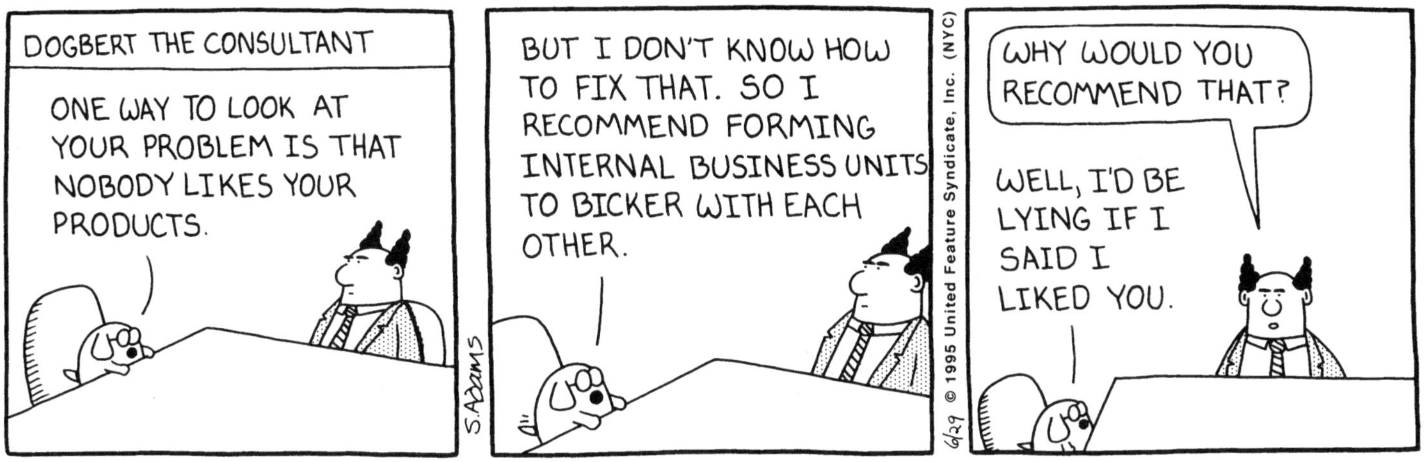
DOGBERT THE CONSULTANT
ONE WAY TO LOOK AT YOUR PROBLEM IS THAT NOBODY LIKES YOUR PRODUCTS.
S. Adams
BUT I DON'T KNOW HOW TO FIX THAT. SO I RECOMMEND FORMING INTERNAL BUSINESS UNITS TO BICKER WITH EACH OTHER.
6/29 © 1995 United Feature Syndicate, Inc. (NYC)
WHY WOULD YOU RECOMMEND THAT?
WELL, I'D BE LYING IF I SAID I LIKED YOU.

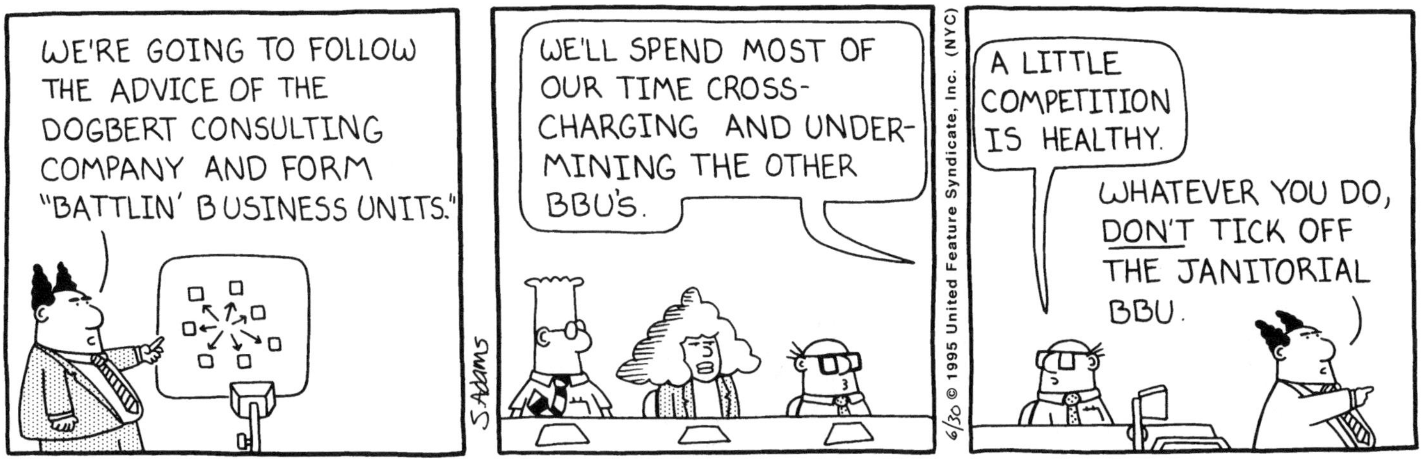
WE'RE GOING TO FOLLOW THE ADVICE OF THE DOGBERT CONSULTING COMPANY AND FORM "BATTLIN' BUSINESS UNITS."
S. Adams
WE'LL SPEND MOST OF OUR TIME CROSS-CHARGING AND UNDER-MINING THE OTHER BBU'S.
6/30 © 1995 United Feature Syndicate, Inc. (NYC)
A LITTLE COMPETITION IS HEALTHY.
WHATEVER YOU DO, DON'T TICK OFF THE JANITORIAL BBU.

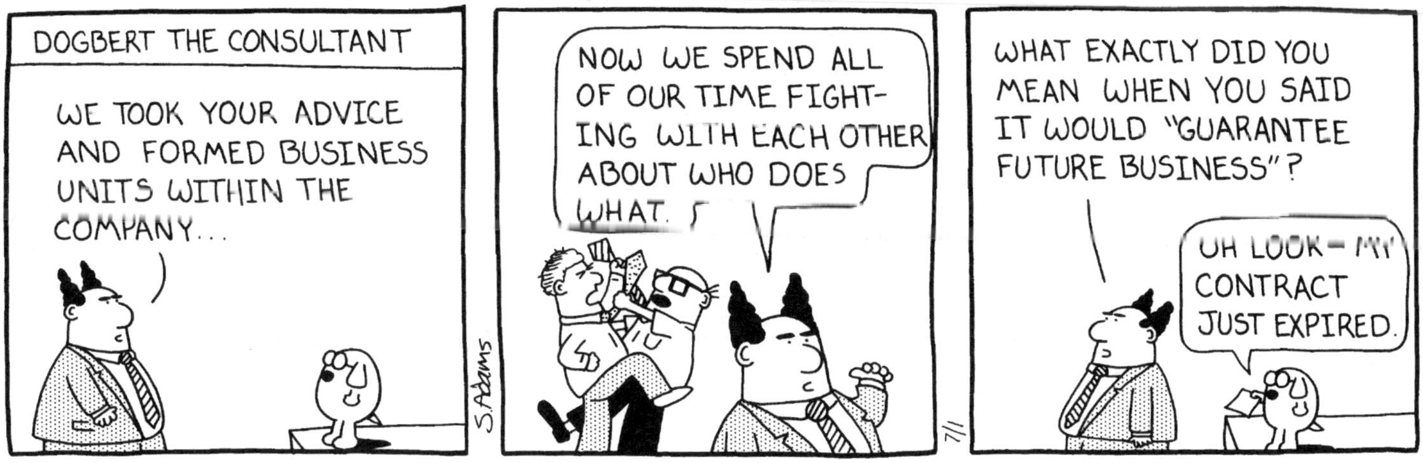
DOGBERT THE CONSULTANT
WE TOOK YOUR ADVICE AND FORMED BUSINESS UNITS WITHIN THE COMPANY...
S. Adams
NOW WE SPEND ALL OF OUR TIME FIGHT-ING WITH EACH OTHER ABOUT WHO DOES WHAT.
7/1
WHAT EXACTLY DID YOU MEAN WHEN YOU SAID IT WOULD "GUARANTEE FUTURE BUSINESS"?
UH LOOK — MY CONTRACT JUST EXPIRED.

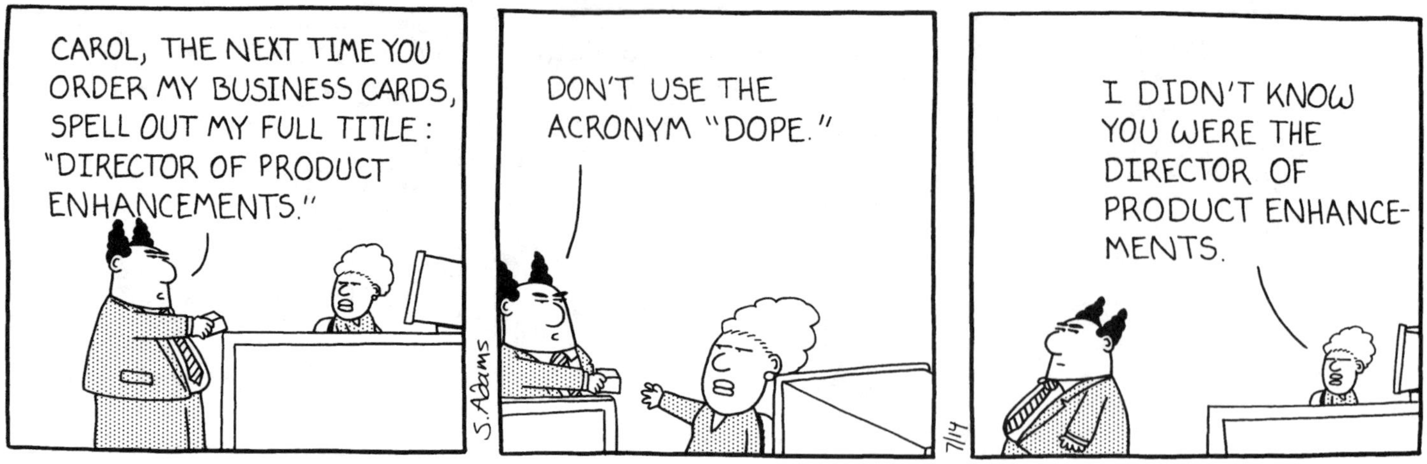
CAROL, THE NEXT TIME YOU ORDER MY BUSINESS CARDS, SPELL OUT MY FULL TITLE: "DIRECTOR OF PRODUCT ENHANCEMENTS."
S. Adams
DON'T USE THE ACRONYM "DOPE."
7/14
I DIDN'T KNOW YOU WERE THE DIRECTOR OF PRODUCT ENHANCEMENTS.

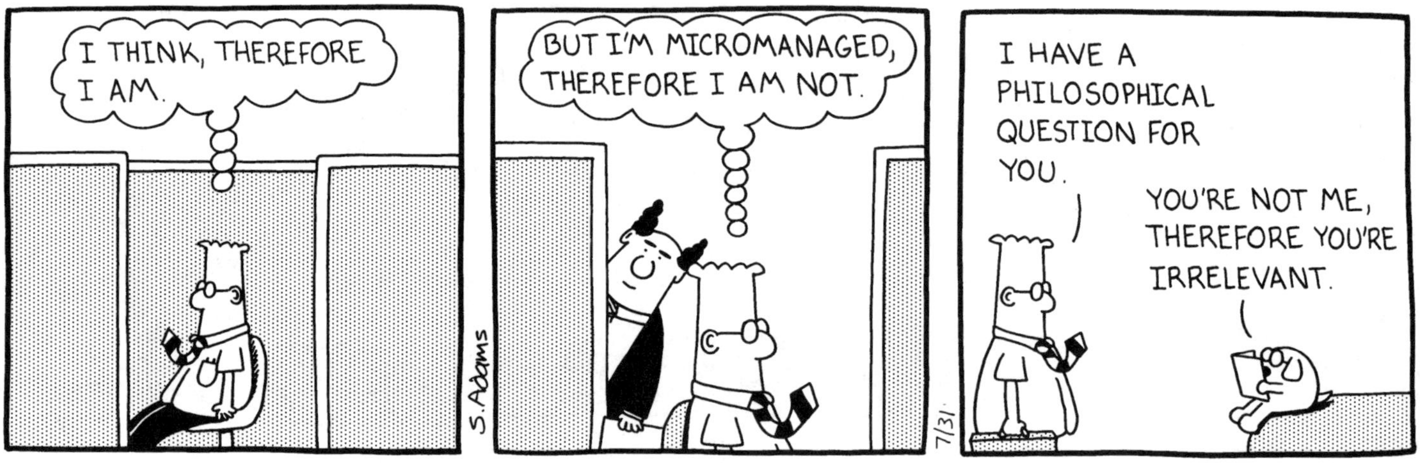
I THINK, THEREFORE I AM.
S. Adams
BUT I'M MICROMANAGED, THEREFORE I AM NOT.
7/31
I HAVE A PHILOSOPHICAL QUESTION FOR YOU.
YOU'RE NOT ME, THEREFORE YOU'RE IRRELEVANT.

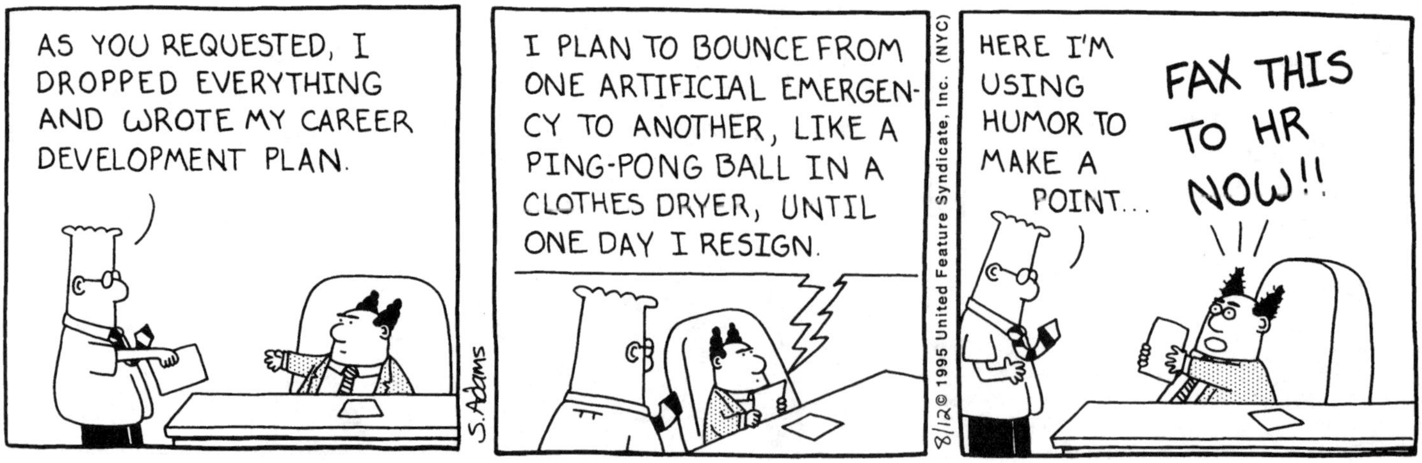
AS YOU REQUESTED, I DROPPED EVERYTHING AND WROTE MY CAREER DEVELOPMENT PLAN.
S. Adams
I PLAN TO BOUNCE FROM ONE ARTIFICIAL EMERGENCY TO ANOTHER, LIKE A PING-PONG BALL IN A CLOTHES DRYER, UNTIL ONE DAY I RESIGN.
8/12 © 1995 United Feature Syndicate, Inc. (NYC)
HERE I'M USING HUMOR TO MAKE A POINT...
FAX THIS TO HR NOW!!

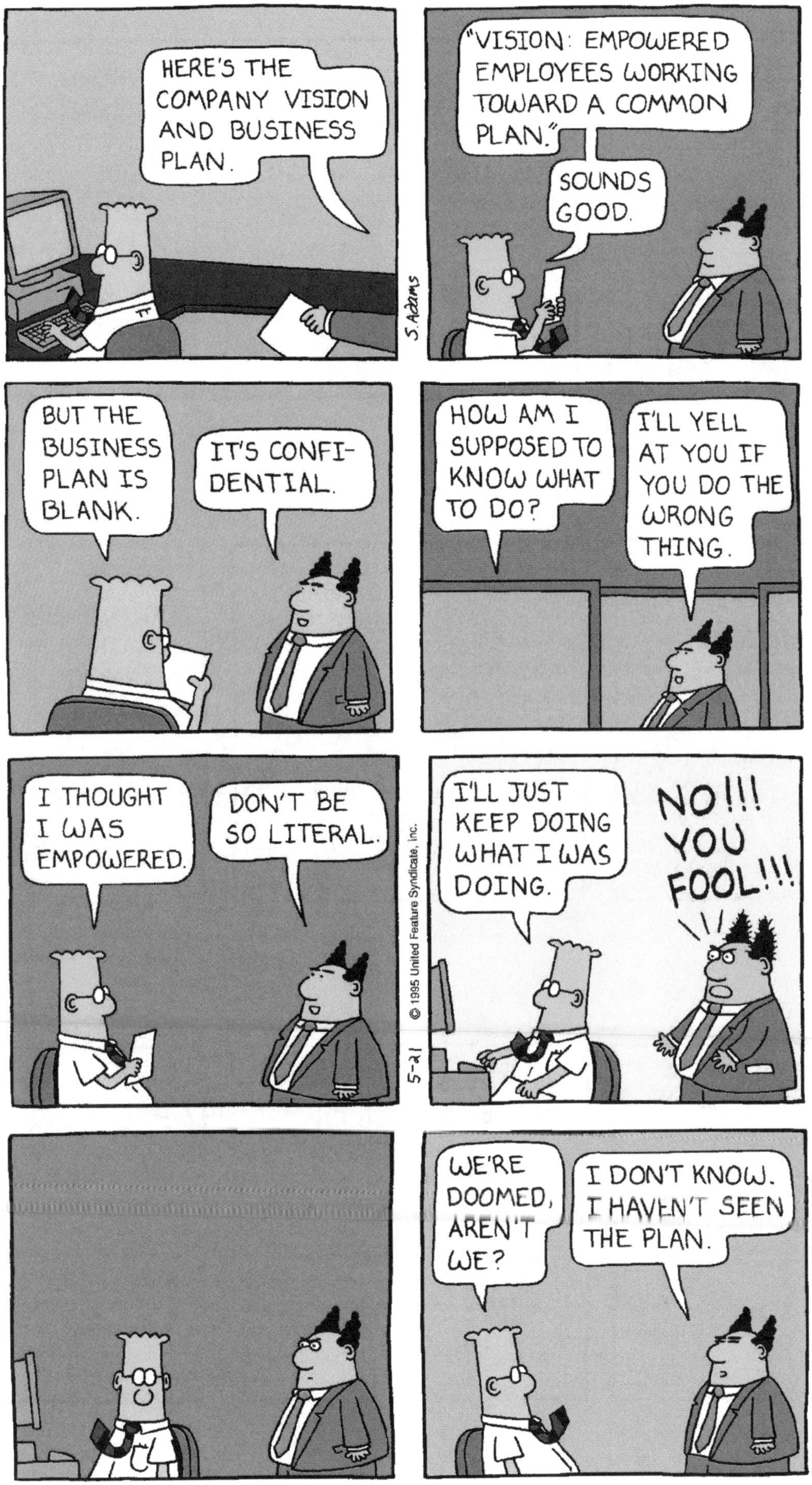
HERE'S THE COMPANY VISION AND BUSINESS PLAN.
S. Adams
"VISION: EMPOWERED EMPLOYEES WORKING TOWARD A COMMON PLAN."
SOUNDS GOOD.
BUT THE BUSINESS PLAN IS BLANK.
IT'S CONFI-DENTIAL.
HOW AM I SUPPOSED TO KNOW WHAT TO DO?
I'LL YELL AT YOU IF YOU DO THE WRONG THING.
I THOUGHT I WAS EMPOWERED.
DON'T BE SO LITERAL.
© 1995 United Feature Syndicate, Inc.
5-21
I'LL JUST KEEP DOING WHAT I WAS DOING.
NO!!! YOU FOOL!!!
WE'RE DOOMED, AREN'T WE?
I DON'T KNOW. I HAVEN'T SEEN THE PLAN.

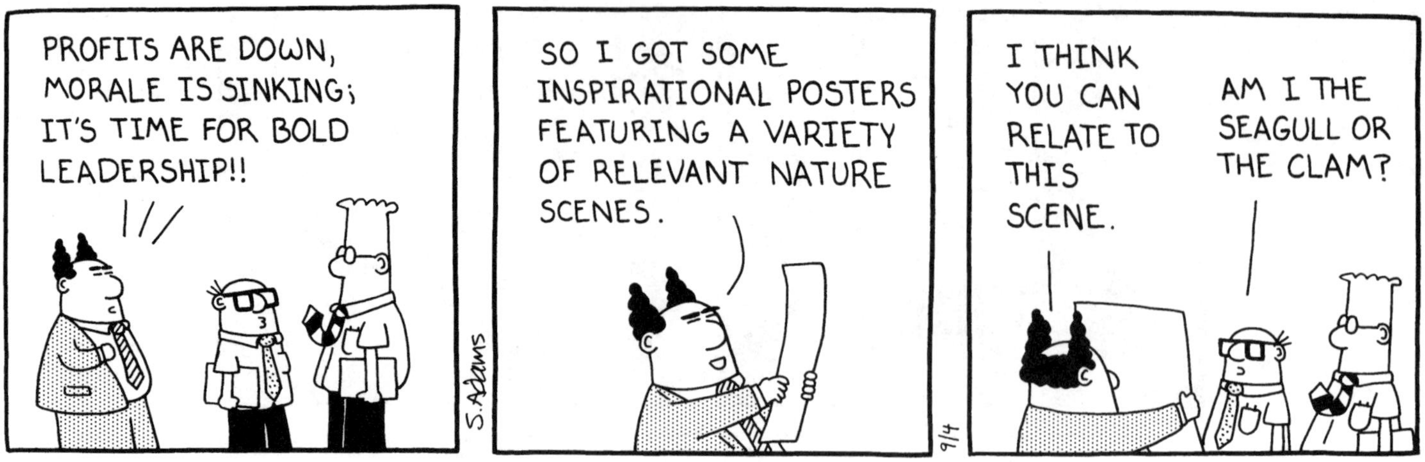
PROFITS ARE DOWN, MORALE IS SINKING; IT'S TIME FOR BOLD LEADERSHIP!!
S. Adams
SO I GOT SOME INSPIRATIONAL POSTERS FEATURING A VARIETY OF RELEVANT NATURE SCENES.
9/4
I THINK YOU CAN RELATE TO THIS SCENE.
AM I THE SEAGULL OR THE CLAM?

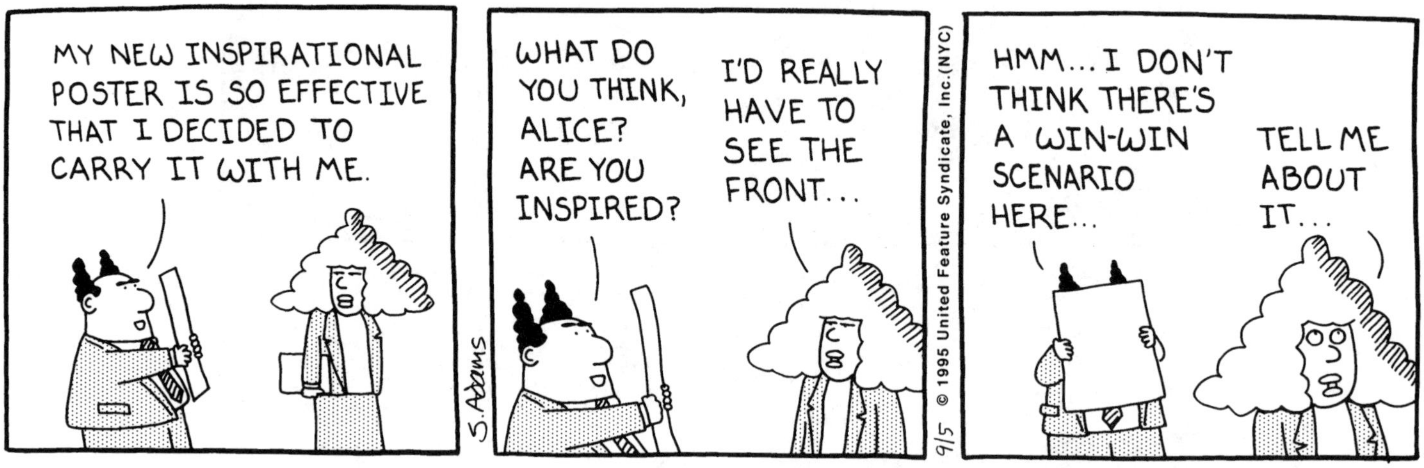
MY NEW INSPIRATIONAL POSTER IS SO EFFECTIVE THAT I DECIDED TO CARRY IT WITH ME.
S. Adams
WHAT DO YOU THINK, ALICE? ARE YOU INSPIRED?
I'D REALLY HAVE TO SEE THE FRONT...
9/5 © 1995 United Feature Syndicate, Inc.(NYC)
HMM... I DON'T THINK THERE'S A WIN-WIN SCENARIO HERE...
TELL ME ABOUT IT...

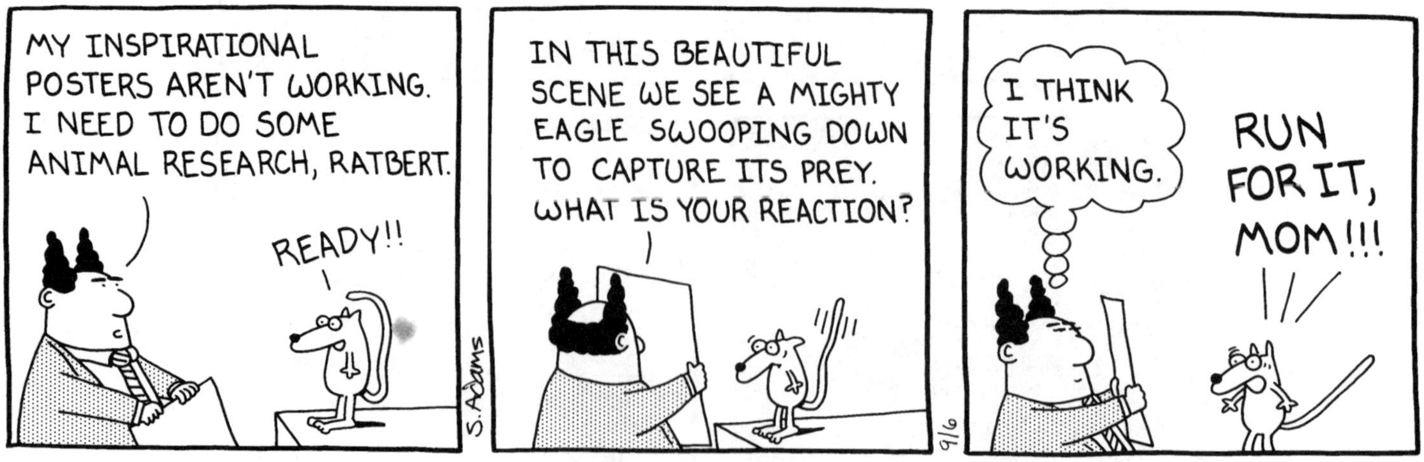
MY INSPIRATIONAL POSTERS AREN'T WORKING. I NEED TO DO SOME ANIMAL RESEARCH, RATBERT.
READY!!
S. Adams
IN THIS BEAUTIFUL SCENE WE SEE A MIGHTY EAGLE SWOOPING DOWN TO CAPTURE ITS PREY. WHAT IS YOUR REACTION?
9/6
I THINK IT'S WORKING.
RUN FOR IT, MOM!!!

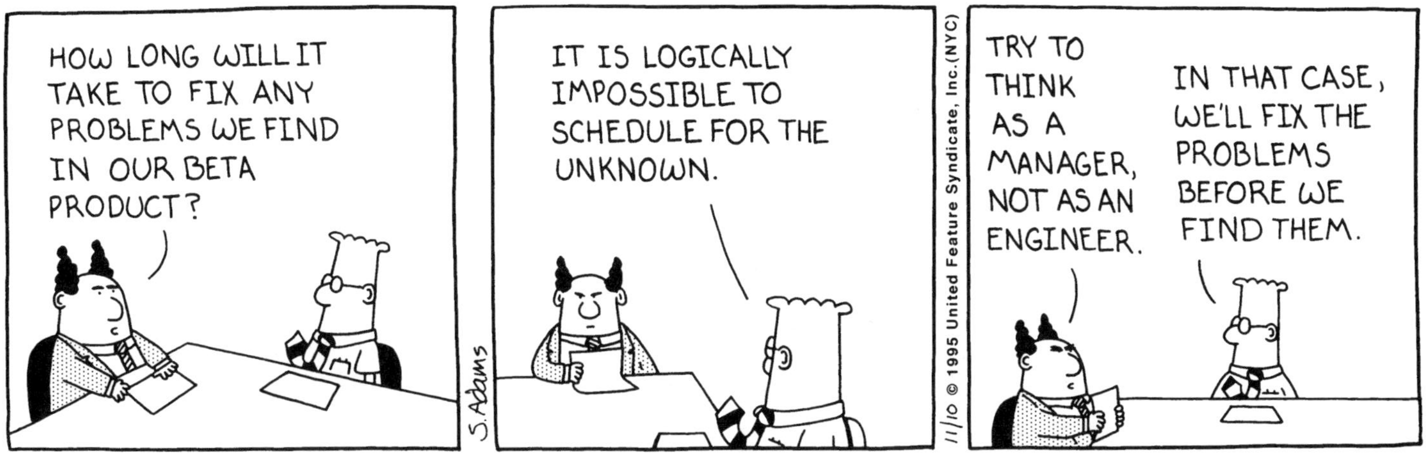
HOW LONG WILL IT TAKE TO FIX ANY PROBLEMS WE FIND IN OUR BETA PRODUCT?
IT IS LOGICALLY IMPOSSIBLE TO SCHEDULE FOR THE UNKNOWN.
S. Adams
11/10 © 1995 United Feature Syndicate, Inc.(NYC)
TRY TO THINK AS A MANAGER, NOT AS AN ENGINEER.
IN THAT CASE, WE'LL FIX THE PROBLEMS BEFORE WE FIND THEM.

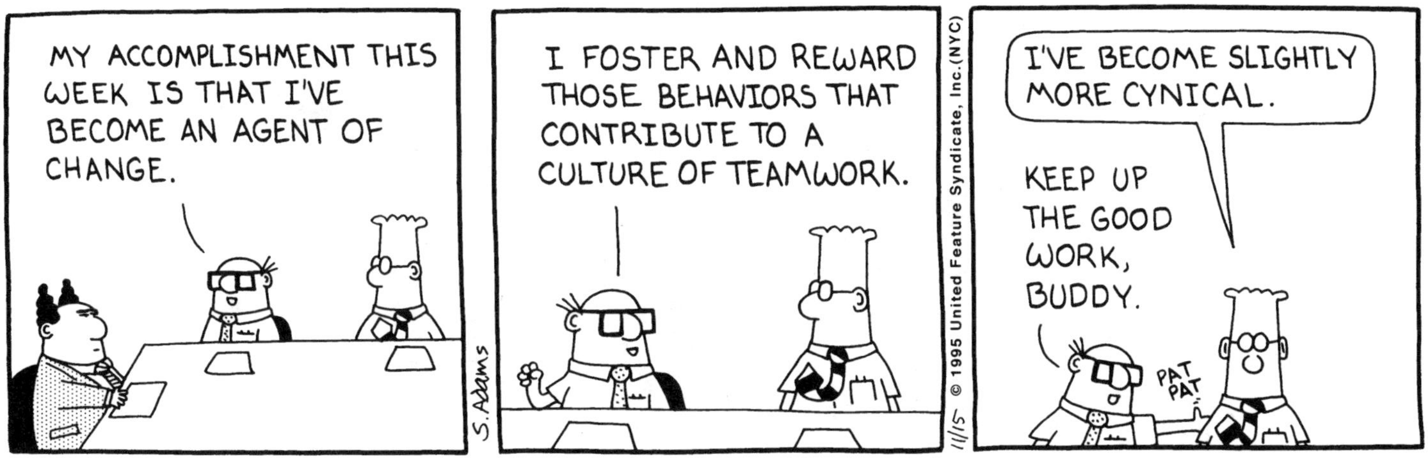
MY ACCOMPLISHMENT THIS WEEK IS THAT I'VE BECOME AN AGENT OF CHANGE.
I FOSTER AND REWARD THOSE BEHAVIORS THAT CONTRIBUTE TO A CULTURE OF TEAMWORK.
S. Adams
11/15 © 1995 United Feature Syndicate, Inc.(NYC)
I'VE BECOME SLIGHTLY MORE CYNICAL.
KEEP UP THE GOOD WORK, BUDDY.
PAT PAT

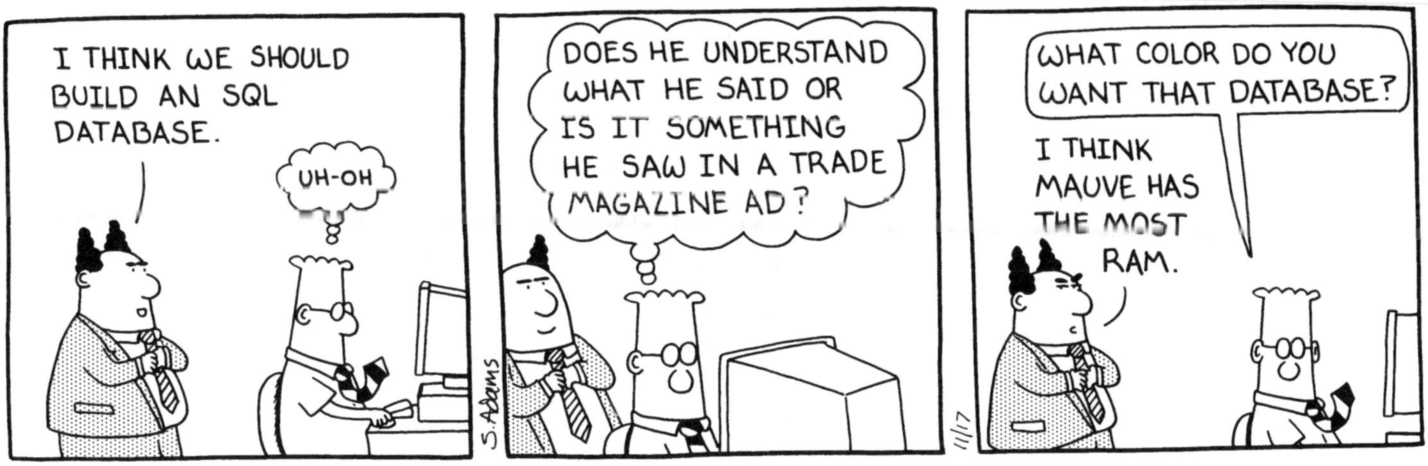
I THINK WE SHOULD BUILD AN SQL DATABASE.
UH-OH
DOES HE UNDERSTAND WHAT HE SAID OR IS IT SOMETHING HE SAW IN A TRADE MAGAZINE AD?
S. Adams
11/17
WHAT COLOR DO YOU WANT THAT DATABASE?
I THINK MAUVE HAS THE MOST RAM.

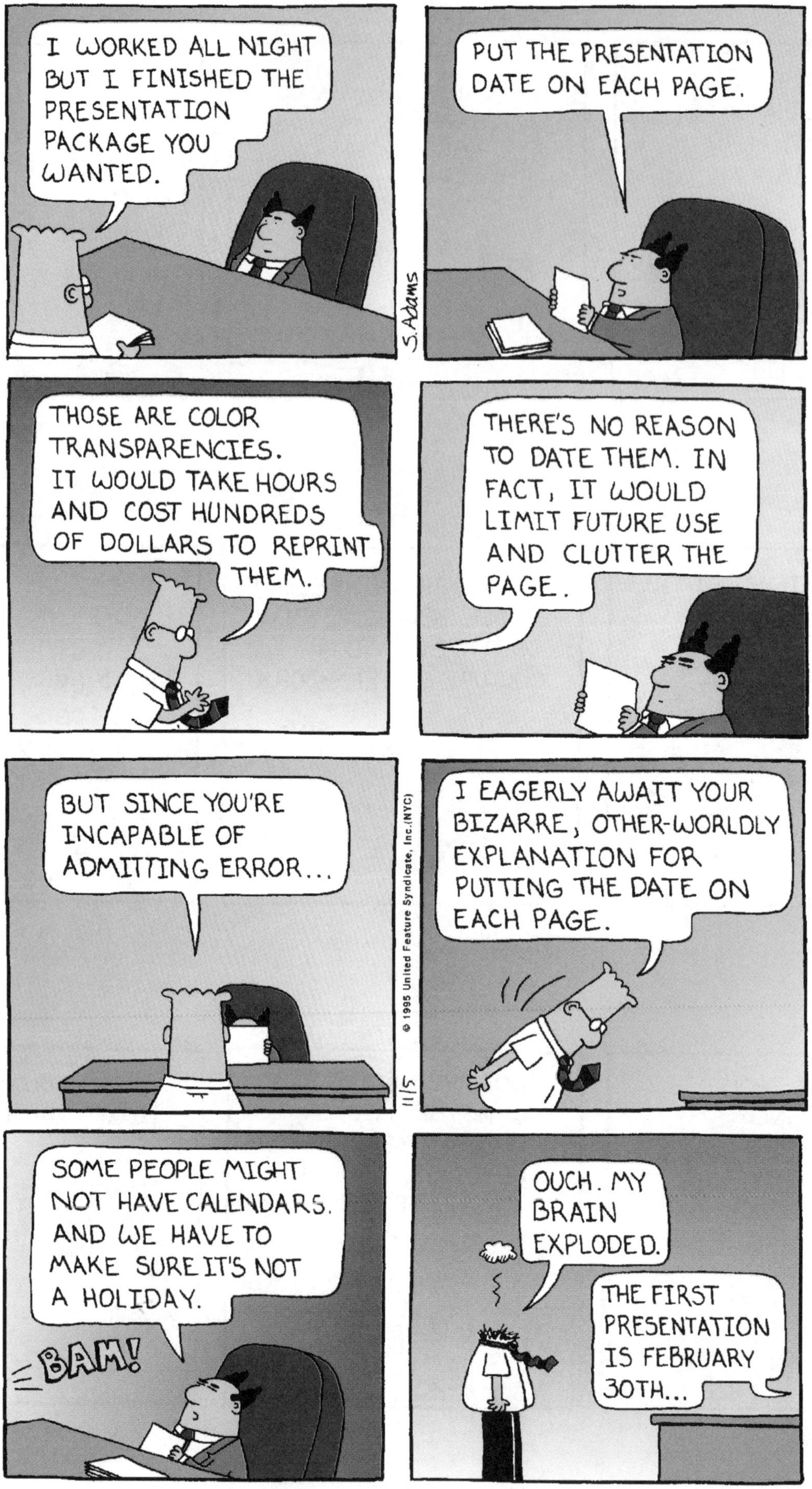

I WORKED ALL NIGHT BUT I FINISHED THE PRESENTATION PACKAGE YOU WANTED.
S. Adams
PUT THE PRESENTATION DATE ON EACH PAGE.
THOSE ARE COLOR TRANSPARENCIES. IT WOULD TAKE HOURS AND COST HUNDREDS OF DOLLARS TO REPRINT THEM.
THERE'S NO REASON TO DATE THEM. IN FACT, IT WOULD LIMIT FUTURE USE AND CLUTTER THE PAGE.
BUT SINCE YOU'RE INCAPABLE OF ADMITTING ERROR...
© 1995 United Feature Syndicate, Inc.(NYC)
11/5
I EAGERLY AWAIT YOUR BIZARRE, OTHER-WORLDLY EXPLANATION FOR PUTTING THE DATE ON EACH PAGE.
SOME PEOPLE MIGHT NOT HAVE CALENDARS. AND WE HAVE TO MAKE SURE IT'S NOT A HOLIDAY.
BAM!
OUCH. MY BRAIN EXPLODED.
THE FIRST PRESENTATION IS FEBRUARY 30TH...

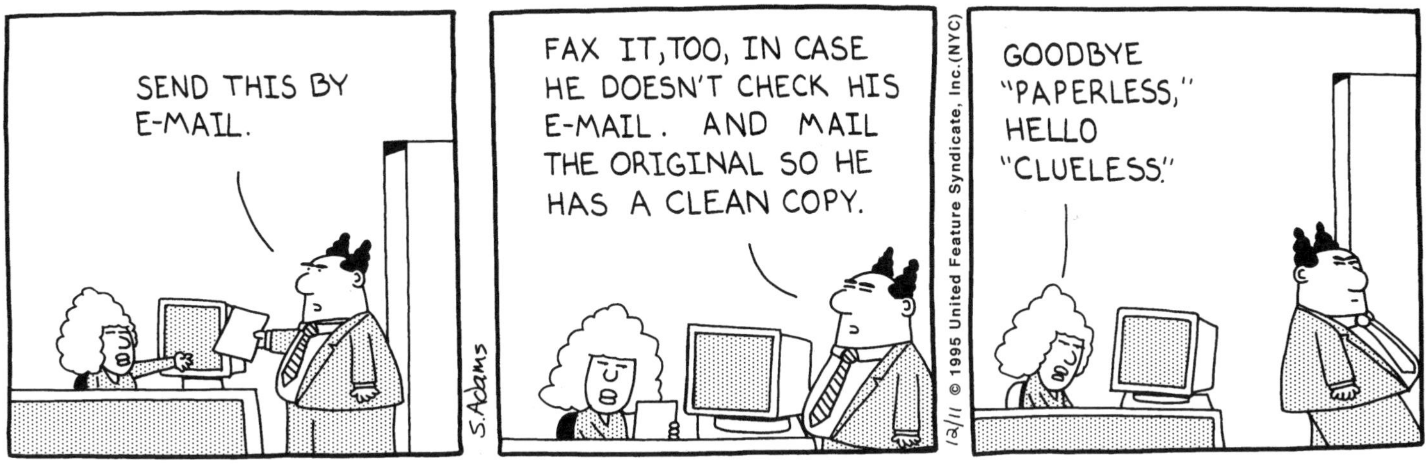
SEND THIS BY E-MAIL.
FAX IT, TOO, IN CASE HE DOESN'T CHECK HIS E-MAIL. AND MAIL THE ORIGINAL SO HE HAS A CLEAN COPY.
GOODBYE "PAPERLESS," HELLO "CLUELESS."
S. Adams
12/11 © 1995 United Feature Syndicate, Inc.(NYC)

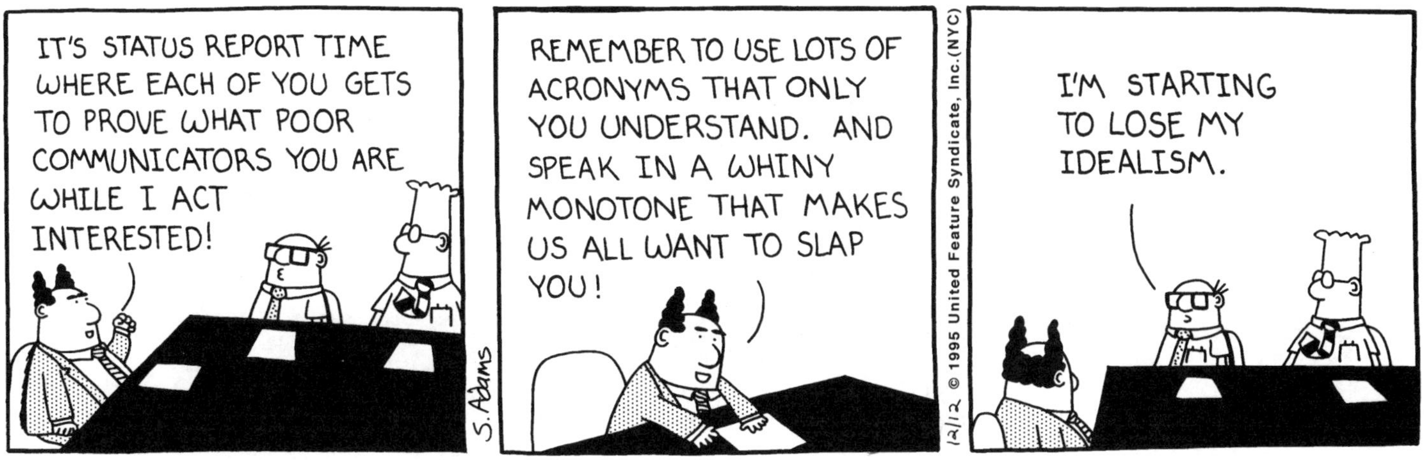
IT'S STATUS REPORT TIME WHERE EACH OF YOU GETS TO PROVE WHAT POOR COMMUNICATORS YOU ARE WHILE I ACT INTERESTED!
REMEMBER TO USE LOTS OF ACRONYMS THAT ONLY YOU UNDERSTAND. AND SPEAK IN A WHINY MONOTONE THAT MAKES US ALL WANT TO SLAP YOU!
I'M STARTING TO LOSE MY IDEALISM.
S. Adams
12/12 © 1995 United Feature Syndicate, Inc.(NYC)

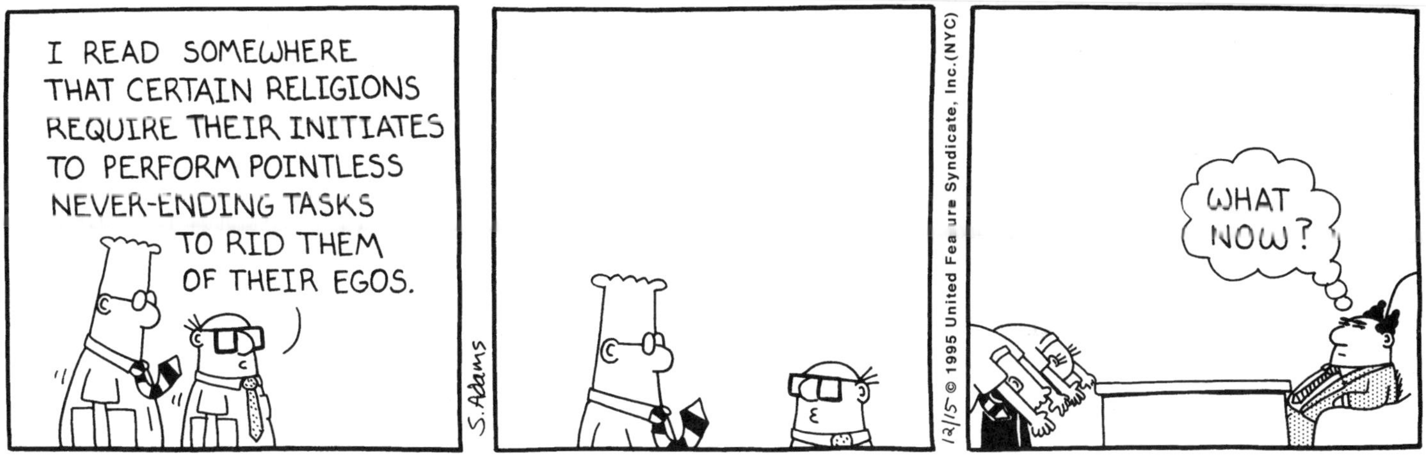
I READ SOMEWHERE THAT CERTAIN RELIGIONS REQUIRE THEIR INITIATES TO PERFORM POINTLESS NEVER-ENDING TASKS TO RID THEM OF THEIR EGOS.
WHAT NOW?
S. Adams
12/15 © 1995 United Feature Syndicate, Inc.(NYC)

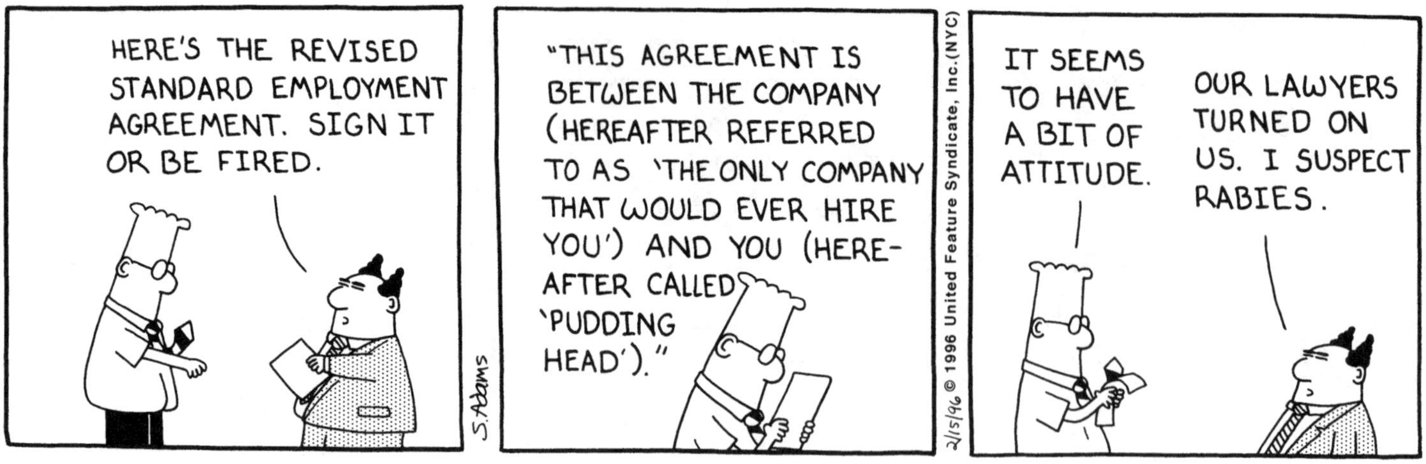
HERE'S THE REVISED STANDARD EMPLOYMENT AGREEMENT. SIGN IT OR BE FIRED.
"THIS AGREEMENT IS BETWEEN THE COMPANY (HEREAFTER REFERRED TO AS 'THE ONLY COMPANY THAT WOULD EVER HIRE YOU') AND YOU (HEREAFTER CALLED 'PUDDING HEAD')."
IT SEEMS TO HAVE A BIT OF ATTITUDE.
OUR LAWYERS TURNED ON US. I SUSPECT RABIES.
S. Adams
2/5/96 © 1996 United Feature Syndicate, Inc.(NYC)

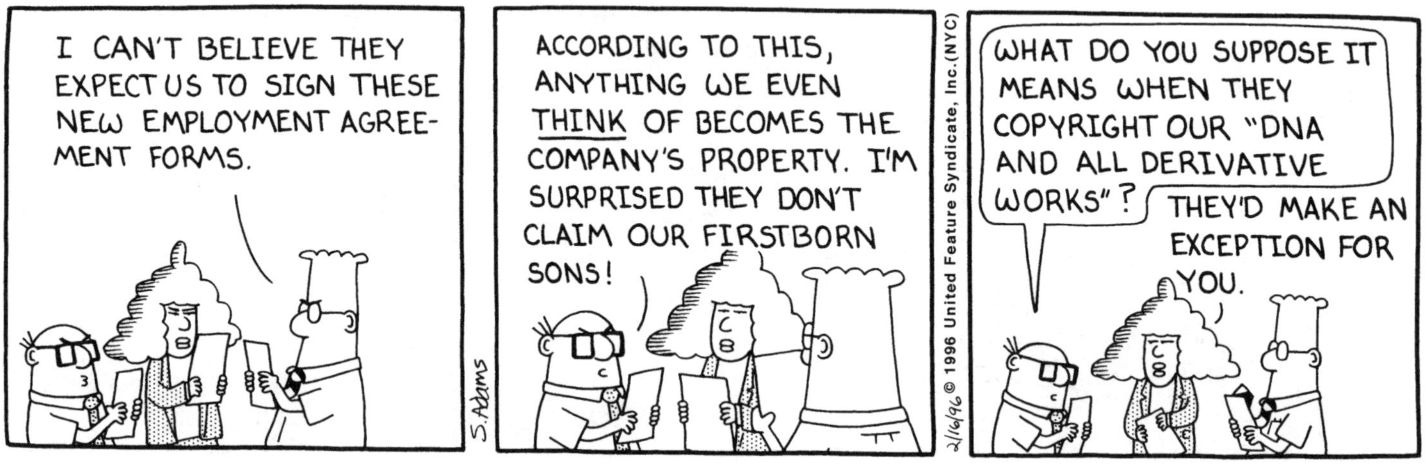
I CAN'T BELIEVE THEY EXPECT US TO SIGN THESE NEW EMPLOYMENT AGREEMENT FORMS.
ACCORDING TO THIS, ANYTHING WE EVEN THINK OF BECOMES THE COMPANY'S PROPERTY. I'M SURPRISED THEY DON'T CLAIM OUR FIRSTBORN SONS!
WHAT DO YOU SUPPOSE IT MEANS WHEN THEY COPYRIGHT OUR "DNA AND ALL DERIVATIVE WORKS"?
THEY'D MAKE AN EXCEPTION FOR YOU.
S. Adams
2/6/96 © 1996 United Feature Syndicate, Inc.(NYC)

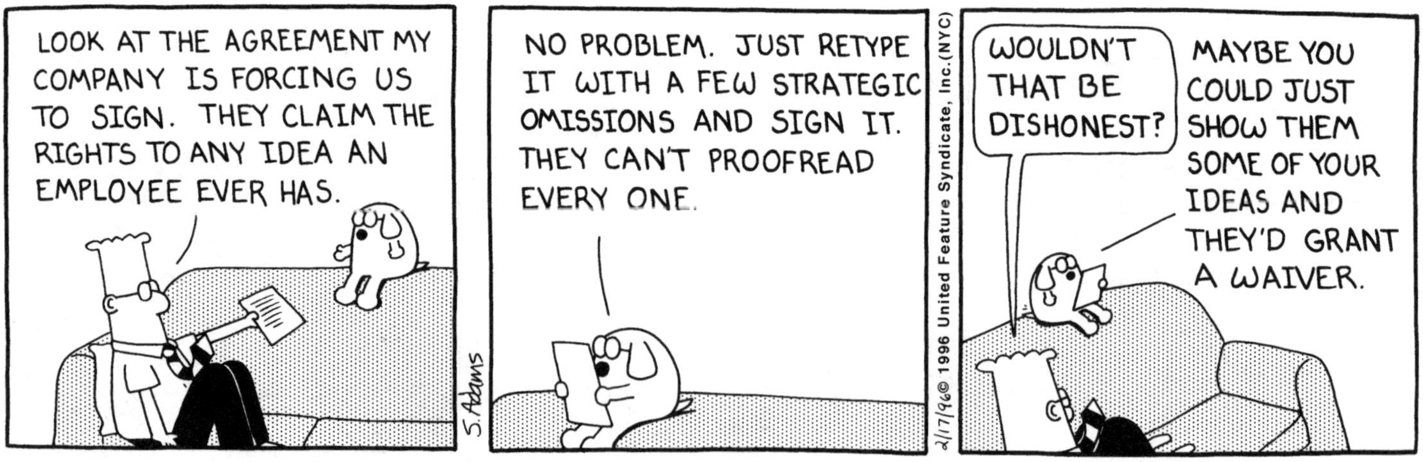
LOOK AT THE AGREEMENT MY COMPANY IS FORCING US TO SIGN. THEY CLAIM THE RIGHTS TO ANY IDEA AN EMPLOYEE EVER HAS.
NO PROBLEM. JUST RETYPE IT WITH A FEW STRATEGIC OMISSIONS AND SIGN IT. THEY CAN'T PROOFREAD EVERY ONE.
WOULDN'T THAT BE DISHONEST?
MAYBE YOU COULD JUST SHOW THEM SOME OF YOUR IDEAS AND THEY'D GRANT A WAIVER.
S. Adams
2/7/96 © 1996 United Feature Syndicate, Inc.(NYC)

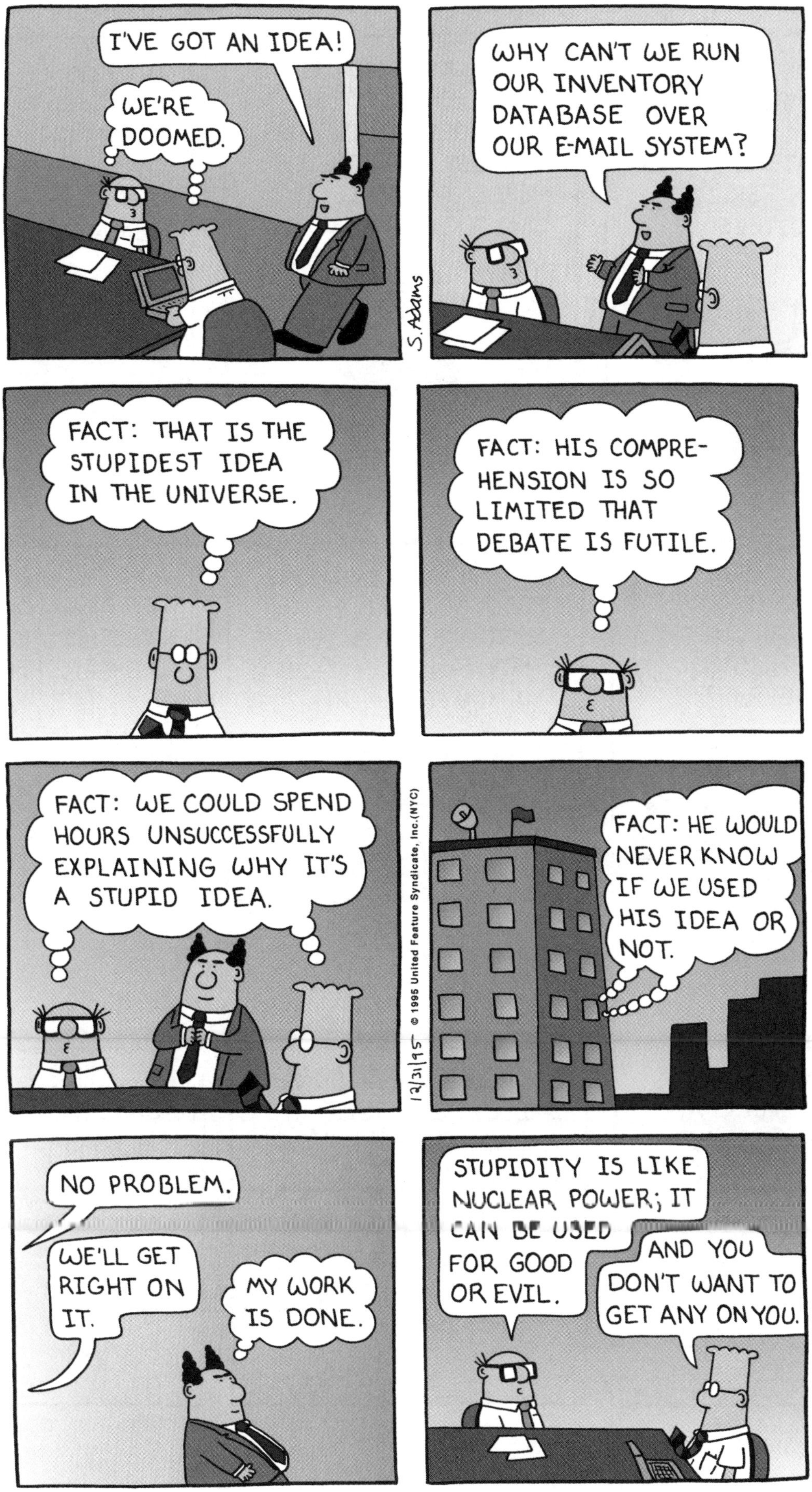
I'VE GOT AN IDEA!
WE'RE DOOMED.
S. Adams
WHY CAN'T WE RUN OUR INVENTORY DATABASE OVER OUR E-MAIL SYSTEM?
FACT: THAT IS THE STUPIDEST IDEA IN THE UNIVERSE.
FACT: HIS COMPRE-HENSION IS SO LIMITED THAT DEBATE IS FUTILE.
FACT: WE COULD SPEND HOURS UNSUCCESSFULLY EXPLAINING WHY IT'S A STUPID IDEA.
12/31/95 © 1995 United Feature Syndicate, Inc.(NYC)
FACT: HE WOULD NEVER KNOW IF WE USED HIS IDEA OR NOT.
NO PROBLEM.
WE'LL GET RIGHT ON IT.
MY WORK IS DONE.
STUPIDITY IS LIKE NUCLEAR POWER; IT CAN BE USED FOR GOOD OR EVIL.
AND YOU DON'T WANT TO GET ANY ON YOU.

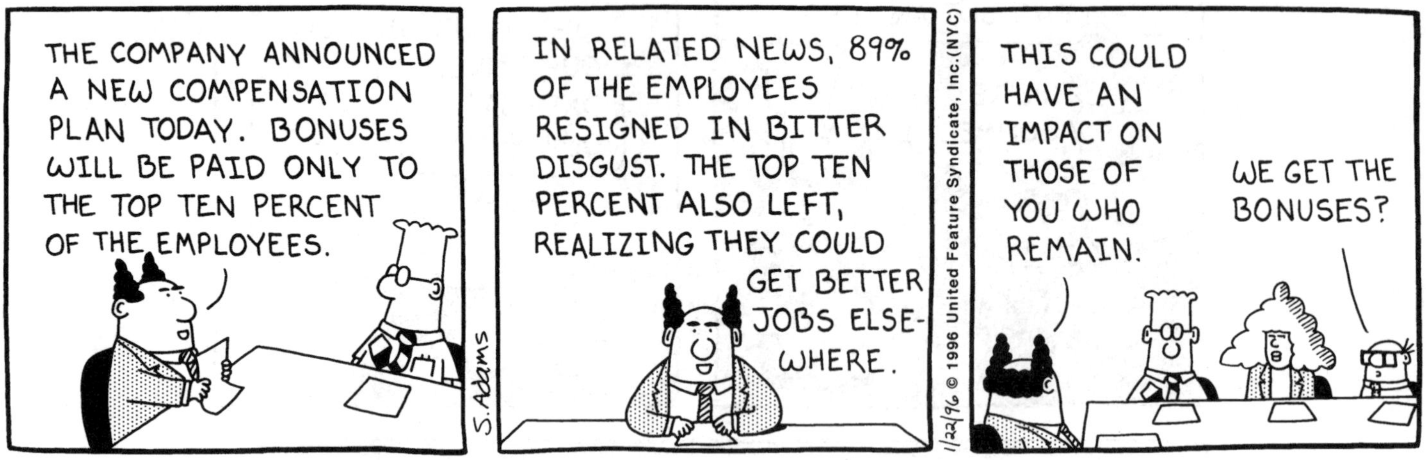
THE COMPANY ANNOUNCED A NEW COMPENSATION PLAN TODAY. BONUSES WILL BE PAID ONLY TO THE TOP TEN PERCENT OF THE EMPLOYEES.
S. Adams
IN RELATED NEWS, 89% OF THE EMPLOYEES RESIGNED IN BITTER DISGUST. THE TOP TEN PERCENT ALSO LEFT, REALIZING THEY COULD GET BETTER JOBS ELSEWHERE.
1/22/96 © 1996 United Feature Syndicate, Inc.(NYC)
THIS COULD HAVE AN IMPACT ON THOSE OF YOU WHO REMAIN.
WE GET THE BONUSES?

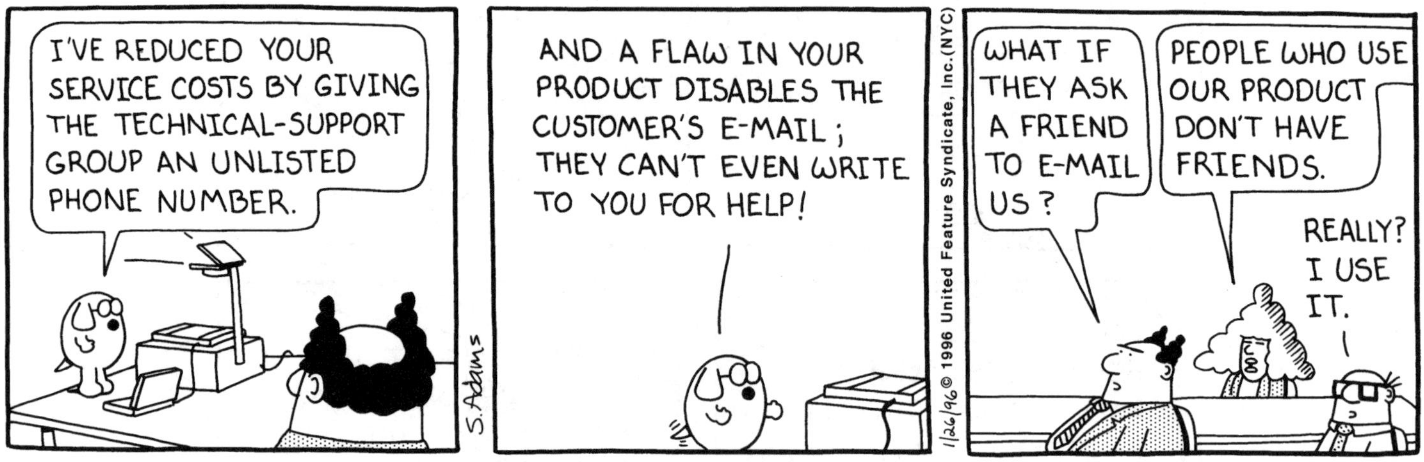
I'VE REDUCED YOUR SERVICE COSTS BY GIVING THE TECHNICAL-SUPPORT GROUP AN UNLISTED PHONE NUMBER.
S. Adams
AND A FLAW IN YOUR PRODUCT DISABLES THE CUSTOMER'S E-MAIL; THEY CAN'T EVEN WRITE TO YOU FOR HELP!
1/26/96 © 1996 United Feature Syndicate, Inc.(NYC)
WHAT IF THEY ASK A FRIEND TO E-MAIL US?
PEOPLE WHO USE OUR PRODUCT DON'T HAVE FRIENDS.
REALLY? I USE IT.

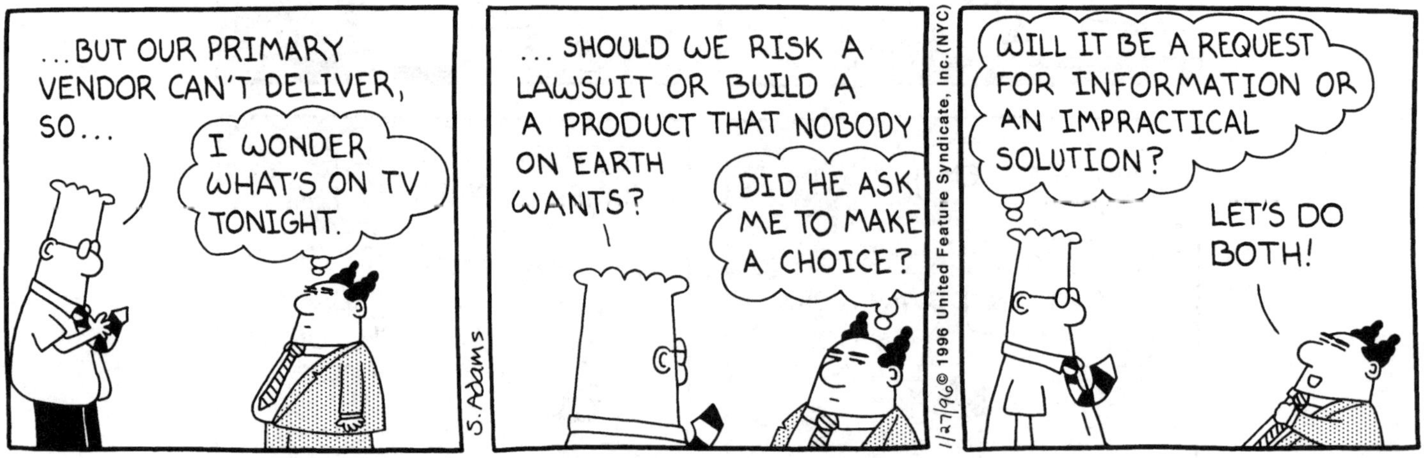
...BUT OUR PRIMARY VENDOR CAN'T DELIVER, SO...
I WONDER WHAT'S ON TV TONIGHT.
S. Adams
...SHOULD WE RISK A LAWSUIT OR BUILD A A PRODUCT THAT NOBODY ON EARTH WANTS?
DID HE ASK ME TO MAKE A CHOICE?
1/27/96 © 1996 United Feature Syndicate, Inc.(NYC)
WILL IT BE A REQUEST FOR INFORMATION OR AN IMPRACTICAL SOLUTION?
LET'S DO BOTH!

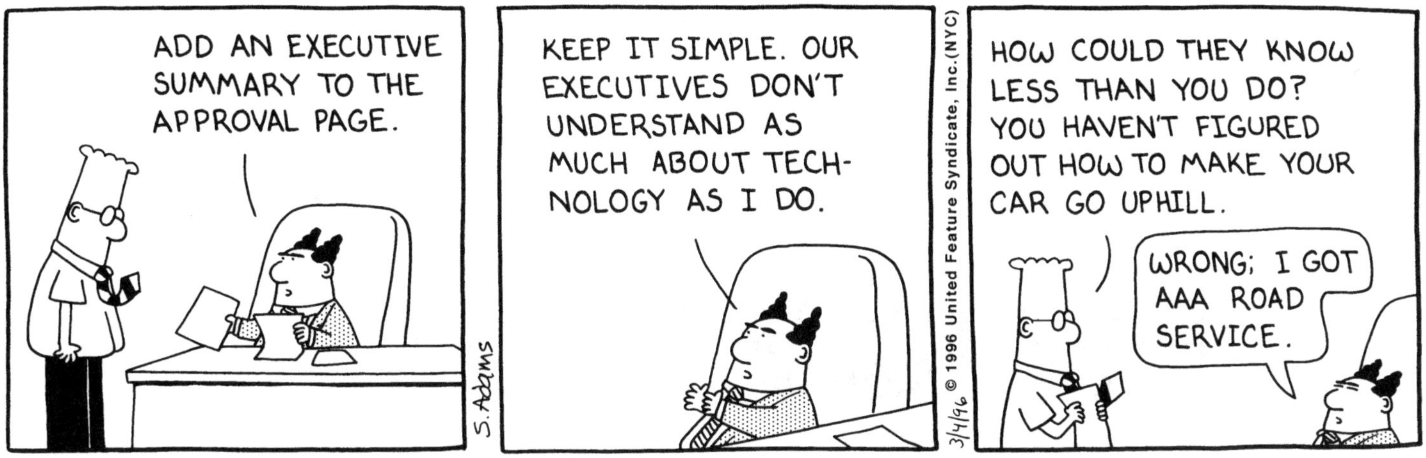
ADD AN EXECUTIVE SUMMARY TO THE APPROVAL PAGE.
S. Adams
KEEP IT SIMPLE. OUR EXECUTIVES DON'T UNDERSTAND AS MUCH ABOUT TECH-NOLOGY AS I DO.
3/4/96 © 1996 United Feature Syndicate, Inc.(NYC)
HOW COULD THEY KNOW LESS THAN YOU DO? YOU HAVEN'T FIGURED OUT HOW TO MAKE YOUR CAR GO UPHILL.
WRONG; I GOT AAA ROAD SERVICE.

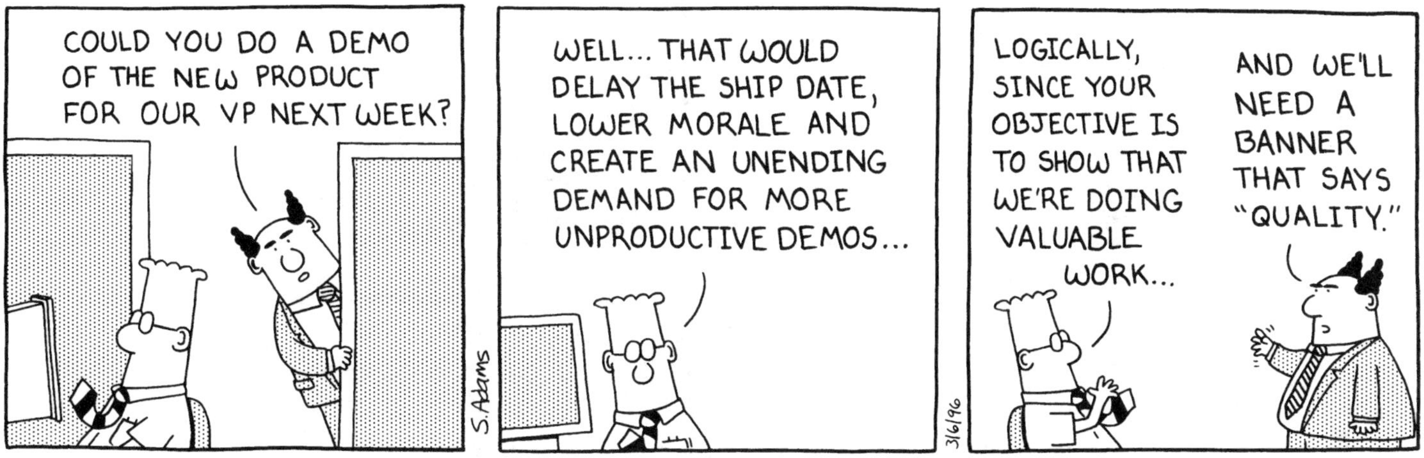
COULD YOU DO A DEMO OF THE NEW PRODUCT FOR OUR VP NEXT WEEK?
S. Adams
WELL... THAT WOULD DELAY THE SHIP DATE, LOWER MORALE AND CREATE AN UNENDING DEMAND FOR MORE UNPRODUCTIVE DEMOS...
3/6/96
LOGICALLY, SINCE YOUR OBJECTIVE IS TO SHOW THAT WE'RE DOING VALUABLE WORK...
AND WE'LL NEED A BANNER THAT SAYS "QUALITY."

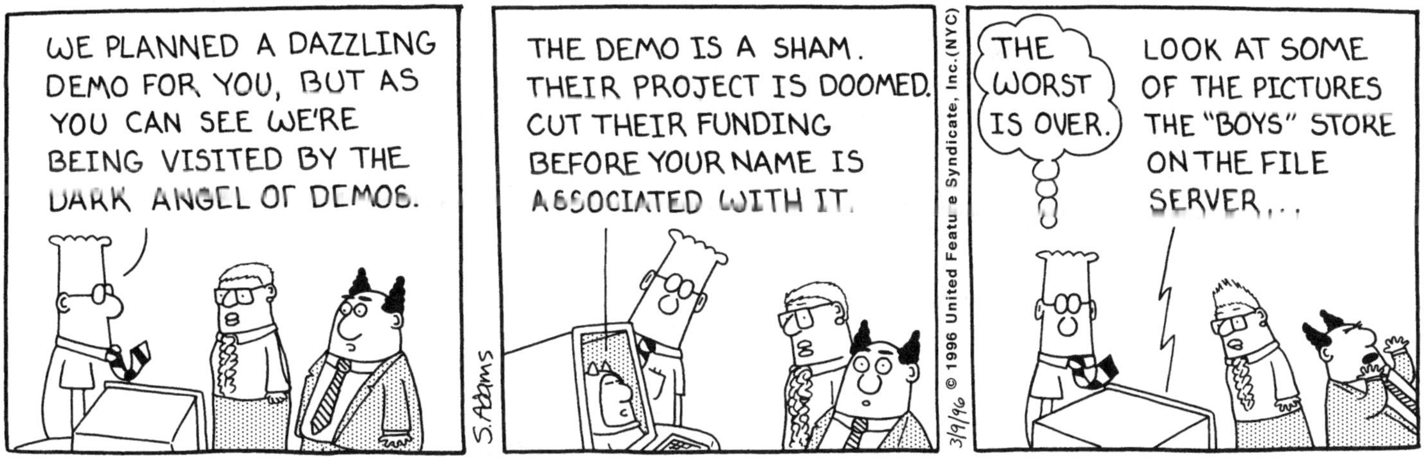
WE PLANNED A DAZZLING DEMO FOR YOU, BUT AS YOU CAN SEE WE'RE BEING VISITED BY THE DARK ANGEL OF DEMOS.
S. Adams
THE DEMO IS A SHAM. THEIR PROJECT IS DOOMED. CUT THEIR FUNDING BEFORE YOUR NAME IS ASSOCIATED WITH IT.
3/9/96 © 1996 United Feature Syndicate, Inc.(NYC)
THE WORST IS OVER.
LOOK AT SOME OF THE PICTURES THE "BOYS" STORE ON THE FILE SERVER...

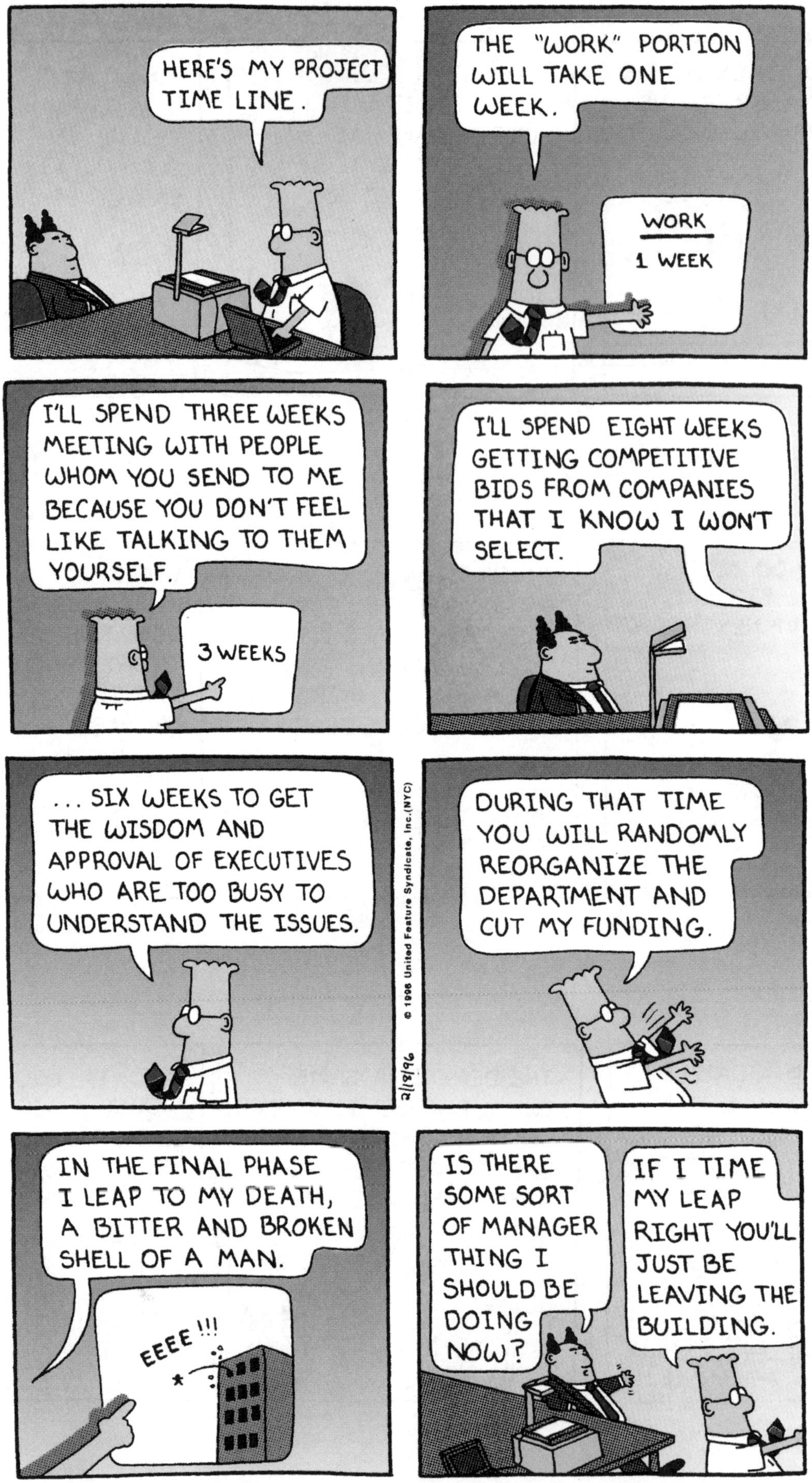
HERE'S MY PROJECT TIME LINE.
THE "WORK" PORTION WILL TAKE ONE WEEK.
WORK
1 WEEK
I'LL SPEND THREE WEEKS MEETING WITH PEOPLE WHOM YOU SEND TO ME BECAUSE YOU DON'T FEEL LIKE TALKING TO THEM YOURSELF.
3 WEEKS
I'LL SPEND EIGHT WEEKS GETTING COMPETITIVE BIDS FROM COMPANIES THAT I KNOW I WON'T SELECT.
... SIX WEEKS TO GET THE WISDOM AND APPROVAL OF EXECUTIVES WHO ARE TOO BUSY TO UNDERSTAND THE ISSUES.
© 1996 United Feature Syndicate, Inc.(NYC)
2/18/96
DURING THAT TIME YOU WILL RANDOMLY REORGANIZE THE DEPARTMENT AND CUT MY FUNDING.
IN THE FINAL PHASE I LEAP TO MY DEATH, A BITTER AND BROKEN SHELL OF A MAN.
EEEE!!!
IS THERE SOME SORT OF MANAGER THING I SHOULD BE DOING NOW?
IF I TIME MY LEAP RIGHT YOU'LL JUST BE LEAVING THE BUILDING.

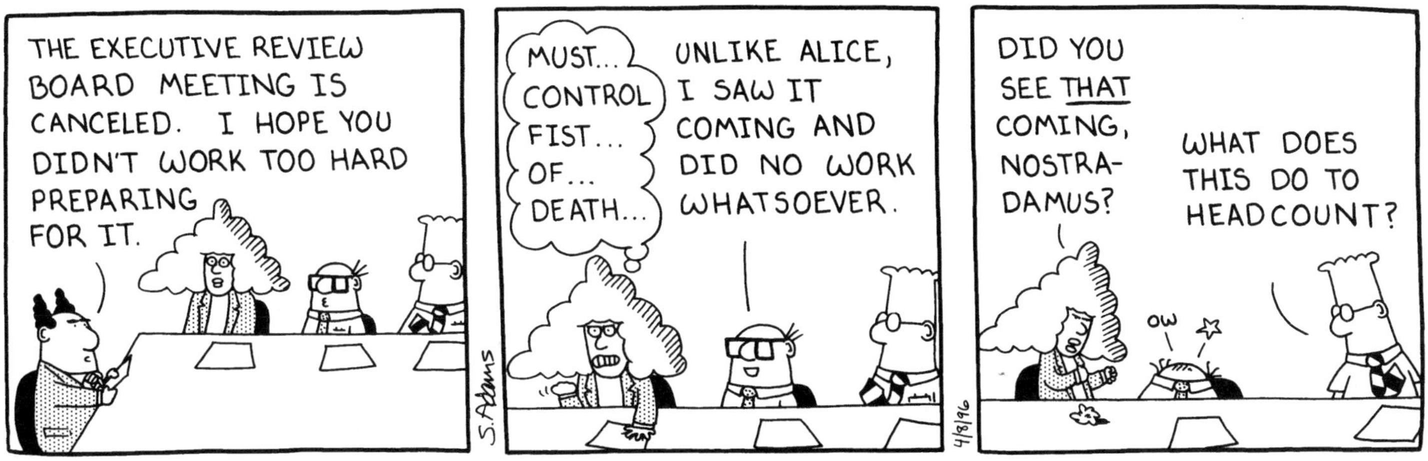
THE EXECUTIVE REVIEW BOARD MEETING IS CANCELED. I HOPE YOU DIDN'T WORK TOO HARD PREPARING FOR IT.
MUST... CONTROL FIST... OF... DEATH...
UNLIKE ALICE, I SAW IT COMING AND DID NO WORK WHATSOEVER.
DID YOU SEE THAT COMING, NOSTRA-DAMUS?
OW
WHAT DOES THIS DO TO HEADCOUNT?
S. Adams
4/8/96

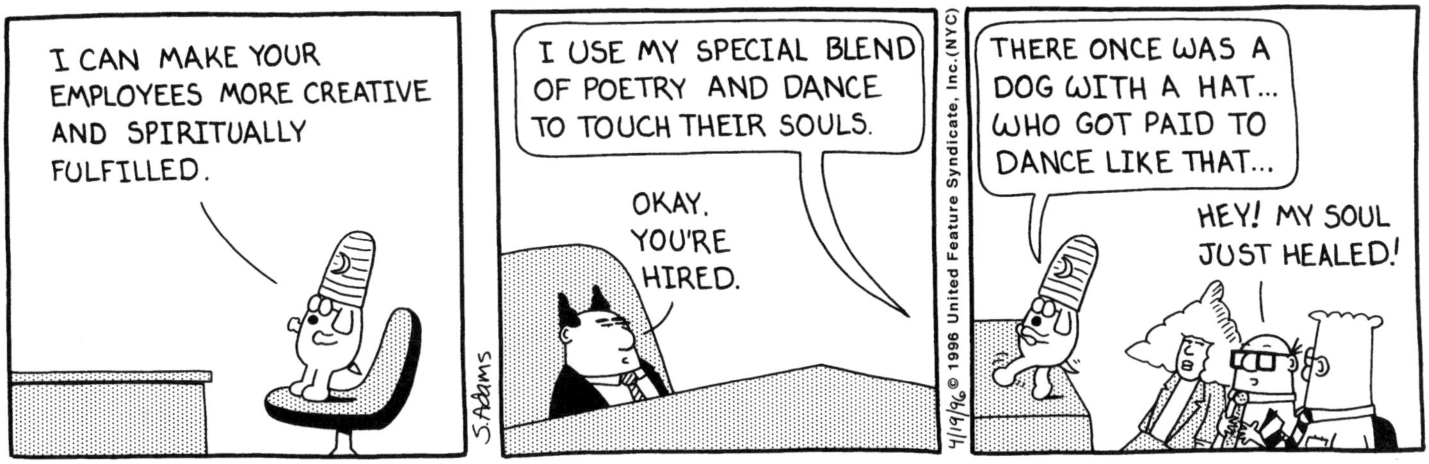
I CAN MAKE YOUR EMPLOYEES MORE CREATIVE AND SPIRITUALLY FULFILLED.
I USE MY SPECIAL BLEND OF POETRY AND DANCE TO TOUCH THEIR SOULS.
OKAY. YOU'RE HIRED.
THERE ONCE WAS A DOG WITH A HAT... WHO GOT PAID TO DANCE LIKE THAT...
HEY! MY SOUL JUST HEALED!
S. Adams
4/19/96 © 1996 United Feature Syndicate, Inc.(NYC)

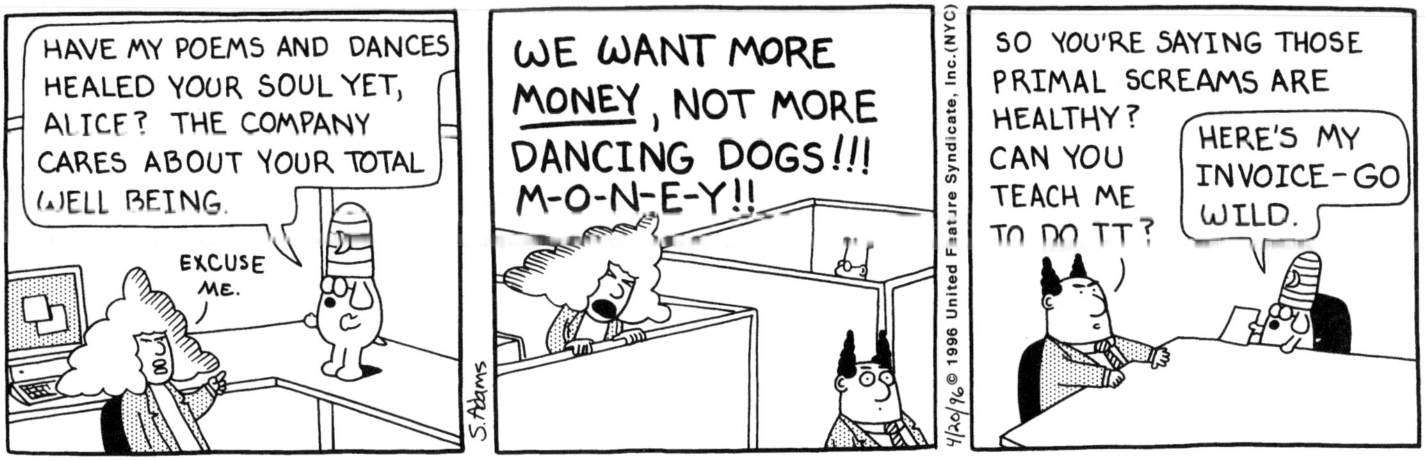
HAVE MY POEMS AND DANCES HEALED YOUR SOUL YET, ALICE? THE COMPANY CARES ABOUT YOUR TOTAL WELL BEING.
EXCUSE ME.
WE WANT MORE MONEY, NOT MORE DANCING DOGS!!! M-O-N-E-Y!!
SO YOU'RE SAYING THOSE PRIMAL SCREAMS ARE HEALTHY? CAN YOU TEACH ME TO DO IT?
HERE'S MY INVOICE-GO WILD.
S. Adams
4/20/96 © 1996 United Feature Syndicate, Inc.(NYC)

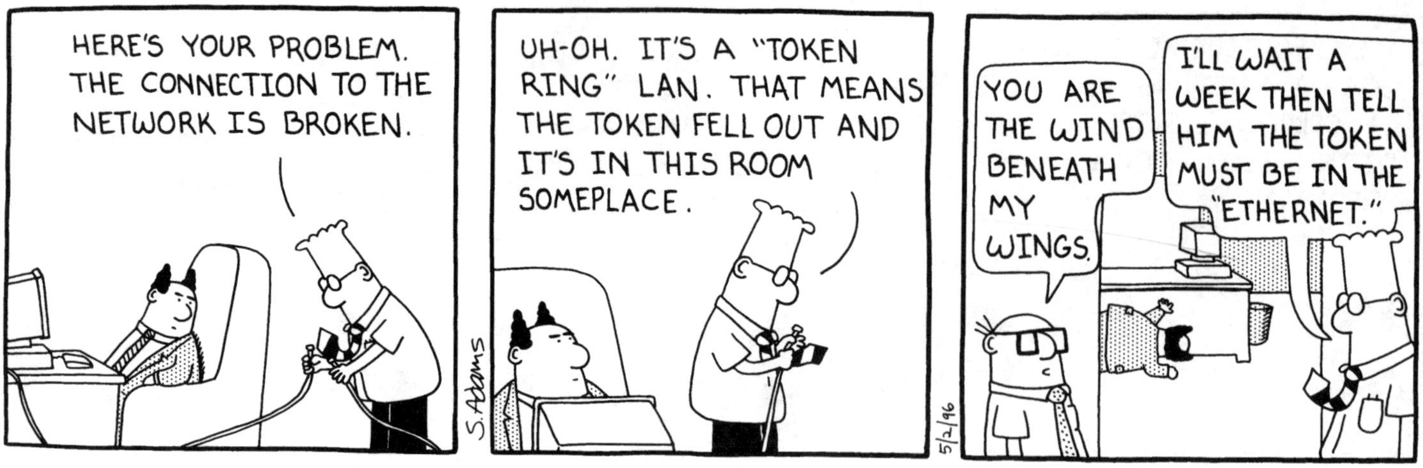
HERE'S YOUR PROBLEM. THE CONNECTION TO THE NETWORK IS BROKEN.
S. Adams
UH-OH. IT'S A "TOKEN RING" LAN. THAT MEANS THE TOKEN FELL OUT AND IT'S IN THIS ROOM SOMEPLACE.
5/2/96
YOU ARE THE WIND BENEATH MY WINGS.
I'LL WAIT A WEEK THEN TELL HIM THE TOKEN MUST BE IN THE "ETHERNET."

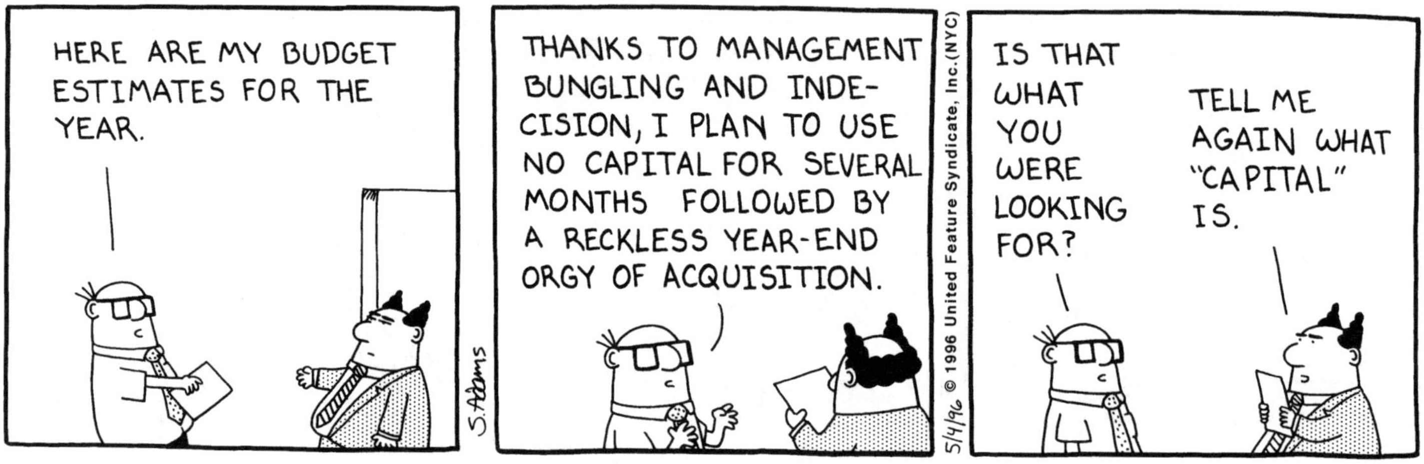
HERE ARE MY BUDGET ESTIMATES FOR THE YEAR.
S. Adams
THANKS TO MANAGEMENT BUNGLING AND INDECISION, I PLAN TO USE NO CAPITAL FOR SEVERAL MONTHS FOLLOWED BY A RECKLESS YEAR-END ORGY OF ACQUISITION.
5/4/96 © 1996 United Feature Syndicate, Inc.(NYC)
IS THAT WHAT YOU WERE LOOKING FOR?
TELL ME AGAIN WHAT "CAPITAL" IS.

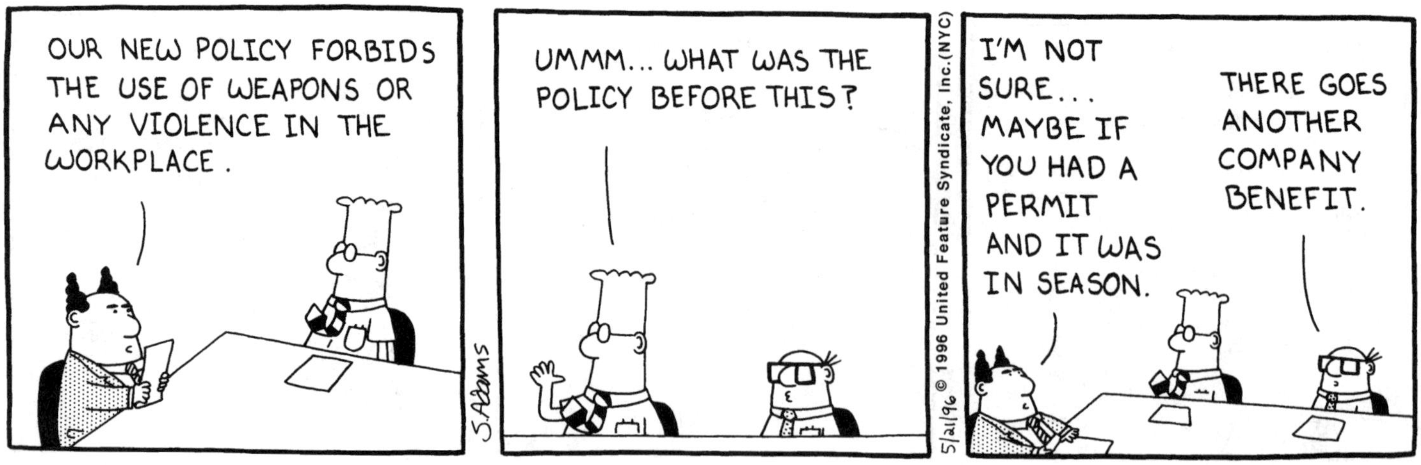
OUR NEW POLICY FORBIDS THE USE OF WEAPONS OR ANY VIOLENCE IN THE WORKPLACE.
S. Adams
UMMM... WHAT WAS THE POLICY BEFORE THIS?
5/21/96 © 1996 United Feature Syndicate, Inc.(NYC)
I'M NOT SURE... MAYBE IF YOU HAD A PERMIT AND IT WAS IN SEASON.
THERE GOES ANOTHER COMPANY BENEFIT.

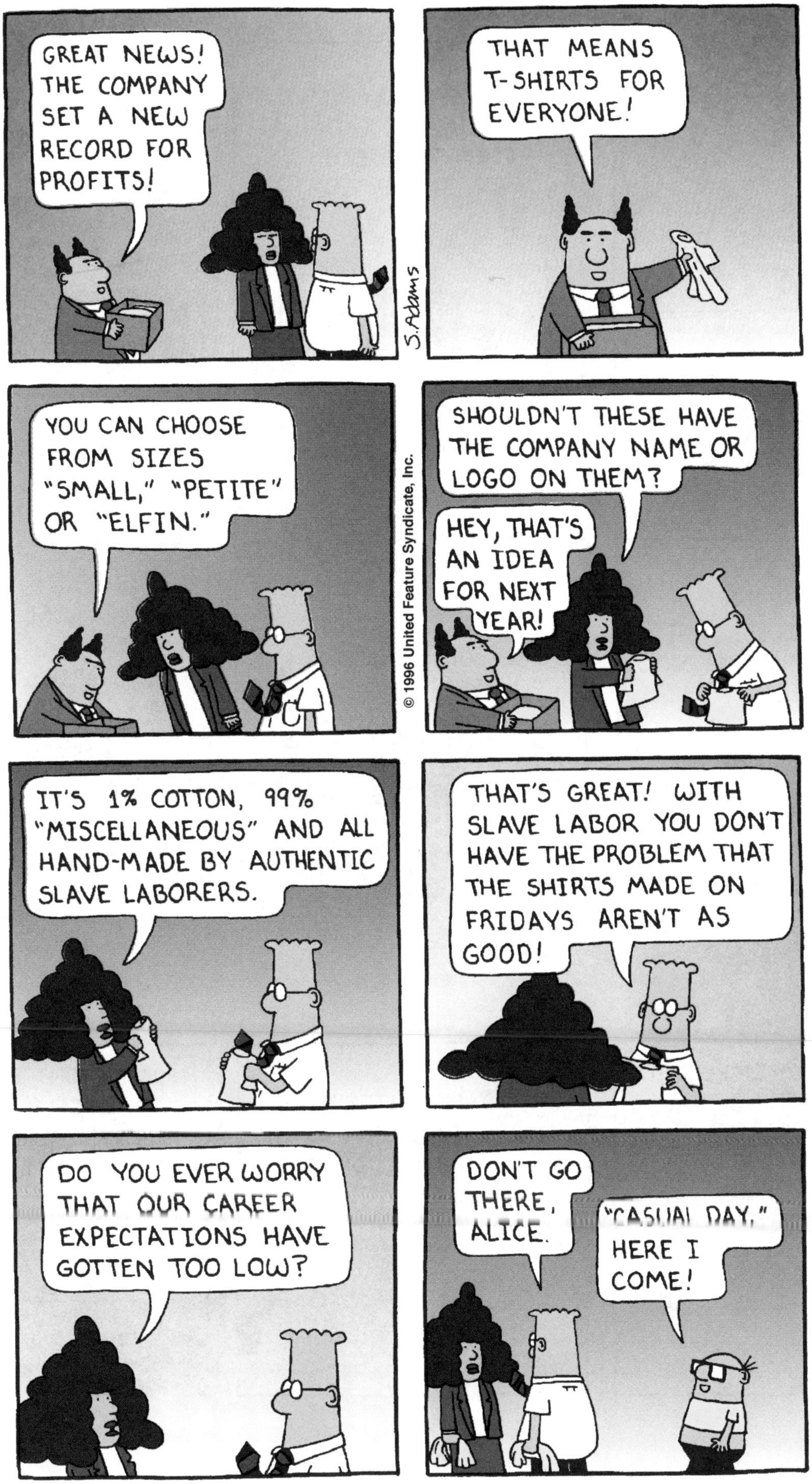
GREAT NEWS! THE COMPANY SET A NEW RECORD FOR PROFITS!
S. Adams
THAT MEANS T-SHIRTS FOR EVERYONE!
YOU CAN CHOOSE FROM SIZES "SMALL," "PETITE" OR "ELFIN."
© 1996 United Feature Syndicate, Inc.
SHOULDN'T THESE HAVE THE COMPANY NAME OR LOGO ON THEM?
HEY, THAT'S AN IDEA FOR NEXT YEAR!
IT'S 1% COTTON, 99% "MISCELLANEOUS" AND ALL HAND-MADE BY AUTHENTIC SLAVE LABORERS.
THAT'S GREAT! WITH SLAVE LABOR YOU DON'T HAVE THE PROBLEM THAT THE SHIRTS MADE ON FRIDAYS AREN'T AS GOOD!
DO YOU EVER WORRY THAT OUR CAREER EXPECTATIONS HAVE GOTTEN TOO LOW?
DON'T GO THERE, ALICE.
"CASUAL DAY," HERE I COME!

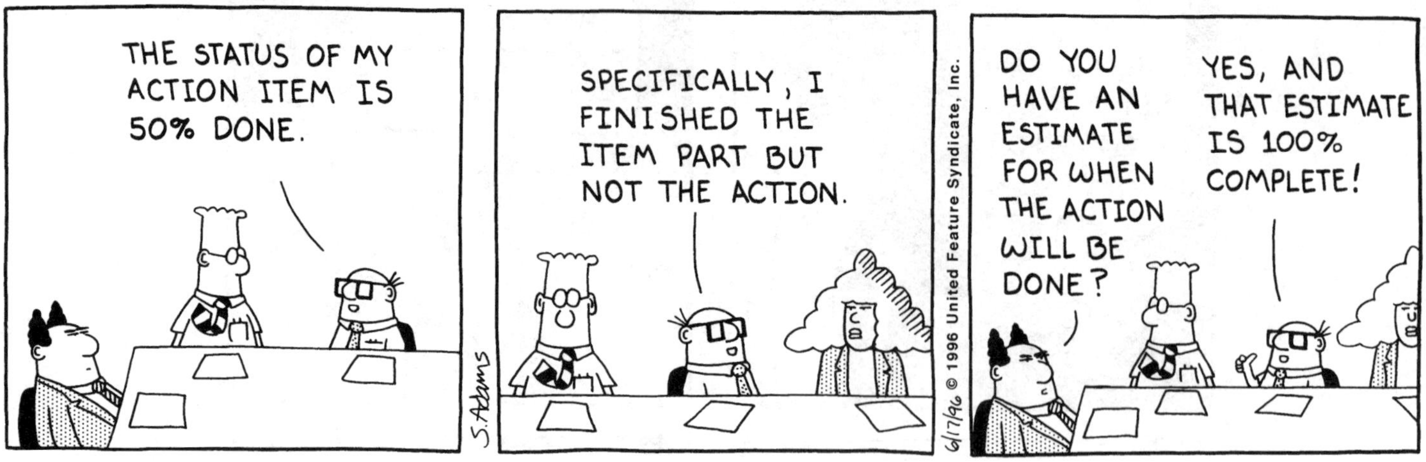
THE STATUS OF MY ACTION ITEM IS 50% DONE.
SPECIFICALLY, I FINISHED THE ITEM PART BUT NOT THE ACTION.
DO YOU HAVE AN ESTIMATE FOR WHEN THE ACTION WILL BE DONE?
YES, AND THAT ESTIMATE IS 100% COMPLETE!
S. Adams
6/17/96 © 1996 United Feature Syndicate, Inc.

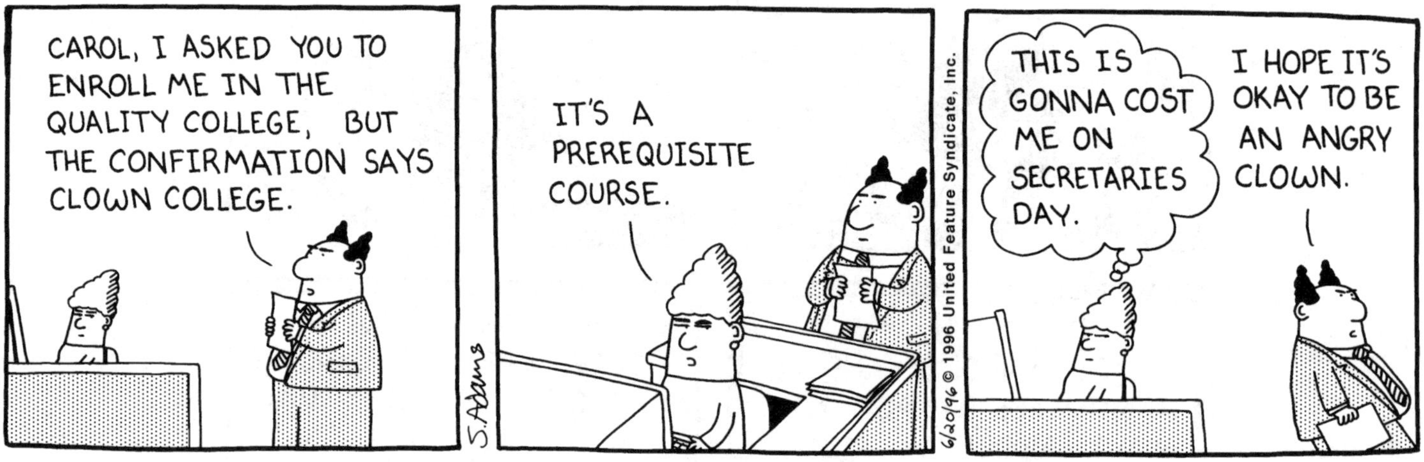
CAROL, I ASKED YOU TO ENROLL ME IN THE QUALITY COLLEGE, BUT THE CONFIRMATION SAYS CLOWN COLLEGE.
IT'S A PREREQUISITE COURSE.
THIS IS GONNA COST ME ON SECRETARIES DAY.
I HOPE IT'S OKAY TO BE AN ANGRY CLOWN.
S. Adams
6/20/96 © 1996 United Feature Syndicate, Inc.

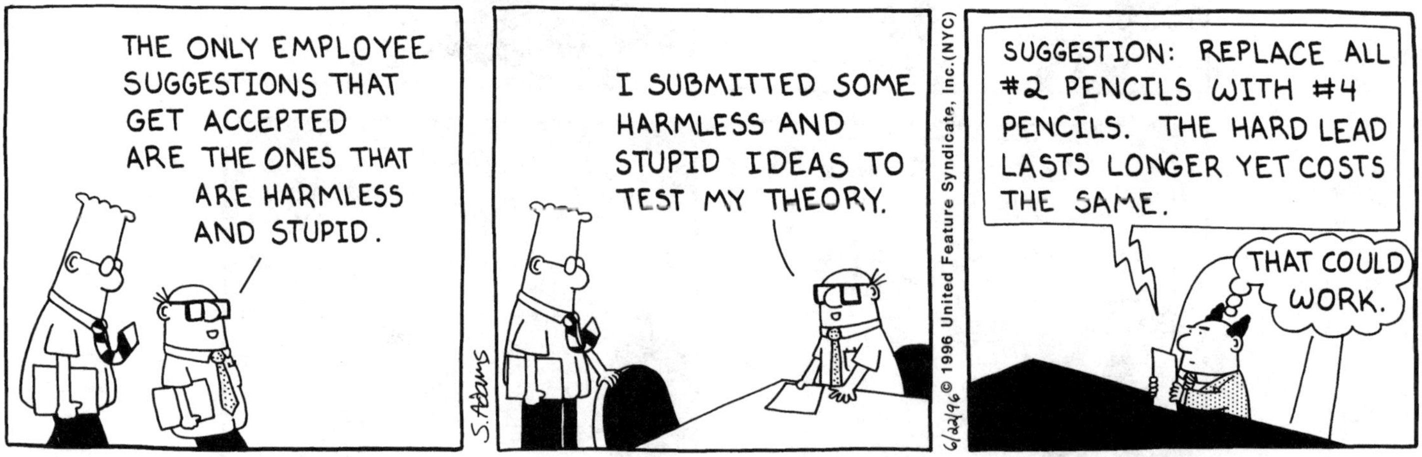
THE ONLY EMPLOYEE SUGGESTIONS THAT GET ACCEPTED ARE THE ONES THAT ARE HARMLESS AND STUPID.
I SUBMITTED SOME HARMLESS AND STUPID IDEAS TO TEST MY THEORY.
SUGGESTION: REPLACE ALL #2 PENCILS WITH #4 PENCILS. THE HARD LEAD LASTS LONGER YET COSTS THE SAME.
THAT COULD WORK.
S. Adams
6/22/96 © 1996 United Feature Syndicate, Inc. (NYC)

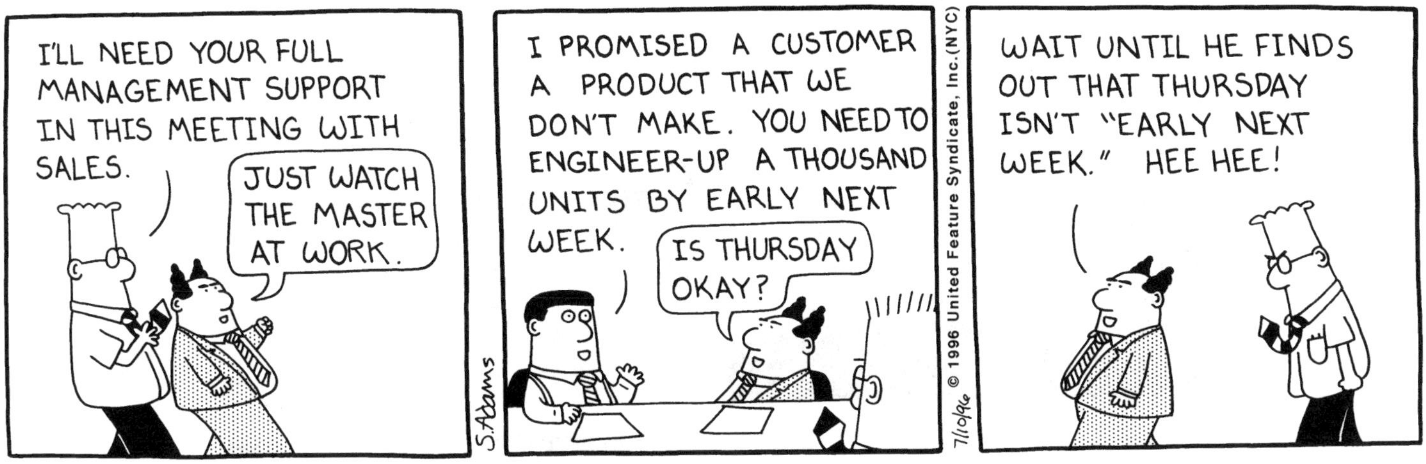
I'LL NEED YOUR FULL MANAGEMENT SUPPORT IN THIS MEETING WITH SALES.
JUST WATCH THE MASTER AT WORK.
I PROMISED A CUSTOMER A PRODUCT THAT WE DON'T MAKE. YOU NEED TO ENGINEER-UP A THOUSAND UNITS BY EARLY NEXT WEEK.
IS THURSDAY OKAY?
WAIT UNTIL HE FINDS OUT THAT THURSDAY ISN'T "EARLY NEXT WEEK." HEE HEE!

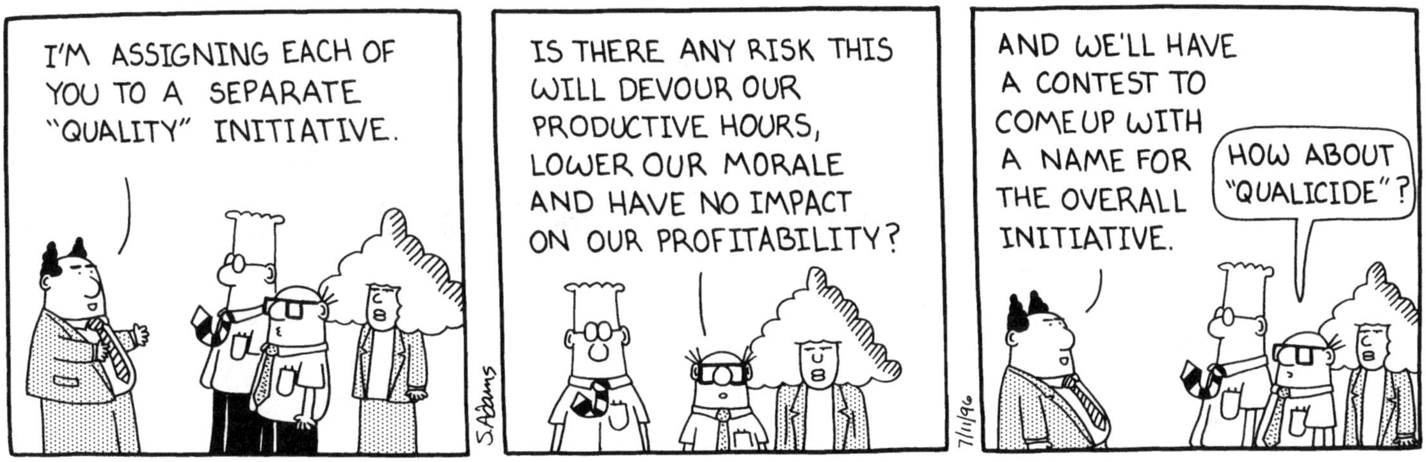
I'M ASSIGNING EACH OF YOU TO A SEPARATE "QUALITY" INITIATIVE.
IS THERE ANY RISK THIS WILL DEVOUR OUR PRODUCTIVE HOURS, LOWER OUR MORALE AND HAVE NO IMPACT ON OUR PROFITABILITY?
AND WE'LL HAVE A CONTEST TO COMEUP WITH A NAME FOR THE OVERALL INITIATIVE.
HOW ABOUT "QUALICIDE"?

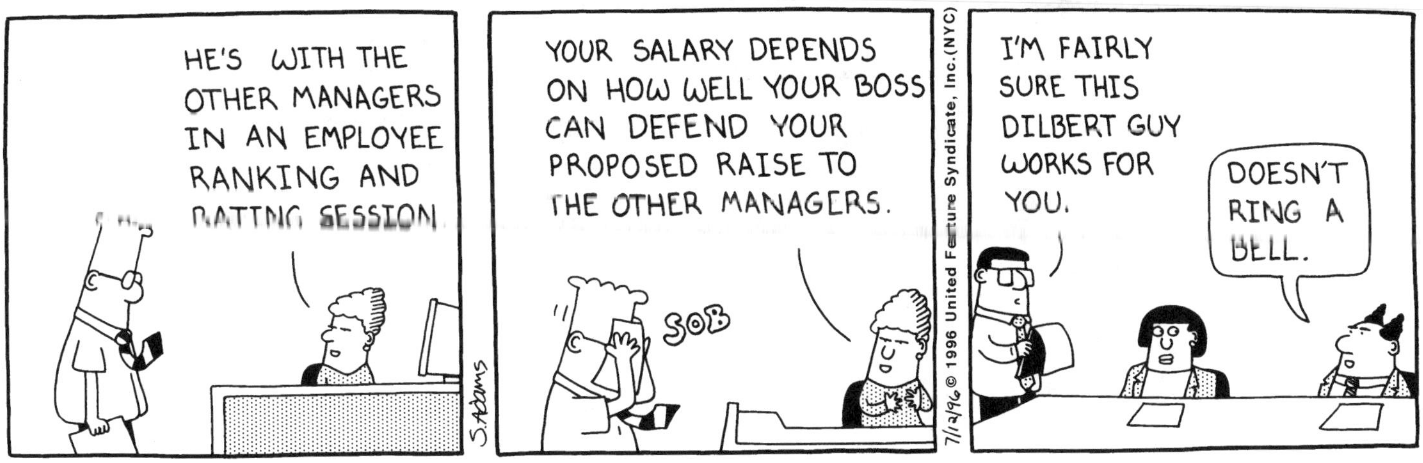
HE'S WITH THE OTHER MANAGERS IN AN EMPLOYEE RANKING AND RATING SESSION.
YOUR SALARY DEPENDS ON HOW WELL YOUR BOSS CAN DEFEND YOUR PROPOSED RAISE TO THE OTHER MANAGERS.
SOB
I'M FAIRLY SURE THIS DILBERT GUY WORKS FOR YOU.
DOESN'T RING A BELL.

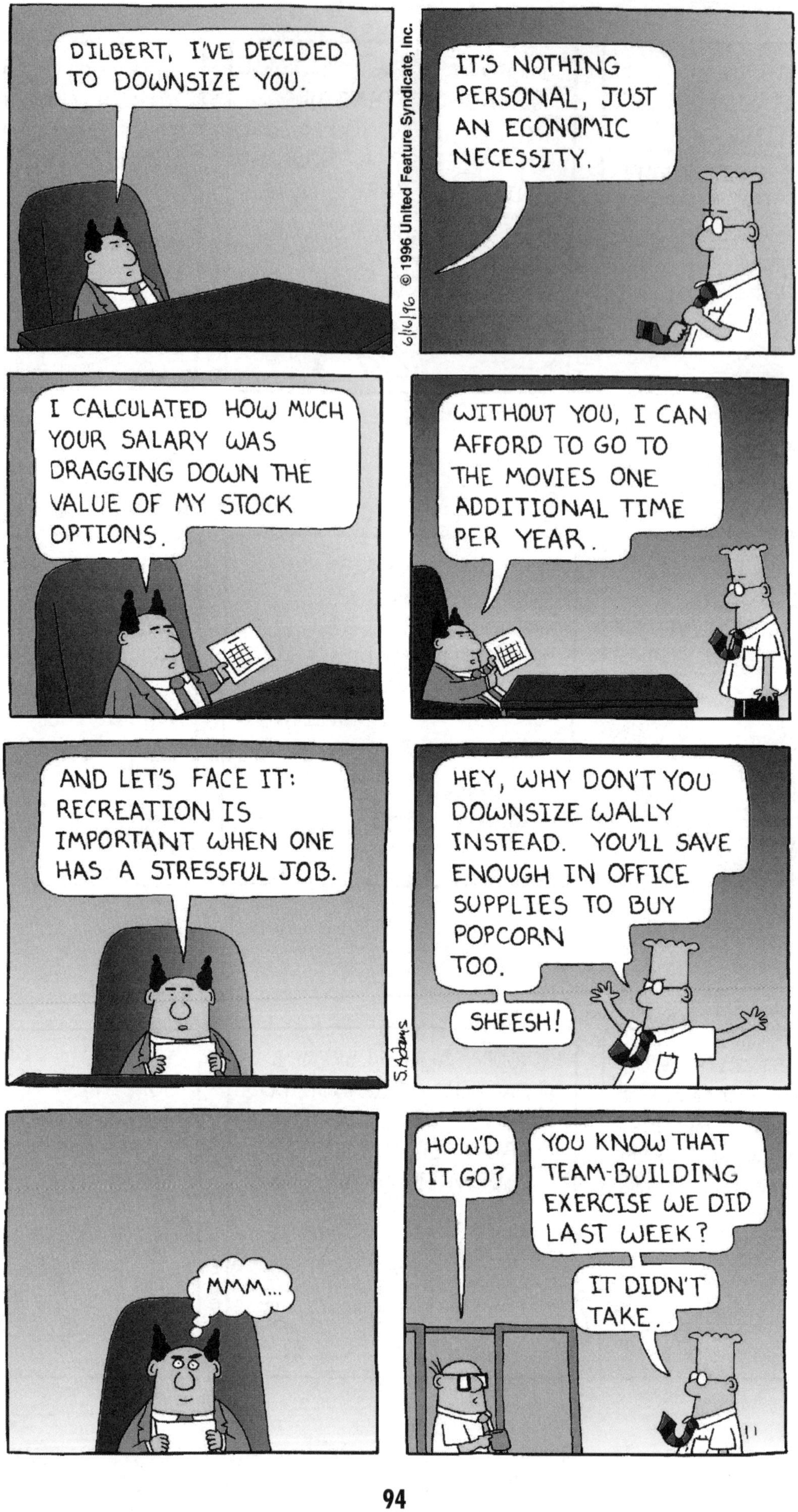
DILBERT, I'VE DECIDED TO DOWNSIZE YOU.
© 1996 United Feature Syndicate, Inc.
6/16/96
IT'S NOTHING PERSONAL, JUST AN ECONOMIC NECESSITY.
I CALCULATED HOW MUCH YOUR SALARY WAS DRAGGING DOWN THE VALUE OF MY STOCK OPTIONS.
WITHOUT YOU, I CAN AFFORD TO GO TO THE MOVIES ONE ADDITIONAL TIME PER YEAR.
AND LET'S FACE IT: RECREATION IS IMPORTANT WHEN ONE HAS A STRESSFUL JOB.
S. Adams
HEY, WHY DON'T YOU DOWNSIZE WALLY INSTEAD. YOU'LL SAVE ENOUGH IN OFFICE SUPPLIES TO BUY POPCORN TOO.
SHEESH!
MMM...
HOW'D IT GO?
YOU KNOW THAT TEAM-BUILDING EXERCISE WE DID LAST WEEK?
IT DIDN'T TAKE.

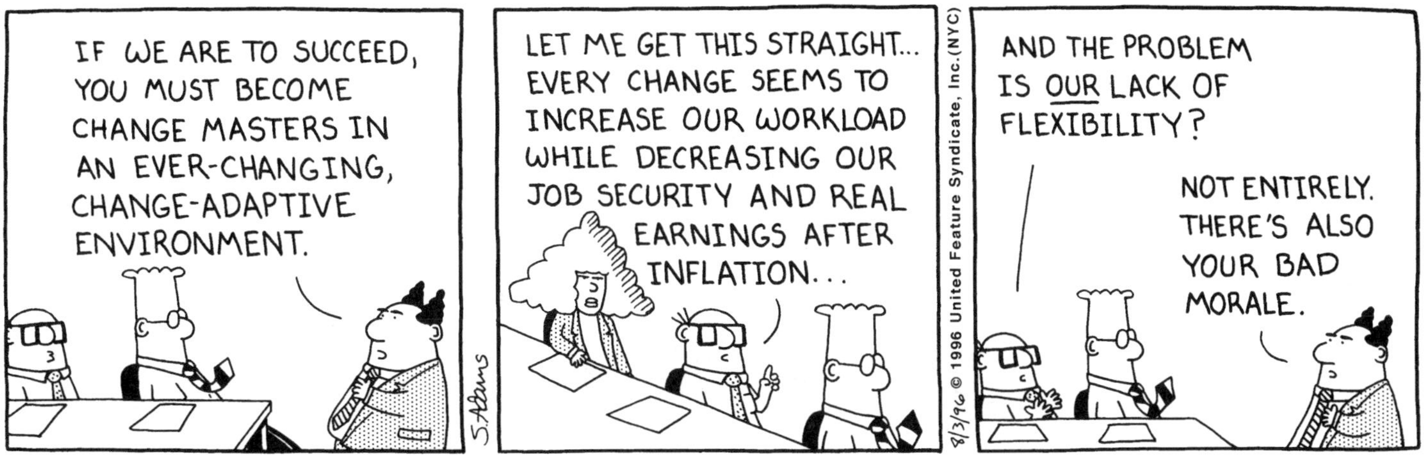
IF WE ARE TO SUCCEED, YOU MUST BECOME CHANGE MASTERS IN AN EVER-CHANGING, CHANGE-ADAPTIVE ENVIRONMENT.
S.Adams
LET ME GET THIS STRAIGHT... EVERY CHANGE SEEMS TO INCREASE OUR WORKLOAD WHILE DECREASING OUR JOB SECURITY AND REAL EARNINGS AFTER INFLATION...
8/3/96 © 1996 United Feature Syndicate, Inc.(NYC)
AND THE PROBLEM IS OUR LACK OF FLEXIBILITY?
NOT ENTIRELY. THERE'S ALSO YOUR BAD MORALE.

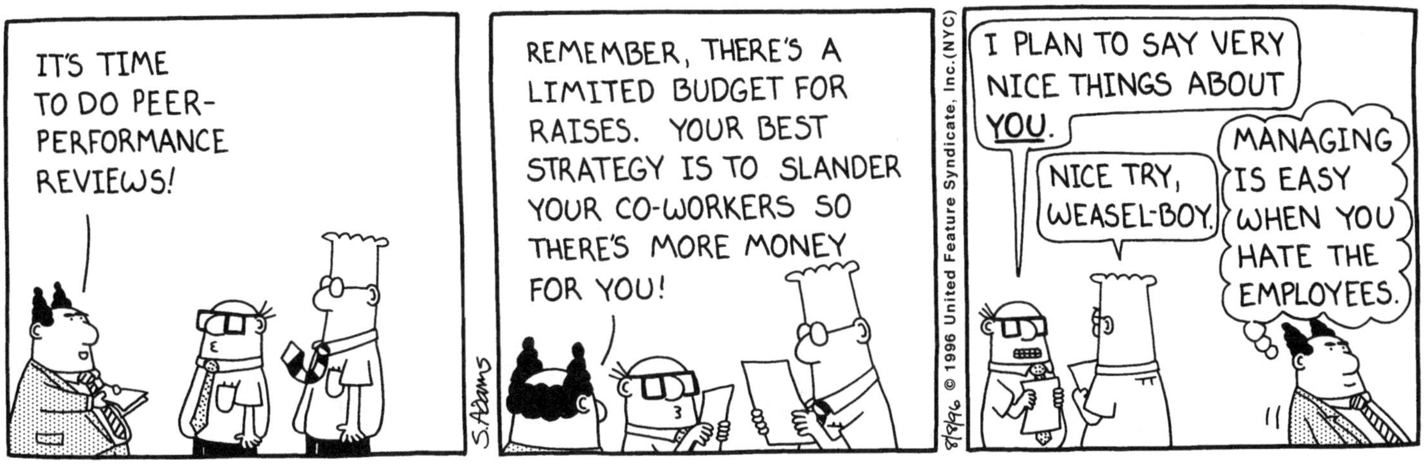
IT'S TIME TO DO PEER-PERFORMANCE REVIEWS!
S.Adams
REMEMBER, THERE'S A LIMITED BUDGET FOR RAISES. YOUR BEST STRATEGY IS TO SLANDER YOUR CO-WORKERS SO THERE'S MORE MONEY FOR YOU!
8/9/96 © 1996 United Feature Syndicate, Inc.(NYC)
I PLAN TO SAY VERY NICE THINGS ABOUT YOU.
NICE TRY, WEASEL-BOY.
MANAGING IS EASY WHEN YOU HATE THE EMPLOYEES.

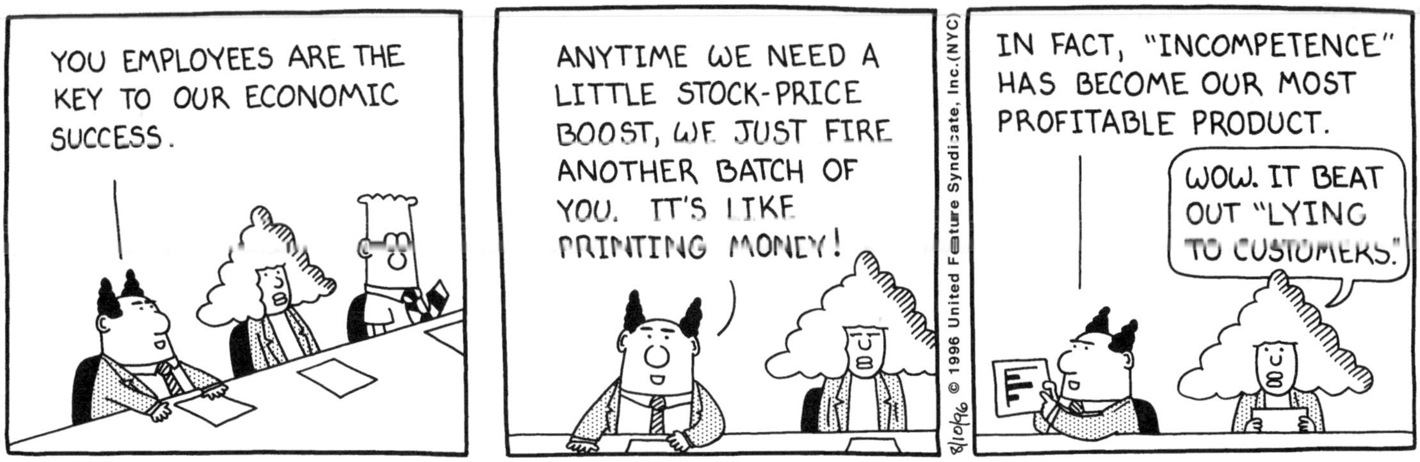
YOU EMPLOYEES ARE THE KEY TO OUR ECONOMIC SUCCESS.
ANYTIME WE NEED A LITTLE STOCK-PRICE BOOST, WE JUST FIRE ANOTHER BATCH OF YOU. IT'S LIKE PRINTING MONEY!
8/10/96 © 1996 United Feature Syndicate, Inc.(NYC)
IN FACT, "INCOMPETENCE" HAS BECOME OUR MOST PROFITABLE PRODUCT.
WOW. IT BEAT OUT "LYING TO CUSTOMERS."

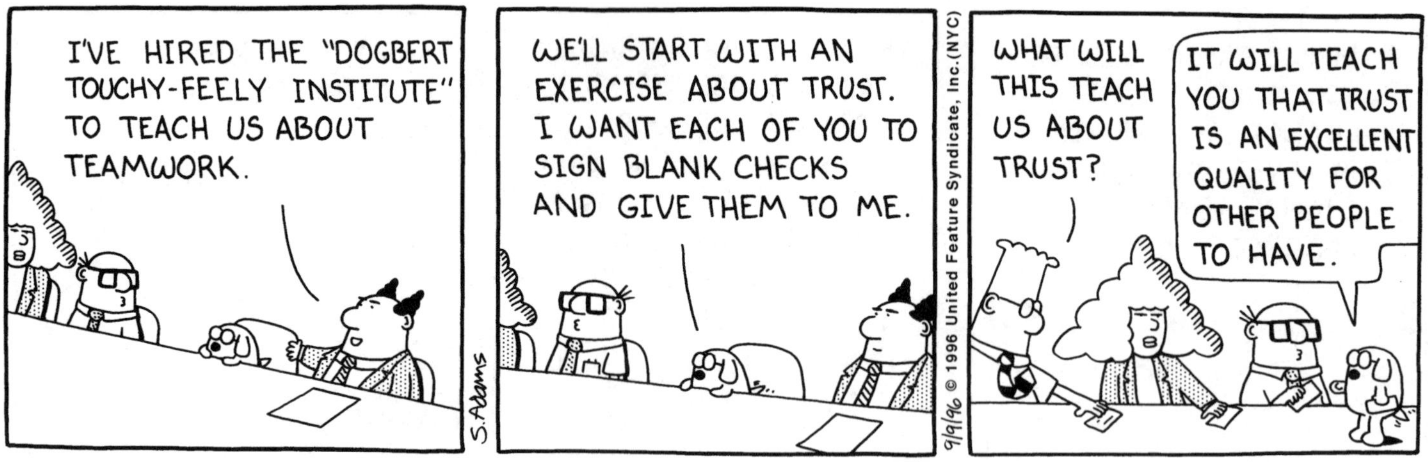
I'VE HIRED THE "DOGBERT TOUCHY-FEELY INSTITUTE" TO TEACH US ABOUT TEAMWORK.
S. Adams
WE'LL START WITH AN EXERCISE ABOUT TRUST. I WANT EACH OF YOU TO SIGN BLANK CHECKS AND GIVE THEM TO ME.
9/9/96 © 1996 United Feature Syndicate, Inc.(NYC)
WHAT WILL THIS TEACH US ABOUT TRUST?
IT WILL TEACH YOU THAT TRUST IS AN EXCELLENT QUALITY FOR OTHER PEOPLE TO HAVE.

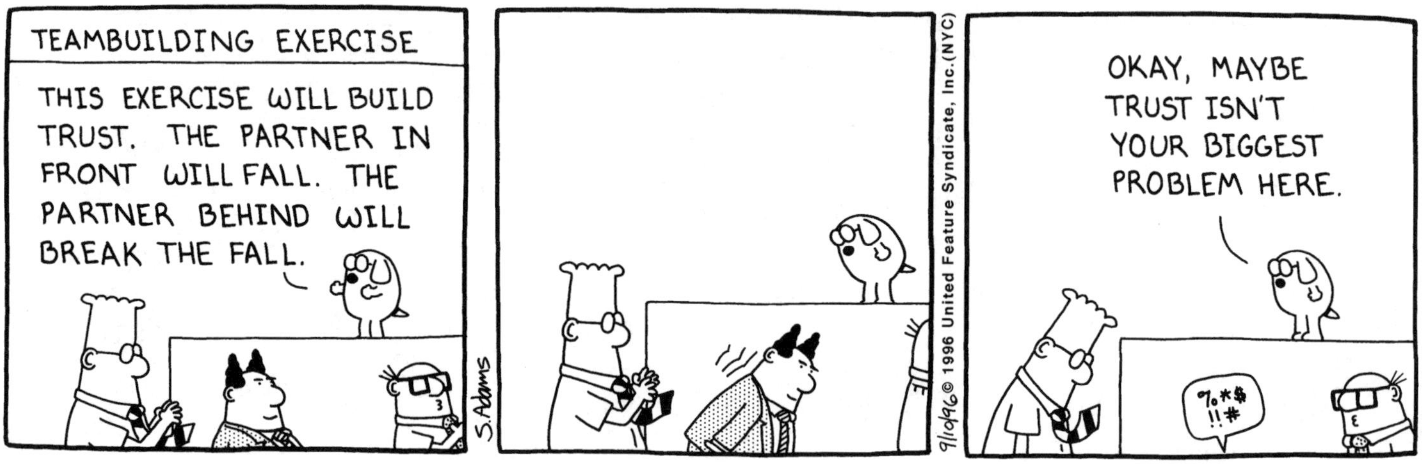
TEAMBUILDING EXERCISE
THIS EXERCISE WILL BUILD TRUST. THE PARTNER IN FRONT WILL FALL. THE PARTNER BEHIND WILL BREAK THE FALL.
S. Adams
9/10/96 © 1996 United Feature Syndicate, Inc.(NYC)
OKAY, MAYBE TRUST ISN'T YOUR BIGGEST PROBLEM HERE.
%*$!!#

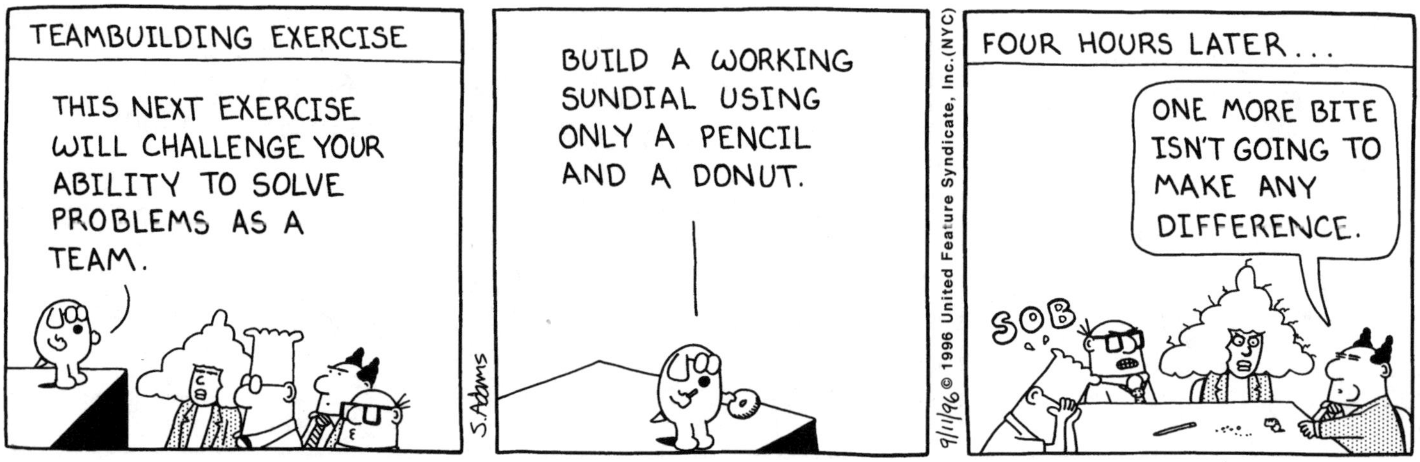
TEAMBUILDING EXERCISE
THIS NEXT EXERCISE WILL CHALLENGE YOUR ABILITY TO SOLVE PROBLEMS AS A TEAM.
S. Adams
BUILD A WORKING SUNDIAL USING ONLY A PENCIL AND A DONUT.
9/11/96 © 1996 United Feature Syndicate, Inc.(NYC)
FOUR HOURS LATER...
ONE MORE BITE ISN'T GOING TO MAKE ANY DIFFERENCE.
SOB

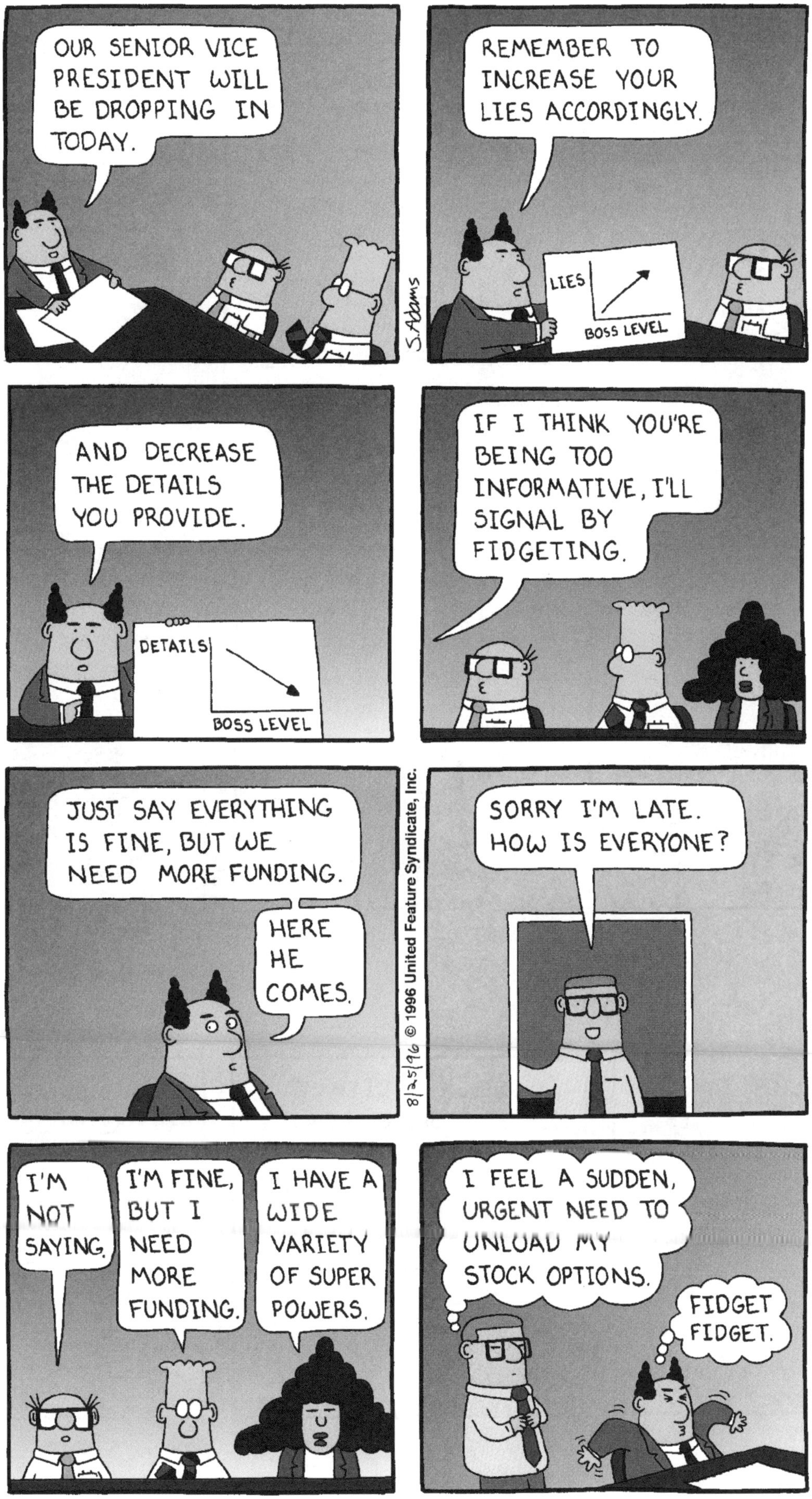
OUR SENIOR VICE PRESIDENT WILL BE DROPPING IN TODAY.
S. Adams
REMEMBER TO INCREASE YOUR LIES ACCORDINGLY.
LIES
BOSS LEVEL
AND DECREASE THE DETAILS YOU PROVIDE.
DETAILS
BOSS LEVEL
IF I THINK YOU'RE BEING TOO INFORMATIVE, I'LL SIGNAL BY FIDGETING.
JUST SAY EVERYTHING IS FINE, BUT WE NEED MORE FUNDING.
HERE HE COMES.
8/25/96 © 1996 United Feature Syndicate, Inc.
SORRY I'M LATE. HOW IS EVERYONE?
I'M NOT SAYING.
I'M FINE, BUT I NEED MORE FUNDING.
I HAVE A WIDE VARIETY OF SUPER POWERS.
I FEEL A SUDDEN, URGENT NEED TO UNLOAD MY STOCK OPTIONS.
FIDGET FIDGET.

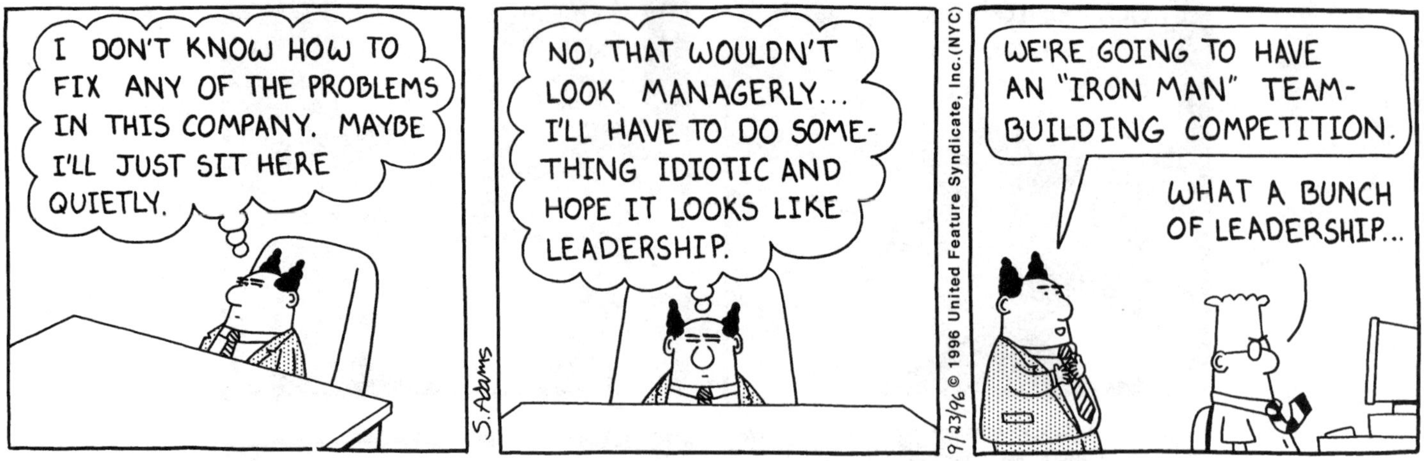
I DON'T KNOW HOW TO FIX ANY OF THE PROBLEMS IN THIS COMPANY. MAYBE I'LL JUST SIT HERE QUIETLY.
NO, THAT WOULDN'T LOOK MANAGERLY... I'LL HAVE TO DO SOMETHING IDIOTIC AND HOPE IT LOOKS LIKE LEADERSHIP.
S. Adams
9/23/96 © 1996 United Feature Syndicate, Inc.(NYC)
WE'RE GOING TO HAVE AN "IRON MAN" TEAM-BUILDING COMPETITION.
WHAT A BUNCH OF LEADERSHIP...

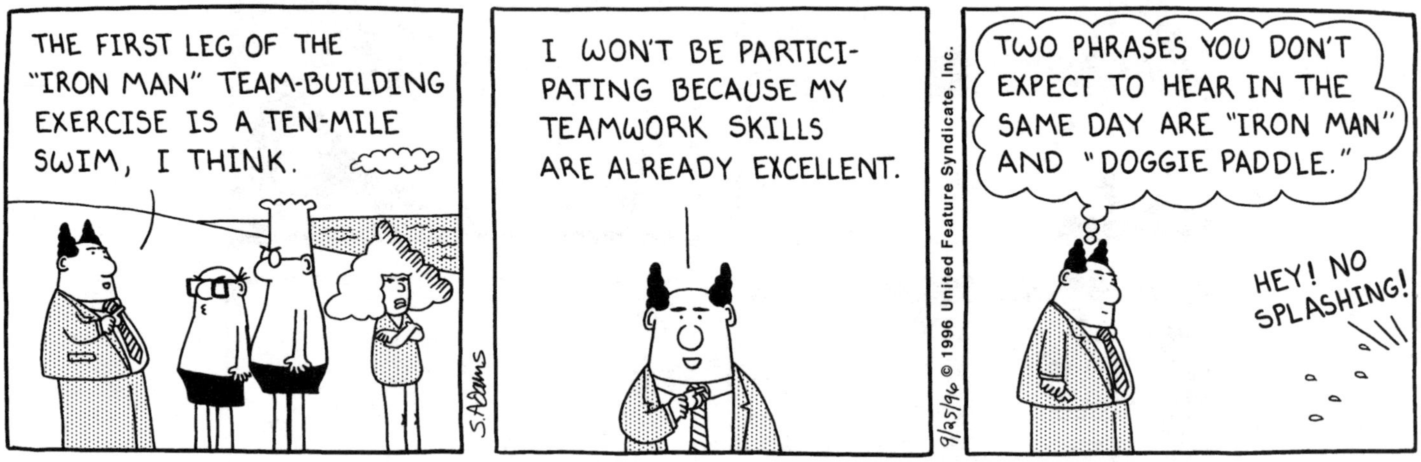
THE FIRST LEG OF THE "IRON MAN" TEAM-BUILDING EXERCISE IS A TEN-MILE SWIM, I THINK.
S. Adams
I WON'T BE PARTICIPATING BECAUSE MY TEAMWORK SKILLS ARE ALREADY EXCELLENT.
9/25/96 © 1996 United Feature Syndicate, Inc.
TWO PHRASES YOU DON'T EXPECT TO HEAR IN THE SAME DAY ARE "IRON MAN" AND "DOGGIE PADDLE."
HEY! NO SPLASHING!

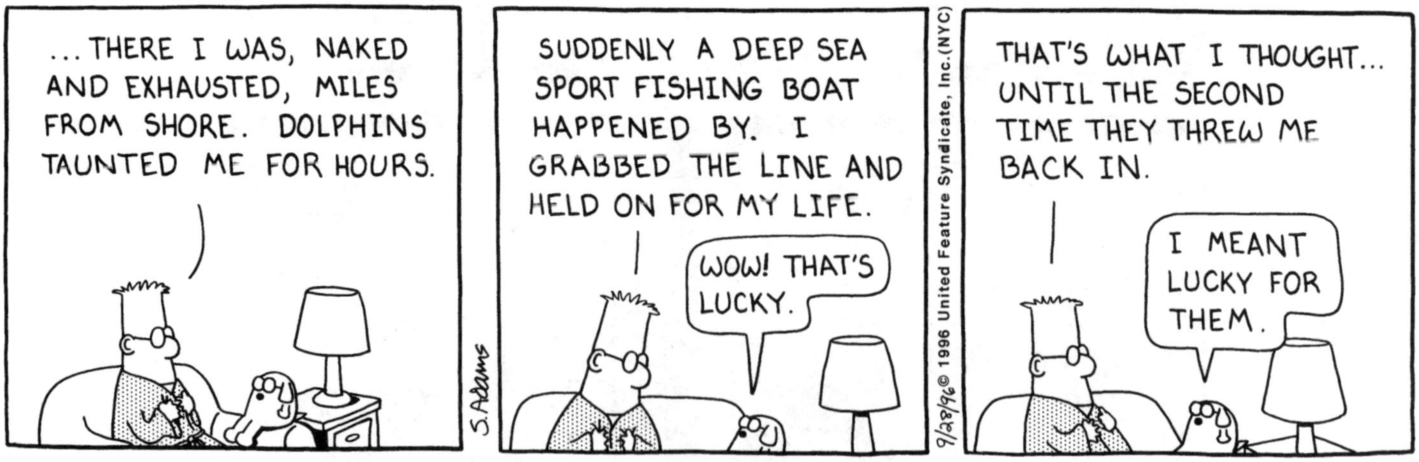
...THERE I WAS, NAKED AND EXHAUSTED, MILES FROM SHORE. DOLPHINS TAUNTED ME FOR HOURS.
S. Adams
SUDDENLY A DEEP SEA SPORT FISHING BOAT HAPPENED BY. I GRABBED THE LINE AND HELD ON FOR MY LIFE.
WOW! THAT'S LUCKY.
9/28/96 © 1996 United Feature Syndicate, Inc.(NYC)
THAT'S WHAT I THOUGHT... UNTIL THE SECOND TIME THEY THREW ME BACK IN.
I MEANT LUCKY FOR THEM.

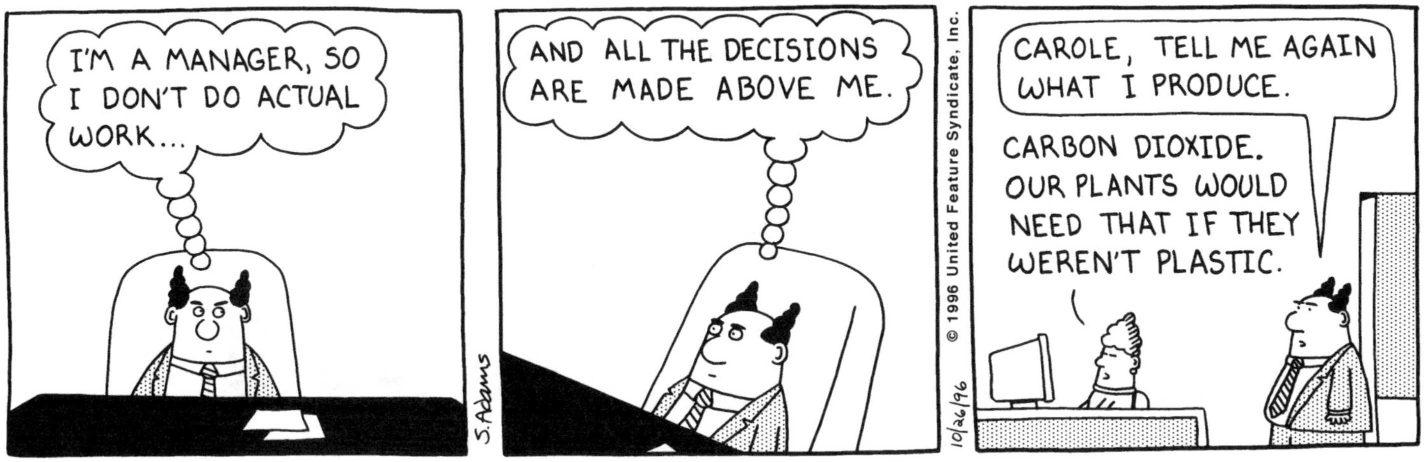
I'M A MANAGER, SO I DON'T DO ACTUAL WORK...
AND ALL THE DECISIONS ARE MADE ABOVE ME.
S. Adams
© 1996 United Feature Syndicate, Inc.
10/26/96
CAROLE, TELL ME AGAIN WHAT I PRODUCE.
CARBON DIOXIDE. OUR PLANTS WOULD NEED THAT IF THEY WEREN'T PLASTIC.

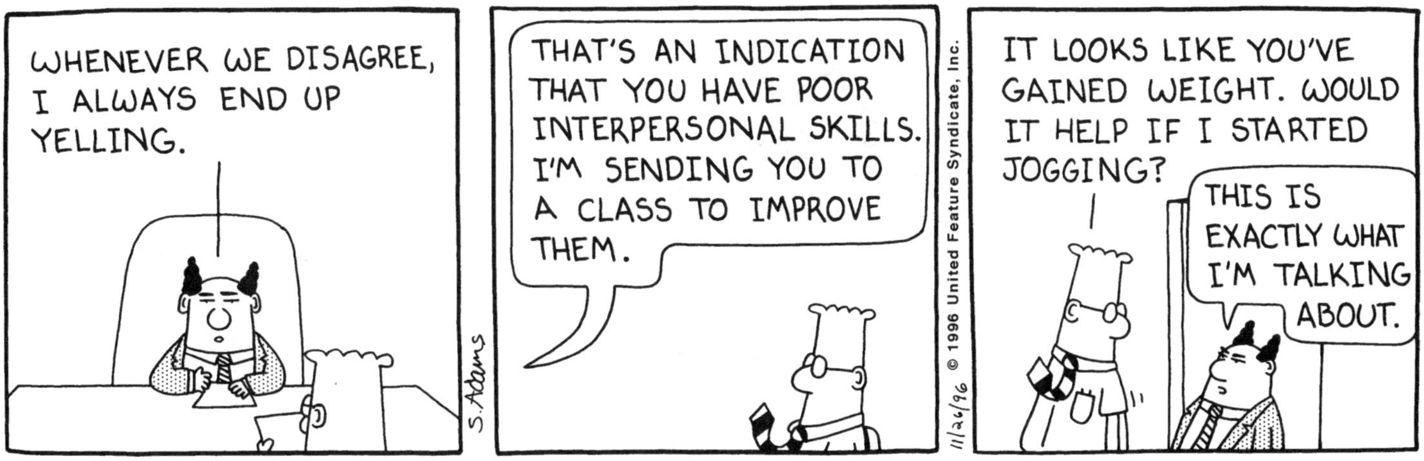
WHENEVER WE DISAGREE, I ALWAYS END UP YELLING.
THAT'S AN INDICATION THAT YOU HAVE POOR INTERPERSONAL SKILLS. I'M SENDING YOU TO A CLASS TO IMPROVE THEM.
S. Adams
© 1996 United Feature Syndicate, Inc.
11/26/96
IT LOOKS LIKE YOU'VE GAINED WEIGHT. WOULD IT HELP IF I STARTED JOGGING?
THIS IS EXACTLY WHAT I'M TALKING ABOUT.

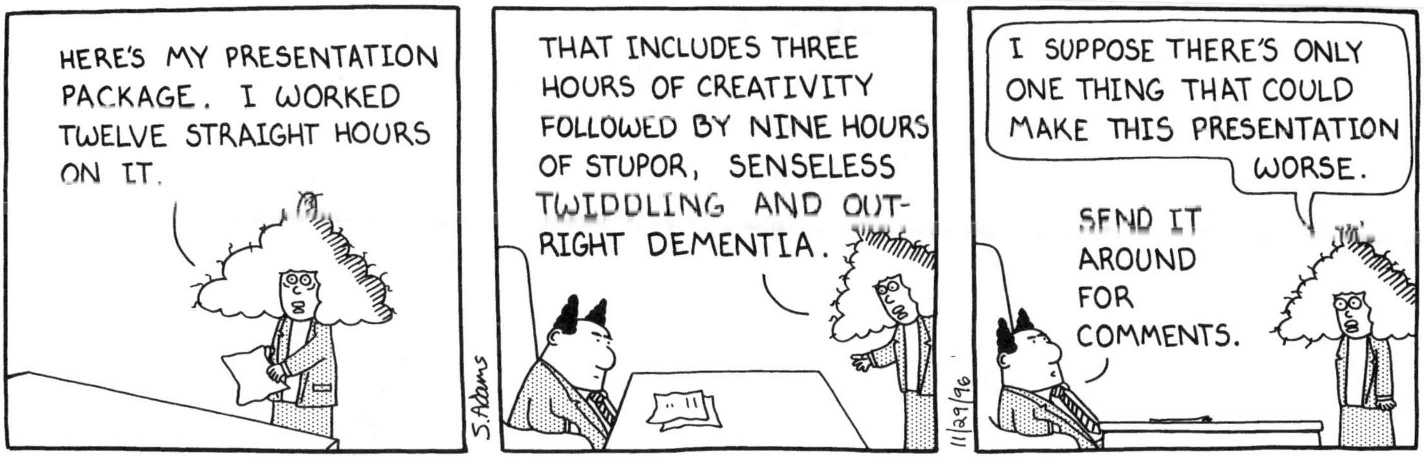
HERE'S MY PRESENTATION PACKAGE. I WORKED TWELVE STRAIGHT HOURS ON IT.
THAT INCLUDES THREE HOURS OF CREATIVITY FOLLOWED BY NINE HOURS OF STUPOR, SENSELESS TWIDDLING AND OUT-RIGHT DEMENTIA.
S. Adams
11/29/96
I SUPPOSE THERE'S ONLY ONE THING THAT COULD MAKE THIS PRESENTATION WORSE.
SEND IT AROUND FOR COMMENTS.

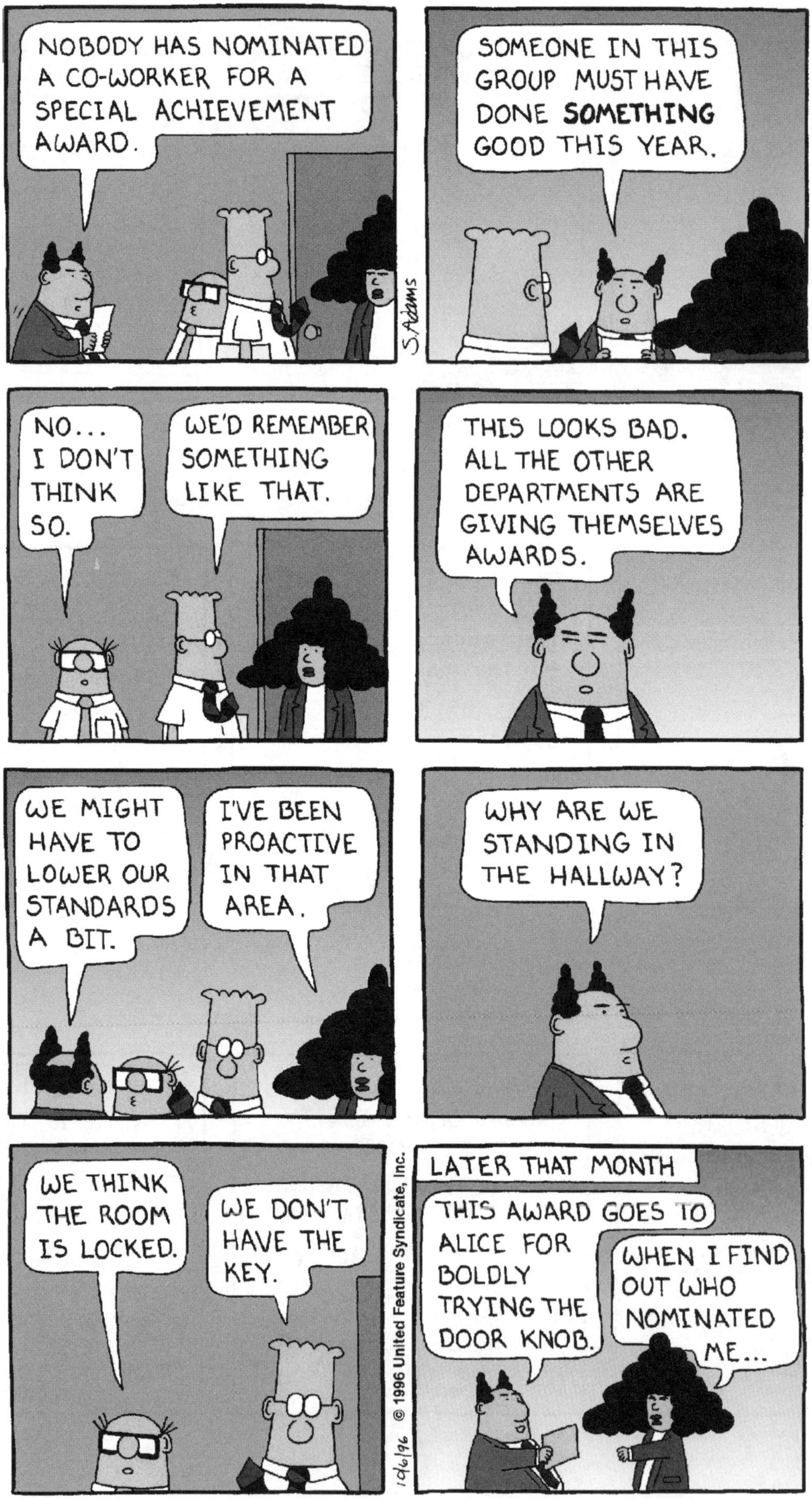
NOBODY HAS NOMINATED A CO-WORKER FOR A SPECIAL ACHIEVEMENT AWARD.
S. Adams
SOMEONE IN THIS GROUP MUST HAVE DONE **SOMETHING** GOOD THIS YEAR.
NO... I DON'T THINK SO.
WE'D REMEMBER SOMETHING LIKE THAT.
THIS LOOKS BAD. ALL THE OTHER DEPARTMENTS ARE GIVING THEMSELVES AWARDS.
WE MIGHT HAVE TO LOWER OUR STANDARDS A BIT.
I'VE BEEN PROACTIVE IN THAT AREA.
WHY ARE WE STANDING IN THE HALLWAY?
WE THINK THE ROOM IS LOCKED.
WE DON'T HAVE THE KEY.
10/6/96 © 1996 United Feature Syndicate, Inc.
LATER THAT MONTH
THIS AWARD GOES TO ALICE FOR BOLDLY TRYING THE DOOR KNOB.
WHEN I FIND OUT WHO NOMINATED ME...

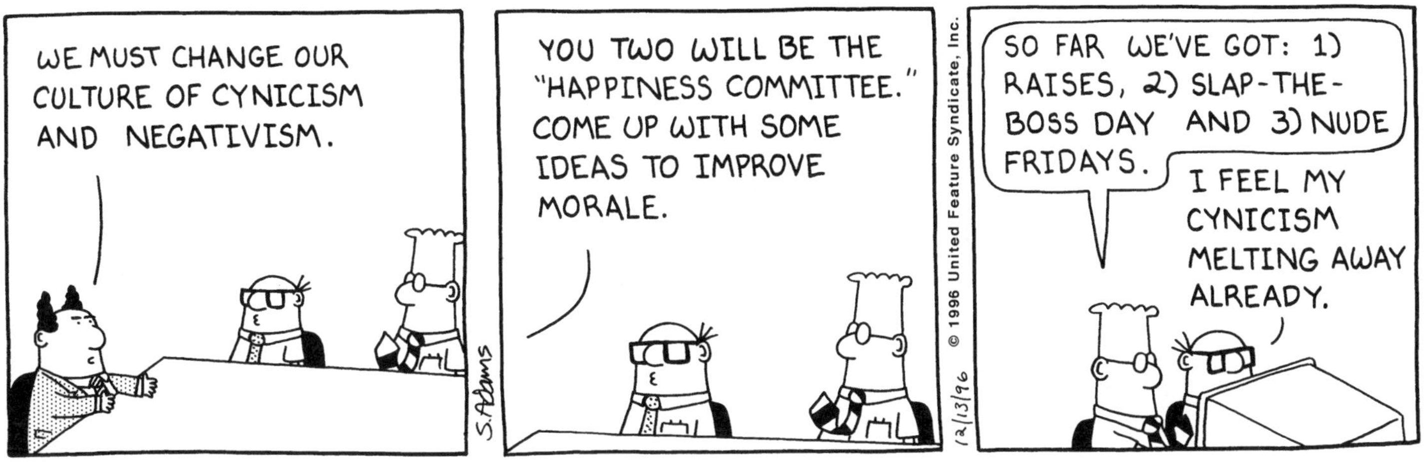
WE MUST CHANGE OUR CULTURE OF CYNICISM AND NEGATIVISM.
S. Adams
YOU TWO WILL BE THE "HAPPINESS COMMITTEE." COME UP WITH SOME IDEAS TO IMPROVE MORALE.
12/13/96
© 1996 United Feature Syndicate, Inc.
SO FAR WE'VE GOT: 1) RAISES, 2) SLAP-THE-BOSS DAY AND 3) NUDE FRIDAYS.
I FEEL MY CYNICISM MELTING AWAY ALREADY.

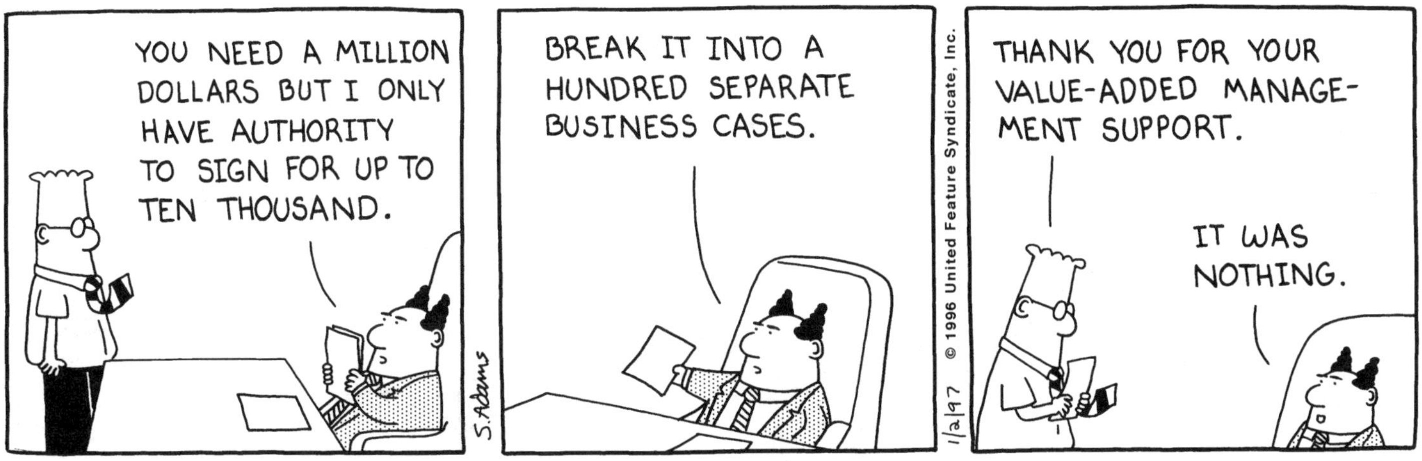
YOU NEED A MILLION DOLLARS BUT I ONLY HAVE AUTHORITY TO SIGN FOR UP TO TEN THOUSAND.
S. Adams
BREAK IT INTO A HUNDRED SEPARATE BUSINESS CASES.
1/2/97
© 1996 United Feature Syndicate, Inc.
THANK YOU FOR YOUR VALUE-ADDED MANAGEMENT SUPPORT.
IT WAS NOTHING.

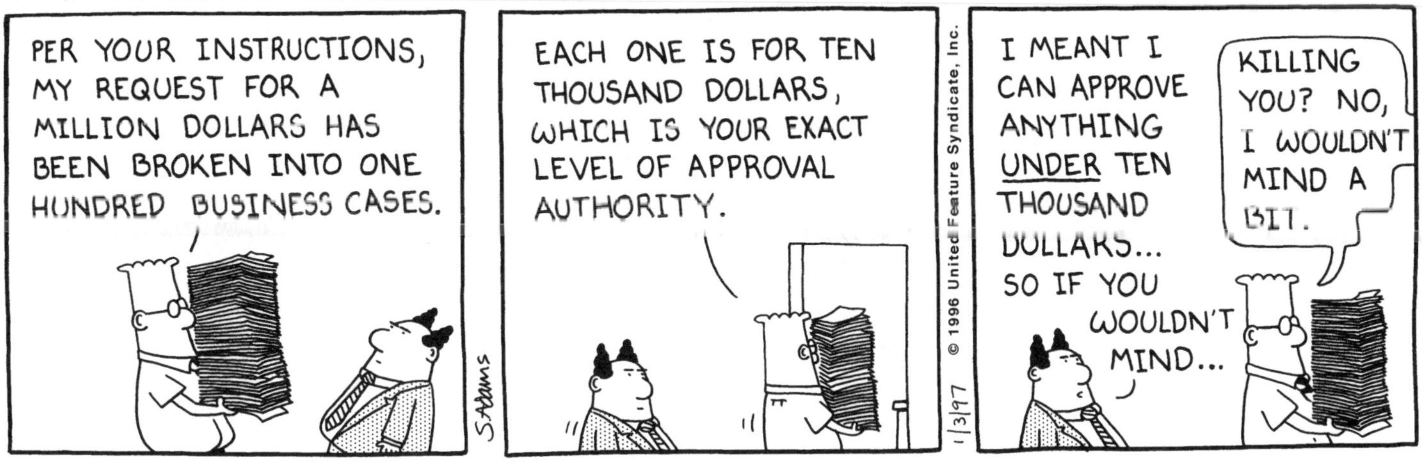
PER YOUR INSTRUCTIONS, MY REQUEST FOR A MILLION DOLLARS HAS BEEN BROKEN INTO ONE HUNDRED BUSINESS CASES.
S. Adams
EACH ONE IS FOR TEN THOUSAND DOLLARS, WHICH IS YOUR EXACT LEVEL OF APPROVAL AUTHORITY.
1/3/97
© 1996 United Feature Syndicate, Inc.
I MEANT I CAN APPROVE ANYTHING UNDER TEN THOUSAND DOLLARS... SO IF YOU WOULDN'T MIND...
KILLING YOU? NO, I WOULDN'T MIND A BIT.

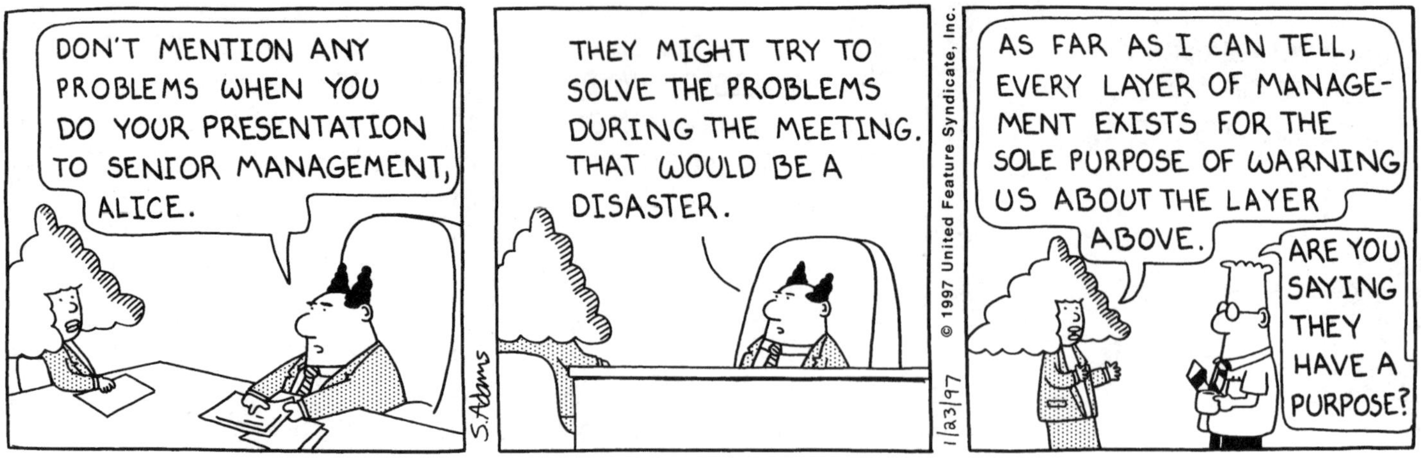
DON'T MENTION ANY PROBLEMS WHEN YOU DO YOUR PRESENTATION TO SENIOR MANAGEMENT, ALICE.
S. Adams
THEY MIGHT TRY TO SOLVE THE PROBLEMS DURING THE MEETING. THAT WOULD BE A DISASTER.
1/23/97
© 1997 United Feature Syndicate, Inc.
AS FAR AS I CAN TELL, EVERY LAYER OF MANAGEMENT EXISTS FOR THE SOLE PURPOSE OF WARNING US ABOUT THE LAYER ABOVE.
ARE YOU SAYING THEY HAVE A PURPOSE?

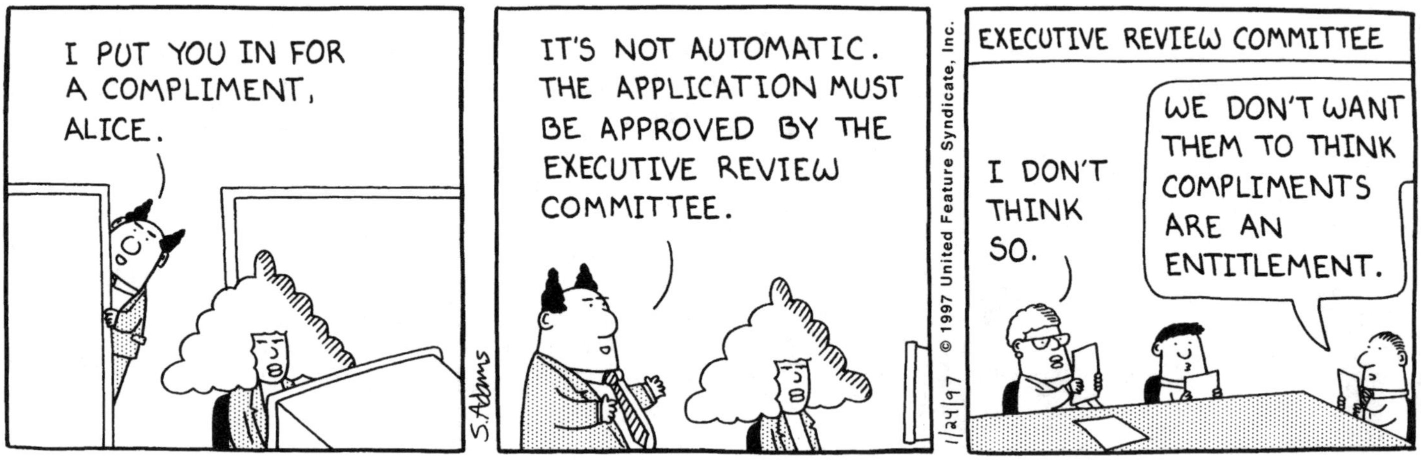
I PUT YOU IN FOR A COMPLIMENT, ALICE.
S. Adams
IT'S NOT AUTOMATIC. THE APPLICATION MUST BE APPROVED BY THE EXECUTIVE REVIEW COMMITTEE.
1/24/97
© 1997 United Feature Syndicate, Inc.
EXECUTIVE REVIEW COMMITTEE
I DON'T THINK SO.
WE DON'T WANT THEM TO THINK COMPLIMENTS ARE AN ENTITLEMENT.

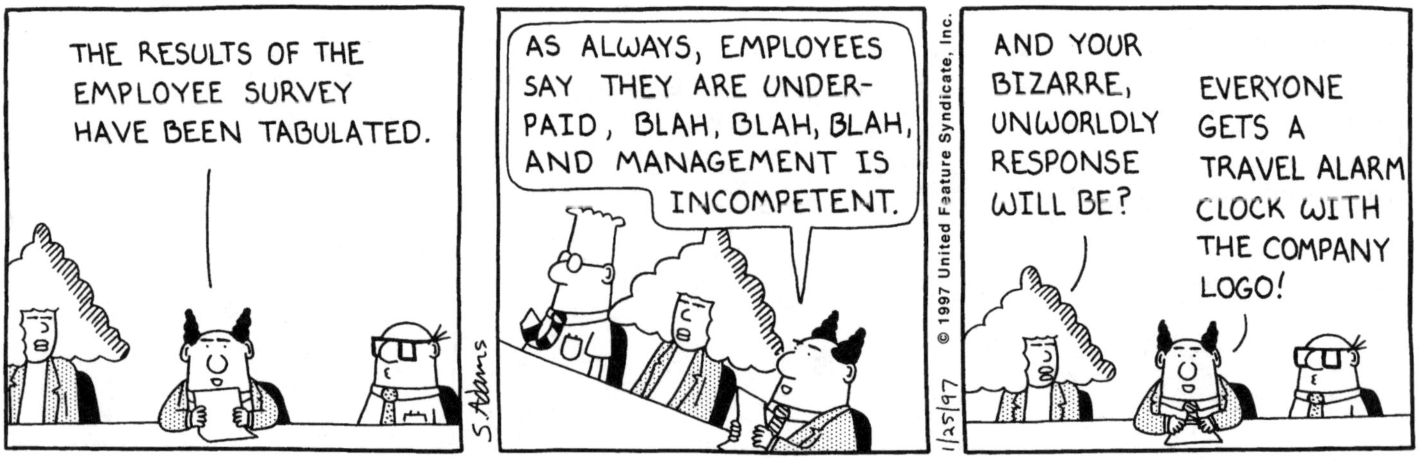
THE RESULTS OF THE EMPLOYEE SURVEY HAVE BEEN TABULATED.
S. Adams
AS ALWAYS, EMPLOYEES SAY THEY ARE UNDERPAID, BLAH, BLAH, BLAH, AND MANAGEMENT IS INCOMPETENT.
1/25/97
© 1997 United Feature Syndicate, Inc.
AND YOUR BIZARRE, UNWORLDLY RESPONSE WILL BE?
EVERYONE GETS A TRAVEL ALARM CLOCK WITH THE COMPANY LOGO!

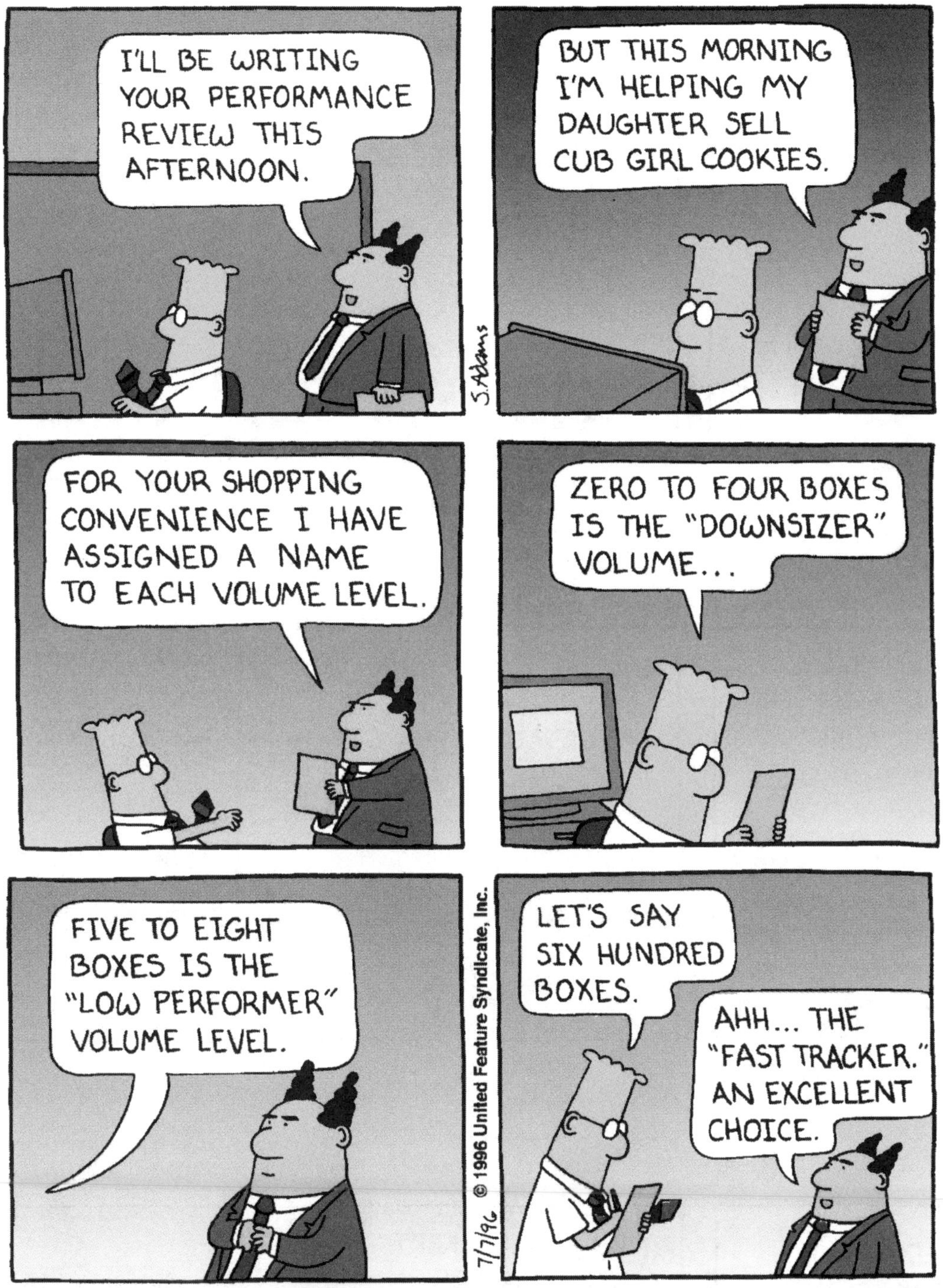
I'LL BE WRITING YOUR PERFORMANCE REVIEW THIS AFTERNOON.
BUT THIS MORNING I'M HELPING MY DAUGHTER SELL CUB GIRL COOKIES.
FOR YOUR SHOPPING CONVENIENCE I HAVE ASSIGNED A NAME TO EACH VOLUME LEVEL.
ZERO TO FOUR BOXES IS THE "DOWNSIZER" VOLUME...
FIVE TO EIGHT BOXES IS THE "LOW PERFORMER" VOLUME LEVEL.
LET'S SAY SIX HUNDRED BOXES.
AHH... THE "FAST TRACKER." AN EXCELLENT CHOICE.
S. Adams
7/7/96
© 1996 United Feature Syndicate, Inc.
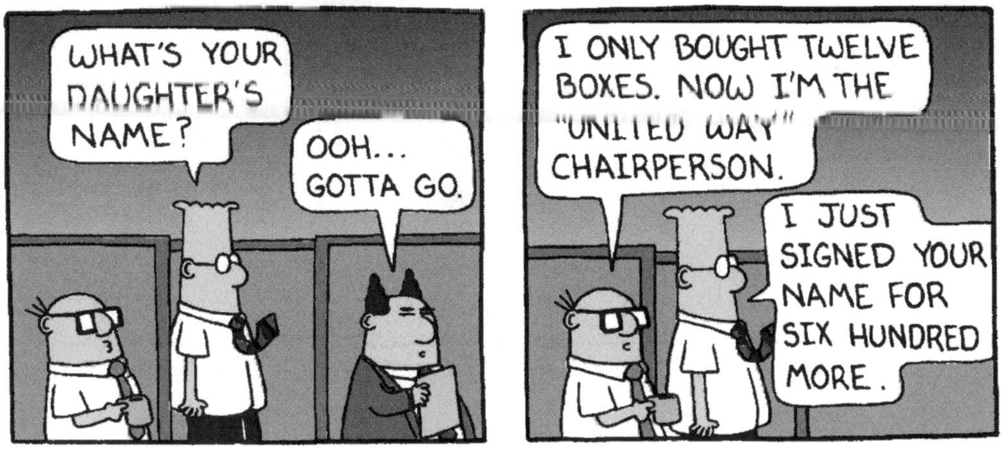
WHAT'S YOUR DAUGHTER'S NAME?
OOH... GOTTA GO.
I ONLY BOUGHT TWELVE BOXES. NOW I'M THE "UNITED WAY" CHAIRPERSON.
I JUST SIGNED YOUR NAME FOR SIX HUNDRED MORE.

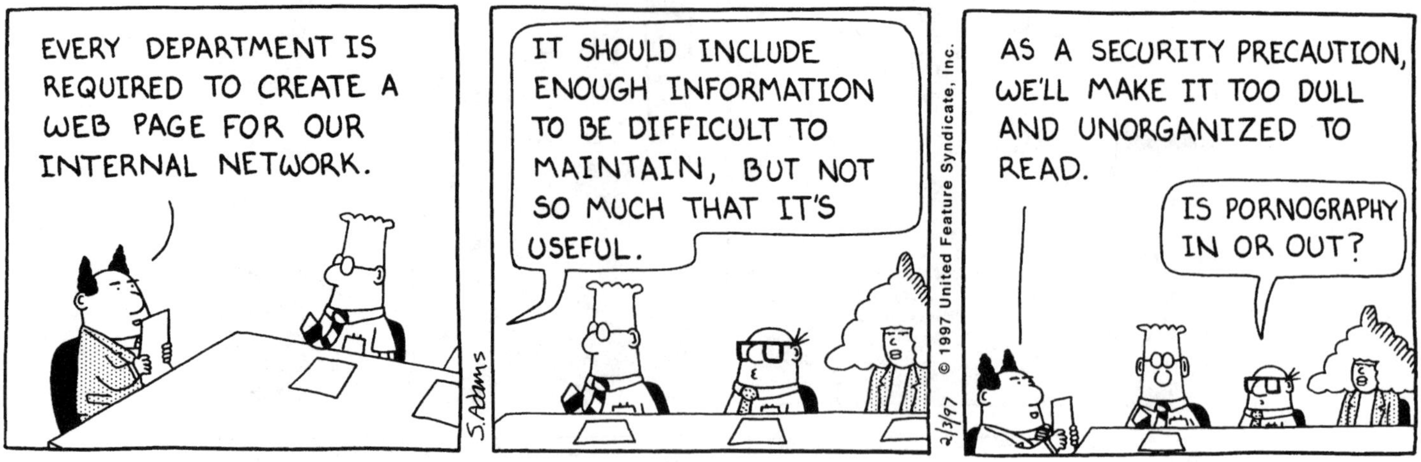
EVERY DEPARTMENT IS REQUIRED TO CREATE A WEB PAGE FOR OUR INTERNAL NETWORK.
S. Adams
IT SHOULD INCLUDE ENOUGH INFORMATION TO BE DIFFICULT TO MAINTAIN, BUT NOT SO MUCH THAT IT'S USEFUL.
2/3/97
© 1997 United Feature Syndicate, Inc.
AS A SECURITY PRECAUTION, WE'LL MAKE IT TOO DULL AND UNORGANIZED TO READ.
IS PORNOGRAPHY IN OR OUT?

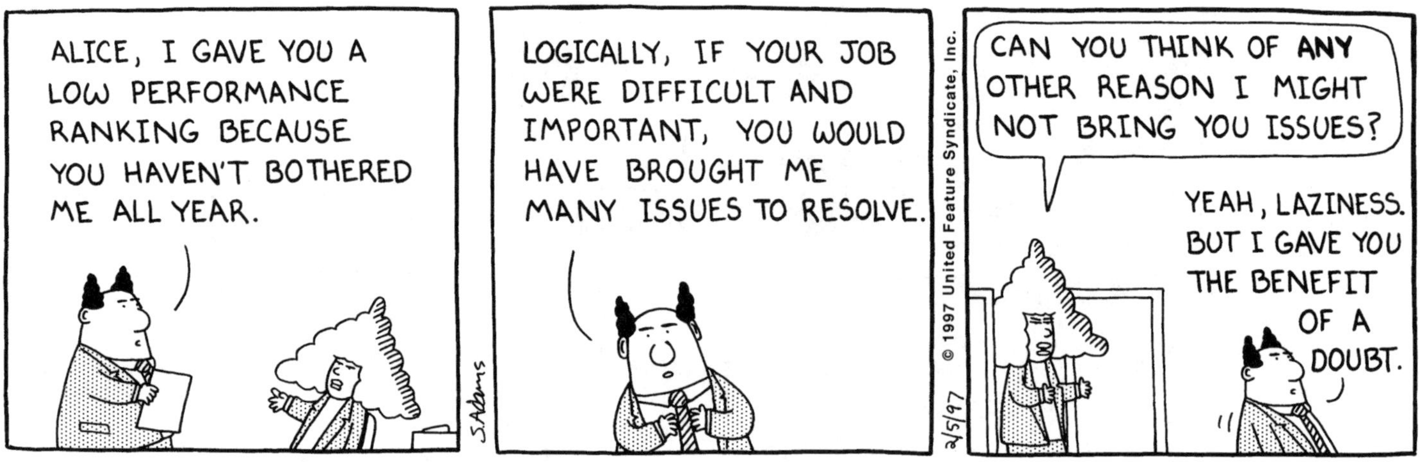
ALICE, I GAVE YOU A LOW PERFORMANCE RANKING BECAUSE YOU HAVEN'T BOTHERED ME ALL YEAR.
S. Adams
LOGICALLY, IF YOUR JOB WERE DIFFICULT AND IMPORTANT, YOU WOULD HAVE BROUGHT ME MANY ISSUES TO RESOLVE.
2/5/97
© 1997 United Feature Syndicate, Inc.
CAN YOU THINK OF **ANY** OTHER REASON I MIGHT NOT BRING YOU ISSUES?
YEAH, LAZINESS. BUT I GAVE YOU THE BENEFIT OF A DOUBT.

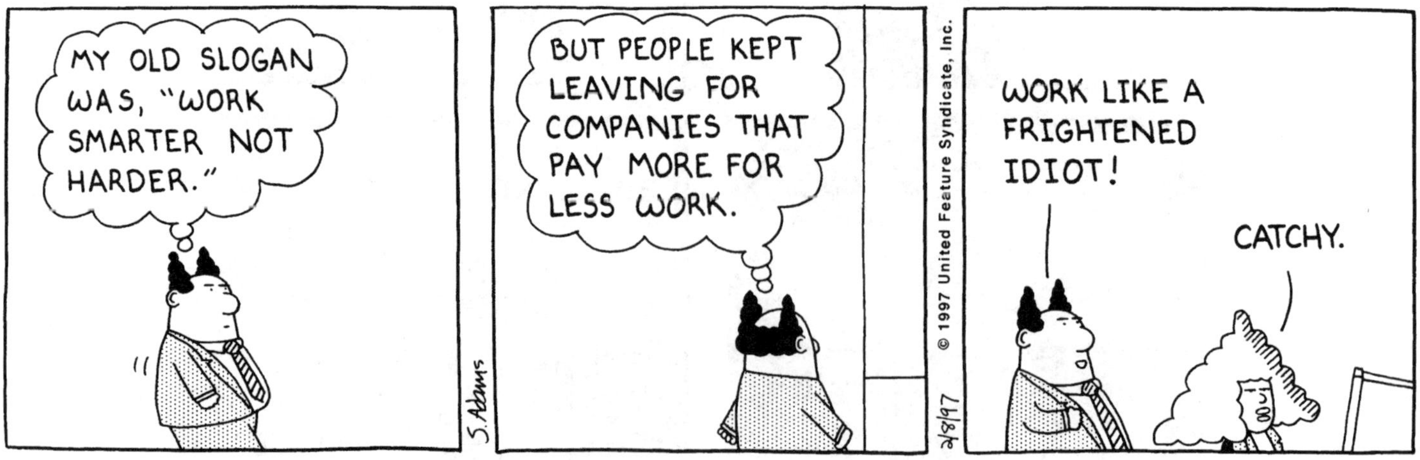
MY OLD SLOGAN WAS, "WORK SMARTER NOT HARDER."
S. Adams
BUT PEOPLE KEPT LEAVING FOR COMPANIES THAT PAY MORE FOR LESS WORK.
2/8/97
© 1997 United Feature Syndicate, Inc.
WORK LIKE A FRIGHTENED IDIOT!
CATCHY.

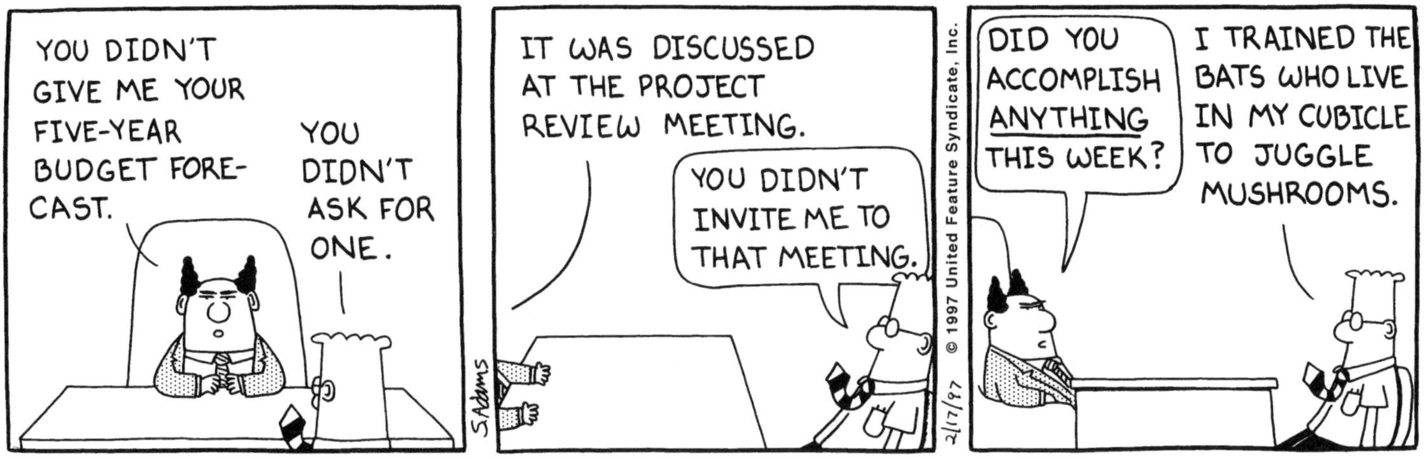
YOU DIDN'T GIVE ME YOUR FIVE-YEAR BUDGET FORECAST.
YOU DIDN'T ASK FOR ONE.
IT WAS DISCUSSED AT THE PROJECT REVIEW MEETING.
YOU DIDN'T INVITE ME TO THAT MEETING.
DID YOU ACCOMPLISH ANYTHING THIS WEEK?
I TRAINED THE BATS WHO LIVE IN MY CUBICLE TO JUGGLE MUSHROOMS.
S.Adams
2/17/97 © 1997 United Feature Syndicate, Inc.

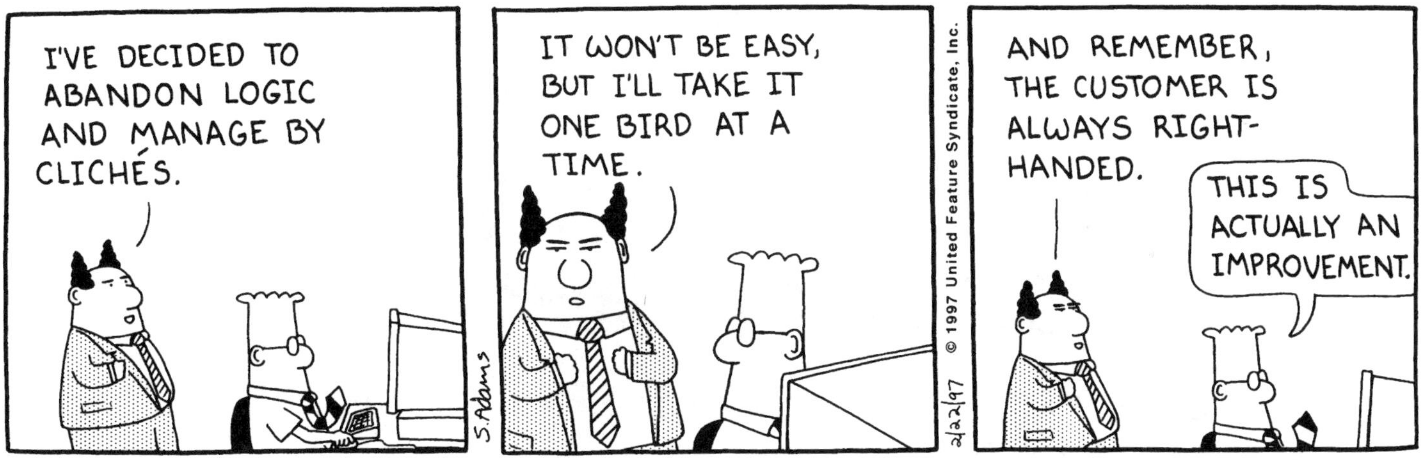
I'VE DECIDED TO ABANDON LOGIC AND MANAGE BY CLICHÉS.
IT WON'T BE EASY, BUT I'LL TAKE IT ONE BIRD AT A TIME.
AND REMEMBER, THE CUSTOMER IS ALWAYS RIGHT-HANDED.
THIS IS ACTUALLY AN IMPROVEMENT.
S.Adams
2/22/97 © 1997 United Feature Syndicate, Inc.

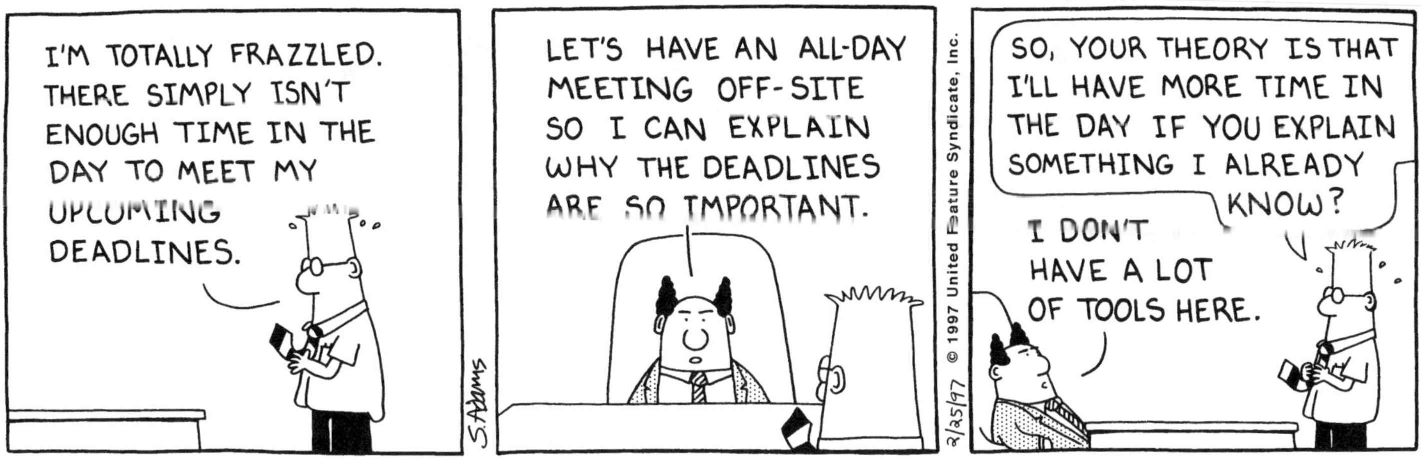
I'M TOTALLY FRAZZLED. THERE SIMPLY ISN'T ENOUGH TIME IN THE DAY TO MEET MY UPCOMING DEADLINES.
LET'S HAVE AN ALL-DAY MEETING OFF-SITE SO I CAN EXPLAIN WHY THE DEADLINES ARE SO IMPORTANT.
SO, YOUR THEORY IS THAT I'LL HAVE MORE TIME IN THE DAY IF YOU EXPLAIN SOMETHING I ALREADY KNOW?
I DON'T HAVE A LOT OF TOOLS HERE.
S.Adams
2/25/97 © 1997 United Feature Syndicate, Inc.

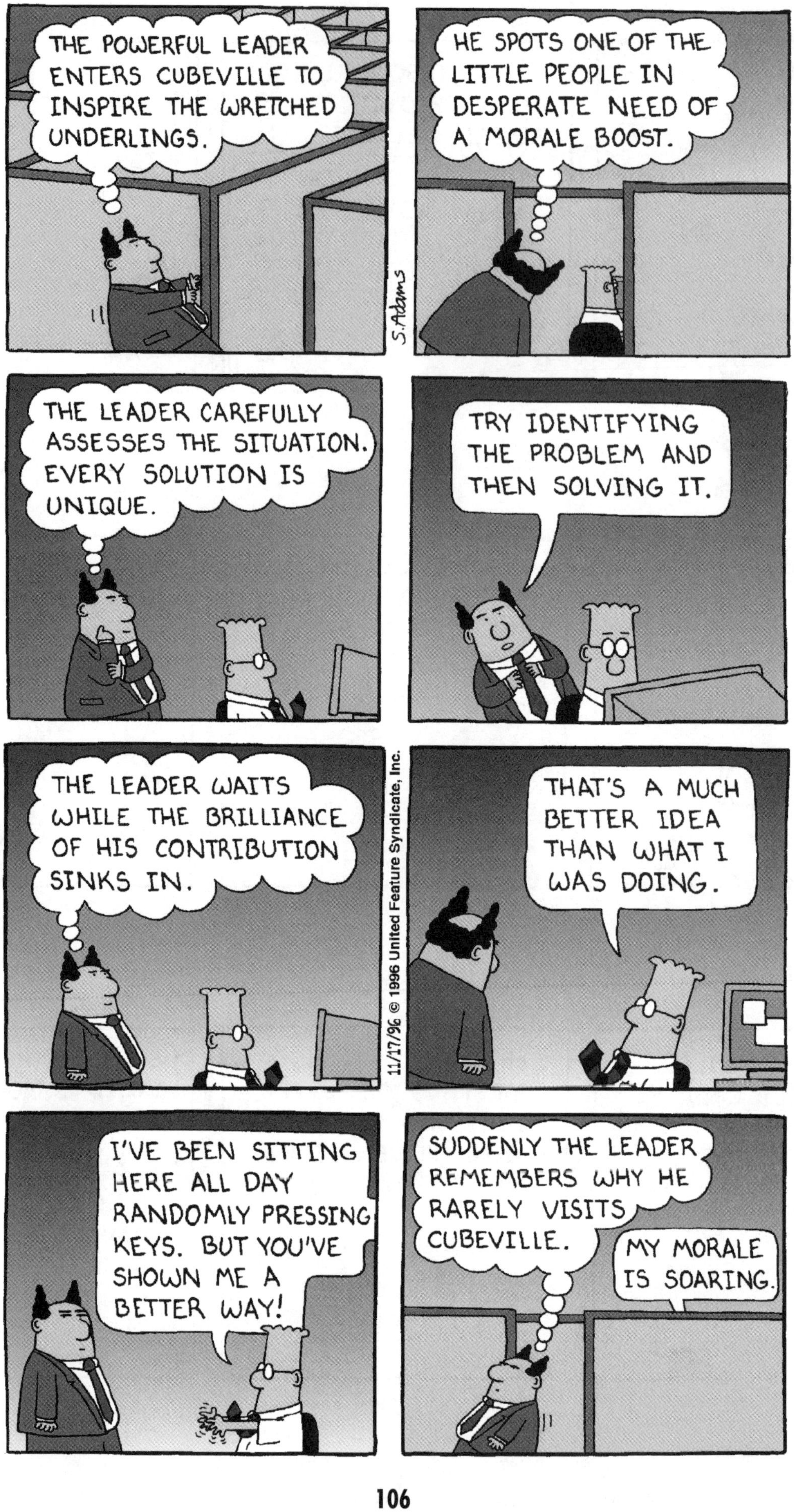
THE POWERFUL LEADER ENTERS CUBEVILLE TO INSPIRE THE WRETCHED UNDERLINGS.
S. Adams
HE SPOTS ONE OF THE LITTLE PEOPLE IN DESPERATE NEED OF A MORALE BOOST.
THE LEADER CAREFULLY ASSESSES THE SITUATION. EVERY SOLUTION IS UNIQUE.
TRY IDENTIFYING THE PROBLEM AND THEN SOLVING IT.
THE LEADER WAITS WHILE THE BRILLIANCE OF HIS CONTRIBUTION SINKS IN.
11/17/96 © 1996 United Feature Syndicate, Inc.
THAT'S A MUCH BETTER IDEA THAN WHAT I WAS DOING.
I'VE BEEN SITTING HERE ALL DAY RANDOMLY PRESSING KEYS. BUT YOU'VE SHOWN ME A BETTER WAY!
SUDDENLY THE LEADER REMEMBERS WHY HE RARELY VISITS CUBEVILLE.
MY MORALE IS SOARING.

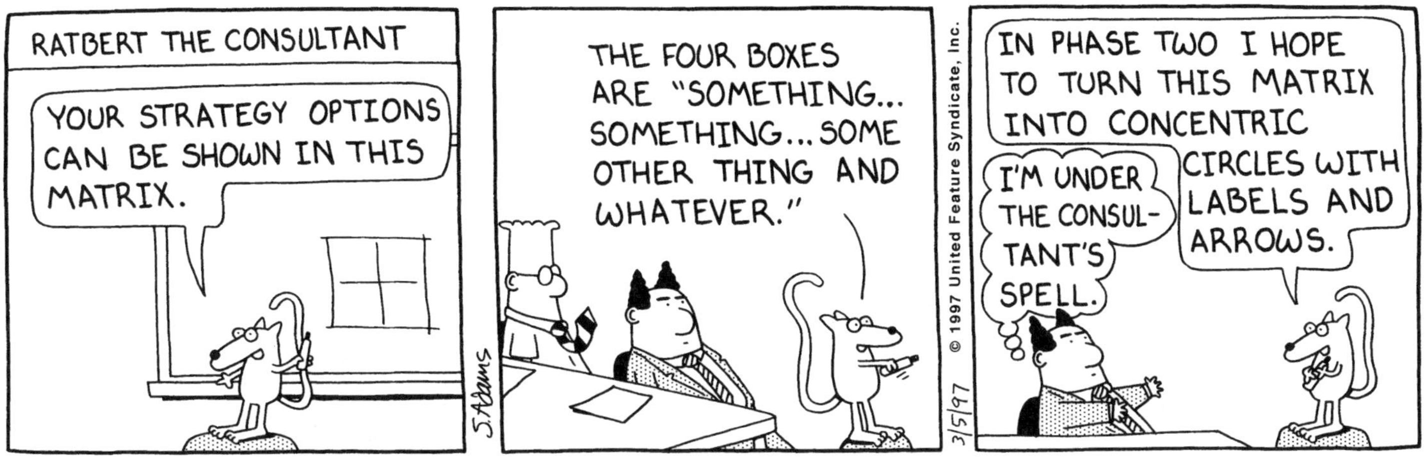
RATBERT THE CONSULTANT
YOUR STRATEGY OPTIONS CAN BE SHOWN IN THIS MATRIX.
S. Adams
THE FOUR BOXES ARE "SOMETHING... SOMETHING... SOME OTHER THING AND WHATEVER."
© 1997 United Feature Syndicate, Inc.
3/5/97
IN PHASE TWO I HOPE TO TURN THIS MATRIX INTO CONCENTRIC CIRCLES WITH LABELS AND ARROWS.
I'M UNDER THE CONSULTANT'S SPELL.

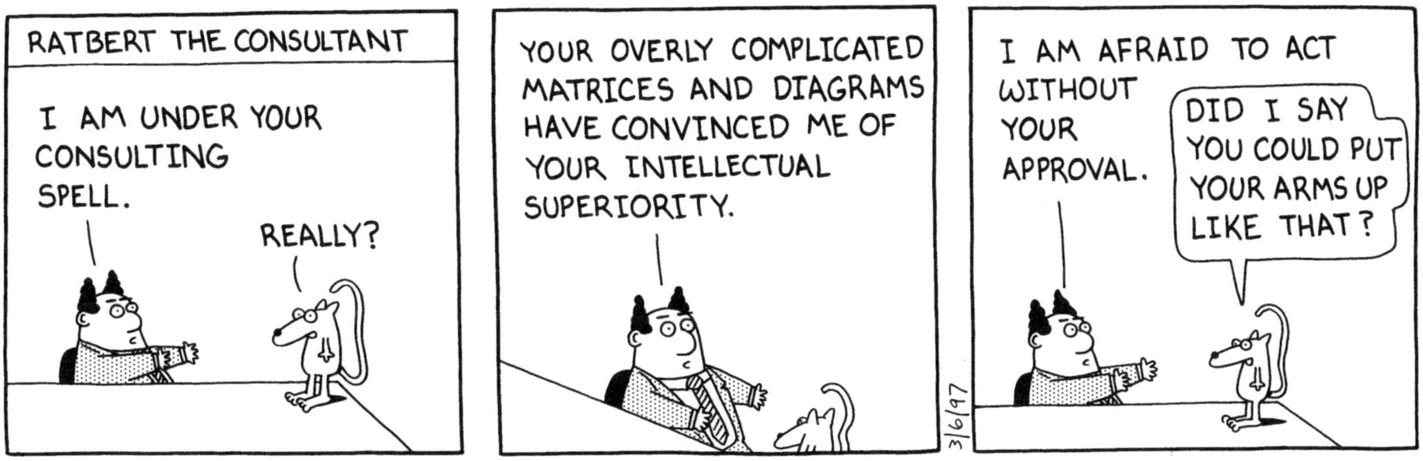
RATBERT THE CONSULTANT
I AM UNDER YOUR CONSULTING SPELL.
REALLY?
YOUR OVERLY COMPLICATED MATRICES AND DIAGRAMS HAVE CONVINCED ME OF YOUR INTELLECTUAL SUPERIORITY.
3/6/97
I AM AFRAID TO ACT WITHOUT YOUR APPROVAL.
DID I SAY YOU COULD PUT YOUR ARMS UP LIKE THAT?

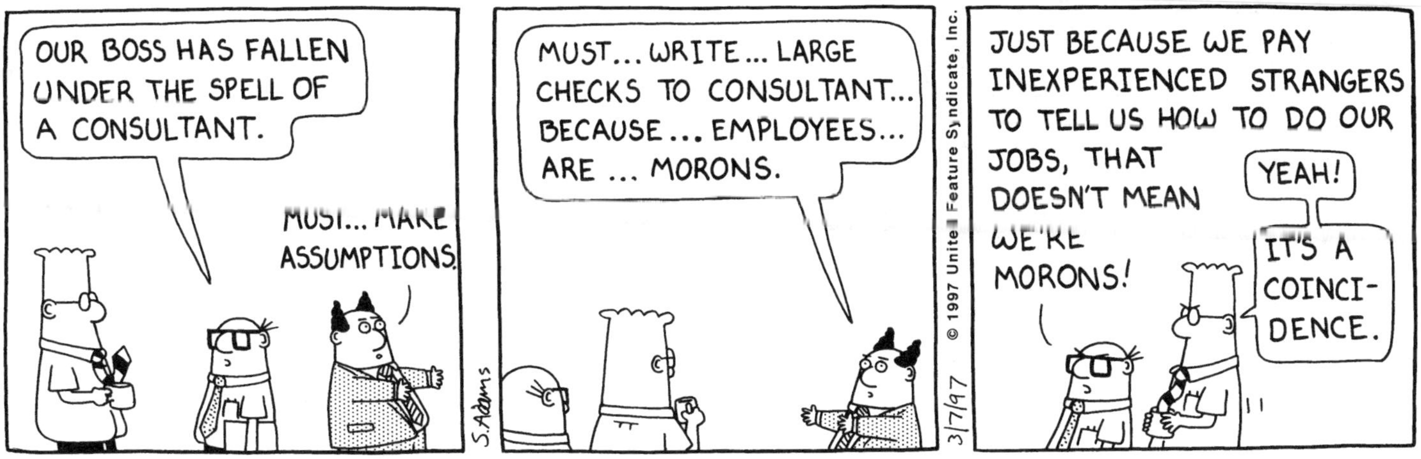
OUR BOSS HAS FALLEN UNDER THE SPELL OF A CONSULTANT.
MUST... MAKE ASSUMPTIONS.
S. Adams
MUST... WRITE... LARGE CHECKS TO CONSULTANT... BECAUSE... EMPLOYEES... ARE ... MORONS.
© 1997 United Feature Syndicate, Inc.
3/7/97
JUST BECAUSE WE PAY INEXPERIENCED STRANGERS TO TELL US HOW TO DO OUR JOBS, THAT DOESN'T MEAN WE'RE MORONS!
YEAH!
IT'S A COINCIDENCE.

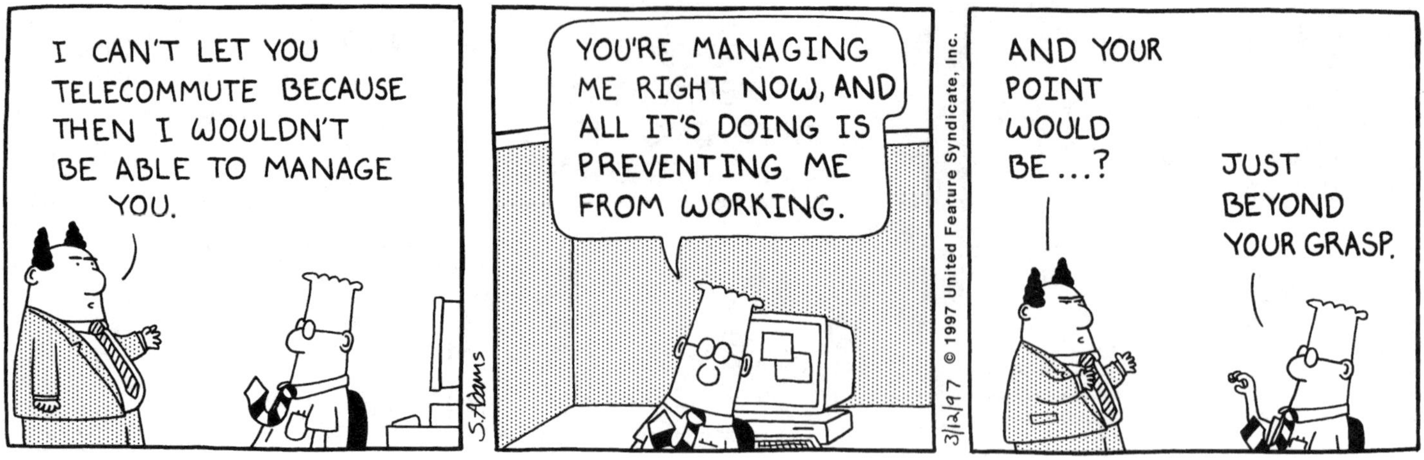
I CAN'T LET YOU TELECOMMUTE BECAUSE THEN I WOULDN'T BE ABLE TO MANAGE YOU.
S. Adams
YOU'RE MANAGING ME RIGHT NOW, AND ALL IT'S DOING IS PREVENTING ME FROM WORKING.
3/12/97 © 1997 United Feature Syndicate, Inc.
AND YOUR POINT WOULD BE...?
JUST BEYOND YOUR GRASP.

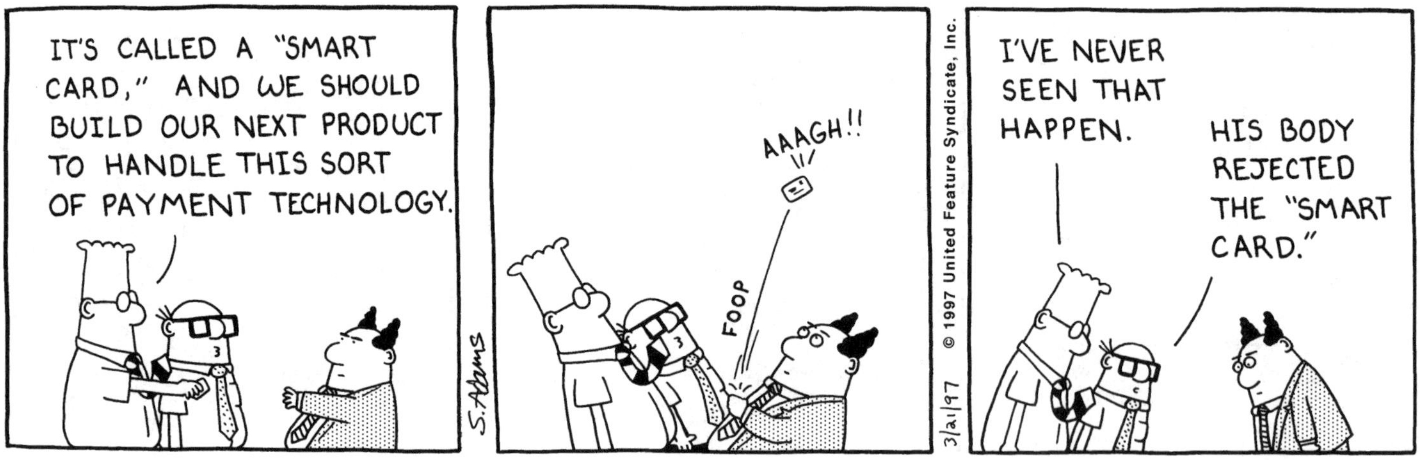
IT'S CALLED A "SMART CARD," AND WE SHOULD BUILD OUR NEXT PRODUCT TO HANDLE THIS SORT OF PAYMENT TECHNOLOGY.
S. Adams
AAAGH!!
FOOP
3/21/97 © 1997 United Feature Syndicate, Inc.
I'VE NEVER SEEN THAT HAPPEN.
HIS BODY REJECTED THE "SMART CARD."

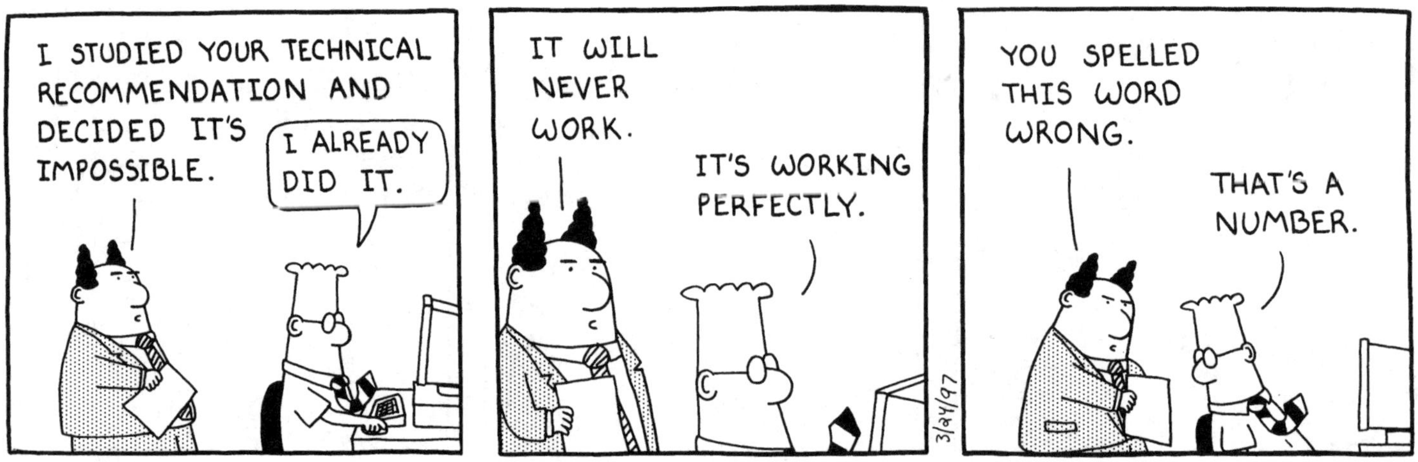
I STUDIED YOUR TECHNICAL RECOMMENDATION AND DECIDED IT'S IMPOSSIBLE.
I ALREADY DID IT.
IT WILL NEVER WORK.
IT'S WORKING PERFECTLY.
3/24/97
YOU SPELLED THIS WORD WRONG.
THAT'S A NUMBER.

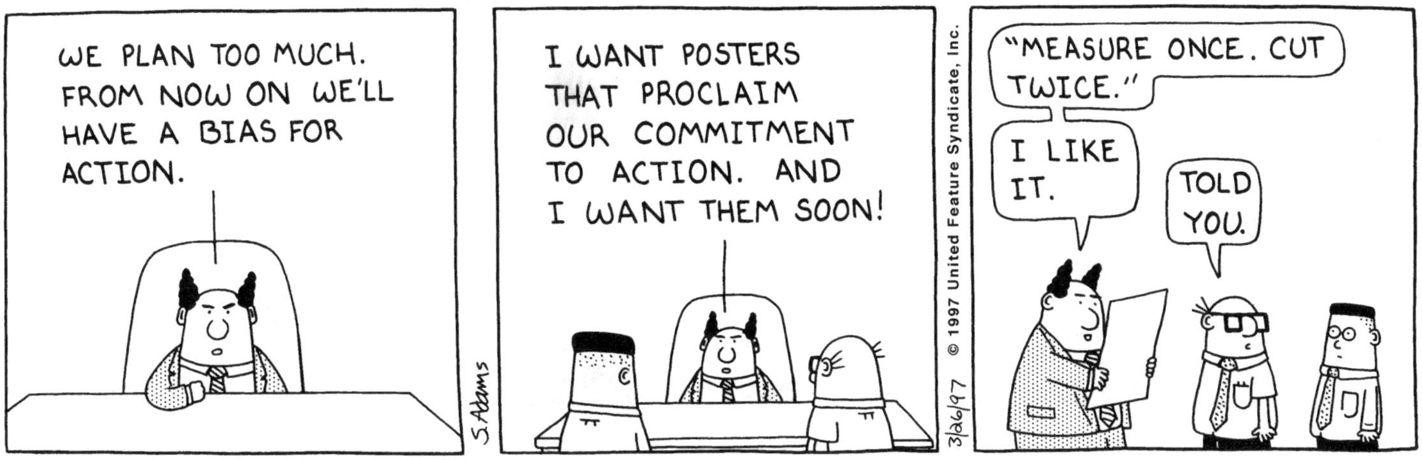
WE PLAN TOO MUCH. FROM NOW ON WE'LL HAVE A BIAS FOR ACTION.
I WANT POSTERS THAT PROCLAIM OUR COMMITMENT TO ACTION. AND I WANT THEM SOON!
"MEASURE ONCE. CUT TWICE."
I LIKE IT.
TOLD YOU.
S. Adams
3/26/97
© 1997 United Feature Syndicate, Inc.

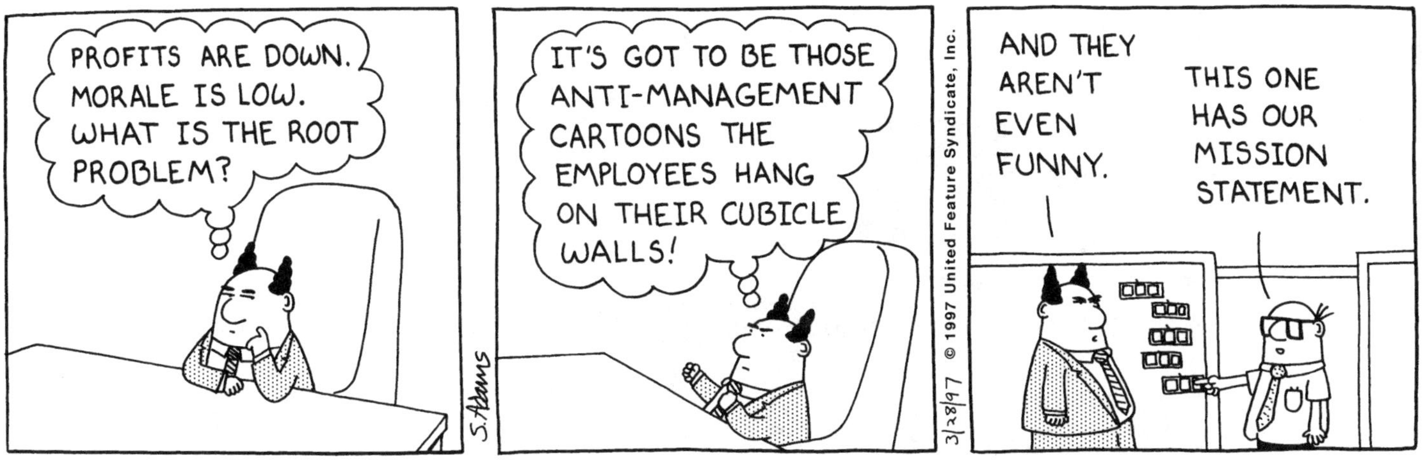
PROFITS ARE DOWN. MORALE IS LOW. WHAT IS THE ROOT PROBLEM?
IT'S GOT TO BE THOSE ANTI-MANAGEMENT CARTOONS THE EMPLOYEES HANG ON THEIR CUBICLE WALLS!
AND THEY AREN'T EVEN FUNNY.
THIS ONE HAS OUR MISSION STATEMENT.
S. Adams
3/28/97
© 1997 United Feature Syndicate, Inc.

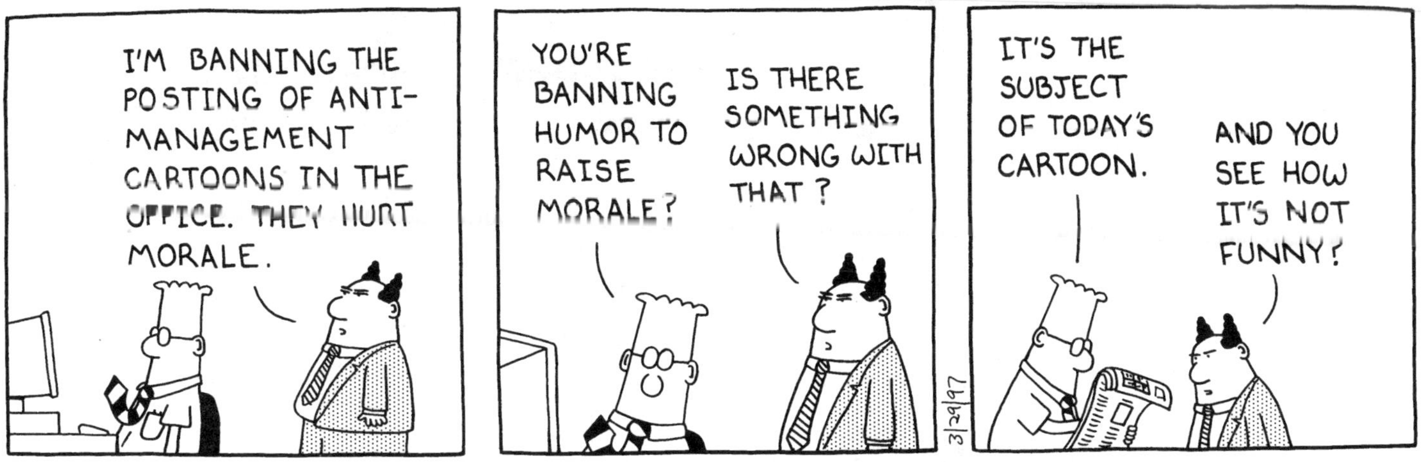
I'M BANNING THE POSTING OF ANTI-MANAGEMENT CARTOONS IN THE OFFICE. THEY HURT MORALE.
YOU'RE BANNING HUMOR TO RAISE MORALE?
IS THERE SOMETHING WRONG WITH THAT?
IT'S THE SUBJECT OF TODAY'S CARTOON.
AND YOU SEE HOW IT'S NOT FUNNY?
3/29/97

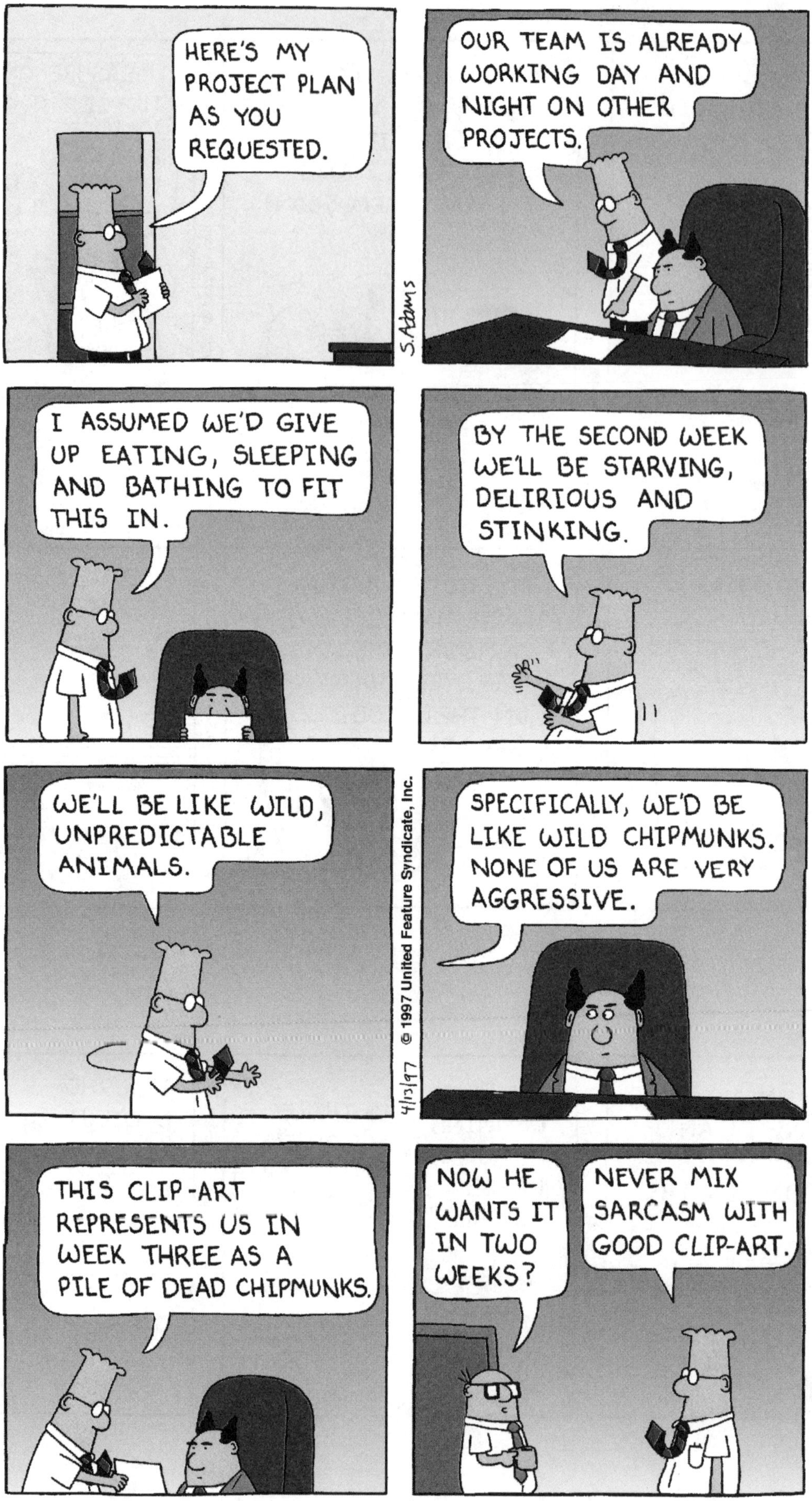
HERE'S MY PROJECT PLAN AS YOU REQUESTED.
S. Adams
OUR TEAM IS ALREADY WORKING DAY AND NIGHT ON OTHER PROJECTS.
I ASSUMED WE'D GIVE UP EATING, SLEEPING AND BATHING TO FIT THIS IN.
BY THE SECOND WEEK WE'LL BE STARVING, DELIRIOUS AND STINKING.
WE'LL BE LIKE WILD, UNPREDICTABLE ANIMALS.
© 1997 United Feature Syndicate, Inc.
4/13/97
SPECIFICALLY, WE'D BE LIKE WILD CHIPMUNKS. NONE OF US ARE VERY AGGRESSIVE.
THIS CLIP-ART REPRESENTS US IN WEEK THREE AS A PILE OF DEAD CHIPMUNKS.
NOW HE WANTS IT IN TWO WEEKS?
NEVER MIX SARCASM WITH GOOD CLIP-ART.

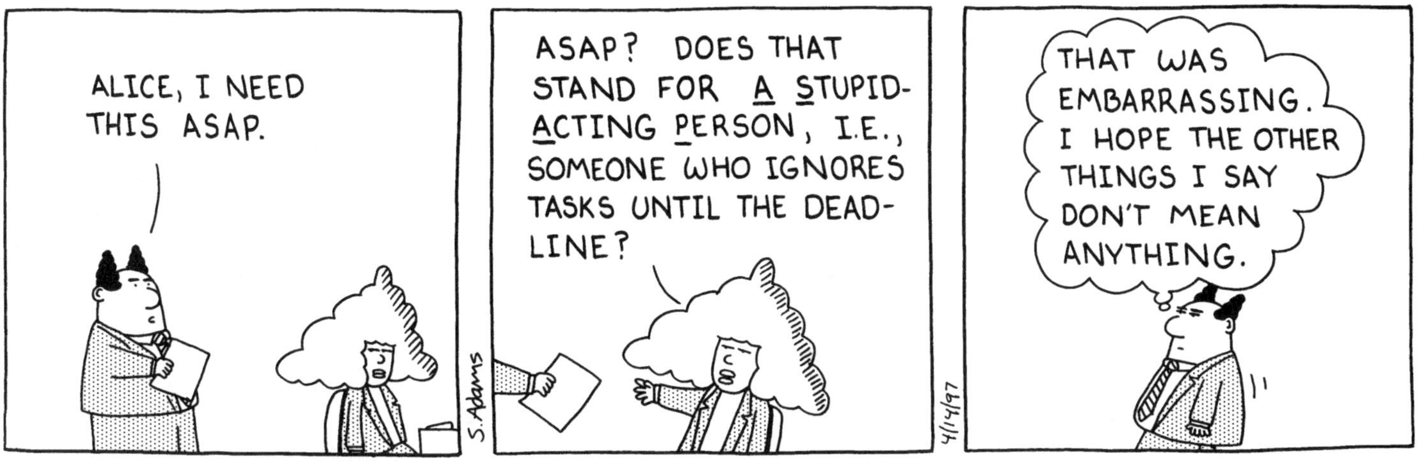
ALICE, I NEED THIS ASAP.
ASAP? DOES THAT STAND FOR A STUPID-ACTING PERSON, I.E., SOMEONE WHO IGNORES TASKS UNTIL THE DEAD-LINE?
THAT WAS EMBARRASSING. I HOPE THE OTHER THINGS I SAY DON'T MEAN ANYTHING.
S. Adams
4/14/97

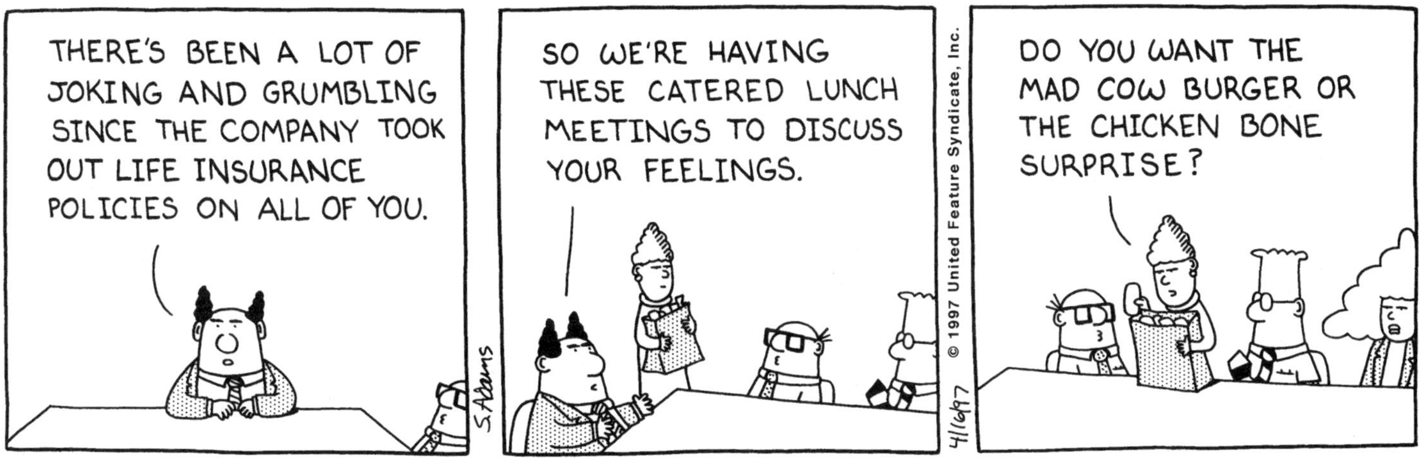
THERE'S BEEN A LOT OF JOKING AND GRUMBLING SINCE THE COMPANY TOOK OUT LIFE INSURANCE POLICIES ON ALL OF YOU.
SO WE'RE HAVING THESE CATERED LUNCH MEETINGS TO DISCUSS YOUR FEELINGS.
DO YOU WANT THE MAD COW BURGER OR THE CHICKEN BONE SURPRISE?
S. Adams
4/16/97
© 1997 United Feature Syndicate, Inc.

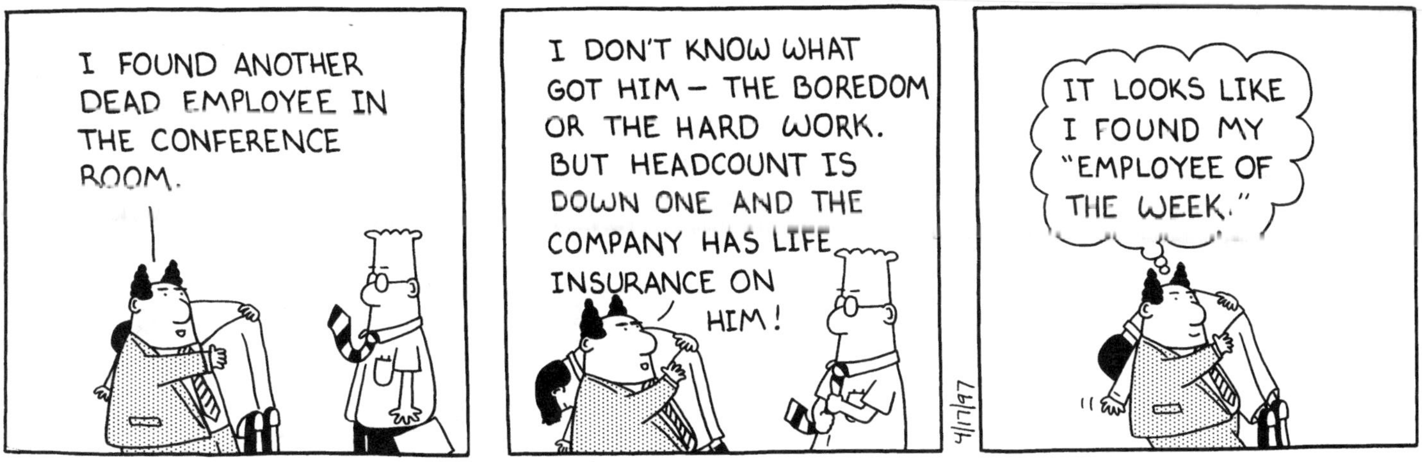
I FOUND ANOTHER DEAD EMPLOYEE IN THE CONFERENCE ROOM.
I DON'T KNOW WHAT GOT HIM – THE BOREDOM OR THE HARD WORK. BUT HEADCOUNT IS DOWN ONE AND THE COMPANY HAS LIFE INSURANCE ON HIM!
IT LOOKS LIKE I FOUND MY "EMPLOYEE OF THE WEEK."
4/17/97

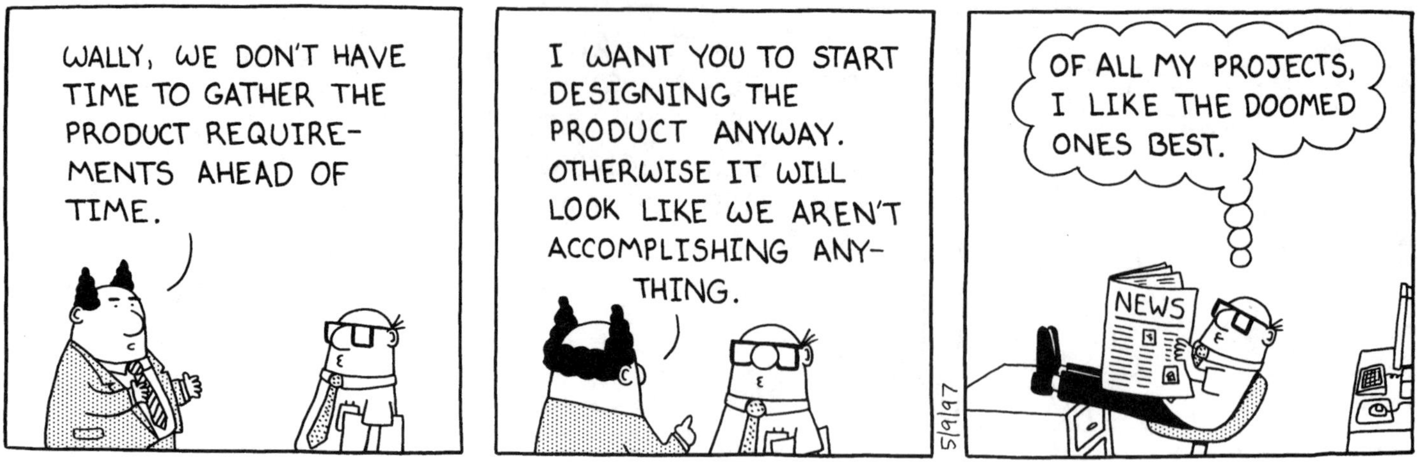
WALLY, WE DON'T HAVE TIME TO GATHER THE PRODUCT REQUIREMENTS AHEAD OF TIME.
I WANT YOU TO START DESIGNING THE PRODUCT ANYWAY. OTHERWISE IT WILL LOOK LIKE WE AREN'T ACCOMPLISHING ANYTHING.
5/9/97
OF ALL MY PROJECTS, I LIKE THE DOOMED ONES BEST.
NEWS

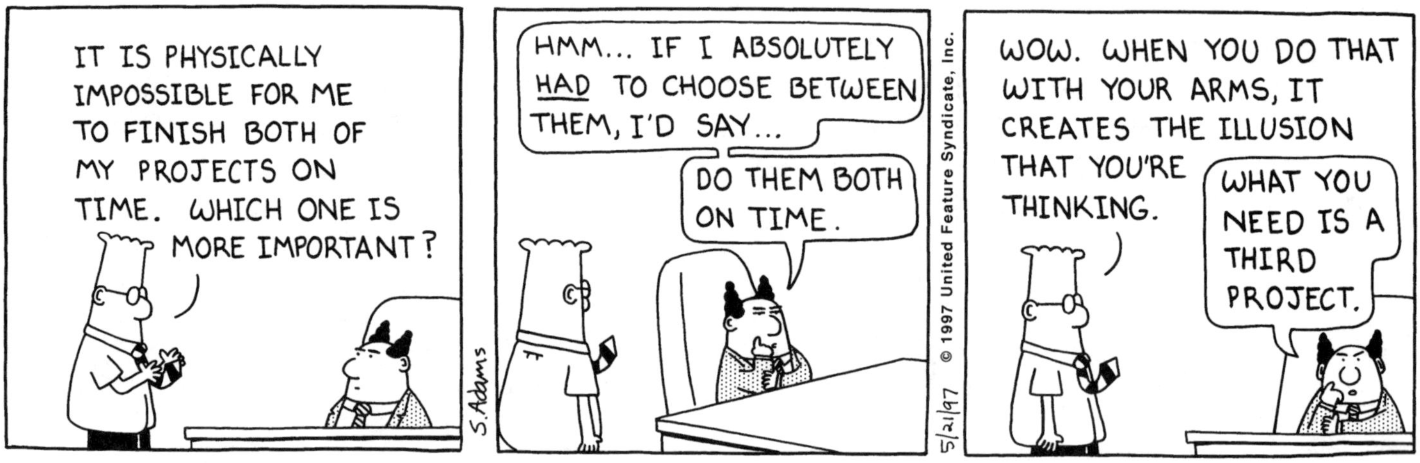
IT IS PHYSICALLY IMPOSSIBLE FOR ME TO FINISH BOTH OF MY PROJECTS ON TIME. WHICH ONE IS MORE IMPORTANT?
S. Adams
HMM... IF I ABSOLUTELY HAD TO CHOOSE BETWEEN THEM, I'D SAY...
DO THEM BOTH ON TIME.
5/21/97
© 1997 United Feature Syndicate, Inc.
WOW. WHEN YOU DO THAT WITH YOUR ARMS, IT CREATES THE ILLUSION THAT YOU'RE THINKING.
WHAT YOU NEED IS A THIRD PROJECT.

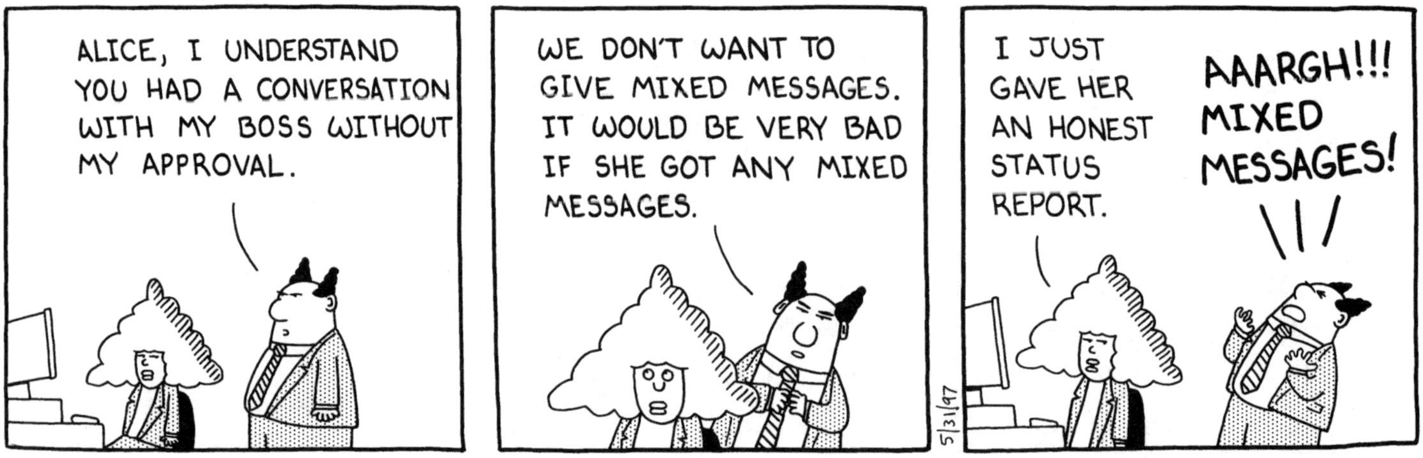
ALICE, I UNDERSTAND YOU HAD A CONVERSATION WITH MY BOSS WITHOUT MY APPROVAL.
WE DON'T WANT TO GIVE MIXED MESSAGES. IT WOULD BE VERY BAD IF SHE GOT ANY MIXED MESSAGES.
5/31/97
I JUST GAVE HER AN HONEST STATUS REPORT.
AAARGH!!! MIXED MESSAGES!

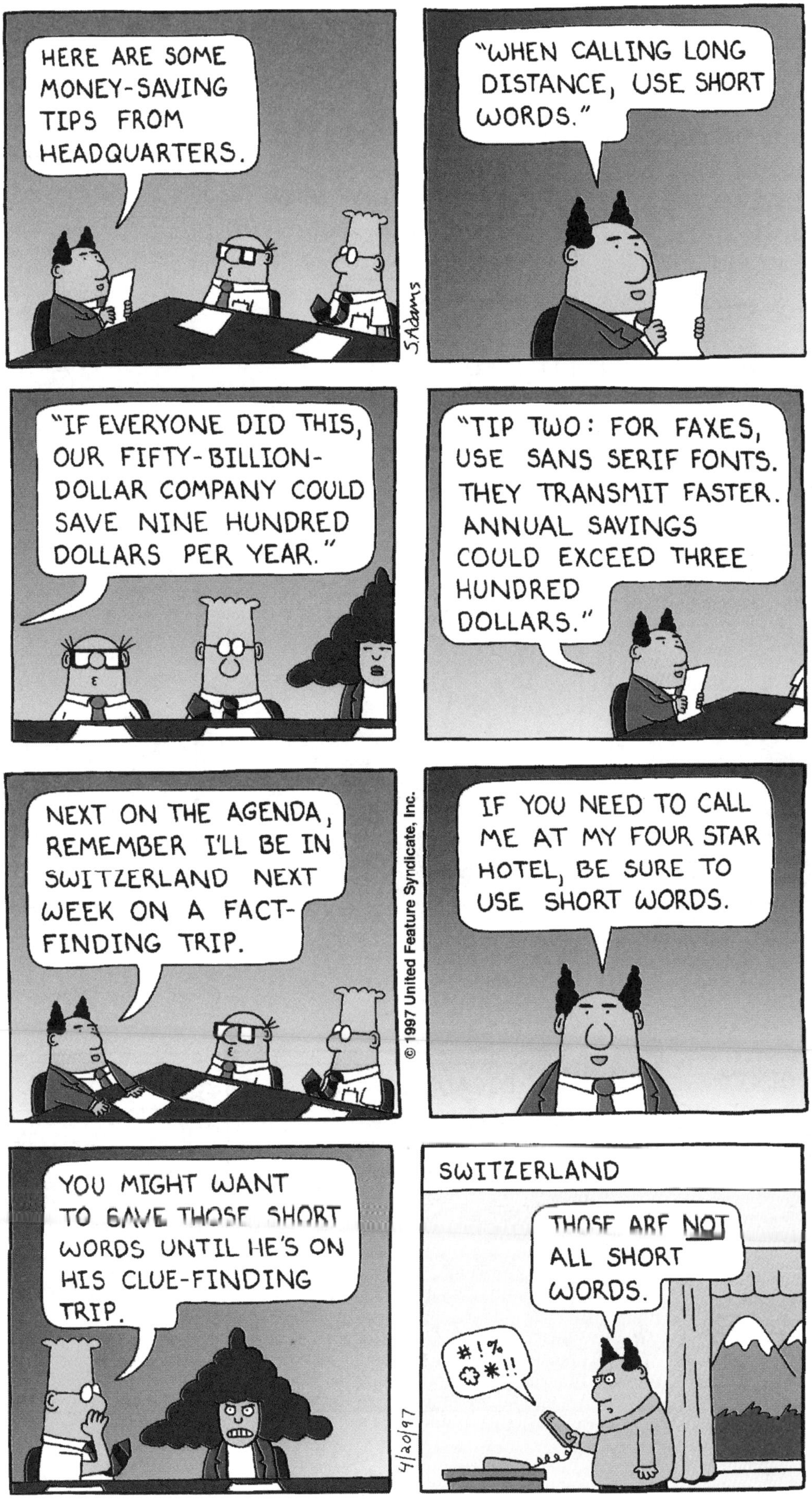
HERE ARE SOME MONEY-SAVING TIPS FROM HEADQUARTERS.
"WHEN CALLING LONG DISTANCE, USE SHORT WORDS."
S.Adams
"IF EVERYONE DID THIS, OUR FIFTY-BILLION-DOLLAR COMPANY COULD SAVE NINE HUNDRED DOLLARS PER YEAR."
"TIP TWO: FOR FAXES, USE SANS SERIF FONTS. THEY TRANSMIT FASTER. ANNUAL SAVINGS COULD EXCEED THREE HUNDRED DOLLARS."
NEXT ON THE AGENDA, REMEMBER I'LL BE IN SWITZERLAND NEXT WEEK ON A FACT-FINDING TRIP.
© 1997 United Feature Syndicate, Inc.
IF YOU NEED TO CALL ME AT MY FOUR STAR HOTEL, BE SURE TO USE SHORT WORDS.
YOU MIGHT WANT TO SAVE THOSE SHORT WORDS UNTIL HE'S ON HIS CLUE-FINDING TRIP.
4/20/97
SWITZERLAND
THOSE ARE NOT ALL SHORT WORDS.
#!%
✿✱!!

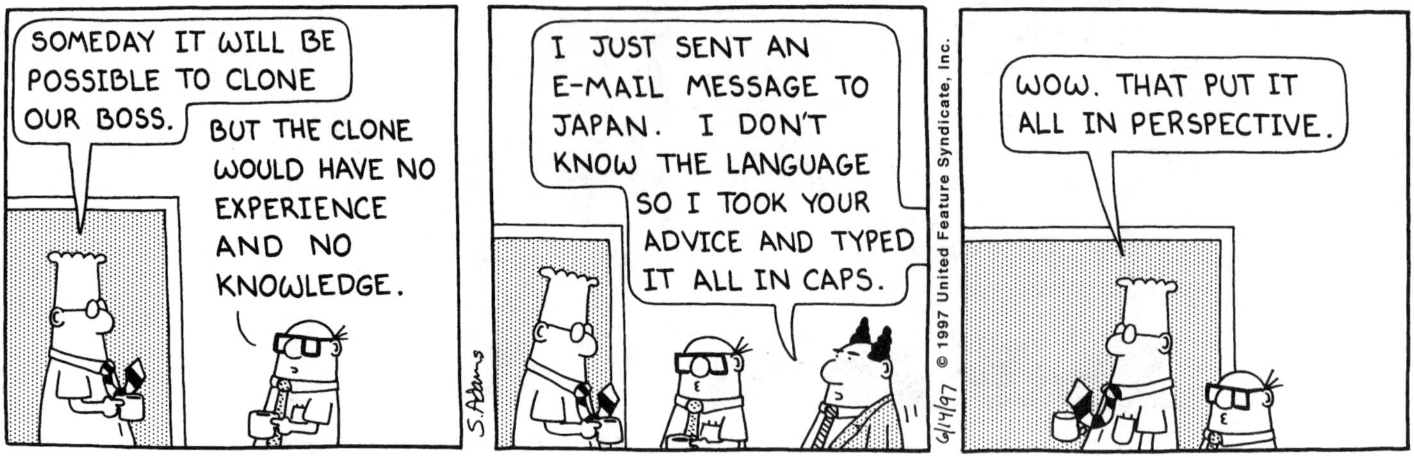
SOMEDAY IT WILL BE POSSIBLE TO CLONE OUR BOSS.
BUT THE CLONE WOULD HAVE NO EXPERIENCE AND NO KNOWLEDGE.
I JUST SENT AN E-MAIL MESSAGE TO JAPAN. I DON'T KNOW THE LANGUAGE SO I TOOK YOUR ADVICE AND TYPED IT ALL IN CAPS.
WOW. THAT PUT IT ALL IN PERSPECTIVE.
6/4/97
© 1997 United Feature Syndicate, Inc.

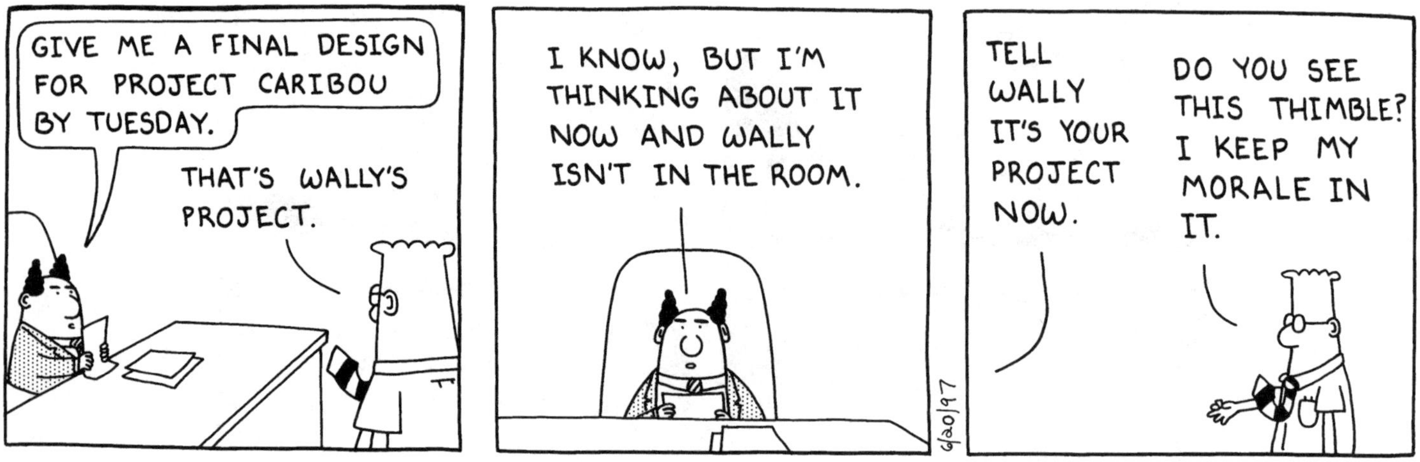
GIVE ME A FINAL DESIGN FOR PROJECT CARIBOU BY TUESDAY.
THAT'S WALLY'S PROJECT.
I KNOW, BUT I'M THINKING ABOUT IT NOW AND WALLY ISN'T IN THE ROOM.
TELL WALLY IT'S YOUR PROJECT NOW.
DO YOU SEE THIS THIMBLE? I KEEP MY MORALE IN IT.
6/20/97

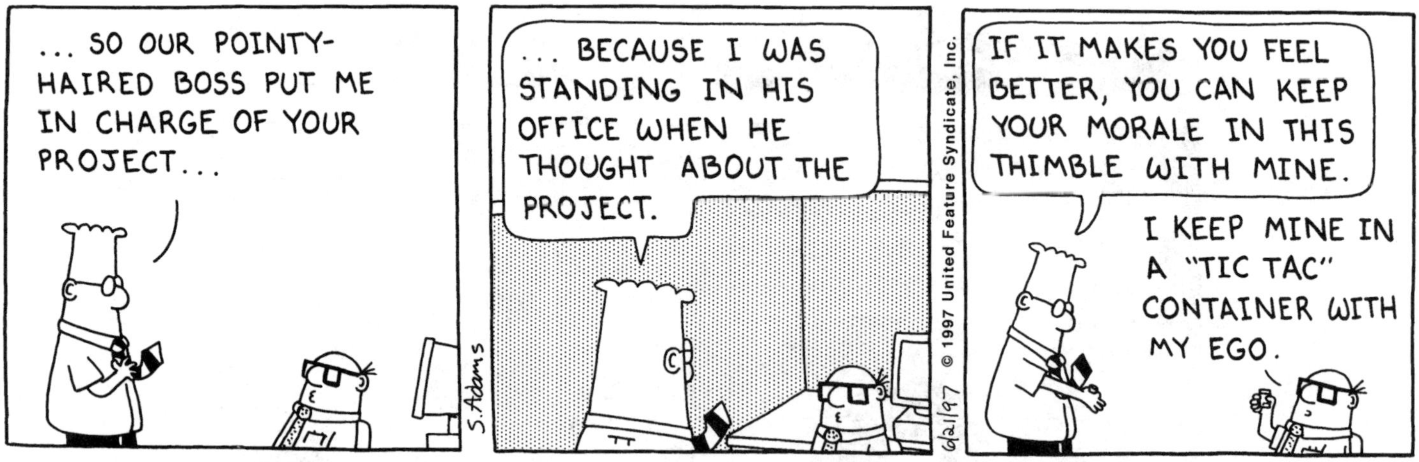
... SO OUR POINTY-HAIRED BOSS PUT ME IN CHARGE OF YOUR PROJECT...
... BECAUSE I WAS STANDING IN HIS OFFICE WHEN HE THOUGHT ABOUT THE PROJECT.
IF IT MAKES YOU FEEL BETTER, YOU CAN KEEP YOUR MORALE IN THIS THIMBLE WITH MINE.
I KEEP MINE IN A "TIC TAC" CONTAINER WITH MY EGO.
6/21/97
© 1997 United Feature Syndicate, Inc.

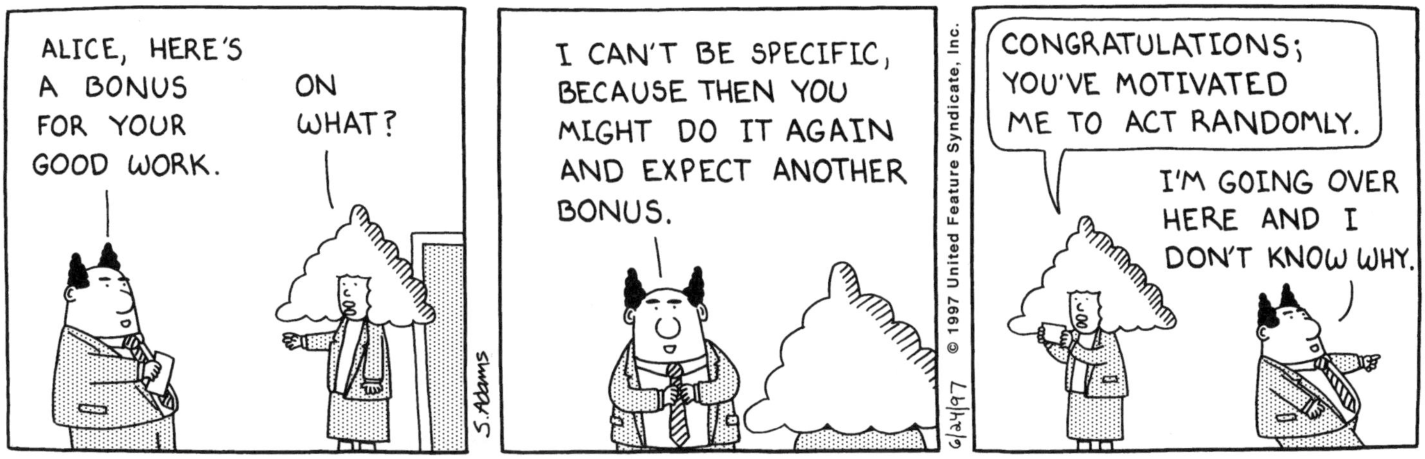
ALICE, HERE'S A BONUS FOR YOUR GOOD WORK.
ON WHAT?
I CAN'T BE SPECIFIC, BECAUSE THEN YOU MIGHT DO IT AGAIN AND EXPECT ANOTHER BONUS.
CONGRATULATIONS; YOU'VE MOTIVATED ME TO ACT RANDOMLY.
I'M GOING OVER HERE AND I DON'T KNOW WHY.
S. Adams
6/24/97
© 1997 United Feature Syndicate, Inc.

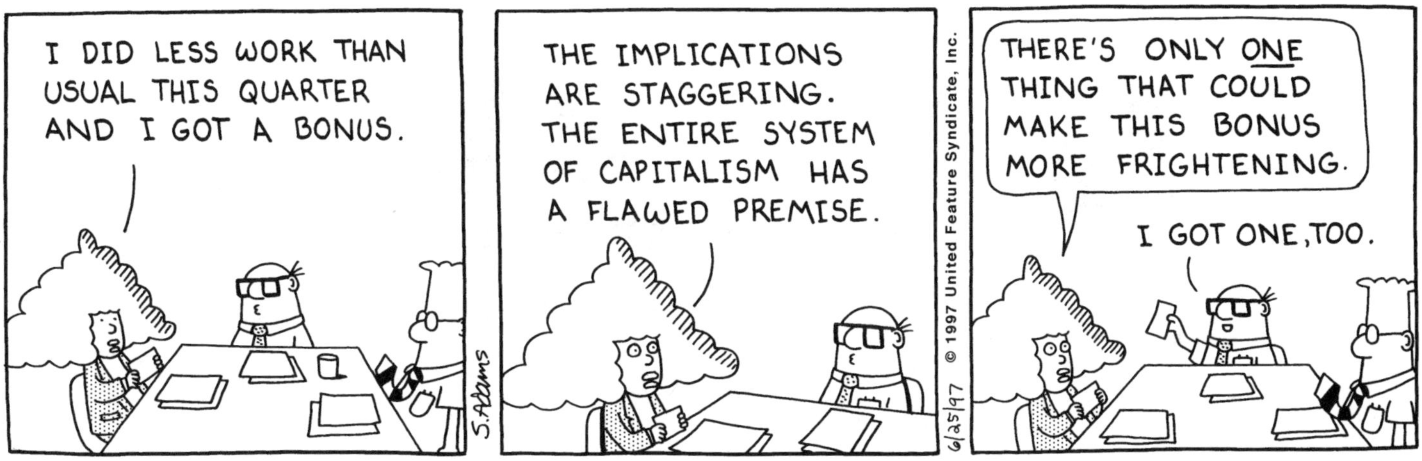
I DID LESS WORK THAN USUAL THIS QUARTER AND I GOT A BONUS.
THE IMPLICATIONS ARE STAGGERING. THE ENTIRE SYSTEM OF CAPITALISM HAS A FLAWED PREMISE.
THERE'S ONLY ONE THING THAT COULD MAKE THIS BONUS MORE FRIGHTENING.
I GOT ONE, TOO.
S. Adams
6/25/97
© 1997 United Feature Syndicate, Inc.

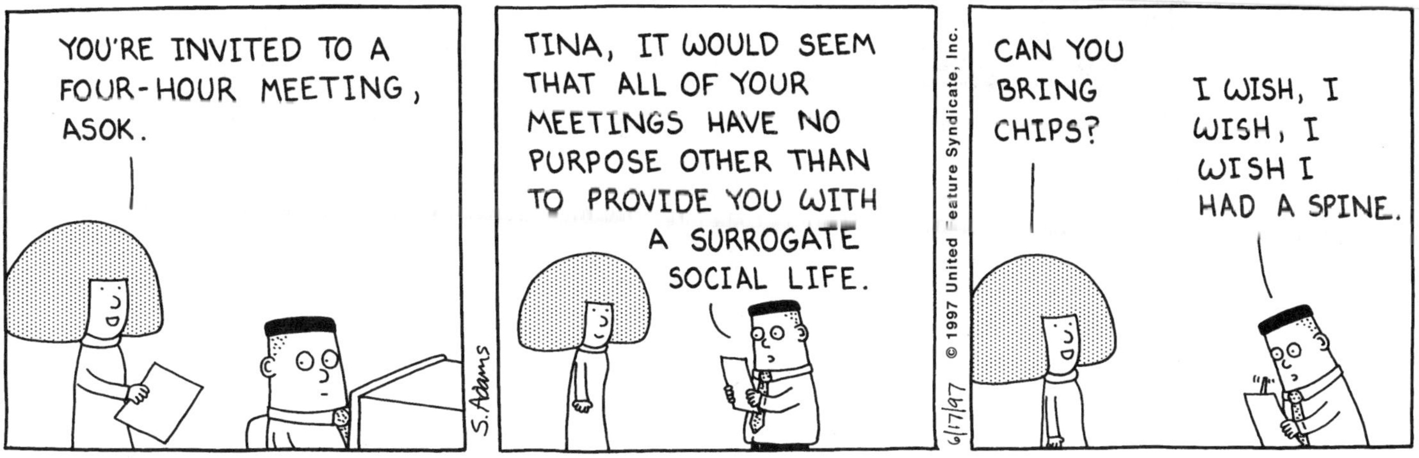
YOU'RE INVITED TO A FOUR-HOUR MEETING, ASOK.
TINA, IT WOULD SEEM THAT ALL OF YOUR MEETINGS HAVE NO PURPOSE OTHER THAN TO PROVIDE YOU WITH A SURROGATE SOCIAL LIFE.
CAN YOU BRING CHIPS?
I WISH, I WISH, I WISH I HAD A SPINE.
S. Adams
6/17/97
© 1997 United Feature Syndicate, Inc.

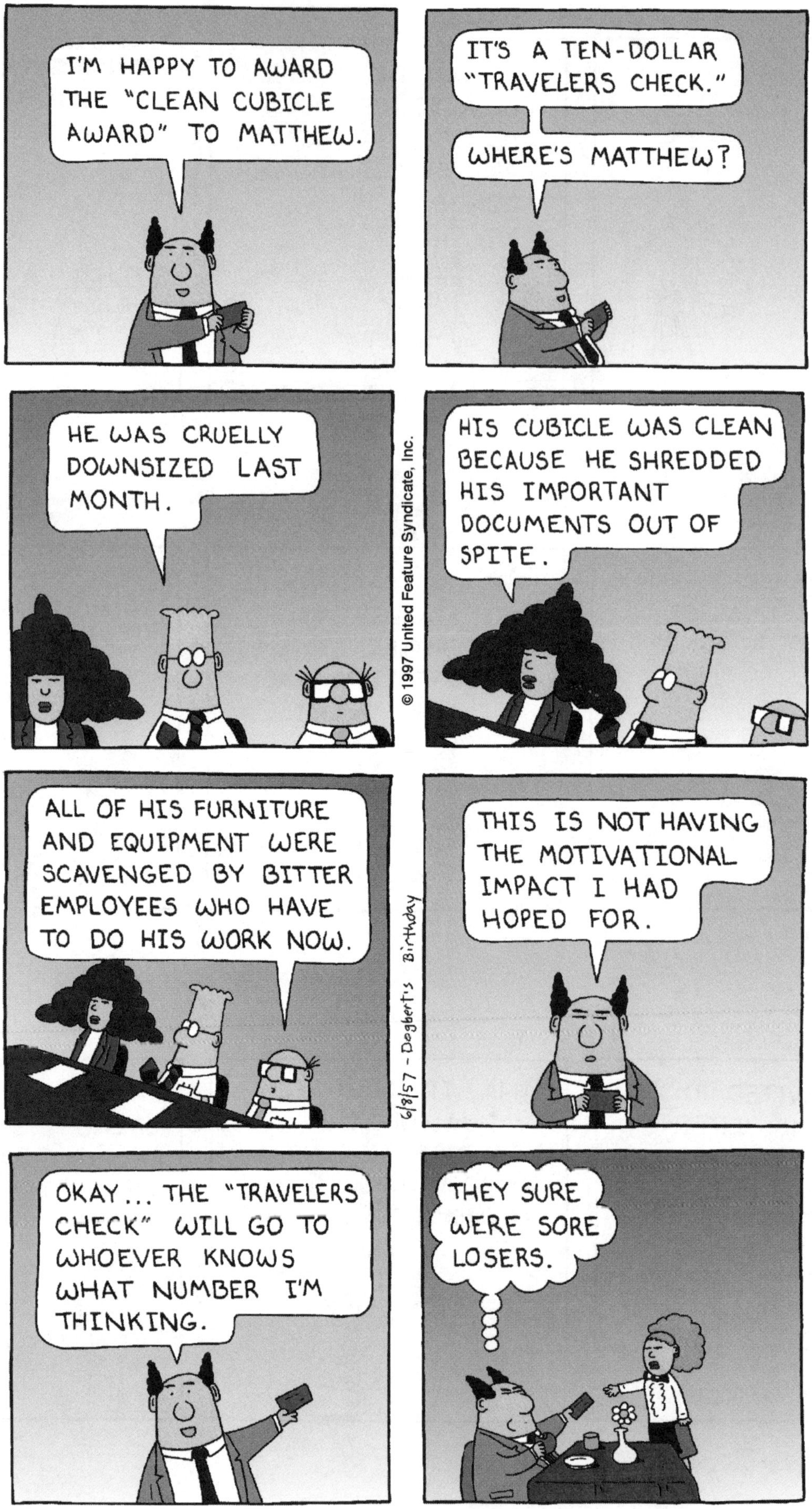
I'M HAPPY TO AWARD THE "CLEAN CUBICLE AWARD" TO MATTHEW.
IT'S A TEN-DOLLAR "TRAVELERS CHECK."
WHERE'S MATTHEW?
HE WAS CRUELLY DOWNSIZED LAST MONTH.
HIS CUBICLE WAS CLEAN BECAUSE HE SHREDDED HIS IMPORTANT DOCUMENTS OUT OF SPITE.
ALL OF HIS FURNITURE AND EQUIPMENT WERE SCAVENGED BY BITTER EMPLOYEES WHO HAVE TO DO HIS WORK NOW.
THIS IS NOT HAVING THE MOTIVATIONAL IMPACT I HAD HOPED FOR.
OKAY... THE "TRAVELERS CHECK" WILL GO TO WHOEVER KNOWS WHAT NUMBER I'M THINKING.
THEY SURE WERE SORE LOSERS.
6/8/57 - Dogbert's Birthday

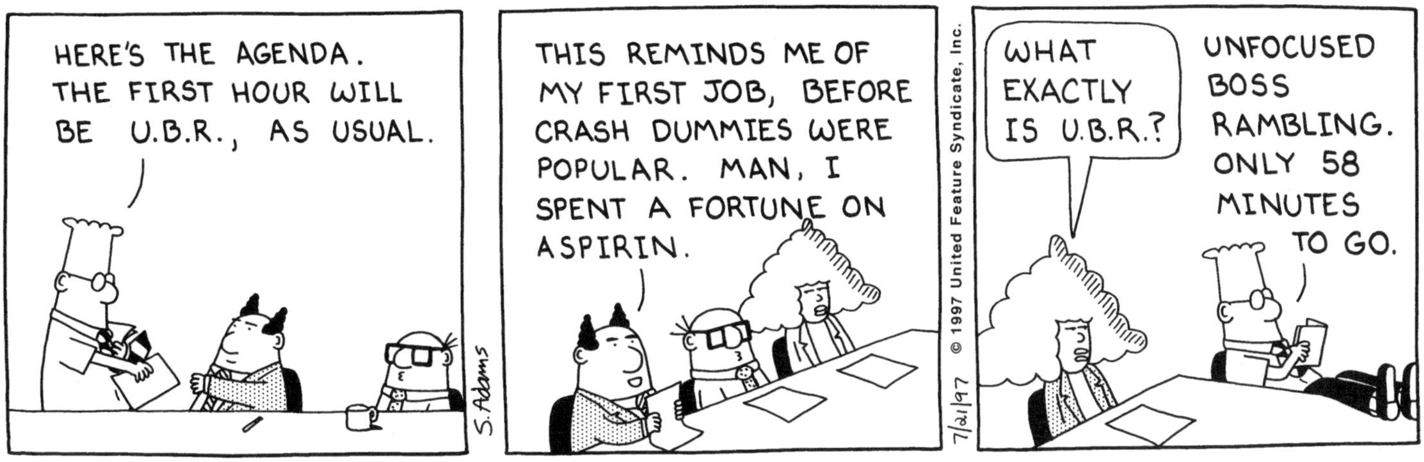
HERE'S THE AGENDA. THE FIRST HOUR WILL BE U.B.R., AS USUAL.
S. Adams
THIS REMINDS ME OF MY FIRST JOB, BEFORE CRASH DUMMIES WERE POPULAR. MAN, I SPENT A FORTUNE ON ASPIRIN.
7/21/97 © 1997 United Feature Syndicate, Inc.
WHAT EXACTLY IS U.B.R.?
UNFOCUSED BOSS RAMBLING. ONLY 58 MINUTES TO GO.

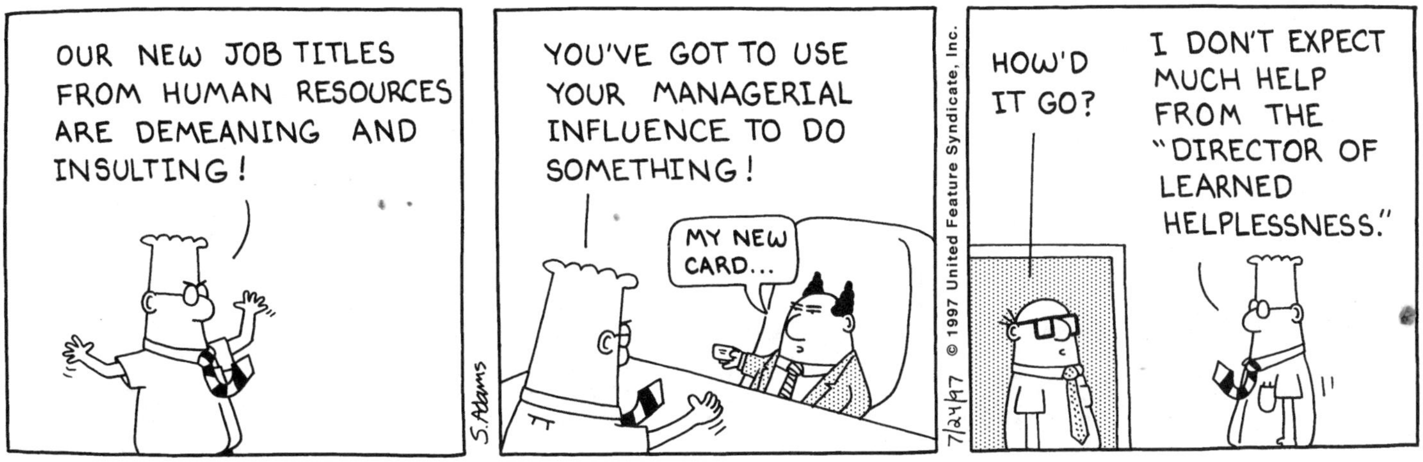
OUR NEW JOB TITLES FROM HUMAN RESOURCES ARE DEMEANING AND INSULTING!
S. Adams
YOU'VE GOT TO USE YOUR MANAGERIAL INFLUENCE TO DO SOMETHING!
MY NEW CARD...
7/24/97 © 1997 United Feature Syndicate, Inc.
HOW'D IT GO?
I DON'T EXPECT MUCH HELP FROM THE "DIRECTOR OF LEARNED HELPLESSNESS."

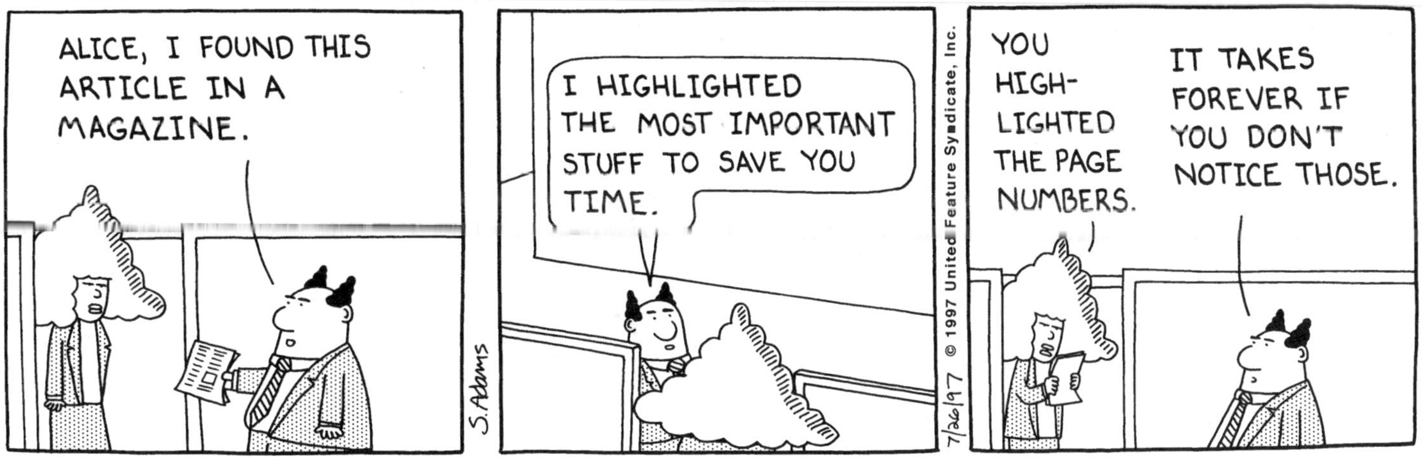
ALICE, I FOUND THIS ARTICLE IN A MAGAZINE.
S. Adams
I HIGHLIGHTED THE MOST IMPORTANT STUFF TO SAVE YOU TIME.
7/26/97 © 1997 United Feature Syndicate, Inc.
YOU HIGH-LIGHTED THE PAGE NUMBERS.
IT TAKES FOREVER IF YOU DON'T NOTICE THOSE.

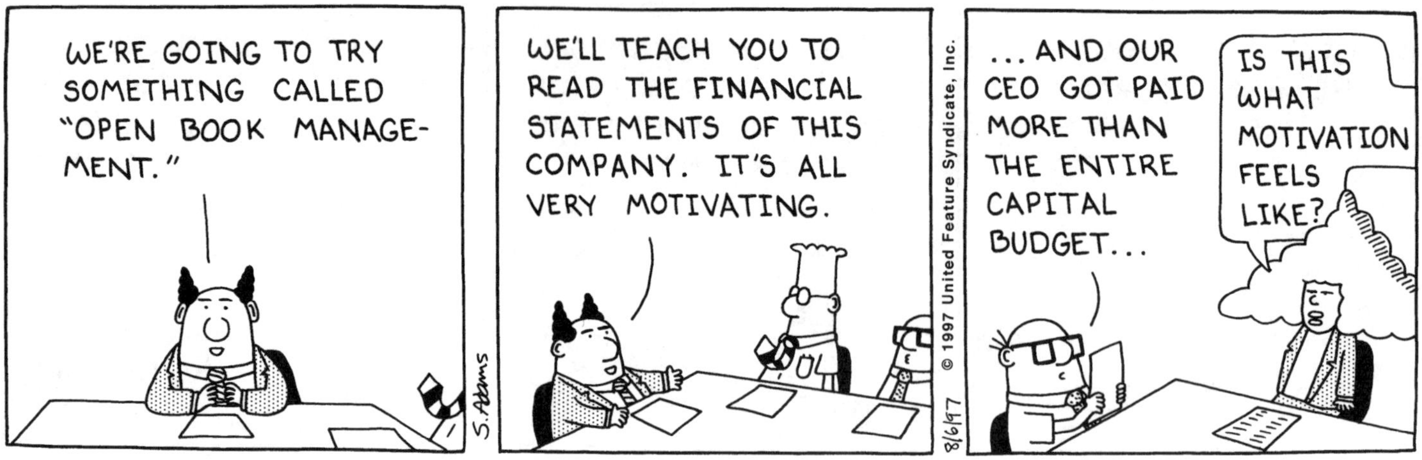
WE'RE GOING TO TRY SOMETHING CALLED "OPEN BOOK MANAGEMENT."
S. Adams
WE'LL TEACH YOU TO READ THE FINANCIAL STATEMENTS OF THIS COMPANY. IT'S ALL VERY MOTIVATING.
8/6/97 © 1997 United Feature Syndicate, Inc.
... AND OUR CEO GOT PAID MORE THAN THE ENTIRE CAPITAL BUDGET...
IS THIS WHAT MOTIVATION FEELS LIKE?

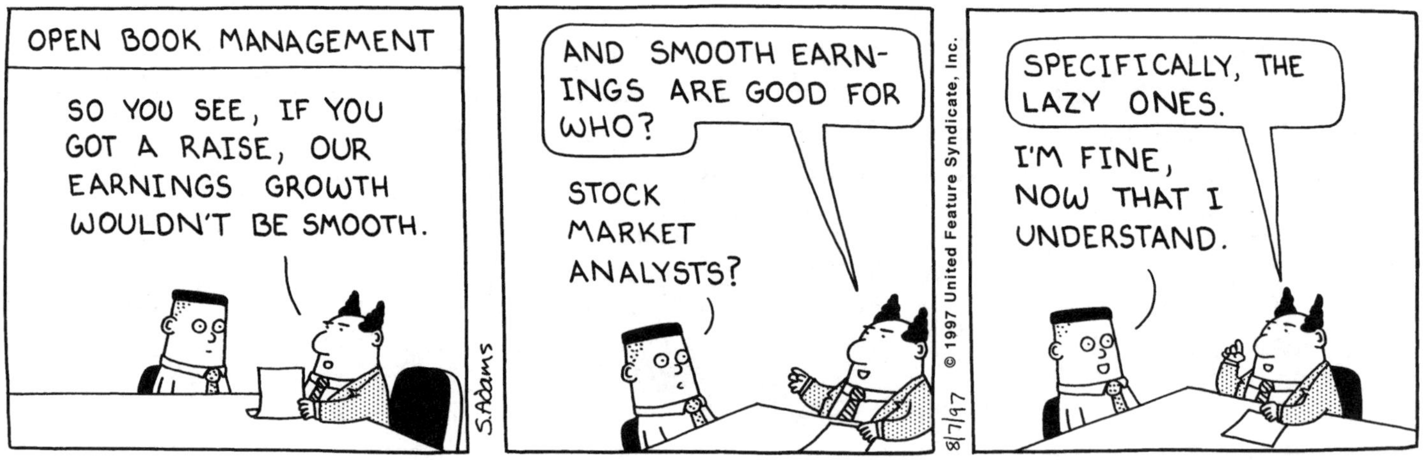
OPEN BOOK MANAGEMENT
SO YOU SEE, IF YOU GOT A RAISE, OUR EARNINGS GROWTH WOULDN'T BE SMOOTH.
S. Adams
AND SMOOTH EARNINGS ARE GOOD FOR WHO?
STOCK MARKET ANALYSTS?
8/7/97 © 1997 United Feature Syndicate, Inc.
SPECIFICALLY, THE LAZY ONES.
I'M FINE, NOW THAT I UNDERSTAND.

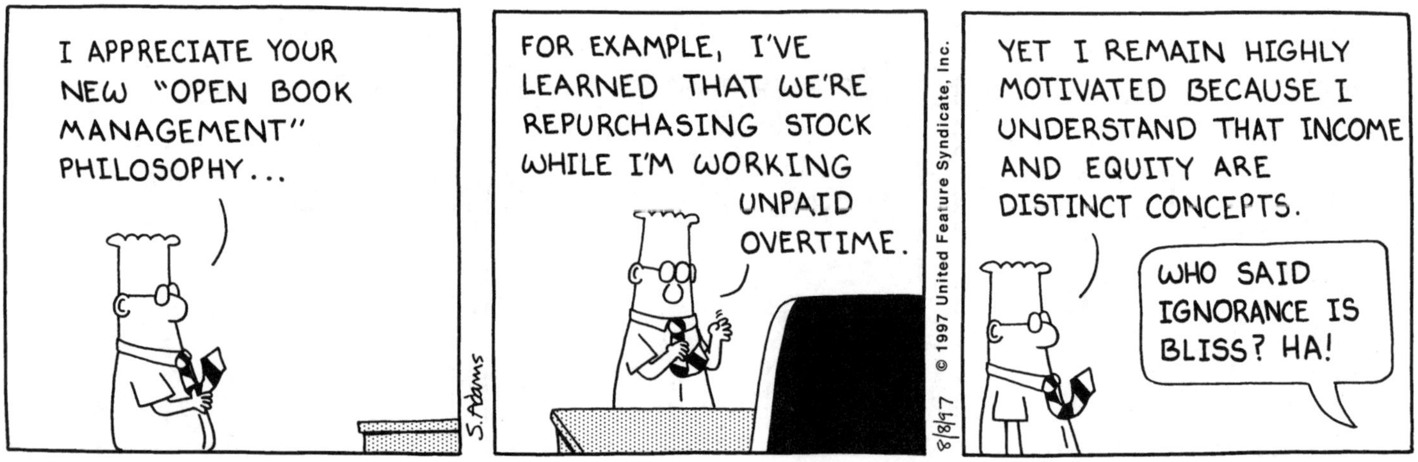
I APPRECIATE YOUR NEW "OPEN BOOK MANAGEMENT" PHILOSOPHY...
S. Adams
FOR EXAMPLE, I'VE LEARNED THAT WE'RE REPURCHASING STOCK WHILE I'M WORKING UNPAID OVERTIME.
8/8/97 © 1997 United Feature Syndicate, Inc.
YET I REMAIN HIGHLY MOTIVATED BECAUSE I UNDERSTAND THAT INCOME AND EQUITY ARE DISTINCT CONCEPTS.
WHO SAID IGNORANCE IS BLISS? HA!

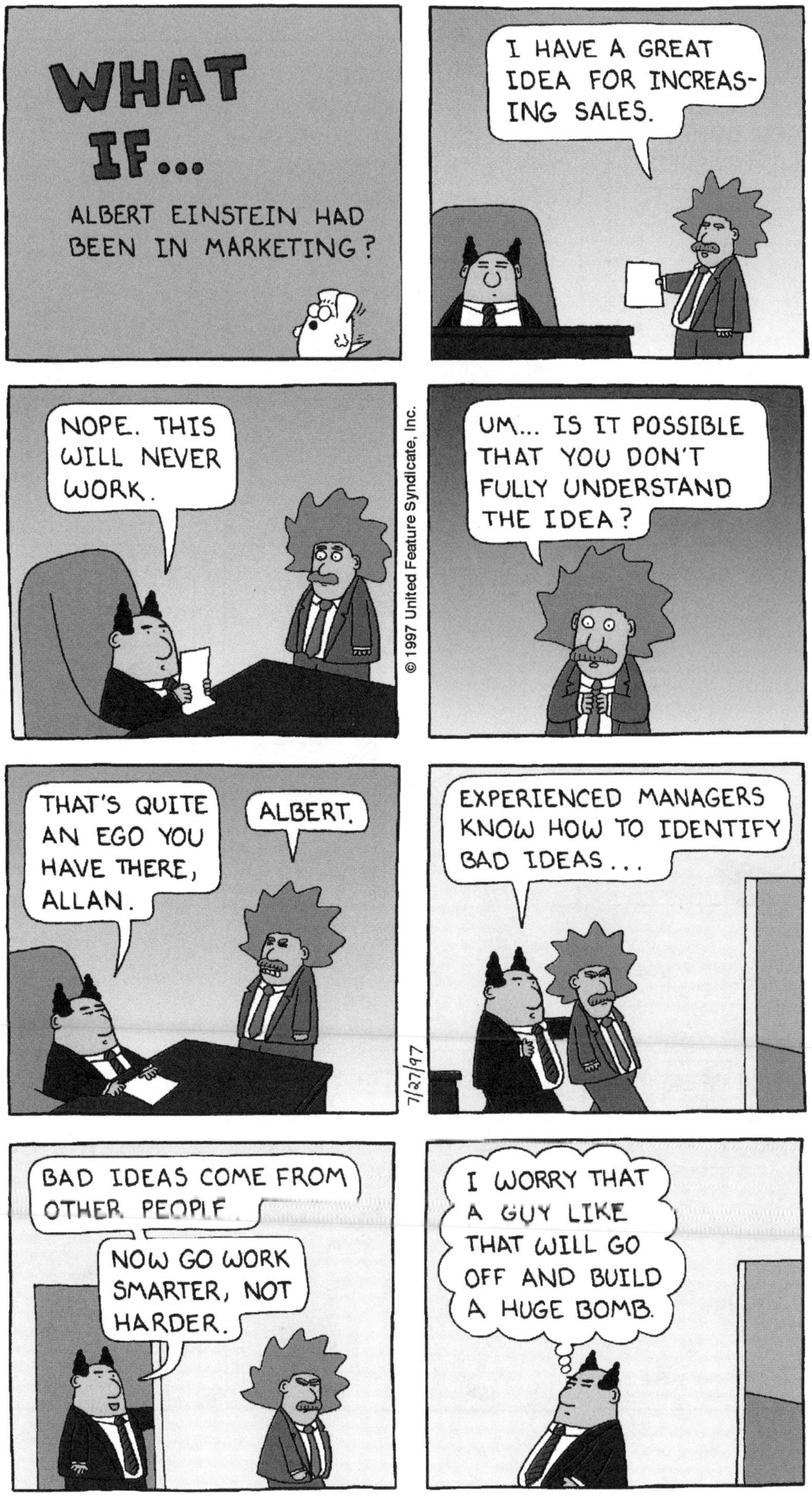
WHAT IF...
ALBERT EINSTEIN HAD BEEN IN MARKETING?
I HAVE A GREAT IDEA FOR INCREAS-ING SALES.
NOPE. THIS WILL NEVER WORK.
© 1997 United Feature Syndicate, Inc.
UM... IS IT POSSIBLE THAT YOU DON'T FULLY UNDERSTAND THE IDEA?
THAT'S QUITE AN EGO YOU HAVE THERE, ALLAN.
ALBERT.
7/27/97
EXPERIENCED MANAGERS KNOW HOW TO IDENTIFY BAD IDEAS...
BAD IDEAS COME FROM OTHER PEOPLE.
NOW GO WORK SMARTER, NOT HARDER.
I WORRY THAT A GUY LIKE THAT WILL GO OFF AND BUILD A HUGE BOMB.

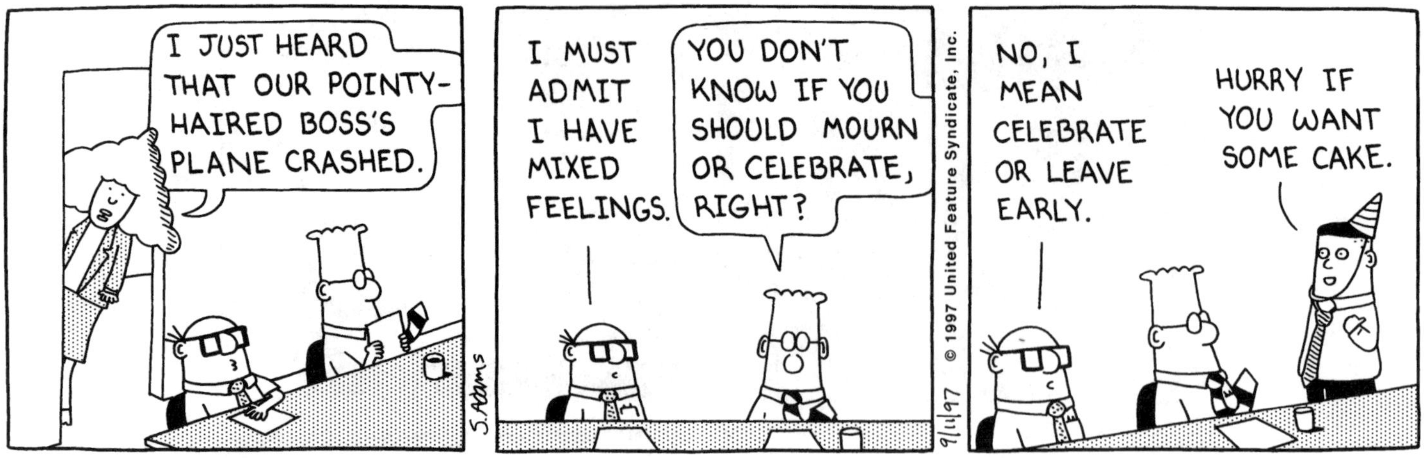
I JUST HEARD THAT OUR POINTY-HAIRED BOSS'S PLANE CRASHED.
S. Adams
I MUST ADMIT I HAVE MIXED FEELINGS.
YOU DON'T KNOW IF YOU SHOULD MOURN OR CELEBRATE, RIGHT?
9/11/97 © 1997 United Feature Syndicate, Inc.
NO, I MEAN CELEBRATE OR LEAVE EARLY.
HURRY IF YOU WANT SOME CAKE.

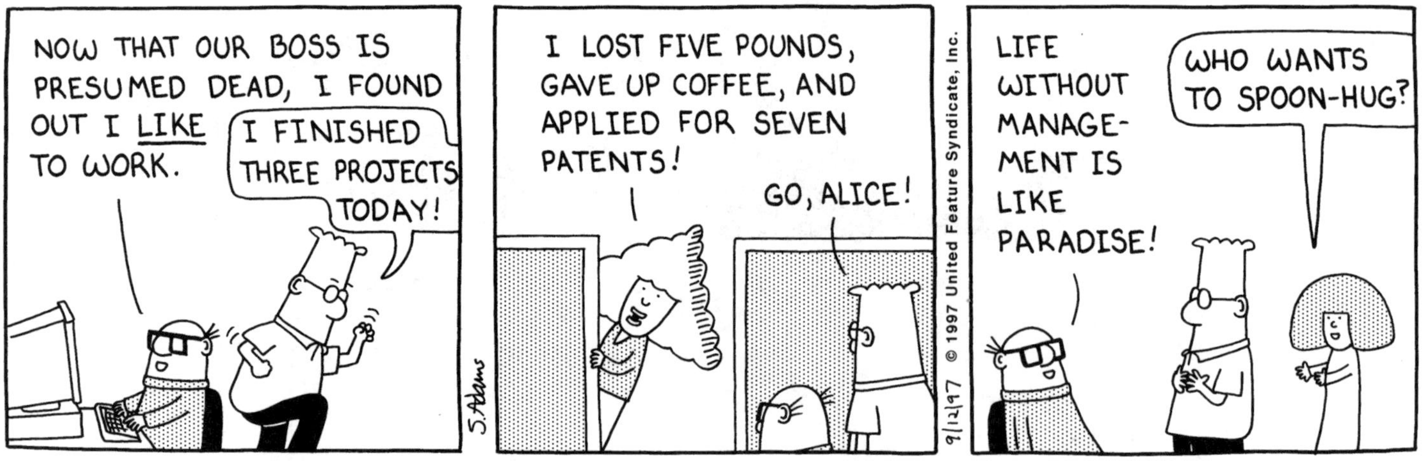
NOW THAT OUR BOSS IS PRESUMED DEAD, I FOUND OUT I LIKE TO WORK.
I FINISHED THREE PROJECTS TODAY!
S. Adams
I LOST FIVE POUNDS, GAVE UP COFFEE, AND APPLIED FOR SEVEN PATENTS!
GO, ALICE!
9/12/97 © 1997 United Feature Syndicate, Inc.
LIFE WITHOUT MANAGEMENT IS LIKE PARADISE!
WHO WANTS TO SPOON-HUG?

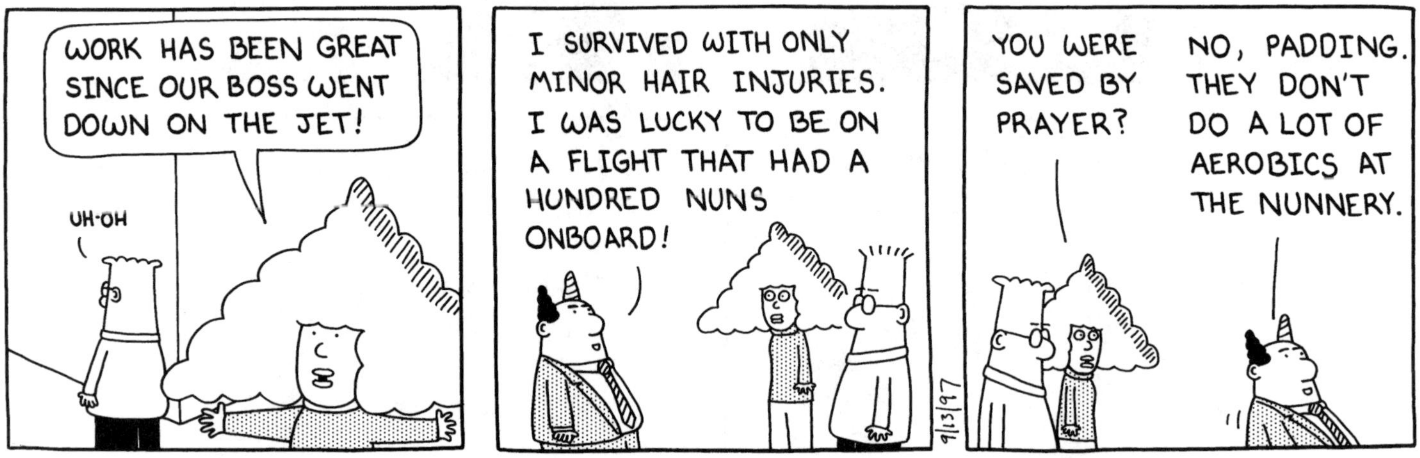
WORK HAS BEEN GREAT SINCE OUR BOSS WENT DOWN ON THE JET!
UH-OH
I SURVIVED WITH ONLY MINOR HAIR INJURIES. I WAS LUCKY TO BE ON A FLIGHT THAT HAD A HUNDRED NUNS ONBOARD!
9/13/97
YOU WERE SAVED BY PRAYER?
NO, PADDING. THEY DON'T DO A LOT OF AEROBICS AT THE NUNNERY.

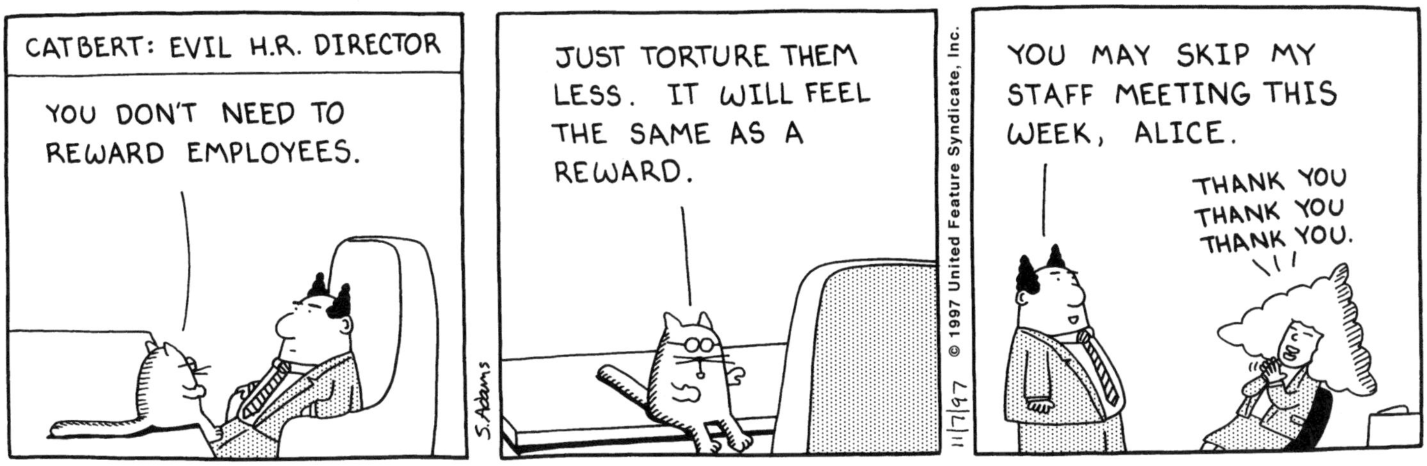
CATBERT: EVIL H.R. DIRECTOR
YOU DON'T NEED TO REWARD EMPLOYEES.
JUST TORTURE THEM LESS. IT WILL FEEL THE SAME AS A REWARD.
YOU MAY SKIP MY STAFF MEETING THIS WEEK, ALICE.
THANK YOU THANK YOU THANK YOU.
S. Adams
11/7/97 © 1997 United Feature Syndicate, Inc.

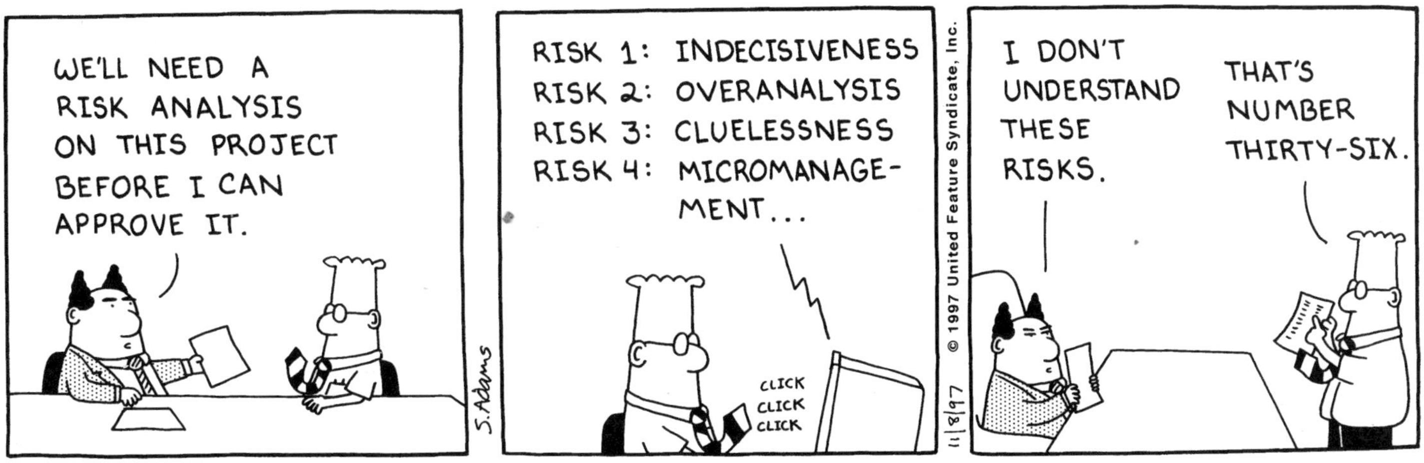
WE'LL NEED A RISK ANALYSIS ON THIS PROJECT BEFORE I CAN APPROVE IT.
RISK 1: INDECISIVENESS
RISK 2: OVERANALYSIS
RISK 3: CLUELESSNESS
RISK 4: MICROMANAGE-MENT...
CLICK CLICK CLICK
I DON'T UNDERSTAND THESE RISKS.
THAT'S NUMBER THIRTY-SIX.
S. Adams
11/8/97 © 1997 United Feature Syndicate, Inc.

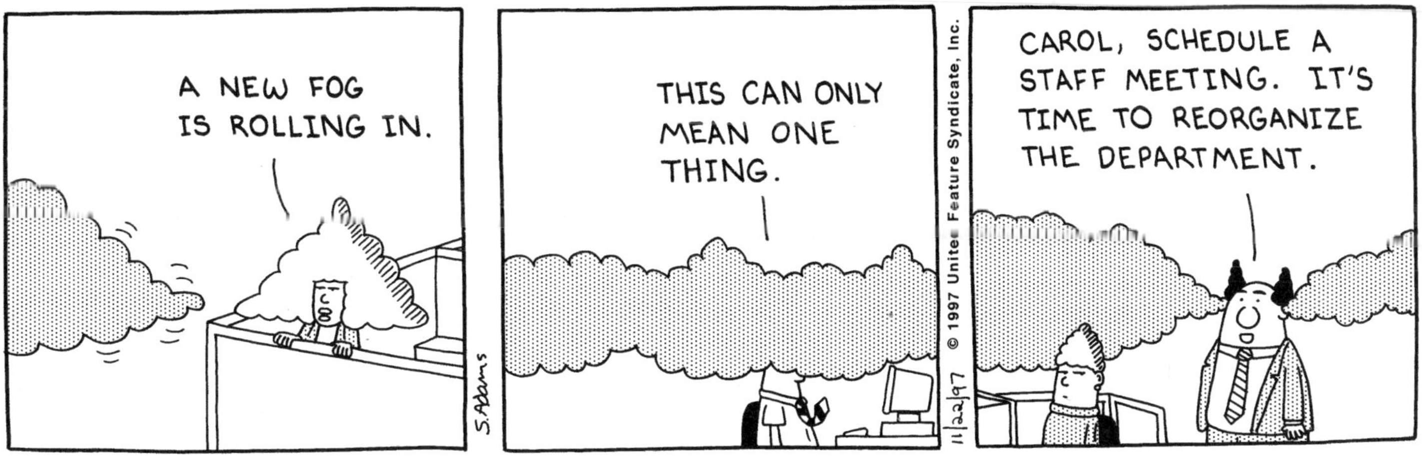
A NEW FOG IS ROLLING IN.
THIS CAN ONLY MEAN ONE THING.
CAROL, SCHEDULE A STAFF MEETING. IT'S TIME TO REORGANIZE THE DEPARTMENT.
S. Adams
11/22/97 © 1997 United Feature Syndicate, Inc.

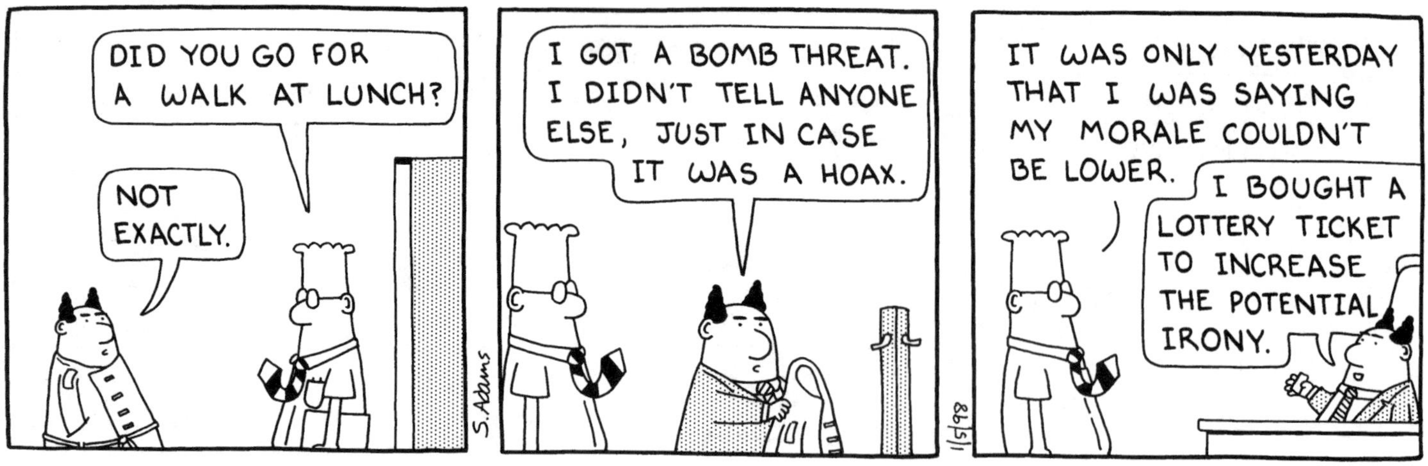
DID YOU GO FOR A WALK AT LUNCH?
NOT EXACTLY.
S. Adams
I GOT A BOMB THREAT. I DIDN'T TELL ANYONE ELSE, JUST IN CASE IT WAS A HOAX.
1/5/98
IT WAS ONLY YESTERDAY THAT I WAS SAYING MY MORALE COULDN'T BE LOWER.
I BOUGHT A LOTTERY TICKET TO INCREASE THE POTENTIAL IRONY.

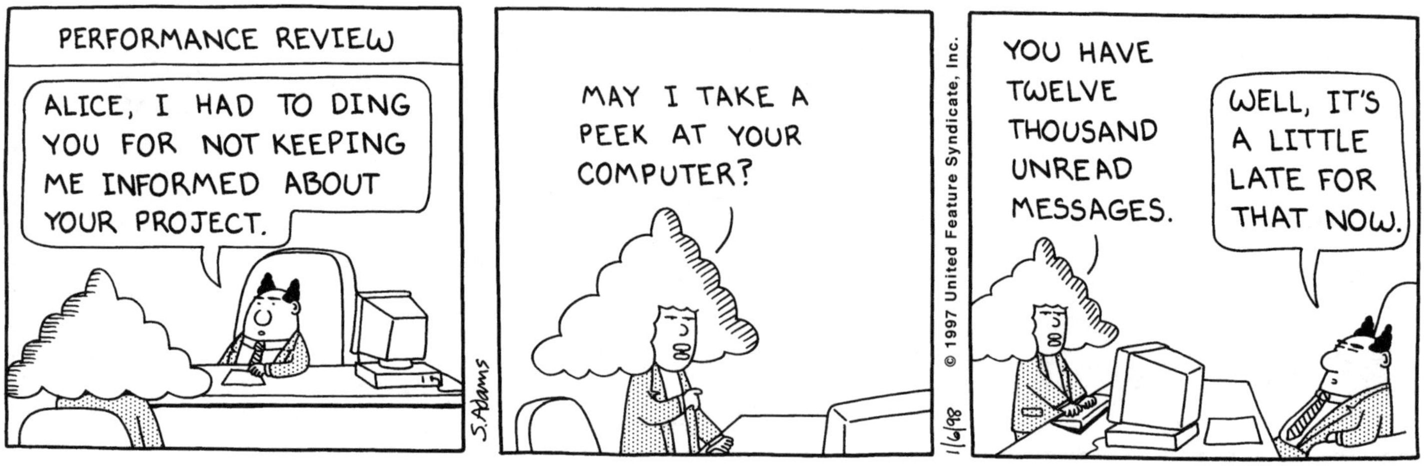
PERFORMANCE REVIEW
ALICE, I HAD TO DING YOU FOR NOT KEEPING ME INFORMED ABOUT YOUR PROJECT.
S. Adams
MAY I TAKE A PEEK AT YOUR COMPUTER?
1/6/98
© 1997 United Feature Syndicate, Inc.
YOU HAVE TWELVE THOUSAND UNREAD MESSAGES.
WELL, IT'S A LITTLE LATE FOR THAT NOW.

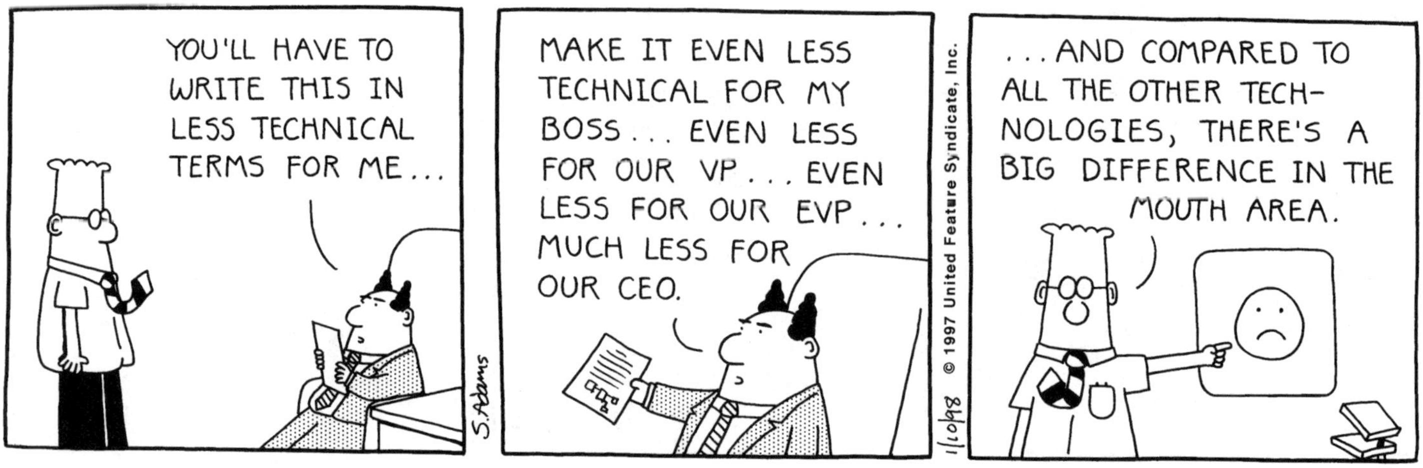
YOU'LL HAVE TO WRITE THIS IN LESS TECHNICAL TERMS FOR ME...
S. Adams
MAKE IT EVEN LESS TECHNICAL FOR MY BOSS... EVEN LESS FOR OUR VP... EVEN LESS FOR OUR EVP... MUCH LESS FOR OUR CEO.
1/10/98
© 1997 United Feature Syndicate, Inc.
...AND COMPARED TO ALL THE OTHER TECH-NOLOGIES, THERE'S A BIG DIFFERENCE IN THE MOUTH AREA.

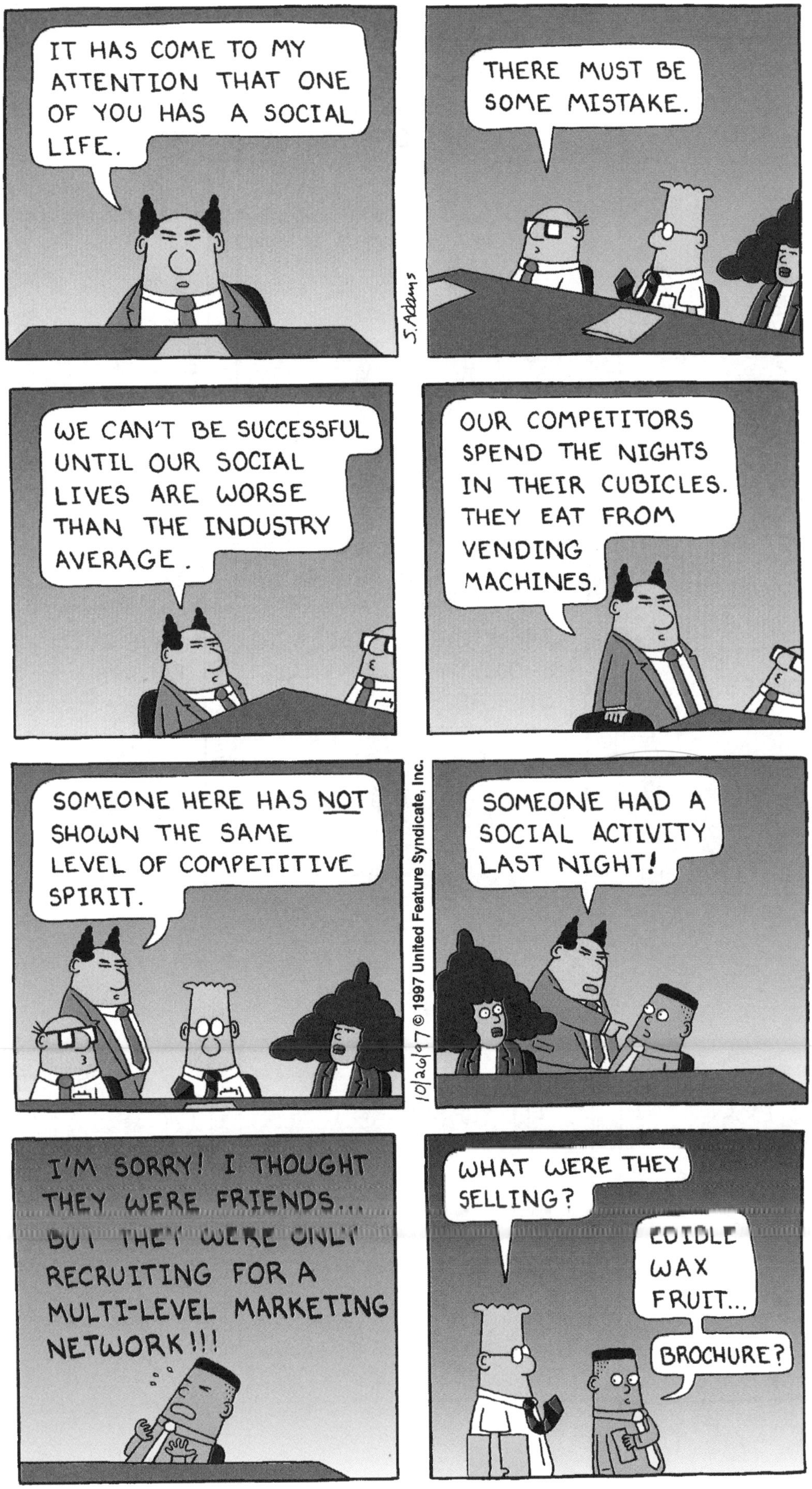
IT HAS COME TO MY ATTENTION THAT ONE OF YOU HAS A SOCIAL LIFE.
S. Adams
THERE MUST BE SOME MISTAKE.
WE CAN'T BE SUCCESSFUL UNTIL OUR SOCIAL LIVES ARE WORSE THAN THE INDUSTRY AVERAGE.
OUR COMPETITORS SPEND THE NIGHTS IN THEIR CUBICLES. THEY EAT FROM VENDING MACHINES.
SOMEONE HERE HAS NOT SHOWN THE SAME LEVEL OF COMPETITIVE SPIRIT.
10/26/97 © 1997 United Feature Syndicate, Inc.
SOMEONE HAD A SOCIAL ACTIVITY LAST NIGHT!
I'M SORRY! I THOUGHT THEY WERE FRIENDS... BUT THEY WERE ONLY RECRUITING FOR A MULTI-LEVEL MARKETING NETWORK!!!
WHAT WERE THEY SELLING?
EDIBLE WAX FRUIT...
BROCHURE?

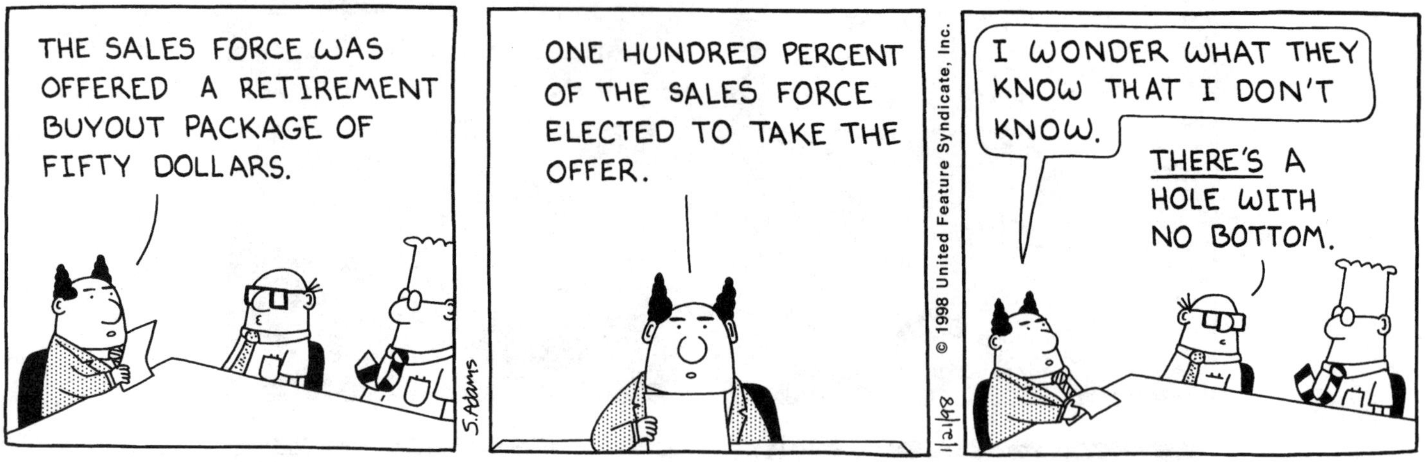
THE SALES FORCE WAS OFFERED A RETIREMENT BUYOUT PACKAGE OF FIFTY DOLLARS.
S. Adams
ONE HUNDRED PERCENT OF THE SALES FORCE ELECTED TO TAKE THE OFFER.
© 1998 United Feature Syndicate, Inc.
1/21/98
I WONDER WHAT THEY KNOW THAT I DON'T KNOW.
THERE'S A HOLE WITH NO BOTTOM.

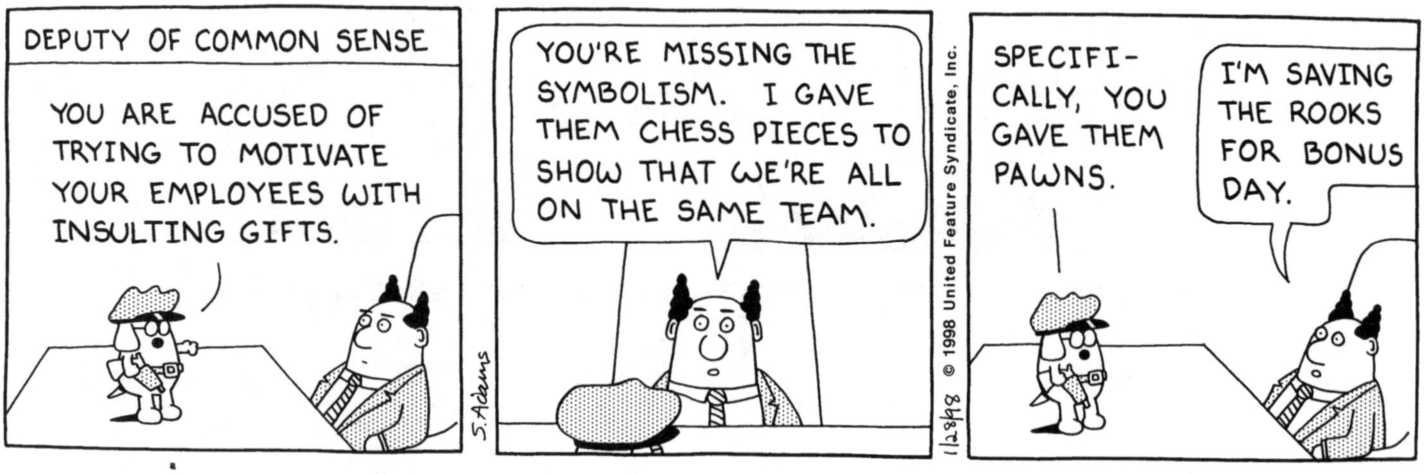
DEPUTY OF COMMON SENSE
YOU ARE ACCUSED OF TRYING TO MOTIVATE YOUR EMPLOYEES WITH INSULTING GIFTS.
S. Adams
YOU'RE MISSING THE SYMBOLISM. I GAVE THEM CHESS PIECES TO SHOW THAT WE'RE ALL ON THE SAME TEAM.
© 1998 United Feature Syndicate, Inc.
1/28/98
SPECIFI- CALLY, YOU GAVE THEM PAWNS.
I'M SAVING THE ROOKS FOR BONUS DAY.

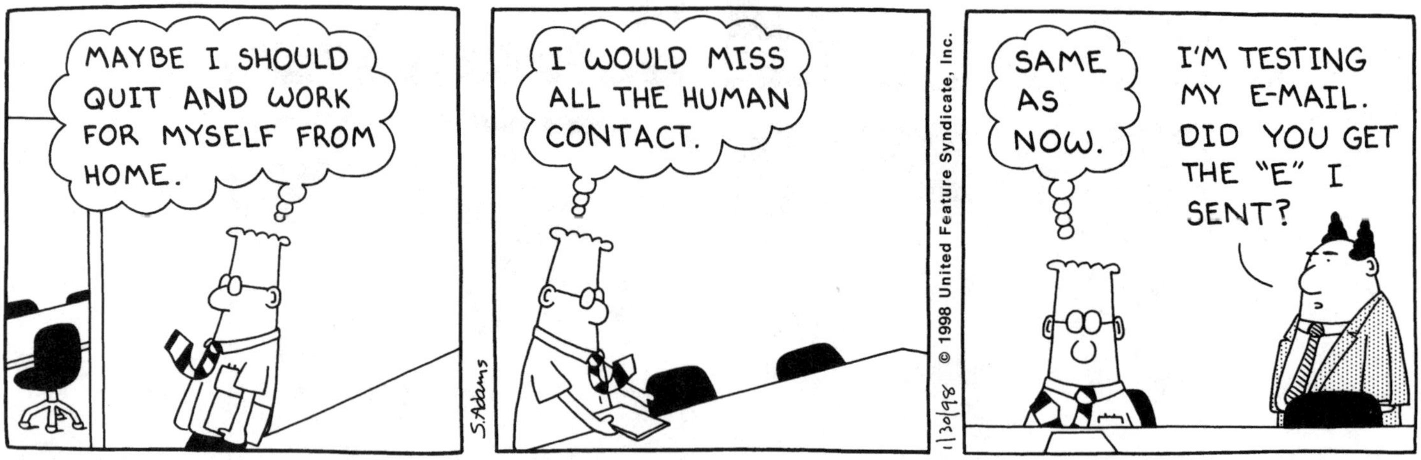
MAYBE I SHOULD QUIT AND WORK FOR MYSELF FROM HOME.
S. Adams
I WOULD MISS ALL THE HUMAN CONTACT.
© 1998 United Feature Syndicate, Inc.
1/30/98
SAME AS NOW.
I'M TESTING MY E-MAIL. DID YOU GET THE "E" I SENT?

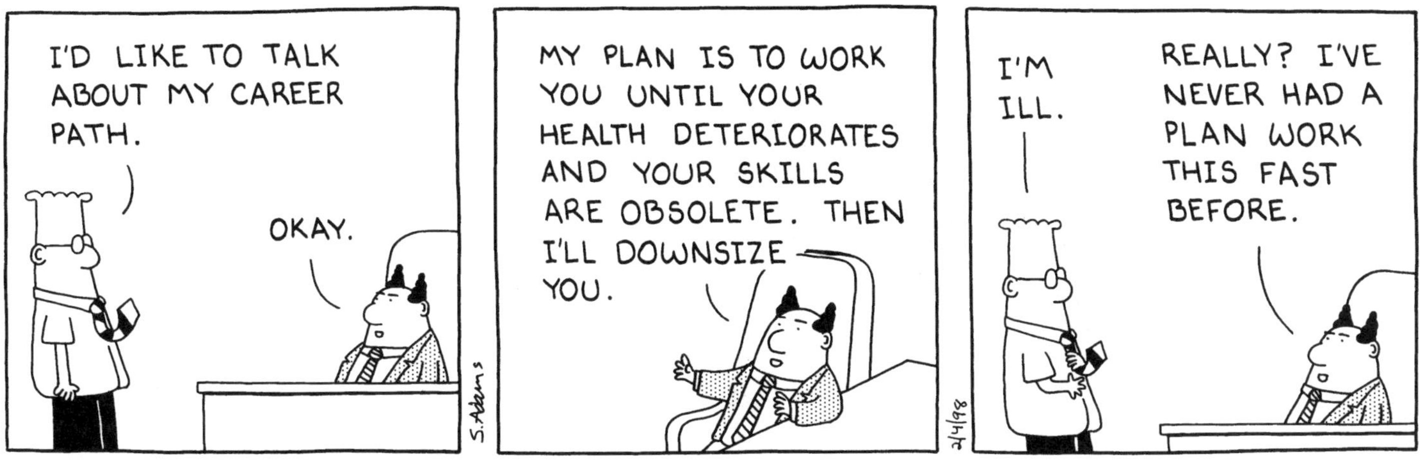
I'D LIKE TO TALK ABOUT MY CAREER PATH.
OKAY.
MY PLAN IS TO WORK YOU UNTIL YOUR HEALTH DETERIORATES AND YOUR SKILLS ARE OBSOLETE. THEN I'LL DOWNSIZE YOU.
I'M ILL.
REALLY? I'VE NEVER HAD A PLAN WORK THIS FAST BEFORE.
S. Adams
2/4/98

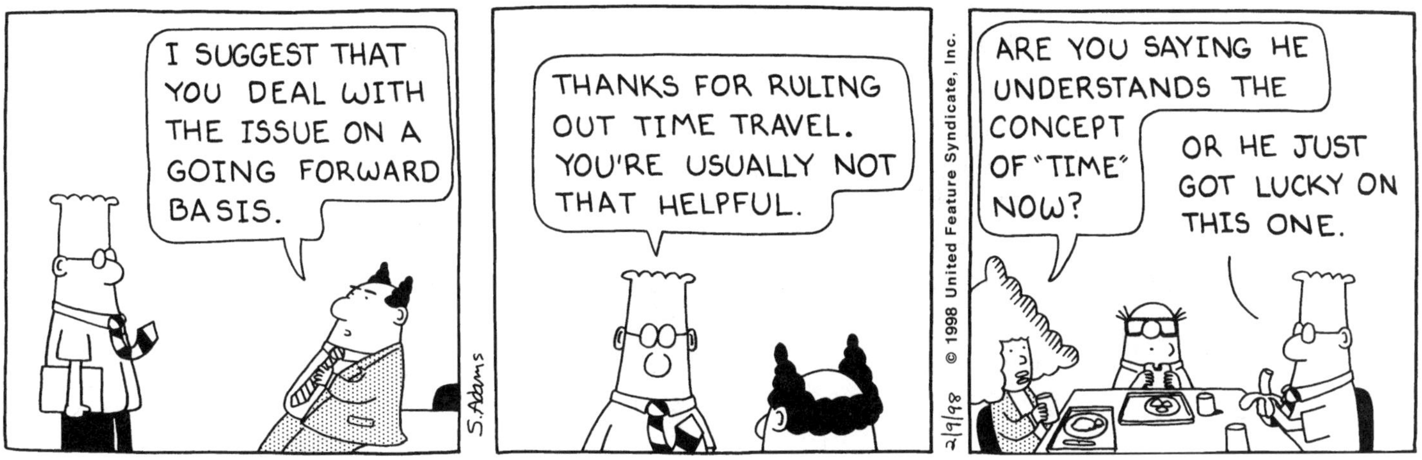
I SUGGEST THAT YOU DEAL WITH THE ISSUE ON A GOING FORWARD BASIS.
THANKS FOR RULING OUT TIME TRAVEL. YOU'RE USUALLY NOT THAT HELPFUL.
ARE YOU SAYING HE UNDERSTANDS THE CONCEPT OF "TIME" NOW?
OR HE JUST GOT LUCKY ON THIS ONE.
S. Adams
2/9/98
© 1998 United Feature Syndicate, Inc.

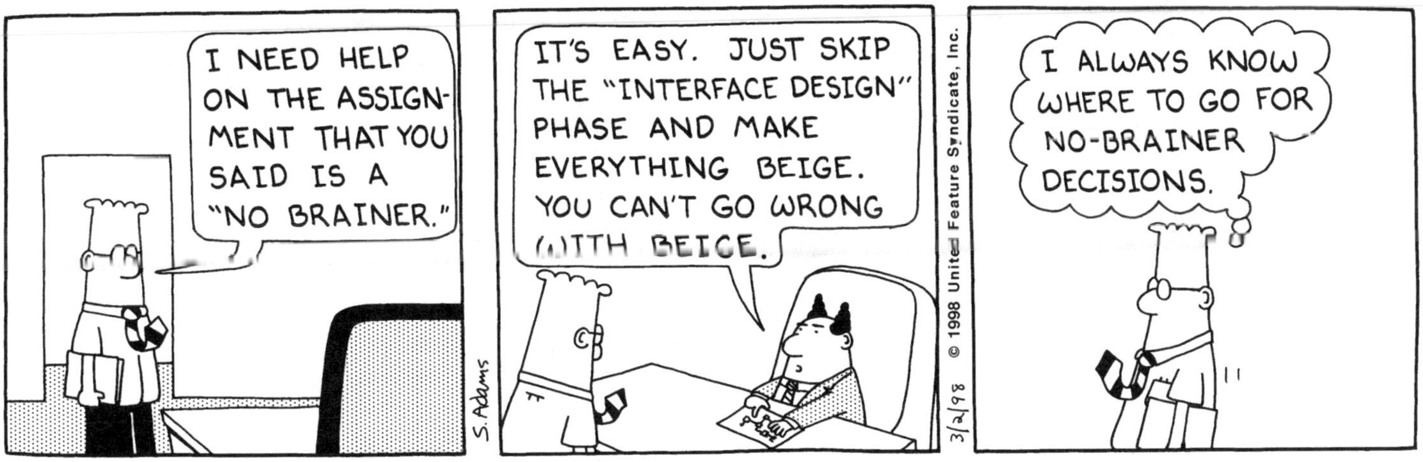
I NEED HELP ON THE ASSIGNMENT THAT YOU SAID IS A "NO BRAINER."
IT'S EASY. JUST SKIP THE "INTERFACE DESIGN" PHASE AND MAKE EVERYTHING BEIGE. YOU CAN'T GO WRONG WITH BEIGE.
I ALWAYS KNOW WHERE TO GO FOR NO-BRAINER DECISIONS.
S. Adams
3/2/98
© 1998 United Feature Syndicate, Inc.

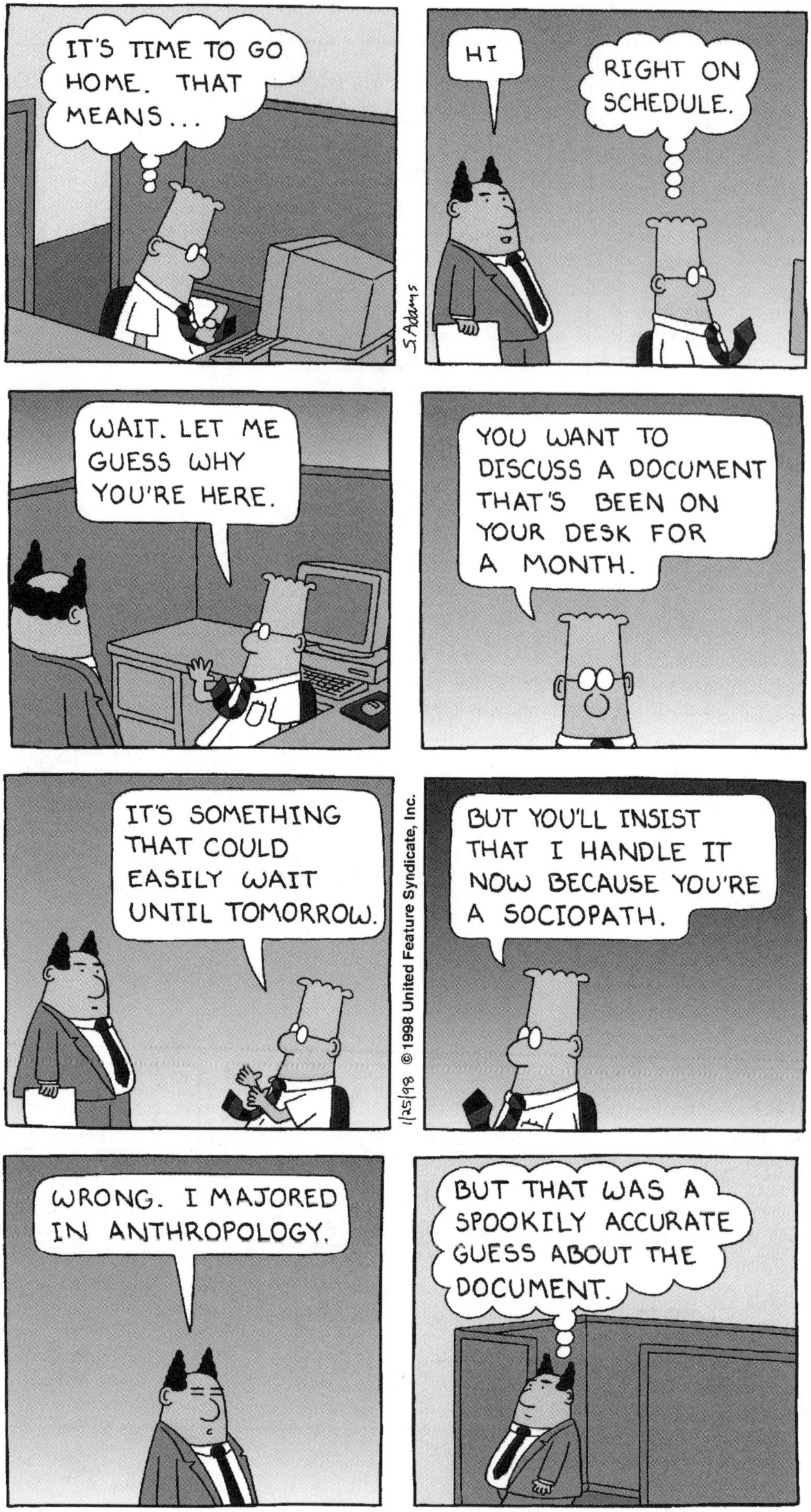
IT'S TIME TO GO HOME. THAT MEANS...
HI
RIGHT ON SCHEDULE.
WAIT. LET ME GUESS WHY YOU'RE HERE.
YOU WANT TO DISCUSS A DOCUMENT THAT'S BEEN ON YOUR DESK FOR A MONTH.
IT'S SOMETHING THAT COULD EASILY WAIT UNTIL TOMORROW.
BUT YOU'LL INSIST THAT I HANDLE IT NOW BECAUSE YOU'RE A SOCIOPATH.
WRONG. I MAJORED IN ANTHROPOLOGY.
BUT THAT WAS A SPOOKILY ACCURATE GUESS ABOUT THE DOCUMENT.
S. Adams
1/25/98 © 1998 United Feature Syndicate, Inc.

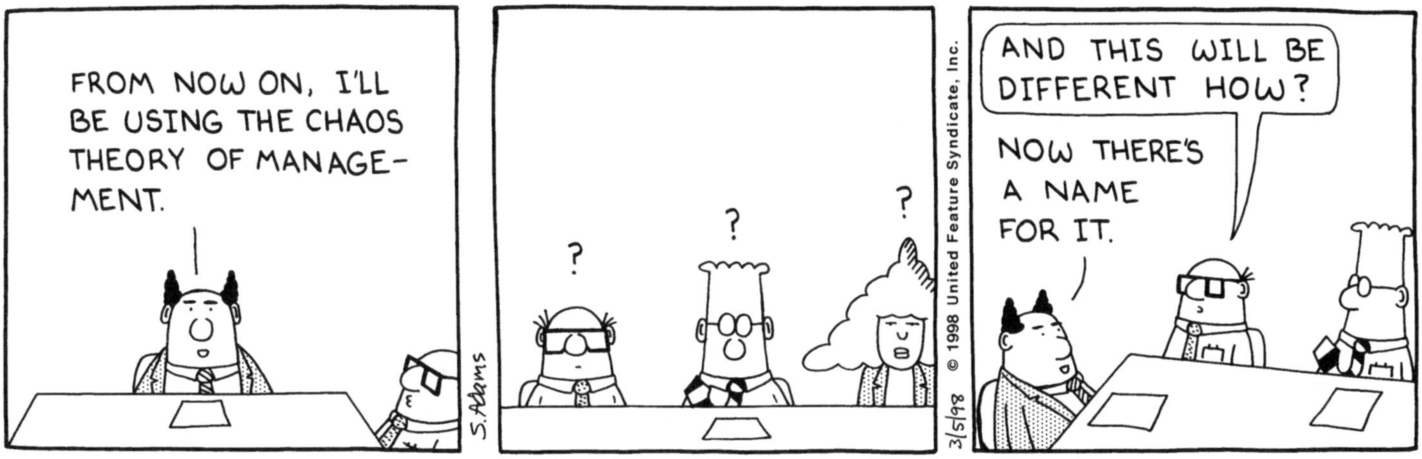
FROM NOW ON, I'LL BE USING THE CHAOS THEORY OF MANAGE-MENT.
?
?
?
AND THIS WILL BE DIFFERENT HOW?
NOW THERE'S A NAME FOR IT.
S. Adams
3/5/98
© 1998 United Feature Syndicate, Inc.

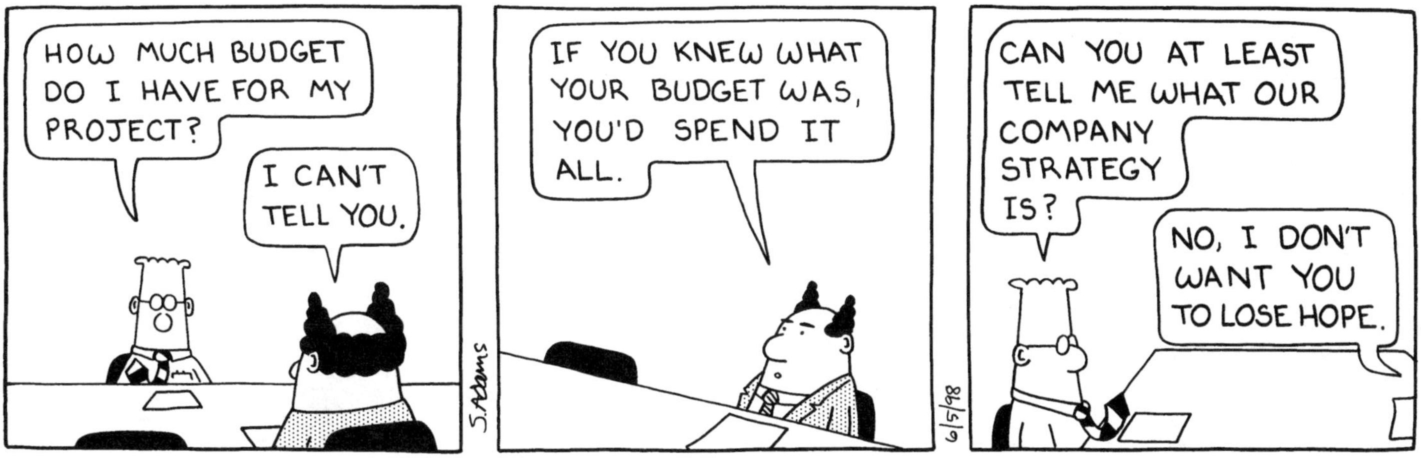
HOW MUCH BUDGET DO I HAVE FOR MY PROJECT?
I CAN'T TELL YOU.
IF YOU KNEW WHAT YOUR BUDGET WAS, YOU'D SPEND IT ALL.
CAN YOU AT LEAST TELL ME WHAT OUR COMPANY STRATEGY IS?
NO, I DON'T WANT YOU TO LOSE HOPE.
S. Adams
6/5/98

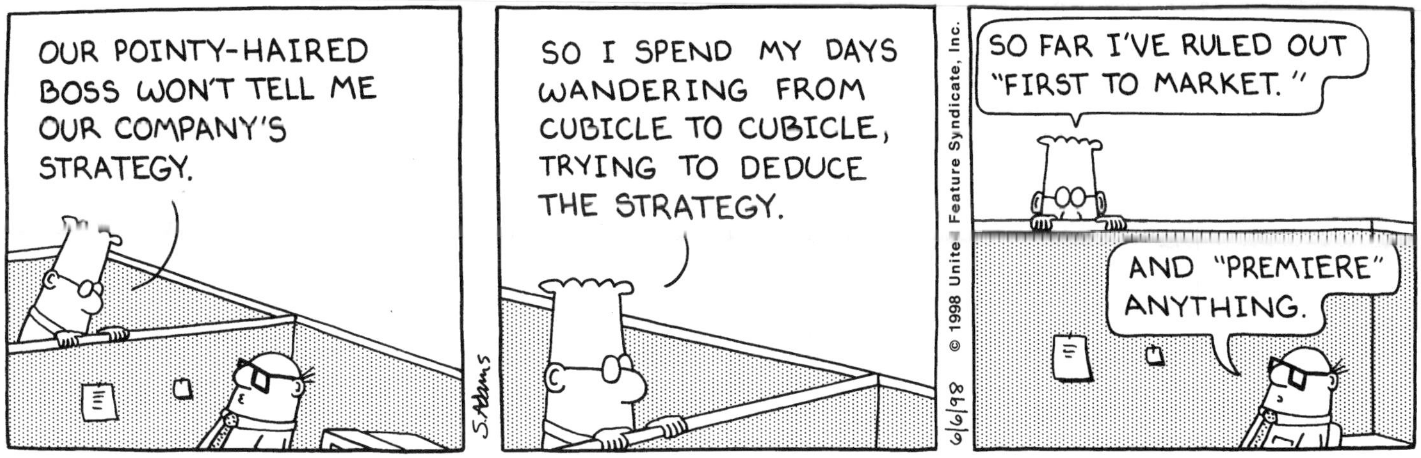
OUR POINTY-HAIRED BOSS WON'T TELL ME OUR COMPANY'S STRATEGY.
SO I SPEND MY DAYS WANDERING FROM CUBICLE TO CUBICLE, TRYING TO DEDUCE THE STRATEGY.
SO FAR I'VE RULED OUT "FIRST TO MARKET."
AND "PREMIERE" ANYTHING.
S. Adams
6/6/98
© 1998 United Feature Syndicate, Inc.

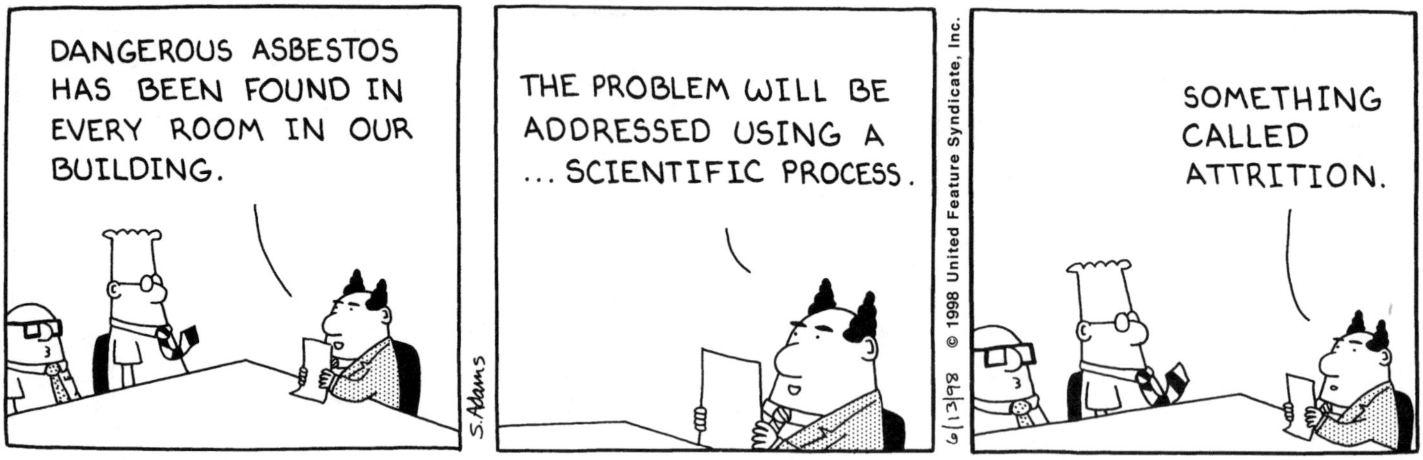
DANGEROUS ASBESTOS HAS BEEN FOUND IN EVERY ROOM IN OUR BUILDING.
S. Adams
THE PROBLEM WILL BE ADDRESSED USING A ... SCIENTIFIC PROCESS.
6/13/98 © 1998 United Feature Syndicate, Inc.
SOMETHING CALLED ATTRITION.

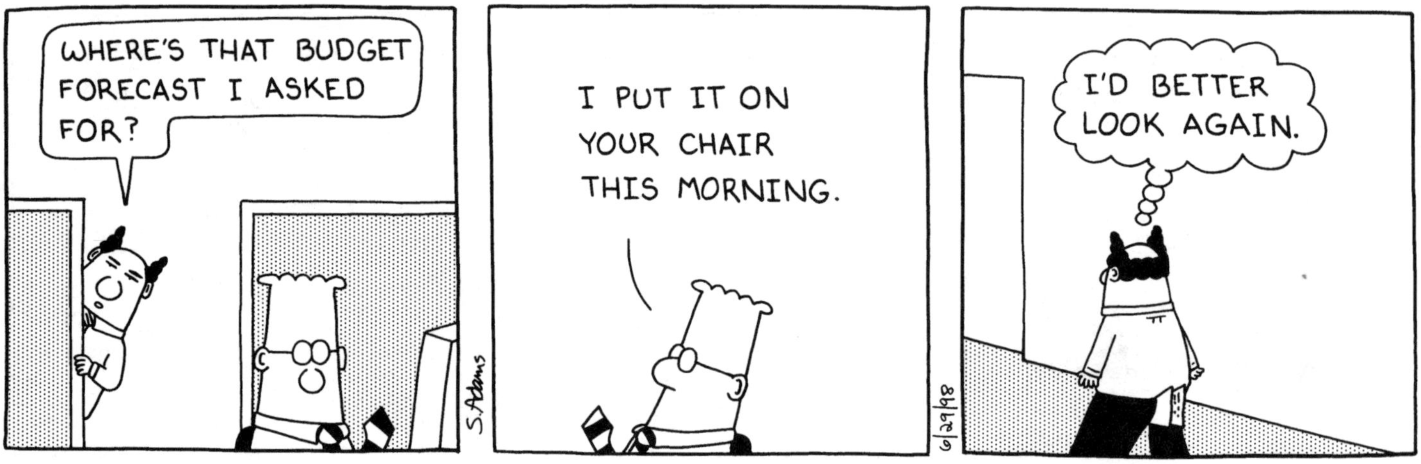
WHERE'S THAT BUDGET FORECAST I ASKED FOR?
S. Adams
I PUT IT ON YOUR CHAIR THIS MORNING.
6/29/98
I'D BETTER LOOK AGAIN.

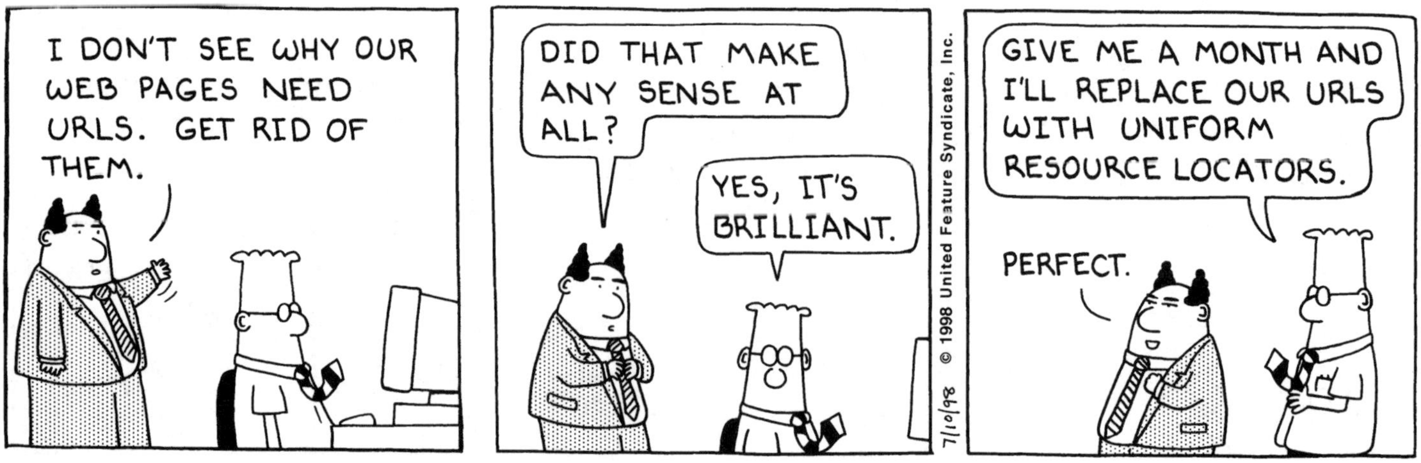
I DON'T SEE WHY OUR WEB PAGES NEED URLS. GET RID OF THEM.
DID THAT MAKE ANY SENSE AT ALL?
YES, IT'S BRILLIANT.
7/10/98 © 1998 United Feature Syndicate, Inc.
GIVE ME A MONTH AND I'LL REPLACE OUR URLS WITH UNIFORM RESOURCE LOCATORS.
PERFECT.

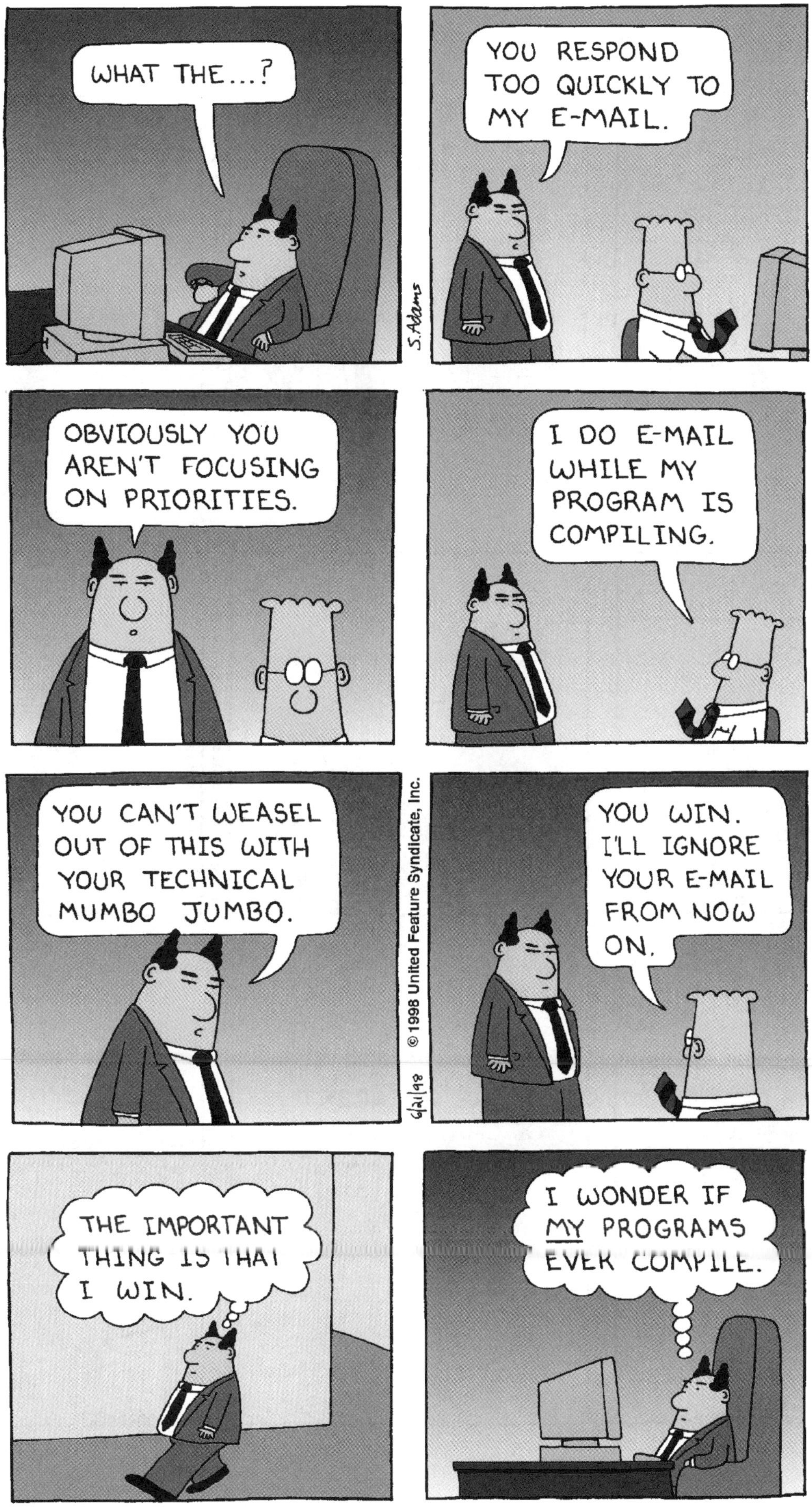
WHAT THE...?
S. Adams
YOU RESPOND TOO QUICKLY TO MY E-MAIL.
OBVIOUSLY YOU AREN'T FOCUSING ON PRIORITIES.
I DO E-MAIL WHILE MY PROGRAM IS COMPILING.
YOU CAN'T WEASEL OUT OF THIS WITH YOUR TECHNICAL MUMBO JUMBO.
© 1998 United Feature Syndicate, Inc.
6/21/98
YOU WIN. I'LL IGNORE YOUR E-MAIL FROM NOW ON.
THE IMPORTANT THING IS THAT I WIN.
I WONDER IF MY PROGRAMS EVER COMPILE.

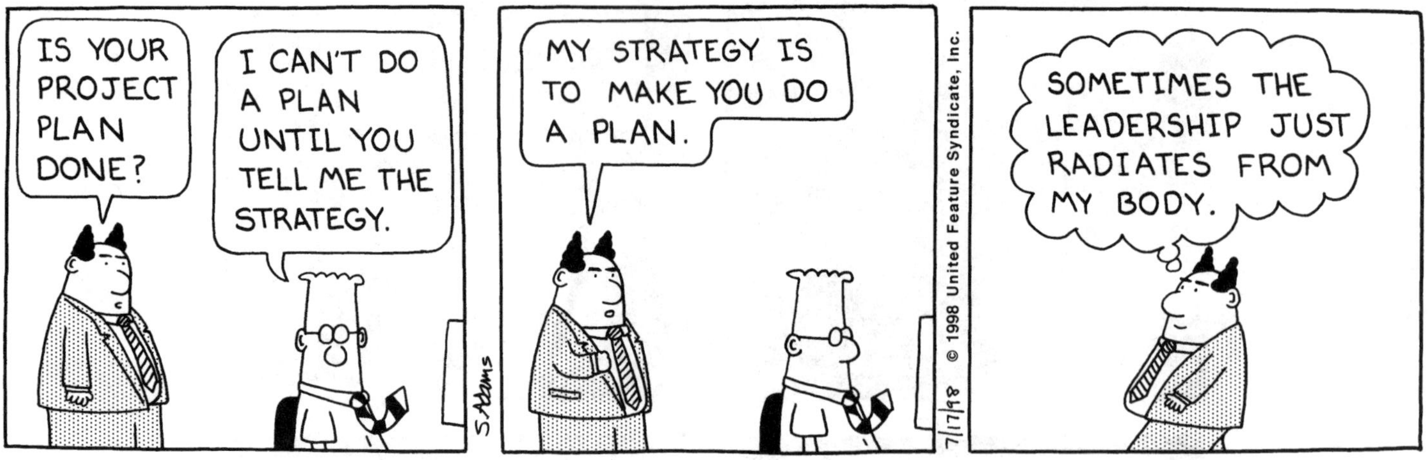
IS YOUR PROJECT PLAN DONE?
I CAN'T DO A PLAN UNTIL YOU TELL ME THE STRATEGY.
MY STRATEGY IS TO MAKE YOU DO A PLAN.
SOMETIMES THE LEADERSHIP JUST RADIATES FROM MY BODY.
S. Adams
7/17/98 © 1998 United Feature Syndicate, Inc.

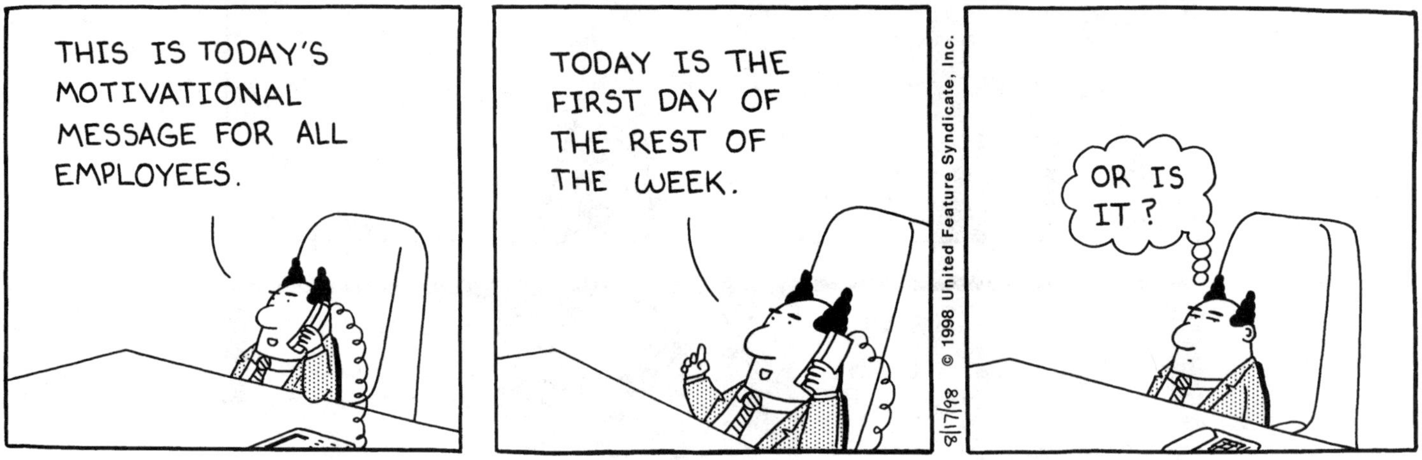
THIS IS TODAY'S MOTIVATIONAL MESSAGE FOR ALL EMPLOYEES.
TODAY IS THE FIRST DAY OF THE REST OF THE WEEK.
OR IS IT?
8/17/98 © 1998 United Feature Syndicate, Inc.

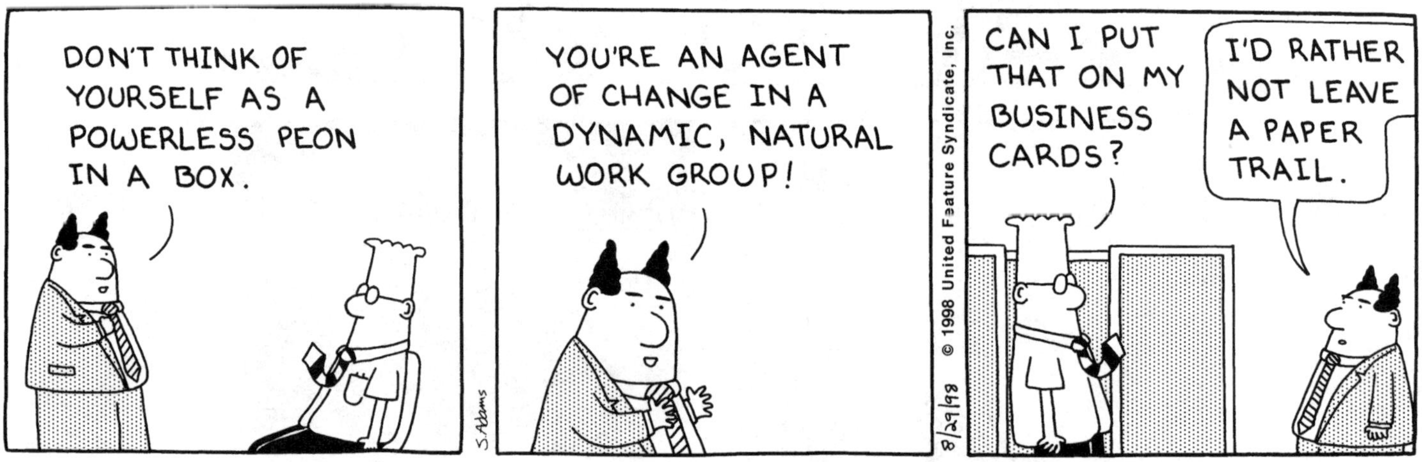
DON'T THINK OF YOURSELF AS A POWERLESS PEON IN A BOX.
YOU'RE AN AGENT OF CHANGE IN A DYNAMIC, NATURAL WORK GROUP!
CAN I PUT THAT ON MY BUSINESS CARDS?
I'D RATHER NOT LEAVE A PAPER TRAIL.
S. Adams
8/29/98 © 1998 United Feature Syndicate, Inc.

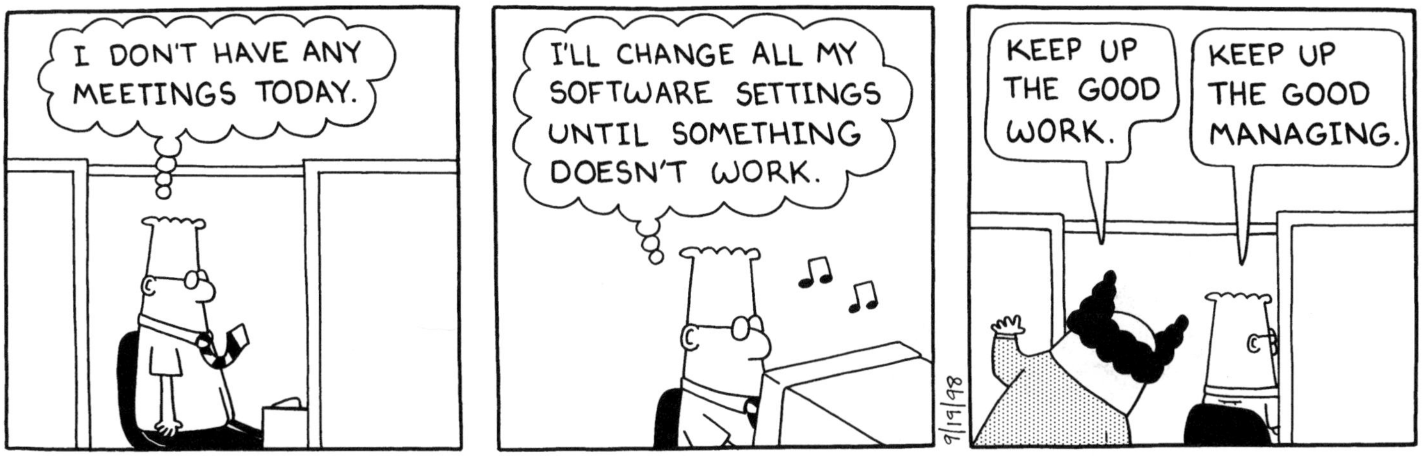
I DON'T HAVE ANY MEETINGS TODAY.
I'LL CHANGE ALL MY SOFTWARE SETTINGS UNTIL SOMETHING DOESN'T WORK.
9/19/98
KEEP UP THE GOOD WORK.
KEEP UP THE GOOD MANAGING.

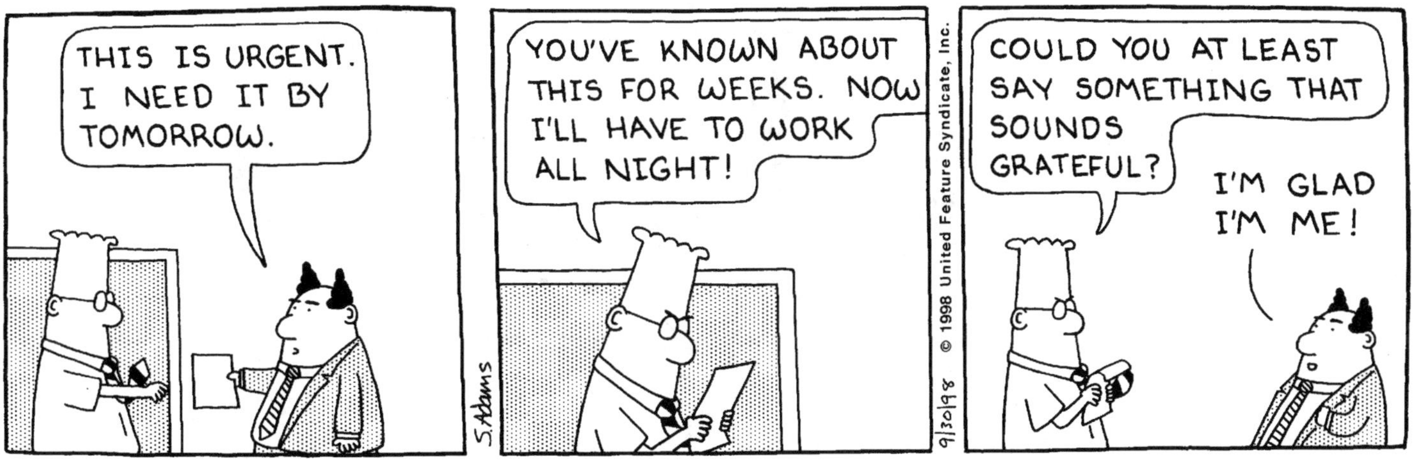
THIS IS URGENT. I NEED IT BY TOMORROW.
S.Adams
YOU'VE KNOWN ABOUT THIS FOR WEEKS. NOW I'LL HAVE TO WORK ALL NIGHT!
9/30/98 © 1998 United Feature Syndicate, Inc.
COULD YOU AT LEAST SAY SOMETHING THAT SOUNDS GRATEFUL?
I'M GLAD I'M ME!

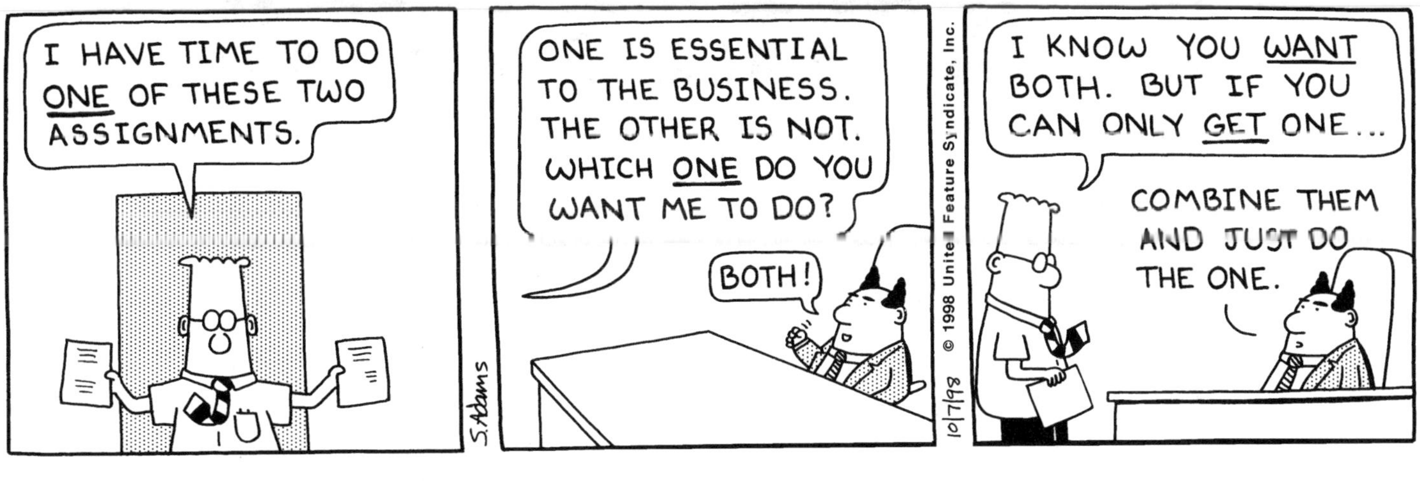
I HAVE TIME TO DO ONE OF THESE TWO ASSIGNMENTS.
S.Adams
ONE IS ESSENTIAL TO THE BUSINESS. THE OTHER IS NOT. WHICH ONE DO YOU WANT ME TO DO?
BOTH!
10/7/98 © 1998 United Feature Syndicate, Inc.
I KNOW YOU WANT BOTH. BUT IF YOU CAN ONLY GET ONE...
COMBINE THEM AND JUST DO THE ONE.

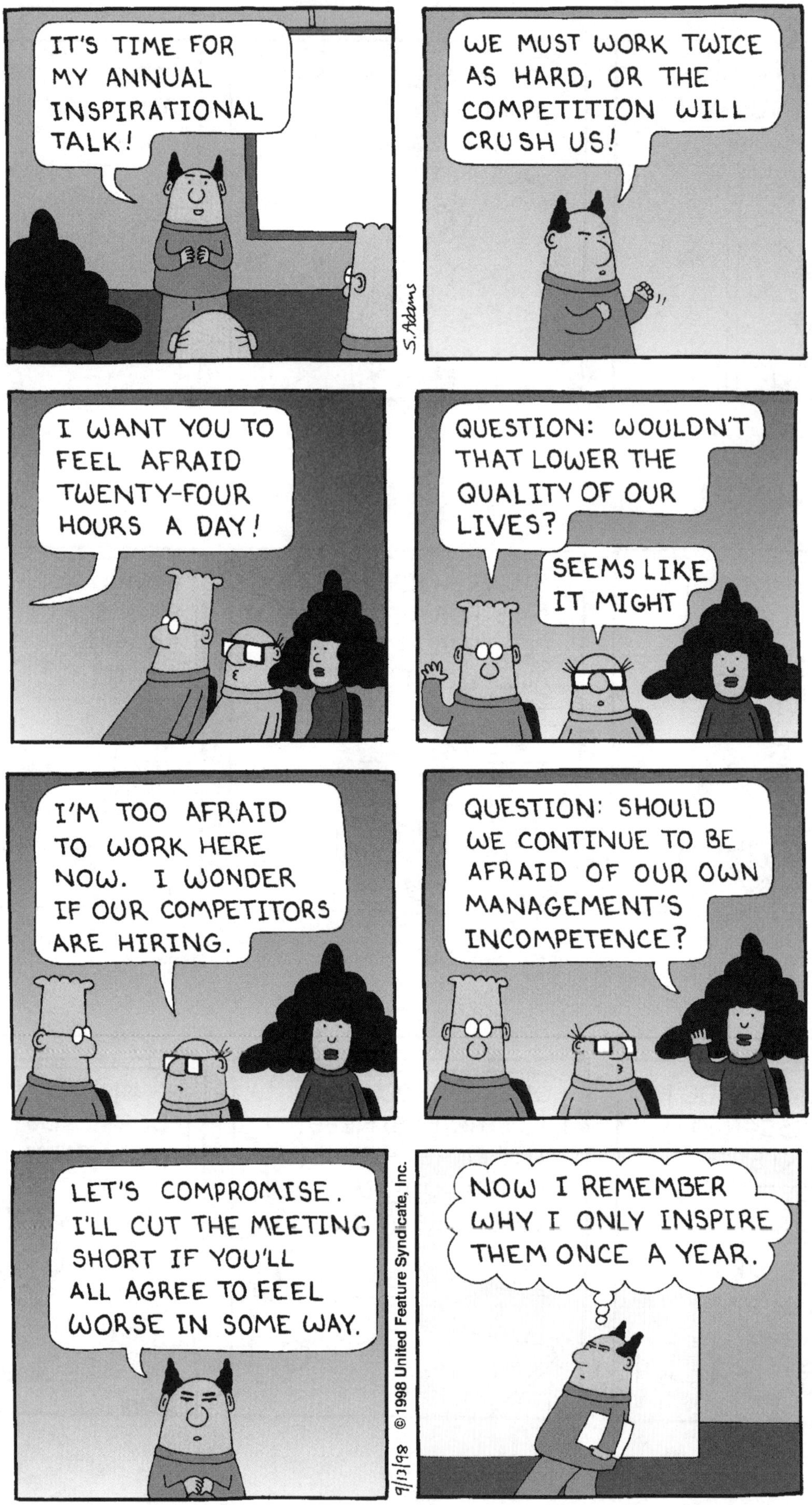
IT'S TIME FOR MY ANNUAL INSPIRATIONAL TALK!
S. Adams
WE MUST WORK TWICE AS HARD, OR THE COMPETITION WILL CRUSH US!
I WANT YOU TO FEEL AFRAID TWENTY-FOUR HOURS A DAY!
QUESTION: WOULDN'T THAT LOWER THE QUALITY OF OUR LIVES?
SEEMS LIKE IT MIGHT
I'M TOO AFRAID TO WORK HERE NOW. I WONDER IF OUR COMPETITORS ARE HIRING.
QUESTION: SHOULD WE CONTINUE TO BE AFRAID OF OUR OWN MANAGEMENT'S INCOMPETENCE?
LET'S COMPROMISE. I'LL CUT THE MEETING SHORT IF YOU'LL ALL AGREE TO FEEL WORSE IN SOME WAY.
9/13/98 © 1998 United Feature Syndicate, Inc.
NOW I REMEMBER WHY I ONLY INSPIRE THEM ONCE A YEAR.

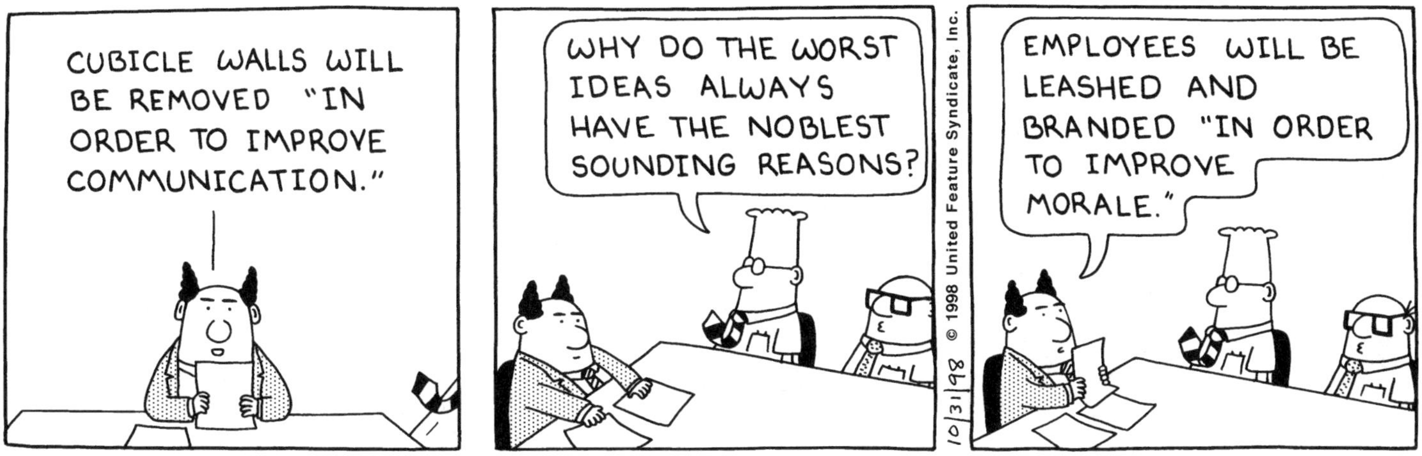
CUBICLE WALLS WILL BE REMOVED "IN ORDER TO IMPROVE COMMUNICATION."
WHY DO THE WORST IDEAS ALWAYS HAVE THE NOBLEST SOUNDING REASONS?
10/31/98 © 1998 United Feature Syndicate, Inc.
EMPLOYEES WILL BE LEASHED AND BRANDED "IN ORDER TO IMPROVE MORALE."

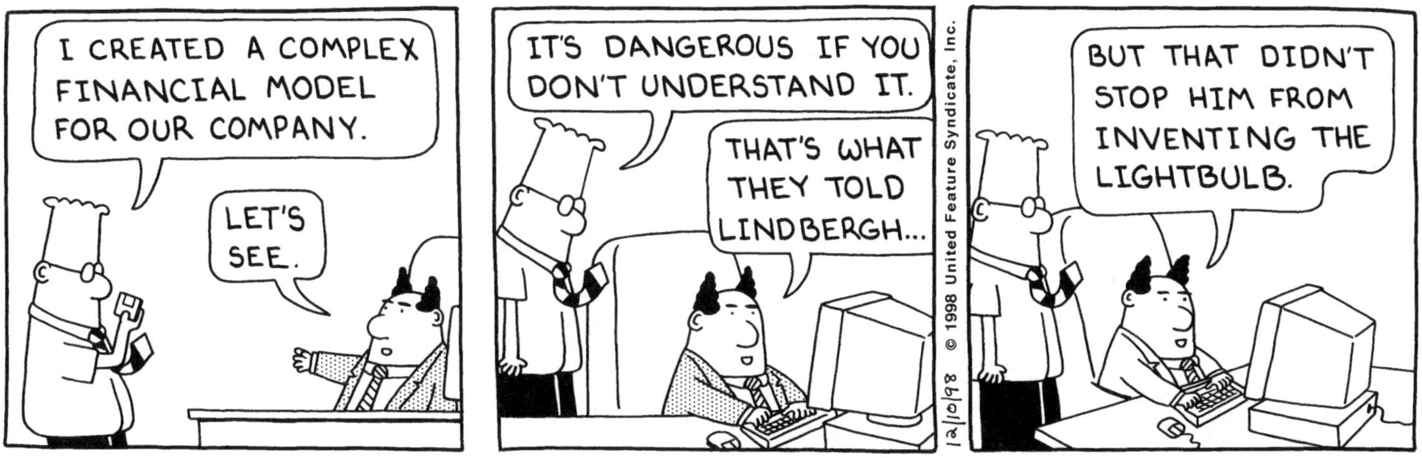
I CREATED A COMPLEX FINANCIAL MODEL FOR OUR COMPANY.
LET'S SEE.
IT'S DANGEROUS IF YOU DON'T UNDERSTAND IT.
THAT'S WHAT THEY TOLD LINDBERGH...
12/10/98 © 1998 United Feature Syndicate, Inc.
BUT THAT DIDN'T STOP HIM FROM INVENTING THE LIGHTBULB.

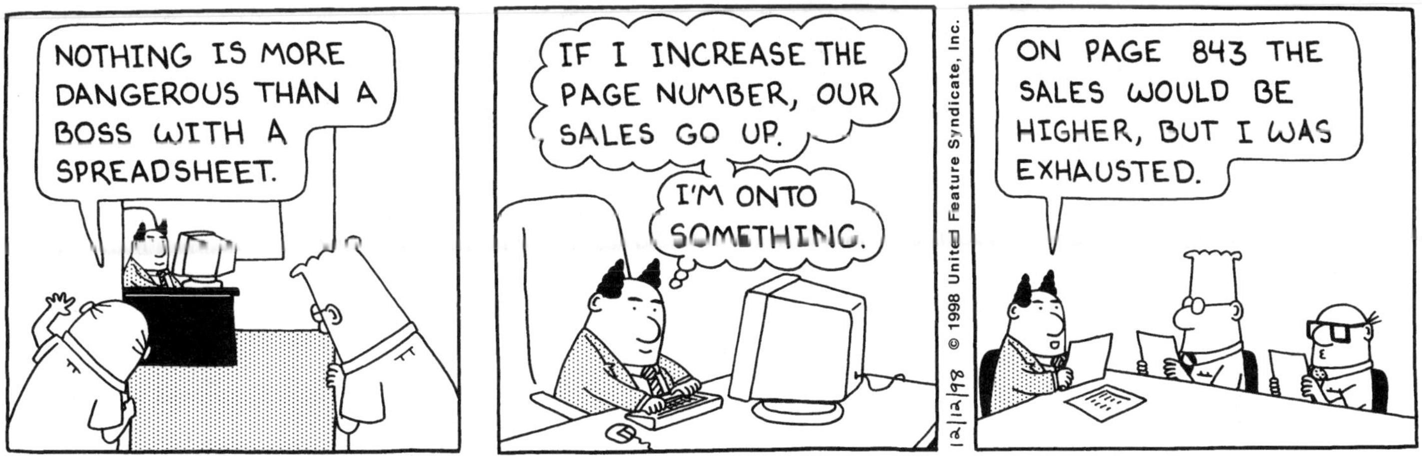
NOTHING IS MORE DANGEROUS THAN A BOSS WITH A SPREADSHEET.
IF I INCREASE THE PAGE NUMBER, OUR SALES GO UP.
I'M ONTO SOMETHING.
12/12/98 © 1998 United Feature Syndicate, Inc.
ON PAGE 843 THE SALES WOULD BE HIGHER, BUT I WAS EXHAUSTED.

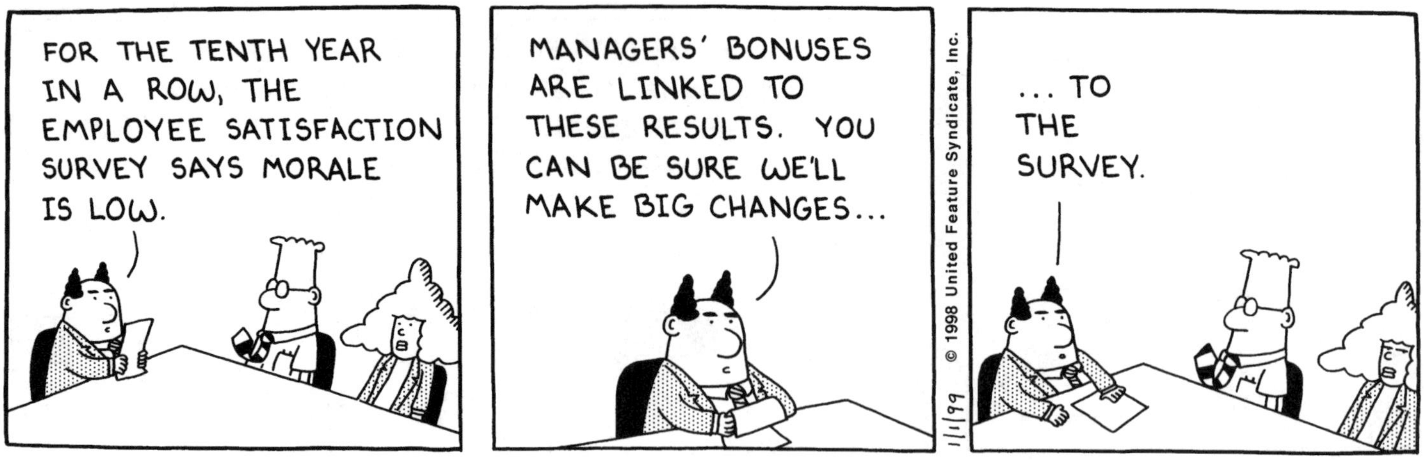
FOR THE TENTH YEAR IN A ROW, THE EMPLOYEE SATISFACTION SURVEY SAYS MORALE IS LOW.
MANAGERS' BONUSES ARE LINKED TO THESE RESULTS. YOU CAN BE SURE WE'LL MAKE BIG CHANGES...
1/1/99 © 1998 United Feature Syndicate, Inc.
... TO THE SURVEY.

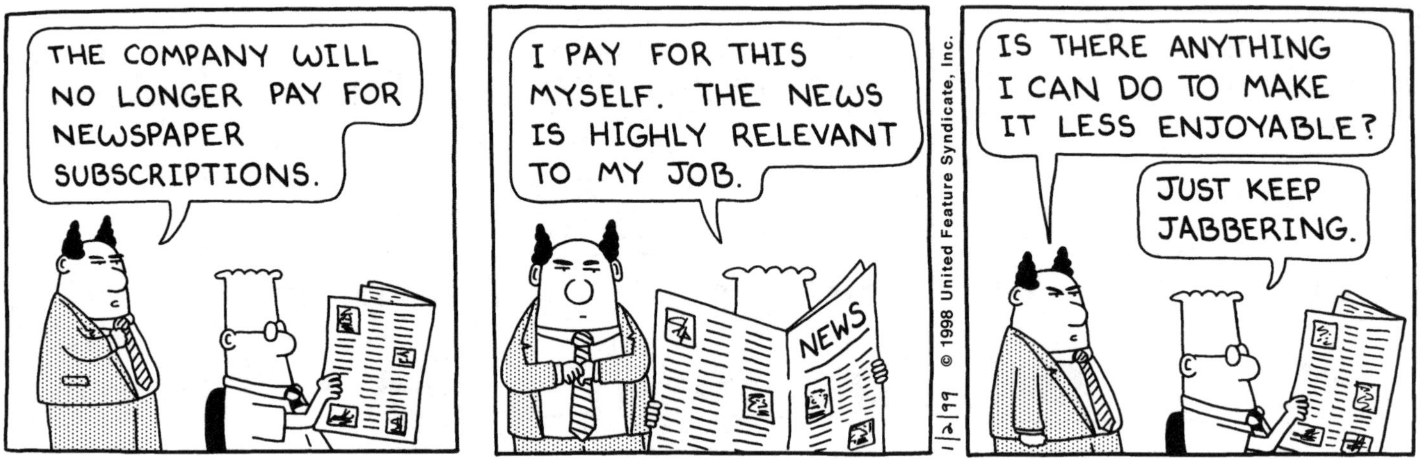
THE COMPANY WILL NO LONGER PAY FOR NEWSPAPER SUBSCRIPTIONS.
I PAY FOR THIS MYSELF. THE NEWS IS HIGHLY RELEVANT TO MY JOB.
NEWS
1/2/99 © 1998 United Feature Syndicate, Inc.
IS THERE ANYTHING I CAN DO TO MAKE IT LESS ENJOYABLE?
JUST KEEP JABBERING.

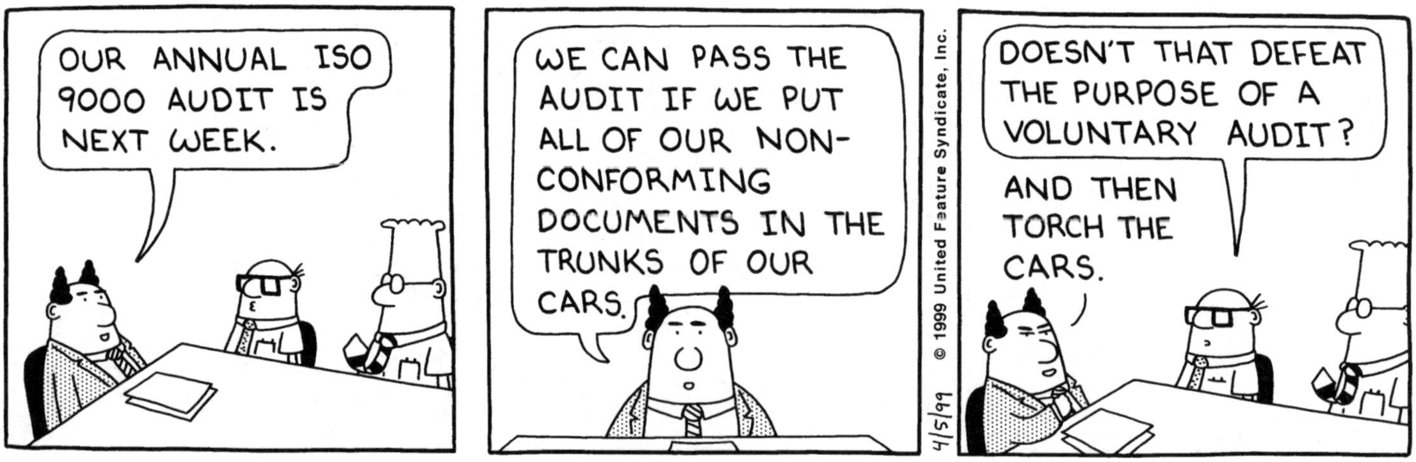
OUR ANNUAL ISO 9000 AUDIT IS NEXT WEEK.
WE CAN PASS THE AUDIT IF WE PUT ALL OF OUR NON-CONFORMING DOCUMENTS IN THE TRUNKS OF OUR CARS.
4/5/99 © 1999 United Feature Syndicate, Inc.
DOESN'T THAT DEFEAT THE PURPOSE OF A VOLUNTARY AUDIT?
AND THEN TORCH THE CARS.

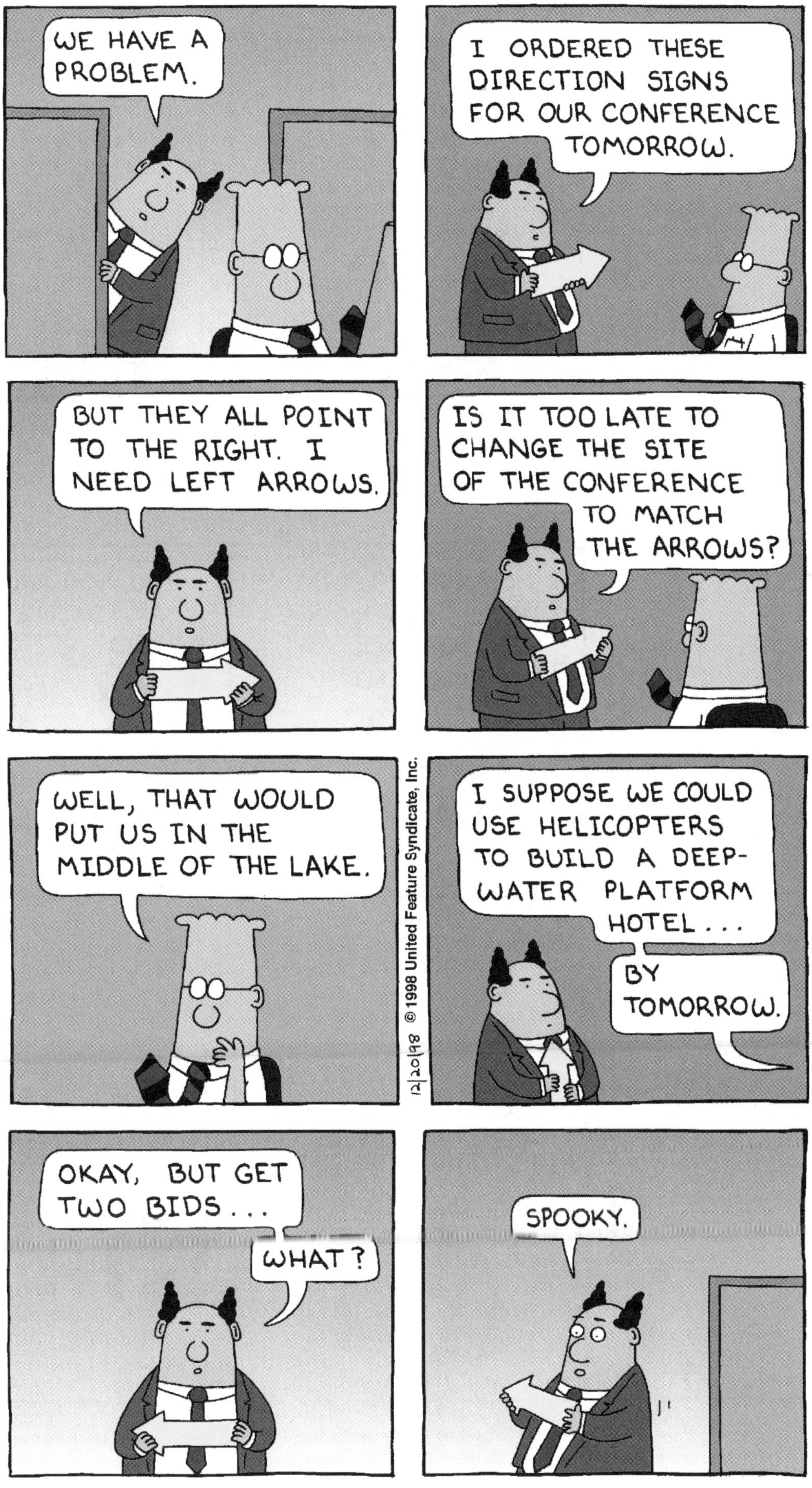
WE HAVE A PROBLEM.
I ORDERED THESE DIRECTION SIGNS FOR OUR CONFERENCE TOMORROW.
BUT THEY ALL POINT TO THE RIGHT. I NEED LEFT ARROWS.
IS IT TOO LATE TO CHANGE THE SITE OF THE CONFERENCE TO MATCH THE ARROWS?
WELL, THAT WOULD PUT US IN THE MIDDLE OF THE LAKE.
I SUPPOSE WE COULD USE HELICOPTERS TO BUILD A DEEP-WATER PLATFORM HOTEL . . .
BY TOMORROW.
OKAY, BUT GET TWO BIDS . . .
WHAT?
SPOOKY.
12/20/98 © 1998 United Feature Syndicate, Inc.

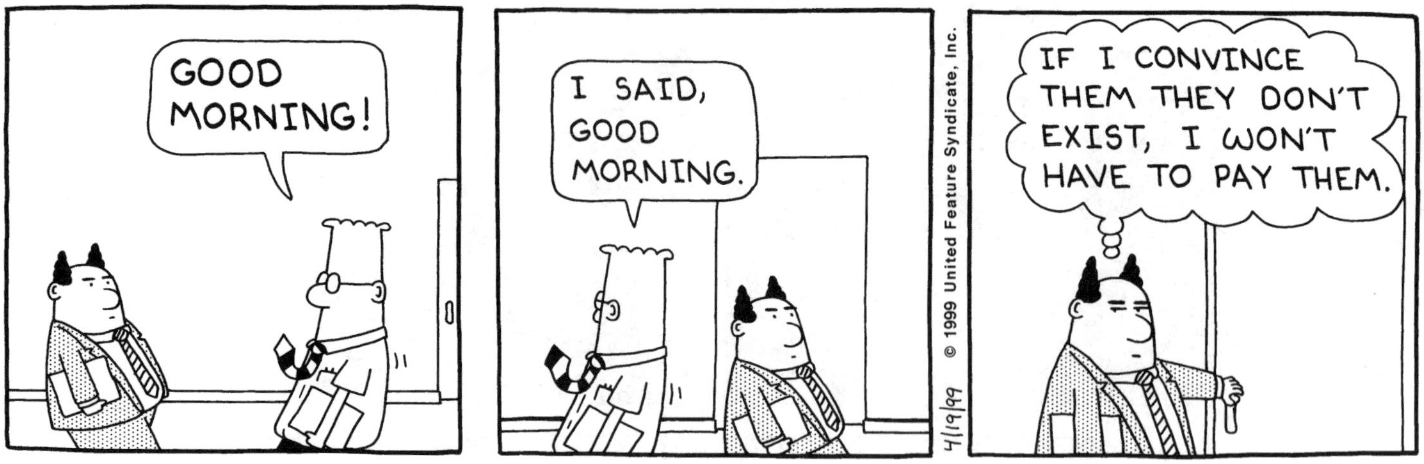
GOOD MORNING!
I SAID, GOOD MORNING.
4/19/99 © 1999 United Feature Syndicate, Inc.
IF I CONVINCE THEM THEY DON'T EXIST, I WON'T HAVE TO PAY THEM.

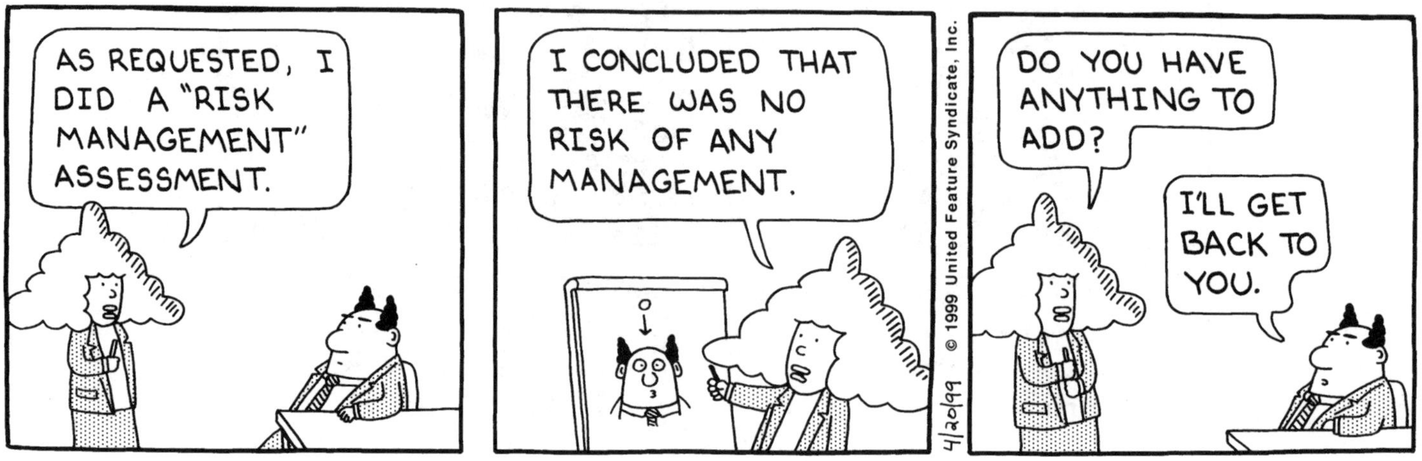
AS REQUESTED, I DID A "RISK MANAGEMENT" ASSESSMENT.
I CONCLUDED THAT THERE WAS NO RISK OF ANY MANAGEMENT.
4/20/99 © 1999 United Feature Syndicate, Inc.
DO YOU HAVE ANYTHING TO ADD?
I'LL GET BACK TO YOU.

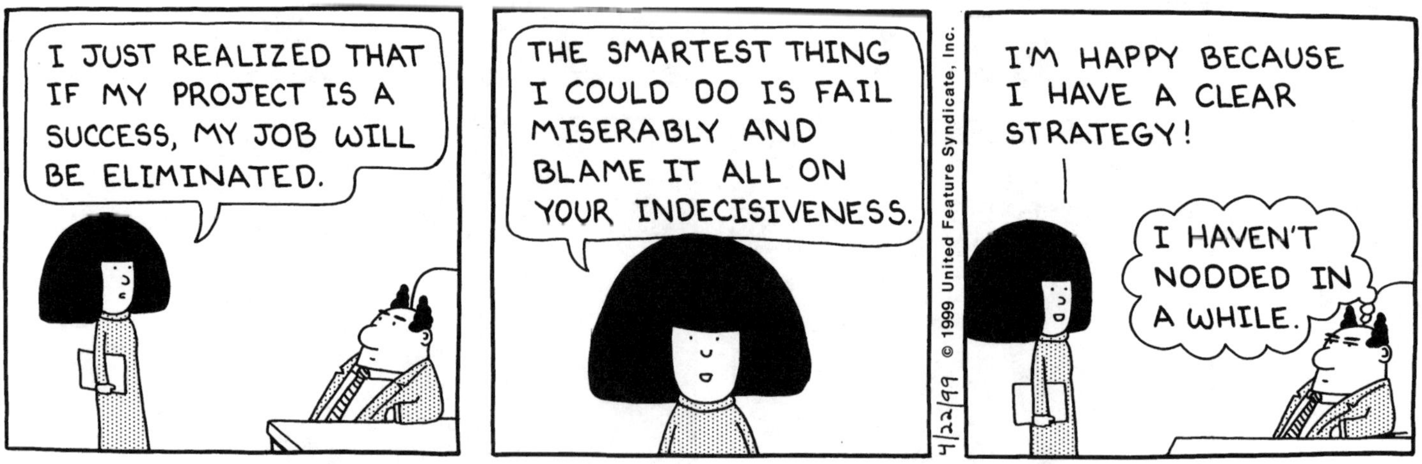
I JUST REALIZED THAT IF MY PROJECT IS A SUCCESS, MY JOB WILL BE ELIMINATED.
THE SMARTEST THING I COULD DO IS FAIL MISERABLY AND BLAME IT ALL ON YOUR INDECISIVENESS.
4/22/99 © 1999 United Feature Syndicate, Inc.
I'M HAPPY BECAUSE I HAVE A CLEAR STRATEGY!
I HAVEN'T NODDED IN A WHILE.

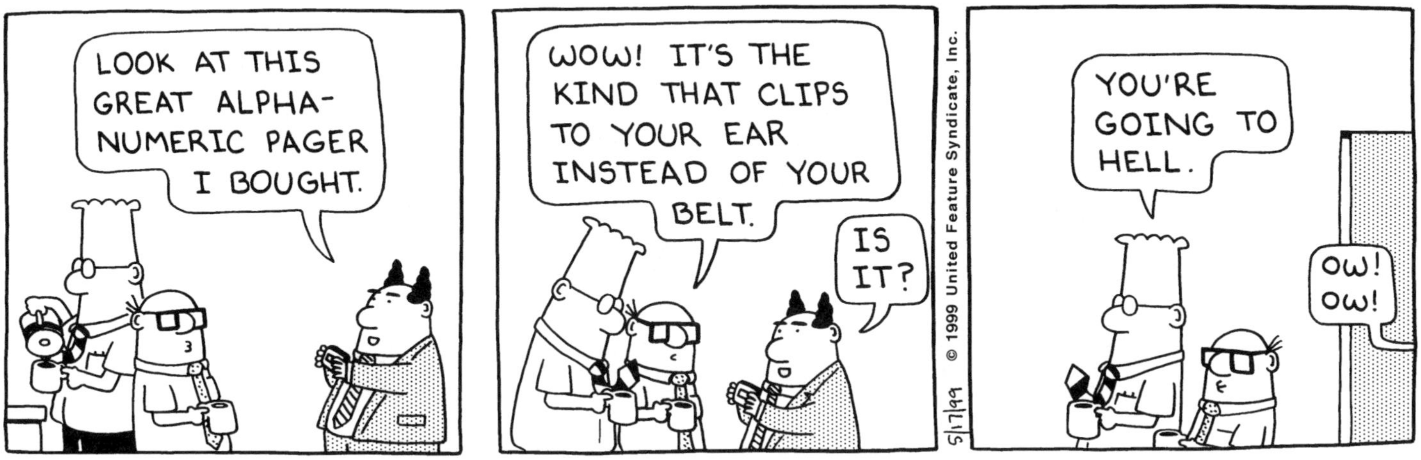
LOOK AT THIS GREAT ALPHA-NUMERIC PAGER I BOUGHT.
WOW! IT'S THE KIND THAT CLIPS TO YOUR EAR INSTEAD OF YOUR BELT.
IS IT?
© 1999 United Feature Syndicate, Inc.
5/17/99
YOU'RE GOING TO HELL.
OW! OW!

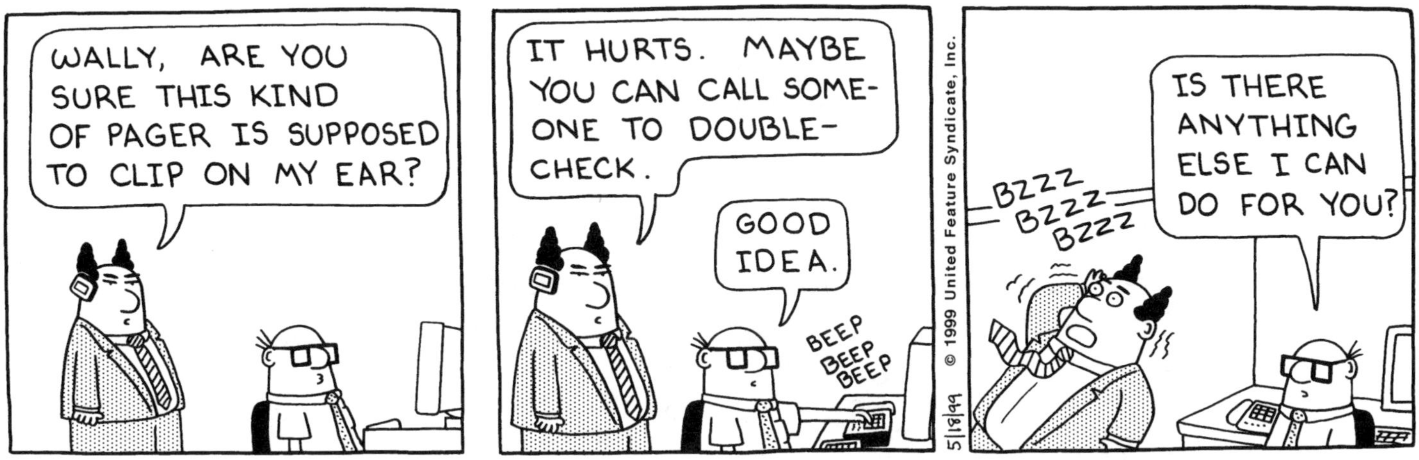
WALLY, ARE YOU SURE THIS KIND OF PAGER IS SUPPOSED TO CLIP ON MY EAR?
IT HURTS. MAYBE YOU CAN CALL SOME-ONE TO DOUBLE-CHECK.
GOOD IDEA.
BEEP BEEP BEEP
© 1999 United Feature Syndicate, Inc.
5/18/99
BZZZ BZZZ BZZZ
IS THERE ANYTHING ELSE I CAN DO FOR YOU?

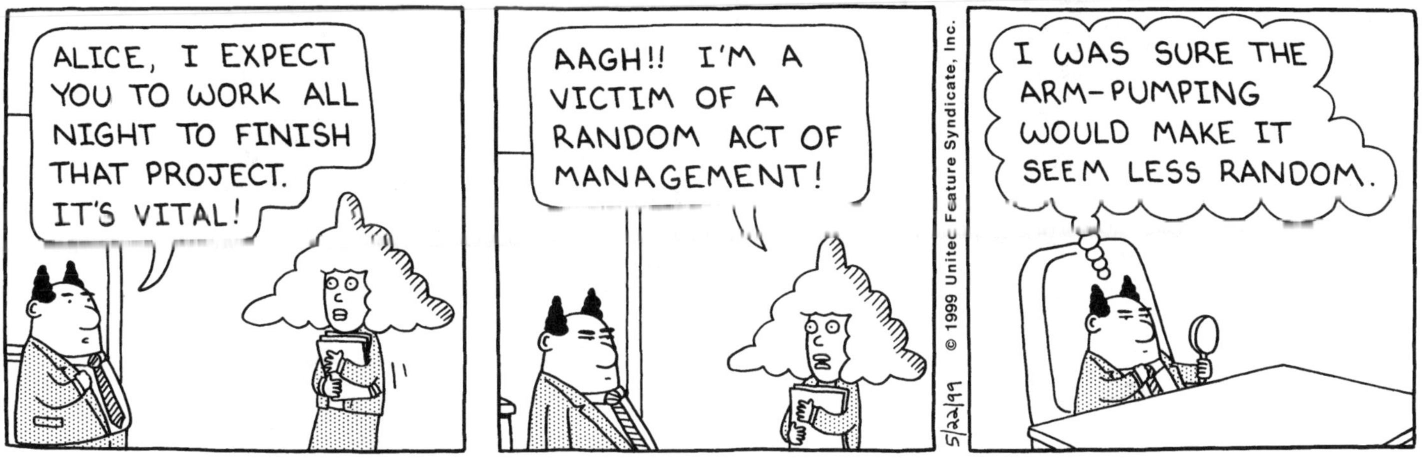
ALICE, I EXPECT YOU TO WORK ALL NIGHT TO FINISH THAT PROJECT. IT'S VITAL!
AAGH!! I'M A VICTIM OF A RANDOM ACT OF MANAGEMENT!
© 1999 United Feature Syndicate, Inc.
5/22/99
I WAS SURE THE ARM-PUMPING WOULD MAKE IT SEEM LESS RANDOM.

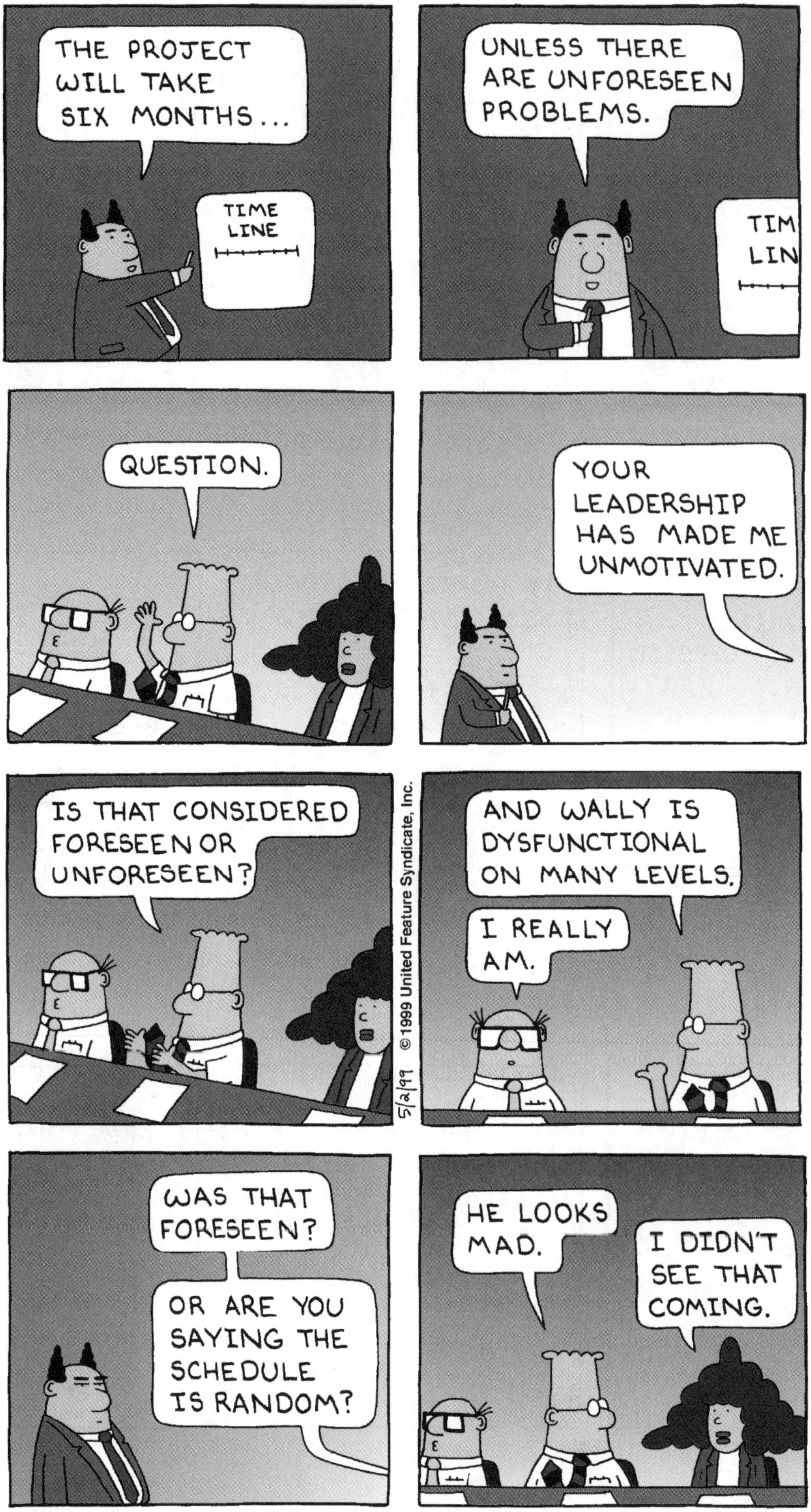
THE PROJECT WILL TAKE SIX MONTHS...
TIME LINE
UNLESS THERE ARE UNFORESEEN PROBLEMS.
QUESTION.
YOUR LEADERSHIP HAS MADE ME UNMOTIVATED.
IS THAT CONSIDERED FORESEEN OR UNFORESEEN?
© 1999 United Feature Syndicate, Inc.
5/2/99
AND WALLY IS DYSFUNCTIONAL ON MANY LEVELS.
I REALLY AM.
WAS THAT FORESEEN?
OR ARE YOU SAYING THE SCHEDULE IS RANDOM?
HE LOOKS MAD.
I DIDN'T SEE THAT COMING.

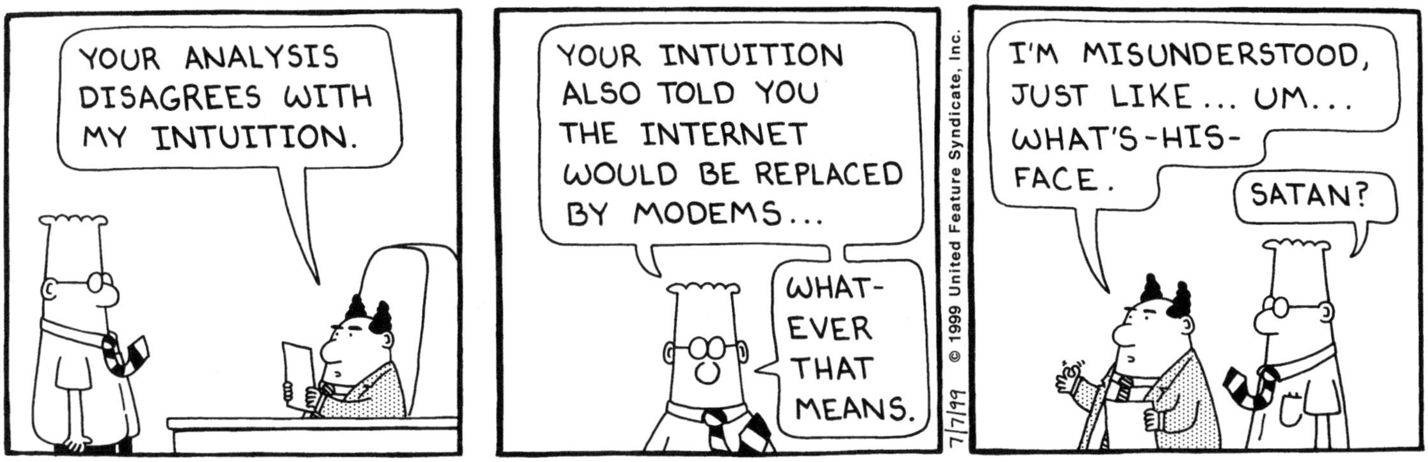
YOUR ANALYSIS DISAGREES WITH MY INTUITION.
YOUR INTUITION ALSO TOLD YOU THE INTERNET WOULD BE REPLACED BY MODEMS...
WHAT-EVER THAT MEANS.
© 1999 United Feature Syndicate, Inc.
7/7/99
I'M MISUNDERSTOOD, JUST LIKE... UM... WHAT'S-HIS-FACE.
SATAN?

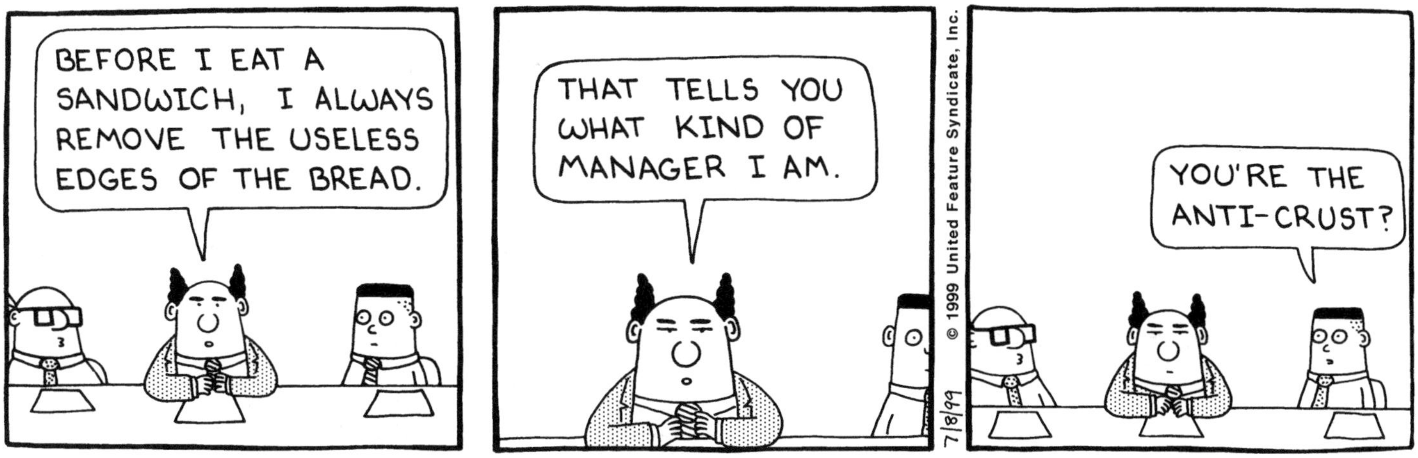
BEFORE I EAT A SANDWICH, I ALWAYS REMOVE THE USELESS EDGES OF THE BREAD.
THAT TELLS YOU WHAT KIND OF MANAGER I AM.
© 1999 United Feature Syndicate, Inc.
7/8/99
YOU'RE THE ANTI-CRUST?

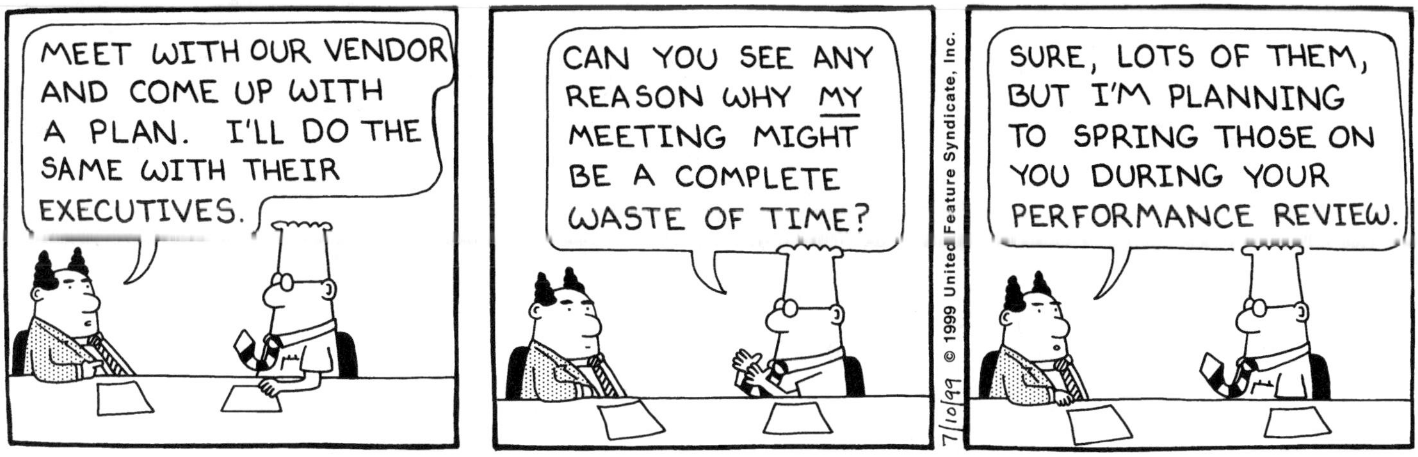
MEET WITH OUR VENDOR AND COME UP WITH A PLAN. I'LL DO THE SAME WITH THEIR EXECUTIVES.
CAN YOU SEE ANY REASON WHY MY MEETING MIGHT BE A COMPLETE WASTE OF TIME?
© 1999 United Feature Syndicate, Inc.
7/10/99
SURE, LOTS OF THEM, BUT I'M PLANNING TO SPRING THOSE ON YOU DURING YOUR PERFORMANCE REVIEW.

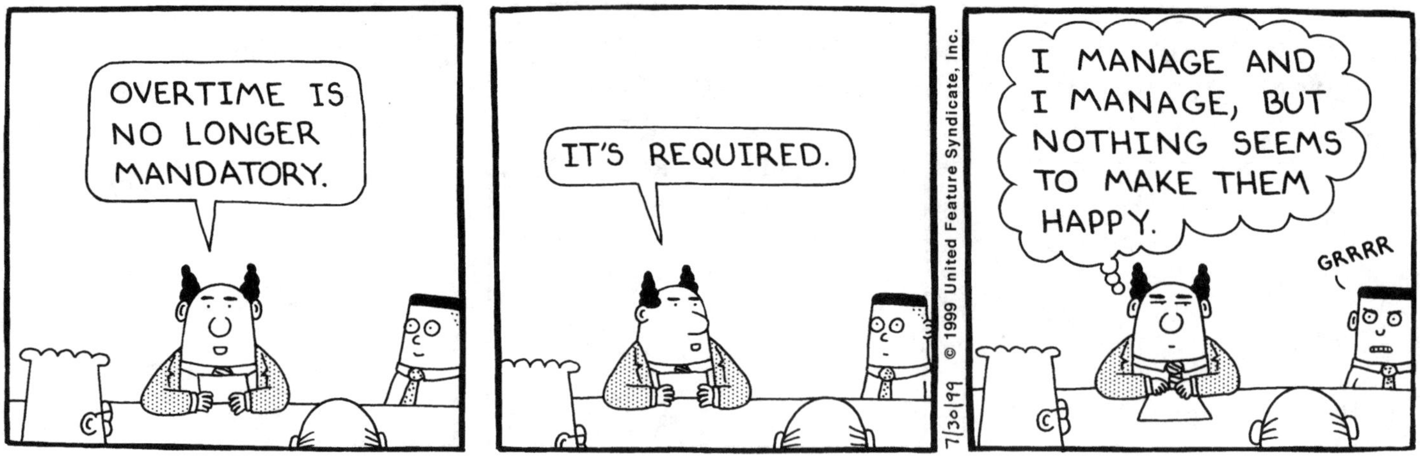
OVERTIME IS NO LONGER MANDATORY.
IT'S REQUIRED.
7/30/99 © 1999 United Feature Syndicate, Inc.
I MANAGE AND I MANAGE, BUT NOTHING SEEMS TO MAKE THEM HAPPY.
GRRRR

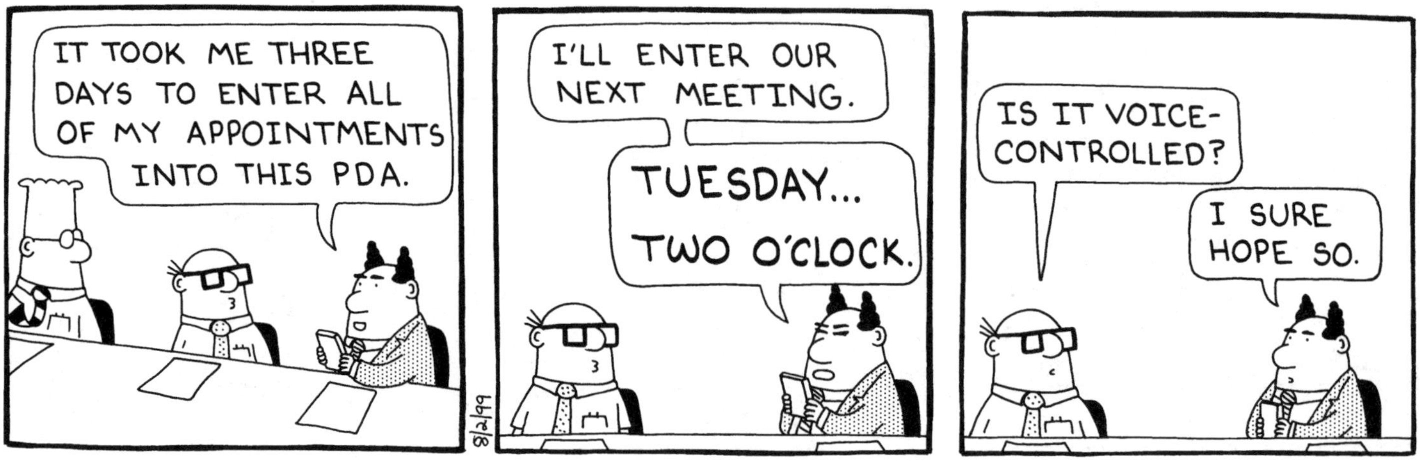
IT TOOK ME THREE DAYS TO ENTER ALL OF MY APPOINTMENTS INTO THIS PDA.
8/2/99
I'LL ENTER OUR NEXT MEETING.
TUESDAY... TWO O'CLOCK.
IS IT VOICE-CONTROLLED?
I SURE HOPE SO.

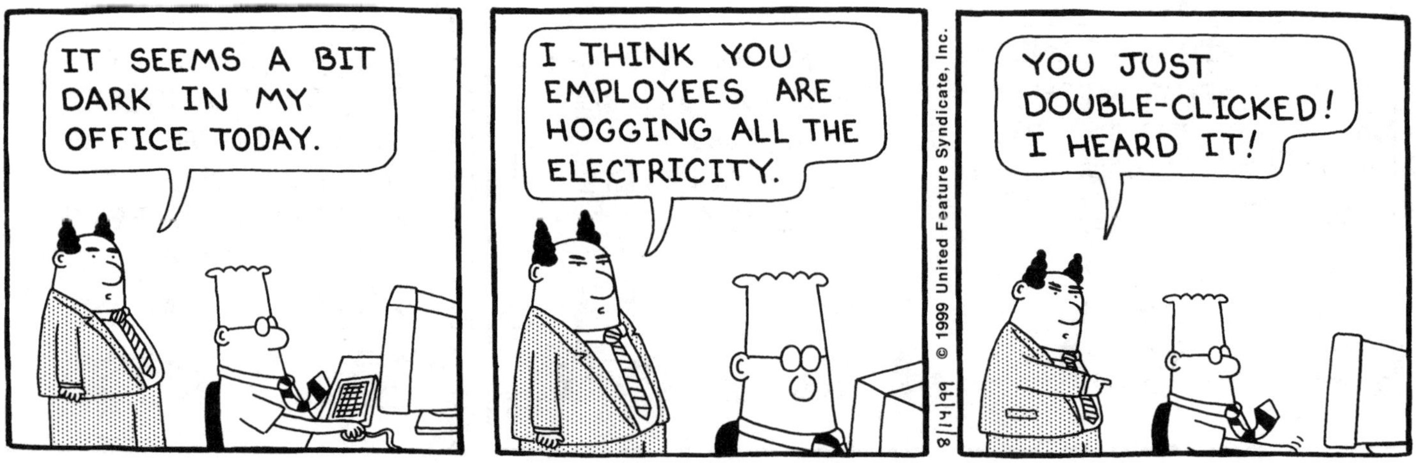
IT SEEMS A BIT DARK IN MY OFFICE TODAY.
I THINK YOU EMPLOYEES ARE HOGGING ALL THE ELECTRICITY.
8/4/99 © 1999 United Feature Syndicate, Inc.
YOU JUST DOUBLE-CLICKED! I HEARD IT!

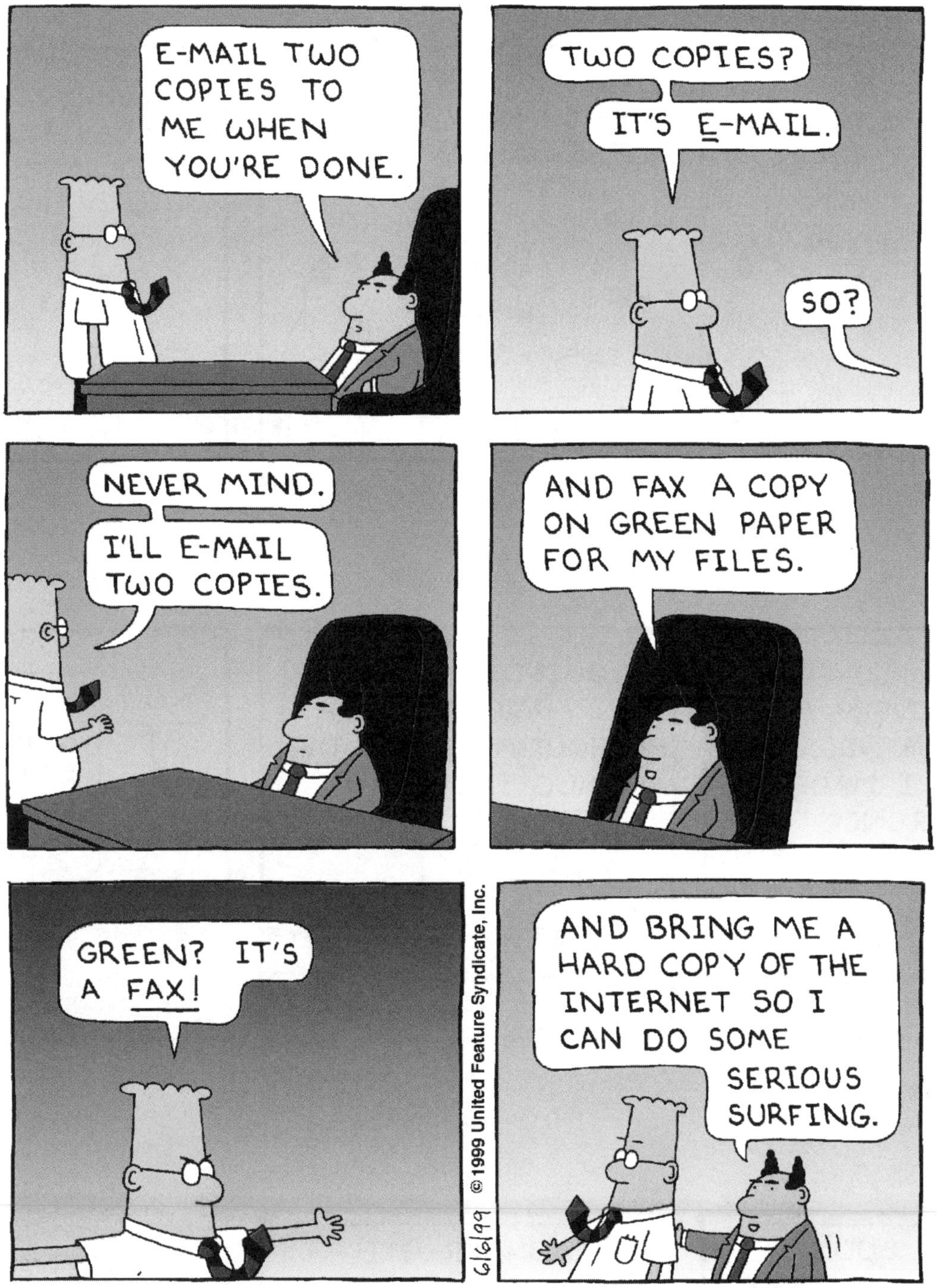
E-MAIL TWO COPIES TO ME WHEN YOU'RE DONE.
TWO COPIES?
IT'S E-MAIL.
SO?
NEVER MIND.
I'LL E-MAIL TWO COPIES.
AND FAX A COPY ON GREEN PAPER FOR MY FILES.
GREEN? IT'S A FAX!
© 1999 United Feature Syndicate, Inc.
6/6/99
AND BRING ME A HARD COPY OF THE INTERNET SO I CAN DO SOME SERIOUS SURFING.

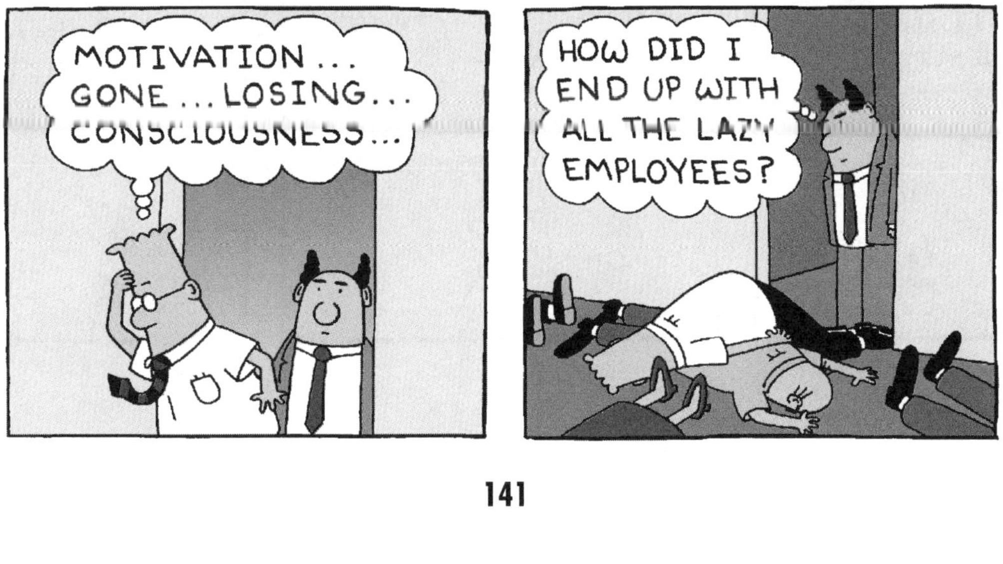
MOTIVATION ... GONE ... LOSING ... CONSCIOUSNESS ...
HOW DID I END UP WITH ALL THE LAZY EMPLOYEES?

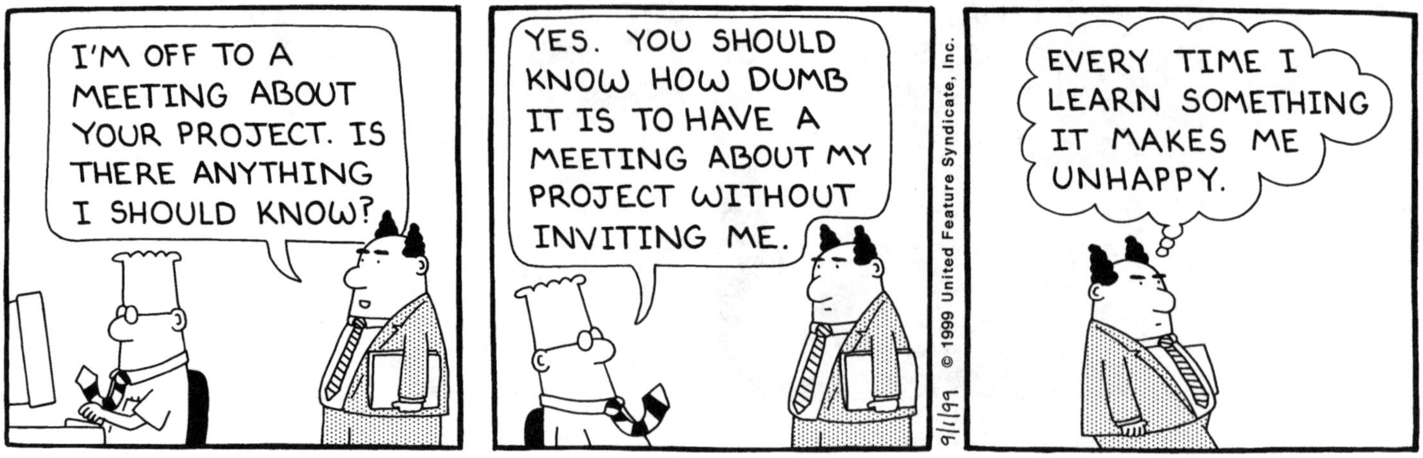

I'M OFF TO A MEETING ABOUT YOUR PROJECT. IS THERE ANYTHING I SHOULD KNOW?
YES. YOU SHOULD KNOW HOW DUMB IT IS TO HAVE A MEETING ABOUT MY PROJECT WITHOUT INVITING ME.
9/1/99
© 1999 United Feature Syndicate, Inc.
EVERY TIME I LEARN SOMETHING IT MAKES ME UNHAPPY.

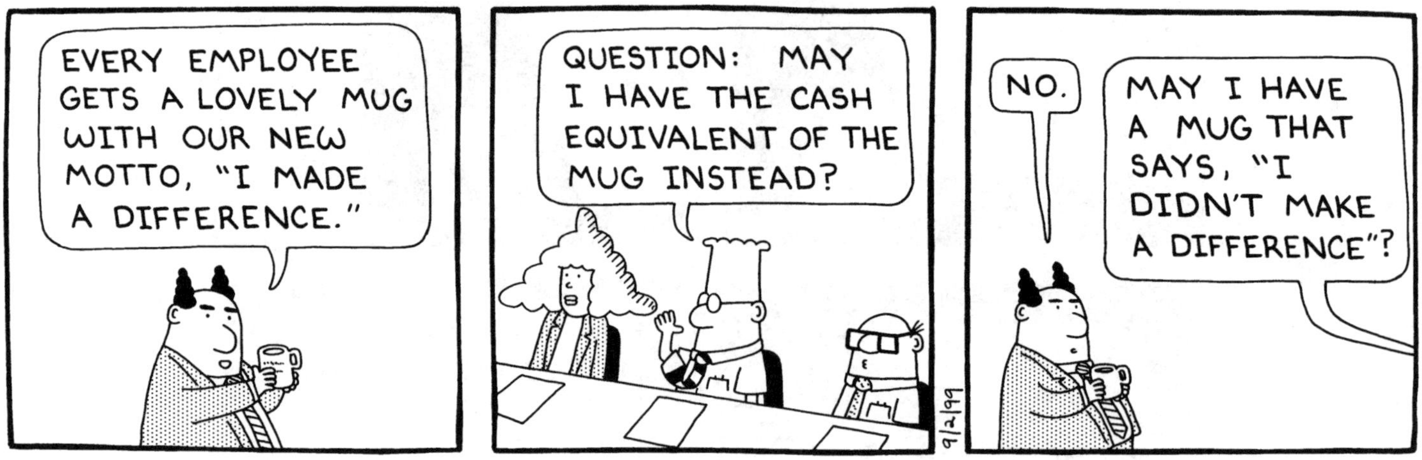

EVERY EMPLOYEE GETS A LOVELY MUG WITH OUR NEW MOTTO, "I MADE A DIFFERENCE."
QUESTION: MAY I HAVE THE CASH EQUIVALENT OF THE MUG INSTEAD?
9/2/99
NO.
MAY I HAVE A MUG THAT SAYS, "I DIDN'T MAKE A DIFFERENCE"?

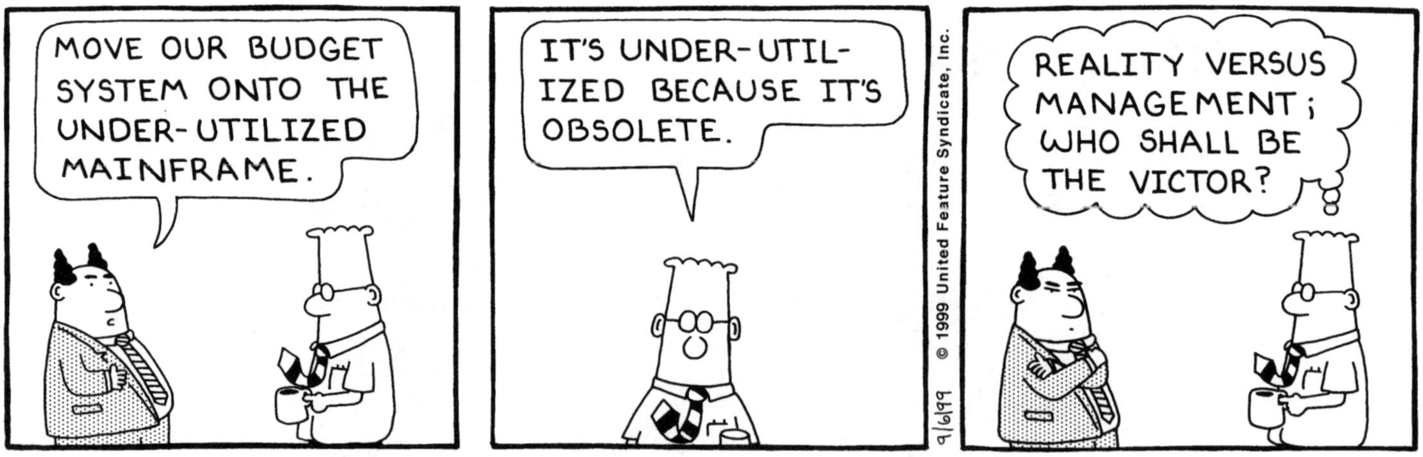

MOVE OUR BUDGET SYSTEM ONTO THE UNDER-UTILIZED MAINFRAME.
IT'S UNDER-UTILIZED BECAUSE IT'S OBSOLETE.
9/6/99
© 1999 United Feature Syndicate, Inc.
REALITY VERSUS MANAGEMENT; WHO SHALL BE THE VICTOR?

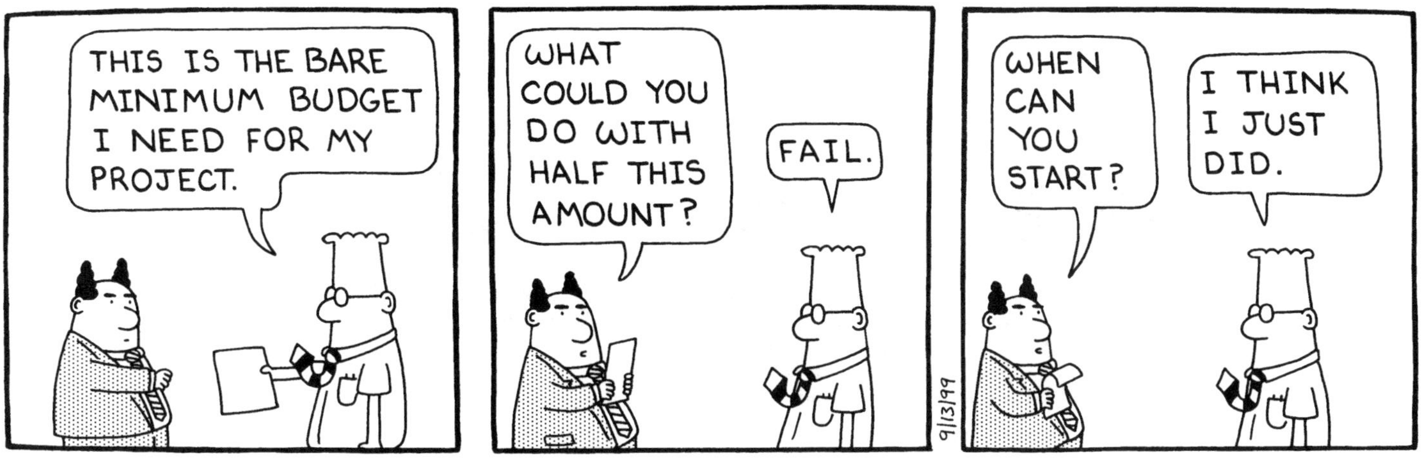
THIS IS THE BARE MINIMUM BUDGET I NEED FOR MY PROJECT.
WHAT COULD YOU DO WITH HALF THIS AMOUNT?
FAIL.
9/13/99
WHEN CAN YOU START?
I THINK I JUST DID.

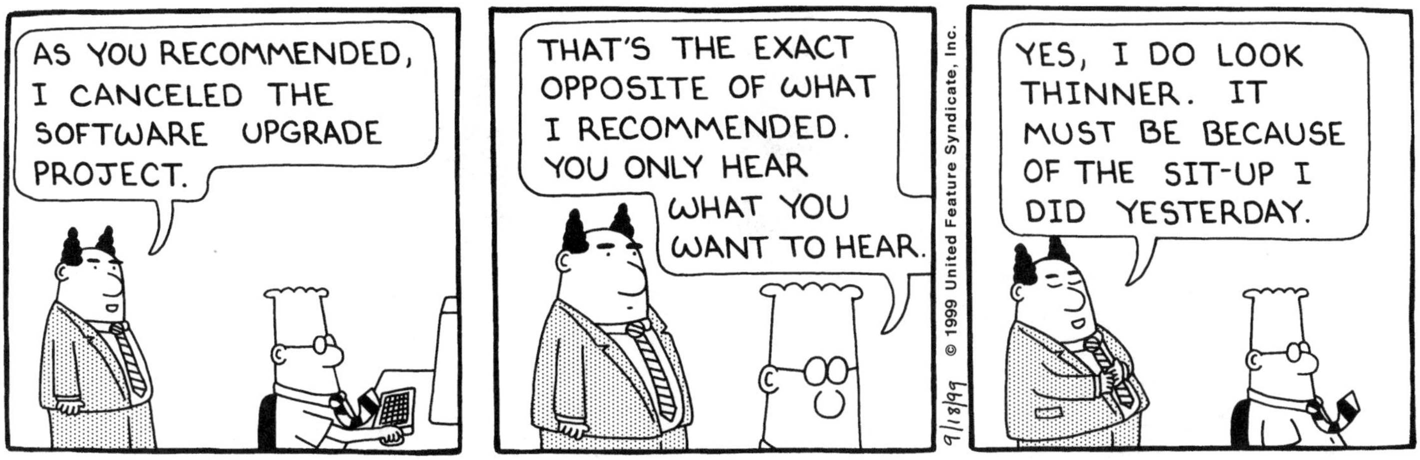
AS YOU RECOMMENDED, I CANCELED THE SOFTWARE UPGRADE PROJECT.
THAT'S THE EXACT OPPOSITE OF WHAT I RECOMMENDED. YOU ONLY HEAR WHAT YOU WANT TO HEAR.
© 1999 United Feature Syndicate, Inc.
9/18/99
YES, I DO LOOK THINNER. IT MUST BE BECAUSE OF THE SIT-UP I DID YESTERDAY.

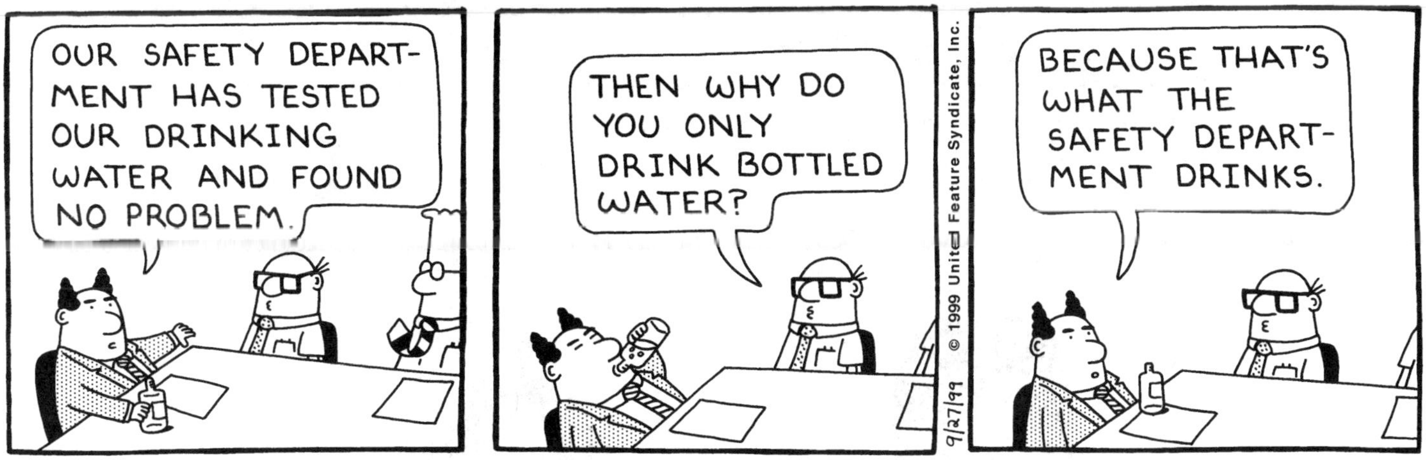
OUR SAFETY DEPARTMENT HAS TESTED OUR DRINKING WATER AND FOUND NO PROBLEM.
THEN WHY DO YOU ONLY DRINK BOTTLED WATER?
© 1999 United Feature Syndicate, Inc.
9/27/99
BECAUSE THAT'S WHAT THE SAFETY DEPARTMENT DRINKS.

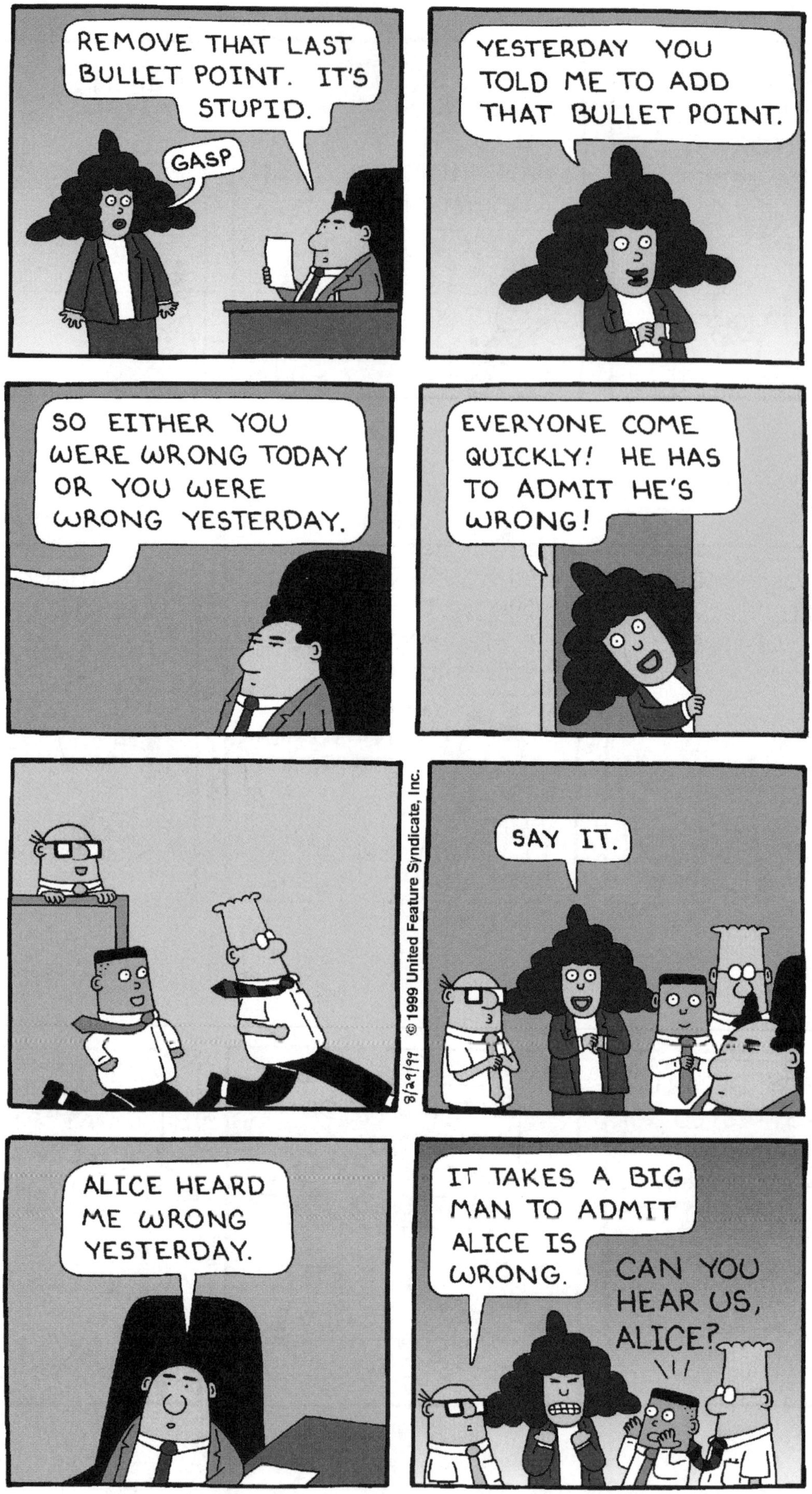

REMOVE THAT LAST BULLET POINT. IT'S STUPID.
GASP
YESTERDAY YOU TOLD ME TO ADD THAT BULLET POINT.
SO EITHER YOU WERE WRONG TODAY OR YOU WERE WRONG YESTERDAY.
EVERYONE COME QUICKLY! HE HAS TO ADMIT HE'S WRONG!
8/29/99 © 1999 United Feature Syndicate, Inc.
SAY IT.
ALICE HEARD ME WRONG YESTERDAY.
IT TAKES A BIG MAN TO ADMIT ALICE IS WRONG.
CAN YOU HEAR US, ALICE?

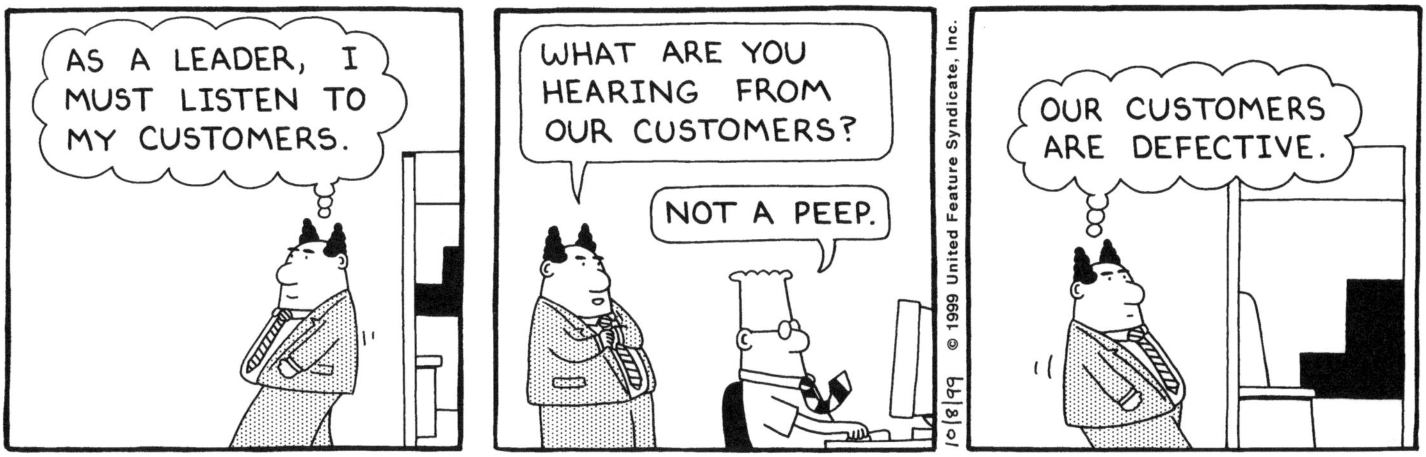
AS A LEADER, I MUST LISTEN TO MY CUSTOMERS.
WHAT ARE YOU HEARING FROM OUR CUSTOMERS?
NOT A PEEP.
10/8/99 © 1999 United Feature Syndicate, Inc.
OUR CUSTOMERS ARE DEFECTIVE.

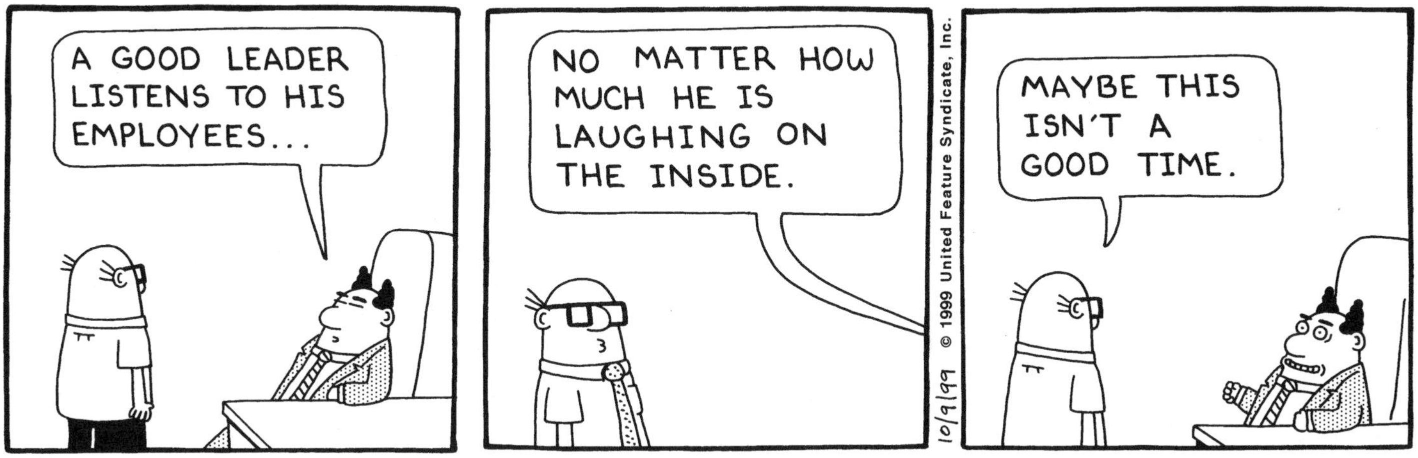
A GOOD LEADER LISTENS TO HIS EMPLOYEES...
NO MATTER HOW MUCH HE IS LAUGHING ON THE INSIDE.
10/9/99 © 1999 United Feature Syndicate, Inc.
MAYBE THIS ISN'T A GOOD TIME.

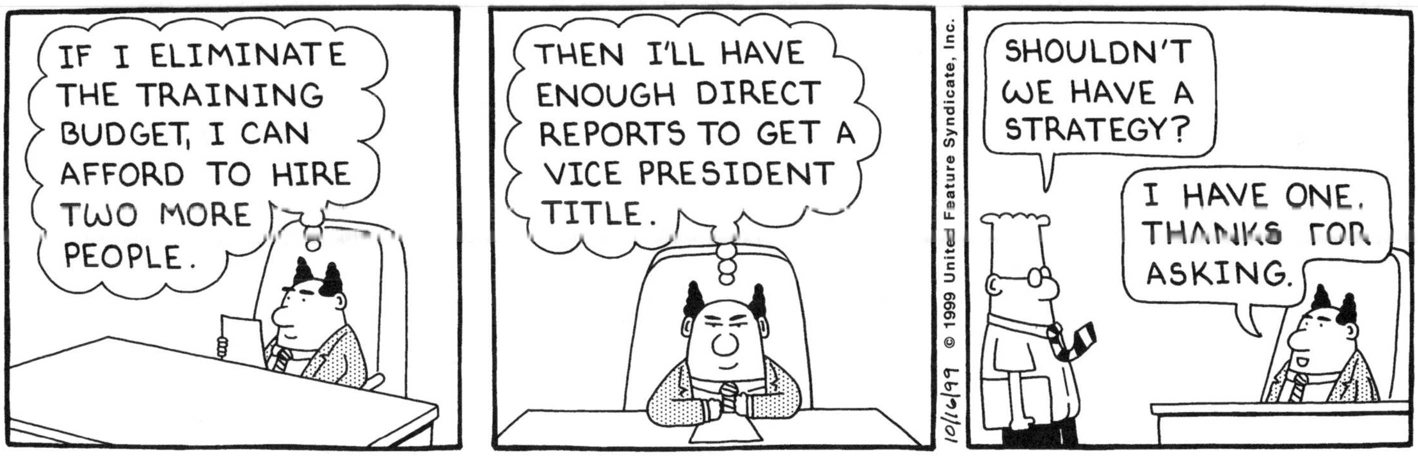
IF I ELIMINATE THE TRAINING BUDGET, I CAN AFFORD TO HIRE TWO MORE PEOPLE.
THEN I'LL HAVE ENOUGH DIRECT REPORTS TO GET A VICE PRESIDENT TITLE.
10/16/99 © 1999 United Feature Syndicate, Inc.
SHOULDN'T WE HAVE A STRATEGY?
I HAVE ONE. THANKS FOR ASKING.

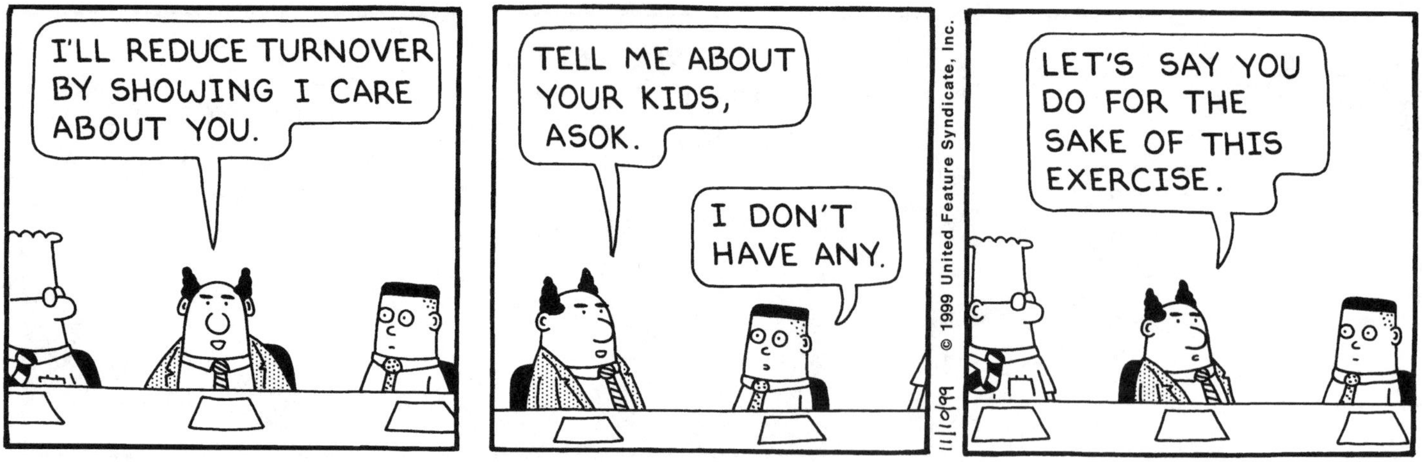
I'LL REDUCE TURNOVER BY SHOWING I CARE ABOUT YOU.
TELL ME ABOUT YOUR KIDS, ASOK.
I DON'T HAVE ANY.
11/10/99 © 1999 United Feature Syndicate, Inc.
LET'S SAY YOU DO FOR THE SAKE OF THIS EXERCISE.

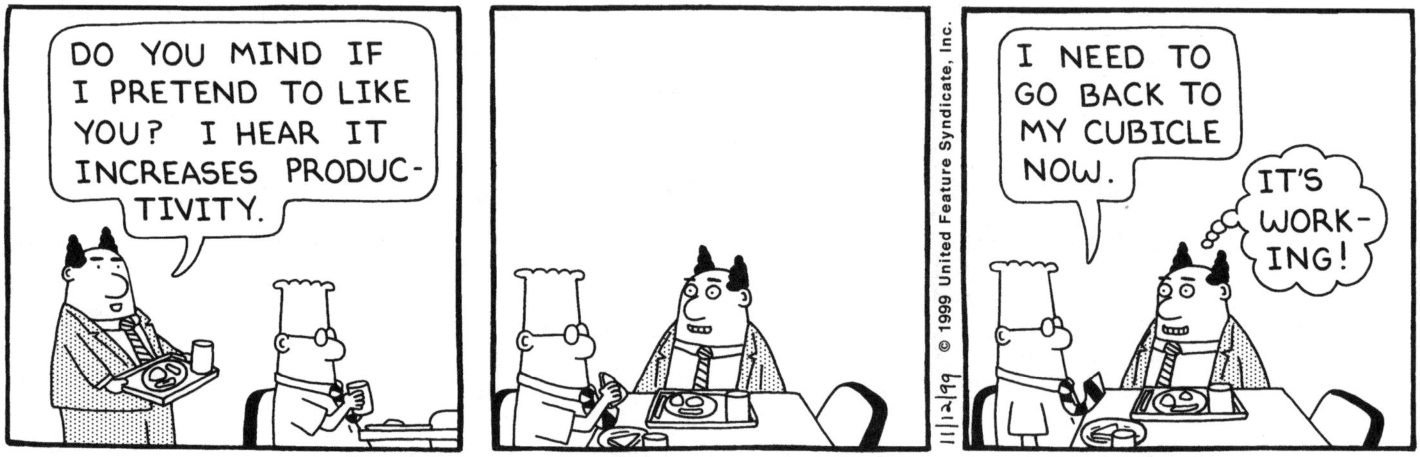
DO YOU MIND IF I PRETEND TO LIKE YOU? I HEAR IT INCREASES PRODUC-TIVITY.
11/12/99 © 1999 United Feature Syndicate, Inc.
I NEED TO GO BACK TO MY CUBICLE NOW.
IT'S WORK-ING!

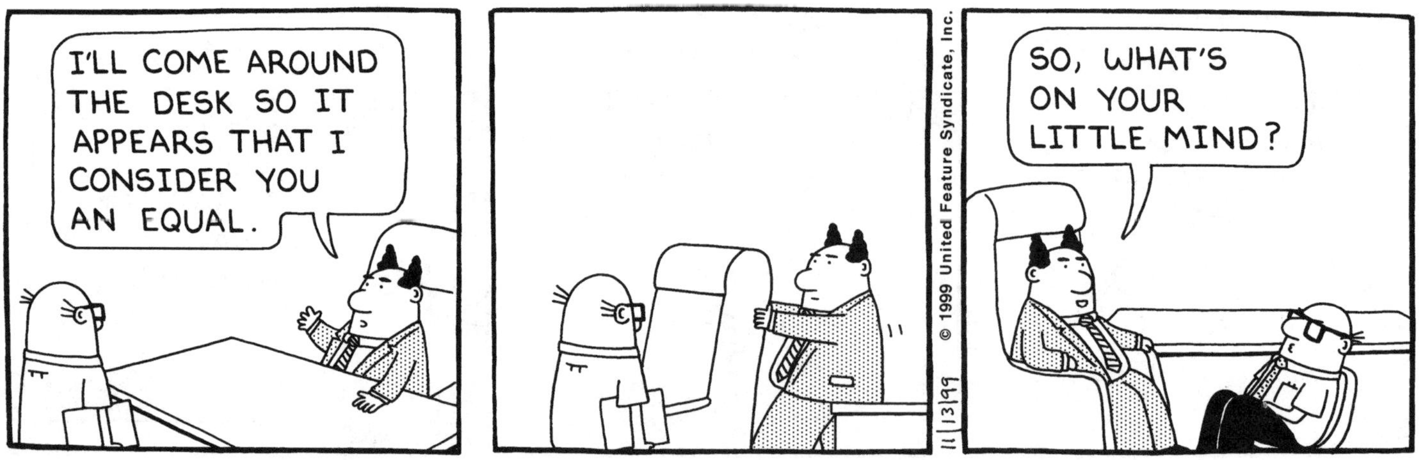
I'LL COME AROUND THE DESK SO IT APPEARS THAT I CONSIDER YOU AN EQUAL.
11/13/99 © 1999 United Feature Syndicate, Inc.
SO, WHAT'S ON YOUR LITTLE MIND?

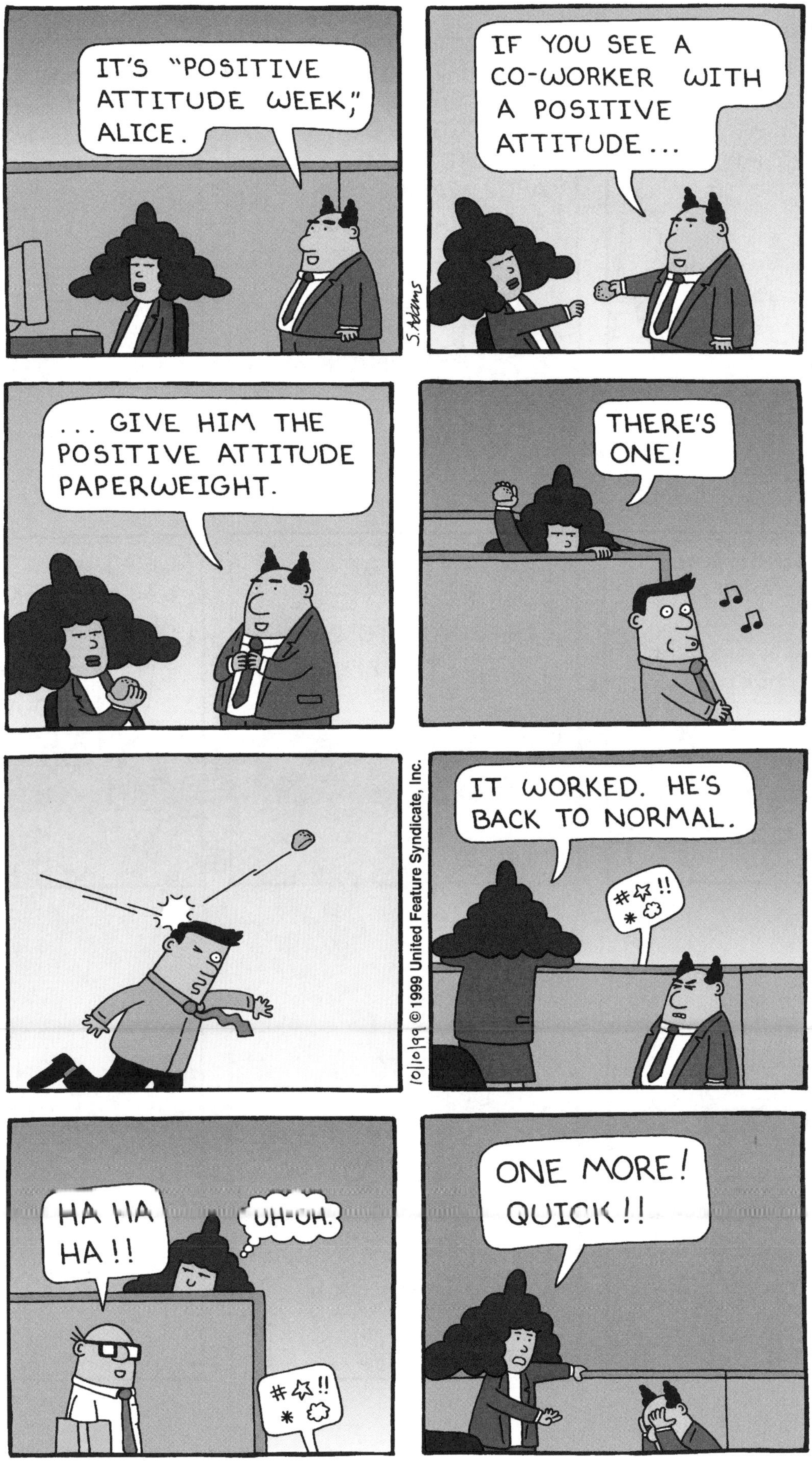
IT'S "POSITIVE ATTITUDE WEEK," ALICE.
IF YOU SEE A CO-WORKER WITH A POSITIVE ATTITUDE...
... GIVE HIM THE POSITIVE ATTITUDE PAPERWEIGHT.
THERE'S ONE!
IT WORKED. HE'S BACK TO NORMAL.
#☆!! * ✿
HA HA HA!!
UH-OH.
#☆!! * ✿
ONE MORE! QUICK!!
S. Adams
10/10/99 © 1999 United Feature Syndicate, Inc.

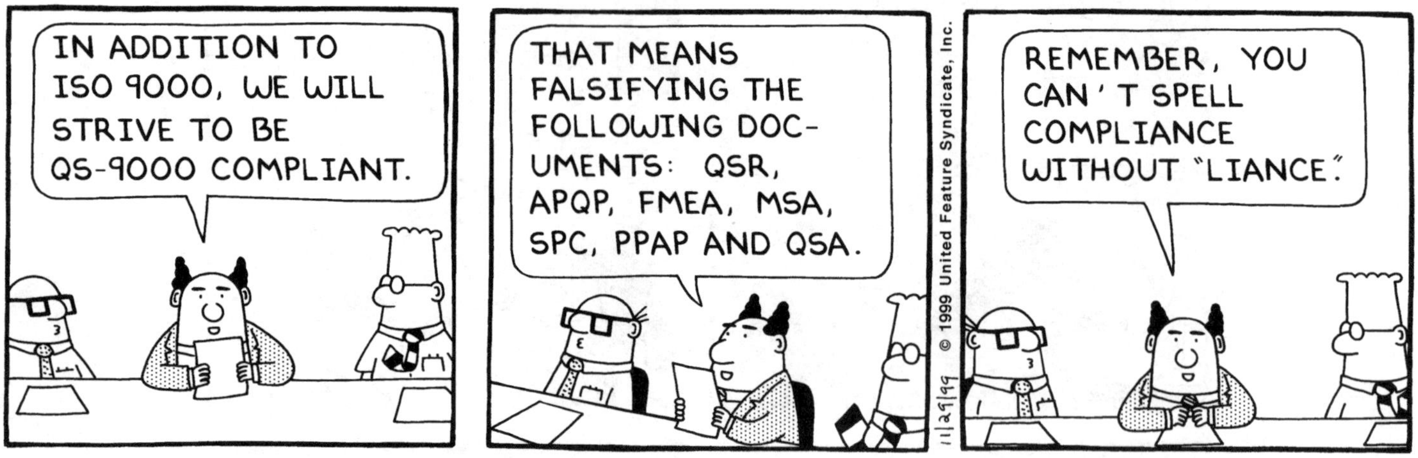
IN ADDITION TO ISO 9000, WE WILL STRIVE TO BE QS-9000 COMPLIANT.
THAT MEANS FALSIFYING THE FOLLOWING DOC-UMENTS: QSR, APQP, FMEA, MSA, SPC, PPAP AND QSA.
11/29/99
© 1999 United Feature Syndicate, Inc.
REMEMBER, YOU CAN'T SPELL COMPLIANCE WITHOUT "LIANCE."

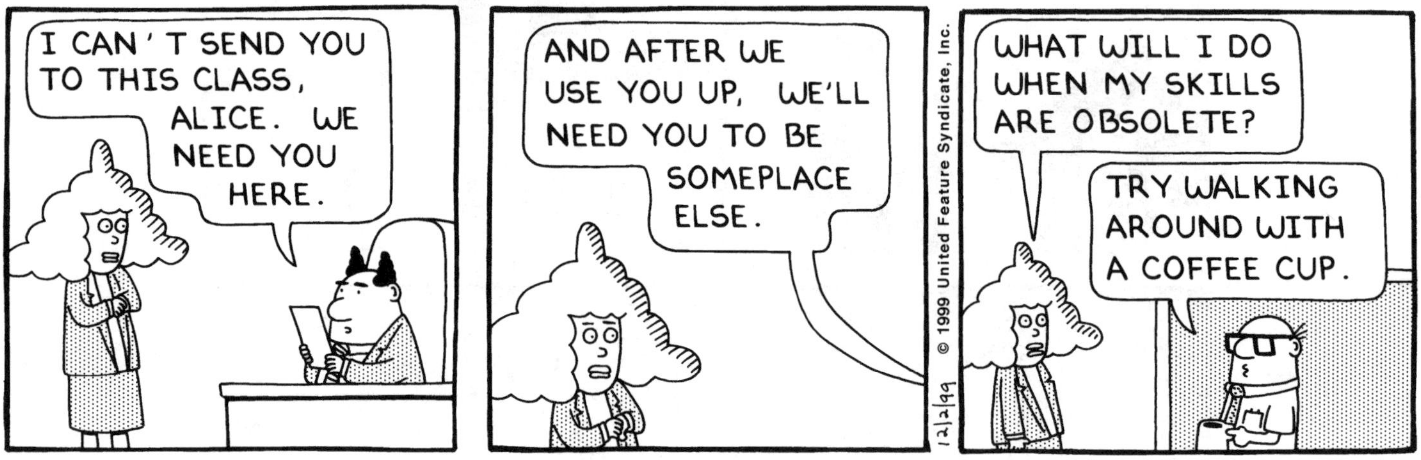
I CAN'T SEND YOU TO THIS CLASS, ALICE. WE NEED YOU HERE.
AND AFTER WE USE YOU UP, WE'LL NEED YOU TO BE SOMEPLACE ELSE.
12/2/99
© 1999 United Feature Syndicate, Inc.
WHAT WILL I DO WHEN MY SKILLS ARE OBSOLETE?
TRY WALKING AROUND WITH A COFFEE CUP.

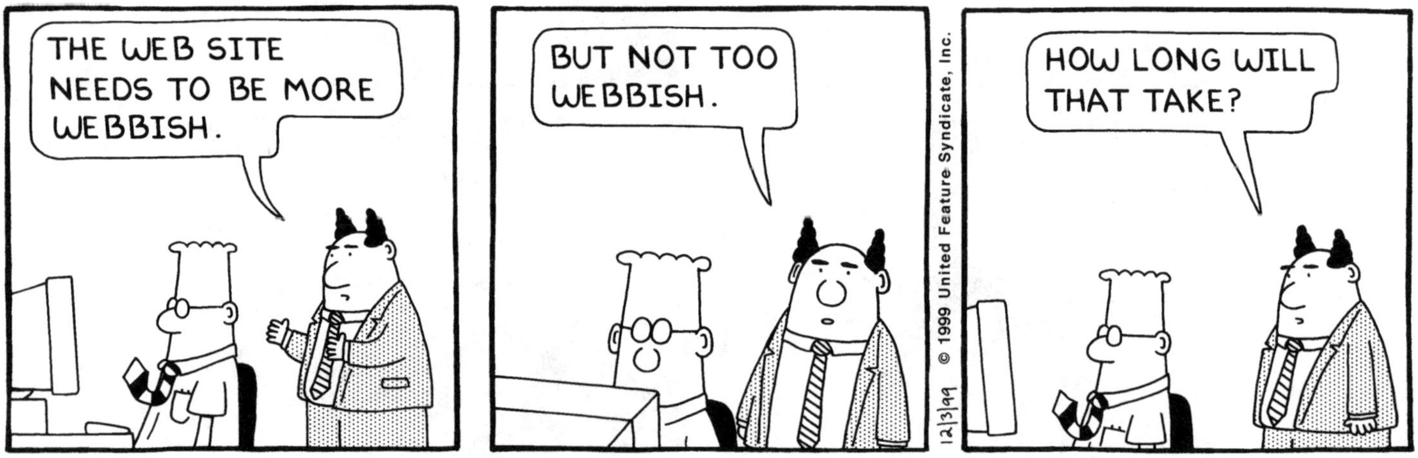
THE WEB SITE NEEDS TO BE MORE WEBBISH.
BUT NOT TOO WEBBISH.
12/3/99
© 1999 United Feature Syndicate, Inc.
HOW LONG WILL THAT TAKE?

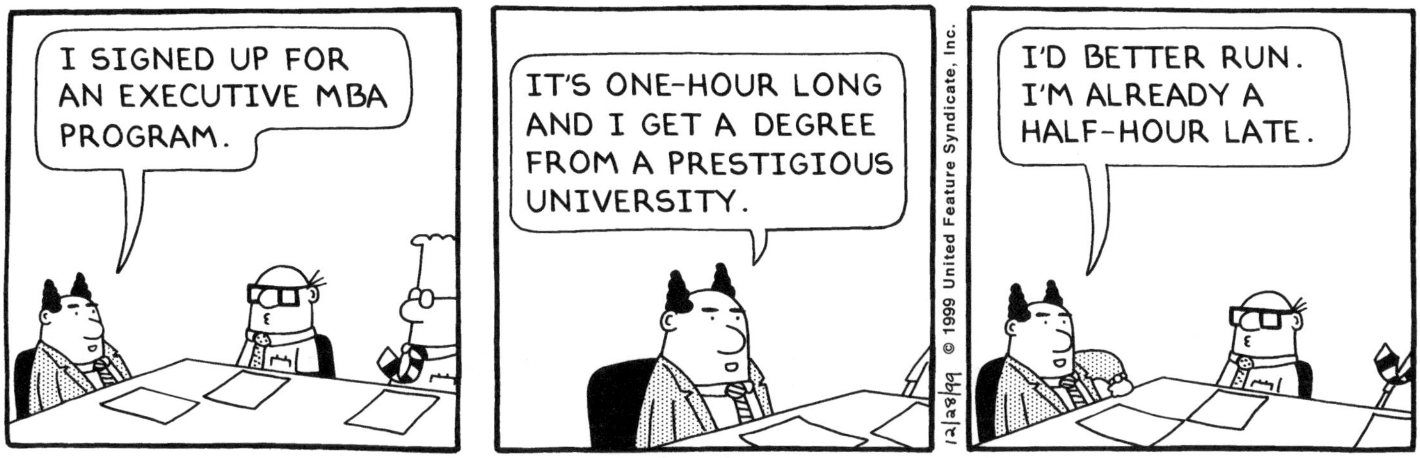
I SIGNED UP FOR AN EXECUTIVE MBA PROGRAM.
IT'S ONE-HOUR LONG AND I GET A DEGREE FROM A PRESTIGIOUS UNIVERSITY.
© 1999 United Feature Syndicate, Inc.
12/28/99
I'D BETTER RUN. I'M ALREADY A HALF-HOUR LATE.

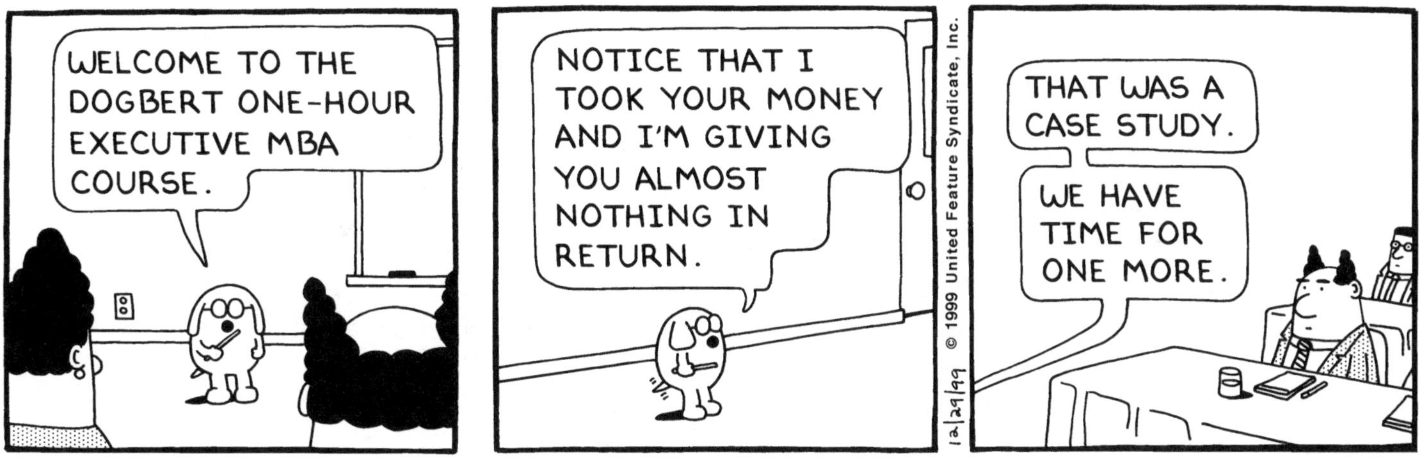
WELCOME TO THE DOGBERT ONE-HOUR EXECUTIVE MBA COURSE.
NOTICE THAT I TOOK YOUR MONEY AND I'M GIVING YOU ALMOST NOTHING IN RETURN.
© 1999 United Feature Syndicate, Inc.
12/29/99
THAT WAS A CASE STUDY.
WE HAVE TIME FOR ONE MORE.

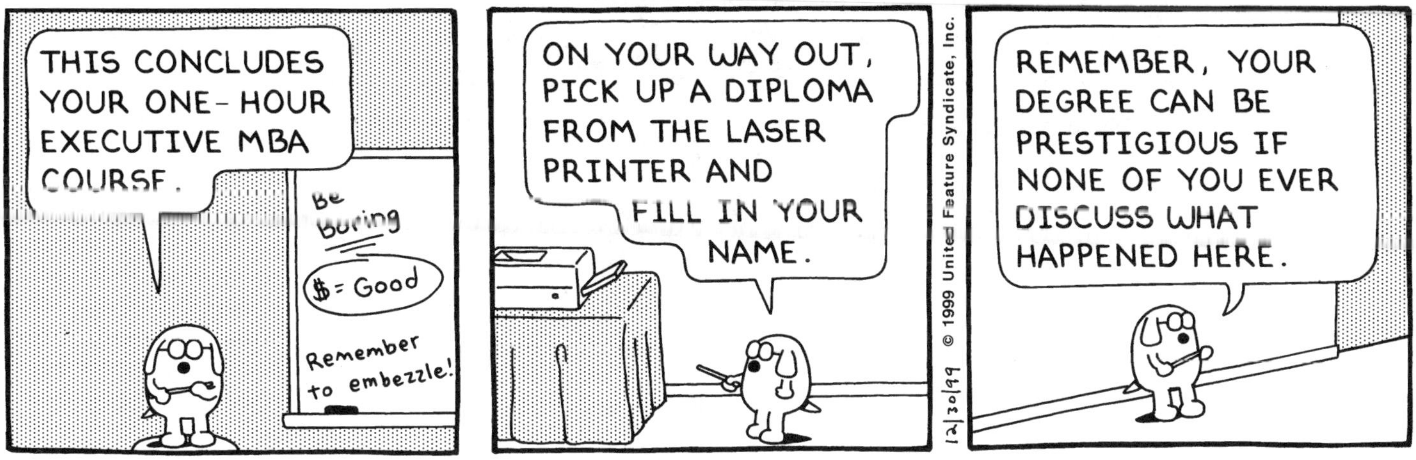
THIS CONCLUDES YOUR ONE-HOUR EXECUTIVE MBA COURSE.
Be Boring
$ = Good
Remember to embezzle!
ON YOUR WAY OUT, PICK UP A DIPLOMA FROM THE LASER PRINTER AND FILL IN YOUR NAME.
© 1999 United Feature Syndicate, Inc.
12/30/99
REMEMBER, YOUR DEGREE CAN BE PRESTIGIOUS IF NONE OF YOU EVER DISCUSS WHAT HAPPENED HERE.

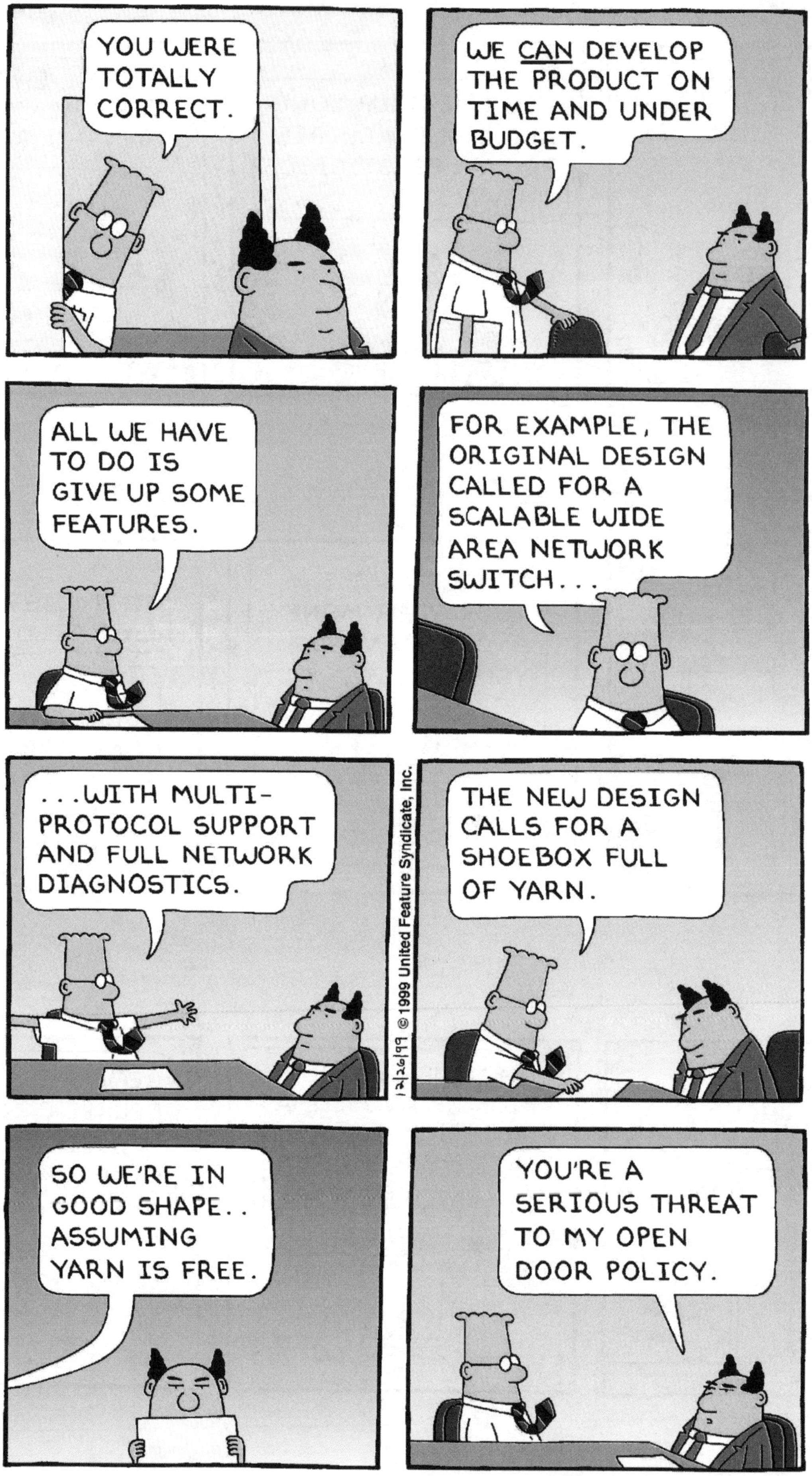
YOU WERE TOTALLY CORRECT.
WE CAN DEVELOP THE PRODUCT ON TIME AND UNDER BUDGET.
ALL WE HAVE TO DO IS GIVE UP SOME FEATURES.
FOR EXAMPLE, THE ORIGINAL DESIGN CALLED FOR A SCALABLE WIDE AREA NETWORK SWITCH...
...WITH MULTI-PROTOCOL SUPPORT AND FULL NETWORK DIAGNOSTICS.
THE NEW DESIGN CALLS FOR A SHOEBOX FULL OF YARN.
SO WE'RE IN GOOD SHAPE.. ASSUMING YARN IS FREE.
YOU'RE A SERIOUS THREAT TO MY OPEN DOOR POLICY.
12/26/99 © 1999 United Feature Syndicate, Inc.

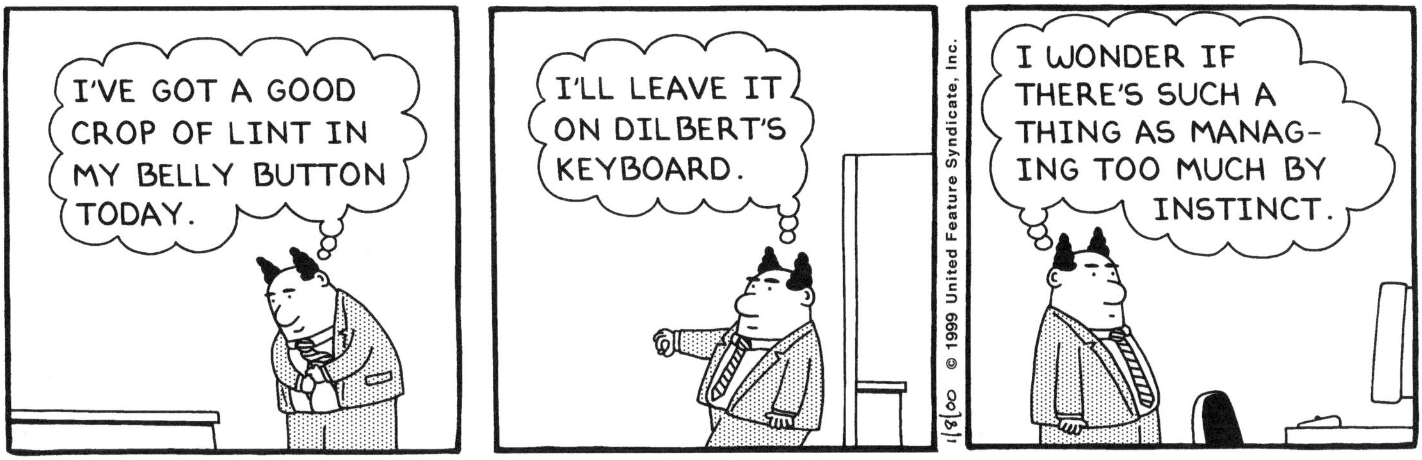
I'VE GOT A GOOD CROP OF LINT IN MY BELLY BUTTON TODAY.
I'LL LEAVE IT ON DILBERT'S KEYBOARD.
I WONDER IF THERE'S SUCH A THING AS MANAGING TOO MUCH BY INSTINCT.
1/8/00 © 1999 United Feature Syndicate, Inc.

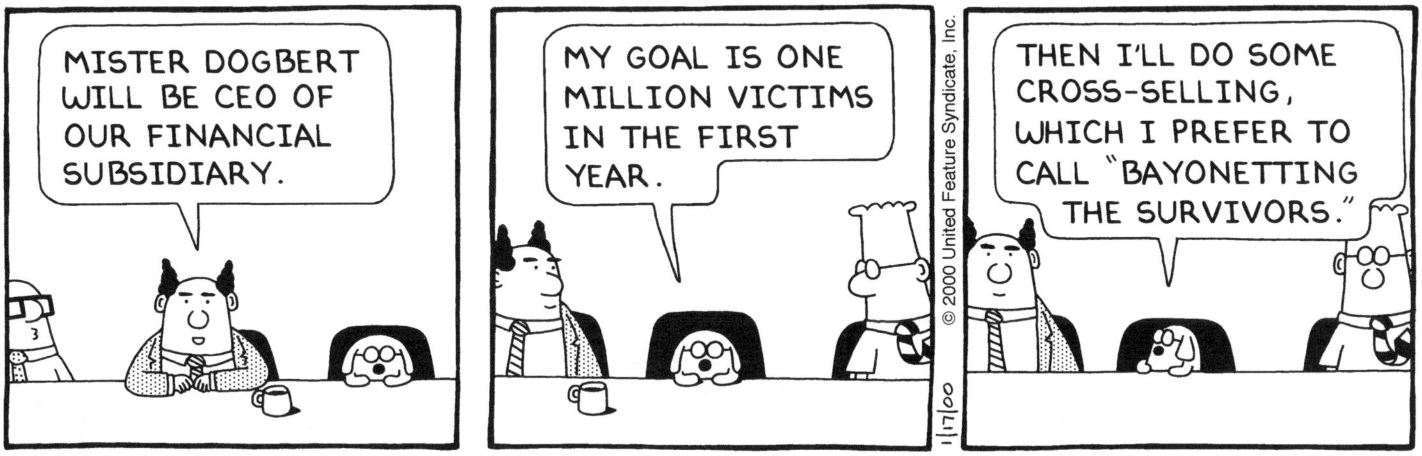
MISTER DOGBERT WILL BE CEO OF OUR FINANCIAL SUBSIDIARY.
MY GOAL IS ONE MILLION VICTIMS IN THE FIRST YEAR.
THEN I'LL DO SOME CROSS-SELLING, WHICH I PREFER TO CALL "BAYONETTING THE SURVIVORS."
1/17/00 © 2000 United Feature Syndicate, Inc.

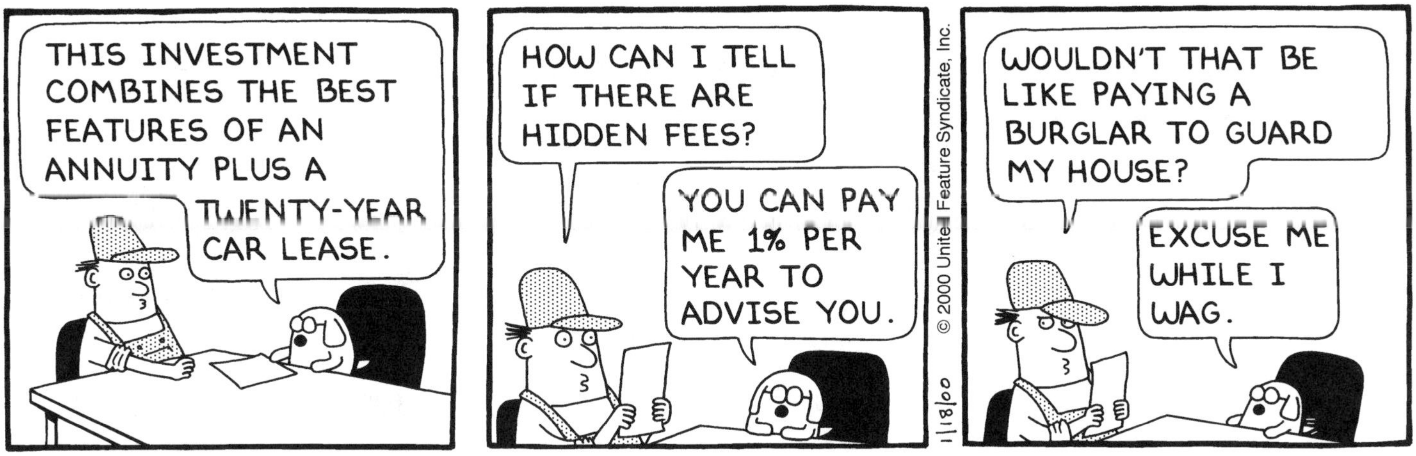
THIS INVESTMENT COMBINES THE BEST FEATURES OF AN ANNUITY PLUS A TWENTY-YEAR CAR LEASE.
HOW CAN I TELL IF THERE ARE HIDDEN FEES?
YOU CAN PAY ME 1% PER YEAR TO ADVISE YOU.
WOULDN'T THAT BE LIKE PAYING A BURGLAR TO GUARD MY HOUSE?
EXCUSE ME WHILE I WAG.
1/18/00 © 2000 United Feature Syndicate, Inc.

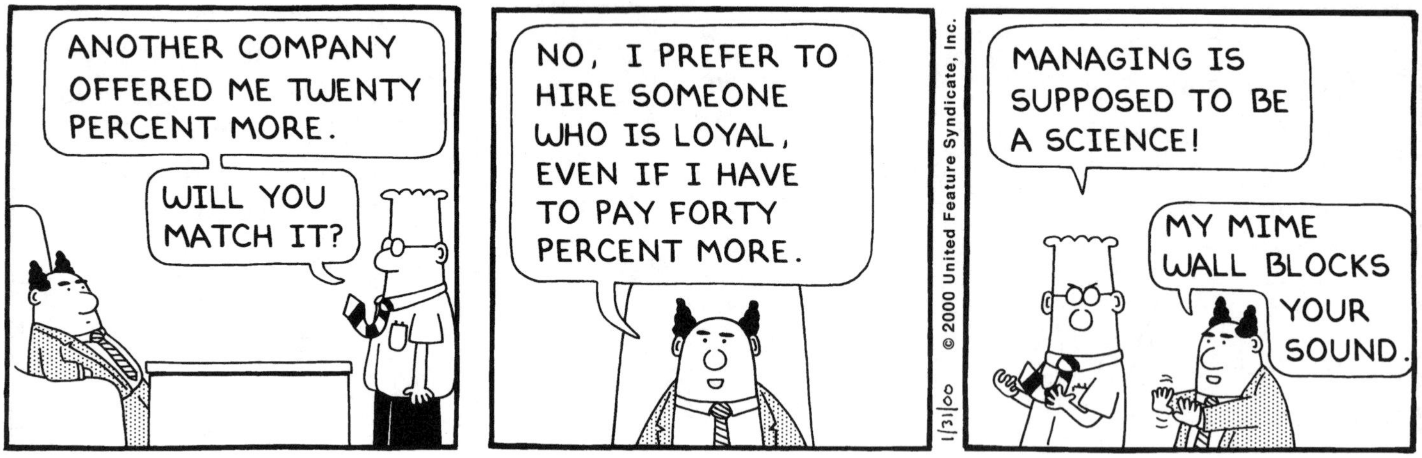
ANOTHER COMPANY OFFERED ME TWENTY PERCENT MORE.
WILL YOU MATCH IT?
NO, I PREFER TO HIRE SOMEONE WHO IS LOYAL, EVEN IF I HAVE TO PAY FORTY PERCENT MORE.
1/31/00 © 2000 United Feature Syndicate, Inc.
MANAGING IS SUPPOSED TO BE A SCIENCE!
MY MIME WALL BLOCKS YOUR SOUND.

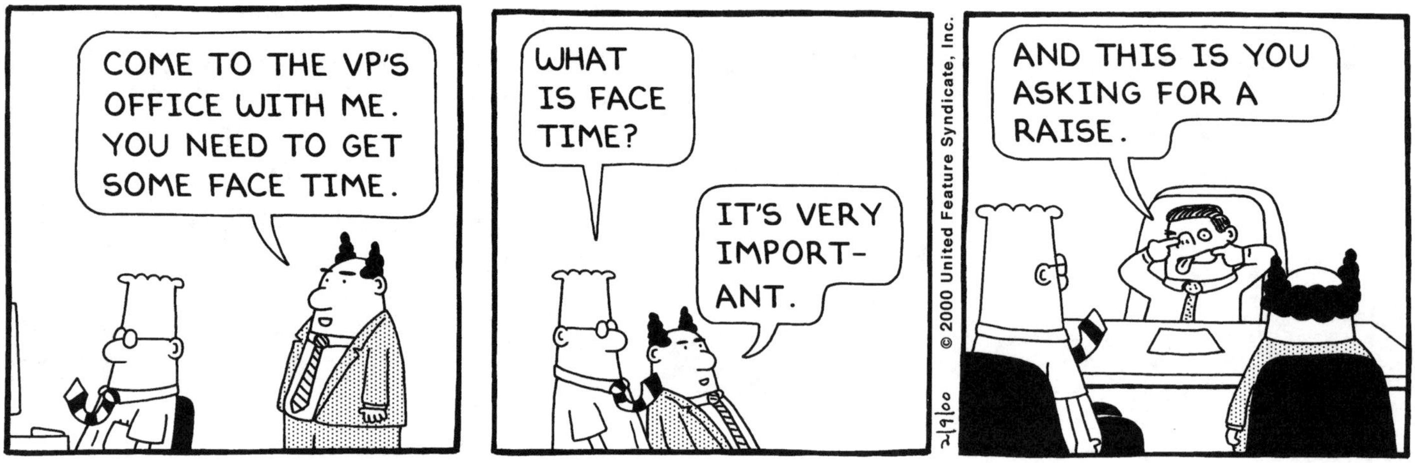
COME TO THE VP'S OFFICE WITH ME. YOU NEED TO GET SOME FACE TIME.
WHAT IS FACE TIME?
IT'S VERY IMPORT-ANT.
2/9/00 © 2000 United Feature Syndicate, Inc.
AND THIS IS YOU ASKING FOR A RAISE.

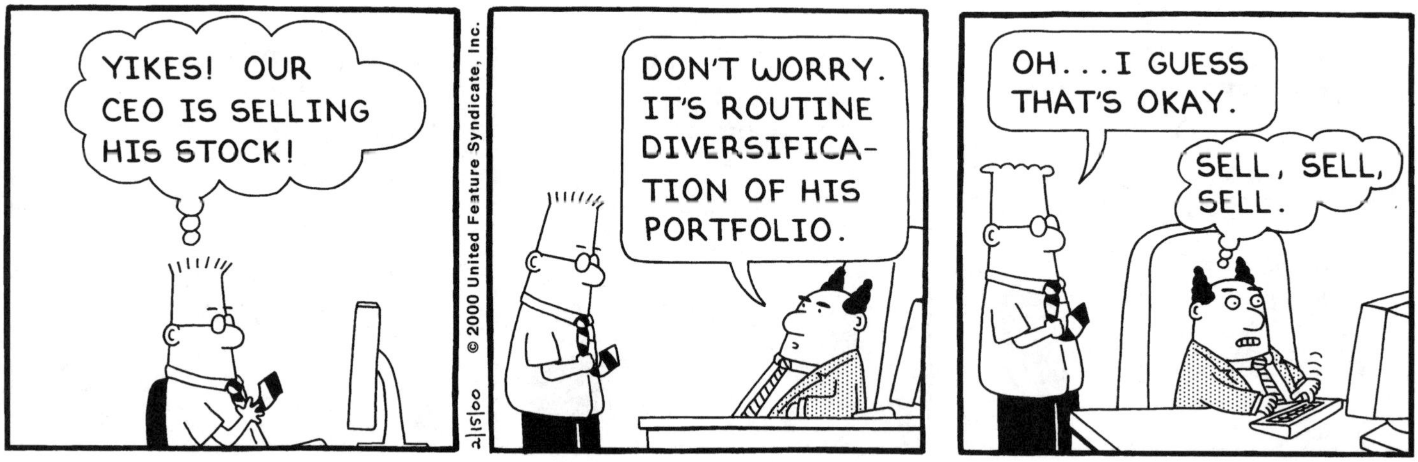
YIKES! OUR CEO IS SELLING HIS STOCK!
2/15/00 © 2000 United Feature Syndicate, Inc.
DON'T WORRY. IT'S ROUTINE DIVERSIFICA-TION OF HIS PORTFOLIO.
OH...I GUESS THAT'S OKAY.
SELL, SELL, SELL.

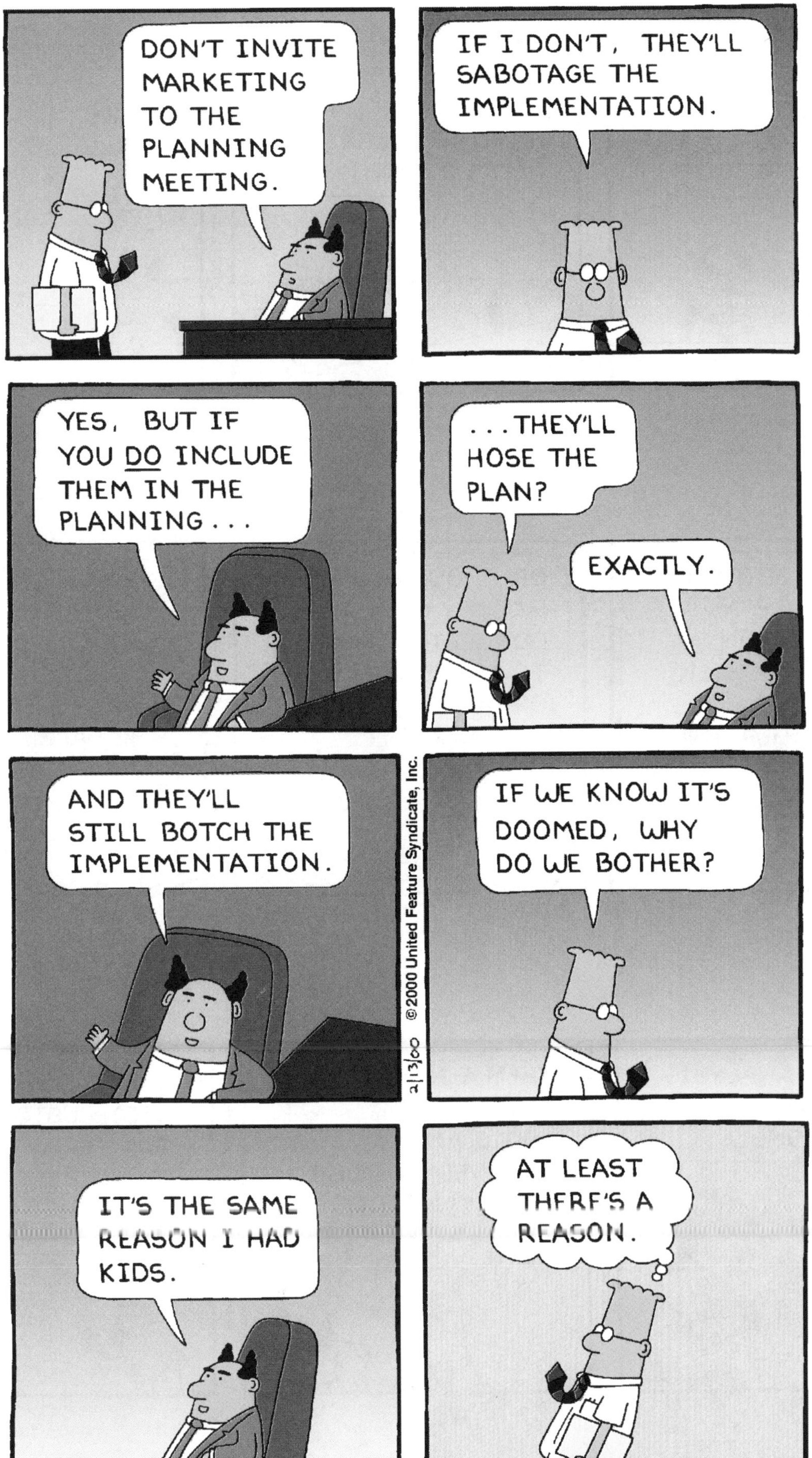
DON'T INVITE MARKETING TO THE PLANNING MEETING.
IF I DON'T, THEY'LL SABOTAGE THE IMPLEMENTATION.
YES, BUT IF YOU DO INCLUDE THEM IN THE PLANNING . . .
. . . THEY'LL HOSE THE PLAN?
EXACTLY.
AND THEY'LL STILL BOTCH THE IMPLEMENTATION.
IF WE KNOW IT'S DOOMED, WHY DO WE BOTHER?
IT'S THE SAME REASON I HAD KIDS.
AT LEAST THERE'S A REASON.
©2000 United Feature Syndicate, Inc.
2/13/00

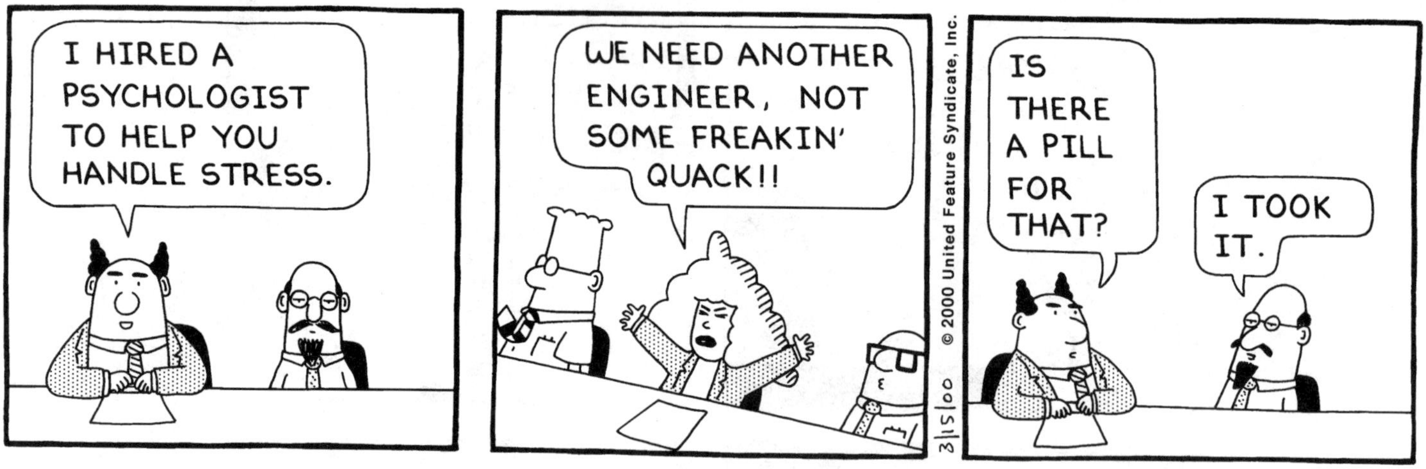
I HIRED A PSYCHOLOGIST TO HELP YOU HANDLE STRESS.
WE NEED ANOTHER ENGINEER, NOT SOME FREAKIN' QUACK!!
3/15/00
© 2000 United Feature Syndicate, Inc.
IS THERE A PILL FOR THAT?
I TOOK IT.

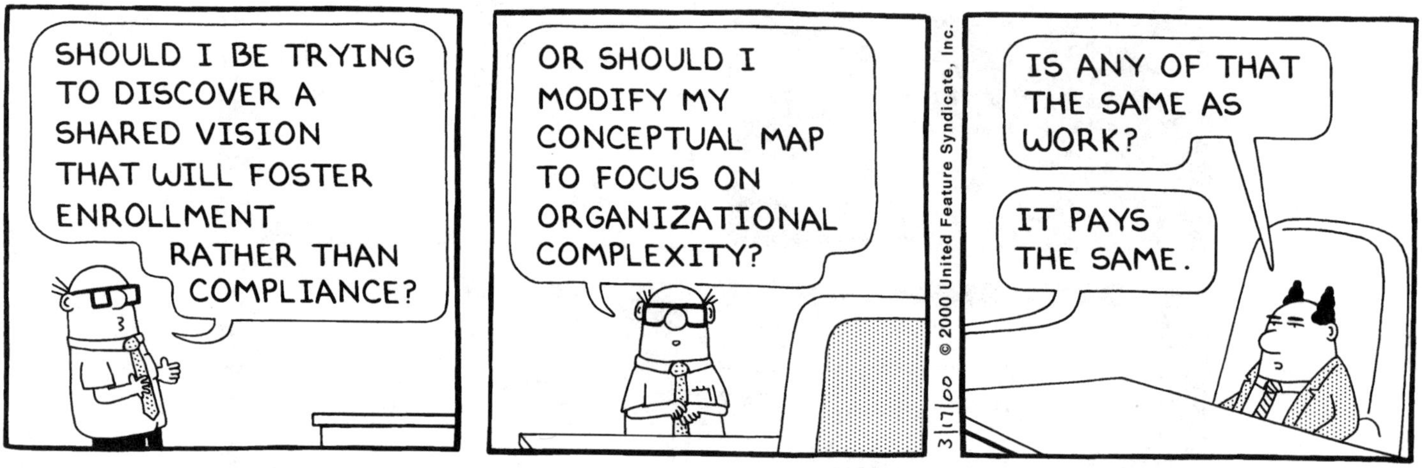
SHOULD I BE TRYING TO DISCOVER A SHARED VISION THAT WILL FOSTER ENROLLMENT RATHER THAN COMPLIANCE?
OR SHOULD I MODIFY MY CONCEPTUAL MAP TO FOCUS ON ORGANIZATIONAL COMPLEXITY?
3/17/00
© 2000 United Feature Syndicate, Inc.
IS ANY OF THAT THE SAME AS WORK?
IT PAYS THE SAME.

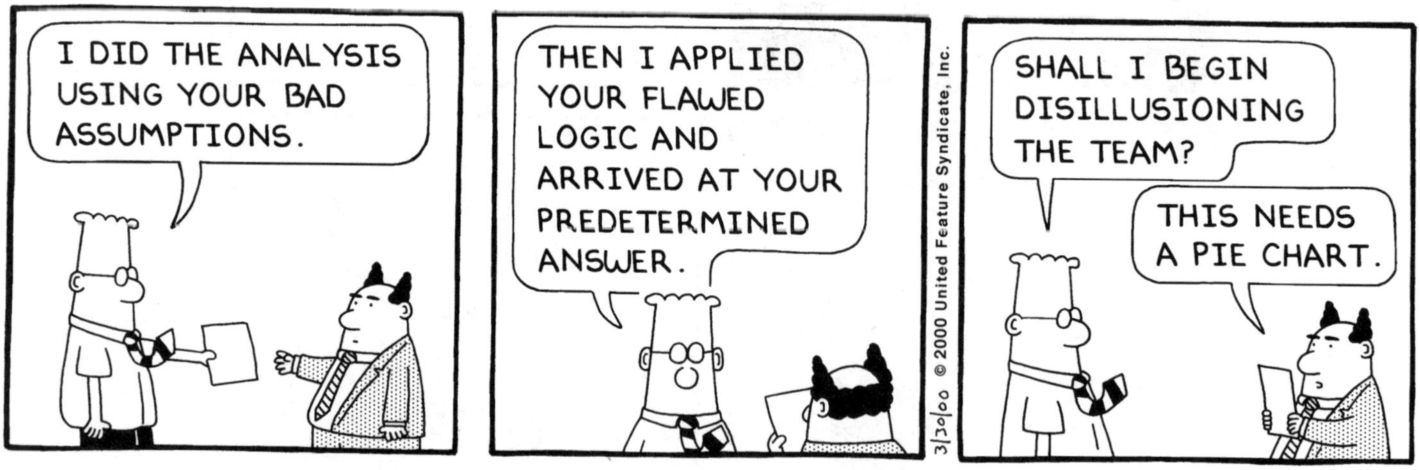
I DID THE ANALYSIS USING YOUR BAD ASSUMPTIONS.
THEN I APPLIED YOUR FLAWED LOGIC AND ARRIVED AT YOUR PREDETERMINED ANSWER.
3/30/00
© 2000 United Feature Syndicate, Inc.
SHALL I BEGIN DISILLUSIONING THE TEAM?
THIS NEEDS A PIE CHART.

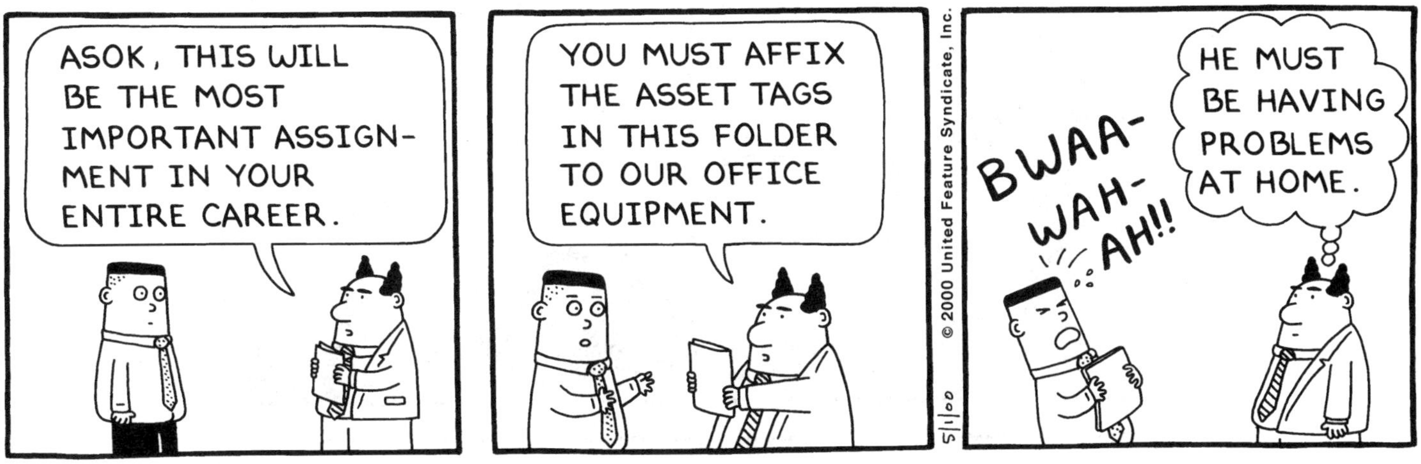
ASOK, THIS WILL BE THE MOST IMPORTANT ASSIGNMENT IN YOUR ENTIRE CAREER.
YOU MUST AFFIX THE ASSET TAGS IN THIS FOLDER TO OUR OFFICE EQUIPMENT.
BWAA-WAH-AH!!
HE MUST BE HAVING PROBLEMS AT HOME.
5/1/00 © 2000 United Feature Syndicate, Inc.

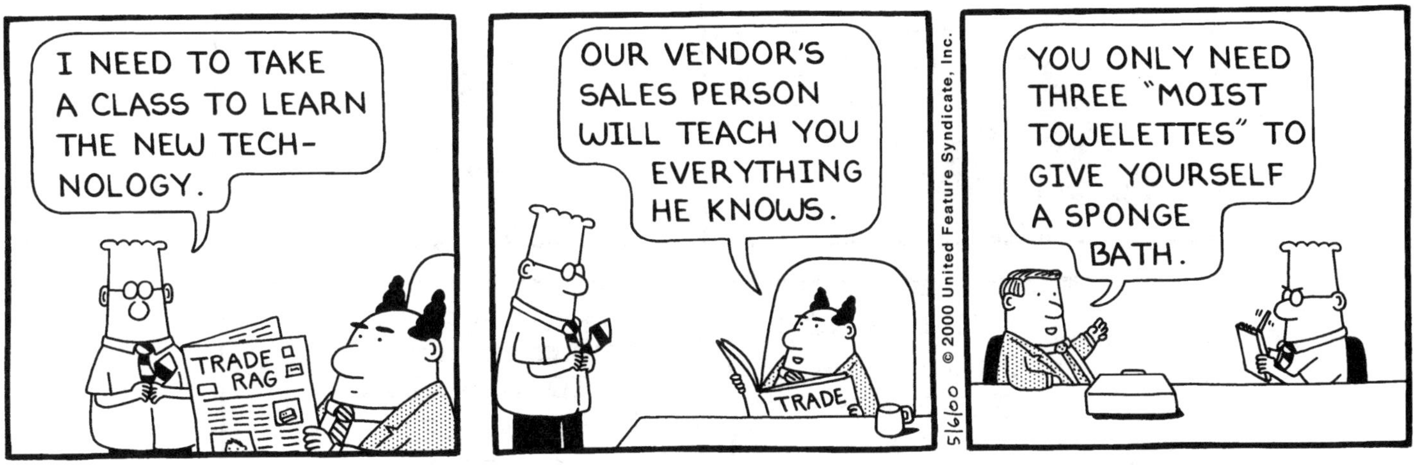
I NEED TO TAKE A CLASS TO LEARN THE NEW TECHNOLOGY.
TRADE RAG
OUR VENDOR'S SALES PERSON WILL TEACH YOU EVERYTHING HE KNOWS.
TRADE
YOU ONLY NEED THREE "MOIST TOWELETTES" TO GIVE YOURSELF A SPONGE BATH.
5/6/00 © 2000 United Feature Syndicate, Inc.

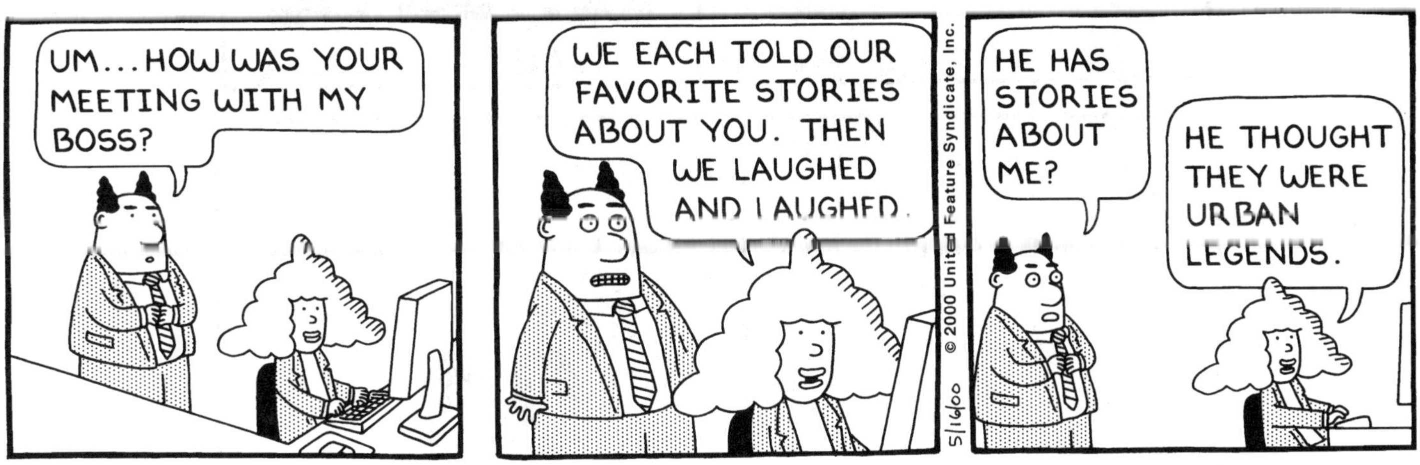
UM... HOW WAS YOUR MEETING WITH MY BOSS?
WE EACH TOLD OUR FAVORITE STORIES ABOUT YOU. THEN WE LAUGHED AND LAUGHED.
HE HAS STORIES ABOUT ME?
HE THOUGHT THEY WERE URBAN LEGENDS.
5/16/00 © 2000 United Feature Syndicate, Inc.

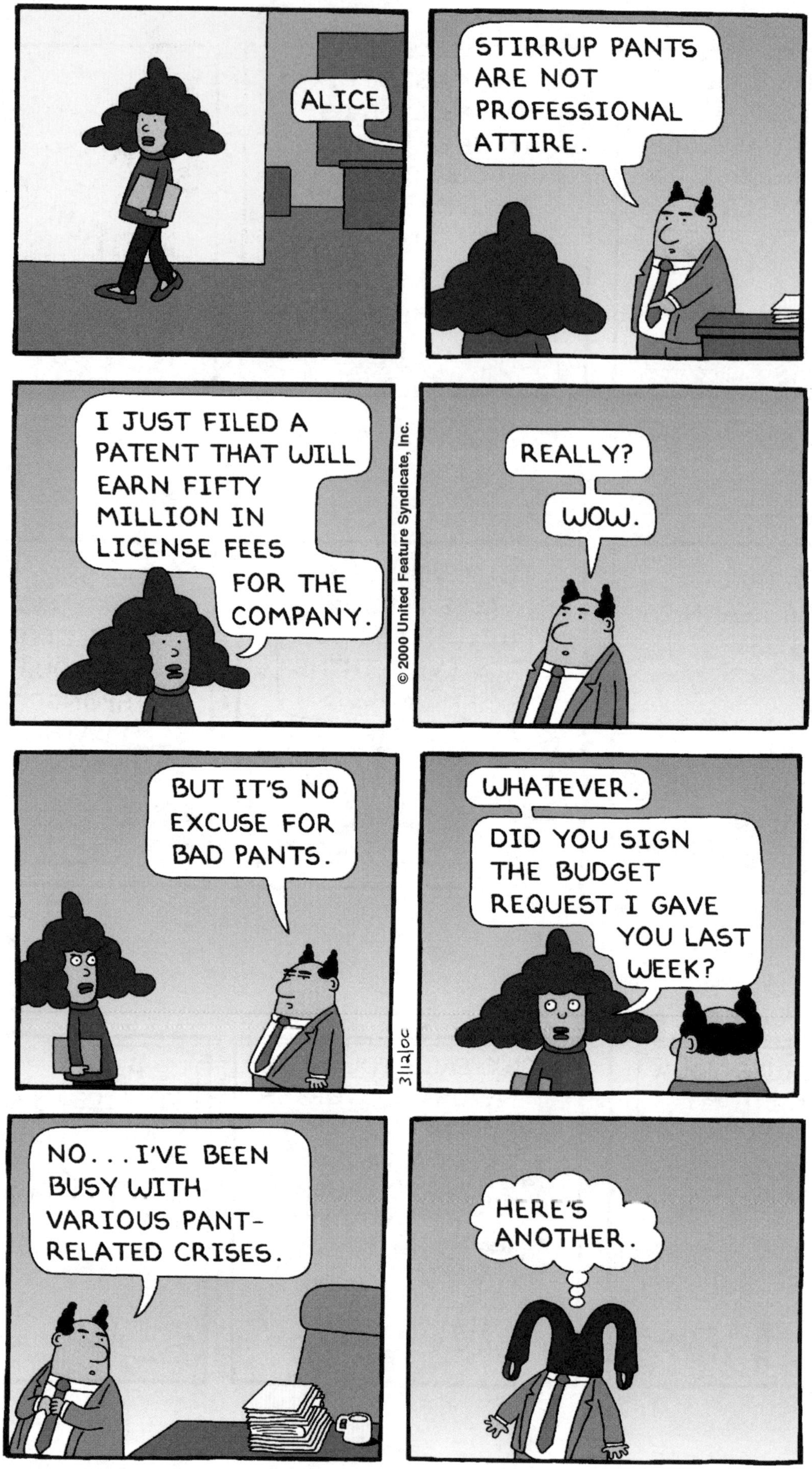
ALICE
STIRRUP PANTS ARE NOT PROFESSIONAL ATTIRE.
I JUST FILED A PATENT THAT WILL EARN FIFTY MILLION IN LICENSE FEES
FOR THE COMPANY.
© 2000 United Feature Syndicate, Inc.
REALLY?
WOW.
BUT IT'S NO EXCUSE FOR BAD PANTS.
3/12/00
WHATEVER.
DID YOU SIGN THE BUDGET REQUEST I GAVE
YOU LAST WEEK?
NO...I'VE BEEN BUSY WITH VARIOUS PANT-RELATED CRISES.
HERE'S ANOTHER.

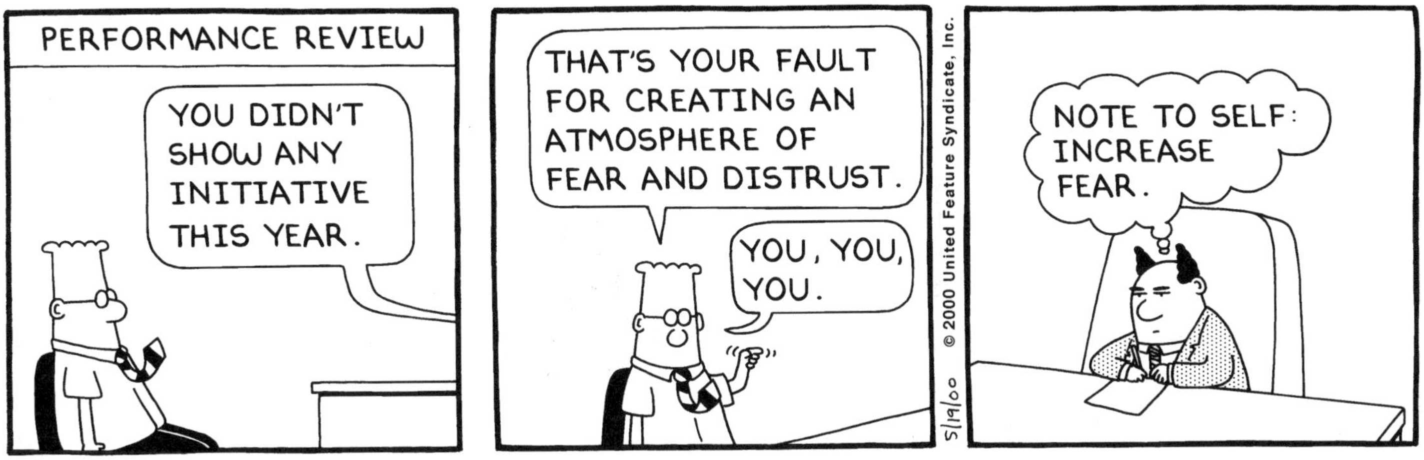
PERFORMANCE REVIEW
YOU DIDN'T SHOW ANY INITIATIVE THIS YEAR.
THAT'S YOUR FAULT FOR CREATING AN ATMOSPHERE OF FEAR AND DISTRUST.
YOU, YOU, YOU.
© 2000 United Feature Syndicate, Inc.
5/19/00
NOTE TO SELF: INCREASE FEAR.

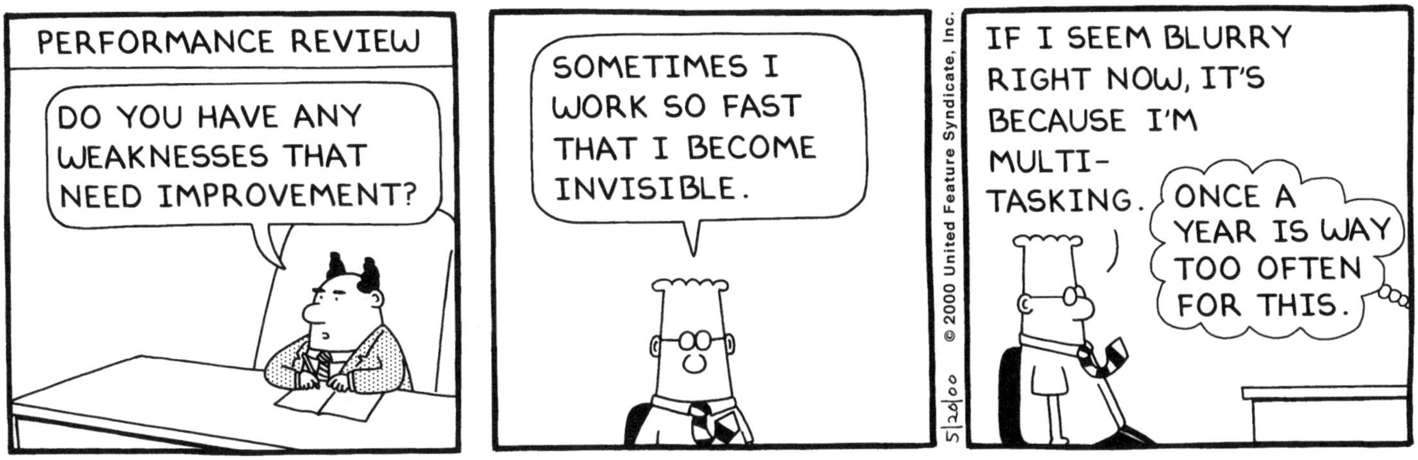
PERFORMANCE REVIEW
DO YOU HAVE ANY WEAKNESSES THAT NEED IMPROVEMENT?
SOMETIMES I WORK SO FAST THAT I BECOME INVISIBLE.
© 2000 United Feature Syndicate, Inc.
5/20/00
IF I SEEM BLURRY RIGHT NOW, IT'S BECAUSE I'M MULTI-TASKING.
ONCE A YEAR IS WAY TOO OFTEN FOR THIS.

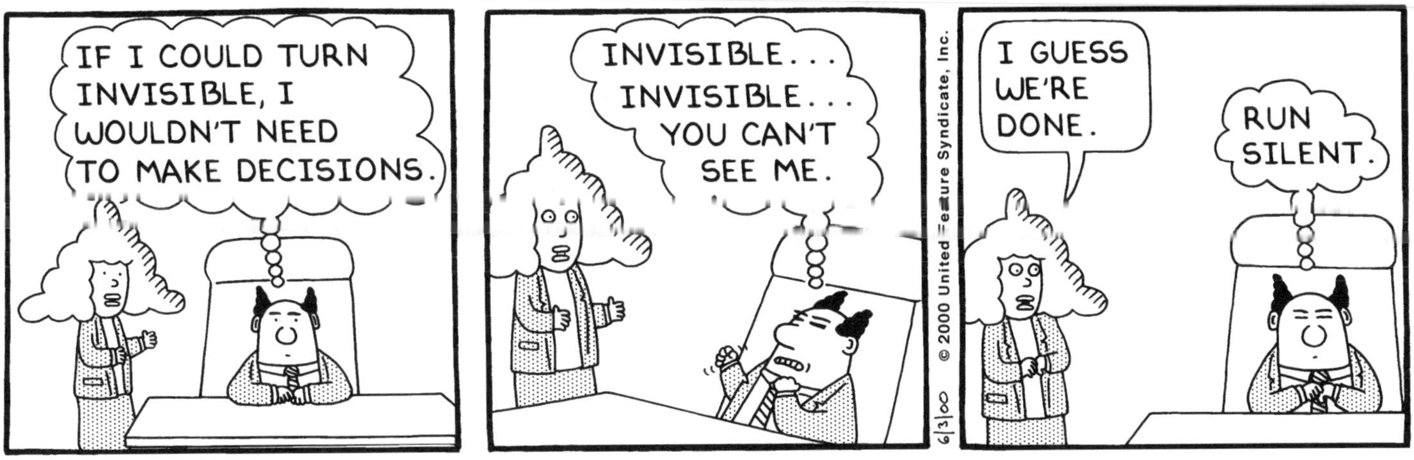
IF I COULD TURN INVISIBLE, I WOULDN'T NEED TO MAKE DECISIONS.
INVISIBLE... INVISIBLE... YOU CAN'T SEE ME.
© 2000 United Feature Syndicate, Inc.
6/3/00
I GUESS WE'RE DONE.
RUN SILENT.

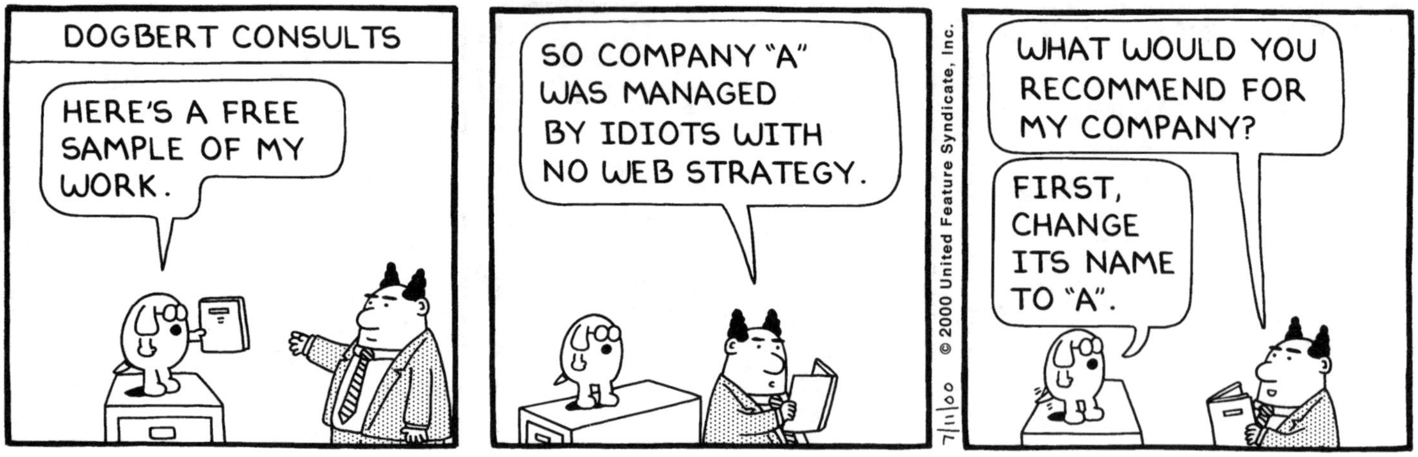
DOGBERT CONSULTS
HERE'S A FREE SAMPLE OF MY WORK.
SO COMPANY "A" WAS MANAGED BY IDIOTS WITH NO WEB STRATEGY.
WHAT WOULD YOU RECOMMEND FOR MY COMPANY?
FIRST, CHANGE ITS NAME TO "A".
7/11/00 © 2000 United Feature Syndicate, Inc.

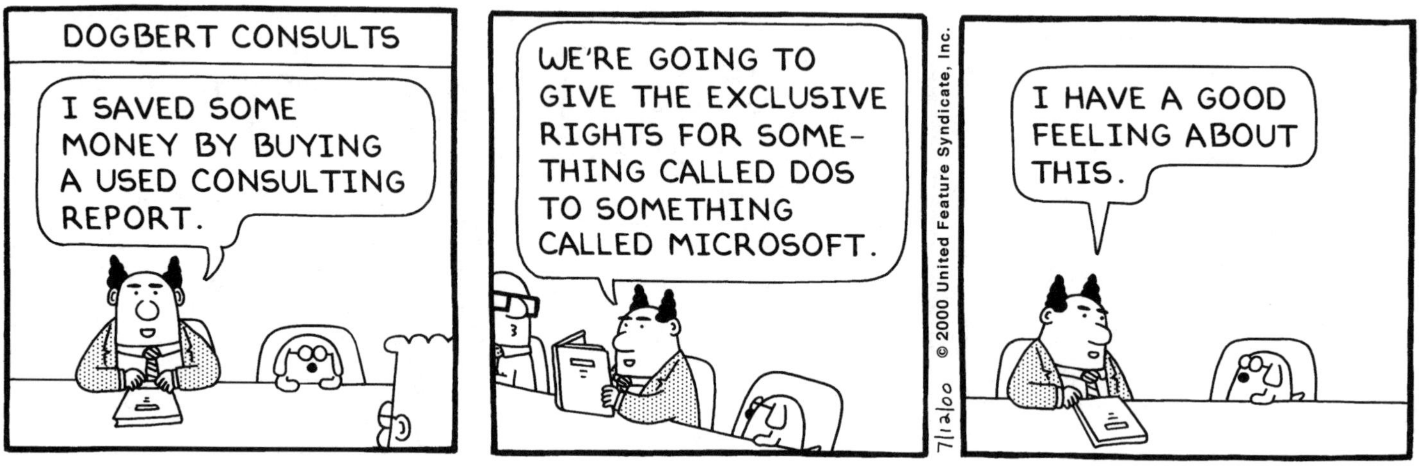
DOGBERT CONSULTS
I SAVED SOME MONEY BY BUYING A USED CONSULTING REPORT.
WE'RE GOING TO GIVE THE EXCLUSIVE RIGHTS FOR SOME-THING CALLED DOS TO SOMETHING CALLED MICROSOFT.
I HAVE A GOOD FEELING ABOUT THIS.
7/12/00 © 2000 United Feature Syndicate, Inc.

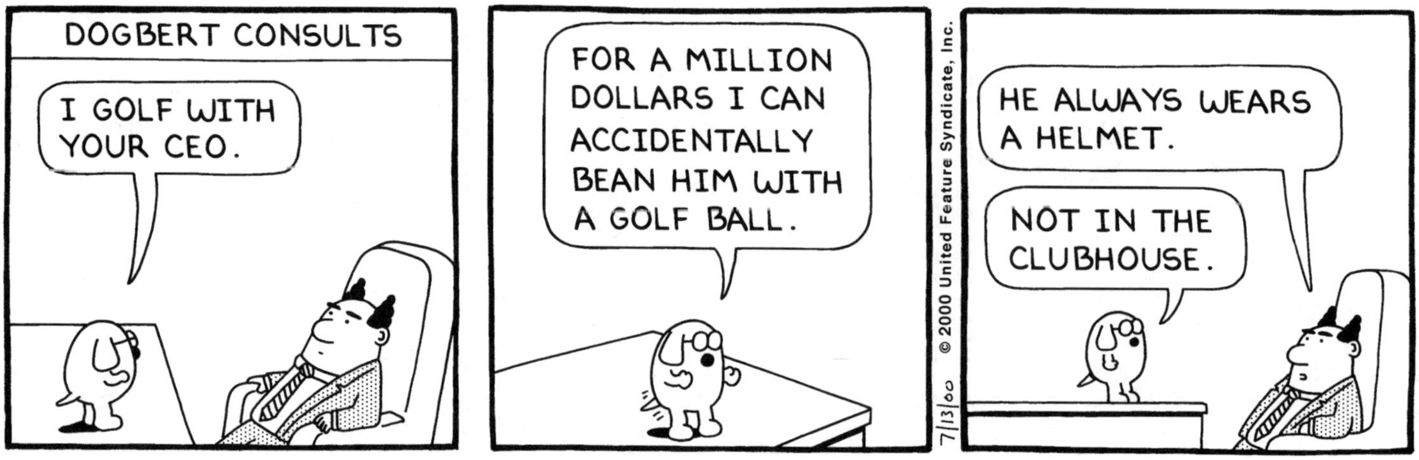
DOGBERT CONSULTS
I GOLF WITH YOUR CEO.
FOR A MILLION DOLLARS I CAN ACCIDENTALLY BEAN HIM WITH A GOLF BALL.
HE ALWAYS WEARS A HELMET.
NOT IN THE CLUBHOUSE.
7/13/00 © 2000 United Feature Syndicate, Inc.

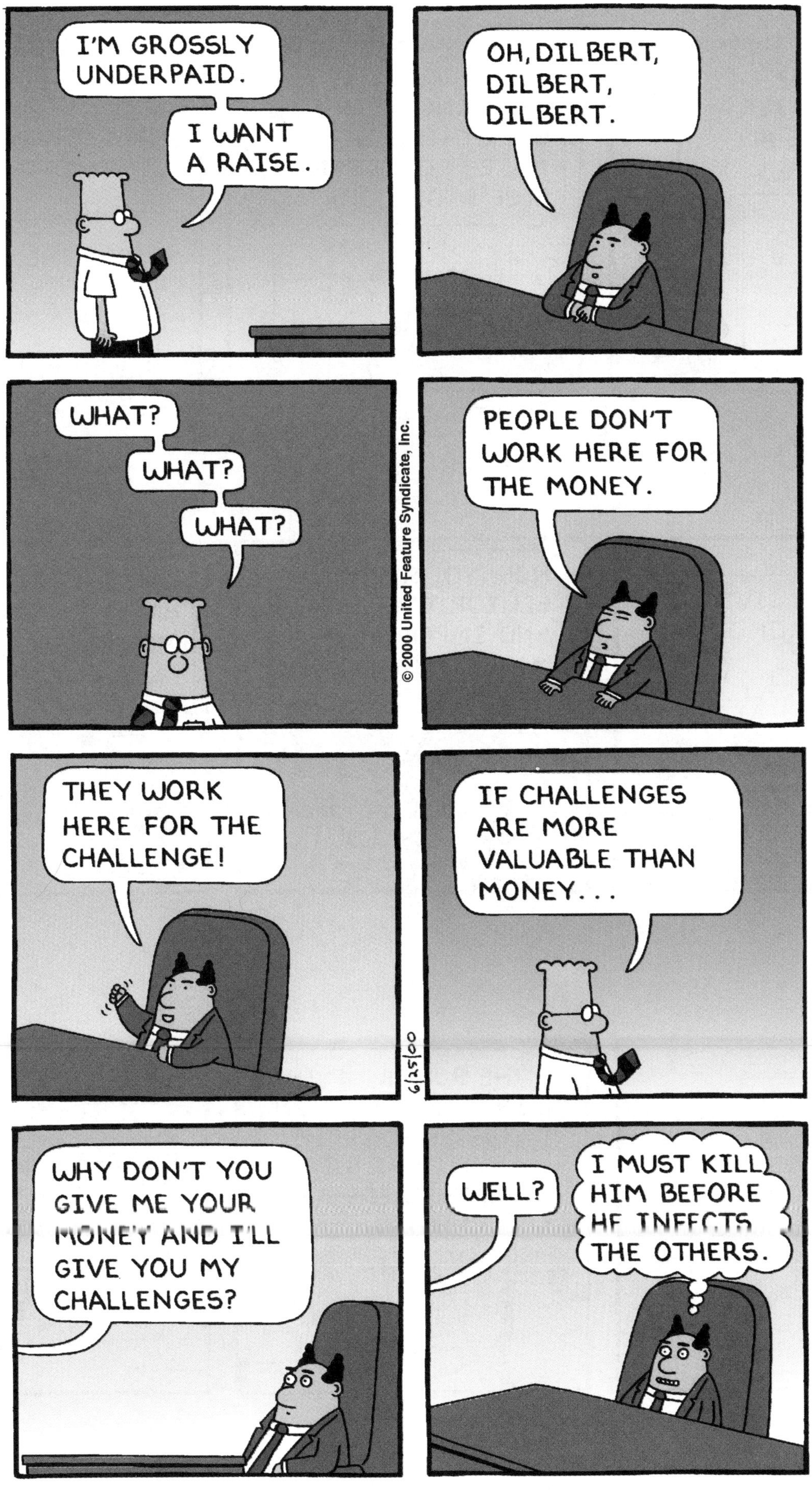
I'M GROSSLY UNDERPAID.
I WANT A RAISE.
OH, DILBERT, DILBERT, DILBERT.
WHAT?
WHAT?
WHAT?
© 2000 United Feature Syndicate, Inc.
PEOPLE DON'T WORK HERE FOR THE MONEY.
THEY WORK HERE FOR THE CHALLENGE!
6/25/00
IF CHALLENGES ARE MORE VALUABLE THAN MONEY...
WHY DON'T YOU GIVE ME YOUR MONEY AND I'LL GIVE YOU MY CHALLENGES?
WELL?
I MUST KILL HIM BEFORE HE INFECTS THE OTHERS.

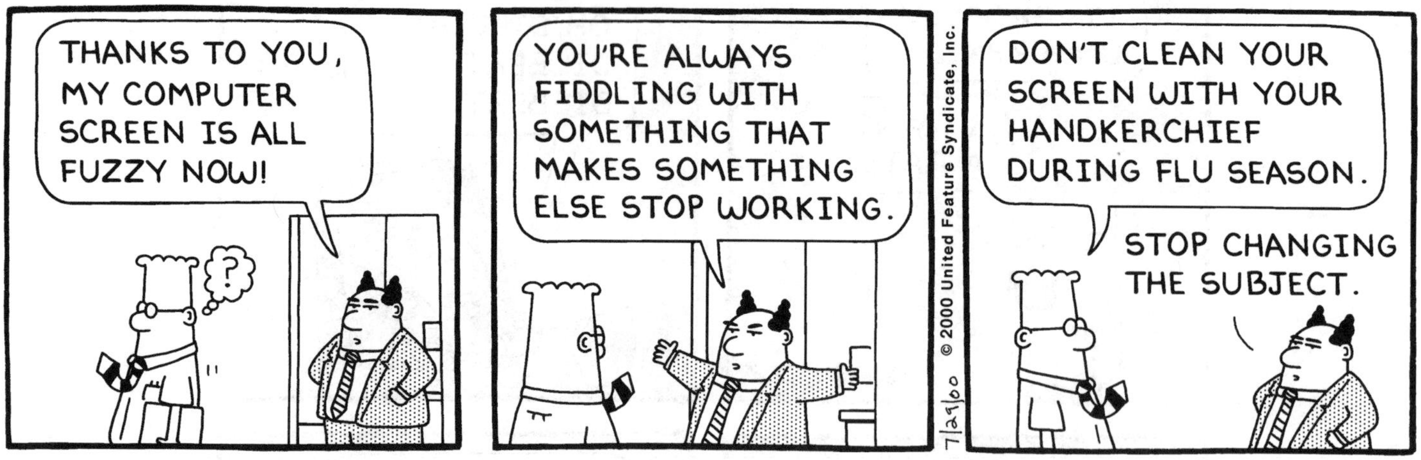
THANKS TO YOU, MY COMPUTER SCREEN IS ALL FUZZY NOW!
?
YOU'RE ALWAYS FIDDLING WITH SOMETHING THAT MAKES SOMETHING ELSE STOP WORKING.
7/29/00 © 2000 United Feature Syndicate, Inc.
DON'T CLEAN YOUR SCREEN WITH YOUR HANDKERCHIEF DURING FLU SEASON.
STOP CHANGING THE SUBJECT.

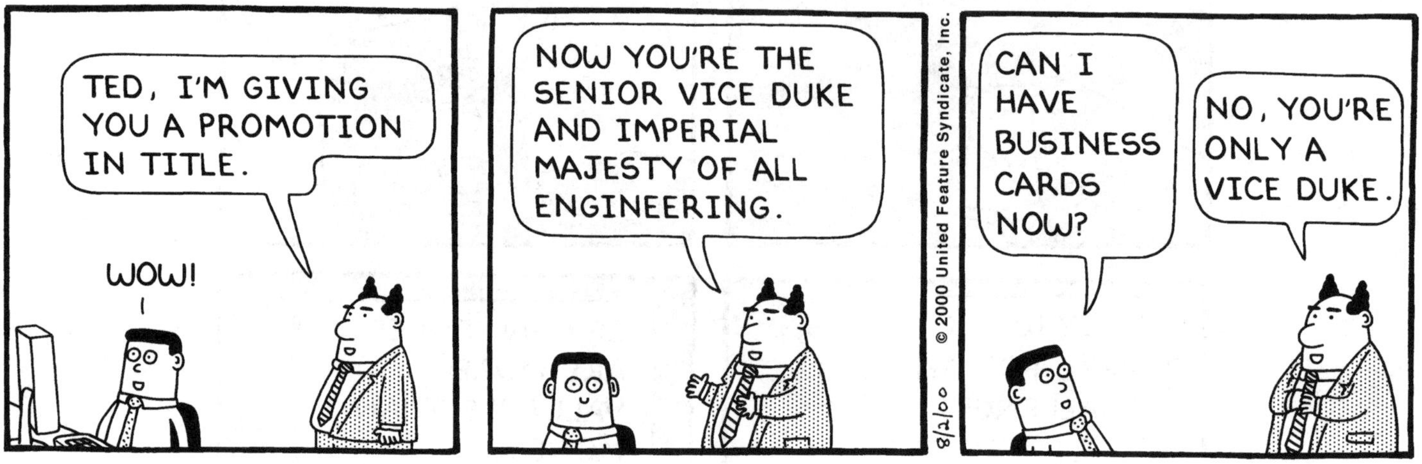
TED, I'M GIVING YOU A PROMOTION IN TITLE.
WOW!
NOW YOU'RE THE SENIOR VICE DUKE AND IMPERIAL MAJESTY OF ALL ENGINEERING.
8/2/00 © 2000 United Feature Syndicate, Inc.
CAN I HAVE BUSINESS CARDS NOW?
NO, YOU'RE ONLY A VICE DUKE.

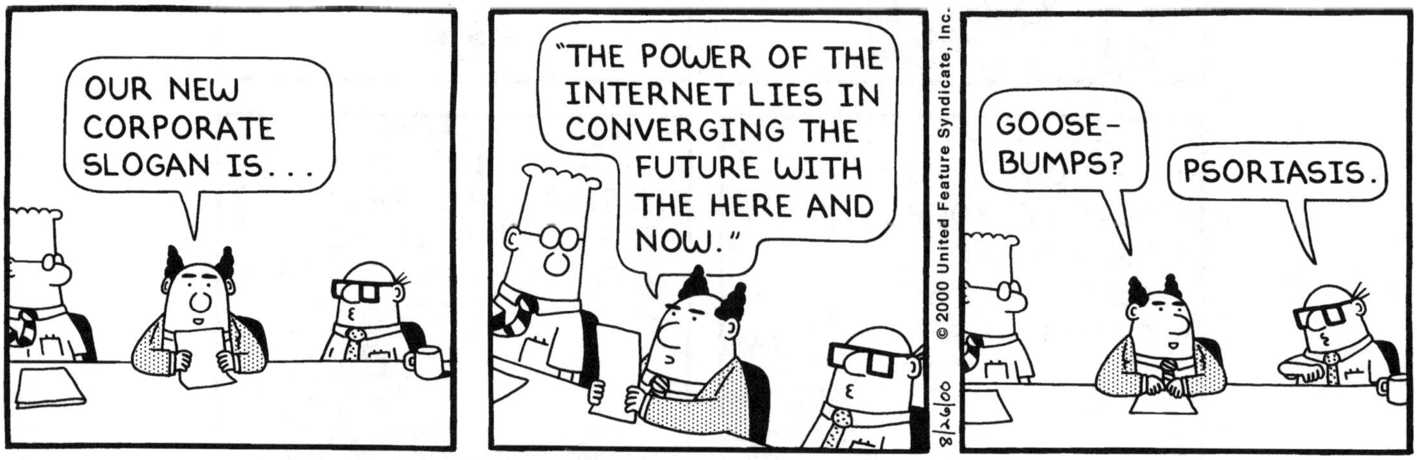
OUR NEW CORPORATE SLOGAN IS...
"THE POWER OF THE INTERNET LIES IN CONVERGING THE FUTURE WITH THE HERE AND NOW."
8/26/00 © 2000 United Feature Syndicate, Inc.
GOOSE-BUMPS?
PSORIASIS.

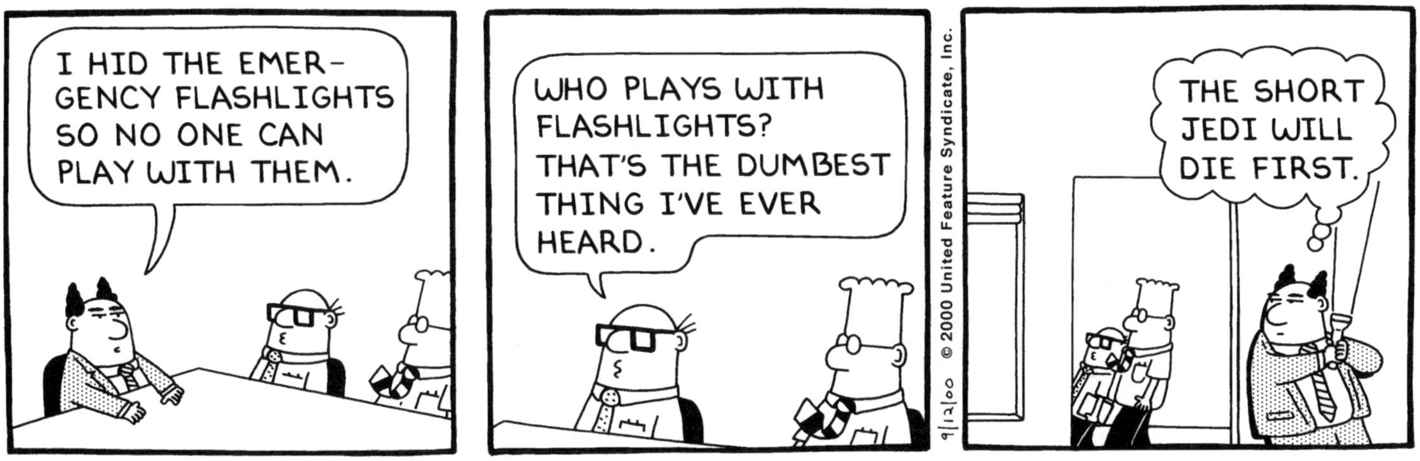
I HID THE EMERGENCY FLASHLIGHTS SO NO ONE CAN PLAY WITH THEM.
WHO PLAYS WITH FLASHLIGHTS? THAT'S THE DUMBEST THING I'VE EVER HEARD.
9/12/00 © 2000 United Feature Syndicate, Inc.
THE SHORT JEDI WILL DIE FIRST.

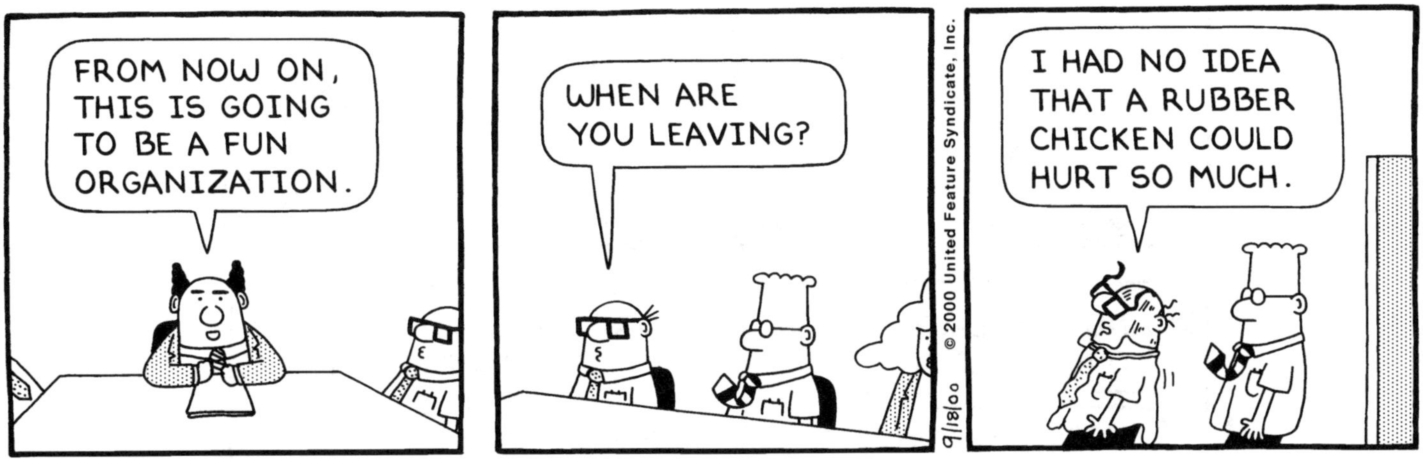
FROM NOW ON, THIS IS GOING TO BE A FUN ORGANIZATION.
WHEN ARE YOU LEAVING?
9/18/00 © 2000 United Feature Syndicate, Inc.
I HAD NO IDEA THAT A RUBBER CHICKEN COULD HURT SO MUCH.

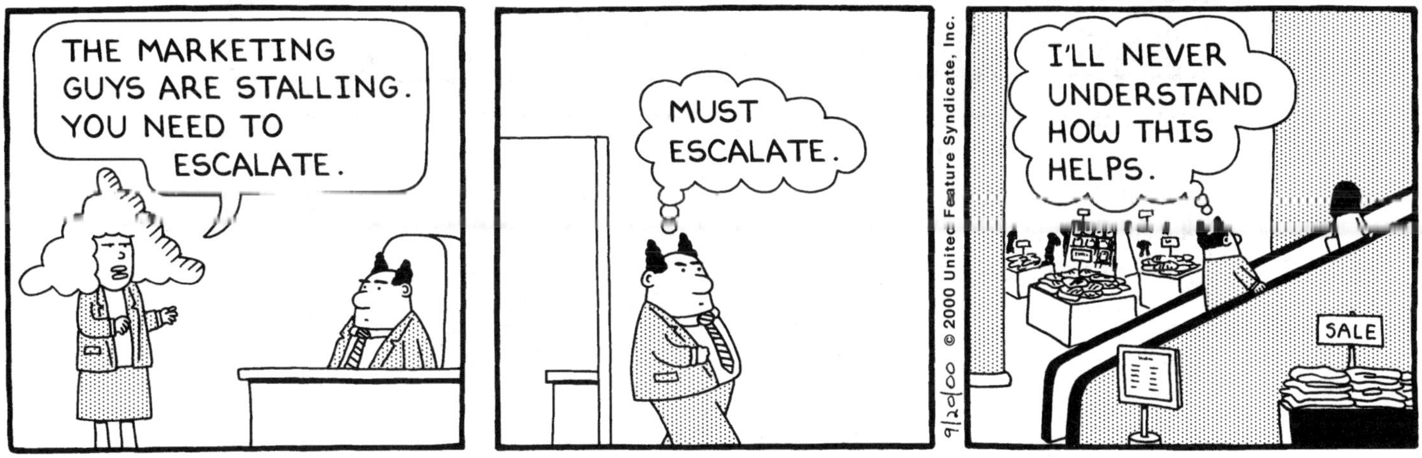
THE MARKETING GUYS ARE STALLING. YOU NEED TO ESCALATE.
MUST ESCALATE.
9/20/00 © 2000 United Feature Syndicate, Inc.
I'LL NEVER UNDERSTAND HOW THIS HELPS.
SALE

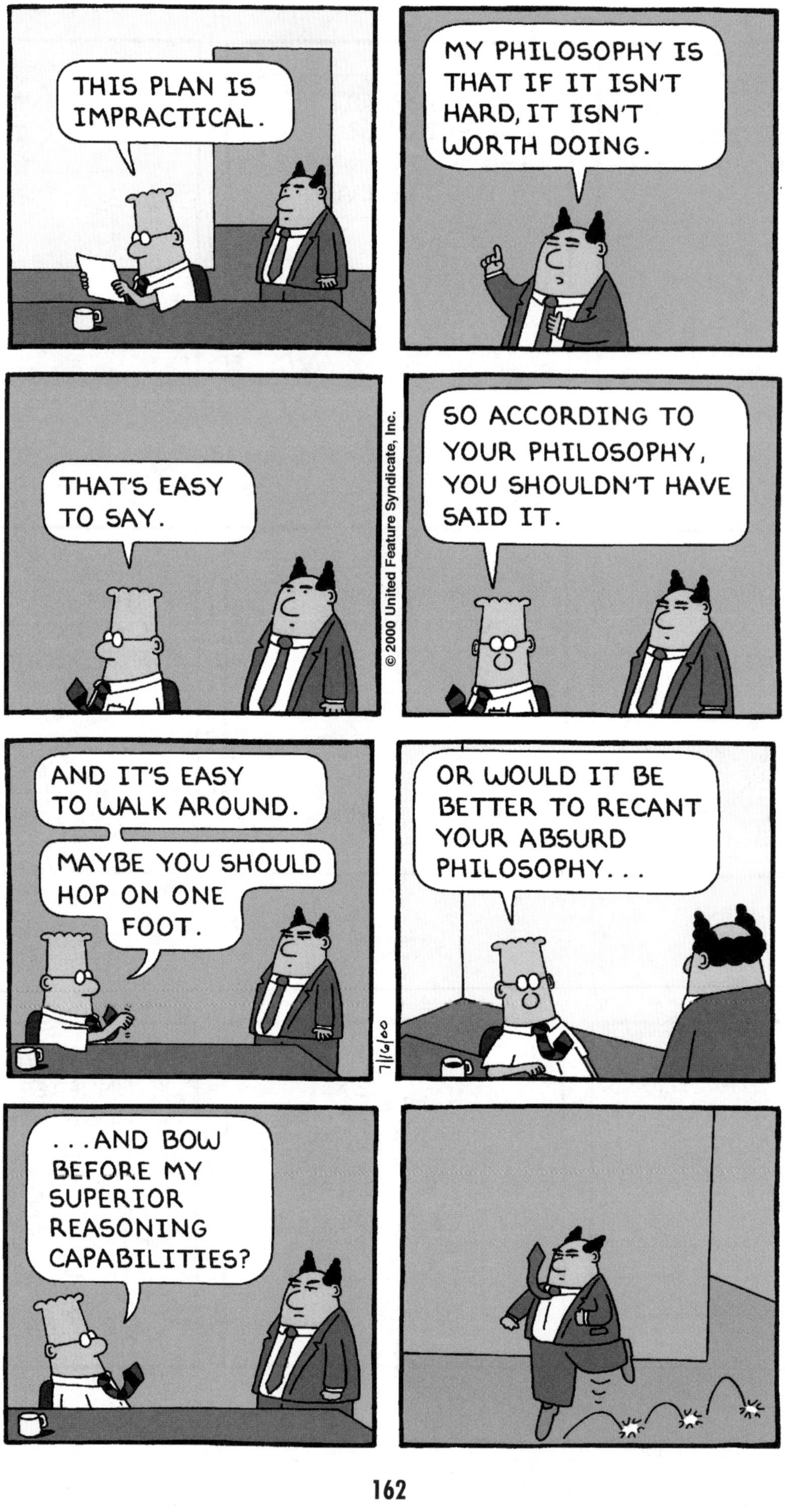
THIS PLAN IS IMPRACTICAL.
MY PHILOSOPHY IS THAT IF IT ISN'T HARD, IT ISN'T WORTH DOING.
THAT'S EASY TO SAY.
SO ACCORDING TO YOUR PHILOSOPHY, YOU SHOULDN'T HAVE SAID IT.
© 2000 United Feature Syndicate, Inc.
AND IT'S EASY TO WALK AROUND.
MAYBE YOU SHOULD HOP ON ONE FOOT.
7/16/00
OR WOULD IT BE BETTER TO RECANT YOUR ABSURD PHILOSOPHY...
...AND BOW BEFORE MY SUPERIOR REASONING CAPABILITIES?

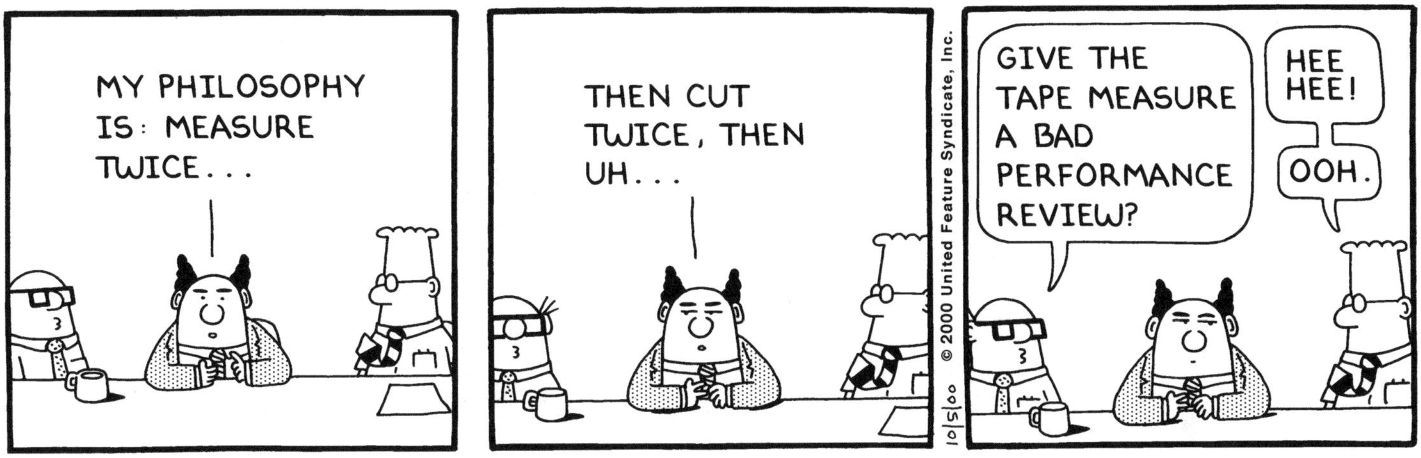
MY PHILOSOPHY IS: MEASURE TWICE...
THEN CUT TWICE, THEN UH...
© 2000 United Feature Syndicate, Inc.
10/5/00
GIVE THE TAPE MEASURE A BAD PERFORMANCE REVIEW?
HEE HEE!
OOH.

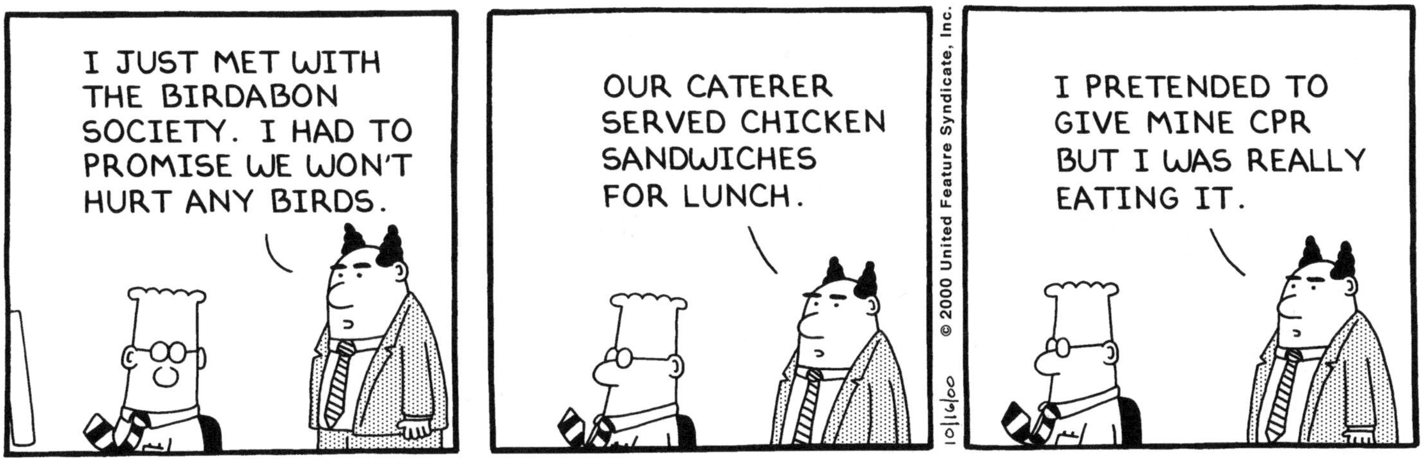
I JUST MET WITH THE BIRDABON SOCIETY. I HAD TO PROMISE WE WON'T HURT ANY BIRDS.
OUR CATERER SERVED CHICKEN SANDWICHES FOR LUNCH.
© 2000 United Feature Syndicate, Inc.
10/16/00
I PRETENDED TO GIVE MINE CPR BUT I WAS REALLY EATING IT.

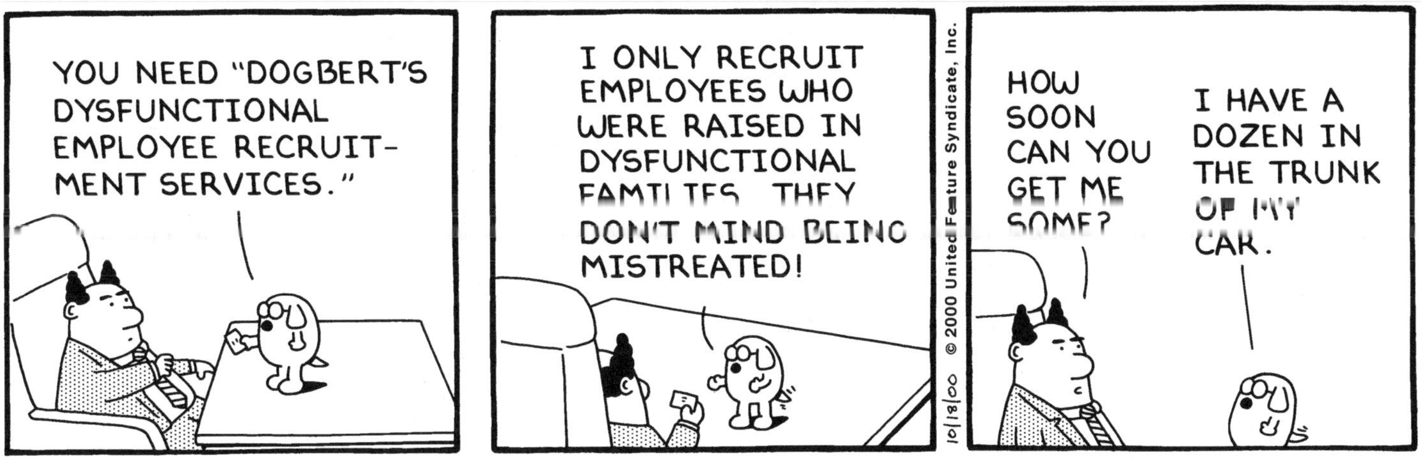
YOU NEED "DOGBERT'S DYSFUNCTIONAL EMPLOYEE RECRUIT-MENT SERVICES."
I ONLY RECRUIT EMPLOYEES WHO WERE RAISED IN DYSFUNCTIONAL FAMILIES. THEY DON'T MIND BEING MISTREATED!
© 2000 United Feature Syndicate, Inc.
10/18/00
HOW SOON CAN YOU GET ME SOME?
I HAVE A DOZEN IN THE TRUNK OF MY CAR.

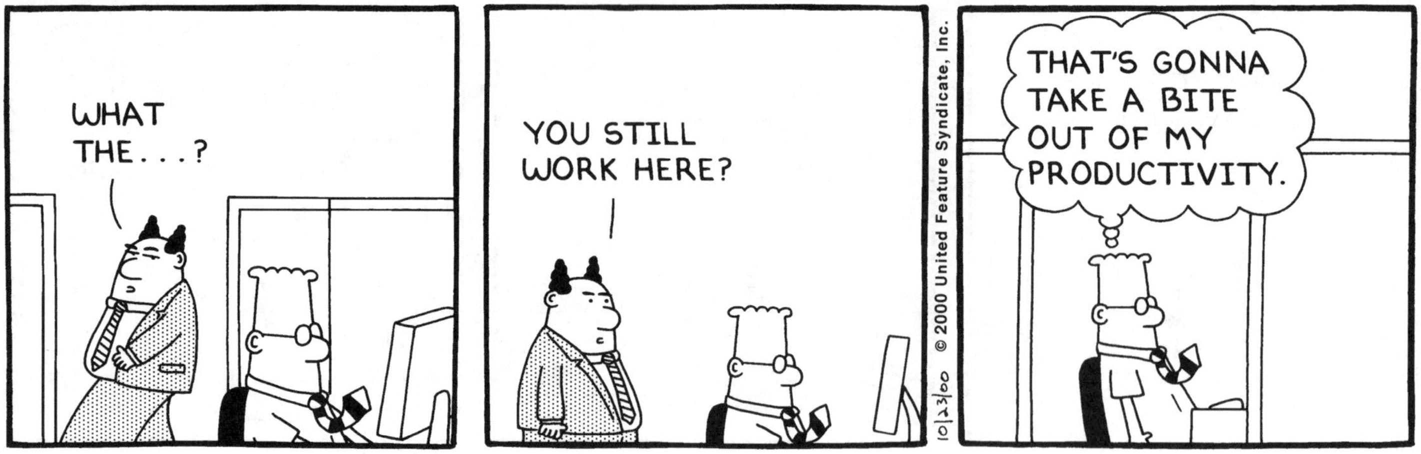
WHAT THE...?
YOU STILL WORK HERE?
© 2000 United Feature Syndicate, Inc.
10/23/00
THAT'S GONNA TAKE A BITE OUT OF MY PRODUCTIVITY.

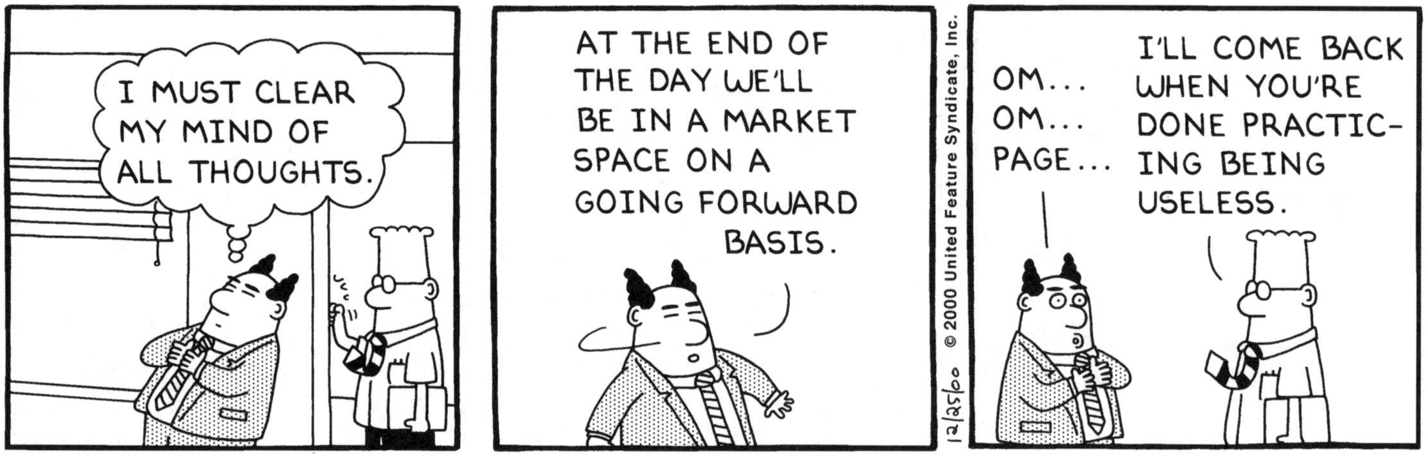
I MUST CLEAR MY MIND OF ALL THOUGHTS.
AT THE END OF THE DAY WE'LL BE IN A MARKET SPACE ON A GOING FORWARD BASIS.
© 2000 United Feature Syndicate, Inc.
12/25/00
OM... OM... PAGE...
I'LL COME BACK WHEN YOU'RE DONE PRACTIC-ING BEING USELESS.

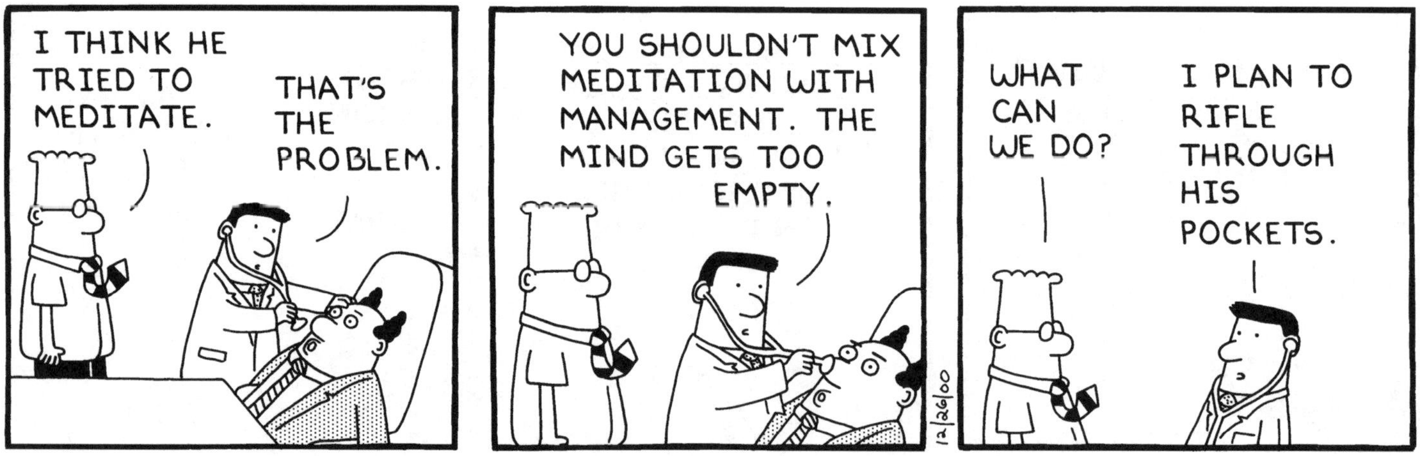
I THINK HE TRIED TO MEDITATE.
THAT'S THE PROBLEM.
YOU SHOULDN'T MIX MEDITATION WITH MANAGEMENT. THE MIND GETS TOO EMPTY.
12/26/00
WHAT CAN WE DO?
I PLAN TO RIFLE THROUGH HIS POCKETS.

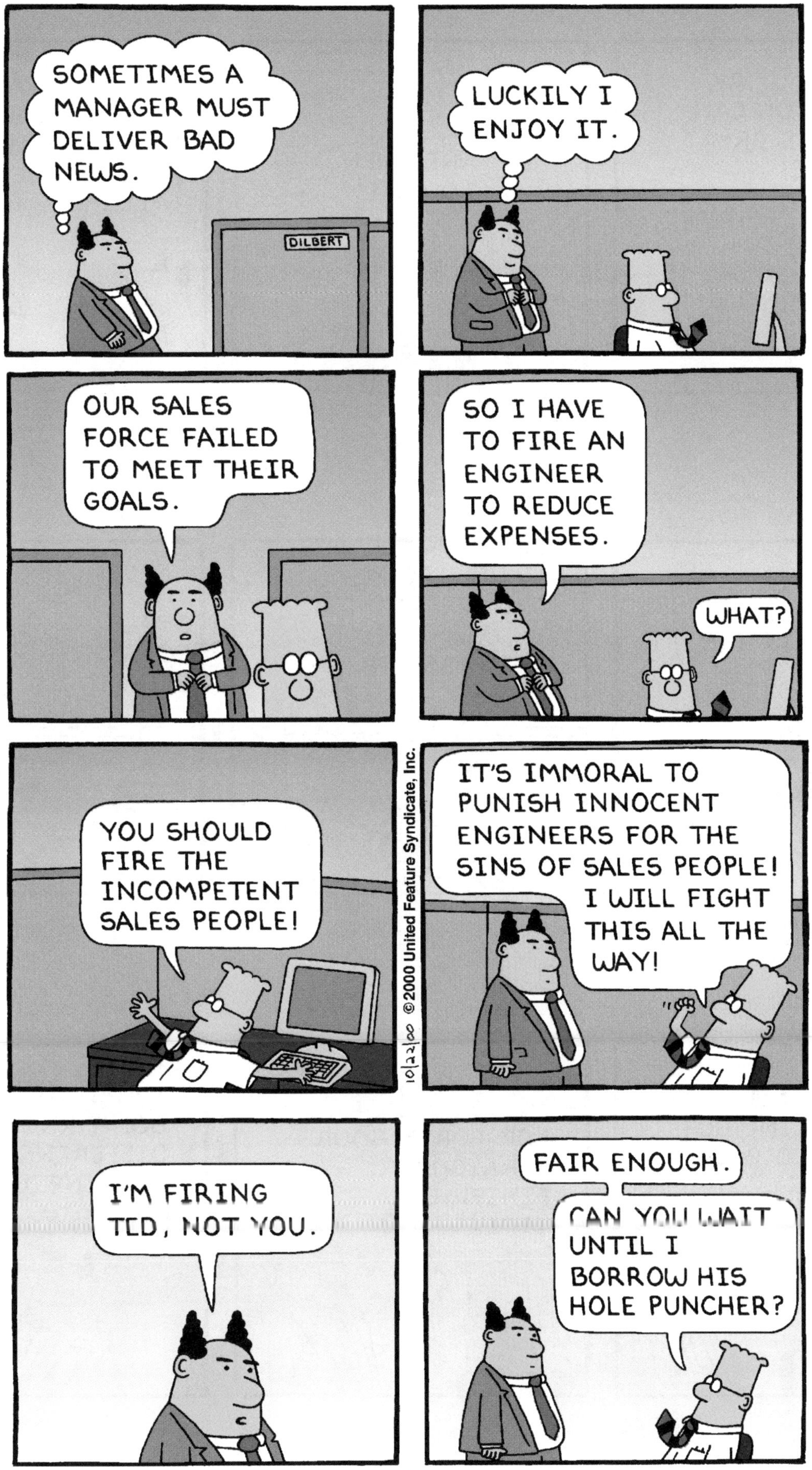
SOMETIMES A MANAGER MUST DELIVER BAD NEWS.
DILBERT
LUCKILY I ENJOY IT.
OUR SALES FORCE FAILED TO MEET THEIR GOALS.
SO I HAVE TO FIRE AN ENGINEER TO REDUCE EXPENSES.
WHAT?
YOU SHOULD FIRE THE INCOMPETENT SALES PEOPLE!
IT'S IMMORAL TO PUNISH INNOCENT ENGINEERS FOR THE SINS OF SALES PEOPLE! I WILL FIGHT THIS ALL THE WAY!
I'M FIRING TED, NOT YOU.
FAIR ENOUGH.
CAN YOU WAIT UNTIL I BORROW HIS HOLE PUNCHER?
10/22/00 ©2000 United Feature Syndicate, Inc.

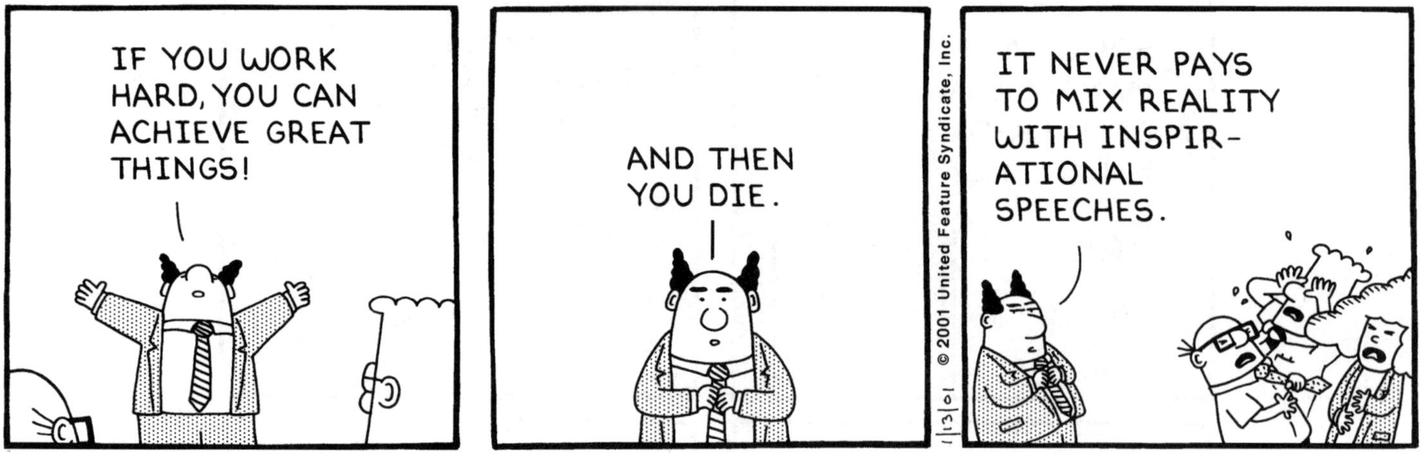
IF YOU WORK HARD, YOU CAN ACHIEVE GREAT THINGS!
AND THEN YOU DIE.
1/13/01 © 2001 United Feature Syndicate, Inc.
IT NEVER PAYS TO MIX REALITY WITH INSPIR-ATIONAL SPEECHES.

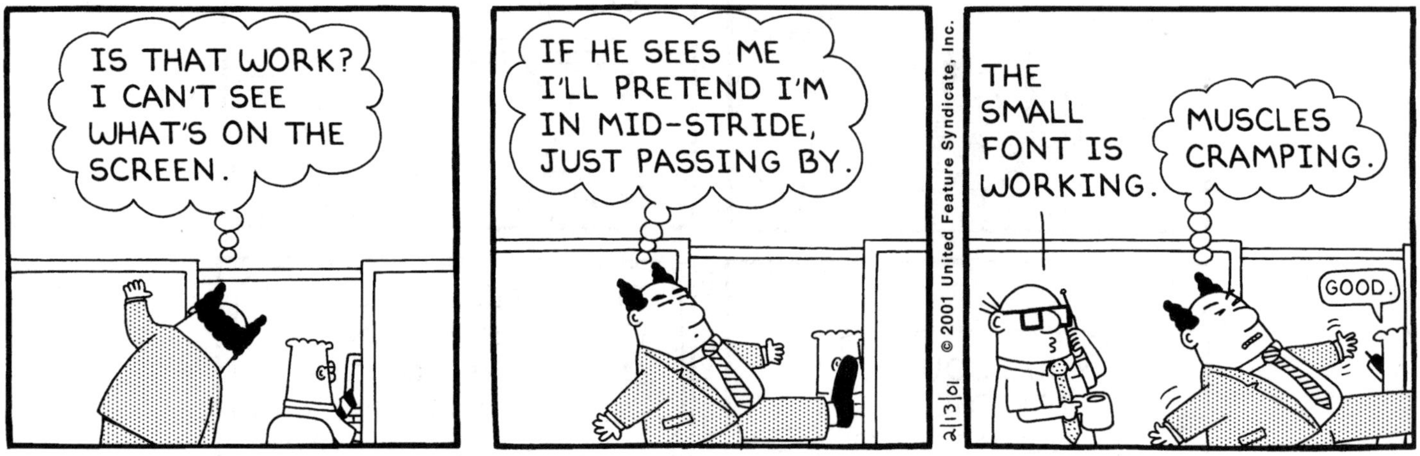
IS THAT WORK? I CAN'T SEE WHAT'S ON THE SCREEN.
IF HE SEES ME I'LL PRETEND I'M IN MID-STRIDE, JUST PASSING BY.
2/13/01 © 2001 United Feature Syndicate, Inc.
THE SMALL FONT IS WORKING.
MUSCLES CRAMPING.
GOOD.

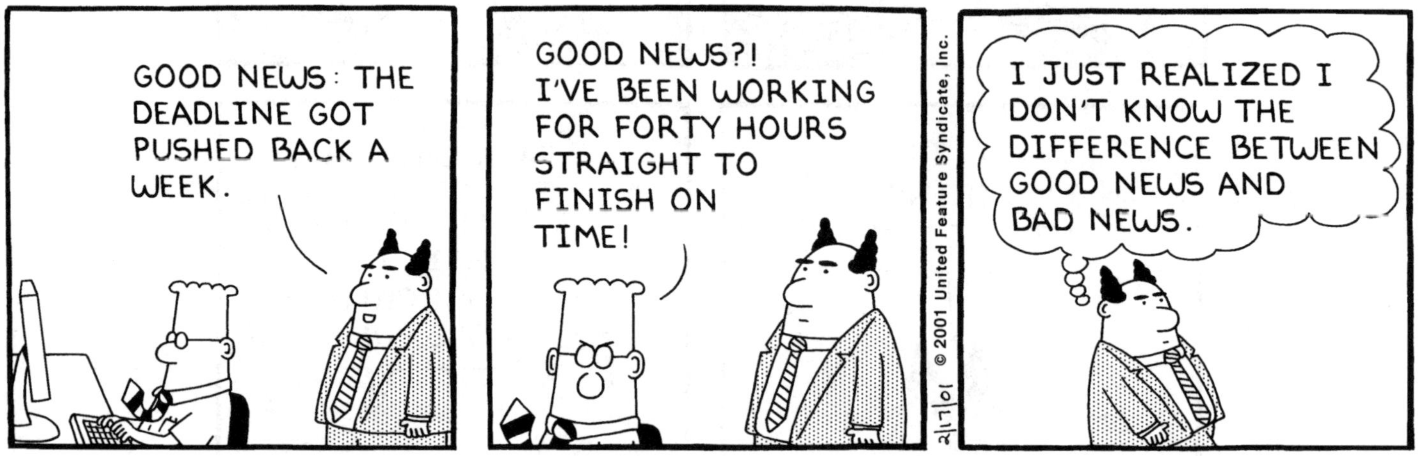
GOOD NEWS: THE DEADLINE GOT PUSHED BACK A WEEK.
GOOD NEWS?! I'VE BEEN WORKING FOR FORTY HOURS STRAIGHT TO FINISH ON TIME!
2/17/01 © 2001 United Feature Syndicate, Inc.
I JUST REALIZED I DON'T KNOW THE DIFFERENCE BETWEEN GOOD NEWS AND BAD NEWS.

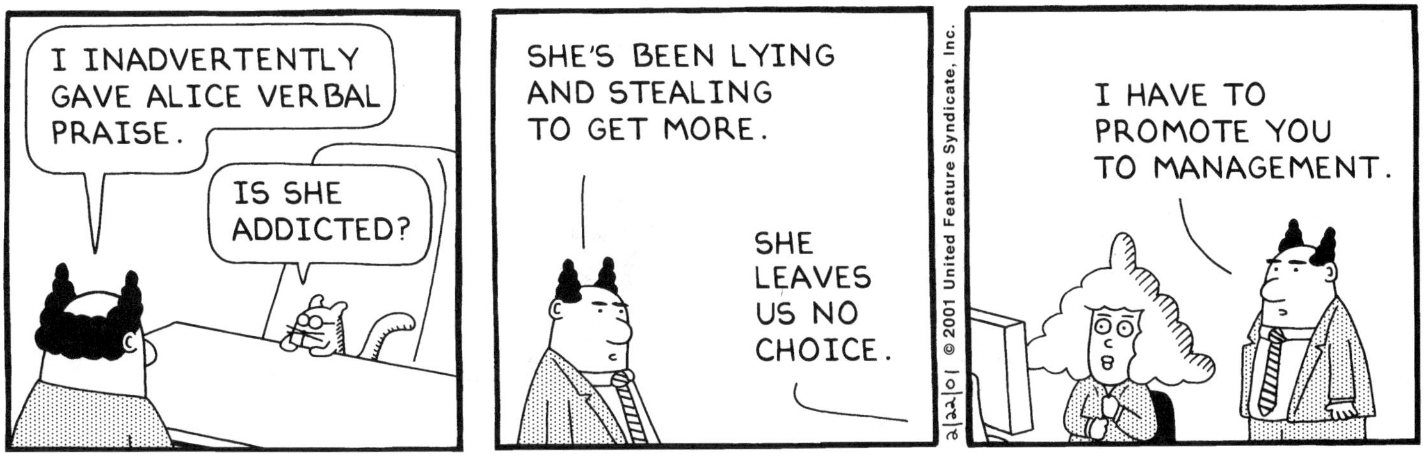
I INADVERTENTLY GAVE ALICE VERBAL PRAISE.
IS SHE ADDICTED?
SHE'S BEEN LYING AND STEALING TO GET MORE.
SHE LEAVES US NO CHOICE.
2/22/01 © 2001 United Feature Syndicate, Inc.
I HAVE TO PROMOTE YOU TO MANAGEMENT.

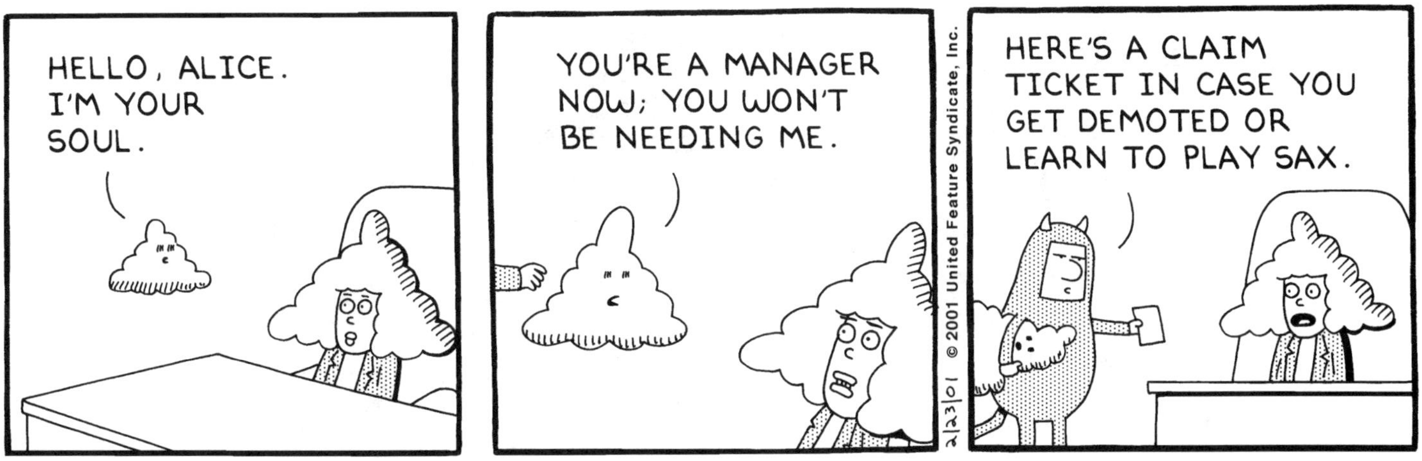
HELLO, ALICE. I'M YOUR SOUL.
YOU'RE A MANAGER NOW; YOU WON'T BE NEEDING ME.
2/23/01 © 2001 United Feature Syndicate, Inc.
HERE'S A CLAIM TICKET IN CASE YOU GET DEMOTED OR LEARN TO PLAY SAX.

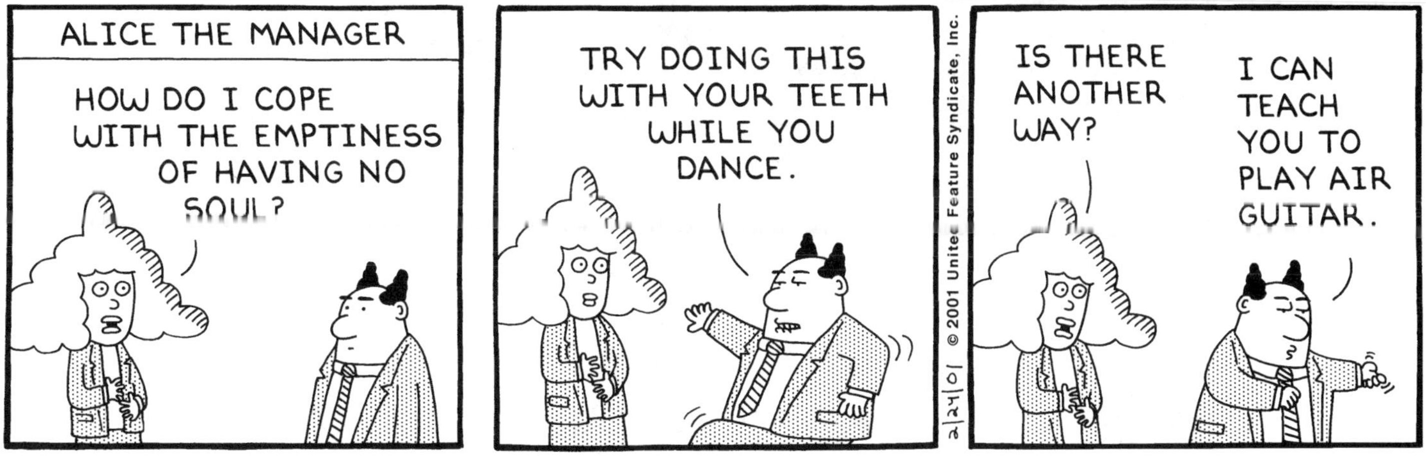
ALICE THE MANAGER
HOW DO I COPE WITH THE EMPTINESS OF HAVING NO SOUL?
TRY DOING THIS WITH YOUR TEETH WHILE YOU DANCE.
2/24/01 © 2001 United Feature Syndicate, Inc.
IS THERE ANOTHER WAY?
I CAN TEACH YOU TO PLAY AIR GUITAR.

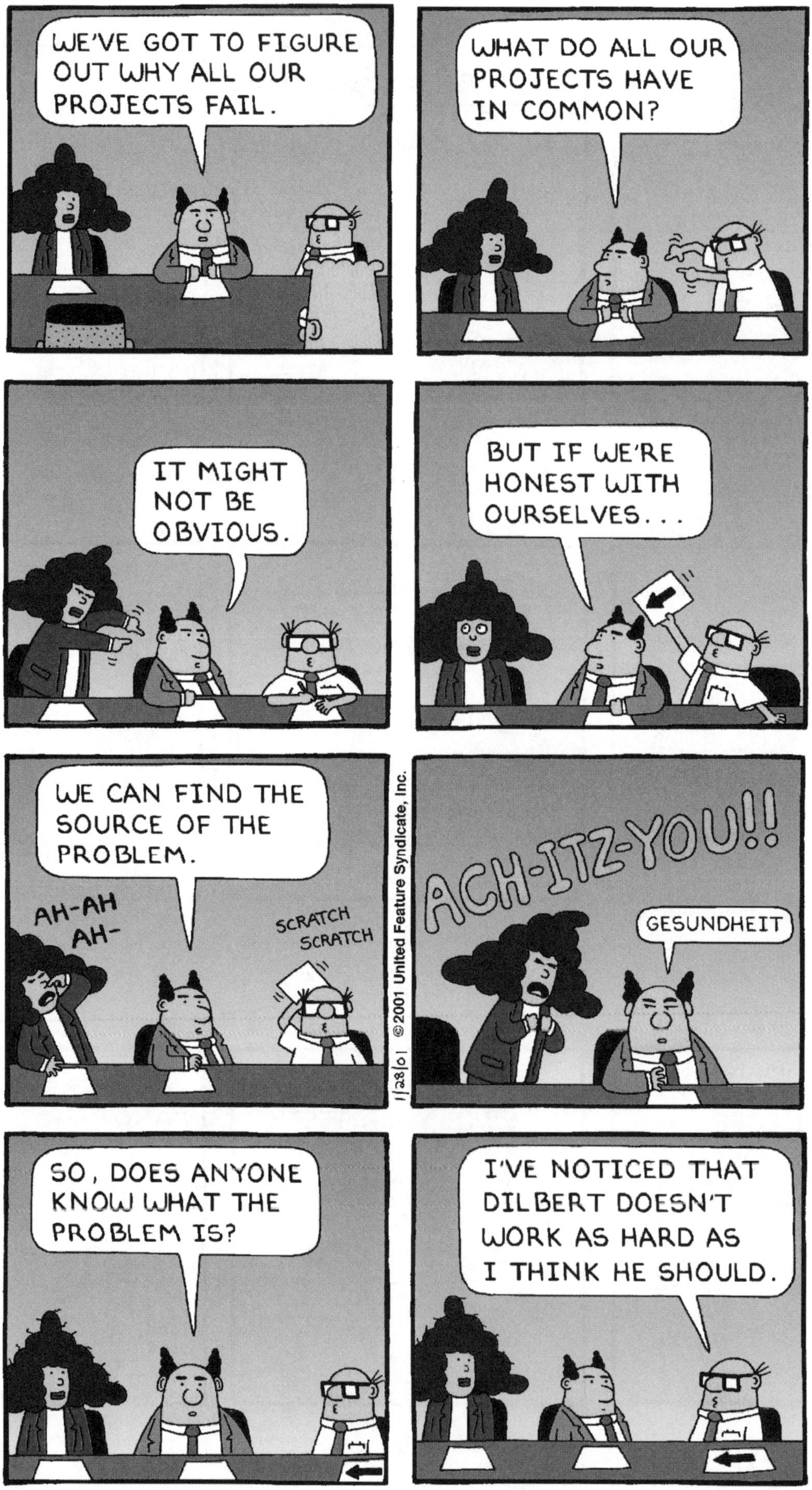
WE'VE GOT TO FIGURE OUT WHY ALL OUR PROJECTS FAIL.
WHAT DO ALL OUR PROJECTS HAVE IN COMMON?
IT MIGHT NOT BE OBVIOUS.
BUT IF WE'RE HONEST WITH OURSELVES...
WE CAN FIND THE SOURCE OF THE PROBLEM.
AH-AH AH-
SCRATCH SCRATCH
ACH-ITZ-YOU!!
GESUNDHEIT
SO, DOES ANYONE KNOW WHAT THE PROBLEM IS?
I'VE NOTICED THAT DILBERT DOESN'T WORK AS HARD AS I THINK HE SHOULD.
1/28/01 ©2001 United Feature Syndicate, Inc.

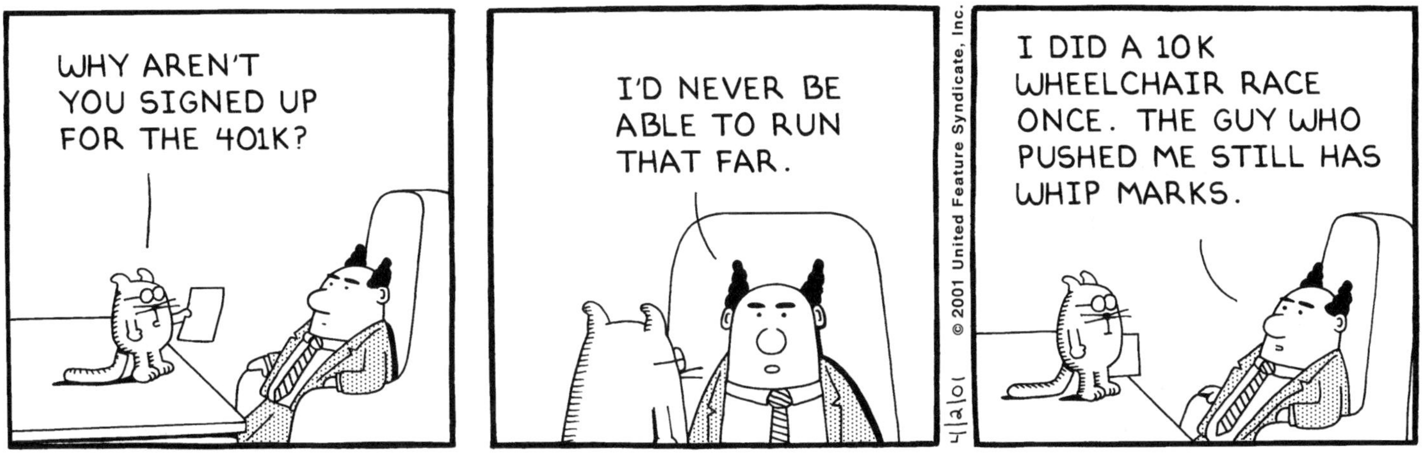
WHY AREN'T YOU SIGNED UP FOR THE 401K?
I'D NEVER BE ABLE TO RUN THAT FAR.
4/2/01
© 2001 United Feature Syndicate, Inc.
I DID A 10K WHEELCHAIR RACE ONCE. THE GUY WHO PUSHED ME STILL HAS WHIP MARKS.

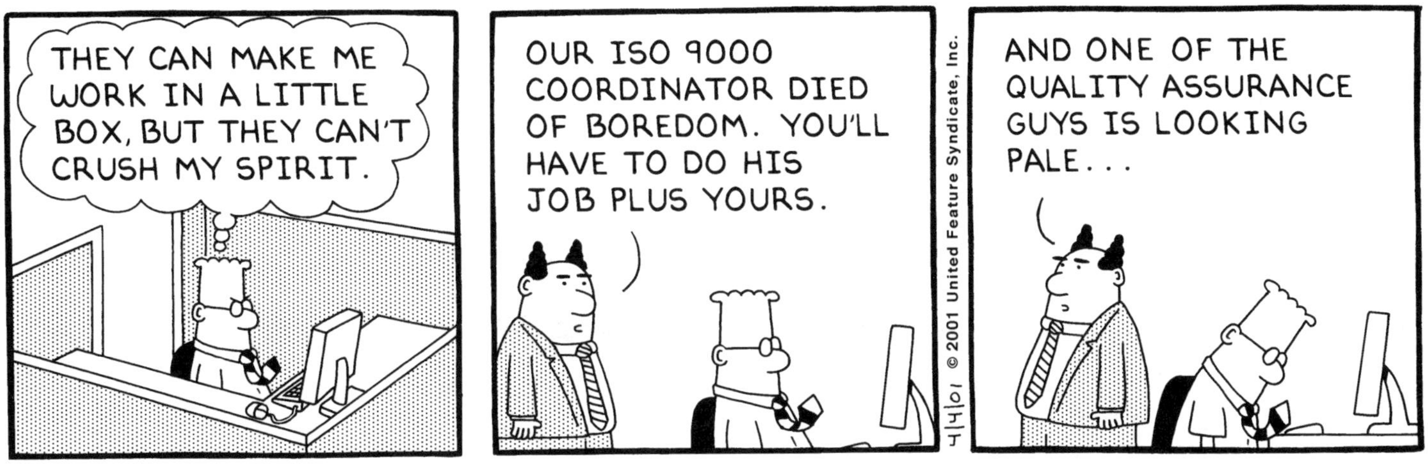
THEY CAN MAKE ME WORK IN A LITTLE BOX, BUT THEY CAN'T CRUSH MY SPIRIT.
OUR ISO 9000 COORDINATOR DIED OF BOREDOM. YOU'LL HAVE TO DO HIS JOB PLUS YOURS.
4/4/01
© 2001 United Feature Syndicate, Inc.
AND ONE OF THE QUALITY ASSURANCE GUYS IS LOOKING PALE...

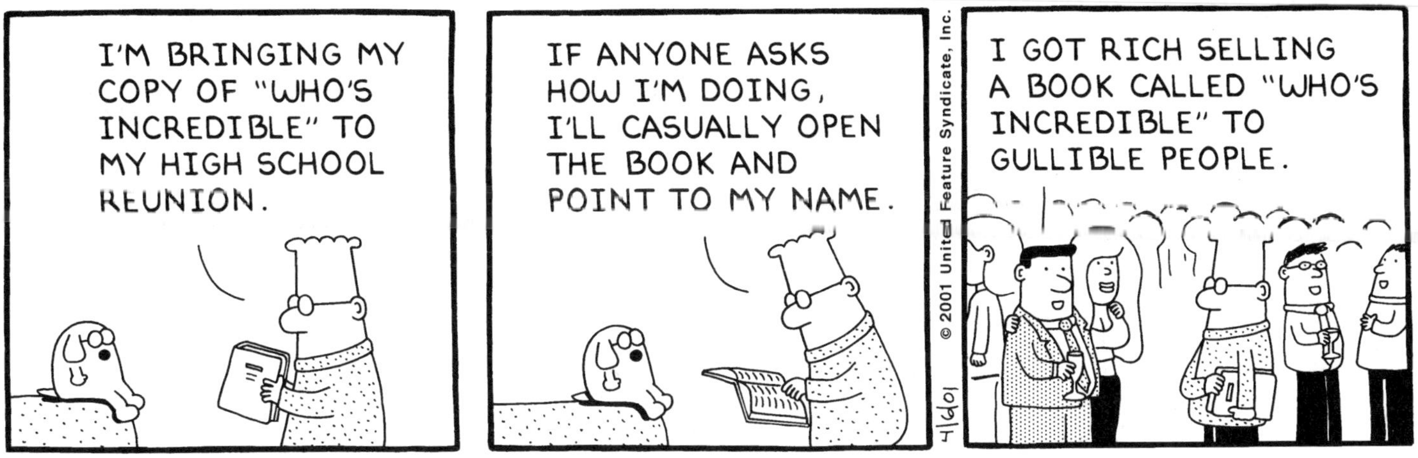
I'M BRINGING MY COPY OF "WHO'S INCREDIBLE" TO MY HIGH SCHOOL REUNION.
IF ANYONE ASKS HOW I'M DOING, I'LL CASUALLY OPEN THE BOOK AND POINT TO MY NAME.
4/6/01
© 2001 United Feature Syndicate, Inc.
I GOT RICH SELLING A BOOK CALLED "WHO'S INCREDIBLE" TO GULLIBLE PEOPLE.

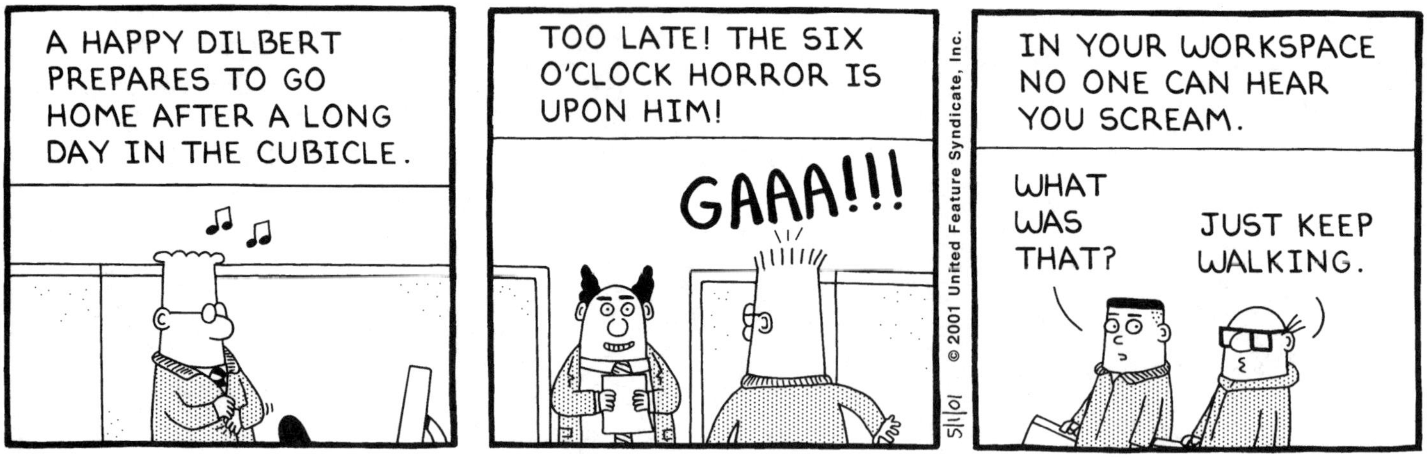
A HAPPY DILBERT PREPARES TO GO HOME AFTER A LONG DAY IN THE CUBICLE.
TOO LATE! THE SIX O'CLOCK HORROR IS UPON HIM!
GAAA!!!
5/1/01
© 2001 United Feature Syndicate, Inc.
IN YOUR WORKSPACE NO ONE CAN HEAR YOU SCREAM.
WHAT WAS THAT?
JUST KEEP WALKING.

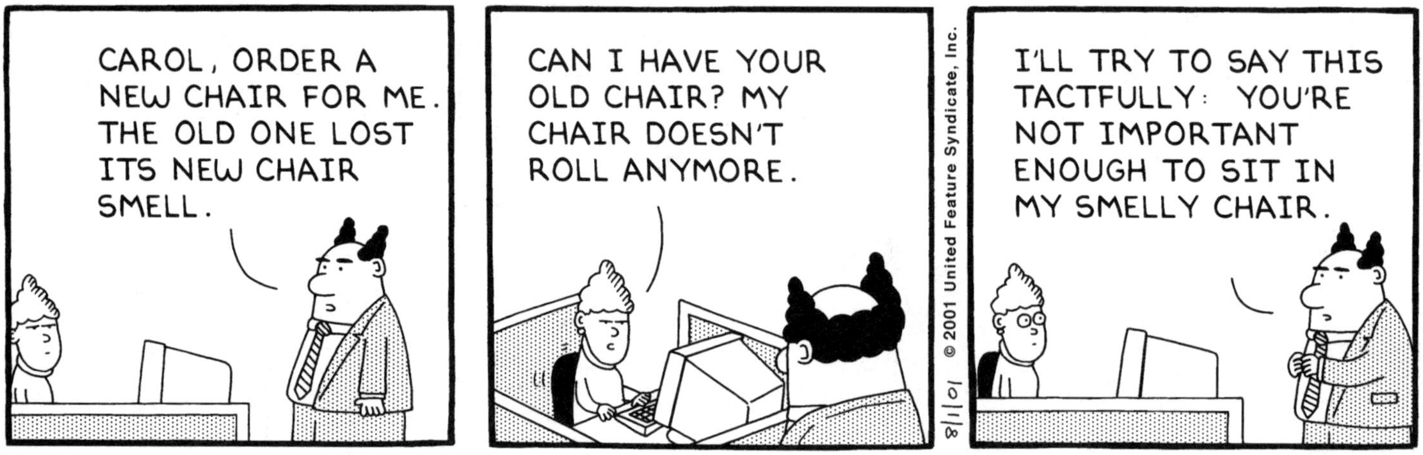
CAROL, ORDER A NEW CHAIR FOR ME. THE OLD ONE LOST ITS NEW CHAIR SMELL.
CAN I HAVE YOUR OLD CHAIR? MY CHAIR DOESN'T ROLL ANYMORE.
8/1/01
© 2001 United Feature Syndicate, Inc.
I'LL TRY TO SAY THIS TACTFULLY: YOU'RE NOT IMPORTANT ENOUGH TO SIT IN MY SMELLY CHAIR.

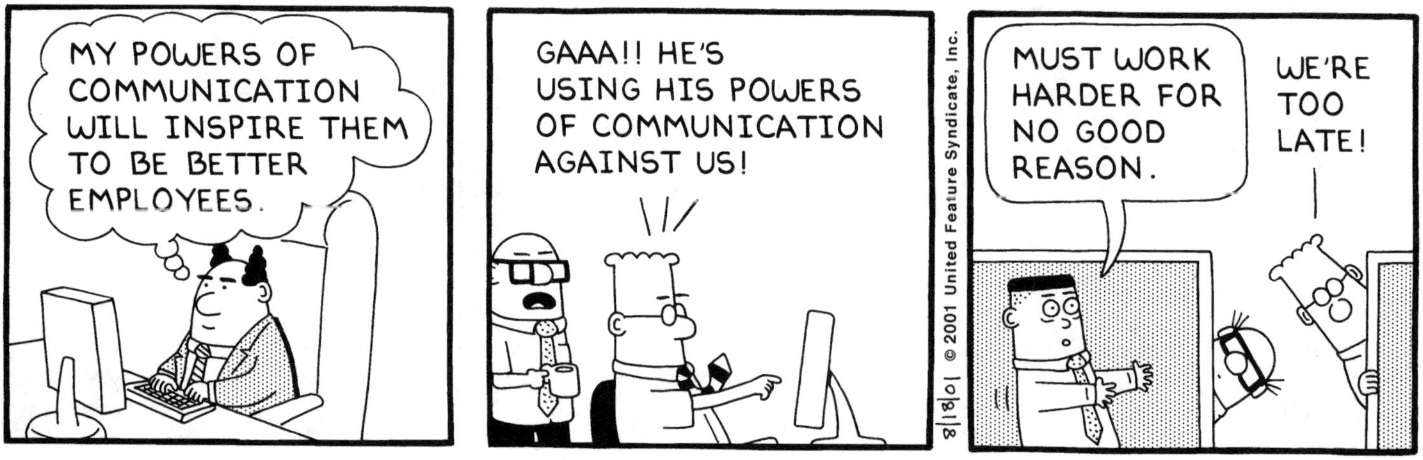
MY POWERS OF COMMUNICATION WILL INSPIRE THEM TO BE BETTER EMPLOYEES.
GAAA!! HE'S USING HIS POWERS OF COMMUNICATION AGAINST US!
8/18/01
© 2001 United Feature Syndicate, Inc.
MUST WORK HARDER FOR NO GOOD REASON.
WE'RE TOO LATE!

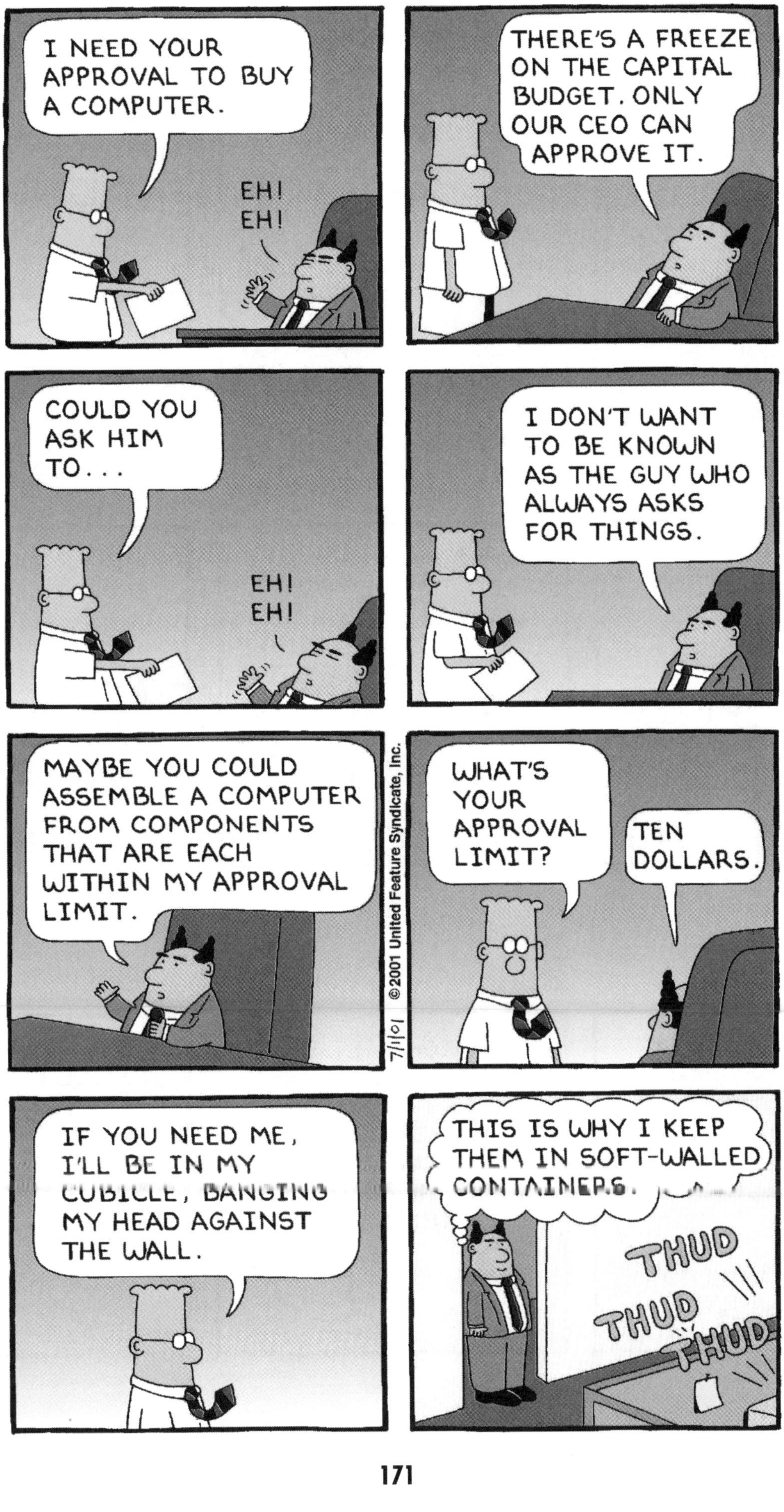
I NEED YOUR APPROVAL TO BUY A COMPUTER.
EH! EH!
THERE'S A FREEZE ON THE CAPITAL BUDGET. ONLY OUR CEO CAN APPROVE IT.
COULD YOU ASK HIM TO...
EH! EH!
I DON'T WANT TO BE KNOWN AS THE GUY WHO ALWAYS ASKS FOR THINGS.
MAYBE YOU COULD ASSEMBLE A COMPUTER FROM COMPONENTS THAT ARE EACH WITHIN MY APPROVAL LIMIT.
©2001 United Feature Syndicate, Inc.
7/1/01
WHAT'S YOUR APPROVAL LIMIT?
TEN DOLLARS.
IF YOU NEED ME, I'LL BE IN MY CUBICLE, BANGING MY HEAD AGAINST THE WALL.
THIS IS WHY I KEEP THEM IN SOFT-WALLED CONTAINERS.
THUD
THUD
THUD

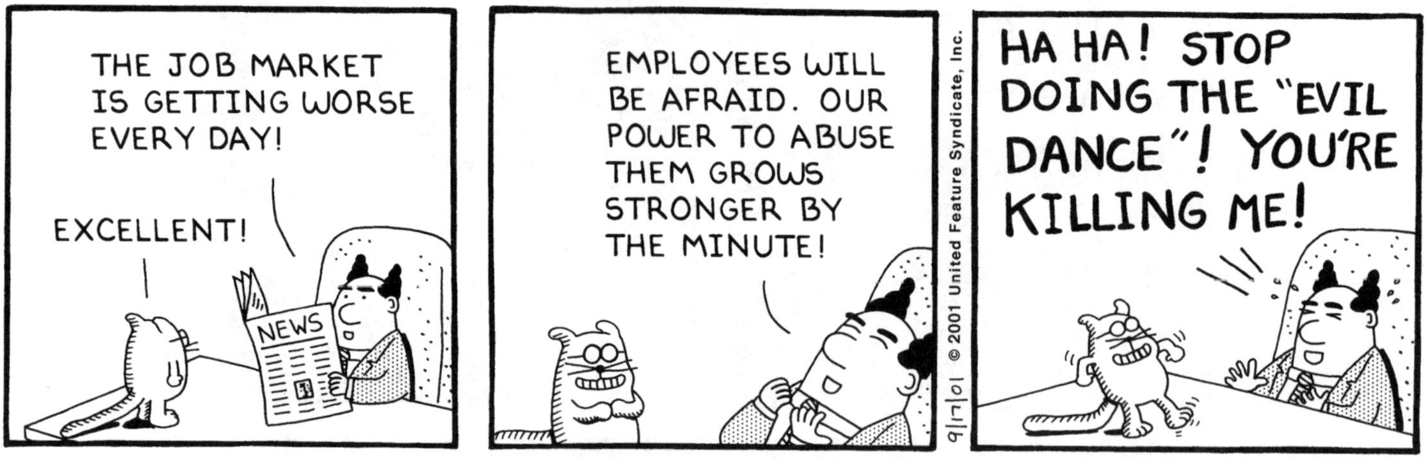
THE JOB MARKET IS GETTING WORSE EVERY DAY!
EXCELLENT!
NEWS
EMPLOYEES WILL BE AFRAID. OUR POWER TO ABUSE THEM GROWS STRONGER BY THE MINUTE!
9/17/01 © 2001 United Feature Syndicate, Inc.
HA HA! STOP DOING THE "EVIL DANCE"! YOU'RE KILLING ME!

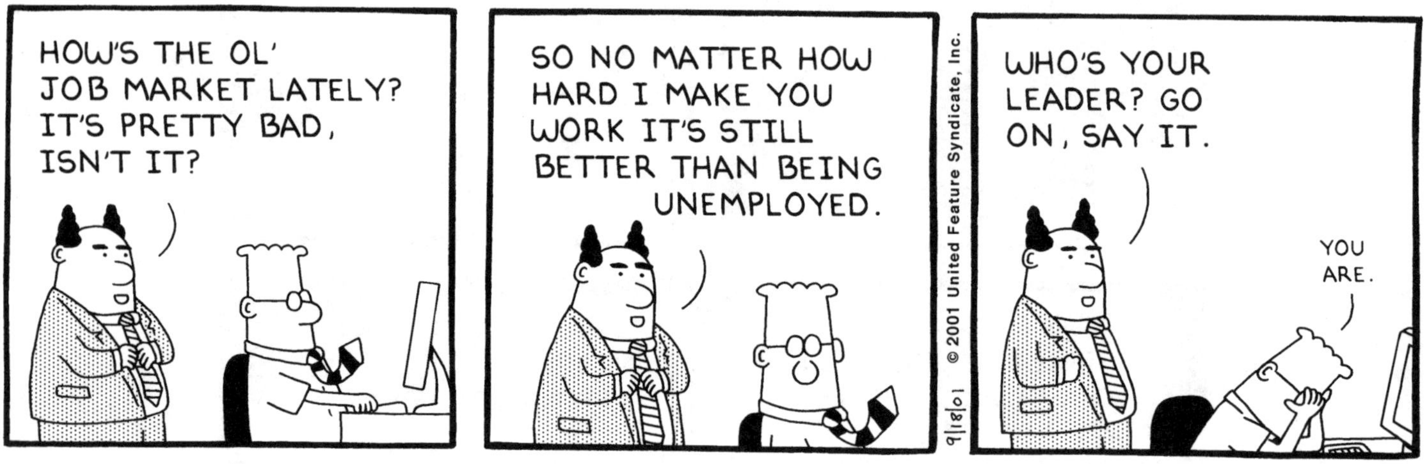
HOW'S THE OL' JOB MARKET LATELY? IT'S PRETTY BAD, ISN'T IT?
SO NO MATTER HOW HARD I MAKE YOU WORK IT'S STILL BETTER THAN BEING UNEMPLOYED.
9/18/01 © 2001 United Feature Syndicate, Inc.
WHO'S YOUR LEADER? GO ON, SAY IT.
YOU ARE.

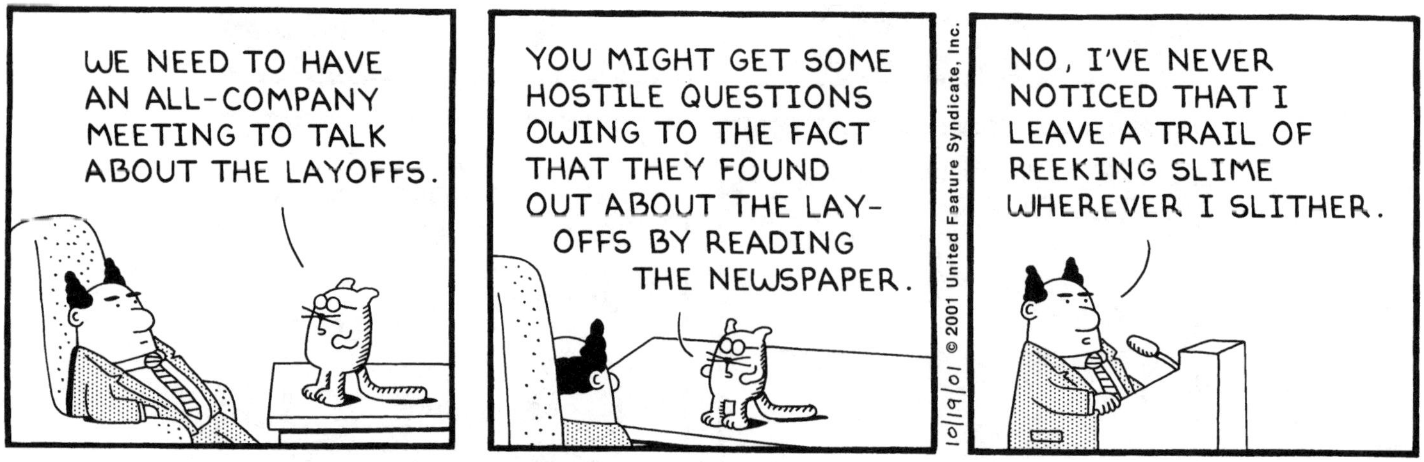
WE NEED TO HAVE AN ALL-COMPANY MEETING TO TALK ABOUT THE LAYOFFS.
YOU MIGHT GET SOME HOSTILE QUESTIONS OWING TO THE FACT THAT THEY FOUND OUT ABOUT THE LAY-OFFS BY READING THE NEWSPAPER.
10/9/01 © 2001 United Feature Syndicate, Inc.
NO, I'VE NEVER NOTICED THAT I LEAVE A TRAIL OF REEKING SLIME WHEREVER I SLITHER.

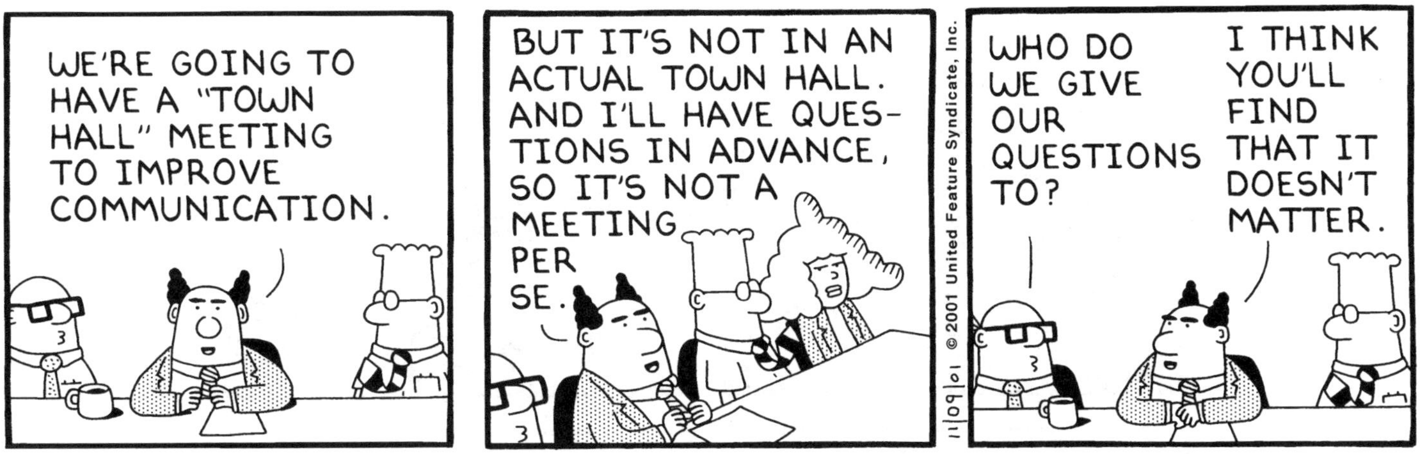
WE'RE GOING TO HAVE A "TOWN HALL" MEETING TO IMPROVE COMMUNICATION.
BUT IT'S NOT IN AN ACTUAL TOWN HALL. AND I'LL HAVE QUESTIONS IN ADVANCE, SO IT'S NOT A MEETING PER SE.
WHO DO WE GIVE OUR QUESTIONS TO?
I THINK YOU'LL FIND THAT IT DOESN'T MATTER.
11/09/01 © 2001 United Feature Syndicate, Inc.

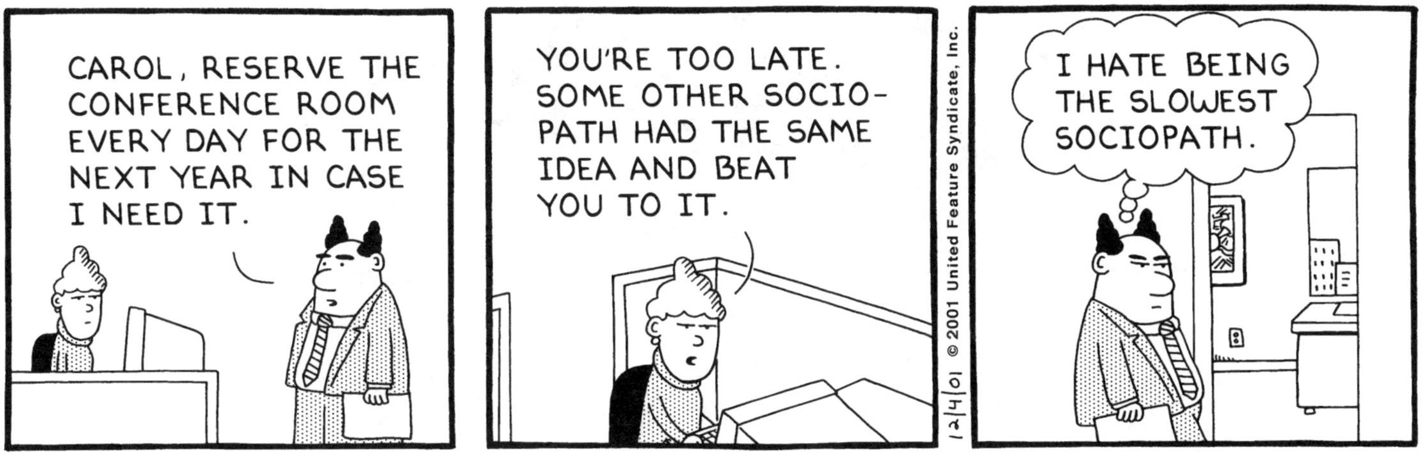
CAROL, RESERVE THE CONFERENCE ROOM EVERY DAY FOR THE NEXT YEAR IN CASE I NEED IT.
YOU'RE TOO LATE. SOME OTHER SOCIOPATH HAD THE SAME IDEA AND BEAT YOU TO IT.
I HATE BEING THE SLOWEST SOCIOPATH.
12/4/01 © 2001 United Feature Syndicate, Inc.

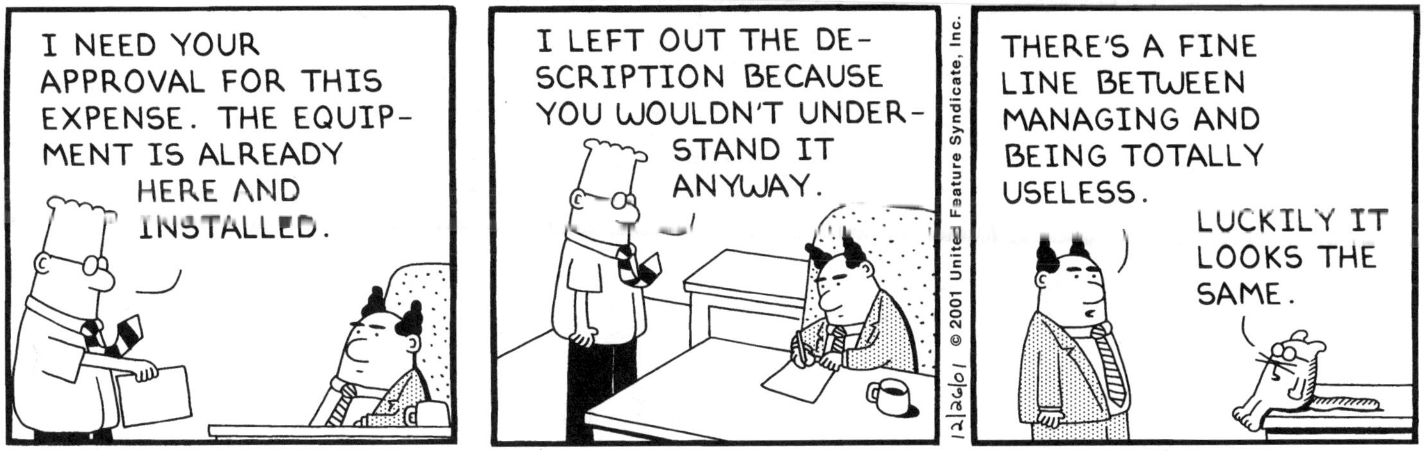
I NEED YOUR APPROVAL FOR THIS EXPENSE. THE EQUIPMENT IS ALREADY HERE AND INSTALLED.
I LEFT OUT THE DESCRIPTION BECAUSE YOU WOULDN'T UNDERSTAND IT ANYWAY.
THERE'S A FINE LINE BETWEEN MANAGING AND BEING TOTALLY USELESS.
LUCKILY IT LOOKS THE SAME.
12/26/01 © 2001 United Feature Syndicate, Inc.

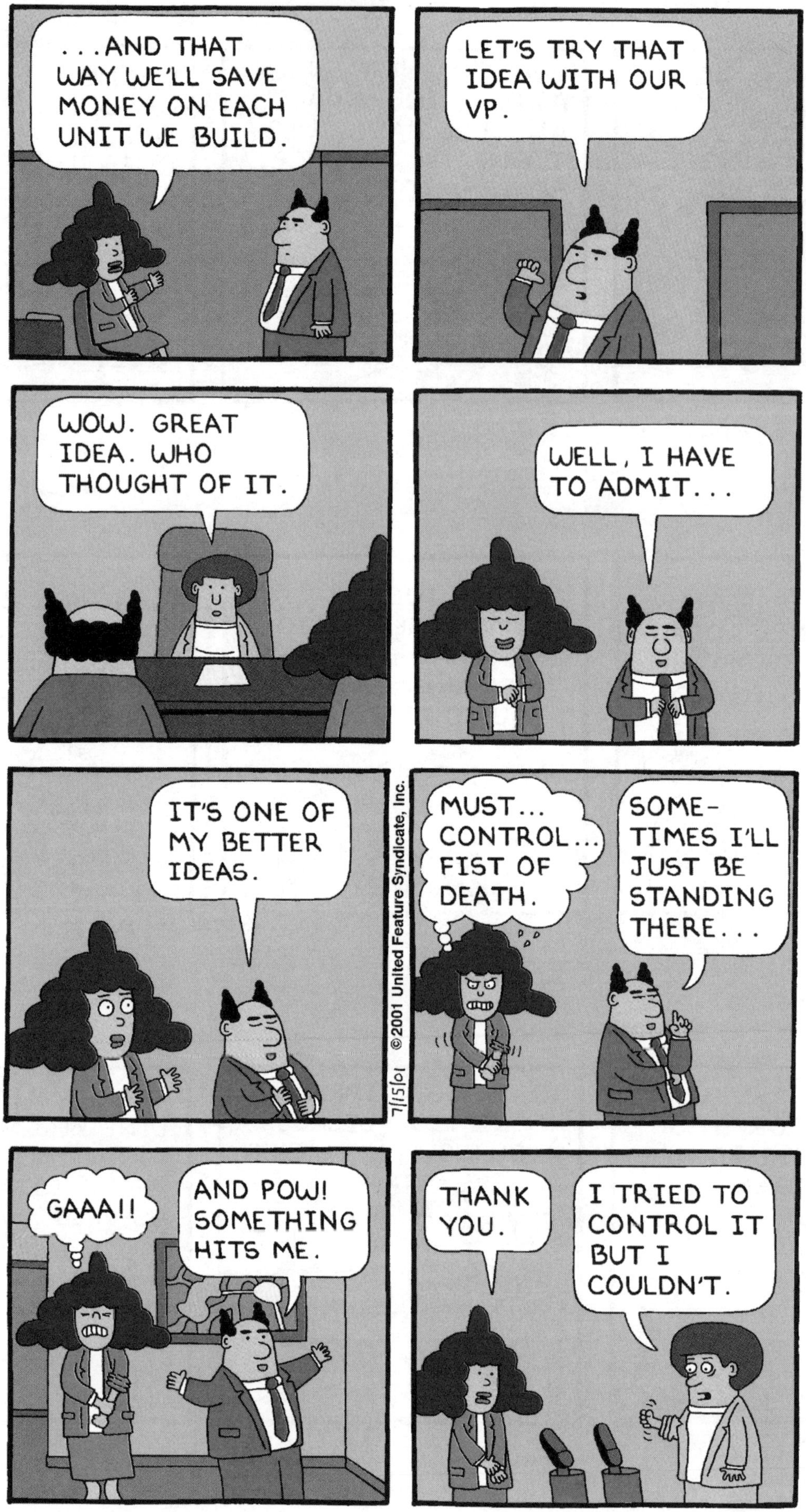
...AND THAT WAY WE'LL SAVE MONEY ON EACH UNIT WE BUILD.
LET'S TRY THAT IDEA WITH OUR VP.
WOW. GREAT IDEA. WHO THOUGHT OF IT.
WELL, I HAVE TO ADMIT...
IT'S ONE OF MY BETTER IDEAS.
© 2001 United Feature Syndicate, Inc.
7/15/01
MUST... CONTROL... FIST OF DEATH.
SOME-TIMES I'LL JUST BE STANDING THERE...
GAAA!!
AND POW! SOMETHING HITS ME.
THANK YOU.
I TRIED TO CONTROL IT BUT I COULDN'T.

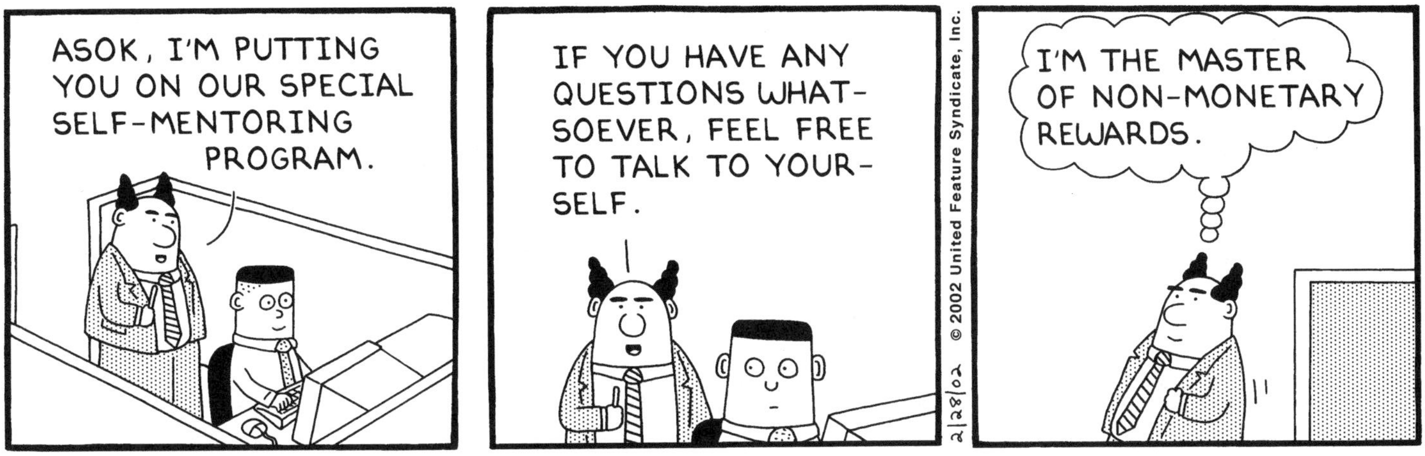
ASOK, I'M PUTTING YOU ON OUR SPECIAL SELF-MENTORING PROGRAM.
IF YOU HAVE ANY QUESTIONS WHATSOEVER, FEEL FREE TO TALK TO YOURSELF.
2/28/02 © 2002 United Feature Syndicate, Inc.
I'M THE MASTER OF NON-MONETARY REWARDS.

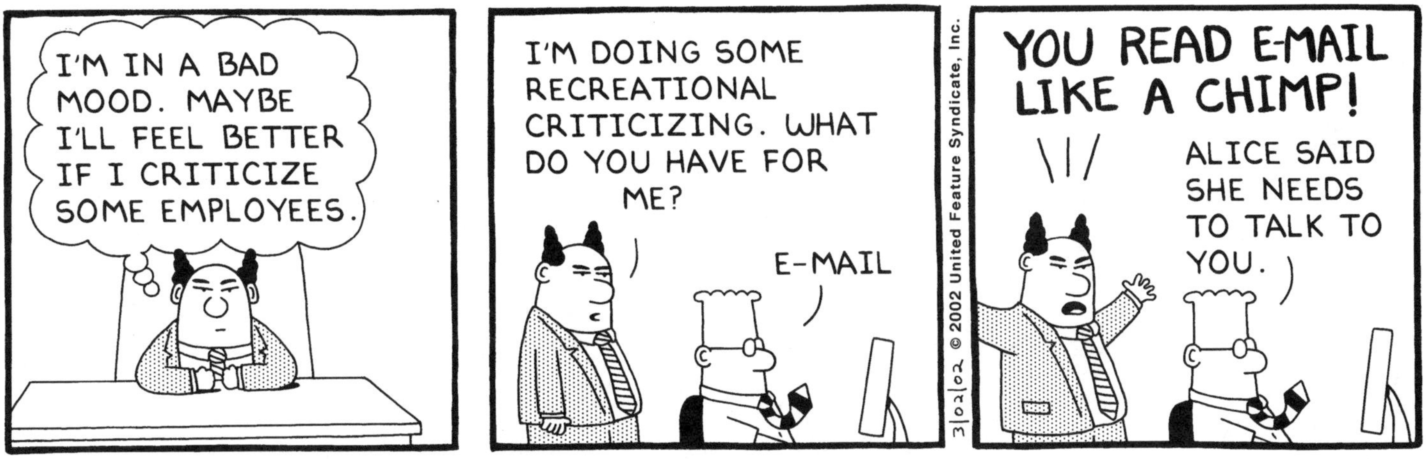
I'M IN A BAD MOOD. MAYBE I'LL FEEL BETTER IF I CRITICIZE SOME EMPLOYEES.
I'M DOING SOME RECREATIONAL CRITICIZING. WHAT DO YOU HAVE FOR ME?
E-MAIL
3/02/02 © 2002 United Feature Syndicate, Inc.
YOU READ E-MAIL LIKE A CHIMP!
ALICE SAID SHE NEEDS TO TALK TO YOU.

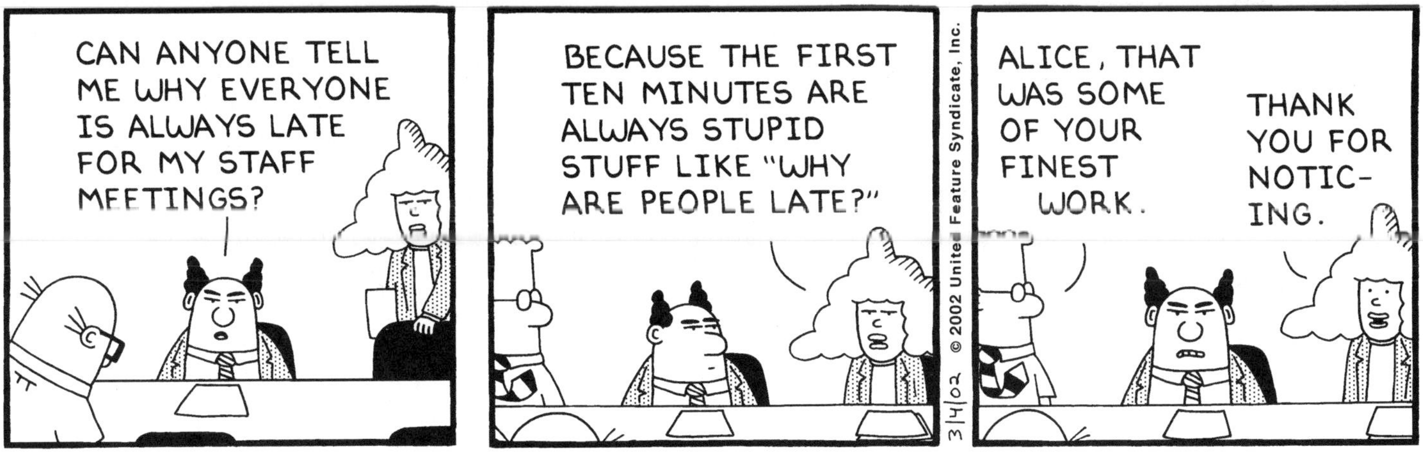
CAN ANYONE TELL ME WHY EVERYONE IS ALWAYS LATE FOR MY STAFF MEETINGS?
BECAUSE THE FIRST TEN MINUTES ARE ALWAYS STUPID STUFF LIKE "WHY ARE PEOPLE LATE?"
3/4/02 © 2002 United Feature Syndicate, Inc.
ALICE, THAT WAS SOME OF YOUR FINEST WORK.
THANK YOU FOR NOTICING.

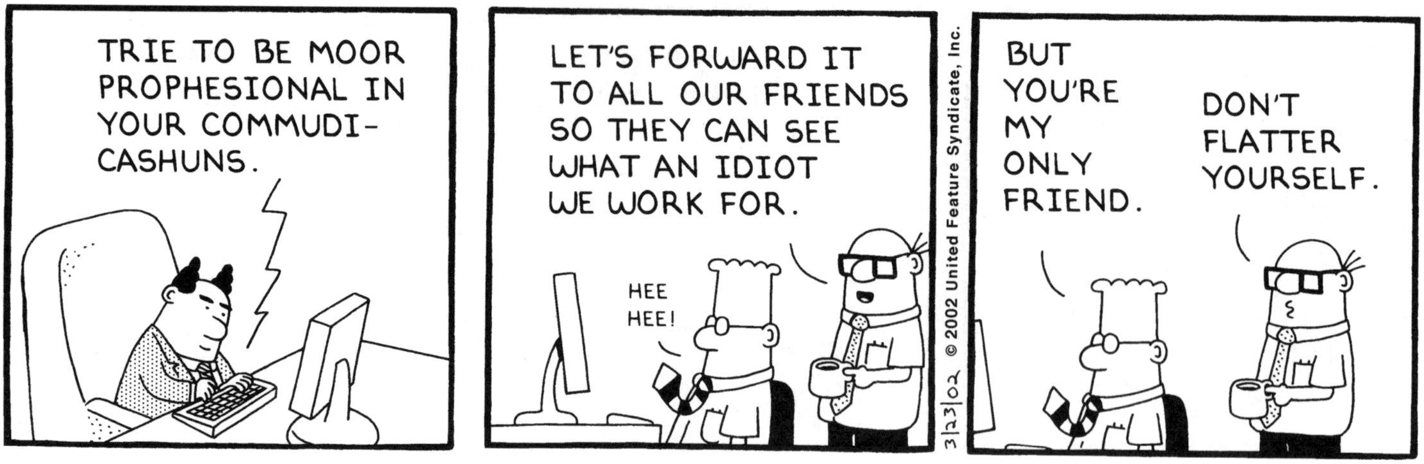
TRIE TO BE MOOR PROPHESIONAL IN YOUR COMMUDI-CASHUNS.
LET'S FORWARD IT TO ALL OUR FRIENDS SO THEY CAN SEE WHAT AN IDIOT WE WORK FOR.
HEE HEE!
3/23/02 © 2002 United Feature Syndicate, Inc.
BUT YOU'RE MY ONLY FRIEND.
DON'T FLATTER YOURSELF.

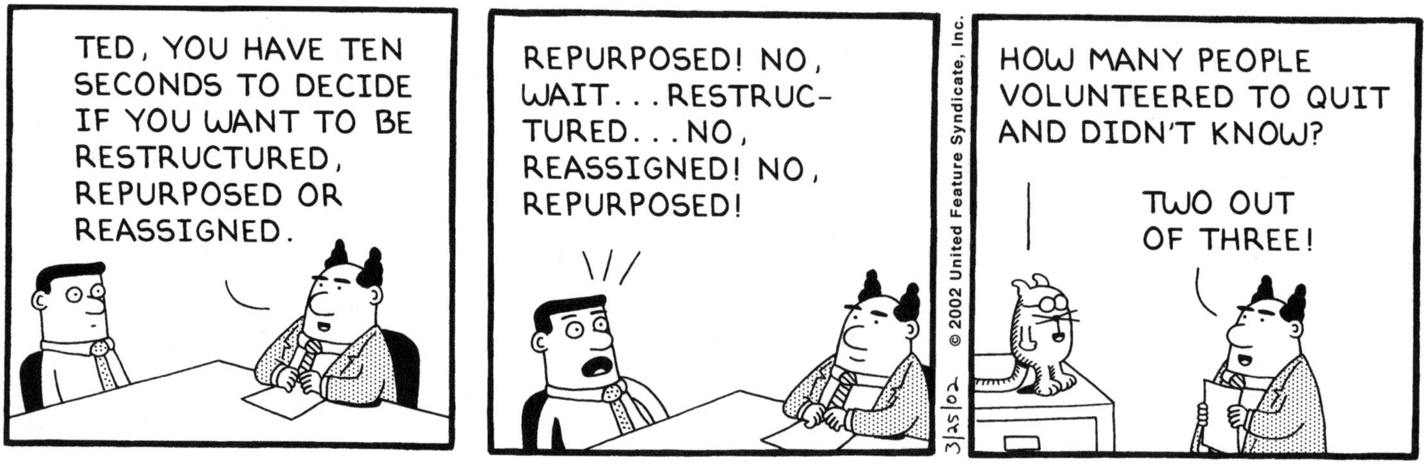
TED, YOU HAVE TEN SECONDS TO DECIDE IF YOU WANT TO BE RESTRUCTURED, REPURPOSED OR REASSIGNED.
REPURPOSED! NO, WAIT... RESTRUC-TURED... NO, REASSIGNED! NO, REPURPOSED!
3/25/02 © 2002 United Feature Syndicate, Inc.
HOW MANY PEOPLE VOLUNTEERED TO QUIT AND DIDN'T KNOW?
TWO OUT OF THREE!

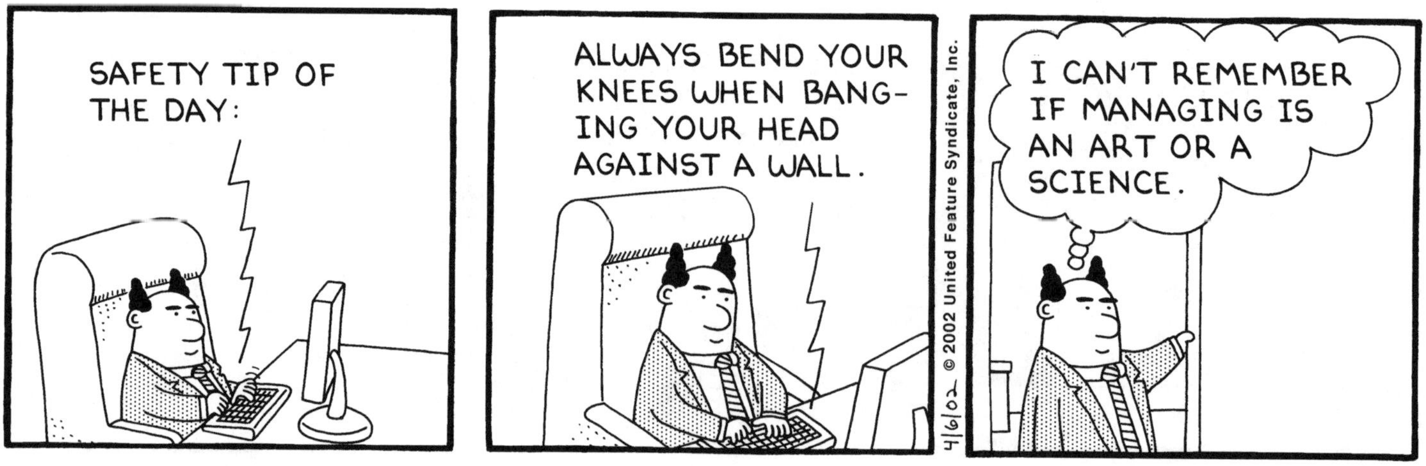
SAFETY TIP OF THE DAY:
ALWAYS BEND YOUR KNEES WHEN BANG-ING YOUR HEAD AGAINST A WALL.
4/6/02 © 2002 United Feature Syndicate, Inc.
I CAN'T REMEMBER IF MANAGING IS AN ART OR A SCIENCE.

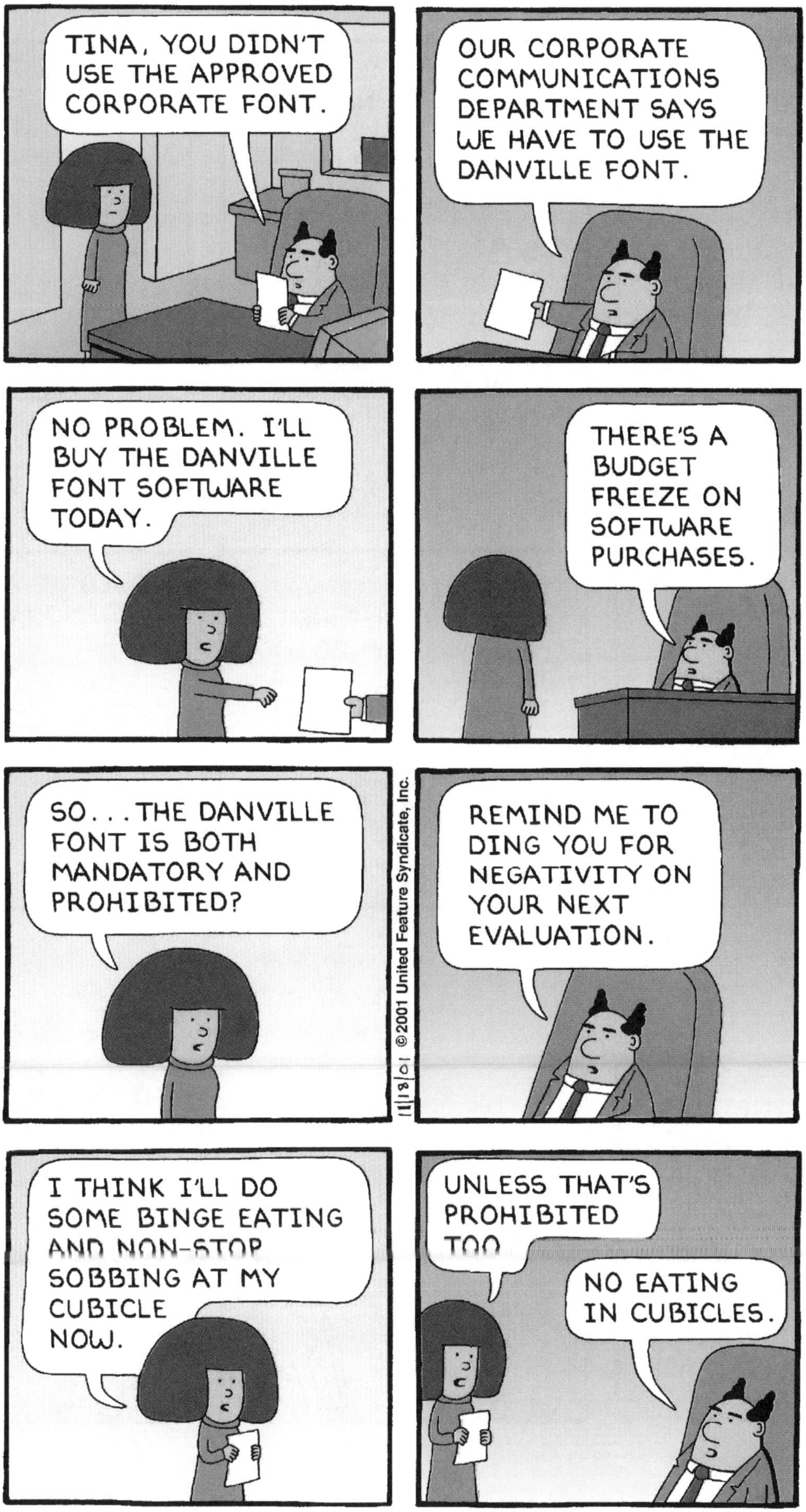
TINA, YOU DIDN'T USE THE APPROVED CORPORATE FONT.
OUR CORPORATE COMMUNICATIONS DEPARTMENT SAYS WE HAVE TO USE THE DANVILLE FONT.
NO PROBLEM. I'LL BUY THE DANVILLE FONT SOFTWARE TODAY.
THERE'S A BUDGET FREEZE ON SOFTWARE PURCHASES.
SO... THE DANVILLE FONT IS BOTH MANDATORY AND PROHIBITED?
REMIND ME TO DING YOU FOR NEGATIVITY ON YOUR NEXT EVALUATION.
I THINK I'LL DO SOME BINGE EATING AND NON-STOP SOBBING AT MY CUBICLE NOW.
UNLESS THAT'S PROHIBITED TOO.
NO EATING IN CUBICLES.
©2001 United Feature Syndicate, Inc.
11/18/01

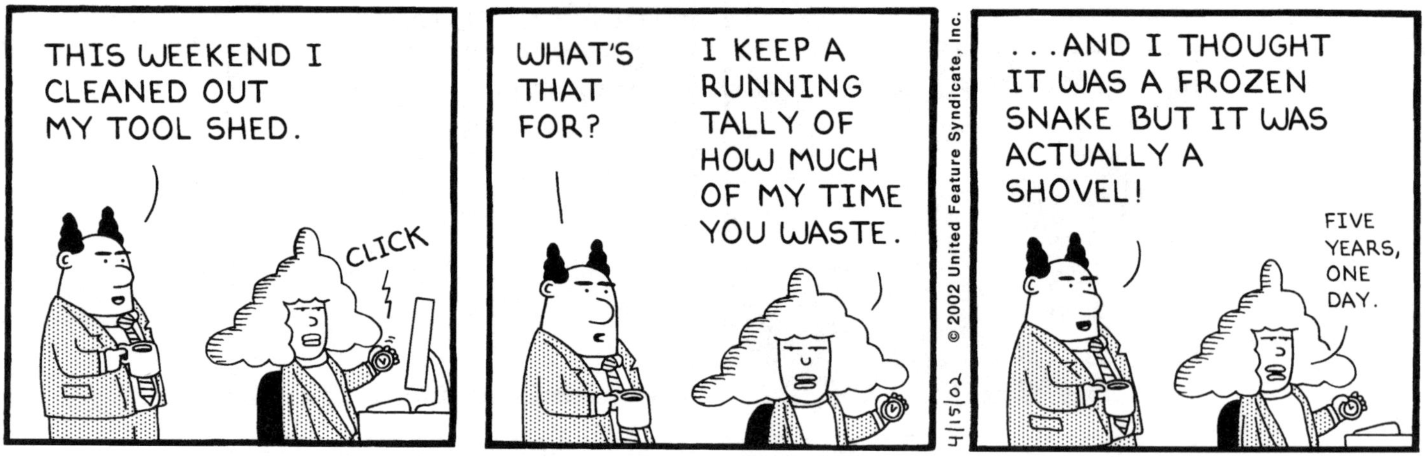
THIS WEEKEND I CLEANED OUT MY TOOL SHED.
CLICK
WHAT'S THAT FOR?
I KEEP A RUNNING TALLY OF HOW MUCH OF MY TIME YOU WASTE.
...AND I THOUGHT IT WAS A FROZEN SNAKE BUT IT WAS ACTUALLY A SHOVEL!
FIVE YEARS, ONE DAY.
4/15/02
© 2002 United Feature Syndicate, Inc.

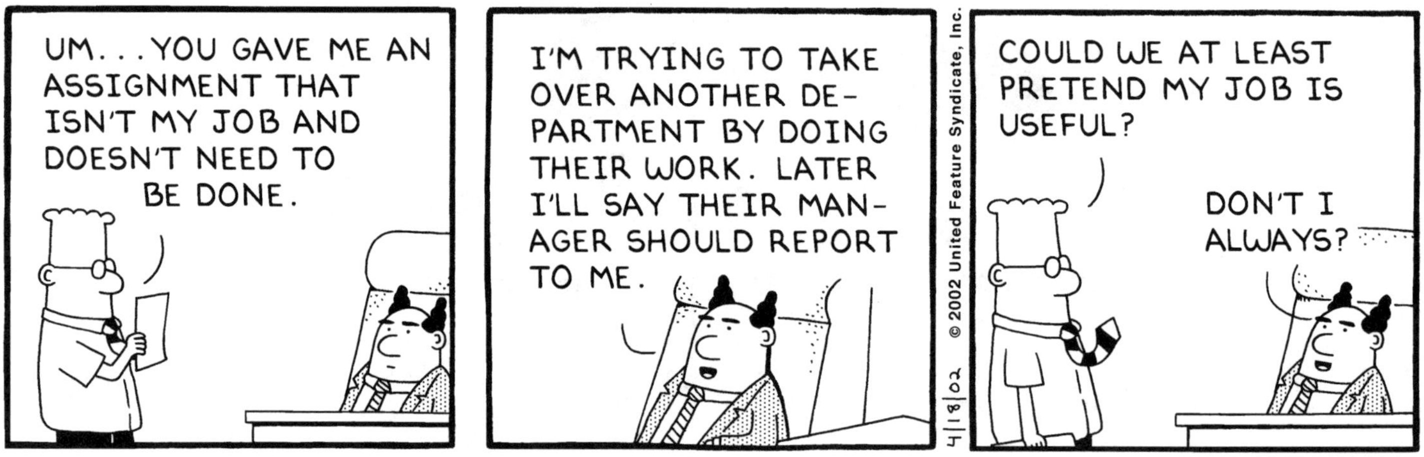
UM...YOU GAVE ME AN ASSIGNMENT THAT ISN'T MY JOB AND DOESN'T NEED TO BE DONE.
I'M TRYING TO TAKE OVER ANOTHER DE-PARTMENT BY DOING THEIR WORK. LATER I'LL SAY THEIR MAN-AGER SHOULD REPORT TO ME.
COULD WE AT LEAST PRETEND MY JOB IS USEFUL?
DON'T I ALWAYS?
4/18/02
© 2002 United Feature Syndicate, Inc.

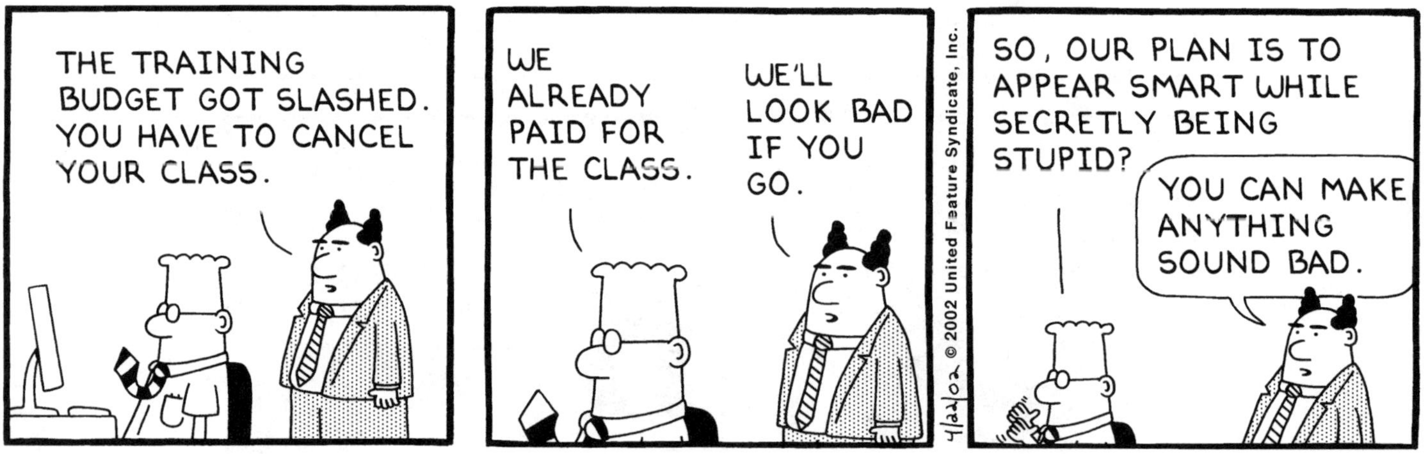
THE TRAINING BUDGET GOT SLASHED. YOU HAVE TO CANCEL YOUR CLASS.
WE ALREADY PAID FOR THE CLASS.
WE'LL LOOK BAD IF YOU GO.
SO, OUR PLAN IS TO APPEAR SMART WHILE SECRETLY BEING STUPID?
YOU CAN MAKE ANYTHING SOUND BAD.
4/22/02
© 2002 United Feature Syndicate, Inc.

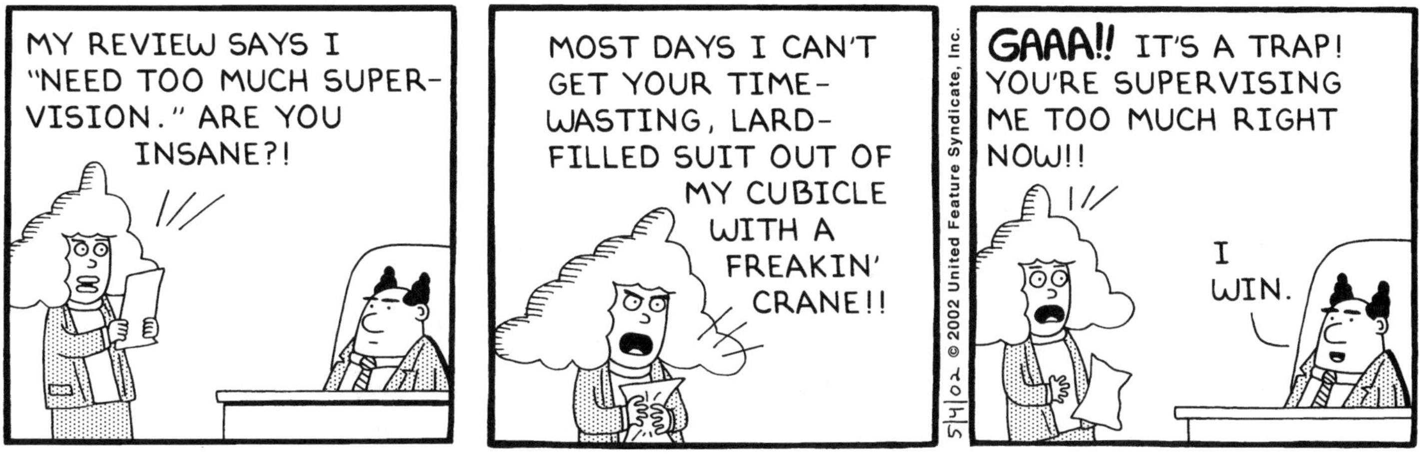
MY REVIEW SAYS I "NEED TOO MUCH SUPER-VISION." ARE YOU INSANE?!
MOST DAYS I CAN'T GET YOUR TIME-WASTING, LARD-FILLED SUIT OUT OF MY CUBICLE WITH A FREAKIN' CRANE!!
5/4/02 © 2002 United Feature Syndicate, Inc.
GAAA!! IT'S A TRAP! YOU'RE SUPERVISING ME TOO MUCH RIGHT NOW!!
I WIN.

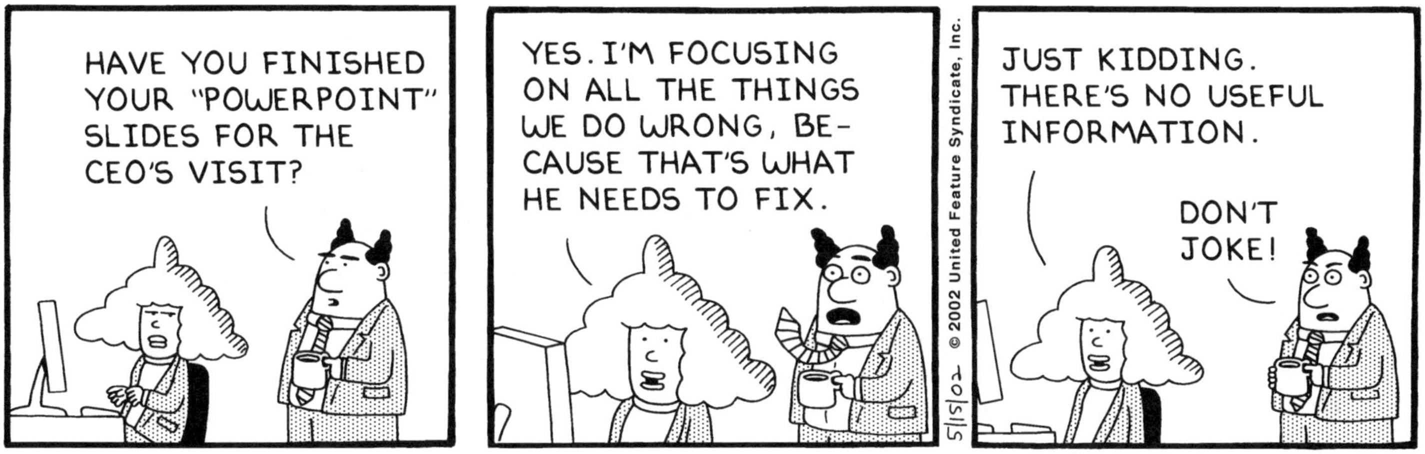
HAVE YOU FINISHED YOUR "POWERPOINT" SLIDES FOR THE CEO'S VISIT?
YES. I'M FOCUSING ON ALL THE THINGS WE DO WRONG, BE-CAUSE THAT'S WHAT HE NEEDS TO FIX.
5/5/02 © 2002 United Feature Syndicate, Inc.
JUST KIDDING. THERE'S NO USEFUL INFORMATION.
DON'T JOKE!

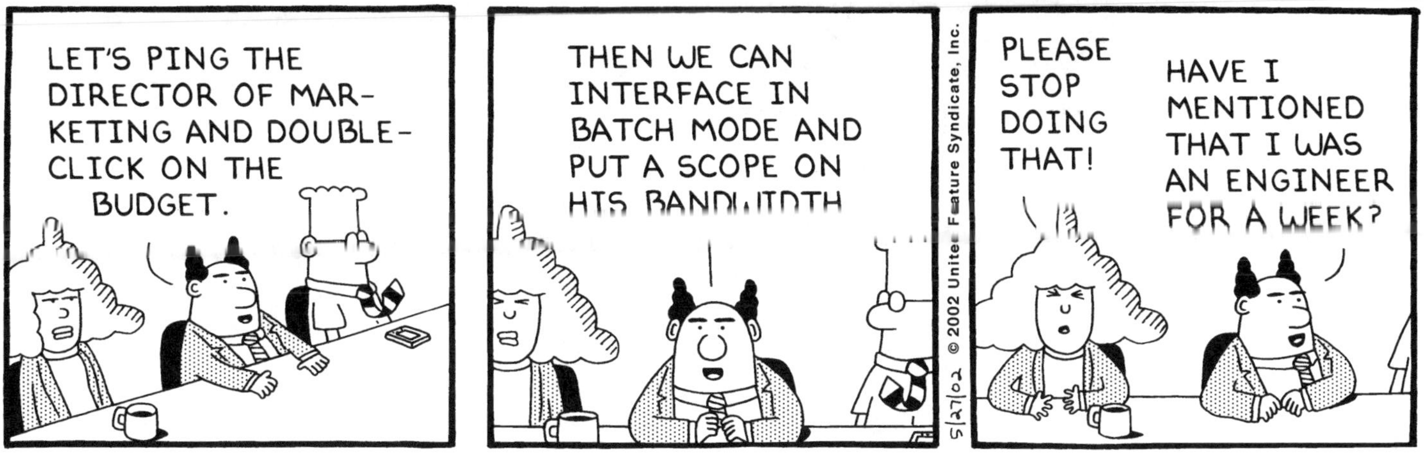
LET'S PING THE DIRECTOR OF MAR-KETING AND DOUBLE-CLICK ON THE BUDGET.
THEN WE CAN INTERFACE IN BATCH MODE AND PUT A SCOPE ON HIS BANDWIDTH
5/27/02 © 2002 United Feature Syndicate, Inc.
PLEASE STOP DOING THAT!
HAVE I MENTIONED THAT I WAS AN ENGINEER FOR A WEEK?

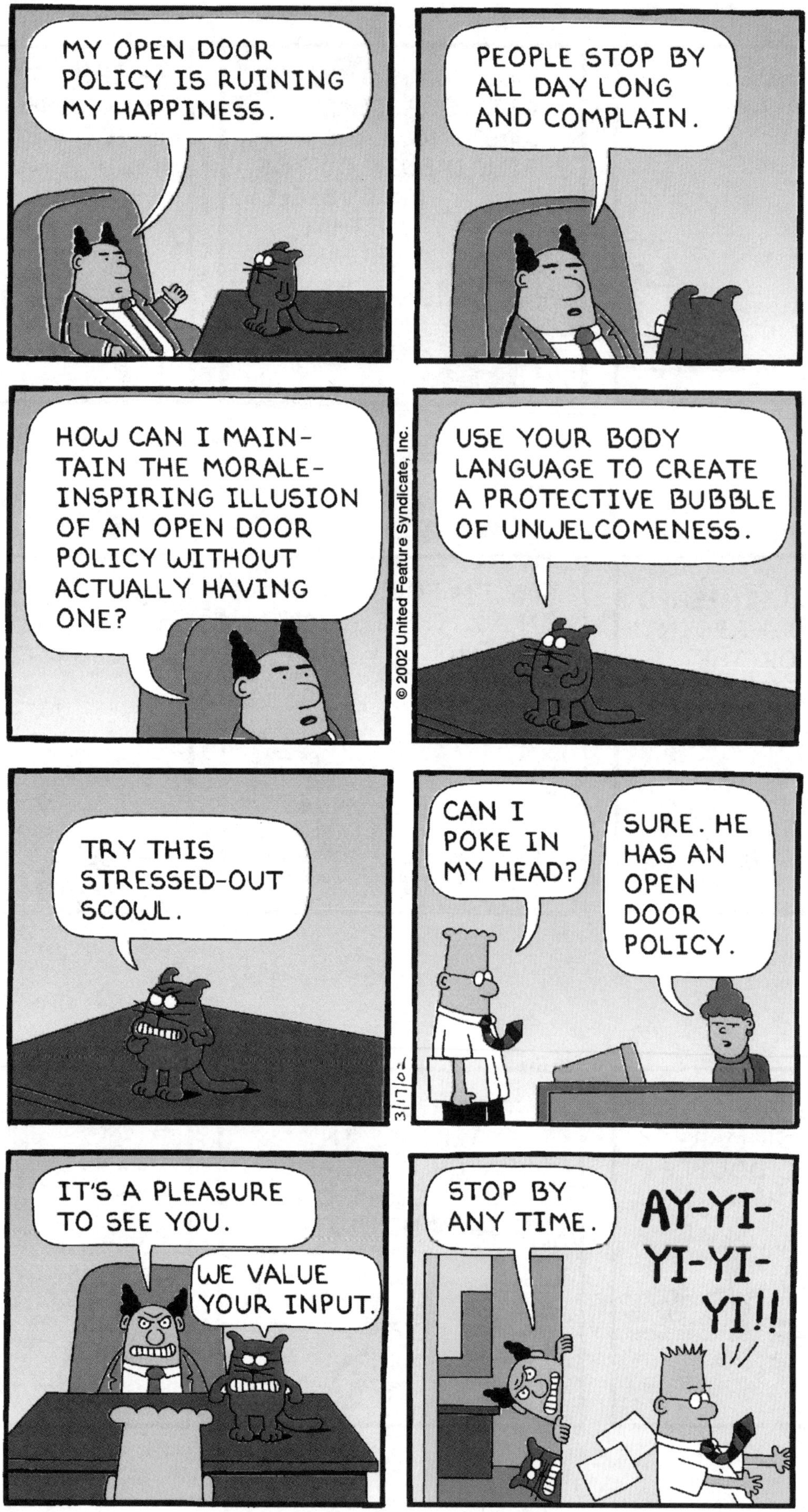
MY OPEN DOOR POLICY IS RUINING MY HAPPINESS.
PEOPLE STOP BY ALL DAY LONG AND COMPLAIN.
HOW CAN I MAIN-TAIN THE MORALE-INSPIRING ILLUSION OF AN OPEN DOOR POLICY WITHOUT ACTUALLY HAVING ONE?
© 2002 United Feature Syndicate, Inc.
USE YOUR BODY LANGUAGE TO CREATE A PROTECTIVE BUBBLE OF UNWELCOMENESS.
TRY THIS STRESSED-OUT SCOWL.
3/17/02
CAN I POKE IN MY HEAD?
SURE. HE HAS AN OPEN DOOR POLICY.
IT'S A PLEASURE TO SEE YOU.
WE VALUE YOUR INPUT.
STOP BY ANY TIME.
AY-YI-YI-YI-YI!!

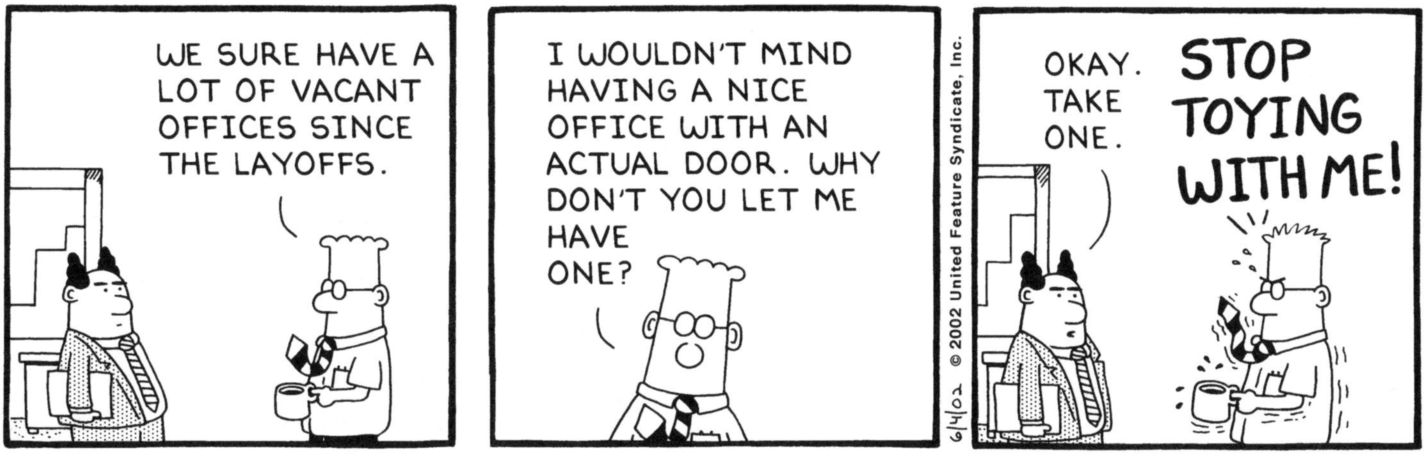
WE SURE HAVE A LOT OF VACANT OFFICES SINCE THE LAYOFFS.
I WOULDN'T MIND HAVING A NICE OFFICE WITH AN ACTUAL DOOR. WHY DON'T YOU LET ME HAVE ONE?
6/4/02 © 2002 United Feature Syndicate, Inc.
OKAY. TAKE ONE.
STOP TOYING WITH ME!

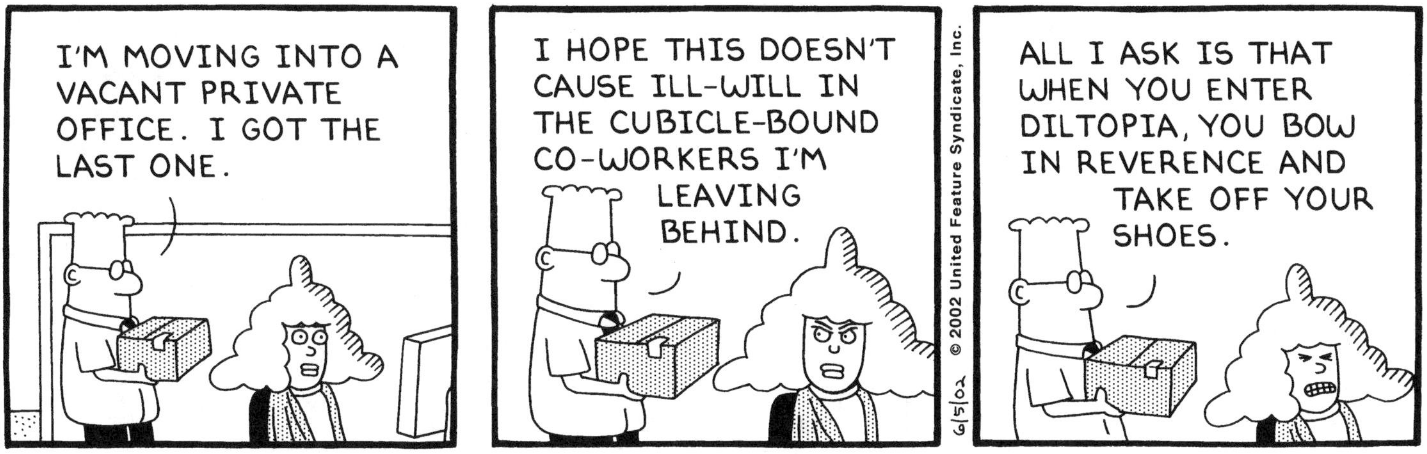
I'M MOVING INTO A VACANT PRIVATE OFFICE. I GOT THE LAST ONE.
I HOPE THIS DOESN'T CAUSE ILL-WILL IN THE CUBICLE-BOUND CO-WORKERS I'M LEAVING BEHIND.
6/5/02 © 2002 United Feature Syndicate, Inc.
ALL I ASK IS THAT WHEN YOU ENTER DILTOPIA, YOU BOW IN REVERENCE AND TAKE OFF YOUR SHOES.

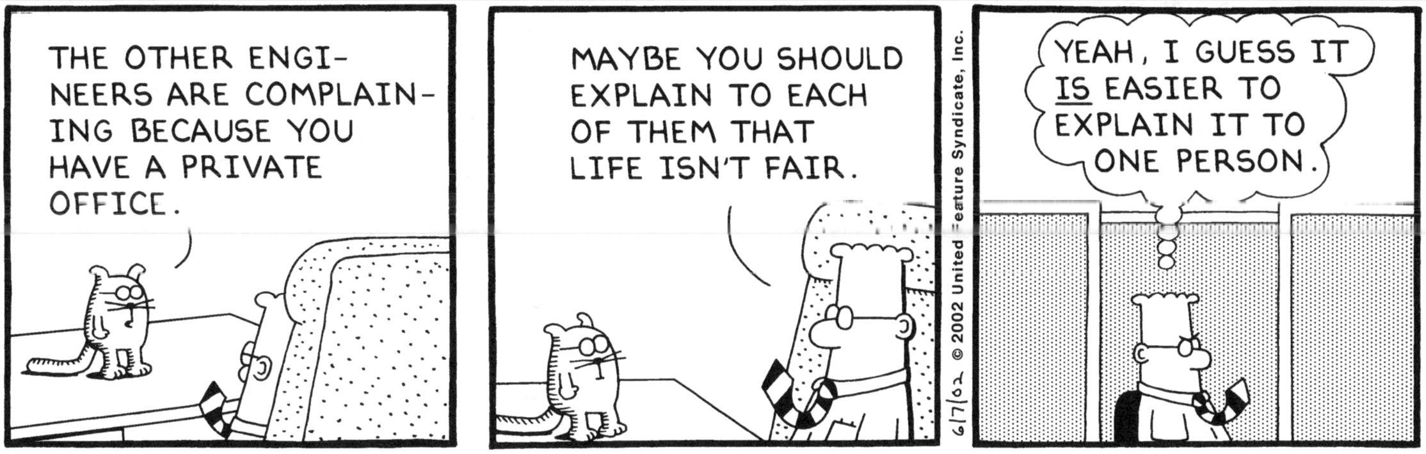
THE OTHER ENGI-NEERS ARE COMPLAIN-ING BECAUSE YOU HAVE A PRIVATE OFFICE.
MAYBE YOU SHOULD EXPLAIN TO EACH OF THEM THAT LIFE ISN'T FAIR.
6/7/02 © 2002 United Feature Syndicate, Inc.
YEAH, I GUESS IT IS EASIER TO EXPLAIN IT TO ONE PERSON.

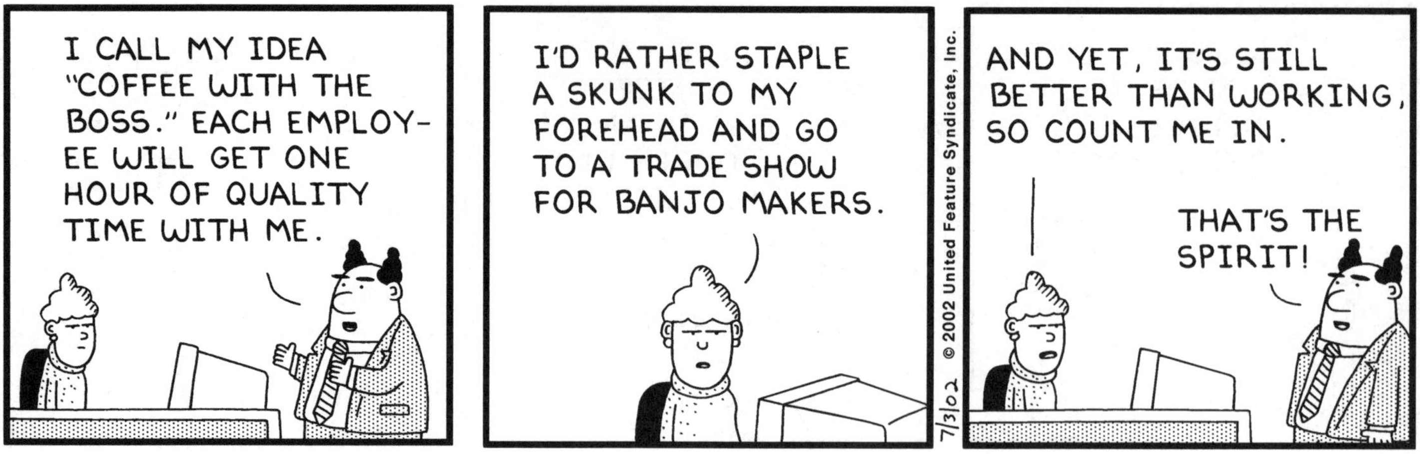
I CALL MY IDEA "COFFEE WITH THE BOSS." EACH EMPLOYEE WILL GET ONE HOUR OF QUALITY TIME WITH ME.
I'D RATHER STAPLE A SKUNK TO MY FOREHEAD AND GO TO A TRADE SHOW FOR BANJO MAKERS.
7/3/02 © 2002 United Feature Syndicate, Inc.
AND YET, IT'S STILL BETTER THAN WORKING, SO COUNT ME IN.
THAT'S THE SPIRIT!

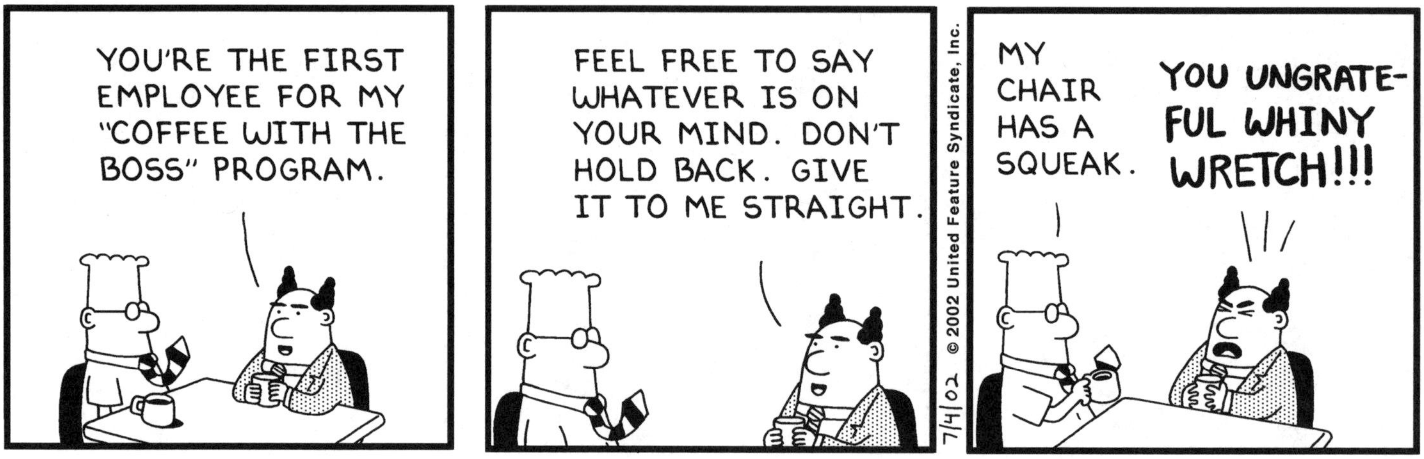
YOU'RE THE FIRST EMPLOYEE FOR MY "COFFEE WITH THE BOSS" PROGRAM.
FEEL FREE TO SAY WHATEVER IS ON YOUR MIND. DON'T HOLD BACK. GIVE IT TO ME STRAIGHT.
7/4/02 © 2002 United Feature Syndicate, Inc.
MY CHAIR HAS A SQUEAK.
YOU UNGRATEFUL WHINY WRETCH!!!

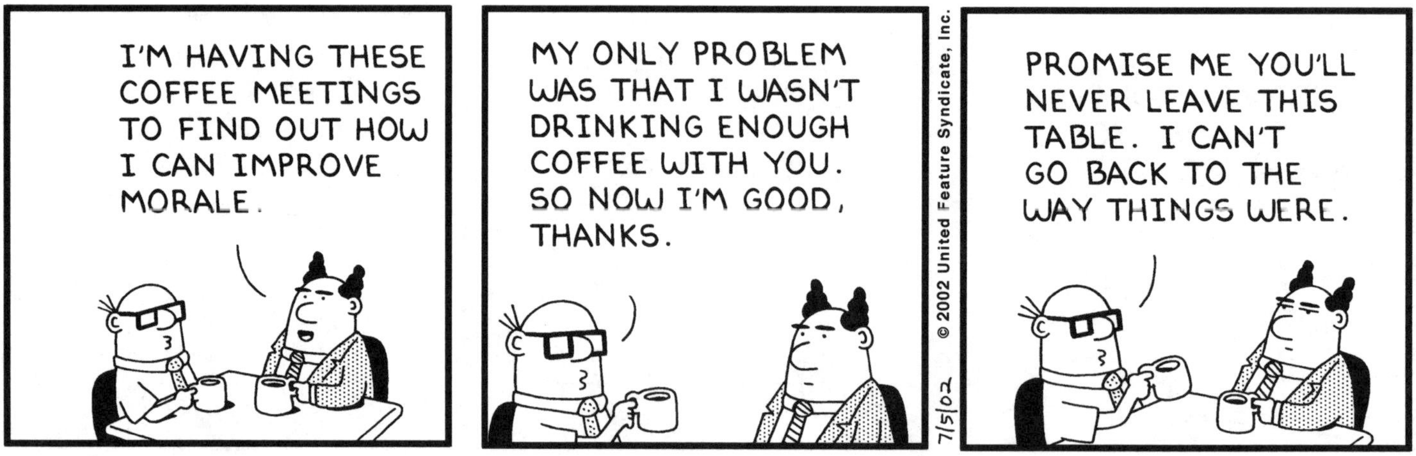
I'M HAVING THESE COFFEE MEETINGS TO FIND OUT HOW I CAN IMPROVE MORALE.
MY ONLY PROBLEM WAS THAT I WASN'T DRINKING ENOUGH COFFEE WITH YOU. SO NOW I'M GOOD, THANKS.
7/5/02 © 2002 United Feature Syndicate, Inc.
PROMISE ME YOU'LL NEVER LEAVE THIS TABLE. I CAN'T GO BACK TO THE WAY THINGS WERE.

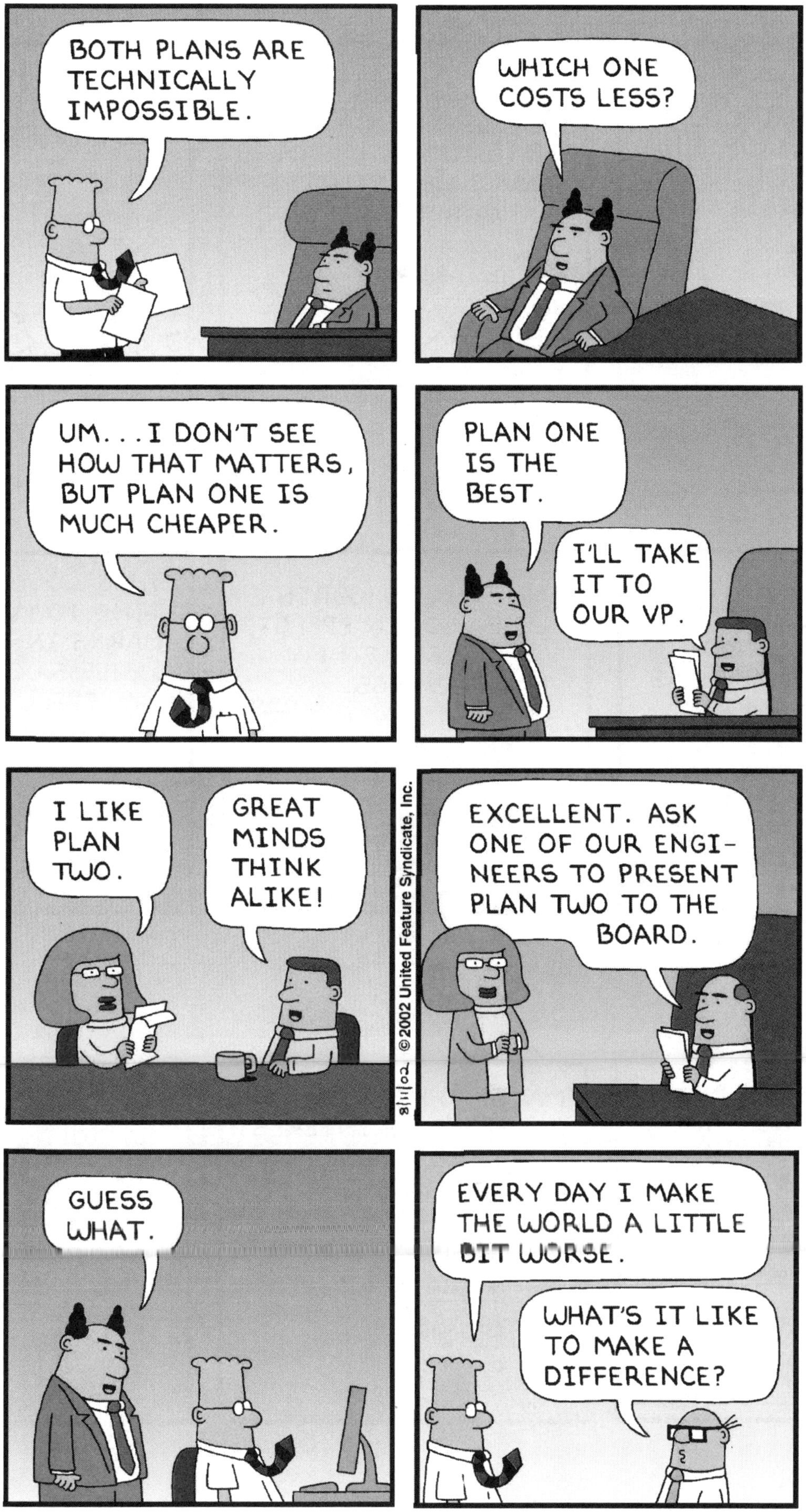

BOTH PLANS ARE TECHNICALLY IMPOSSIBLE.
WHICH ONE COSTS LESS?
UM...I DON'T SEE HOW THAT MATTERS, BUT PLAN ONE IS MUCH CHEAPER.
PLAN ONE IS THE BEST.
I'LL TAKE IT TO OUR VP.
I LIKE PLAN TWO.
GREAT MINDS THINK ALIKE!
EXCELLENT. ASK ONE OF OUR ENGINEERS TO PRESENT PLAN TWO TO THE BOARD.
GUESS WHAT.
EVERY DAY I MAKE THE WORLD A LITTLE BIT WORSE.
WHAT'S IT LIKE TO MAKE A DIFFERENCE?
© 2002 United Feature Syndicate, Inc.
8/11/02

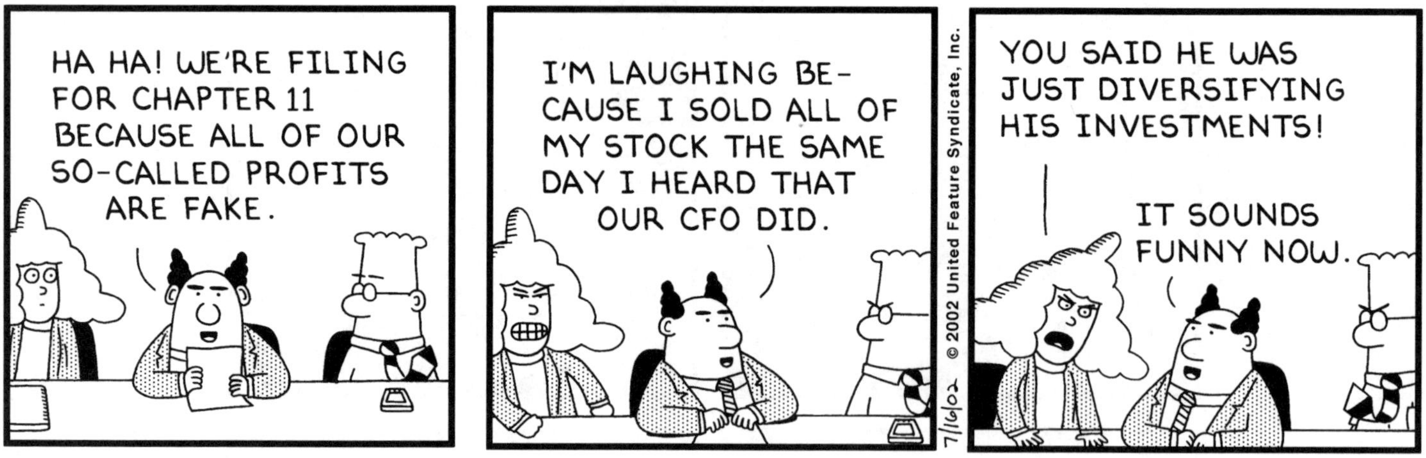
HA HA! WE'RE FILING FOR CHAPTER 11 BECAUSE ALL OF OUR SO-CALLED PROFITS ARE FAKE.
I'M LAUGHING BECAUSE I SOLD ALL OF MY STOCK THE SAME DAY I HEARD THAT OUR CFO DID.
7/16/02 © 2002 United Feature Syndicate, Inc.
YOU SAID HE WAS JUST DIVERSIFYING HIS INVESTMENTS!
IT SOUNDS FUNNY NOW.

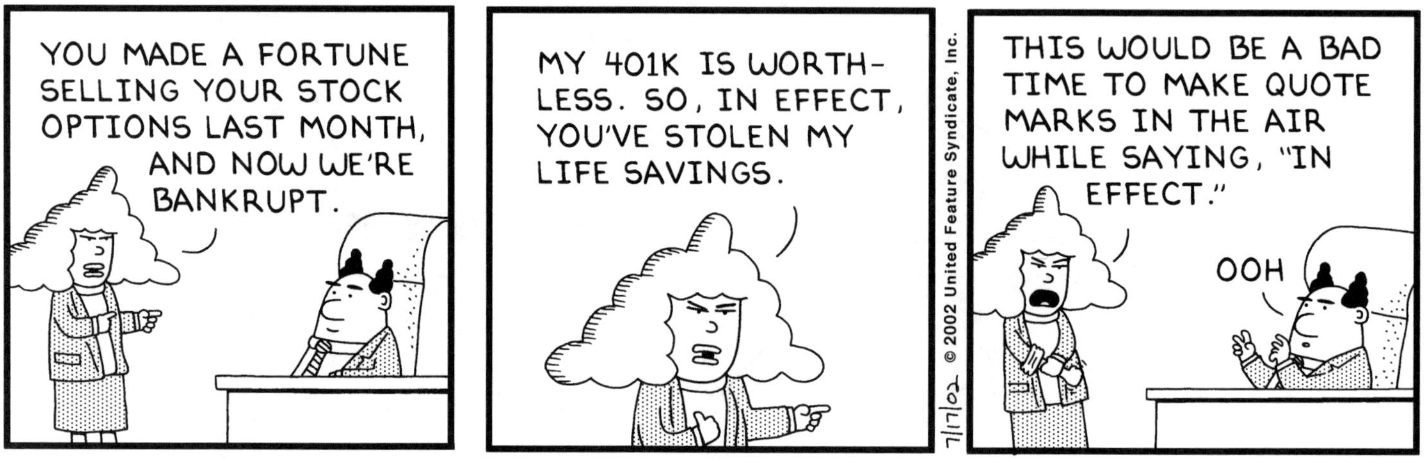
YOU MADE A FORTUNE SELLING YOUR STOCK OPTIONS LAST MONTH, AND NOW WE'RE BANKRUPT.
MY 401K IS WORTHLESS. SO, IN EFFECT, YOU'VE STOLEN MY LIFE SAVINGS.
7/17/02 © 2002 United Feature Syndicate, Inc.
THIS WOULD BE A BAD TIME TO MAKE QUOTE MARKS IN THE AIR WHILE SAYING, "IN EFFECT."
OOH

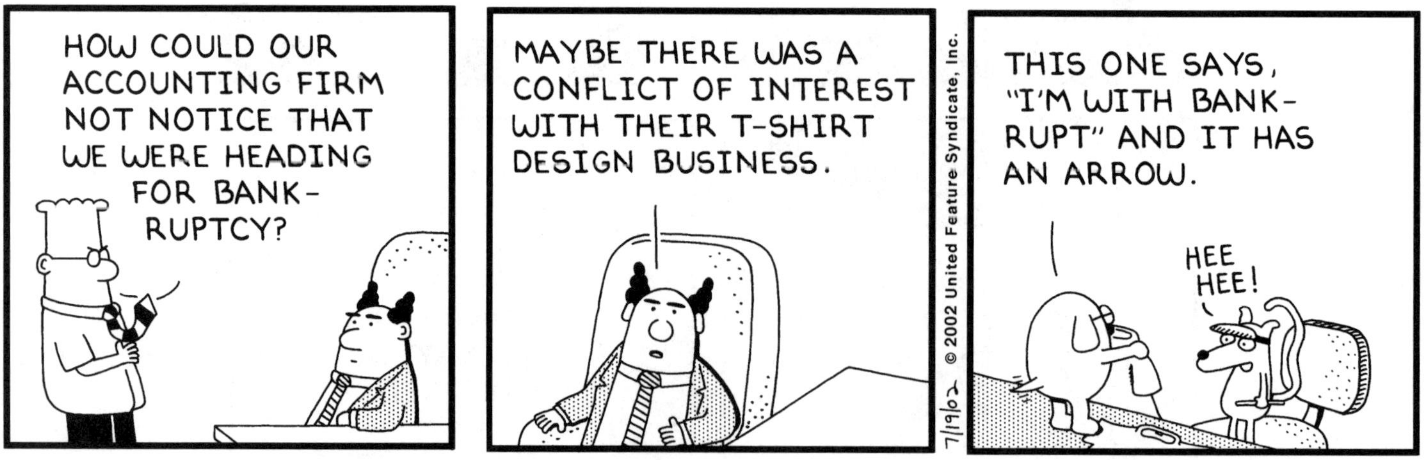
HOW COULD OUR ACCOUNTING FIRM NOT NOTICE THAT WE WERE HEADING FOR BANKRUPTCY?
MAYBE THERE WAS A CONFLICT OF INTEREST WITH THEIR T-SHIRT DESIGN BUSINESS.
7/19/02 © 2002 United Feature Syndicate, Inc.
THIS ONE SAYS, "I'M WITH BANKRUPT" AND IT HAS AN ARROW.
HEE HEE!

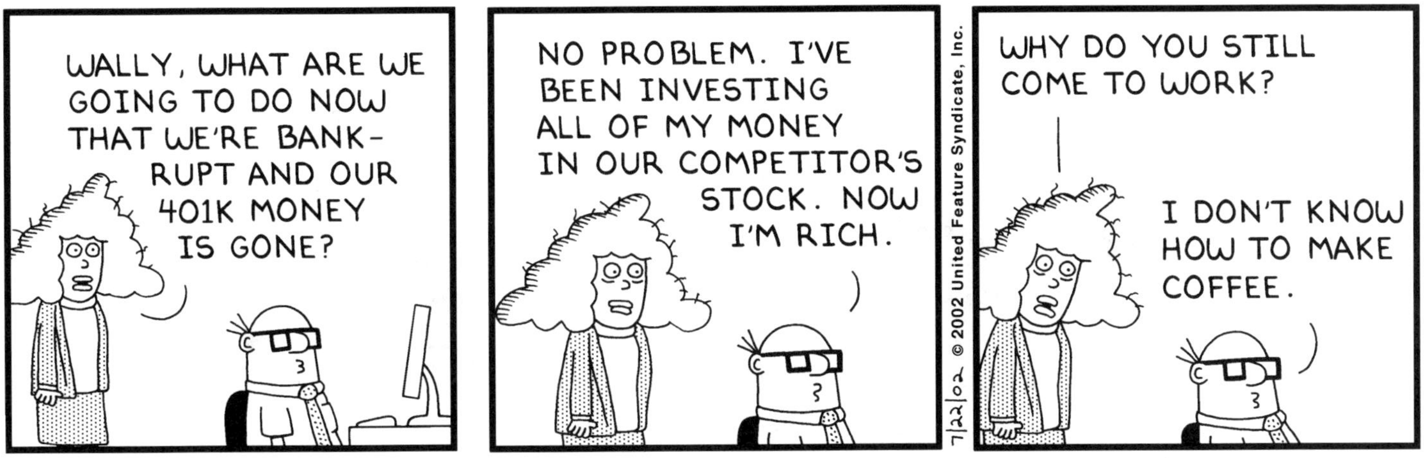
WALLY, WHAT ARE WE GOING TO DO NOW THAT WE'RE BANK-RUPT AND OUR 401K MONEY IS GONE?
NO PROBLEM. I'VE BEEN INVESTING ALL OF MY MONEY IN OUR COMPETITOR'S STOCK. NOW I'M RICH.
7/22/02 © 2002 United Feature Syndicate, Inc.
WHY DO YOU STILL COME TO WORK?
I DON'T KNOW HOW TO MAKE COFFEE.

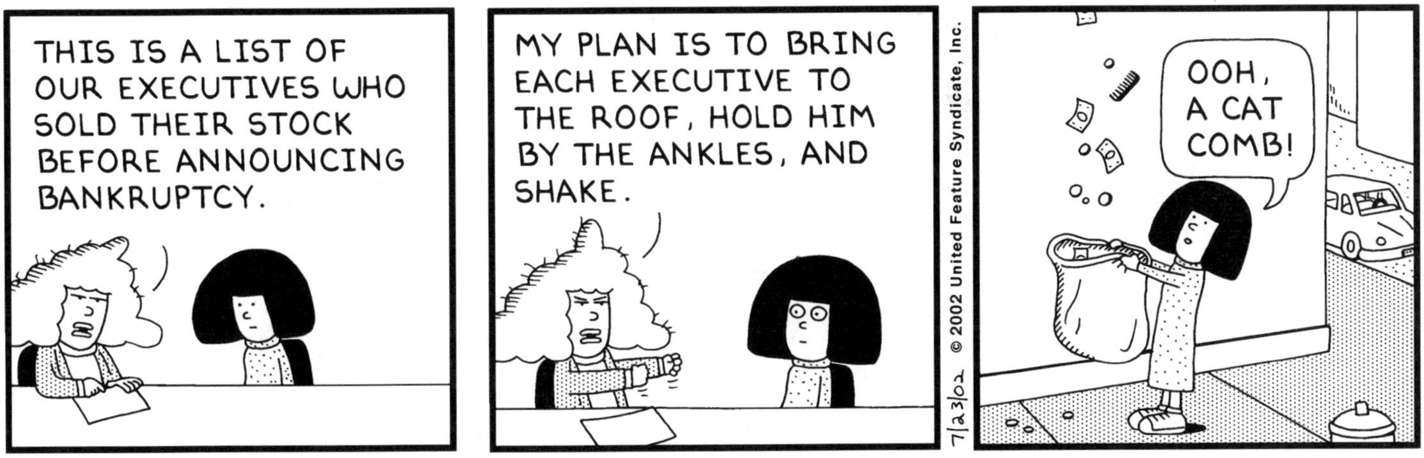
THIS IS A LIST OF OUR EXECUTIVES WHO SOLD THEIR STOCK BEFORE ANNOUNCING BANKRUPTCY.
MY PLAN IS TO BRING EACH EXECUTIVE TO THE ROOF, HOLD HIM BY THE ANKLES, AND SHAKE.
7/23/02 © 2002 United Feature Syndicate, Inc.
OOH, A CAT COMB!

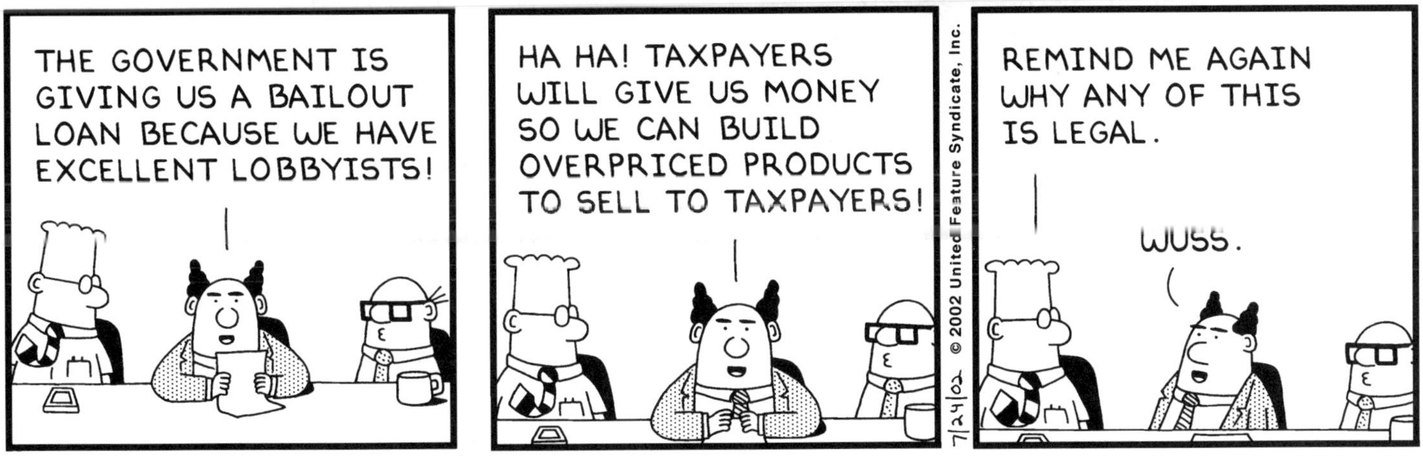
THE GOVERNMENT IS GIVING US A BAILOUT LOAN BECAUSE WE HAVE EXCELLENT LOBBYISTS!
HA HA! TAXPAYERS WILL GIVE US MONEY SO WE CAN BUILD OVERPRICED PRODUCTS TO SELL TO TAXPAYERS!
7/24/02 © 2002 United Feature Syndicate, Inc.
REMIND ME AGAIN WHY ANY OF THIS IS LEGAL.
WUSS.

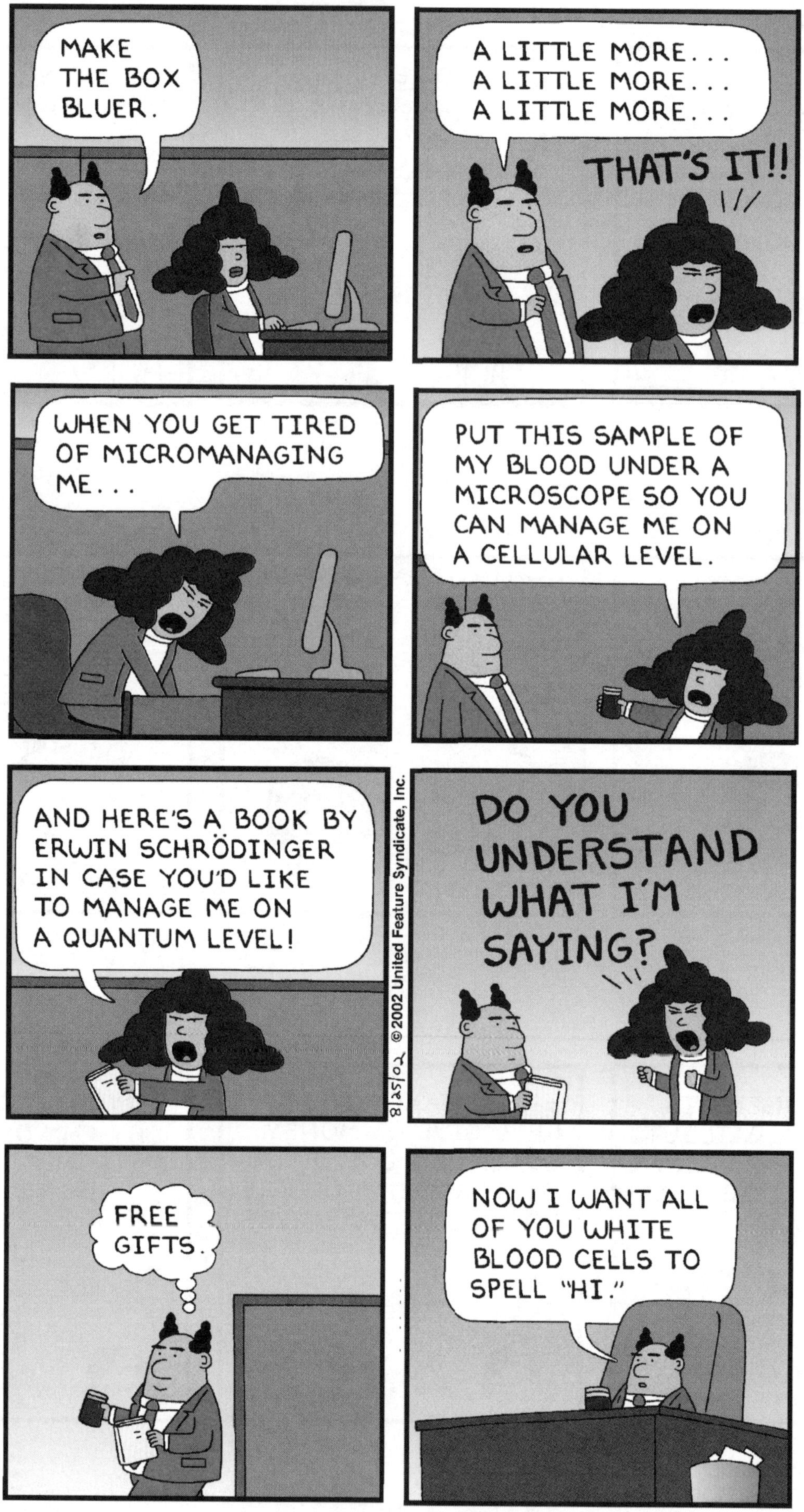
MAKE THE BOX BLUER.
A LITTLE MORE... A LITTLE MORE... A LITTLE MORE...
THAT'S IT!!
WHEN YOU GET TIRED OF MICROMANAGING ME...
PUT THIS SAMPLE OF MY BLOOD UNDER A MICROSCOPE SO YOU CAN MANAGE ME ON A CELLULAR LEVEL.
AND HERE'S A BOOK BY ERWIN SCHRÖDINGER IN CASE YOU'D LIKE TO MANAGE ME ON A QUANTUM LEVEL!
8/25/02 ©2002 United Feature Syndicate, Inc.
DO YOU UNDERSTAND WHAT I'M SAYING?
FREE GIFTS.
NOW I WANT ALL OF YOU WHITE BLOOD CELLS TO SPELL "HI."

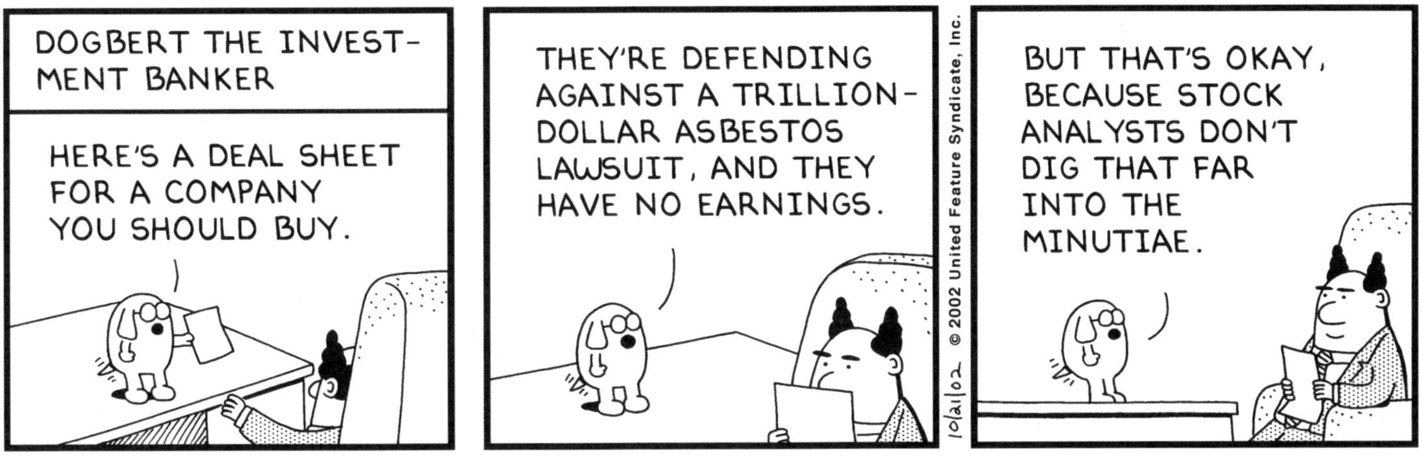
DOGBERT THE INVESTMENT BANKER
HERE'S A DEAL SHEET FOR A COMPANY YOU SHOULD BUY.
THEY'RE DEFENDING AGAINST A TRILLION-DOLLAR ASBESTOS LAWSUIT, AND THEY HAVE NO EARNINGS.
10/21/02 © 2002 United Feature Syndicate, Inc.
BUT THAT'S OKAY, BECAUSE STOCK ANALYSTS DON'T DIG THAT FAR INTO THE MINUTIAE.

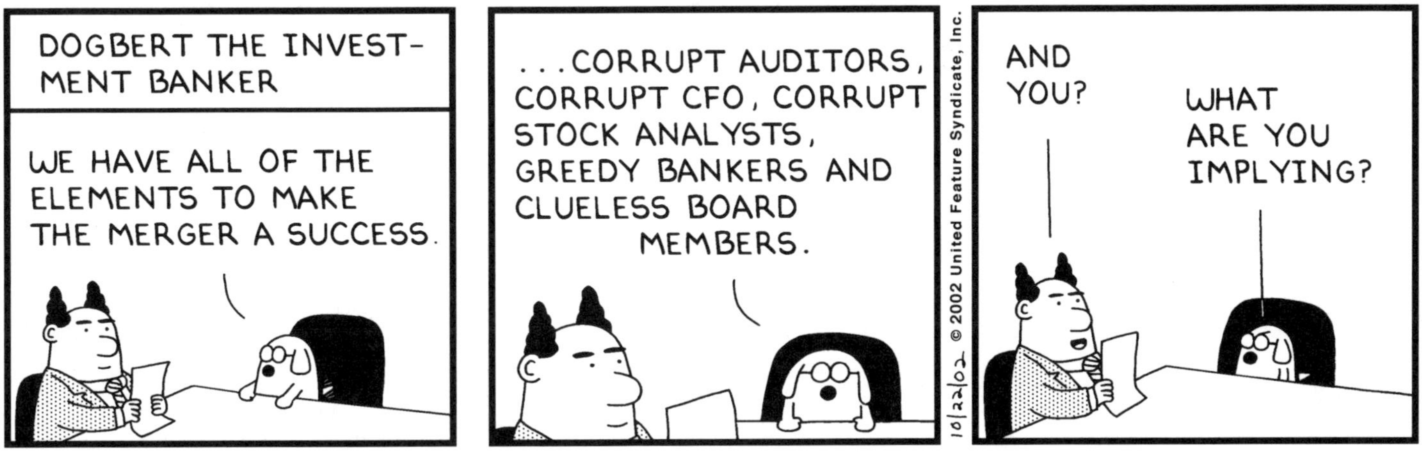
DOGBERT THE INVESTMENT BANKER
WE HAVE ALL OF THE ELEMENTS TO MAKE THE MERGER A SUCCESS.
...CORRUPT AUDITORS, CORRUPT CFO, CORRUPT STOCK ANALYSTS, GREEDY BANKERS AND CLUELESS BOARD MEMBERS.
10/22/02 © 2002 United Feature Syndicate, Inc.
AND YOU?
WHAT ARE YOU IMPLYING?

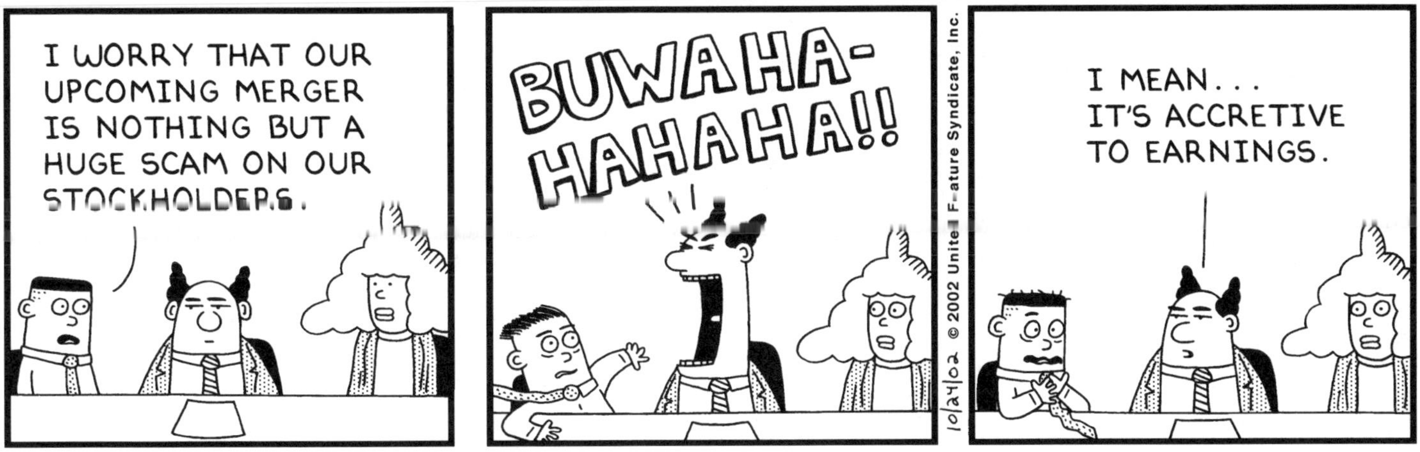
I WORRY THAT OUR UPCOMING MERGER IS NOTHING BUT A HUGE SCAM ON OUR STOCKHOLDERS.
BUWAHA-HAHAHA!!
10/24/02
I MEAN... IT'S ACCRETIVE TO EARNINGS.

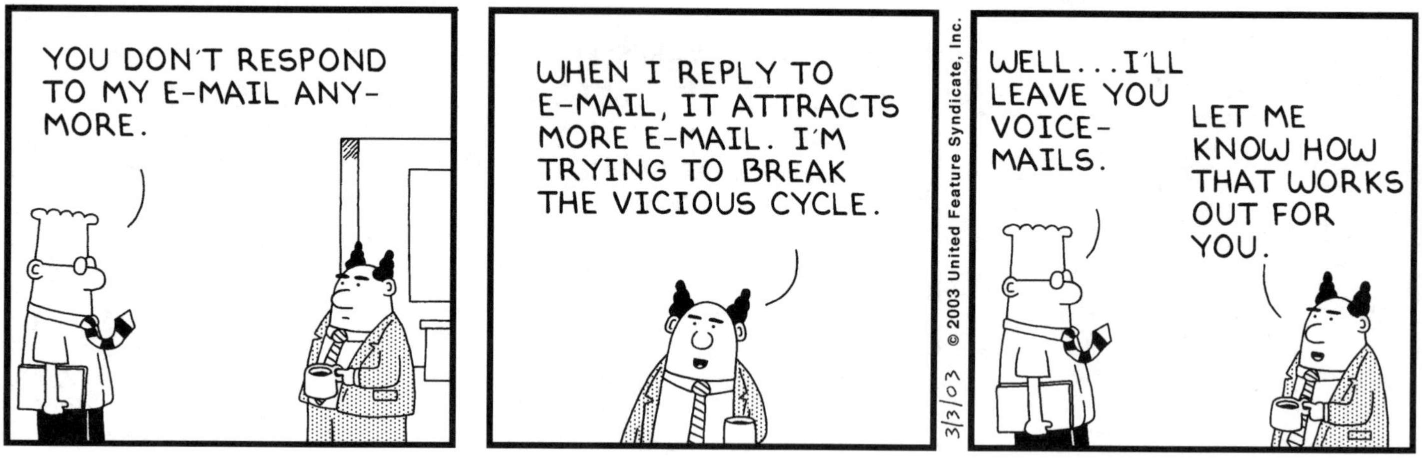
YOU DON'T RESPOND TO MY E-MAIL ANYMORE.
WHEN I REPLY TO E-MAIL, IT ATTRACTS MORE E-MAIL. I'M TRYING TO BREAK THE VICIOUS CYCLE.
3/3/03 © 2003 United Feature Syndicate, Inc.
WELL...I'LL LEAVE YOU VOICE-MAILS.
LET ME KNOW HOW THAT WORKS OUT FOR YOU.

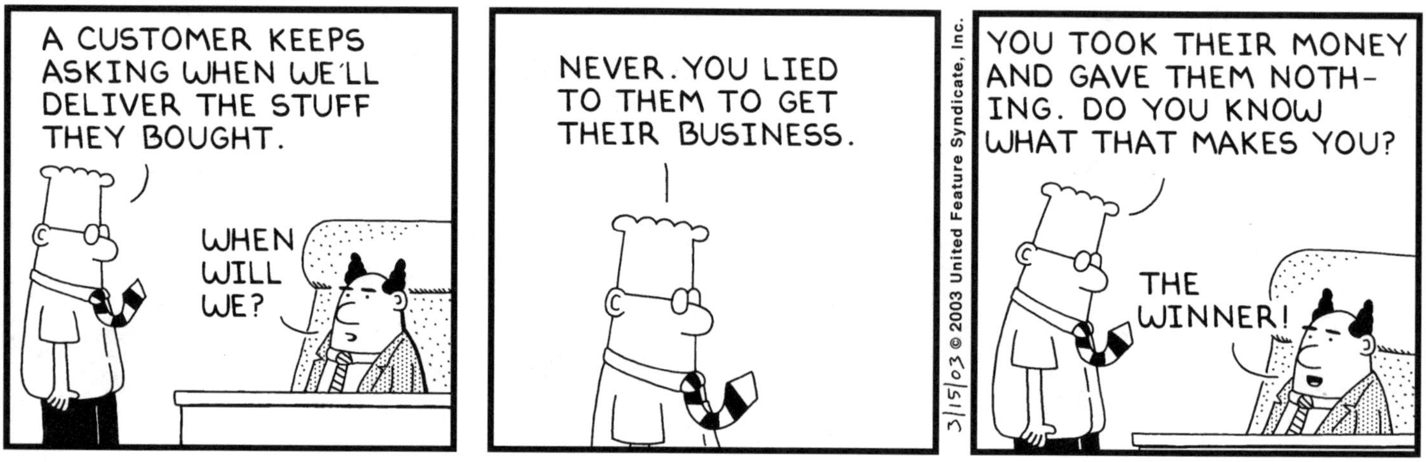
A CUSTOMER KEEPS ASKING WHEN WE'LL DELIVER THE STUFF THEY BOUGHT.
WHEN WILL WE?
NEVER. YOU LIED TO THEM TO GET THEIR BUSINESS.
3/15/03 © 2003 United Feature Syndicate, Inc.
YOU TOOK THEIR MONEY AND GAVE THEM NOTHING. DO YOU KNOW WHAT THAT MAKES YOU?
THE WINNER!

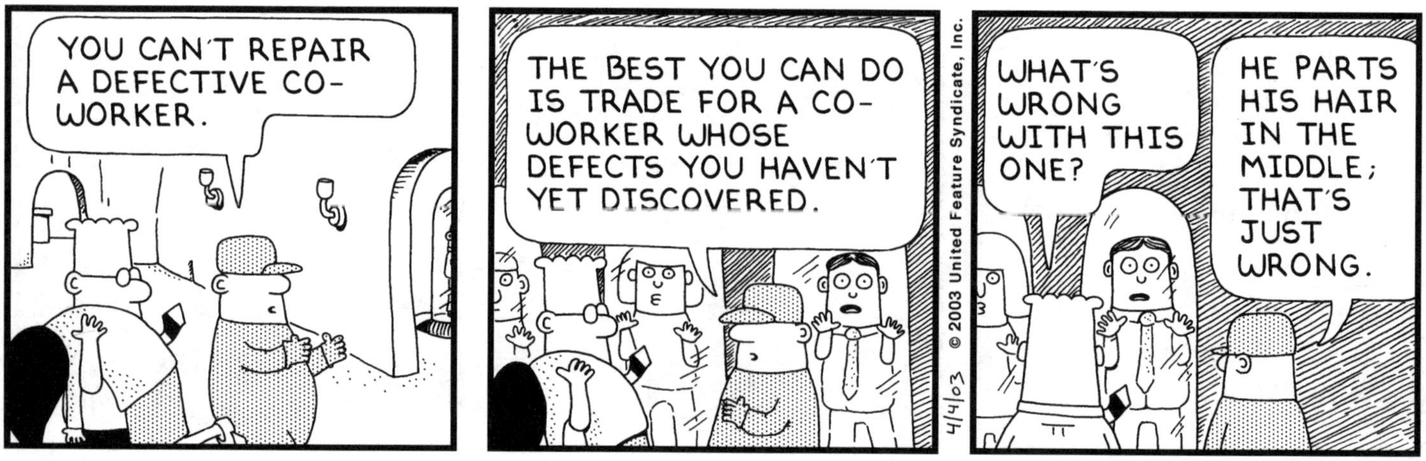
YOU CAN'T REPAIR A DEFECTIVE CO-WORKER.
THE BEST YOU CAN DO IS TRADE FOR A CO-WORKER WHOSE DEFECTS YOU HAVEN'T YET DISCOVERED.
4/4/03 © 2003 United Feature Syndicate, Inc.
WHAT'S WRONG WITH THIS ONE?
HE PARTS HIS HAIR IN THE MIDDLE; THAT'S JUST WRONG.

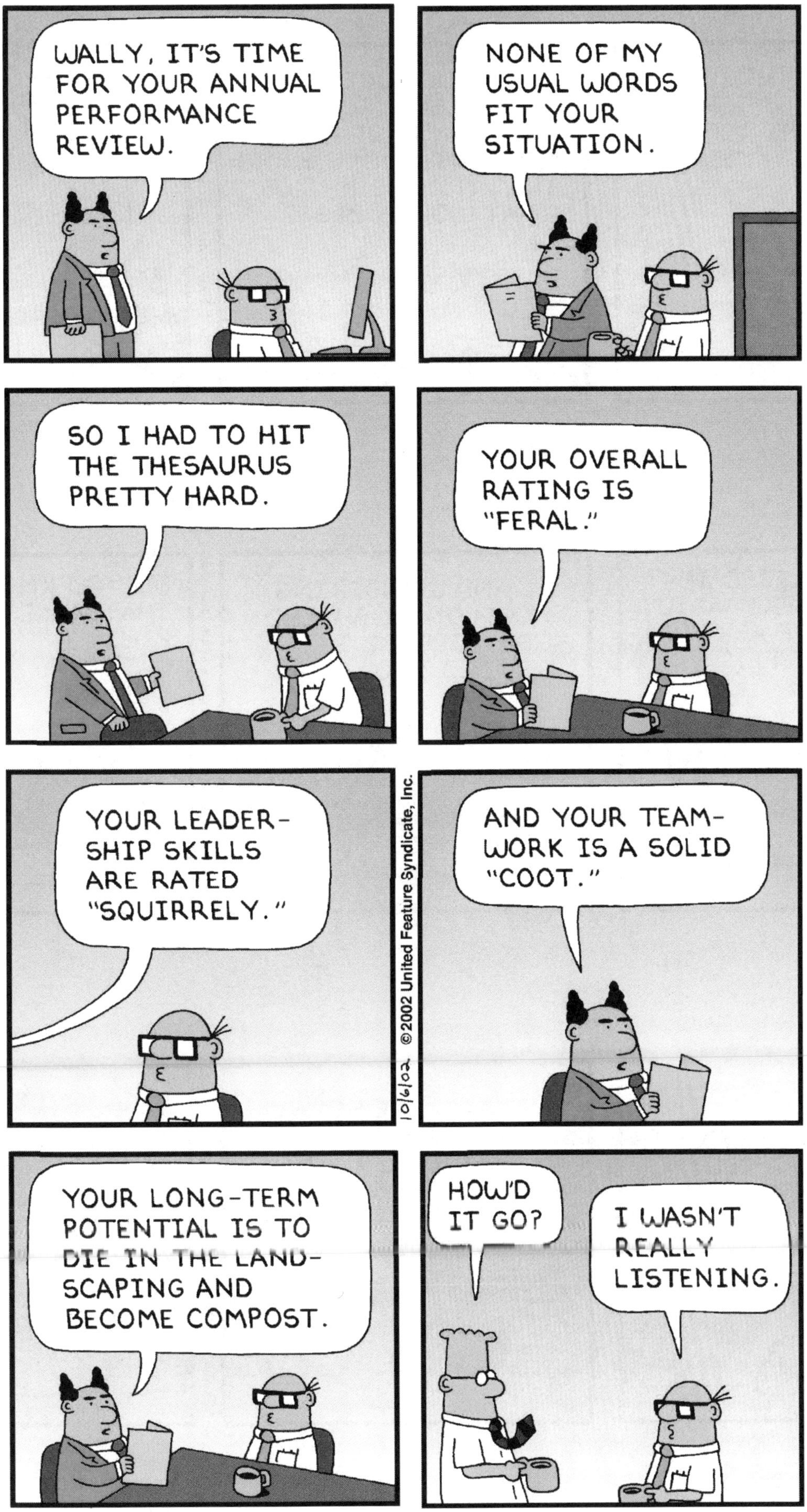
WALLY, IT'S TIME FOR YOUR ANNUAL PERFORMANCE REVIEW.
NONE OF MY USUAL WORDS FIT YOUR SITUATION.
SO I HAD TO HIT THE THESAURUS PRETTY HARD.
YOUR OVERALL RATING IS "FERAL."
YOUR LEADER-SHIP SKILLS ARE RATED "SQUIRRELY."
AND YOUR TEAM-WORK IS A SOLID "COOT."
YOUR LONG-TERM POTENTIAL IS TO DIE IN THE LAND-SCAPING AND BECOME COMPOST.
HOW'D IT GO?
I WASN'T REALLY LISTENING.
10/6/02 © 2002 United Feature Syndicate, Inc.

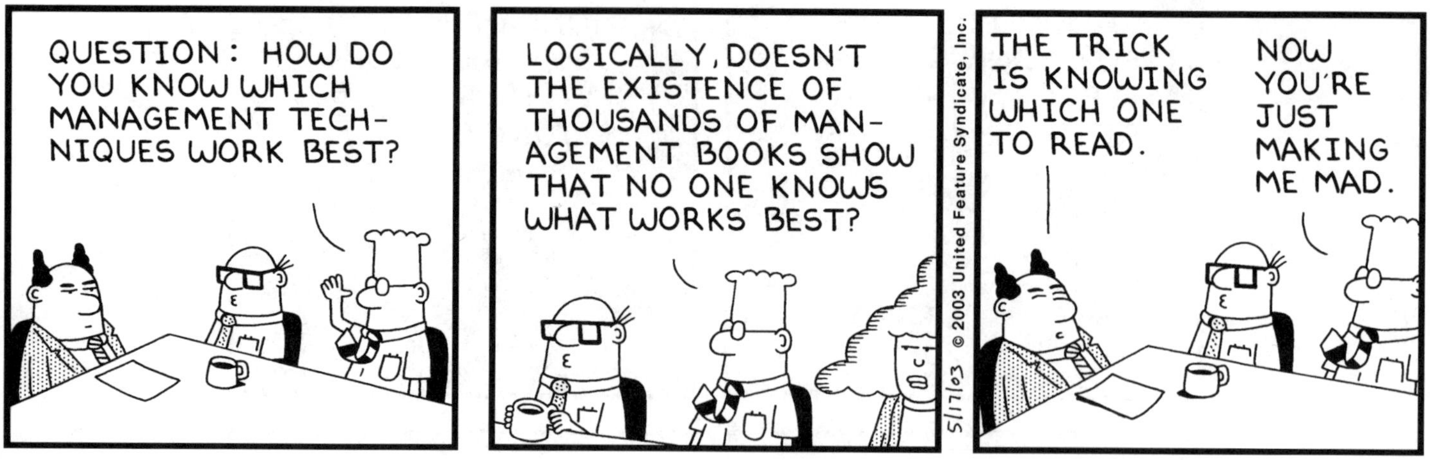
QUESTION: HOW DO YOU KNOW WHICH MANAGEMENT TECHNIQUES WORK BEST?
LOGICALLY, DOESN'T THE EXISTENCE OF THOUSANDS OF MANAGEMENT BOOKS SHOW THAT NO ONE KNOWS WHAT WORKS BEST?
5/17/03 © 2003 United Feature Syndicate, Inc.
THE TRICK IS KNOWING WHICH ONE TO READ.
NOW YOU'RE JUST MAKING ME MAD.

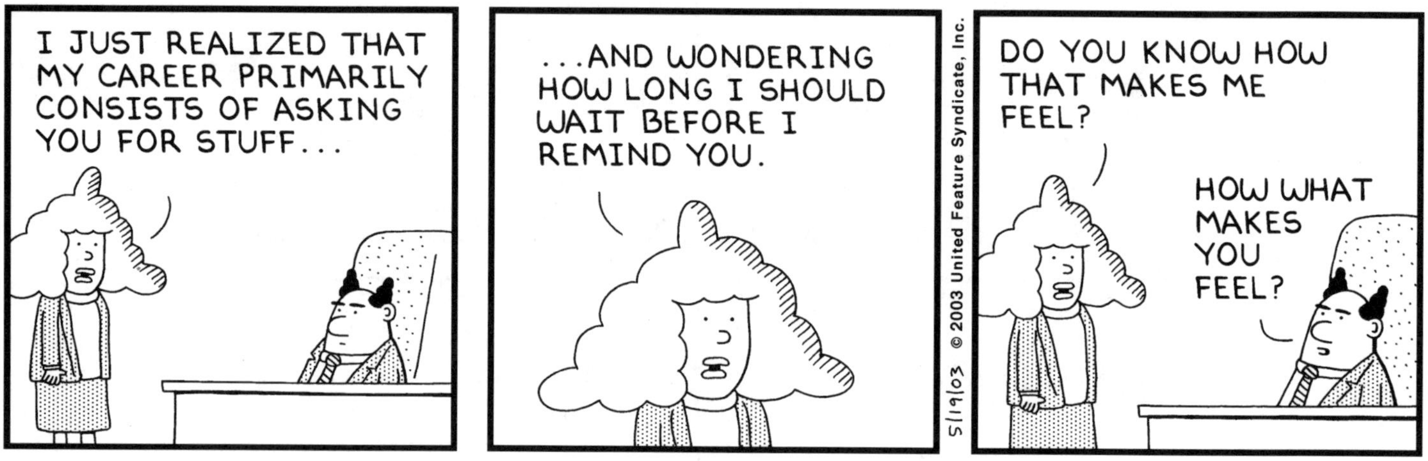
I JUST REALIZED THAT MY CAREER PRIMARILY CONSISTS OF ASKING YOU FOR STUFF...
...AND WONDERING HOW LONG I SHOULD WAIT BEFORE I REMIND YOU.
5/19/03 © 2003 United Feature Syndicate, Inc.
DO YOU KNOW HOW THAT MAKES ME FEEL?
HOW WHAT MAKES YOU FEEL?

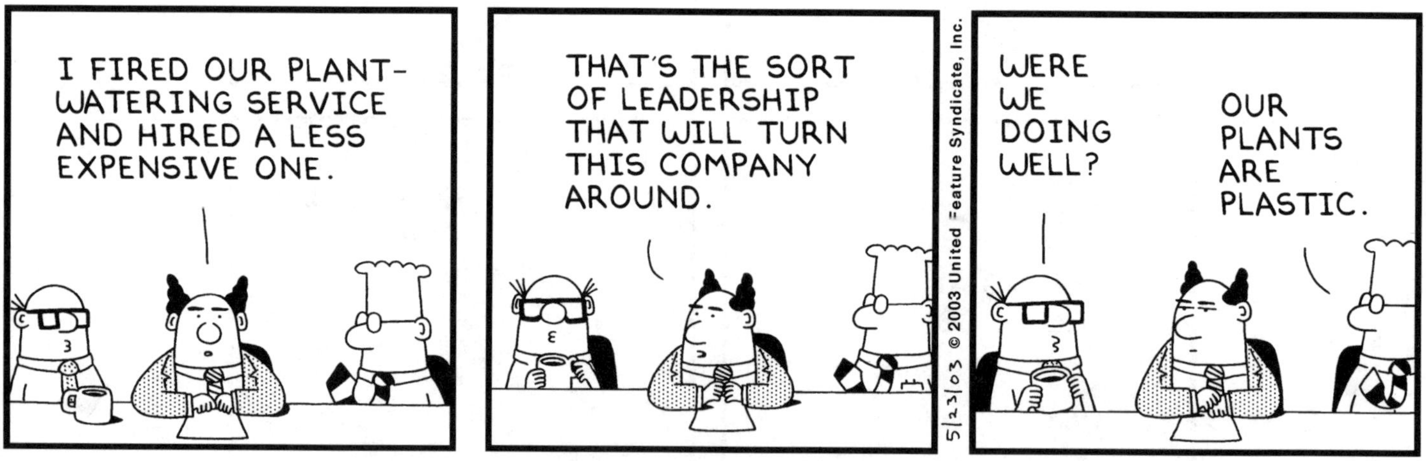
I FIRED OUR PLANT-WATERING SERVICE AND HIRED A LESS EXPENSIVE ONE.
THAT'S THE SORT OF LEADERSHIP THAT WILL TURN THIS COMPANY AROUND.
5/23/03 © 2003 United Feature Syndicate, Inc.
WERE WE DOING WELL?
OUR PLANTS ARE PLASTIC.

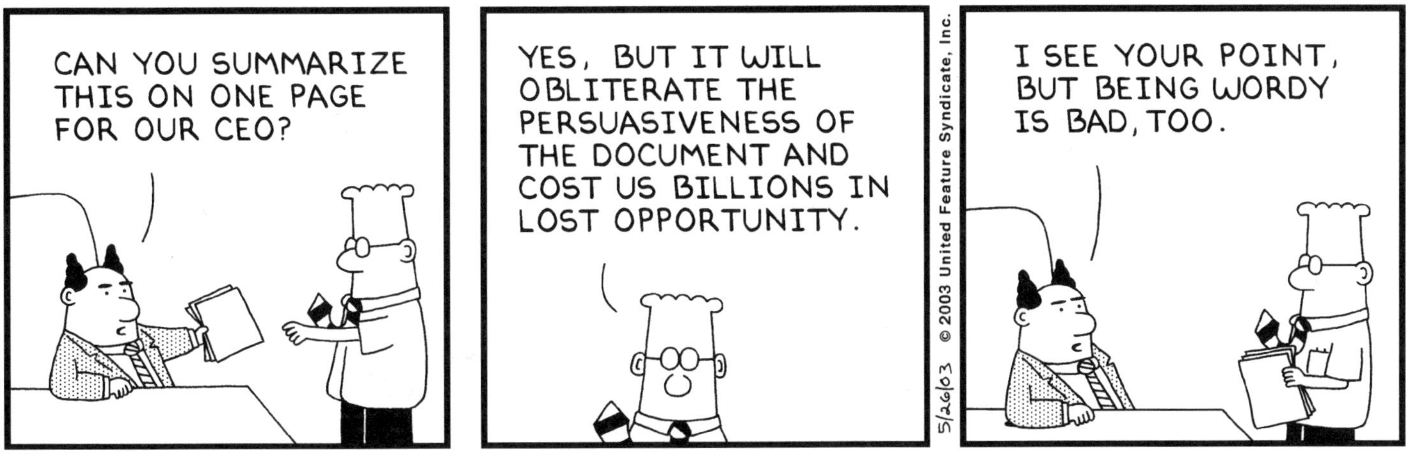
CAN YOU SUMMARIZE THIS ON ONE PAGE FOR OUR CEO?
YES, BUT IT WILL OBLITERATE THE PERSUASIVENESS OF THE DOCUMENT AND COST US BILLIONS IN LOST OPPORTUNITY.
5/26/03 © 2003 United Feature Syndicate, Inc.
I SEE YOUR POINT, BUT BEING WORDY IS BAD, TOO.

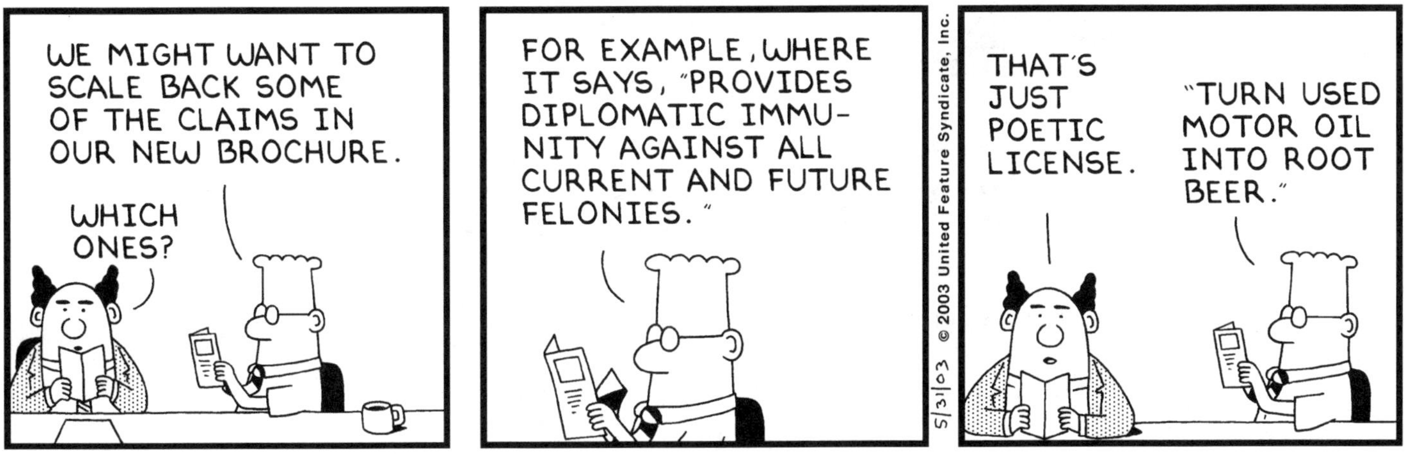
WE MIGHT WANT TO SCALE BACK SOME OF THE CLAIMS IN OUR NEW BROCHURE.
WHICH ONES?
FOR EXAMPLE, WHERE IT SAYS, "PROVIDES DIPLOMATIC IMMUNITY AGAINST ALL CURRENT AND FUTURE FELONIES."
5/31/03 © 2003 United Feature Syndicate, Inc.
THAT'S JUST POETIC LICENSE.
"TURN USED MOTOR OIL INTO ROOT BEER."

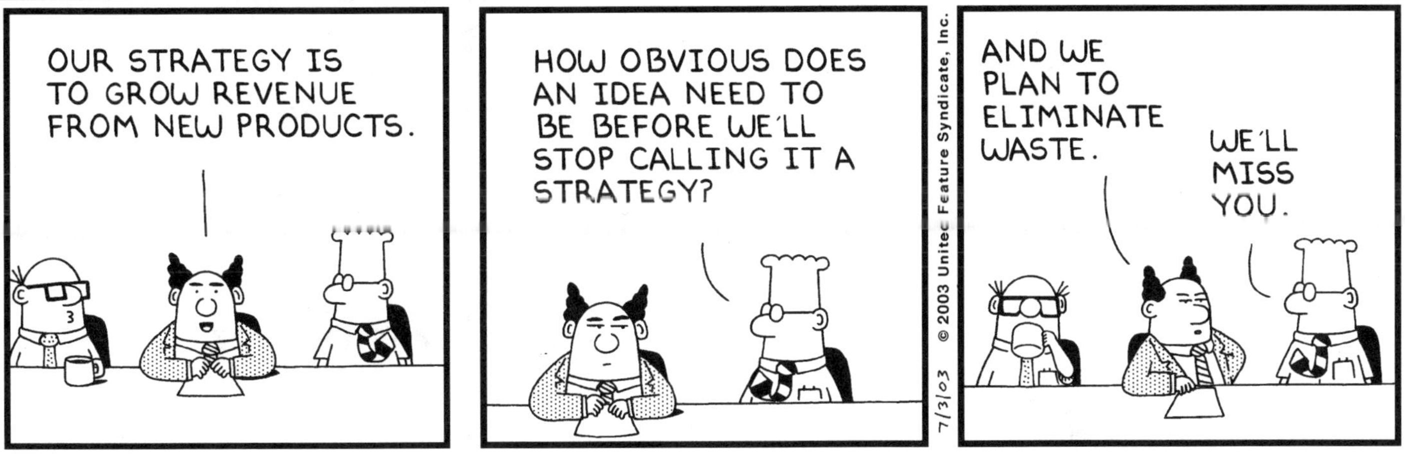
OUR STRATEGY IS TO GROW REVENUE FROM NEW PRODUCTS.
HOW OBVIOUS DOES AN IDEA NEED TO BE BEFORE WE'LL STOP CALLING IT A STRATEGY?
7/3/03 © 2003 United Feature Syndicate, Inc.
AND WE PLAN TO ELIMINATE WASTE.
WE'LL MISS YOU.

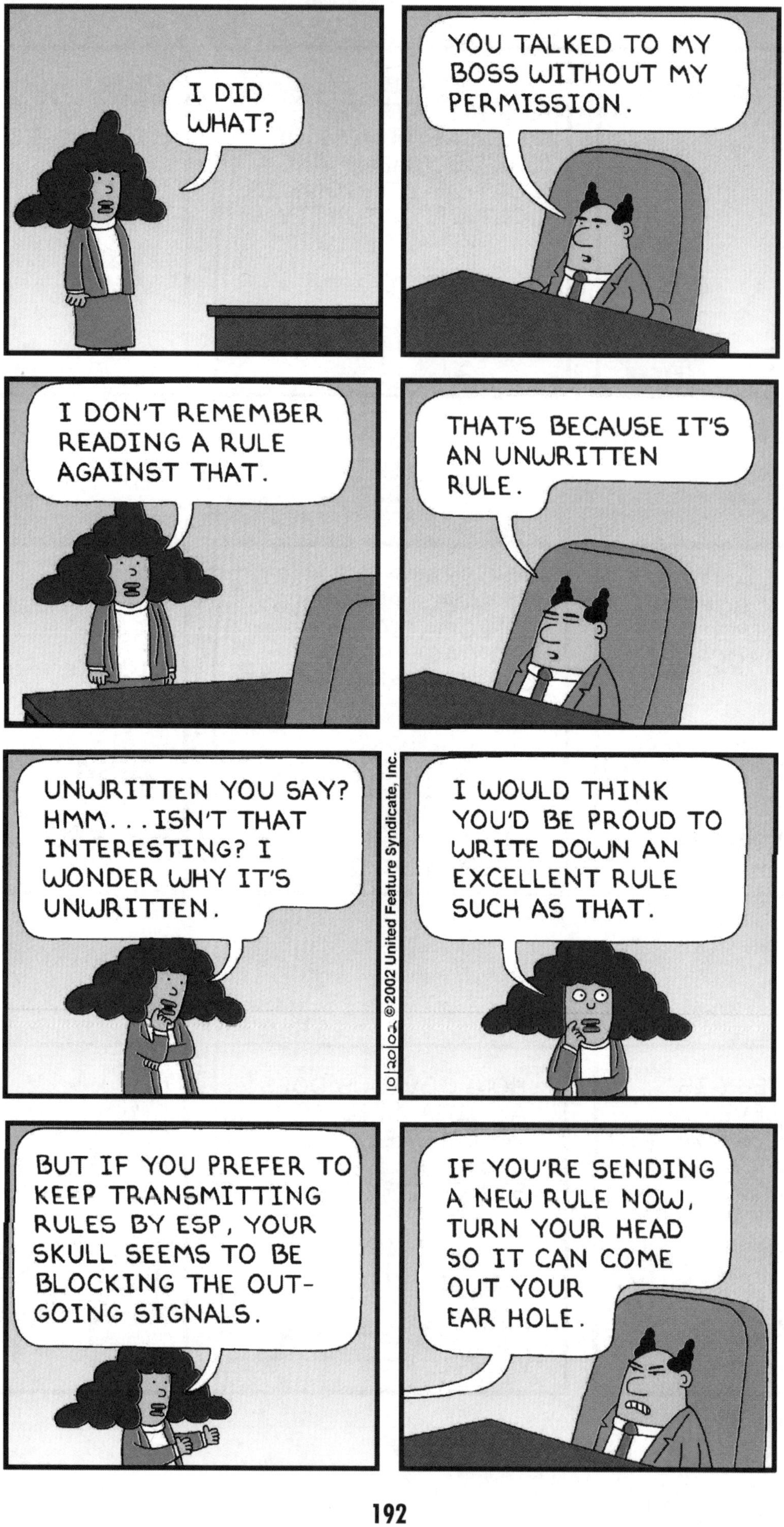
I DID WHAT?
YOU TALKED TO MY BOSS WITHOUT MY PERMISSION.
I DON'T REMEMBER READING A RULE AGAINST THAT.
THAT'S BECAUSE IT'S AN UNWRITTEN RULE.
UNWRITTEN YOU SAY? HMM. . . ISN'T THAT INTERESTING? I WONDER WHY IT'S UNWRITTEN.
I WOULD THINK YOU'D BE PROUD TO WRITE DOWN AN EXCELLENT RULE SUCH AS THAT.
BUT IF YOU PREFER TO KEEP TRANSMITTING RULES BY ESP, YOUR SKULL SEEMS TO BE BLOCKING THE OUT-GOING SIGNALS.
IF YOU'RE SENDING A NEW RULE NOW, TURN YOUR HEAD SO IT CAN COME OUT YOUR EAR HOLE.
10/20/02 ©2002 United Feature Syndicate, Inc.

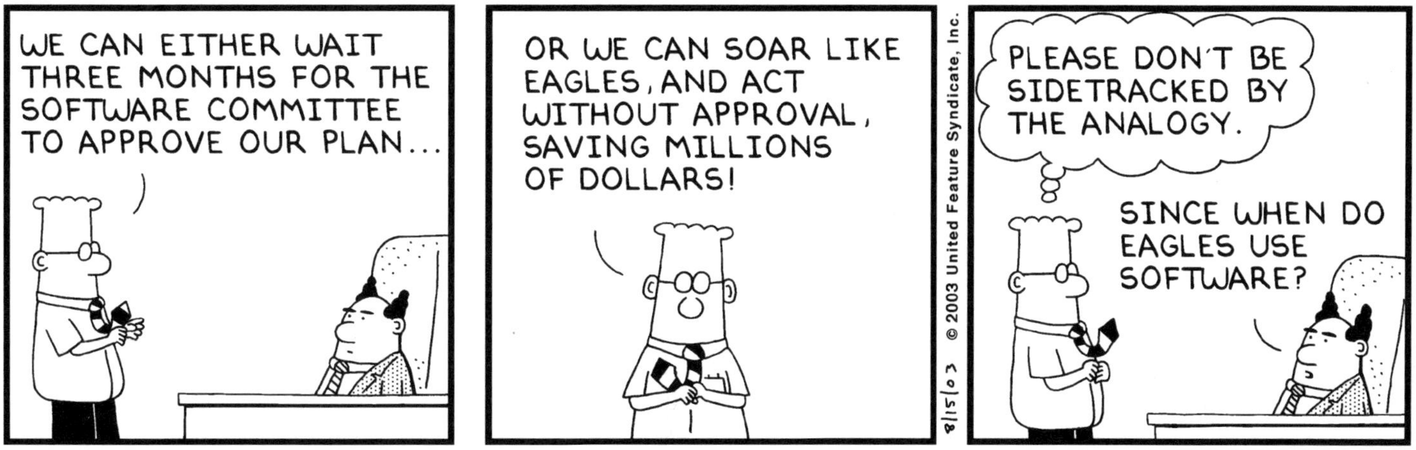
WE CAN EITHER WAIT THREE MONTHS FOR THE SOFTWARE COMMITTEE TO APPROVE OUR PLAN...
OR WE CAN SOAR LIKE EAGLES, AND ACT WITHOUT APPROVAL, SAVING MILLIONS OF DOLLARS!
8/15/03 © 2003 United Feature Syndicate, Inc.
PLEASE DON'T BE SIDETRACKED BY THE ANALOGY.
SINCE WHEN DO EAGLES USE SOFTWARE?

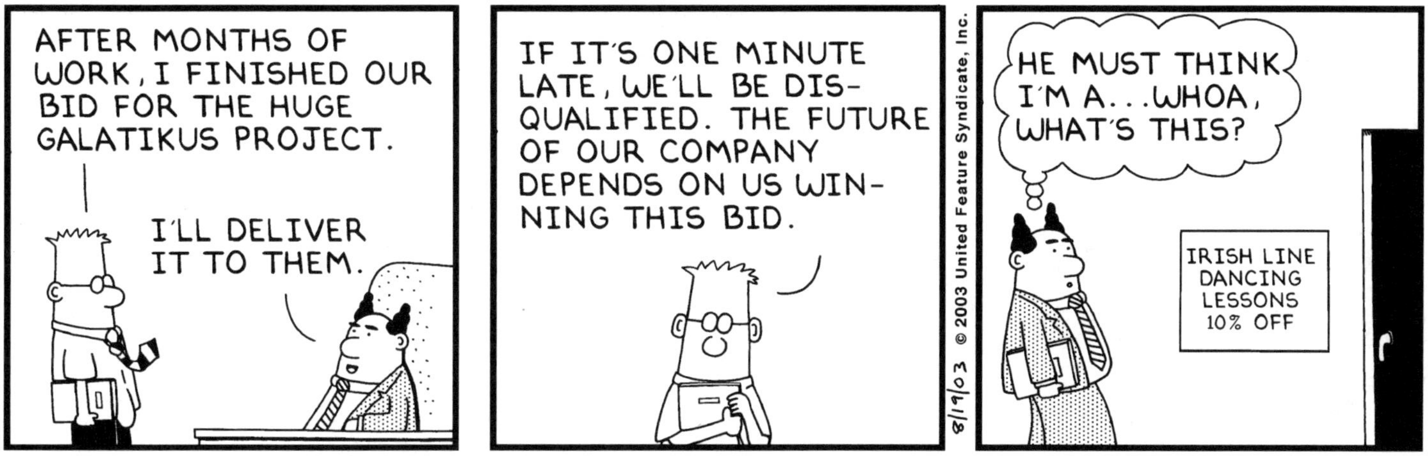
AFTER MONTHS OF WORK, I FINISHED OUR BID FOR THE HUGE GALATIKUS PROJECT.
I'LL DELIVER IT TO THEM.
IF IT'S ONE MINUTE LATE, WE'LL BE DIS-QUALIFIED. THE FUTURE OF OUR COMPANY DEPENDS ON US WIN-NING THIS BID.
8/19/03 © 2003 United Feature Syndicate, Inc.
HE MUST THINK I'M A...WHOA, WHAT'S THIS?
IRISH LINE DANCING LESSONS 10% OFF

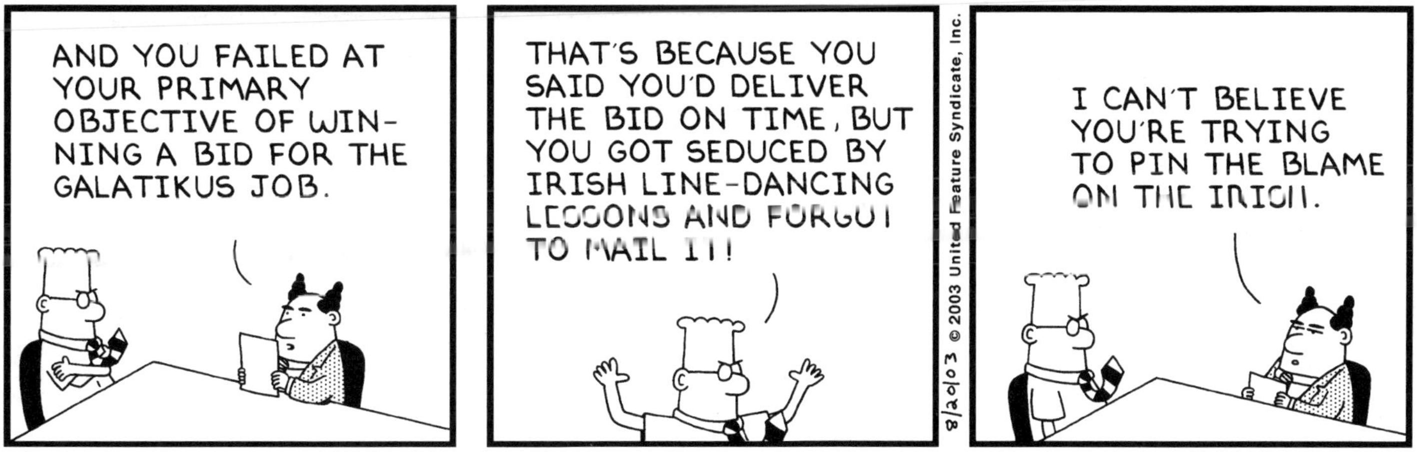
AND YOU FAILED AT YOUR PRIMARY OBJECTIVE OF WIN-NING A BID FOR THE GALATIKUS JOB.
THAT'S BECAUSE YOU SAID YOU'D DELIVER THE BID ON TIME, BUT YOU GOT SEDUCED BY IRISH LINE-DANCING LESSONS AND FORGOT TO MAIL IT!
8/20/03 © 2003 United Feature Syndicate, Inc.
I CAN'T BELIEVE YOU'RE TRYING TO PIN THE BLAME ON THE IRISH.

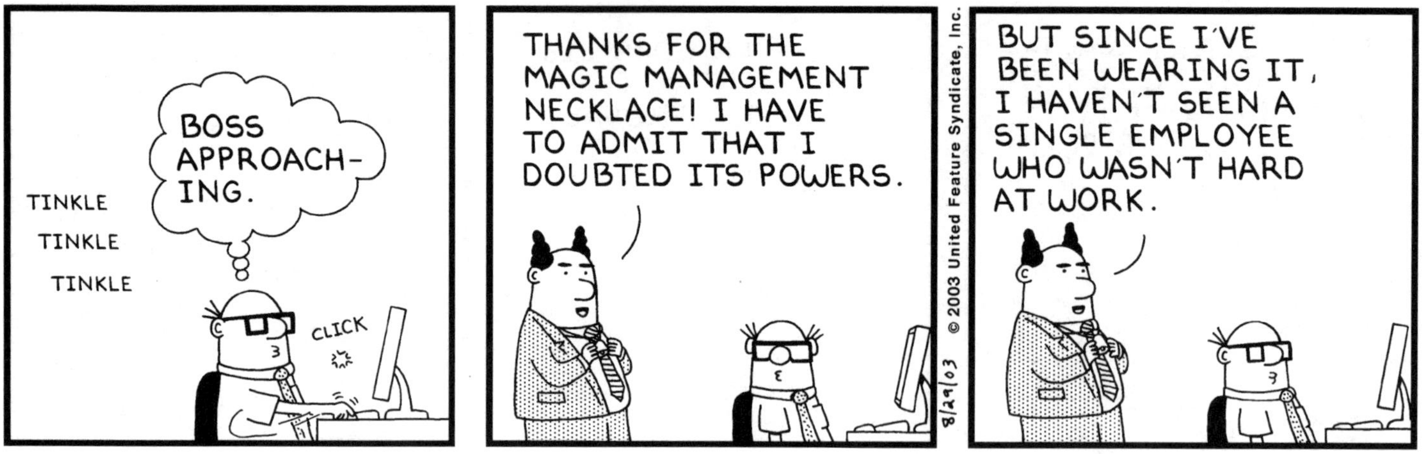
TINKLE
TINKLE
TINKLE
BOSS APPROACH-ING.
CLICK
THANKS FOR THE MAGIC MANAGEMENT NECKLACE! I HAVE TO ADMIT THAT I DOUBTED ITS POWERS.
8/29/03
© 2003 United Feature Syndicate, Inc.
BUT SINCE I'VE BEEN WEARING IT, I HAVEN'T SEEN A SINGLE EMPLOYEE WHO WASN'T HARD AT WORK.

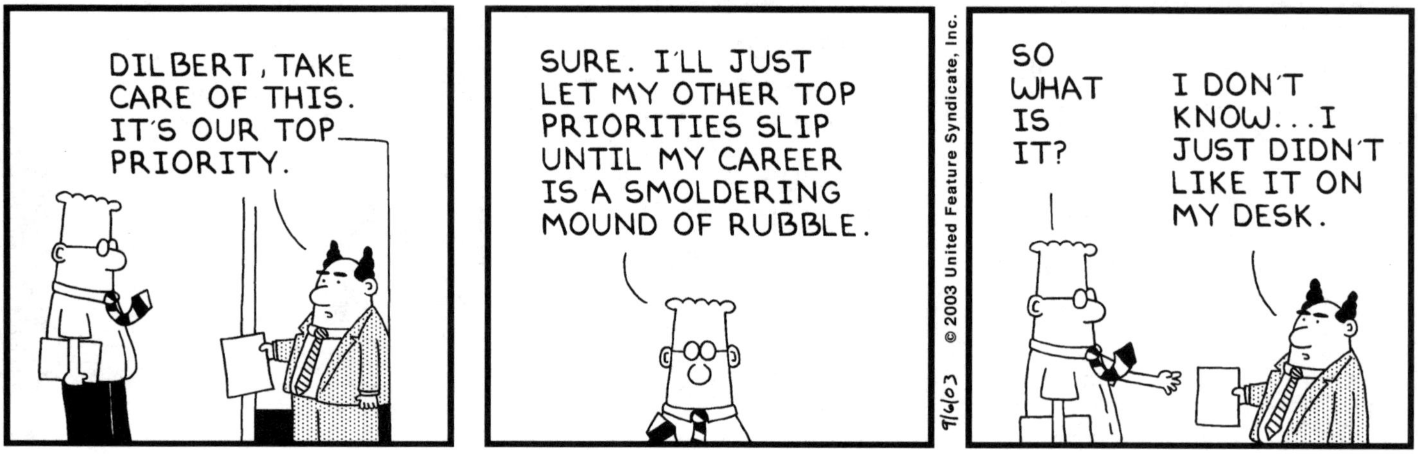
DILBERT, TAKE CARE OF THIS. IT'S OUR TOP PRIORITY.
SURE. I'LL JUST LET MY OTHER TOP PRIORITIES SLIP UNTIL MY CAREER IS A SMOLDERING MOUND OF RUBBLE.
9/6/03
© 2003 United Feature Syndicate, Inc.
SO WHAT IS IT?
I DON'T KNOW... I JUST DIDN'T LIKE IT ON MY DESK.

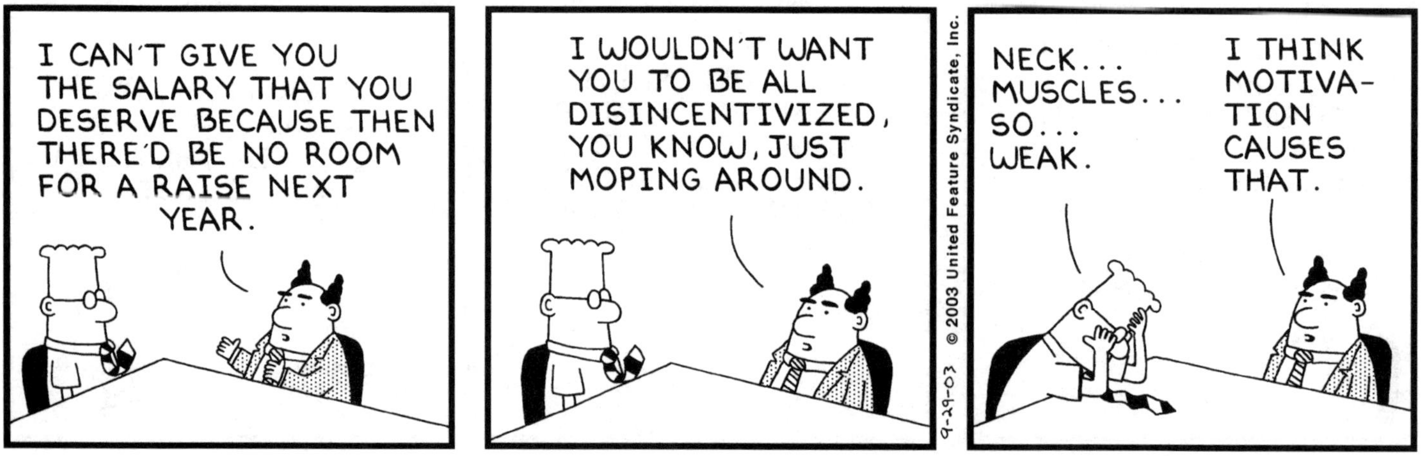
I CAN'T GIVE YOU THE SALARY THAT YOU DESERVE BECAUSE THEN THERE'D BE NO ROOM FOR A RAISE NEXT YEAR.
I WOULDN'T WANT YOU TO BE ALL DISINCENTIVIZED, YOU KNOW, JUST MOPING AROUND.
9-29-03
© 2003 United Feature Syndicate, Inc.
NECK... MUSCLES... SO... WEAK.
I THINK MOTIVA-TION CAUSES THAT.

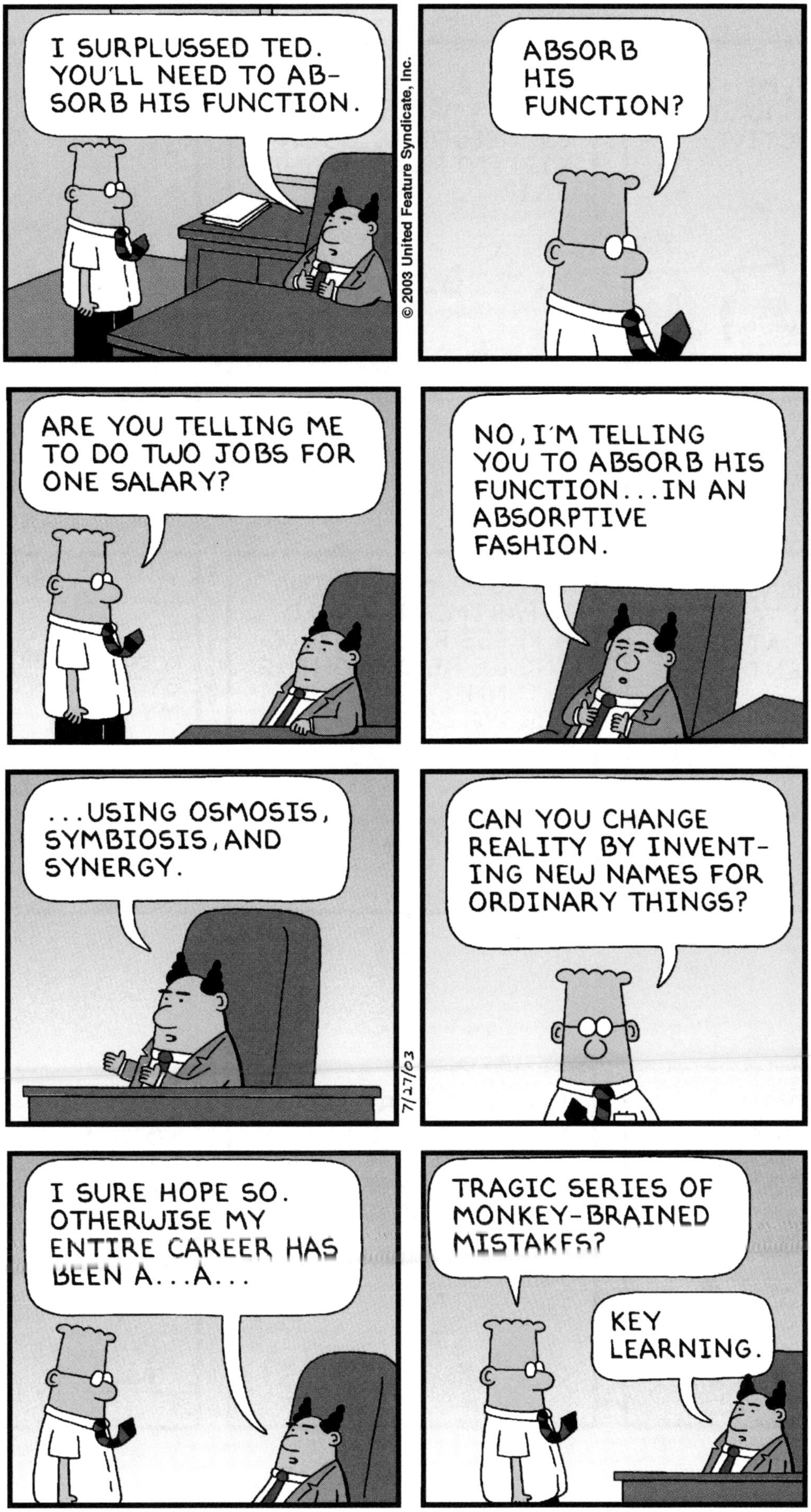
I SURPLUSSED TED. YOU'LL NEED TO ABSORB HIS FUNCTION.
© 2003 United Feature Syndicate, Inc.
ABSORB HIS FUNCTION?
ARE YOU TELLING ME TO DO TWO JOBS FOR ONE SALARY?
NO, I'M TELLING YOU TO ABSORB HIS FUNCTION...IN AN ABSORPTIVE FASHION.
...USING OSMOSIS, SYMBIOSIS, AND SYNERGY.
7/27/03
CAN YOU CHANGE REALITY BY INVENTING NEW NAMES FOR ORDINARY THINGS?
I SURE HOPE SO. OTHERWISE MY ENTIRE CAREER HAS BEEN A...A...
TRAGIC SERIES OF MONKEY-BRAINED MISTAKES?
KEY LEARNING.

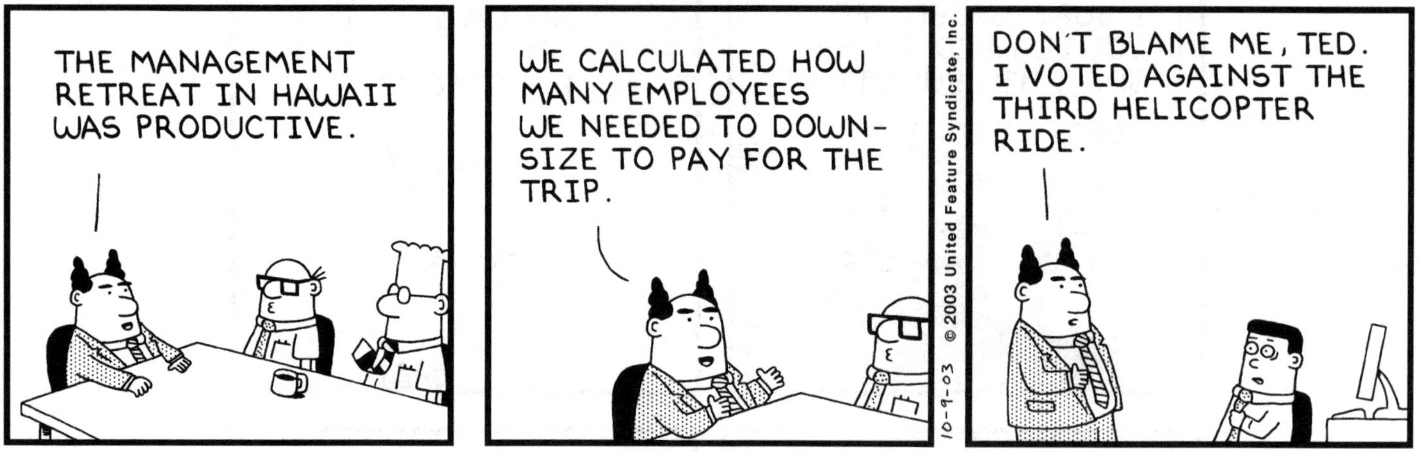
THE MANAGEMENT RETREAT IN HAWAII WAS PRODUCTIVE.
WE CALCULATED HOW MANY EMPLOYEES WE NEEDED TO DOWN-SIZE TO PAY FOR THE TRIP.
10-9-03 © 2003 United Feature Syndicate, Inc.
DON'T BLAME ME, TED. I VOTED AGAINST THE THIRD HELICOPTER RIDE.

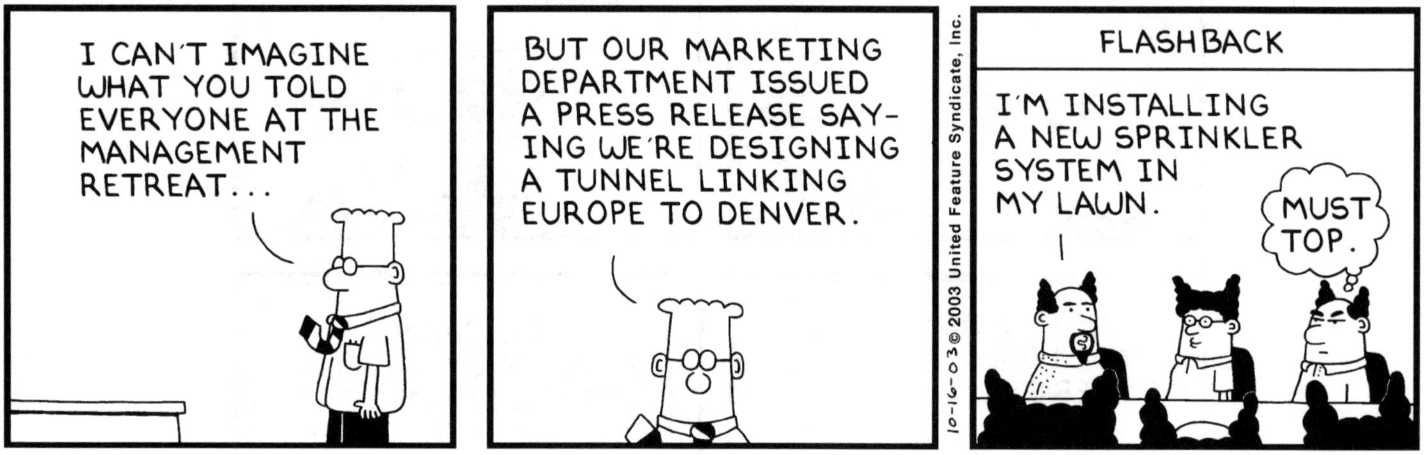
I CAN'T IMAGINE WHAT YOU TOLD EVERYONE AT THE MANAGEMENT RETREAT...
BUT OUR MARKETING DEPARTMENT ISSUED A PRESS RELEASE SAY-ING WE'RE DESIGNING A TUNNEL LINKING EUROPE TO DENVER.
10-16-03 © 2003 United Feature Syndicate, Inc.
FLASHBACK
I'M INSTALLING A NEW SPRINKLER SYSTEM IN MY LAWN.
MUST TOP.

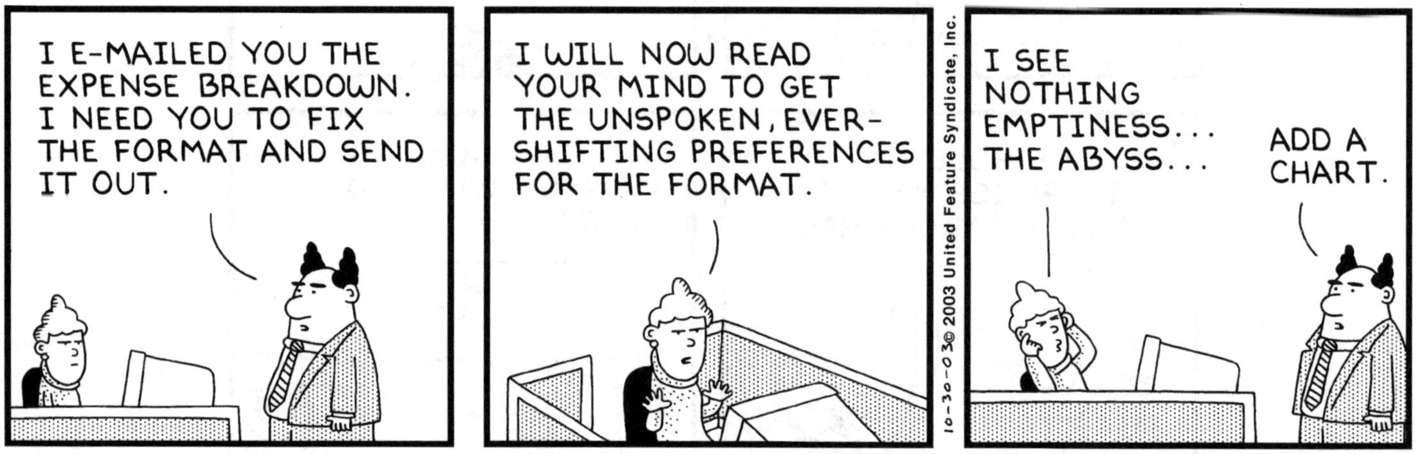
I E-MAILED YOU THE EXPENSE BREAKDOWN. I NEED YOU TO FIX THE FORMAT AND SEND IT OUT.
I WILL NOW READ YOUR MIND TO GET THE UNSPOKEN, EVER-SHIFTING PREFERENCES FOR THE FORMAT.
10-30-03 © 2003 United Feature Syndicate, Inc.
I SEE NOTHING EMPTINESS... THE ABYSS...
ADD A CHART.

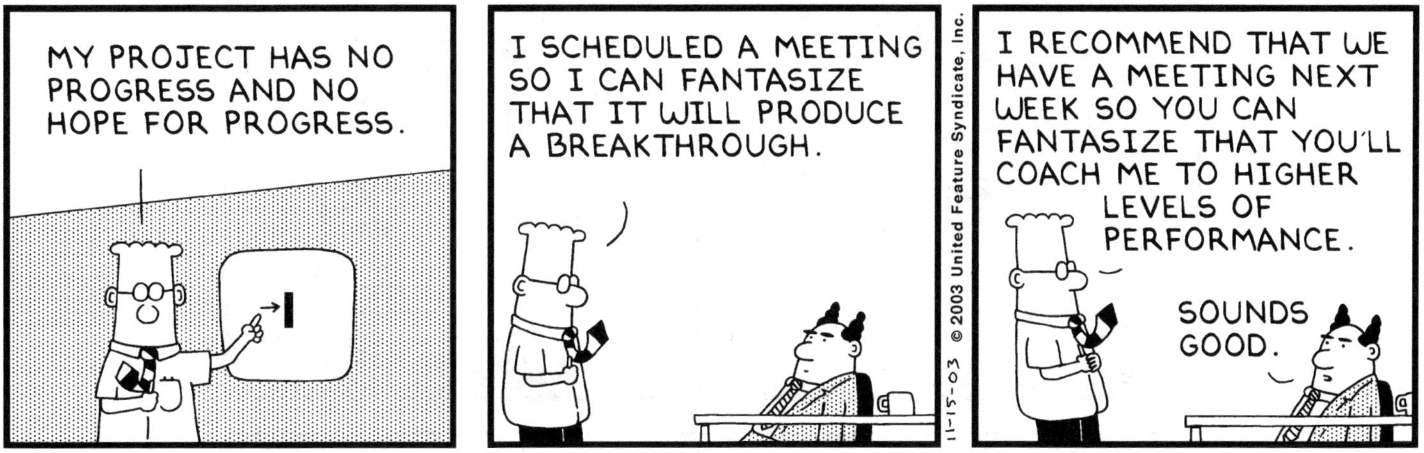
MY PROJECT HAS NO PROGRESS AND NO HOPE FOR PROGRESS.
I SCHEDULED A MEETING SO I CAN FANTASIZE THAT IT WILL PRODUCE A BREAKTHROUGH.
11-15-03 © 2003 United Feature Syndicate, Inc.
I RECOMMEND THAT WE HAVE A MEETING NEXT WEEK SO YOU CAN FANTASIZE THAT YOU'LL COACH ME TO HIGHER LEVELS OF PERFORMANCE.
SOUNDS GOOD.

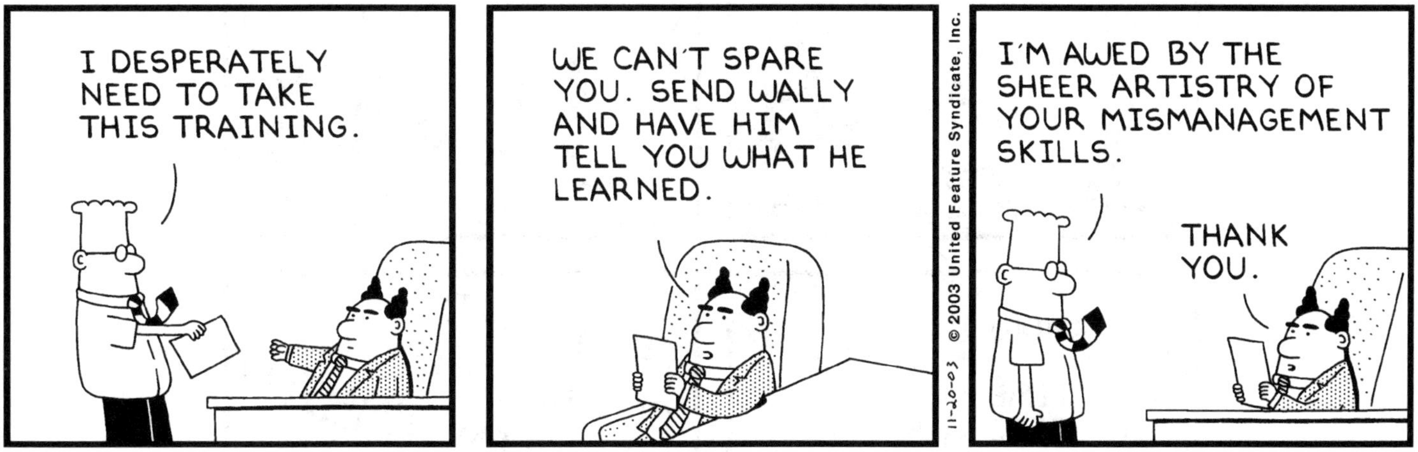
I DESPERATELY NEED TO TAKE THIS TRAINING.
WE CAN'T SPARE YOU. SEND WALLY AND HAVE HIM TELL YOU WHAT HE LEARNED.
11-20-03 © 2003 United Feature Syndicate, Inc.
I'M AWED BY THE SHEER ARTISTRY OF YOUR MISMANAGEMENT SKILLS.
THANK YOU.

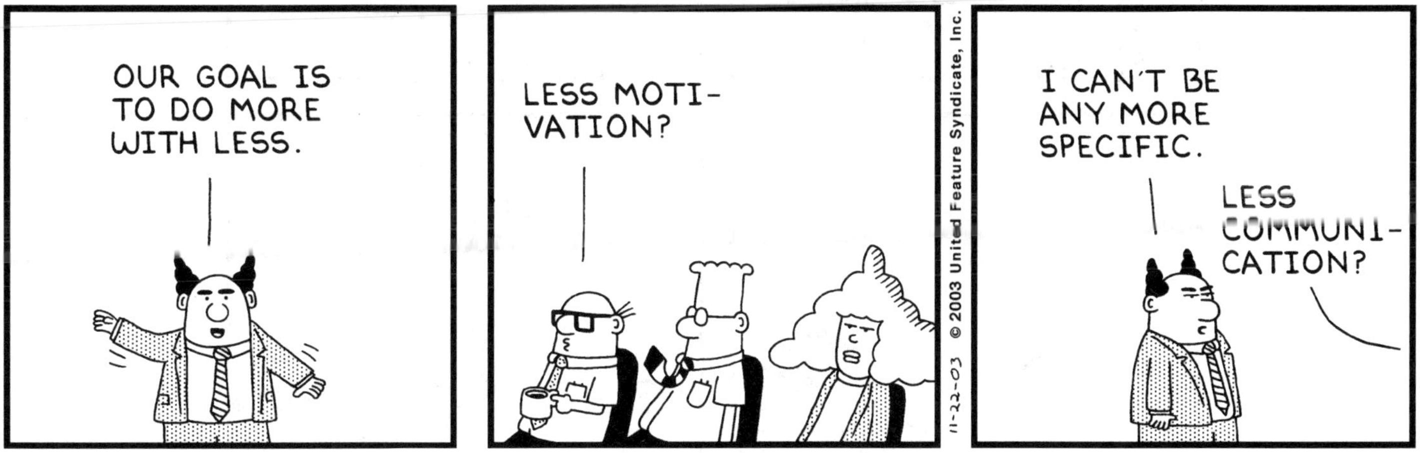
OUR GOAL IS TO DO MORE WITH LESS.
LESS MOTI- VATION?
11-22-03 © 2003 United Feature Syndicate, Inc.
I CAN'T BE ANY MORE SPECIFIC.
LESS COMMUNI- CATION?

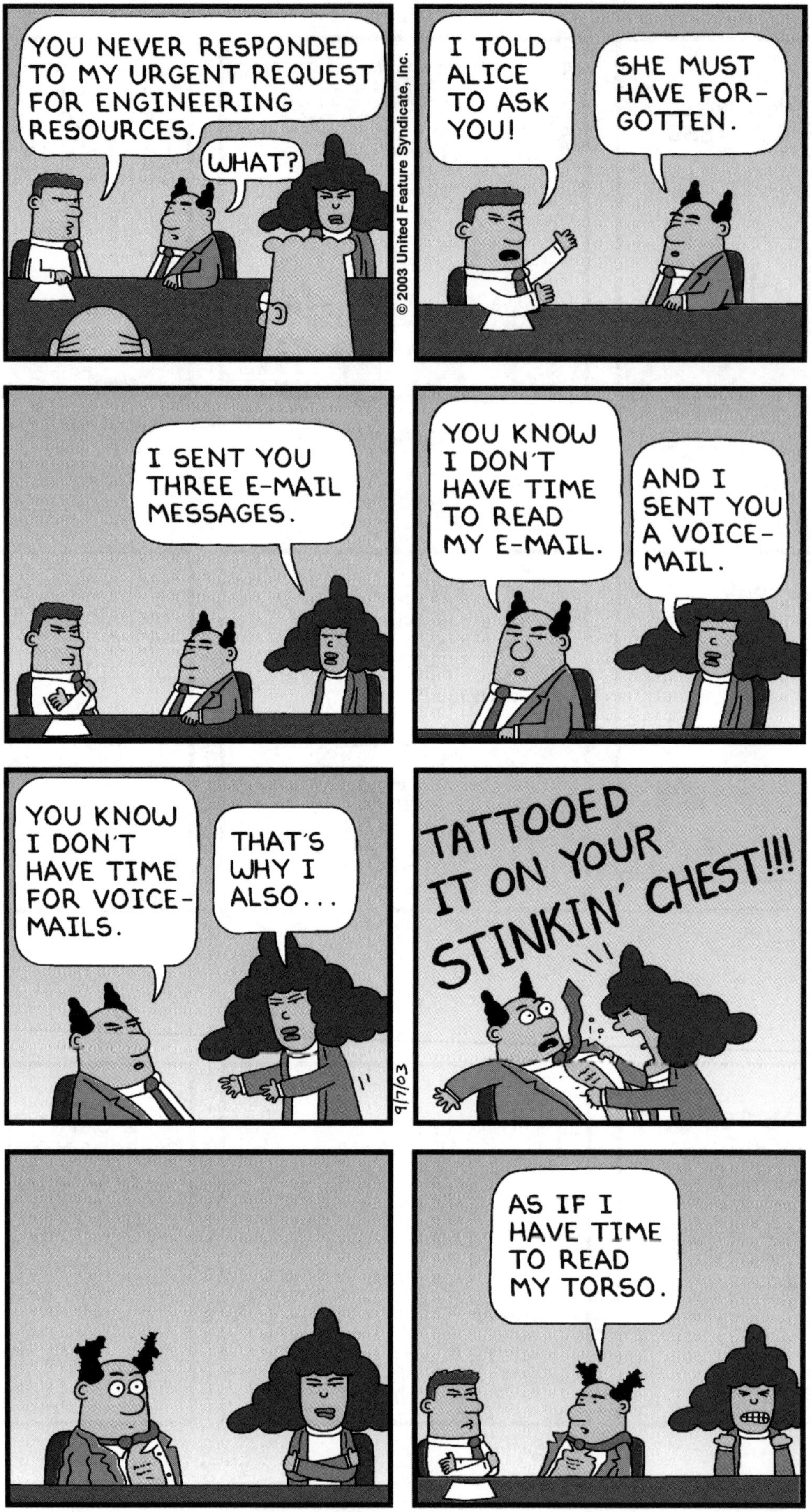
YOU NEVER RESPONDED TO MY URGENT REQUEST FOR ENGINEERING RESOURCES.
WHAT?
© 2003 United Feature Syndicate, Inc.
I TOLD ALICE TO ASK YOU!
SHE MUST HAVE FOR-GOTTEN.
I SENT YOU THREE E-MAIL MESSAGES.
YOU KNOW I DON'T HAVE TIME TO READ MY E-MAIL.
AND I SENT YOU A VOICE-MAIL.
YOU KNOW I DON'T HAVE TIME FOR VOICE-MAILS.
THAT'S WHY I ALSO...
9/7/03
TATTOOED IT ON YOUR STINKIN' CHEST!!!
AS IF I HAVE TIME TO READ MY TORSO.

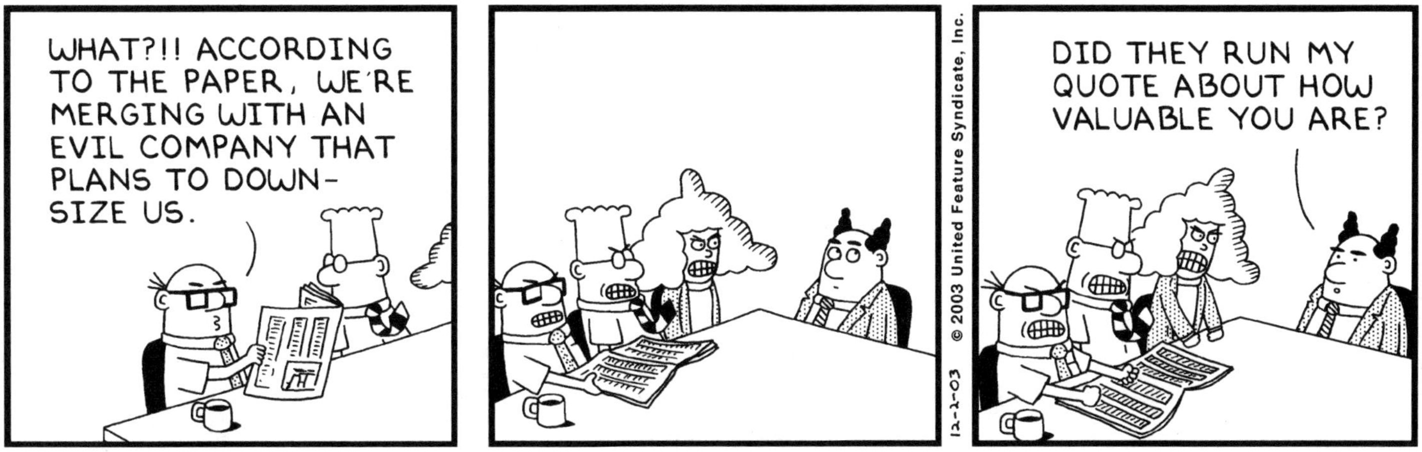
WHAT?!! ACCORDING TO THE PAPER, WE'RE MERGING WITH AN EVIL COMPANY THAT PLANS TO DOWN-SIZE US.
12-2-03
© 2003 United Feature Syndicate, Inc.
DID THEY RUN MY QUOTE ABOUT HOW VALUABLE YOU ARE?

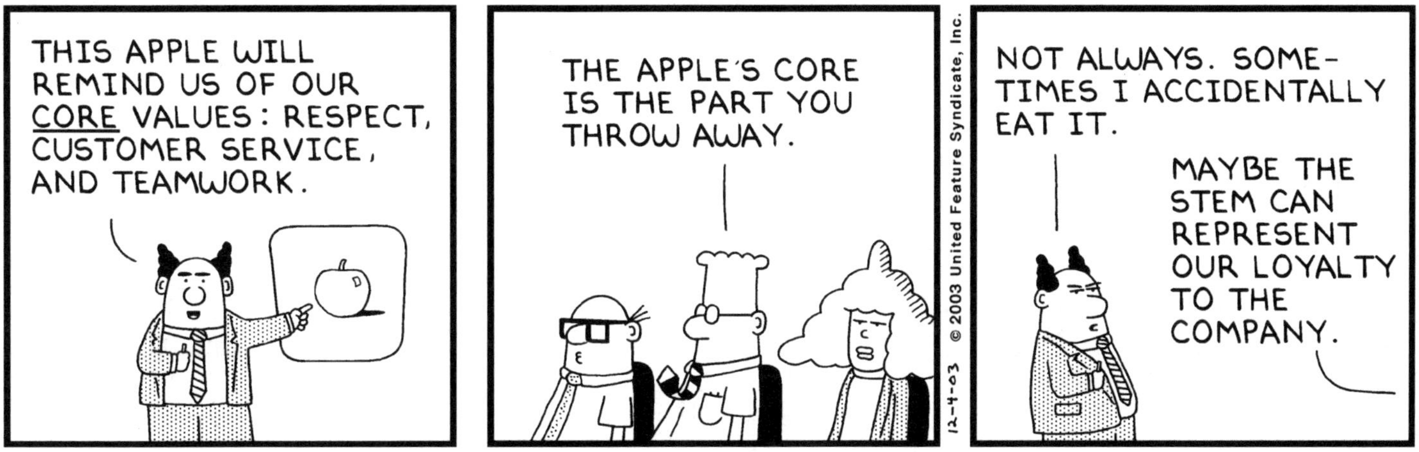
THIS APPLE WILL REMIND US OF OUR CORE VALUES: RESPECT, CUSTOMER SERVICE, AND TEAMWORK.
THE APPLE'S CORE IS THE PART YOU THROW AWAY.
12-4-03
© 2003 United Feature Syndicate, Inc.
NOT ALWAYS. SOME-TIMES I ACCIDENTALLY EAT IT.
MAYBE THE STEM CAN REPRESENT OUR LOYALTY TO THE COMPANY.

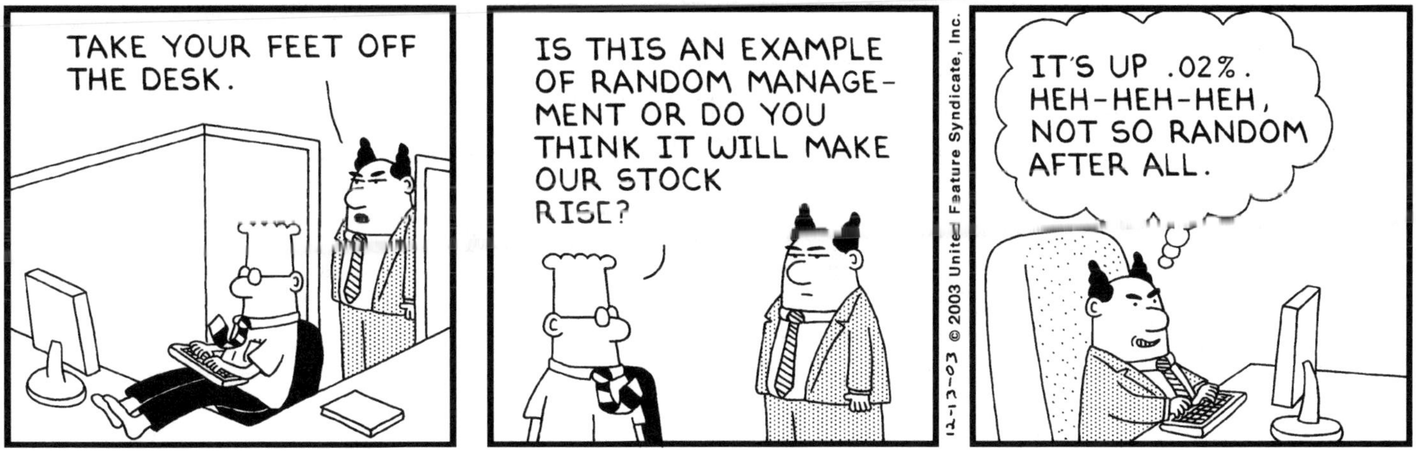
TAKE YOUR FEET OFF THE DESK.
IS THIS AN EXAMPLE OF RANDOM MANAGE-MENT OR DO YOU THINK IT WILL MAKE OUR STOCK RISE?
12-13-03
© 2003 United Feature Syndicate, Inc.
IT'S UP .02%. HEH-HEH-HEH, NOT SO RANDOM AFTER ALL.

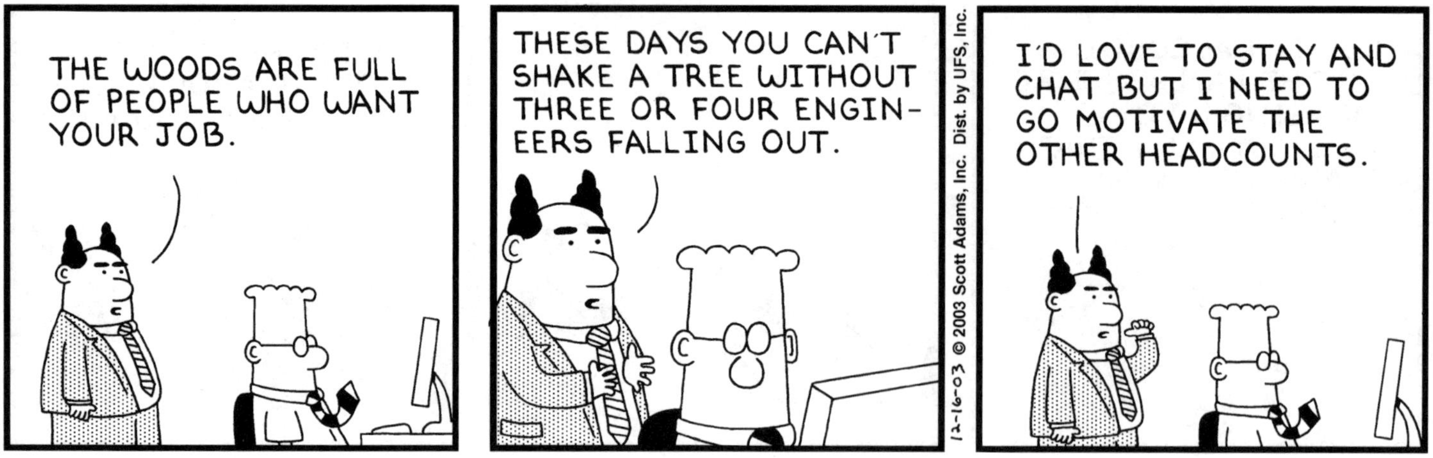
THE WOODS ARE FULL OF PEOPLE WHO WANT YOUR JOB.
THESE DAYS YOU CAN'T SHAKE A TREE WITHOUT THREE OR FOUR ENGIN-EERS FALLING OUT.
12-16-03 © 2003 Scott Adams, Inc. Dist. by UFS, Inc.
I'D LOVE TO STAY AND CHAT BUT I NEED TO GO MOTIVATE THE OTHER HEADCOUNTS.

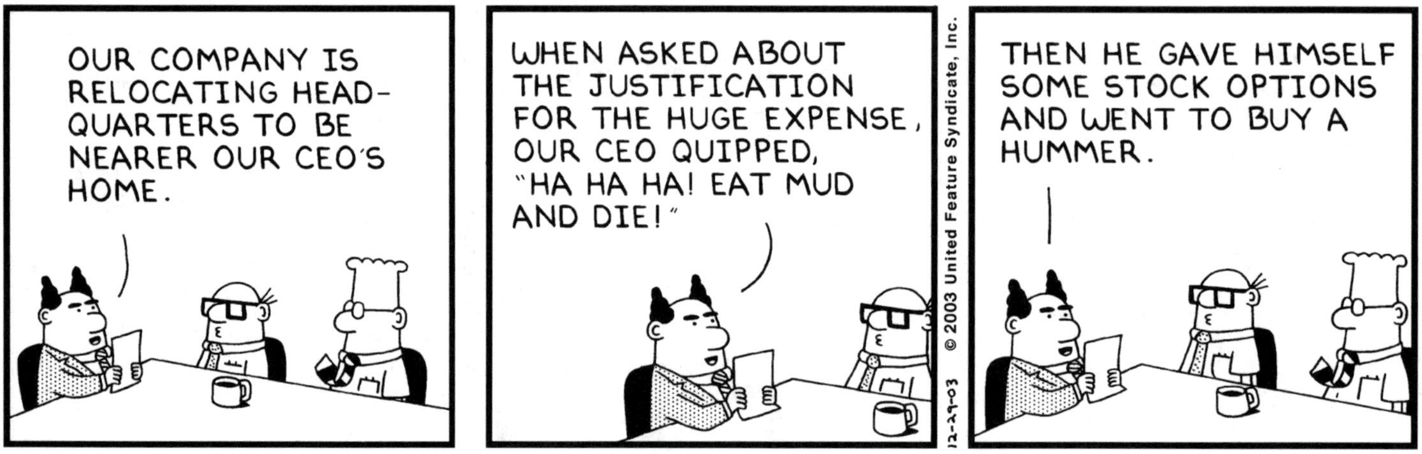
OUR COMPANY IS RELOCATING HEAD-QUARTERS TO BE NEARER OUR CEO'S HOME.
WHEN ASKED ABOUT THE JUSTIFICATION FOR THE HUGE EXPENSE, OUR CEO QUIPPED, "HA HA HA! EAT MUD AND DIE!"
12-29-03 © 2003 United Feature Syndicate, Inc.
THEN HE GAVE HIMSELF SOME STOCK OPTIONS AND WENT TO BUY A HUMMER.

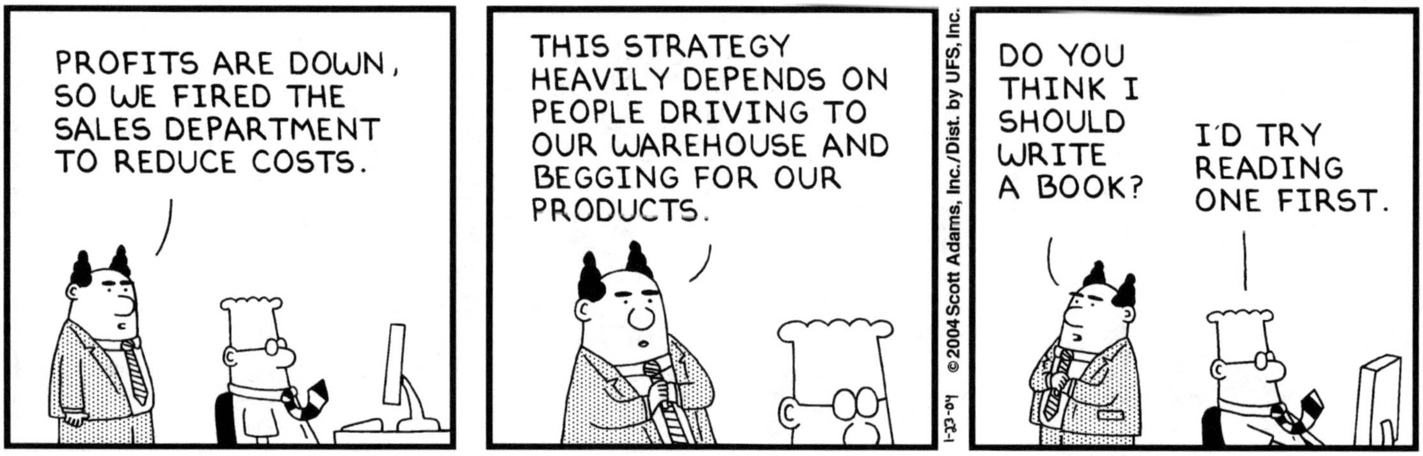
PROFITS ARE DOWN, SO WE FIRED THE SALES DEPARTMENT TO REDUCE COSTS.
THIS STRATEGY HEAVILY DEPENDS ON PEOPLE DRIVING TO OUR WAREHOUSE AND BEGGING FOR OUR PRODUCTS.
1-23-04 © 2004 Scott Adams, Inc./Dist. by UFS, Inc.
DO YOU THINK I SHOULD WRITE A BOOK?
I'D TRY READING ONE FIRST.

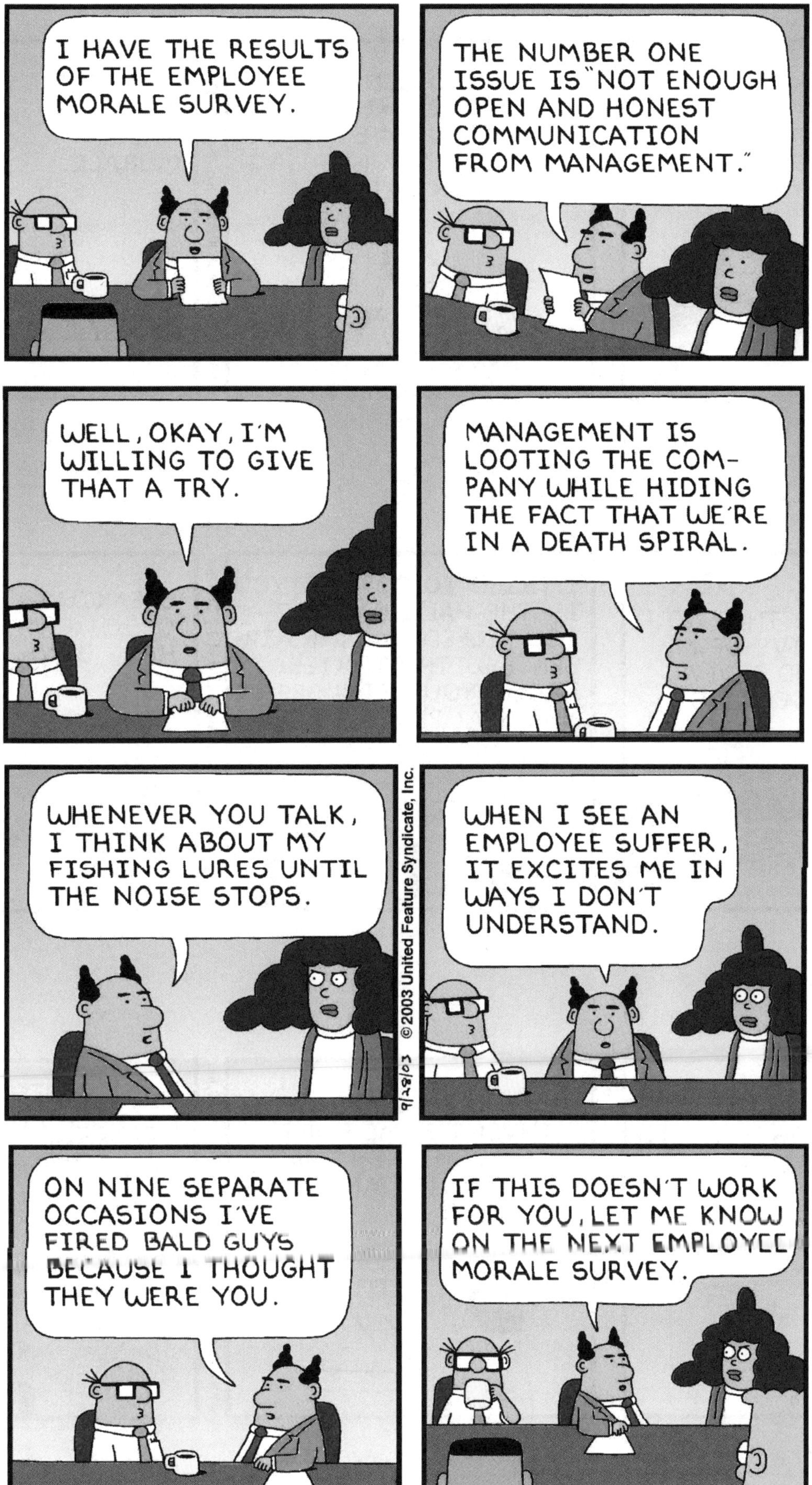
I HAVE THE RESULTS OF THE EMPLOYEE MORALE SURVEY.
THE NUMBER ONE ISSUE IS "NOT ENOUGH OPEN AND HONEST COMMUNICATION FROM MANAGEMENT."
WELL, OKAY, I'M WILLING TO GIVE THAT A TRY.
MANAGEMENT IS LOOTING THE COMPANY WHILE HIDING THE FACT THAT WE'RE IN A DEATH SPIRAL.
WHENEVER YOU TALK, I THINK ABOUT MY FISHING LURES UNTIL THE NOISE STOPS.
©2003 United Feature Syndicate, Inc.
9/28/03
WHEN I SEE AN EMPLOYEE SUFFER, IT EXCITES ME IN WAYS I DON'T UNDERSTAND.
ON NINE SEPARATE OCCASIONS I'VE FIRED BALD GUYS BECAUSE I THOUGHT THEY WERE YOU.
IF THIS DOESN'T WORK FOR YOU, LET ME KNOW ON THE NEXT EMPLOYEE MORALE SURVEY.

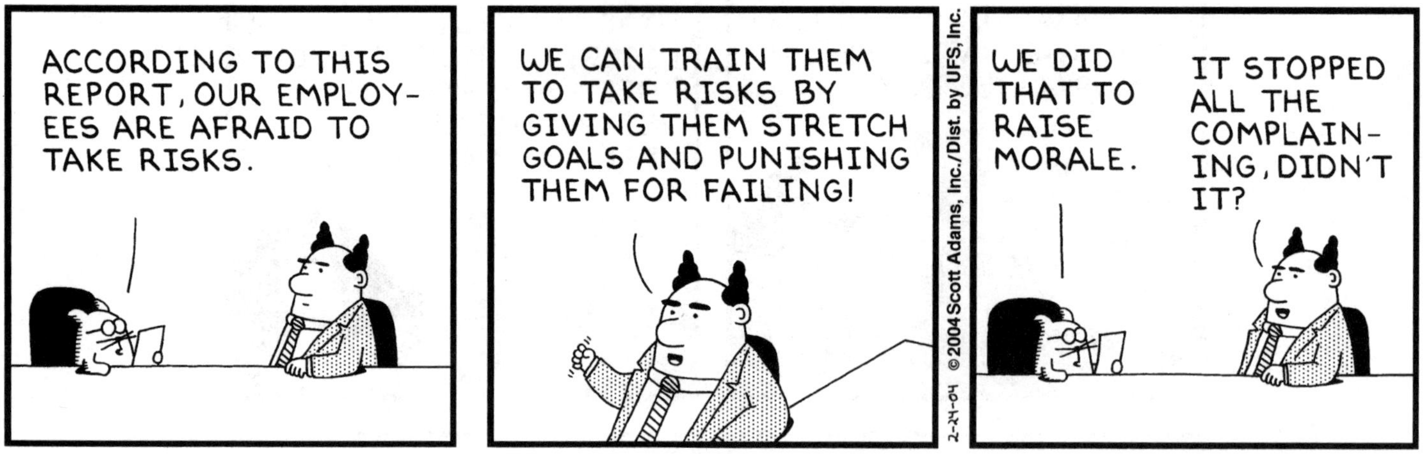
ACCORDING TO THIS REPORT, OUR EMPLOYEES ARE AFRAID TO TAKE RISKS.
WE CAN TRAIN THEM TO TAKE RISKS BY GIVING THEM STRETCH GOALS AND PUNISHING THEM FOR FAILING!
2-24-04 © 2004 Scott Adams, Inc./Dist. by UFS, Inc.
WE DID THAT TO RAISE MORALE.
IT STOPPED ALL THE COMPLAINING, DIDN'T IT?

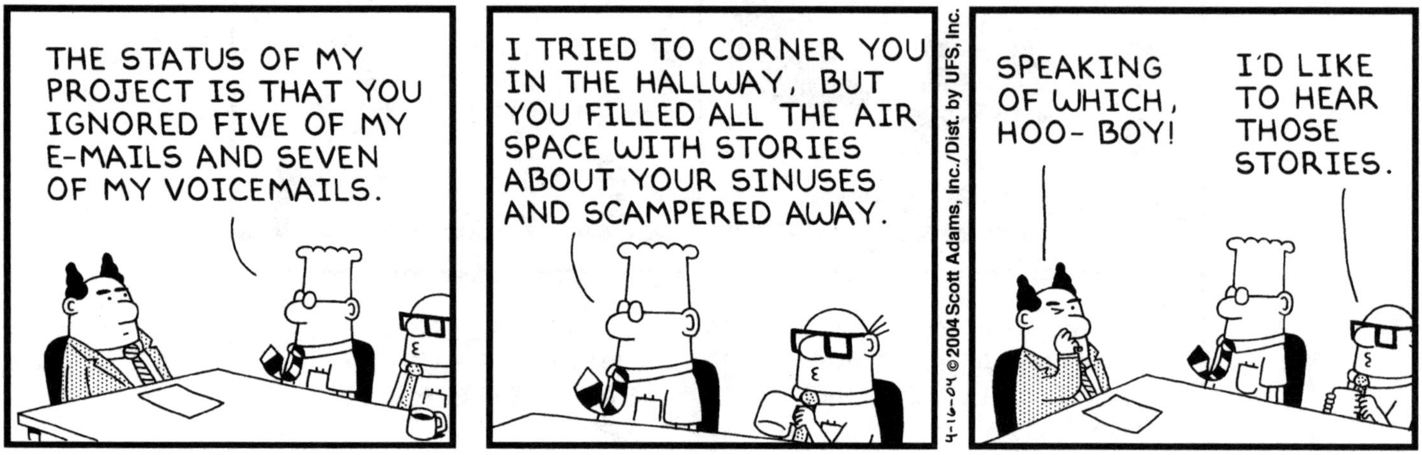
THE STATUS OF MY PROJECT IS THAT YOU IGNORED FIVE OF MY E-MAILS AND SEVEN OF MY VOICEMAILS.
I TRIED TO CORNER YOU IN THE HALLWAY, BUT YOU FILLED ALL THE AIR SPACE WITH STORIES ABOUT YOUR SINUSES AND SCAMPERED AWAY.
4-16-04 © 2004 Scott Adams, Inc./Dist. by UFS, Inc.
SPEAKING OF WHICH, HOO- BOY!
I'D LIKE TO HEAR THOSE STORIES.

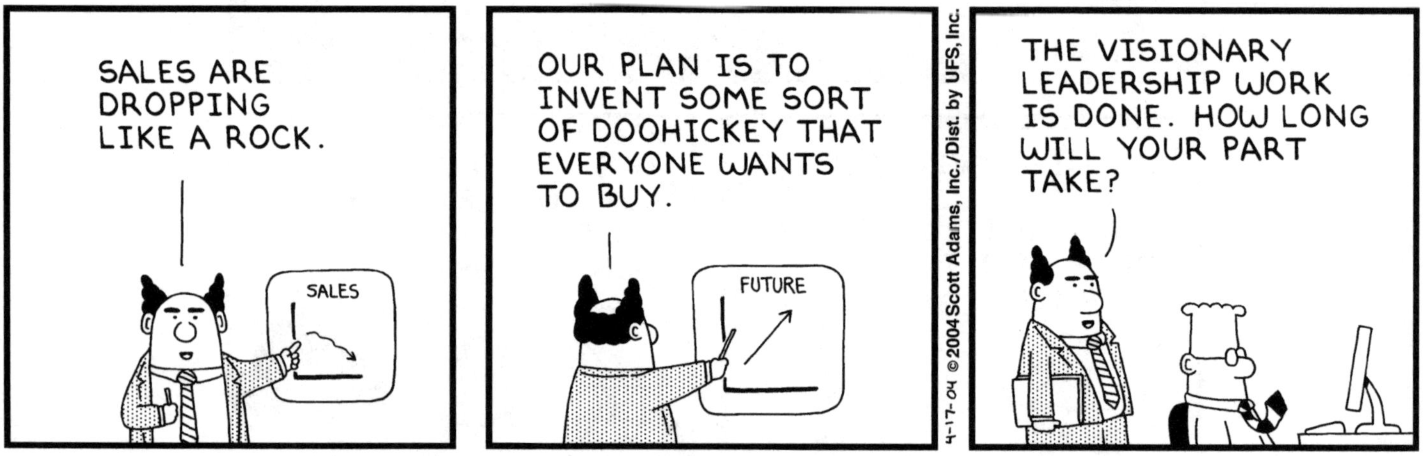
SALES ARE DROPPING LIKE A ROCK.
SALES
OUR PLAN IS TO INVENT SOME SORT OF DOOHICKEY THAT EVERYONE WANTS TO BUY.
FUTURE
4-17-04 © 2004 Scott Adams, Inc./Dist. by UFS, Inc.
THE VISIONARY LEADERSHIP WORK IS DONE. HOW LONG WILL YOUR PART TAKE?

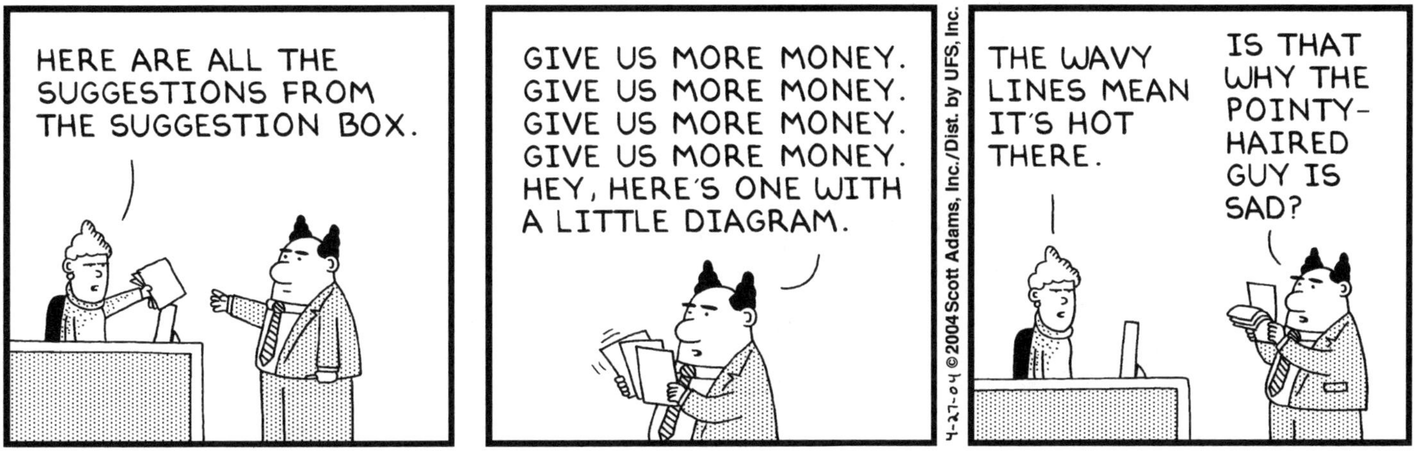
HERE ARE ALL THE SUGGESTIONS FROM THE SUGGESTION BOX.
GIVE US MORE MONEY. GIVE US MORE MONEY. GIVE US MORE MONEY. GIVE US MORE MONEY. HEY, HERE'S ONE WITH A LITTLE DIAGRAM.
4-27-04 © 2004 Scott Adams, Inc./Dist. by UFS, Inc.
THE WAVY LINES MEAN IT'S HOT THERE.
IS THAT WHY THE POINTY-HAIRED GUY IS SAD?

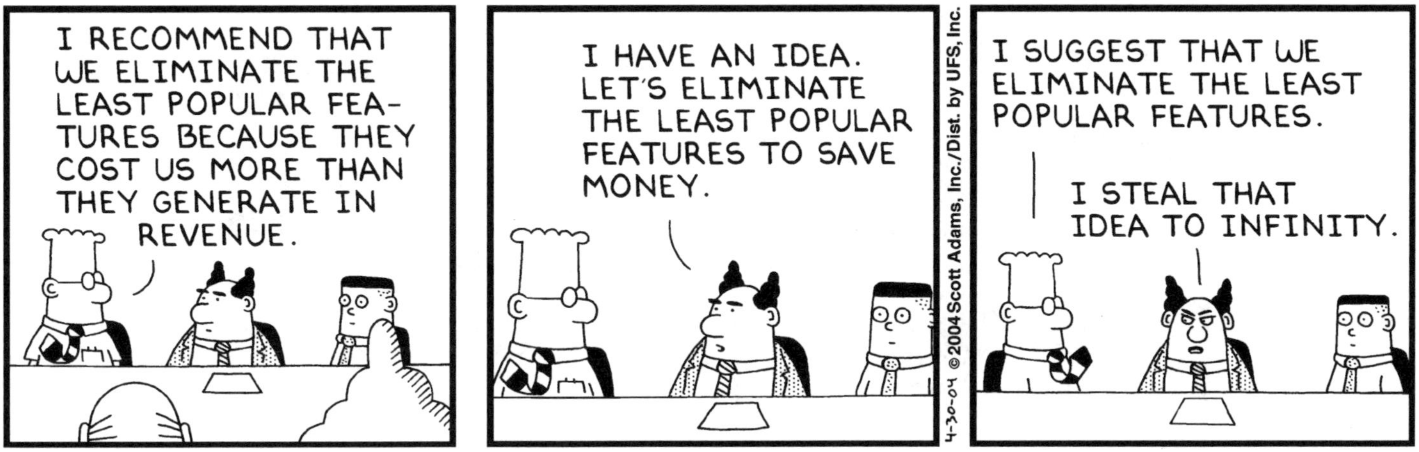
I RECOMMEND THAT WE ELIMINATE THE LEAST POPULAR FEA-TURES BECAUSE THEY COST US MORE THAN THEY GENERATE IN REVENUE.
I HAVE AN IDEA. LET'S ELIMINATE THE LEAST POPULAR FEATURES TO SAVE MONEY.
4-30-04 © 2004 Scott Adams, Inc./Dist. by UFS, Inc.
I SUGGEST THAT WE ELIMINATE THE LEAST POPULAR FEATURES.
I STEAL THAT IDEA TO INFINITY.

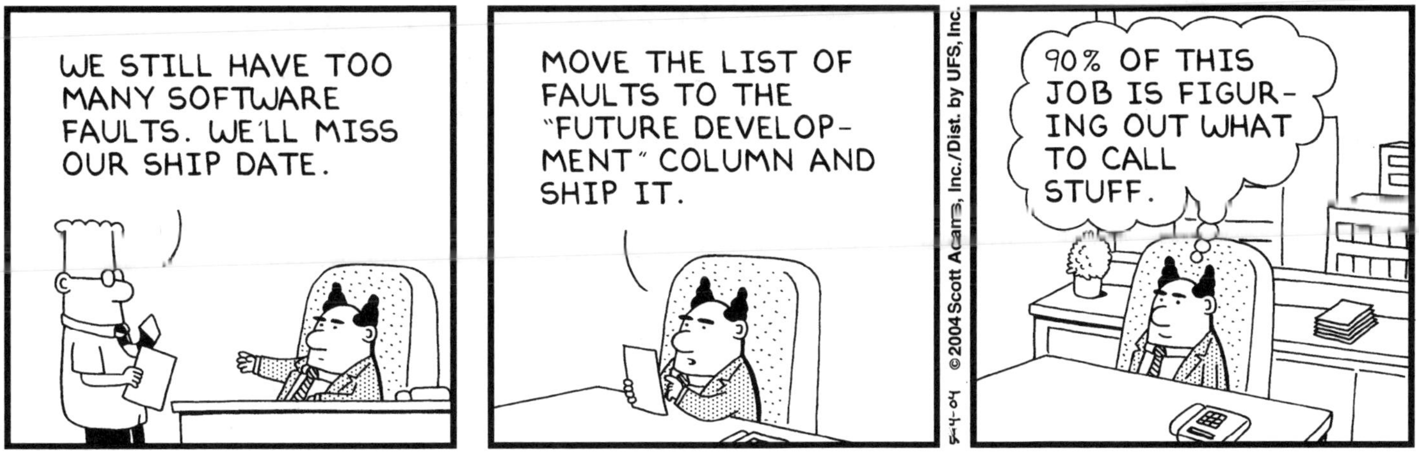
WE STILL HAVE TOO MANY SOFTWARE FAULTS. WE'LL MISS OUR SHIP DATE.
MOVE THE LIST OF FAULTS TO THE "FUTURE DEVELOP-MENT" COLUMN AND SHIP IT.
5-4-04 © 2004 Scott Adams, Inc./Dist. by UFS, Inc.
90% OF THIS JOB IS FIGUR-ING OUT WHAT TO CALL STUFF.

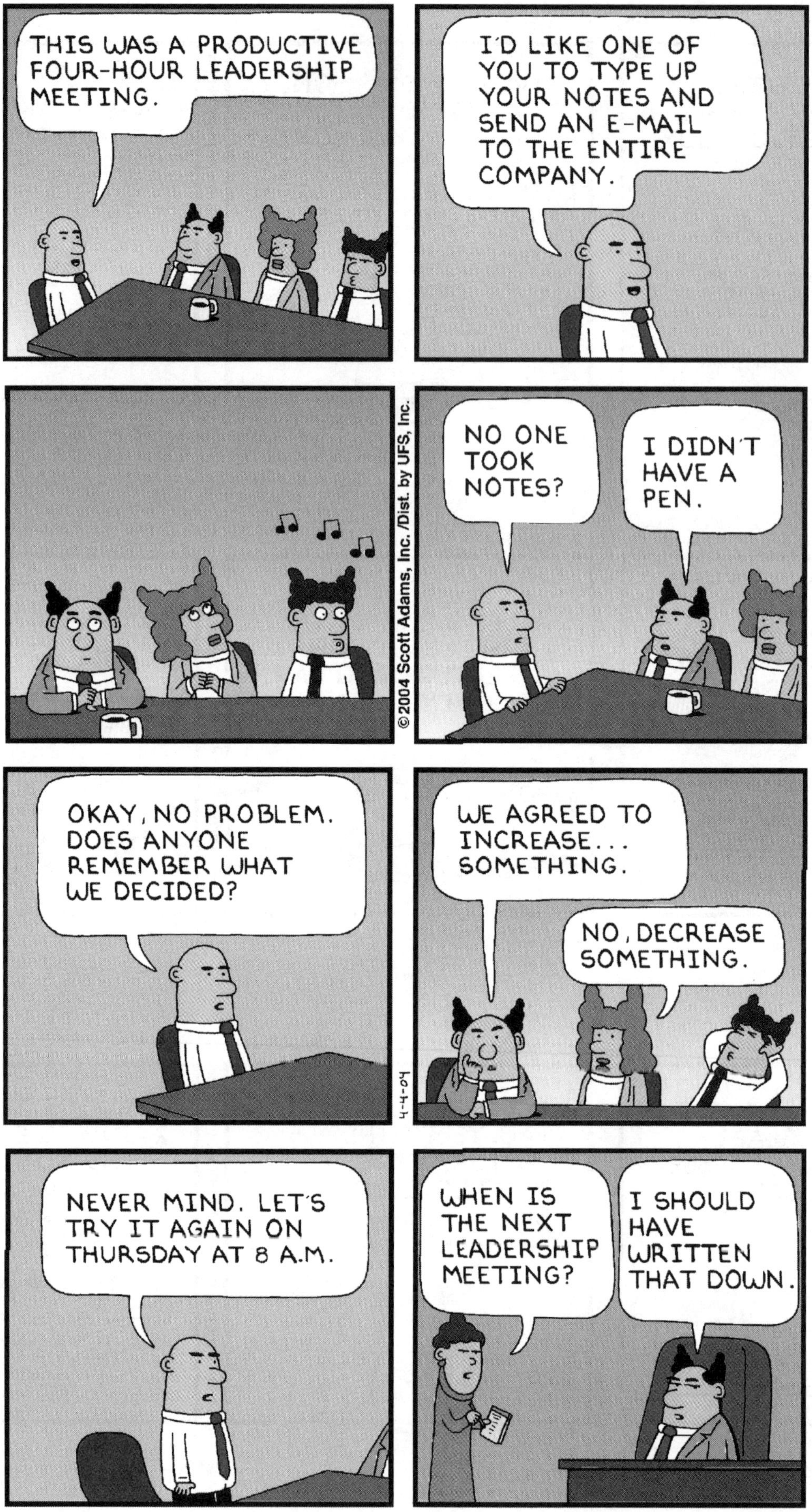
THIS WAS A PRODUCTIVE FOUR-HOUR LEADERSHIP MEETING.
I'D LIKE ONE OF YOU TO TYPE UP YOUR NOTES AND SEND AN E-MAIL TO THE ENTIRE COMPANY.
©2004 Scott Adams, Inc./Dist. by UFS, Inc.
NO ONE TOOK NOTES?
I DIDN'T HAVE A PEN.
OKAY, NO PROBLEM. DOES ANYONE REMEMBER WHAT WE DECIDED?
4-4-04
WE AGREED TO INCREASE... SOMETHING.
NO, DECREASE SOMETHING.
NEVER MIND. LET'S TRY IT AGAIN ON THURSDAY AT 8 A.M.
WHEN IS THE NEXT LEADERSHIP MEETING?
I SHOULD HAVE WRITTEN THAT DOWN.

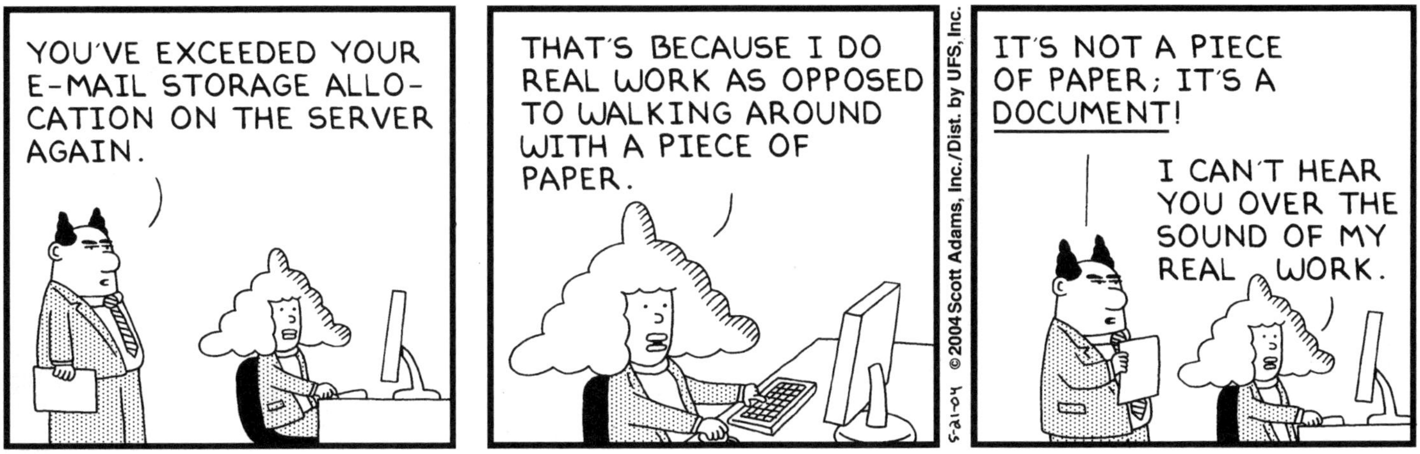
YOU'VE EXCEEDED YOUR E-MAIL STORAGE ALLOCATION ON THE SERVER AGAIN.
THAT'S BECAUSE I DO REAL WORK AS OPPOSED TO WALKING AROUND WITH A PIECE OF PAPER.
5-21-04 © 2004 Scott Adams, Inc./Dist. by UFS, Inc.
IT'S NOT A PIECE OF PAPER; IT'S A DOCUMENT!
I CAN'T HEAR YOU OVER THE SOUND OF MY REAL WORK.

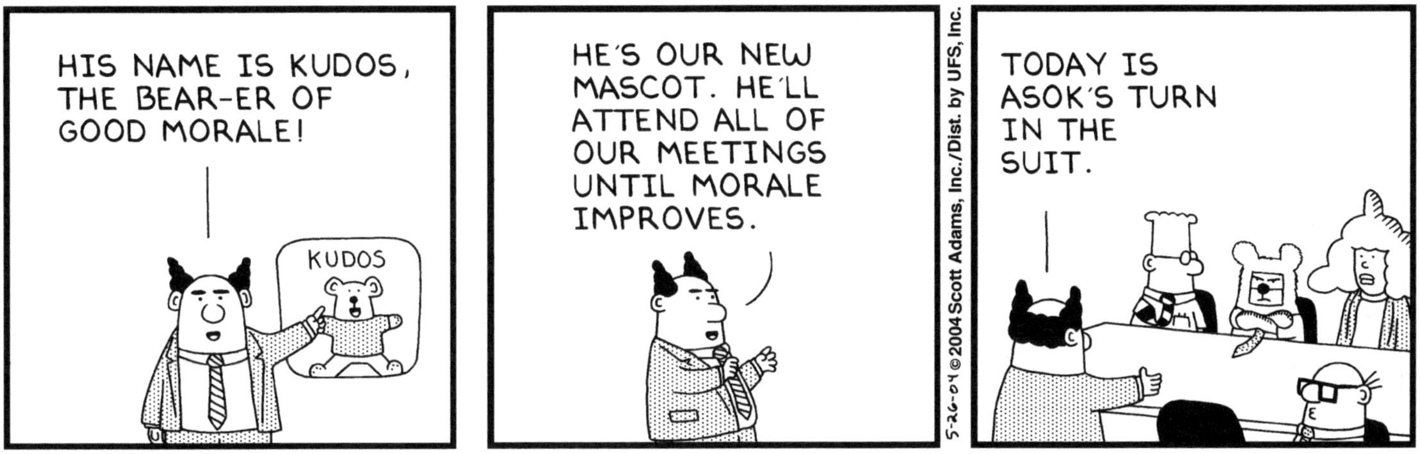
HIS NAME IS KUDOS, THE BEAR-ER OF GOOD MORALE!
KUDOS
HE'S OUR NEW MASCOT. HE'LL ATTEND ALL OF OUR MEETINGS UNTIL MORALE IMPROVES.
5-26-04 © 2004 Scott Adams, Inc./Dist. by UFS, Inc.
TODAY IS ASOK'S TURN IN THE SUIT.

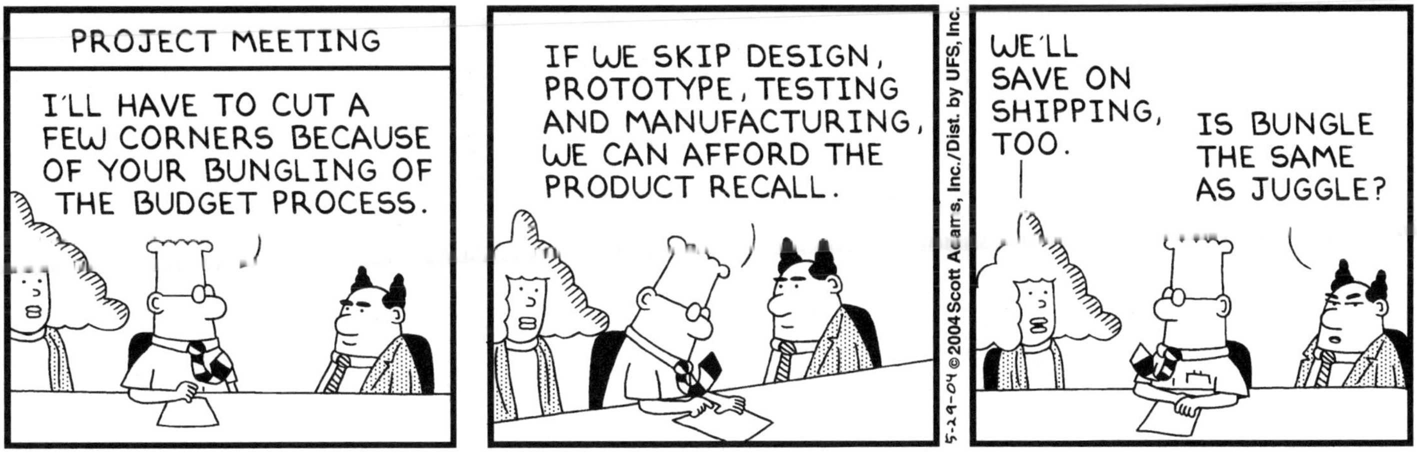
PROJECT MEETING
I'LL HAVE TO CUT A FEW CORNERS BECAUSE OF YOUR BUNGLING OF THE BUDGET PROCESS.
IF WE SKIP DESIGN, PROTOTYPE, TESTING AND MANUFACTURING, WE CAN AFFORD THE PRODUCT RECALL.
5-29-04 © 2004 Scott Adams, Inc./Dist. by UFS, Inc.
WE'LL SAVE ON SHIPPING, TOO.
IS BUNGLE THE SAME AS JUGGLE?

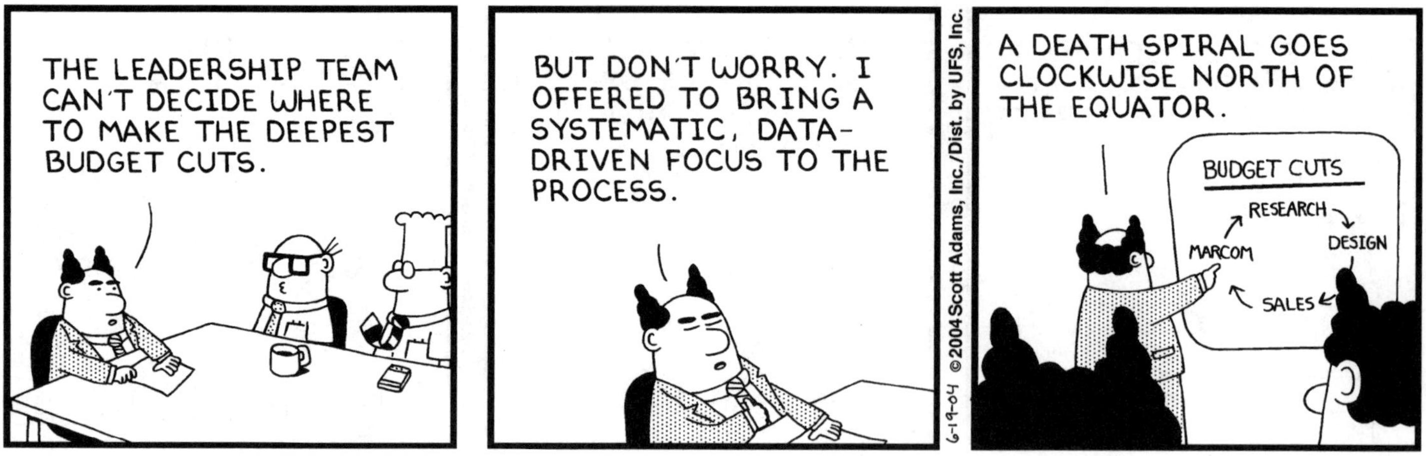
THE LEADERSHIP TEAM CAN'T DECIDE WHERE TO MAKE THE DEEPEST BUDGET CUTS.
BUT DON'T WORRY. I OFFERED TO BRING A SYSTEMATIC, DATA-DRIVEN FOCUS TO THE PROCESS.
6-19-04 ©2004 Scott Adams, Inc./Dist. by UFS, Inc.
A DEATH SPIRAL GOES CLOCKWISE NORTH OF THE EQUATOR.
BUDGET CUTS
RESEARCH
DESIGN
MARCOM
SALES

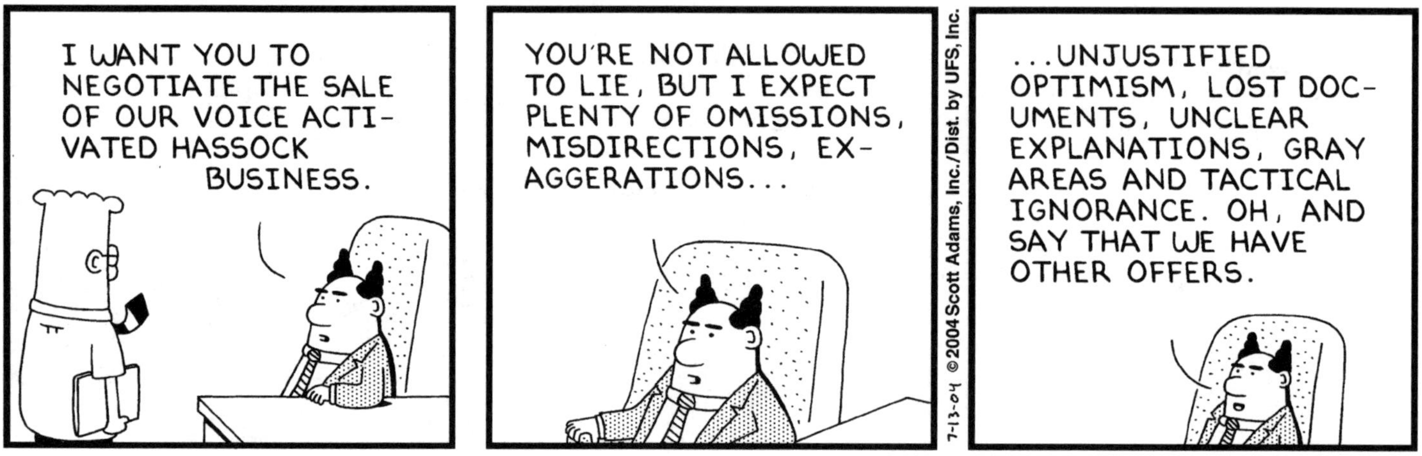
I WANT YOU TO NEGOTIATE THE SALE OF OUR VOICE ACTIVATED HASSOCK BUSINESS.
YOU'RE NOT ALLOWED TO LIE, BUT I EXPECT PLENTY OF OMISSIONS, MISDIRECTIONS, EXAGGERATIONS...
7-13-04 ©2004 Scott Adams, Inc./Dist. by UFS, Inc.
...UNJUSTIFIED OPTIMISM, LOST DOCUMENTS, UNCLEAR EXPLANATIONS, GRAY AREAS AND TACTICAL IGNORANCE. OH, AND SAY THAT WE HAVE OTHER OFFERS.

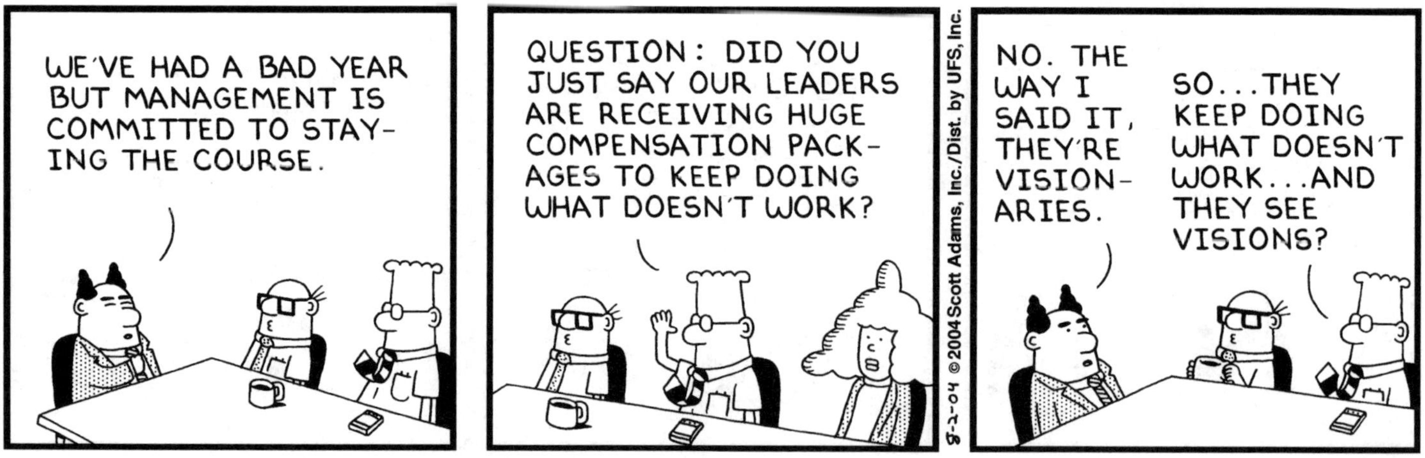
WE'VE HAD A BAD YEAR BUT MANAGEMENT IS COMMITTED TO STAYING THE COURSE.
QUESTION: DID YOU JUST SAY OUR LEADERS ARE RECEIVING HUGE COMPENSATION PACKAGES TO KEEP DOING WHAT DOESN'T WORK?
8-2-04 ©2004 Scott Adams, Inc./Dist. by UFS, Inc.
NO. THE WAY I SAID IT, THEY'RE VISIONARIES.
SO...THEY KEEP DOING WHAT DOESN'T WORK...AND THEY SEE VISIONS?

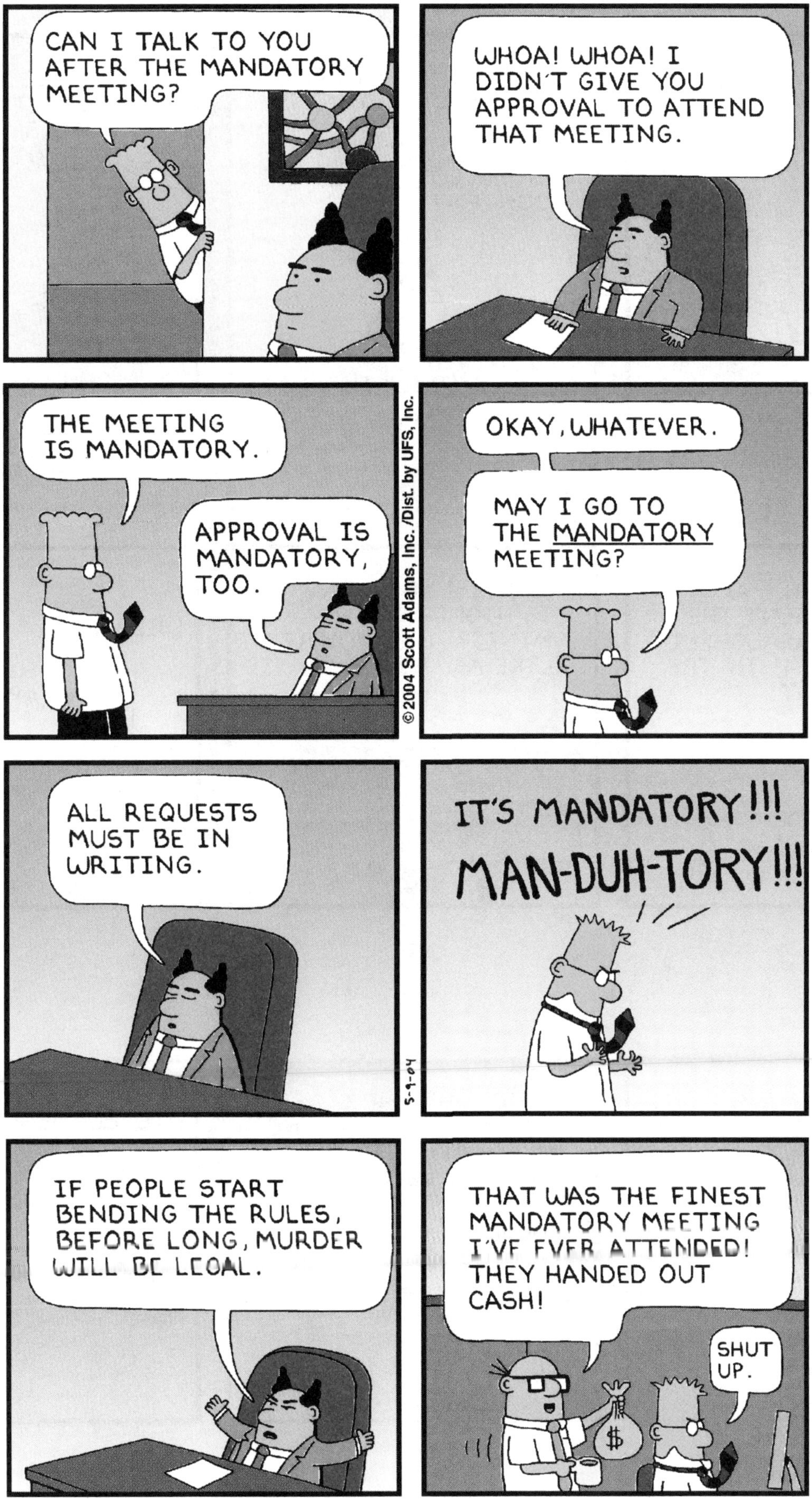
CAN I TALK TO YOU AFTER THE MANDATORY MEETING?
WHOA! WHOA! I DIDN'T GIVE YOU APPROVAL TO ATTEND THAT MEETING.
THE MEETING IS MANDATORY.
APPROVAL IS MANDATORY, TOO.
©2004 Scott Adams, Inc./Dist. by UFS, Inc.
OKAY, WHATEVER.
MAY I GO TO THE MANDATORY MEETING?
ALL REQUESTS MUST BE IN WRITING.
5-9-04
IT'S MANDATORY!!!
MAN-DUH-TORY!!!
IF PEOPLE START BENDING THE RULES, BEFORE LONG, MURDER WILL BE LEGAL.
THAT WAS THE FINEST MANDATORY MEETING I'VE EVER ATTENDED! THEY HANDED OUT CASH!
SHUT UP.

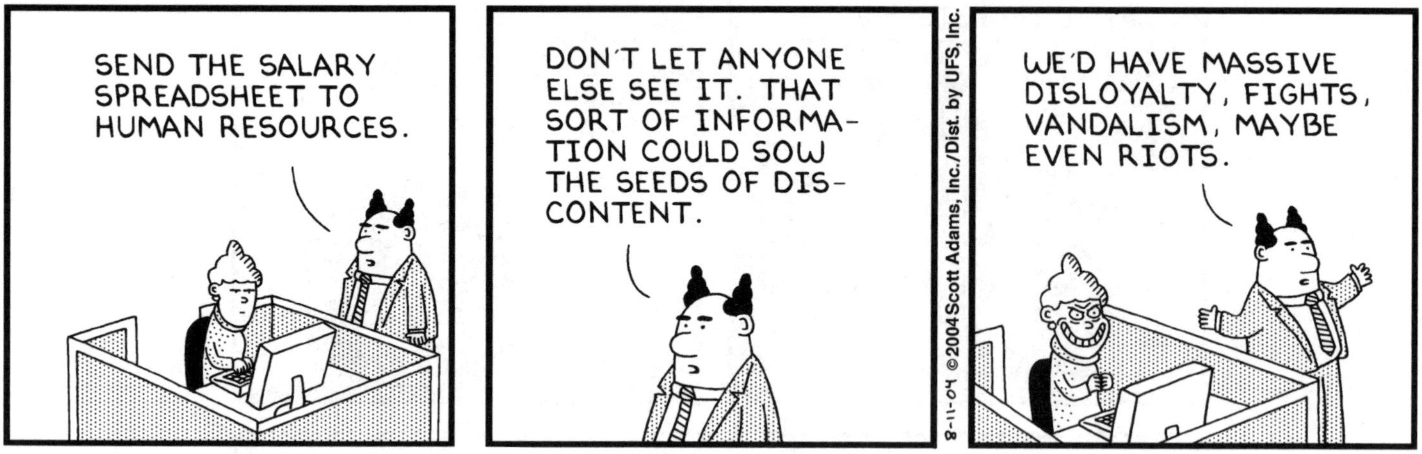
SEND THE SALARY SPREADSHEET TO HUMAN RESOURCES.
DON'T LET ANYONE ELSE SEE IT. THAT SORT OF INFORMATION COULD SOW THE SEEDS OF DISCONTENT.
8-11-04 © 2004 Scott Adams, Inc./Dist. by UFS, Inc.
WE'D HAVE MASSIVE DISLOYALTY, FIGHTS, VANDALISM, MAYBE EVEN RIOTS.

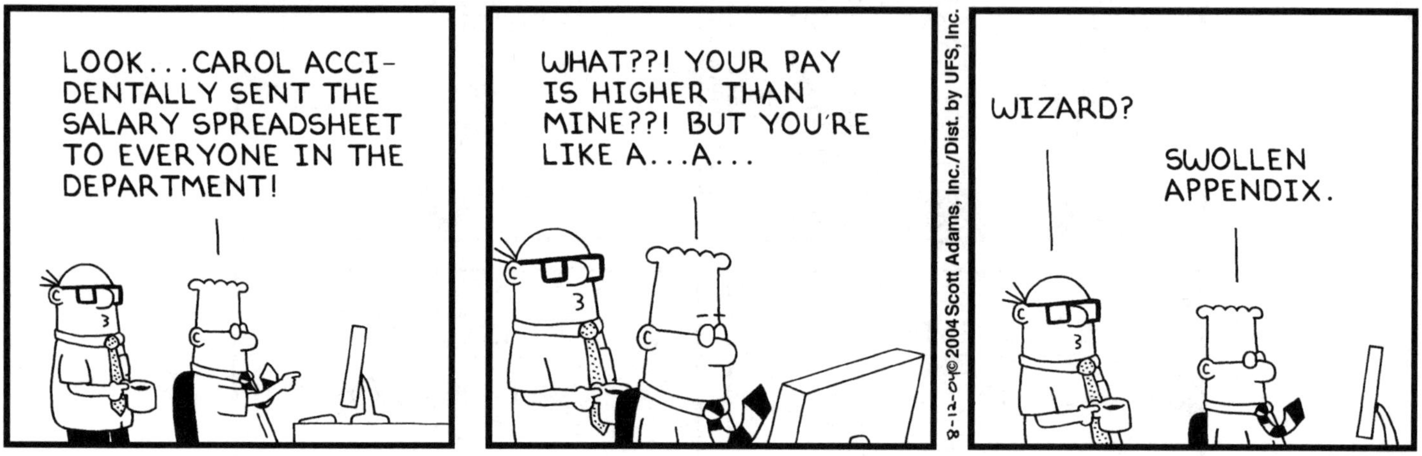
LOOK...CAROL ACCIDENTALLY SENT THE SALARY SPREADSHEET TO EVERYONE IN THE DEPARTMENT!
WHAT??! YOUR PAY IS HIGHER THAN MINE??! BUT YOU'RE LIKE A...A...
8-12-04 © 2004 Scott Adams, Inc./Dist. by UFS, Inc.
WIZARD?
SWOLLEN APPENDIX.

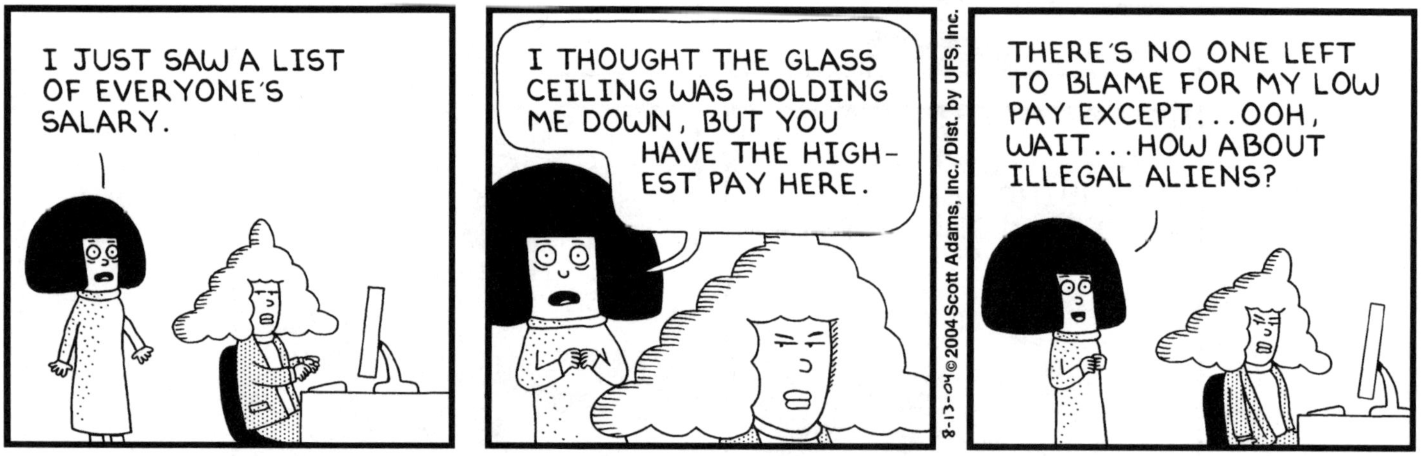
I JUST SAW A LIST OF EVERYONE'S SALARY.
I THOUGHT THE GLASS CEILING WAS HOLDING ME DOWN, BUT YOU HAVE THE HIGHEST PAY HERE.
8-13-04 © 2004 Scott Adams, Inc./Dist. by UFS, Inc.
THERE'S NO ONE LEFT TO BLAME FOR MY LOW PAY EXCEPT...OOH, WAIT...HOW ABOUT ILLEGAL ALIENS?

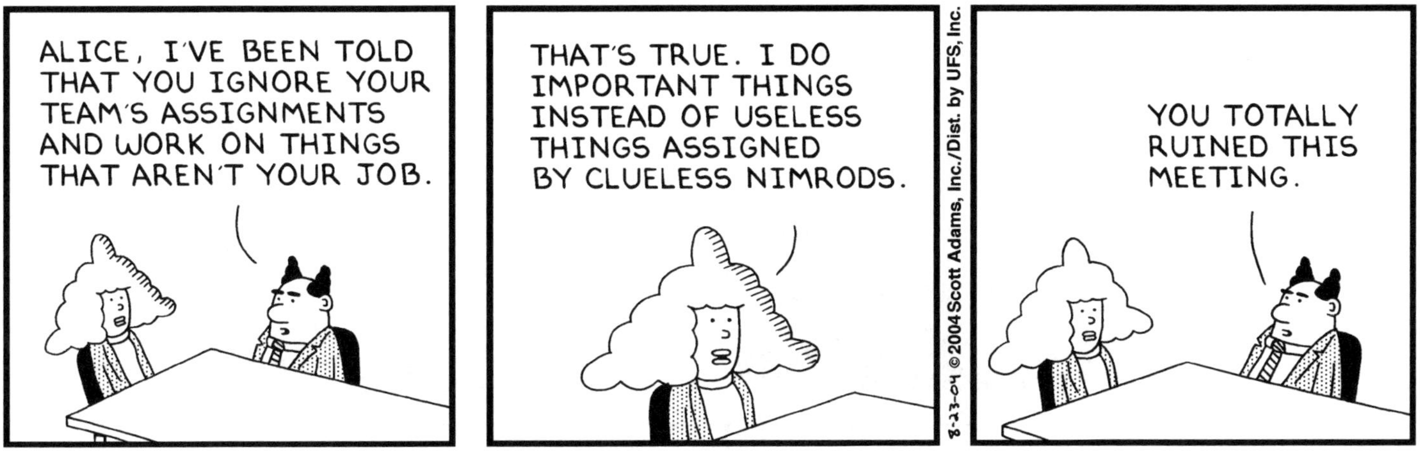
ALICE, I'VE BEEN TOLD THAT YOU IGNORE YOUR TEAM'S ASSIGNMENTS AND WORK ON THINGS THAT AREN'T YOUR JOB.
THAT'S TRUE. I DO IMPORTANT THINGS INSTEAD OF USELESS THINGS ASSIGNED BY CLUELESS NIMRODS.
8-23-04 © 2004 Scott Adams, Inc./Dist. by UFS, Inc.
YOU TOTALLY RUINED THIS MEETING.

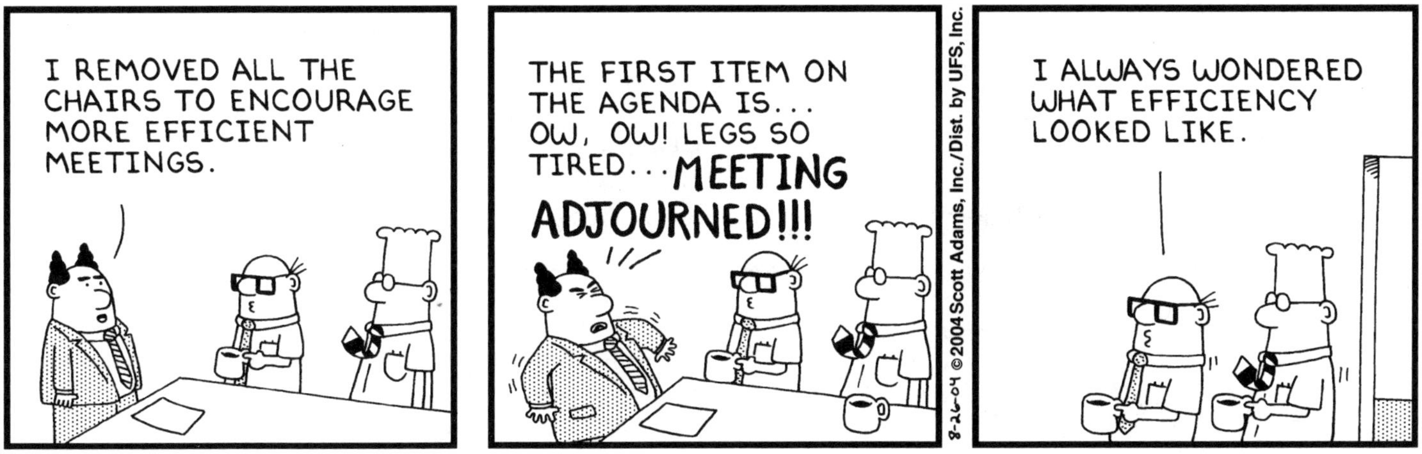
I REMOVED ALL THE CHAIRS TO ENCOURAGE MORE EFFICIENT MEETINGS.
THE FIRST ITEM ON THE AGENDA IS... OW, OW! LEGS SO TIRED... MEETING ADJOURNED!!!
8-26-04 © 2004 Scott Adams, Inc./Dist. by UFS, Inc.
I ALWAYS WONDERED WHAT EFFICIENCY LOOKED LIKE.

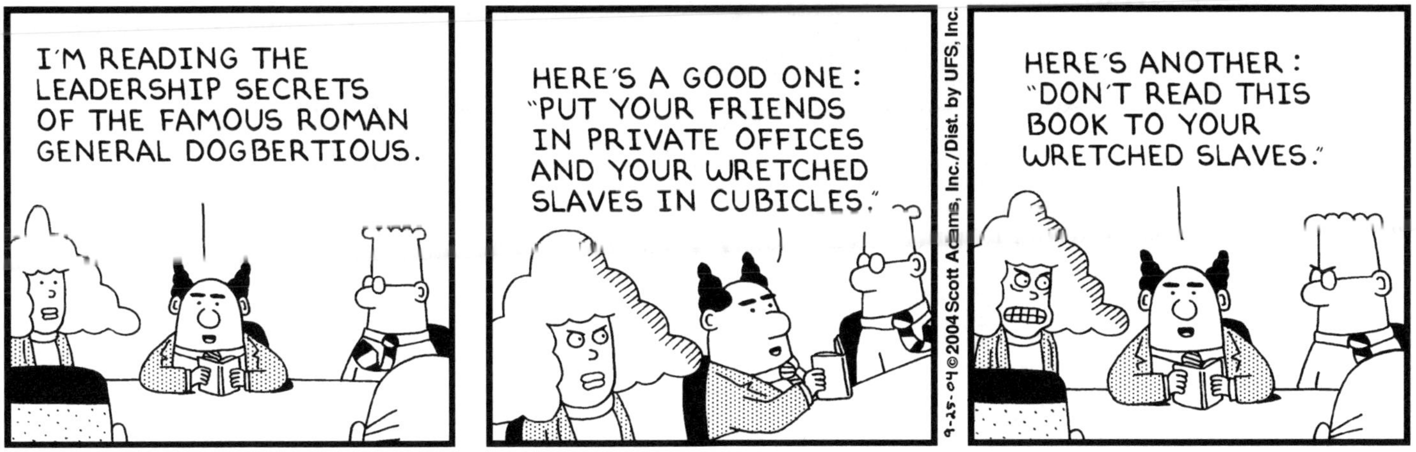
I'M READING THE LEADERSHIP SECRETS OF THE FAMOUS ROMAN GENERAL DOGBERTIOUS.
HERE'S A GOOD ONE: "PUT YOUR FRIENDS IN PRIVATE OFFICES AND YOUR WRETCHED SLAVES IN CUBICLES."
9-25-04 © 2004 Scott Adams, Inc./Dist. by UFS, Inc.
HERE'S ANOTHER: "DON'T READ THIS BOOK TO YOUR WRETCHED SLAVES."

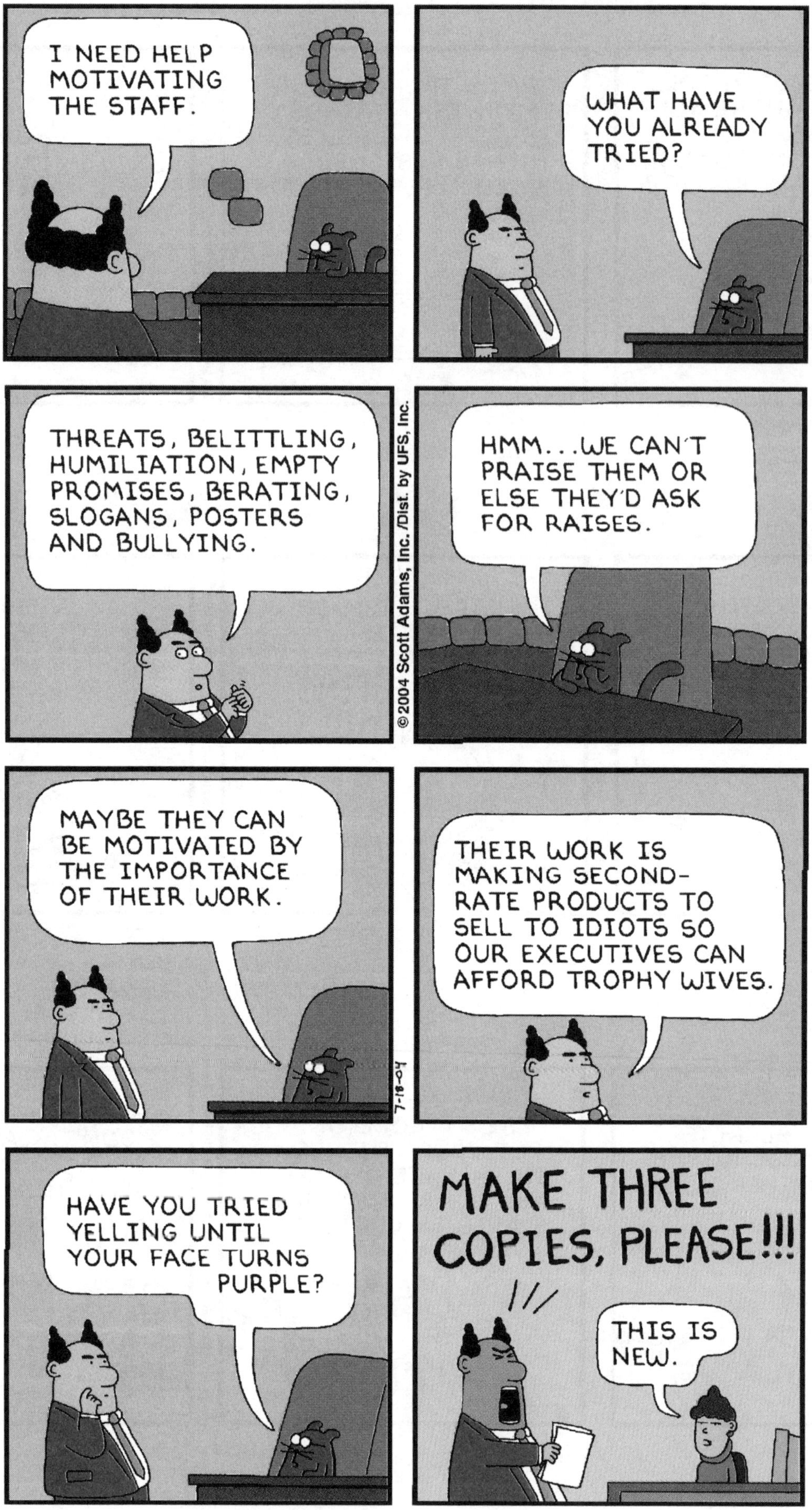

I NEED HELP MOTIVATING THE STAFF.
WHAT HAVE YOU ALREADY TRIED?
THREATS, BELITTLING, HUMILIATION, EMPTY PROMISES, BERATING, SLOGANS, POSTERS AND BULLYING.
©2004 Scott Adams, Inc./Dist. by UFS, Inc.
HMM...WE CAN'T PRAISE THEM OR ELSE THEY'D ASK FOR RAISES.
MAYBE THEY CAN BE MOTIVATED BY THE IMPORTANCE OF THEIR WORK.
7-18-04
THEIR WORK IS MAKING SECOND-RATE PRODUCTS TO SELL TO IDIOTS SO OUR EXECUTIVES CAN AFFORD TROPHY WIVES.
HAVE YOU TRIED YELLING UNTIL YOUR FACE TURNS PURPLE?
MAKE THREE COPIES, PLEASE!!!
THIS IS NEW.

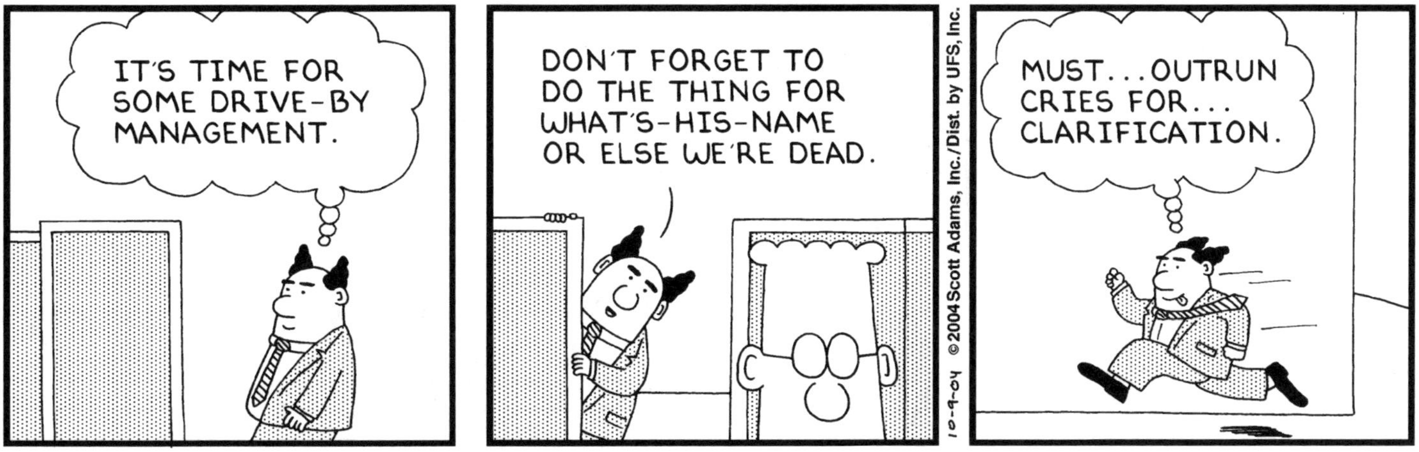
IT'S TIME FOR SOME DRIVE-BY MANAGEMENT.
DON'T FORGET TO DO THE THING FOR WHAT'S-HIS-NAME OR ELSE WE'RE DEAD.
MUST...OUTRUN CRIES FOR... CLARIFICATION.
© 2004 Scott Adams, Inc./Dist. by UFS, Inc.
10-9-04

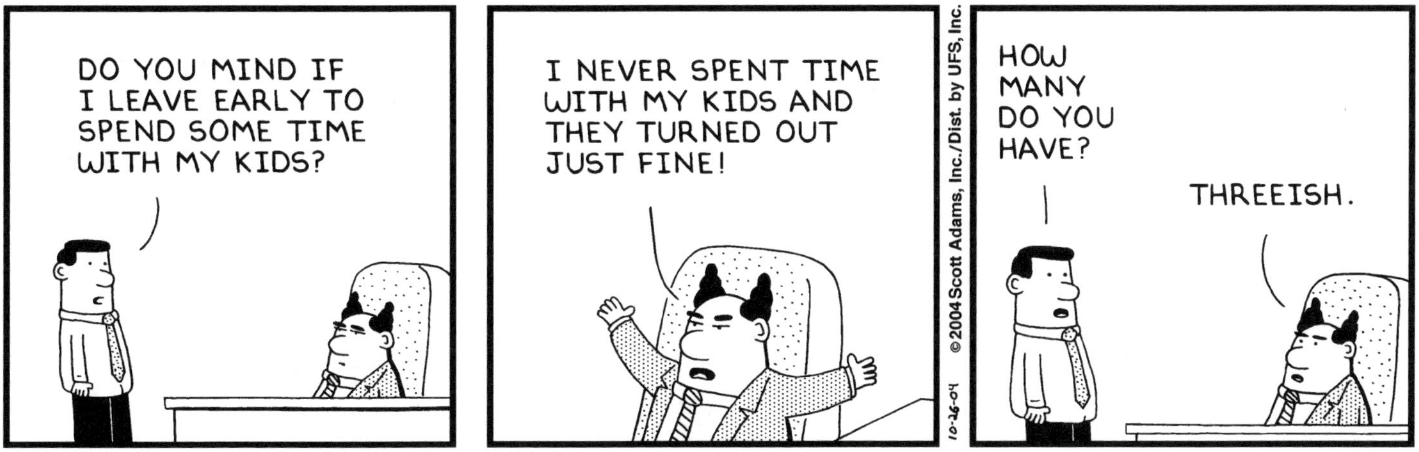
DO YOU MIND IF I LEAVE EARLY TO SPEND SOME TIME WITH MY KIDS?
I NEVER SPENT TIME WITH MY KIDS AND THEY TURNED OUT JUST FINE!
HOW MANY DO YOU HAVE?
THREEISH.
© 2004 Scott Adams, Inc./Dist. by UFS, Inc.

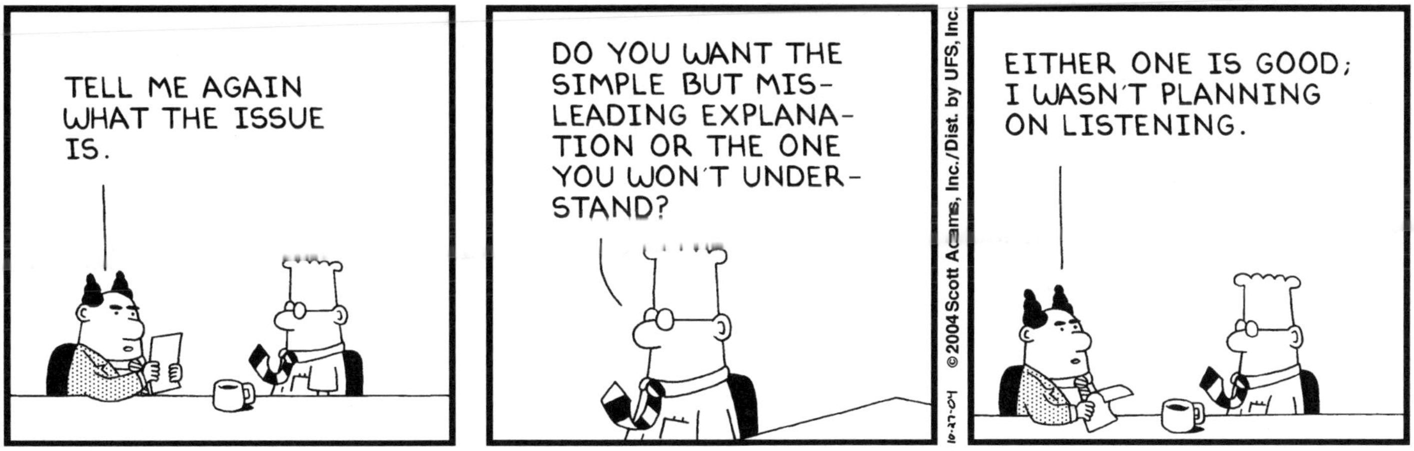
TELL ME AGAIN WHAT THE ISSUE IS.
DO YOU WANT THE SIMPLE BUT MIS-LEADING EXPLANA-TION OR THE ONE YOU WON'T UNDER-STAND?
EITHER ONE IS GOOD; I WASN'T PLANNING ON LISTENING.
© 2004 Scott Adams, Inc./Dist. by UFS, Inc.

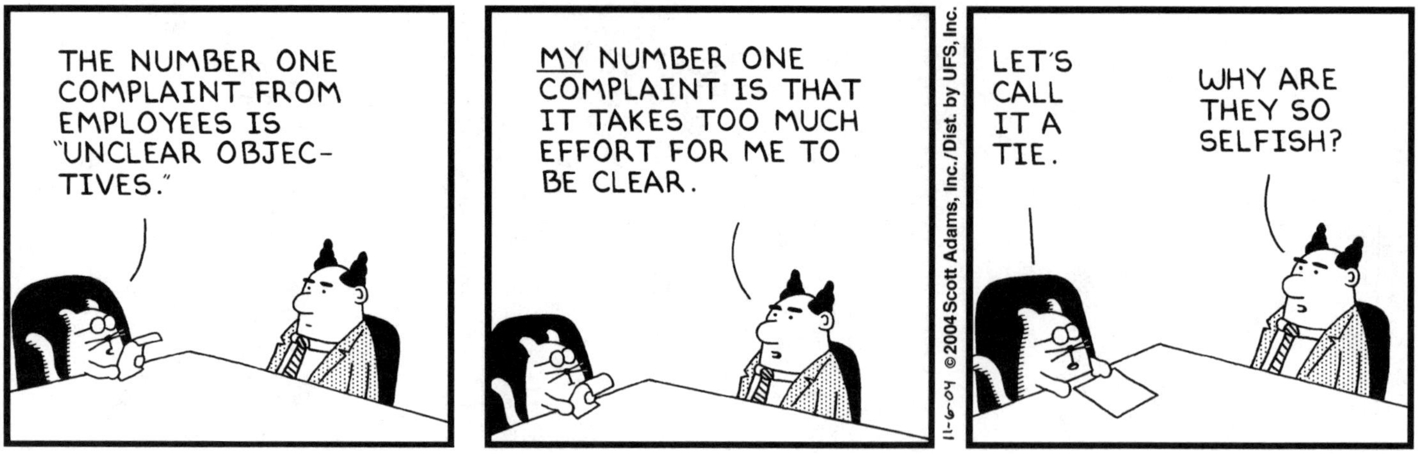
THE NUMBER ONE COMPLAINT FROM EMPLOYEES IS "UNCLEAR OBJEC-TIVES."
MY NUMBER ONE COMPLAINT IS THAT IT TAKES TOO MUCH EFFORT FOR ME TO BE CLEAR.
11-6-04 © 2004 Scott Adams, Inc./Dist. by UFS, Inc.
LET'S CALL IT A TIE.
WHY ARE THEY SO SELFISH?

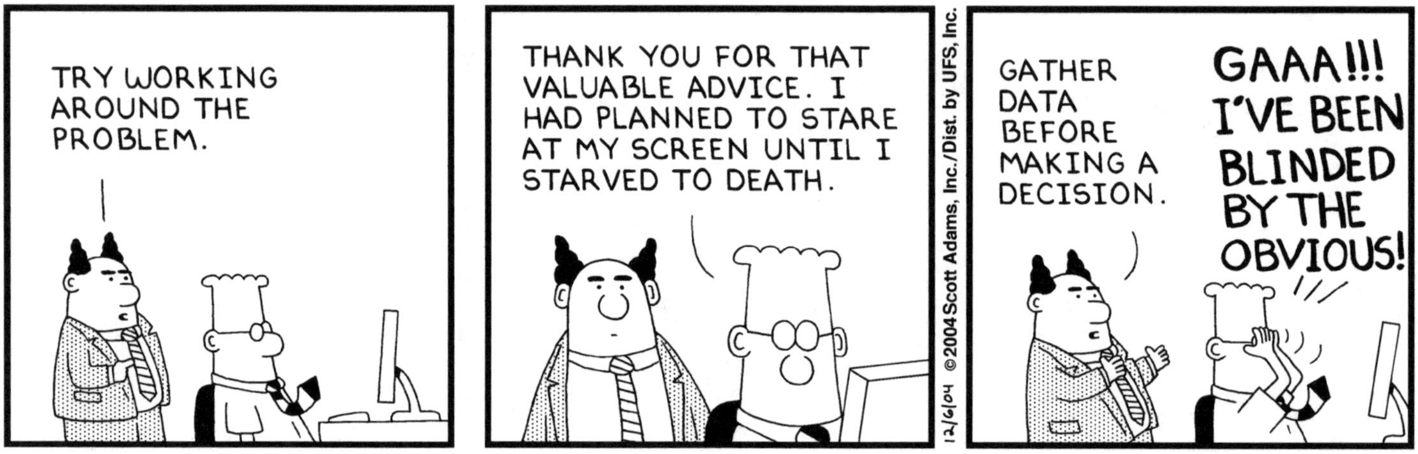
TRY WORKING AROUND THE PROBLEM.
THANK YOU FOR THAT VALUABLE ADVICE. I HAD PLANNED TO STARE AT MY SCREEN UNTIL I STARVED TO DEATH.
12/6/04 © 2004 Scott Adams, Inc./Dist. by UFS, Inc.
GATHER DATA BEFORE MAKING A DECISION.
GAAA!!! I'VE BEEN BLINDED BY THE OBVIOUS!

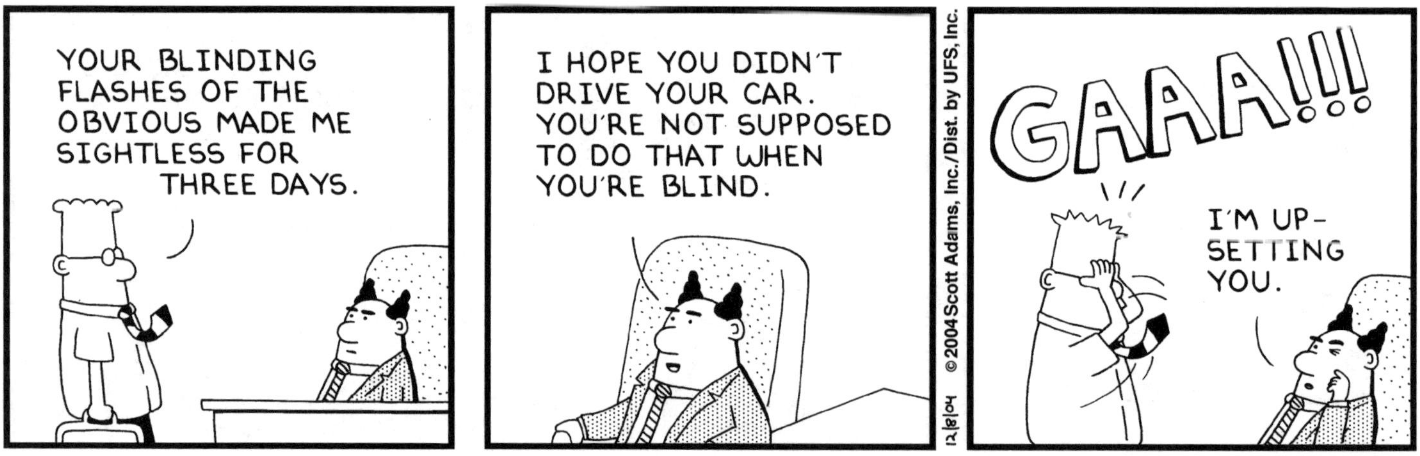
YOUR BLINDING FLASHES OF THE OBVIOUS MADE ME SIGHTLESS FOR THREE DAYS.
I HOPE YOU DIDN'T DRIVE YOUR CAR. YOU'RE NOT SUPPOSED TO DO THAT WHEN YOU'RE BLIND.
12/8/04 © 2004 Scott Adams, Inc./Dist. by UFS, Inc.
GAAA!!!
I'M UP-SETTING YOU.

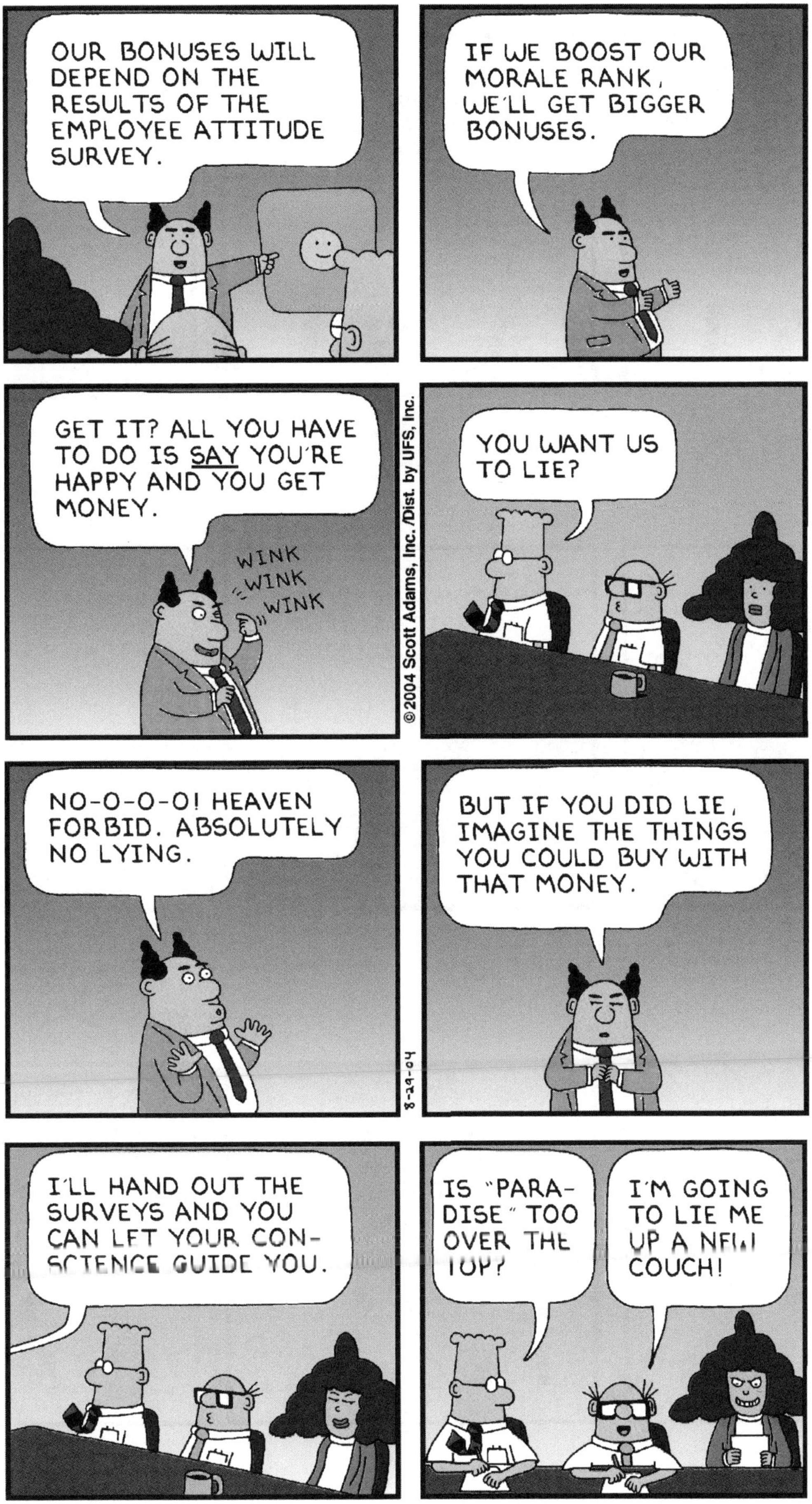
OUR BONUSES WILL DEPEND ON THE RESULTS OF THE EMPLOYEE ATTITUDE SURVEY.
IF WE BOOST OUR MORALE RANK, WE'LL GET BIGGER BONUSES.
GET IT? ALL YOU HAVE TO DO IS SAY YOU'RE HAPPY AND YOU GET MONEY.
WINK WINK WINK
©2004 Scott Adams, Inc./Dist. by UFS, Inc.
YOU WANT US TO LIE?
NO-O-O-O! HEAVEN FORBID. ABSOLUTELY NO LYING.
8-29-04
BUT IF YOU DID LIE, IMAGINE THE THINGS YOU COULD BUY WITH THAT MONEY.
I'LL HAND OUT THE SURVEYS AND YOU CAN LET YOUR CON- SCIENCE GUIDE YOU.
IS "PARA- DISE" TOO OVER THE TOP?
I'M GOING TO LIE ME UP A NEW COUCH!

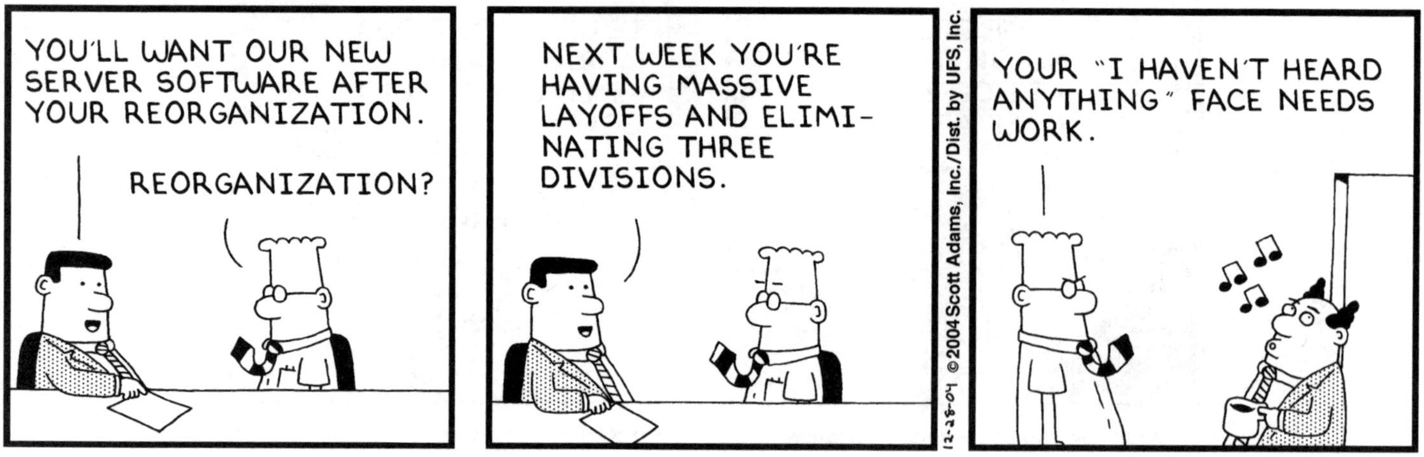
YOU'LL WANT OUR NEW SERVER SOFTWARE AFTER YOUR REORGANIZATION.
REORGANIZATION?
NEXT WEEK YOU'RE HAVING MASSIVE LAYOFFS AND ELIMI-NATING THREE DIVISIONS.
12-28-04 ©2004 Scott Adams, Inc./Dist. by UFS, Inc.
YOUR "I HAVEN'T HEARD ANYTHING" FACE NEEDS WORK.

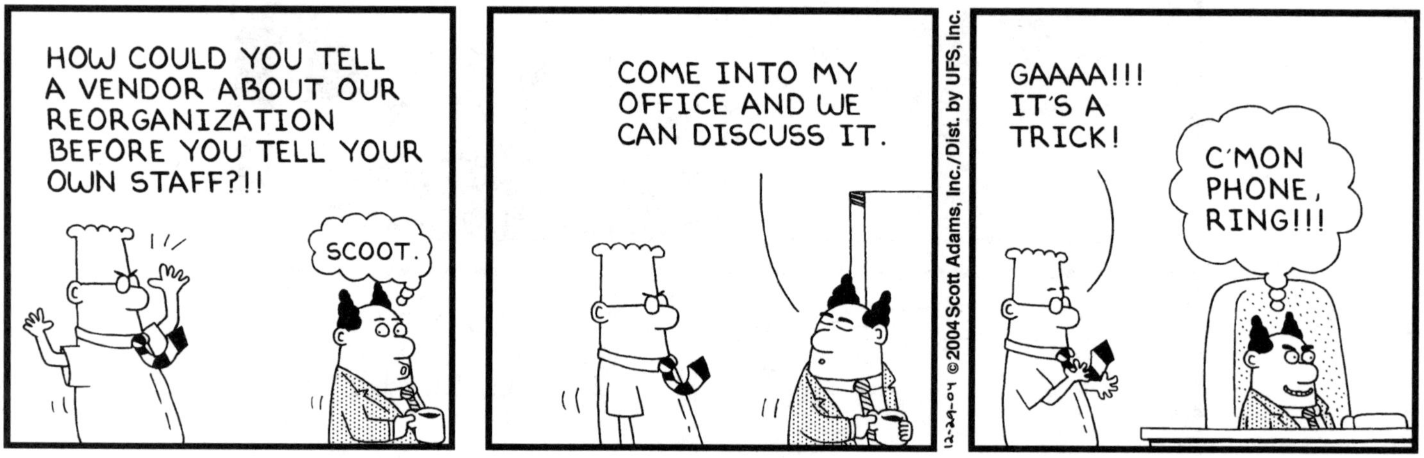
HOW COULD YOU TELL A VENDOR ABOUT OUR REORGANIZATION BEFORE YOU TELL YOUR OWN STAFF?!!
SCOOT.
COME INTO MY OFFICE AND WE CAN DISCUSS IT.
12-29-04 ©2004 Scott Adams, Inc./Dist. by UFS, Inc.
GAAAA!!! IT'S A TRICK!
C'MON PHONE, RING!!!

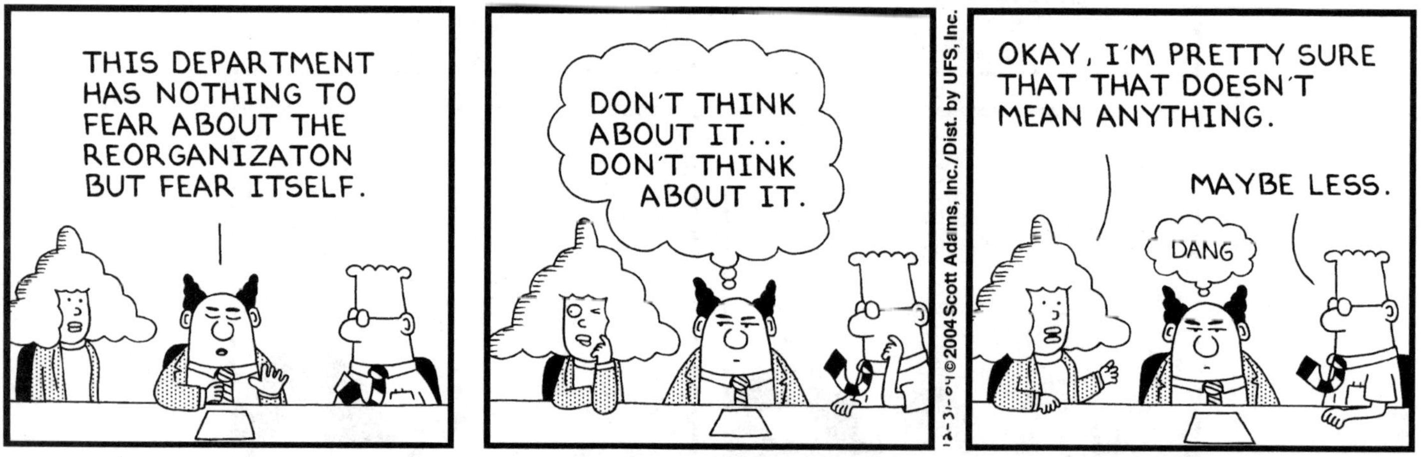
THIS DEPARTMENT HAS NOTHING TO FEAR ABOUT THE REORGANIZATON BUT FEAR ITSELF.
DON'T THINK ABOUT IT... DON'T THINK ABOUT IT.
12-31-04 ©2004 Scott Adams, Inc./Dist. by UFS, Inc.
OKAY, I'M PRETTY SURE THAT THAT DOESN'T MEAN ANYTHING.
MAYBE LESS.
DANG

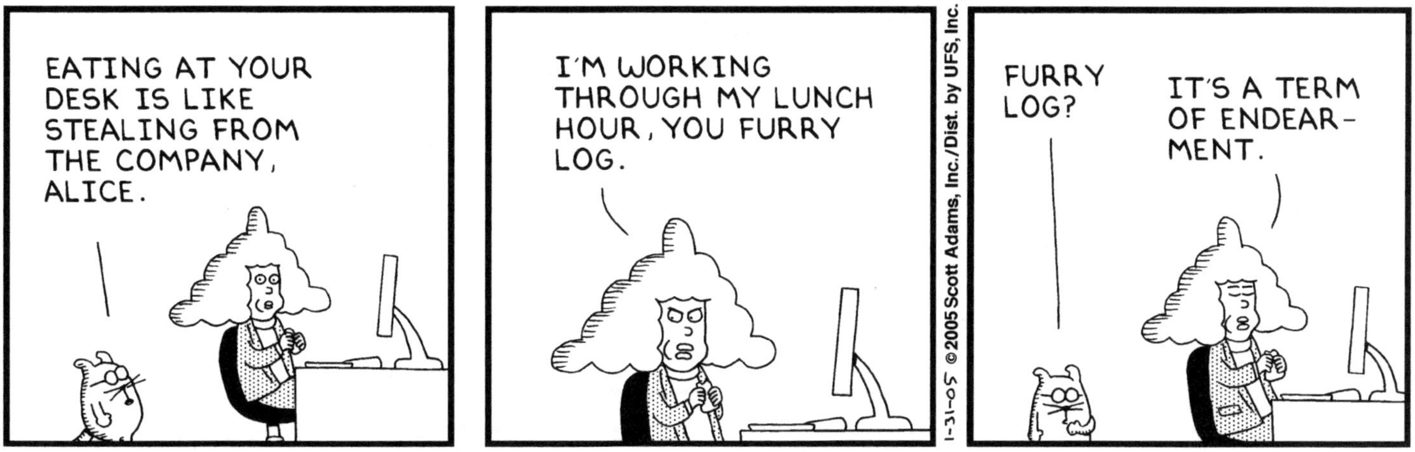
EATING AT YOUR DESK IS LIKE STEALING FROM THE COMPANY, ALICE.
I'M WORKING THROUGH MY LUNCH HOUR, YOU FURRY LOG.
1-31-05 © 2005 Scott Adams, Inc./Dist. by UFS, Inc.
FURRY LOG?
IT'S A TERM OF ENDEARMENT.

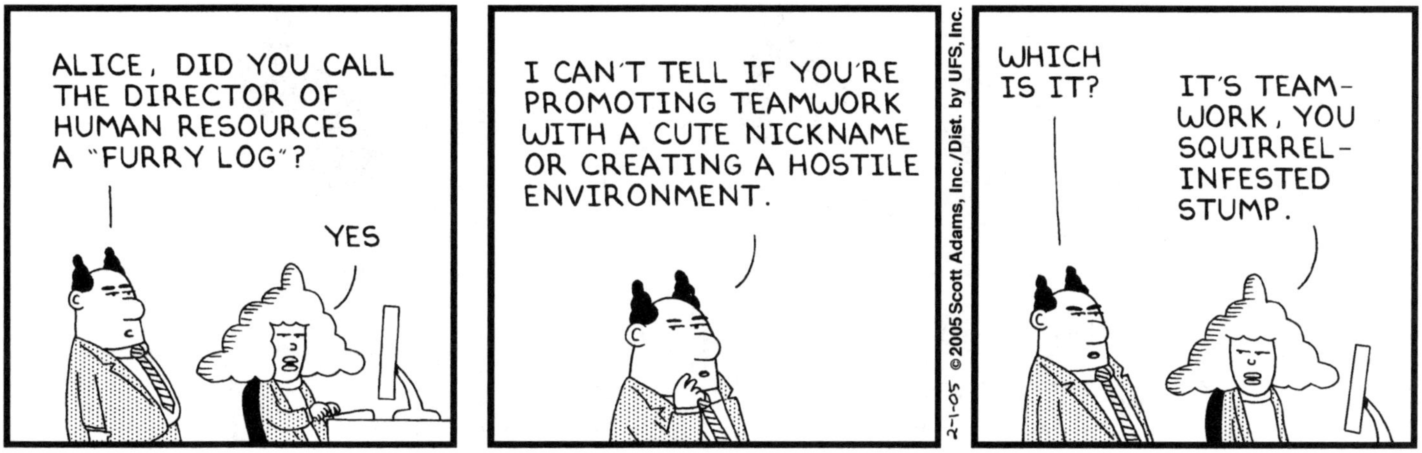
ALICE, DID YOU CALL THE DIRECTOR OF HUMAN RESOURCES A "FURRY LOG"?
YES
I CAN'T TELL IF YOU'RE PROMOTING TEAMWORK WITH A CUTE NICKNAME OR CREATING A HOSTILE ENVIRONMENT.
2-1-05 © 2005 Scott Adams, Inc./Dist. by UFS, Inc.
WHICH IS IT?
IT'S TEAMWORK, YOU SQUIRREL-INFESTED STUMP.

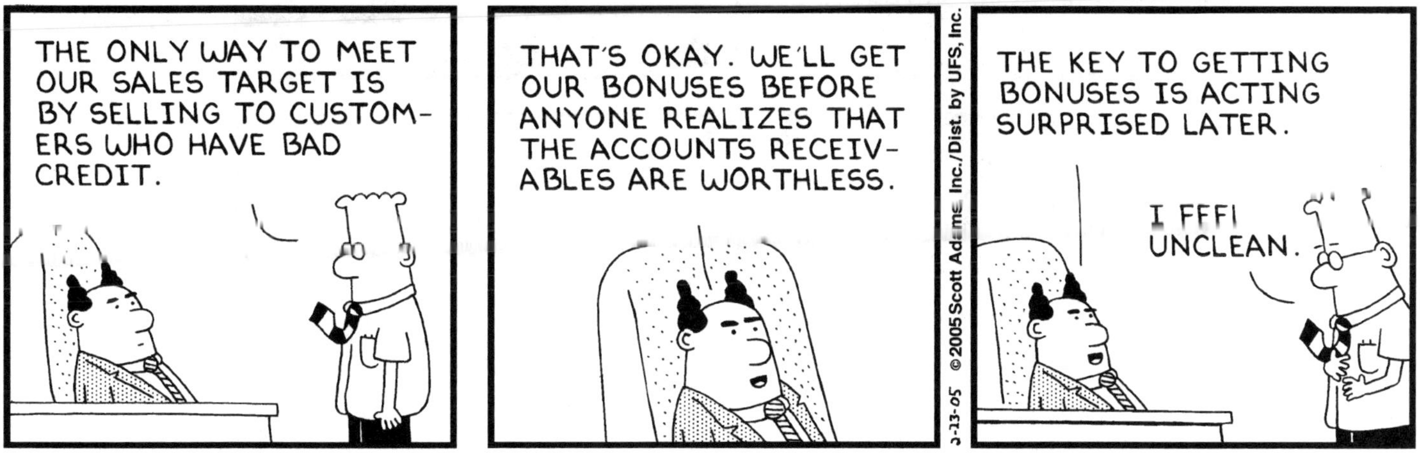
THE ONLY WAY TO MEET OUR SALES TARGET IS BY SELLING TO CUSTOMERS WHO HAVE BAD CREDIT.
THAT'S OKAY. WE'LL GET OUR BONUSES BEFORE ANYONE REALIZES THAT THE ACCOUNTS RECEIVABLES ARE WORTHLESS.
© 2005 Scott Adams Inc./Dist. by UFS, Inc.
THE KEY TO GETTING BONUSES IS ACTING SURPRISED LATER.
I FEEL UNCLEAN.

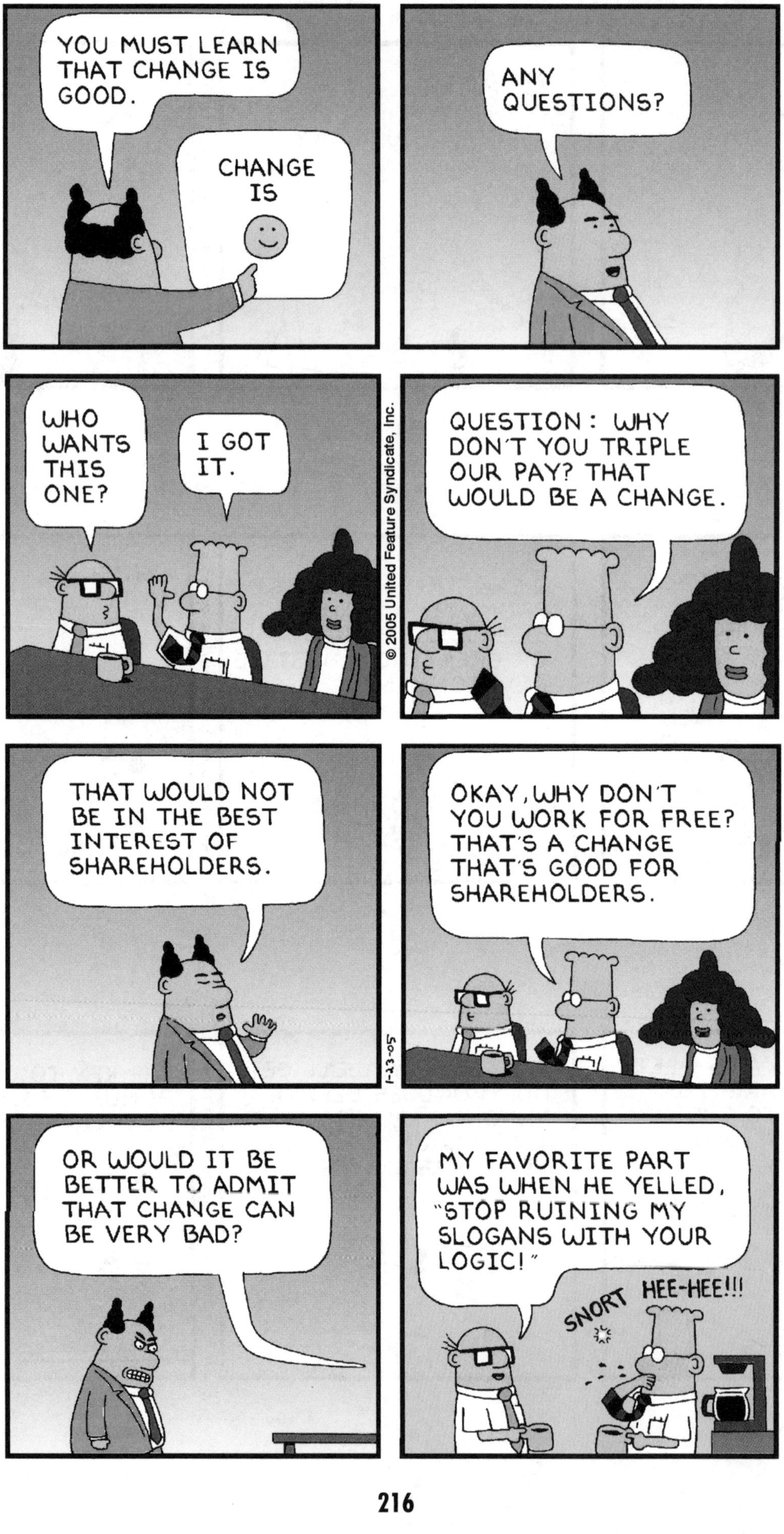
YOU MUST LEARN THAT CHANGE IS GOOD.
CHANGE IS
ANY QUESTIONS?
WHO WANTS THIS ONE?
I GOT IT.
© 2005 United Feature Syndicate, Inc.
QUESTION: WHY DON'T YOU TRIPLE OUR PAY? THAT WOULD BE A CHANGE.
THAT WOULD NOT BE IN THE BEST INTEREST OF SHAREHOLDERS.
1-23-05
OKAY, WHY DON'T YOU WORK FOR FREE? THAT'S A CHANGE THAT'S GOOD FOR SHAREHOLDERS.
OR WOULD IT BE BETTER TO ADMIT THAT CHANGE CAN BE VERY BAD?
MY FAVORITE PART WAS WHEN HE YELLED, "STOP RUINING MY SLOGANS WITH YOUR LOGIC!"
SNORT
HEE-HEE!!!

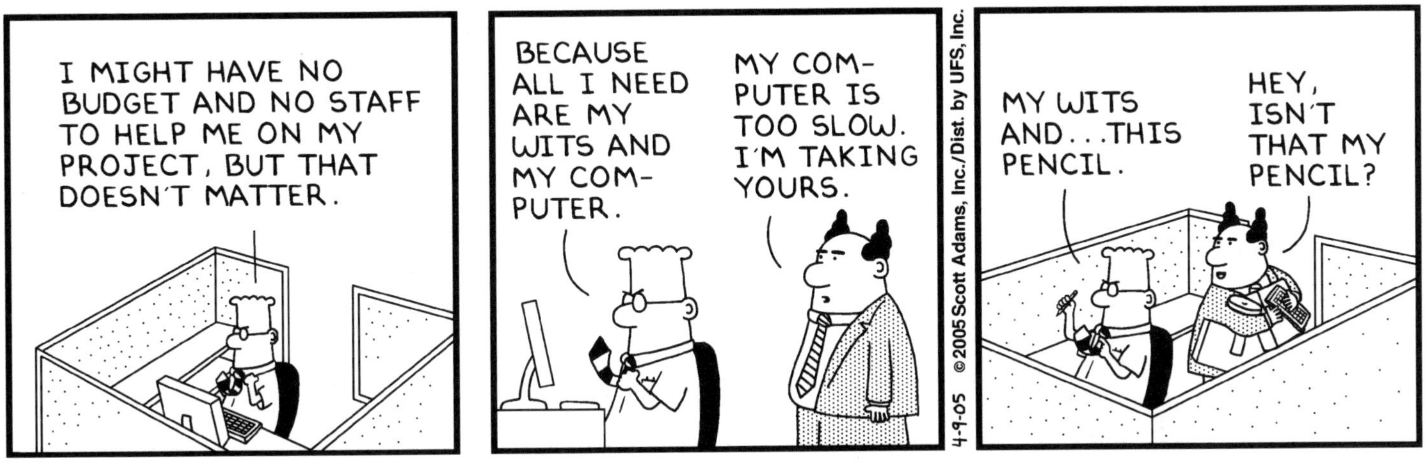
I MIGHT HAVE NO BUDGET AND NO STAFF TO HELP ME ON MY PROJECT, BUT THAT DOESN'T MATTER.
BECAUSE ALL I NEED ARE MY WITS AND MY COMPUTER.
MY COMPUTER IS TOO SLOW. I'M TAKING YOURS.
4-9-05 © 2005 Scott Adams, Inc./Dist. by UFS, Inc.
MY WITS AND...THIS PENCIL.
HEY, ISN'T THAT MY PENCIL?

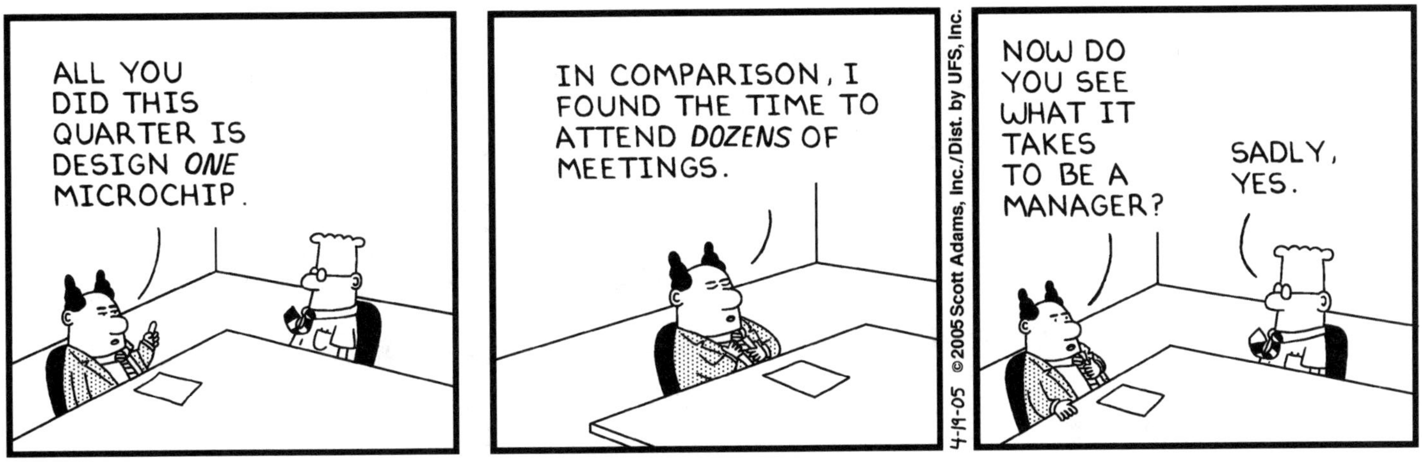
ALL YOU DID THIS QUARTER IS DESIGN *ONE* MICROCHIP.
IN COMPARISON, I FOUND THE TIME TO ATTEND *DOZENS* OF MEETINGS.
4-19-05 © 2005 Scott Adams, Inc./Dist. by UFS, Inc.
NOW DO YOU SEE WHAT IT TAKES TO BE A MANAGER?
SADLY, YES.

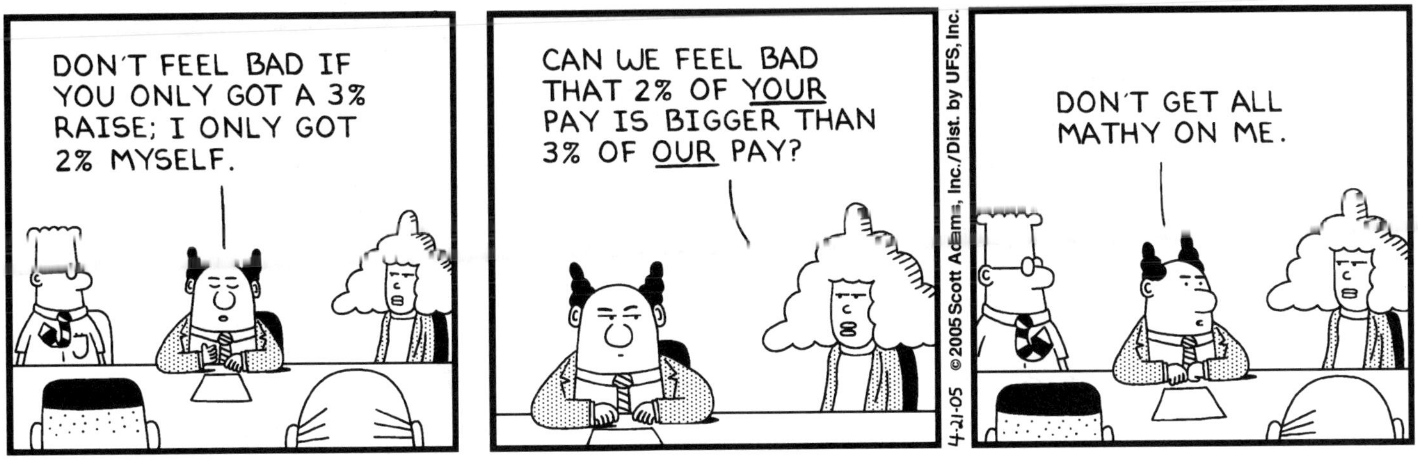
DON'T FEEL BAD IF YOU ONLY GOT A 3% RAISE; I ONLY GOT 2% MYSELF.
CAN WE FEEL BAD THAT 2% OF YOUR PAY IS BIGGER THAN 3% OF OUR PAY?
4-21-05 © 2005 Scott Adams, Inc./Dist. by UFS, Inc.
DON'T GET ALL MATHY ON ME.

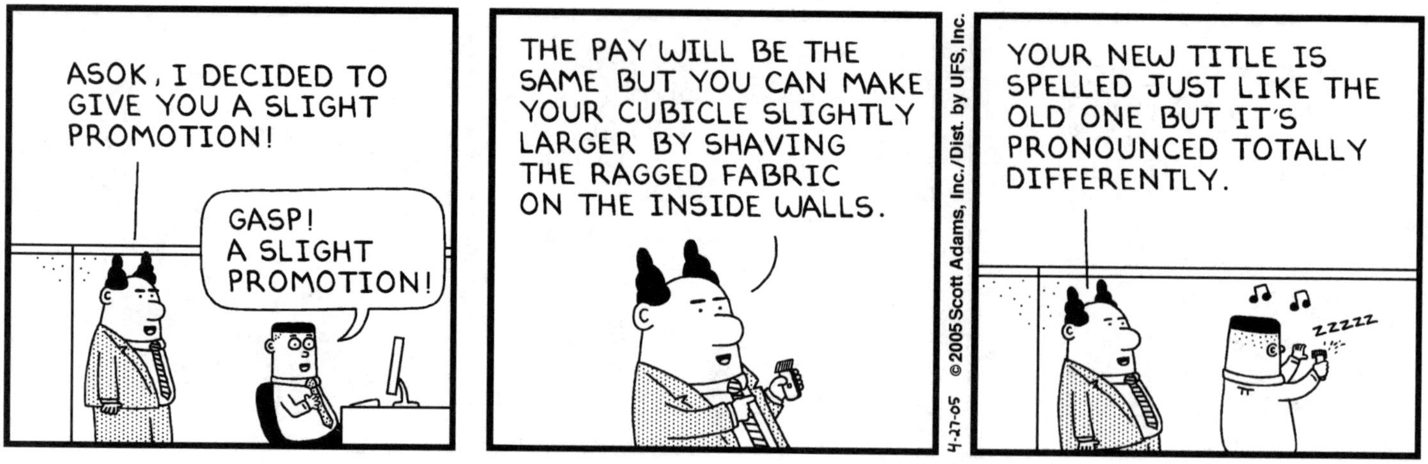
ASOK, I DECIDED TO GIVE YOU A SLIGHT PROMOTION!
GASP! A SLIGHT PROMOTION!
THE PAY WILL BE THE SAME BUT YOU CAN MAKE YOUR CUBICLE SLIGHTLY LARGER BY SHAVING THE RAGGED FABRIC ON THE INSIDE WALLS.
YOUR NEW TITLE IS SPELLED JUST LIKE THE OLD ONE BUT IT'S PRONOUNCED TOTALLY DIFFERENTLY.
ZZZZZ
4-27-05 © 2005 Scott Adams, Inc./Dist. by UFS, Inc.

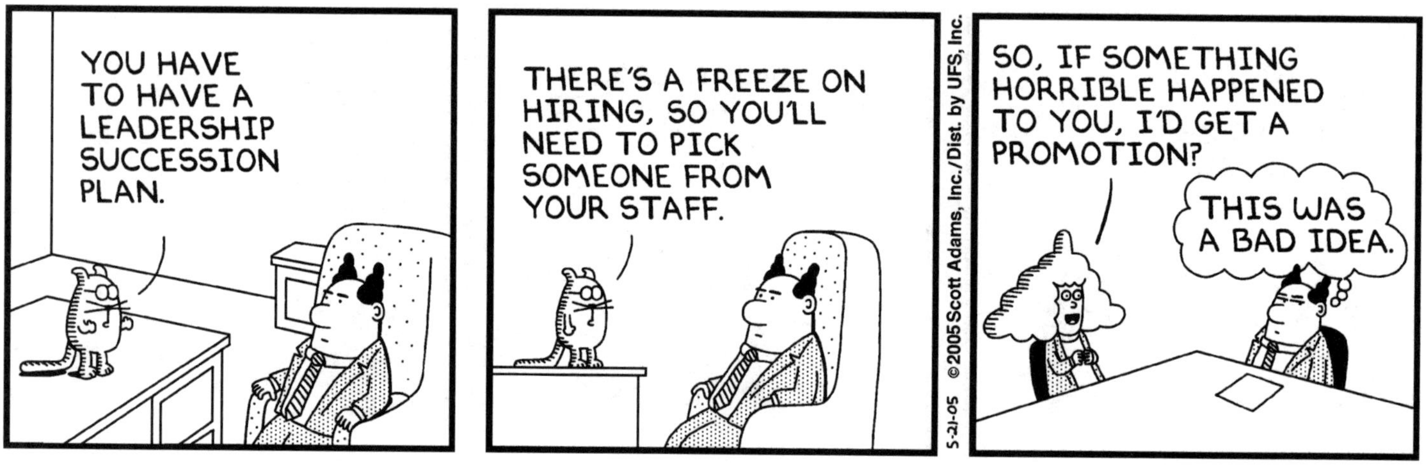
YOU HAVE TO HAVE A LEADERSHIP SUCCESSION PLAN.
THERE'S A FREEZE ON HIRING, SO YOU'LL NEED TO PICK SOMEONE FROM YOUR STAFF.
SO, IF SOMETHING HORRIBLE HAPPENED TO YOU, I'D GET A PROMOTION?
THIS WAS A BAD IDEA.
5-21-05 © 2005 Scott Adams, Inc./Dist. by UFS, Inc.

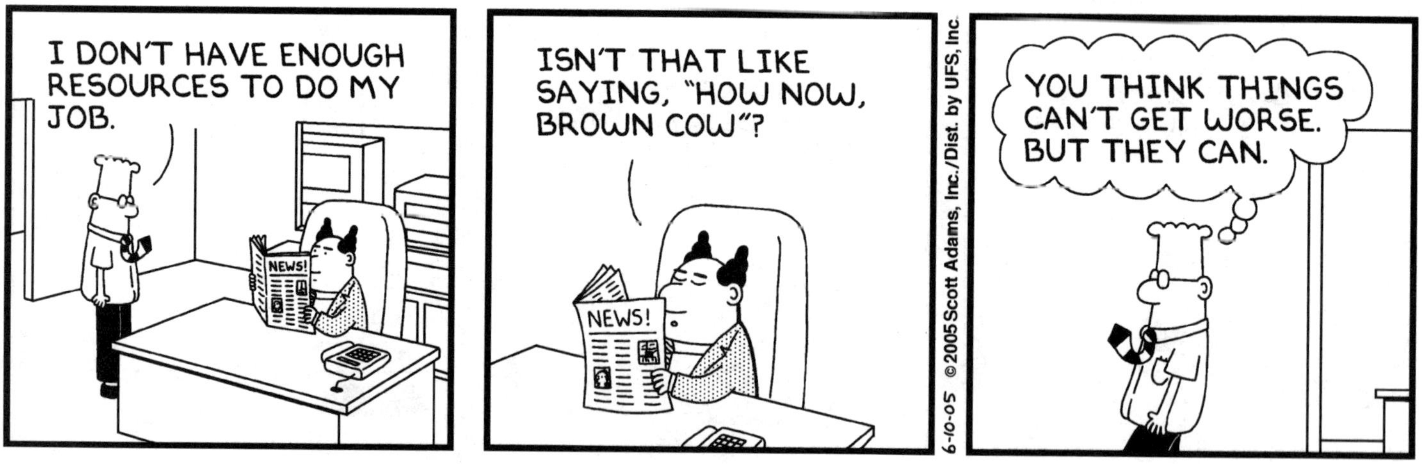
I DON'T HAVE ENOUGH RESOURCES TO DO MY JOB.
NEWS!
ISN'T THAT LIKE SAYING, "HOW NOW, BROWN COW"?
NEWS!
YOU THINK THINGS CAN'T GET WORSE. BUT THEY CAN.
6-10-05 © 2005 Scott Adams, Inc./Dist. by UFS, Inc.

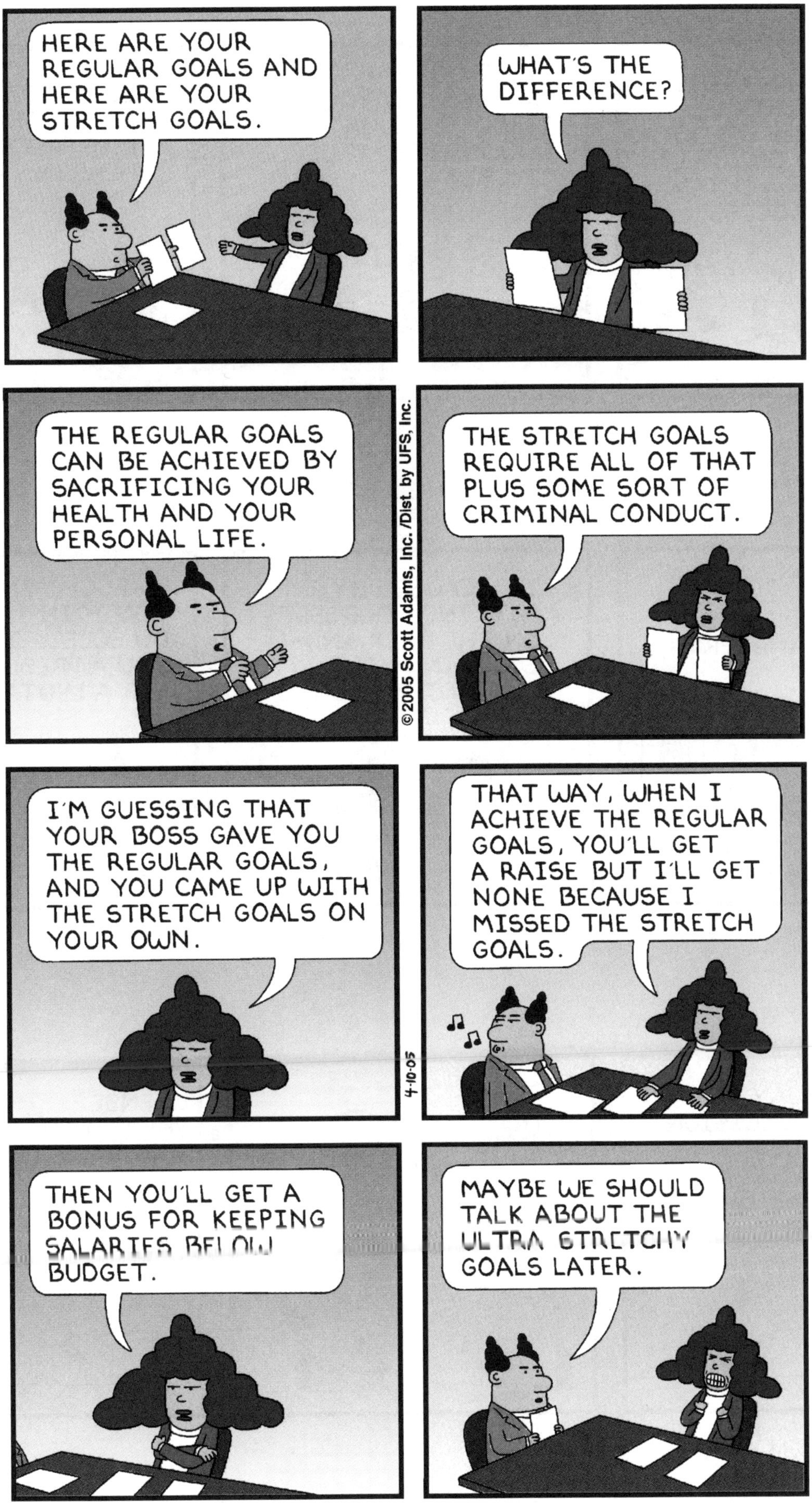
HERE ARE YOUR REGULAR GOALS AND HERE ARE YOUR STRETCH GOALS.
WHAT'S THE DIFFERENCE?
THE REGULAR GOALS CAN BE ACHIEVED BY SACRIFICING YOUR HEALTH AND YOUR PERSONAL LIFE.
©2005 Scott Adams, Inc./Dist. by UFS, Inc.
THE STRETCH GOALS REQUIRE ALL OF THAT PLUS SOME SORT OF CRIMINAL CONDUCT.
I'M GUESSING THAT YOUR BOSS GAVE YOU THE REGULAR GOALS, AND YOU CAME UP WITH THE STRETCH GOALS ON YOUR OWN.
4-10-05
THAT WAY, WHEN I ACHIEVE THE REGULAR GOALS, YOU'LL GET A RAISE BUT I'LL GET NONE BECAUSE I MISSED THE STRETCH GOALS.
THEN YOU'LL GET A BONUS FOR KEEPING SALARIES BELOW BUDGET.
MAYBE WE SHOULD TALK ABOUT THE ULTRA STRETCHY GOALS LATER.

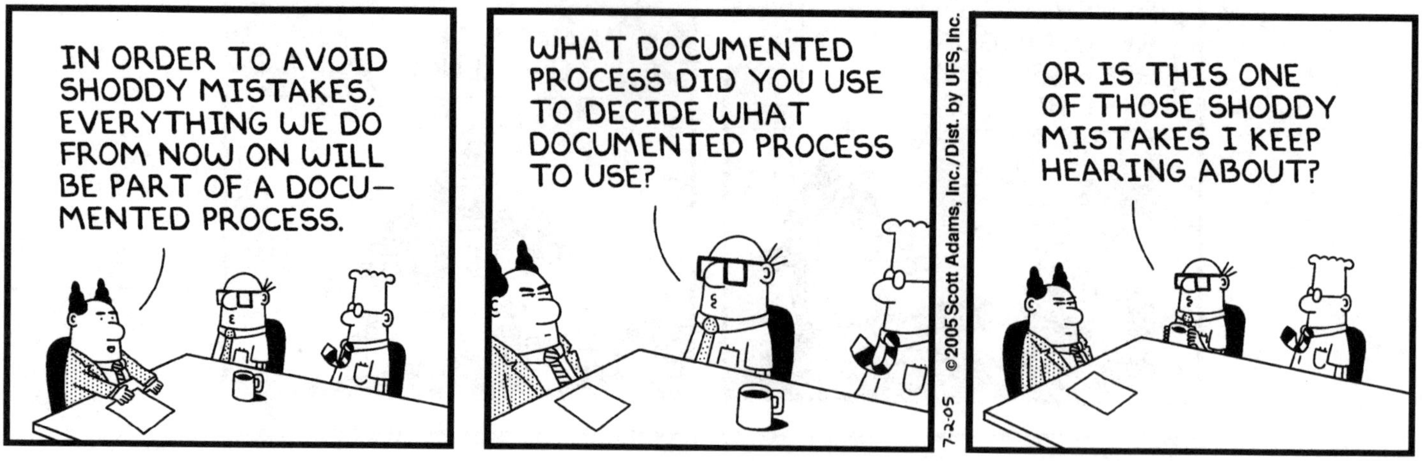
IN ORDER TO AVOID SHODDY MISTAKES, EVERYTHING WE DO FROM NOW ON WILL BE PART OF A DOCU– MENTED PROCESS.
WHAT DOCUMENTED PROCESS DID YOU USE TO DECIDE WHAT DOCUMENTED PROCESS TO USE?
7-2-05 © 2005 Scott Adams, Inc./Dist. by UFS, Inc.
OR IS THIS ONE OF THOSE SHODDY MISTAKES I KEEP HEARING ABOUT?

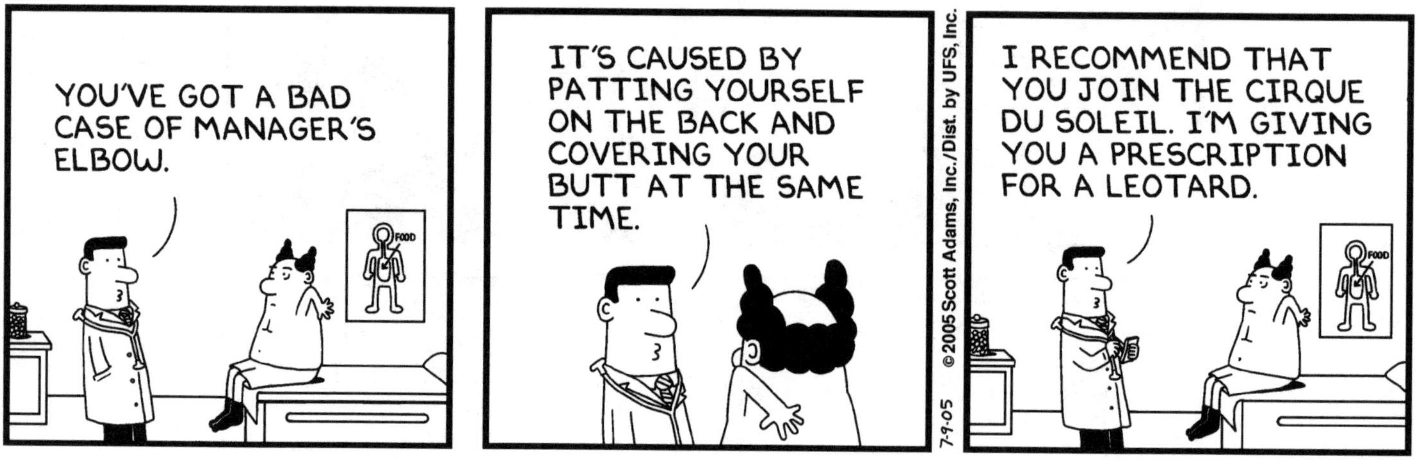
YOU'VE GOT A BAD CASE OF MANAGER'S ELBOW.
FOOD
IT'S CAUSED BY PATTING YOURSELF ON THE BACK AND COVERING YOUR BUTT AT THE SAME TIME.
7-9-05 © 2005 Scott Adams, Inc./Dist. by UFS, Inc.
I RECOMMEND THAT YOU JOIN THE CIRQUE DU SOLEIL. I'M GIVING YOU A PRESCRIPTION FOR A LEOTARD.
FOOD

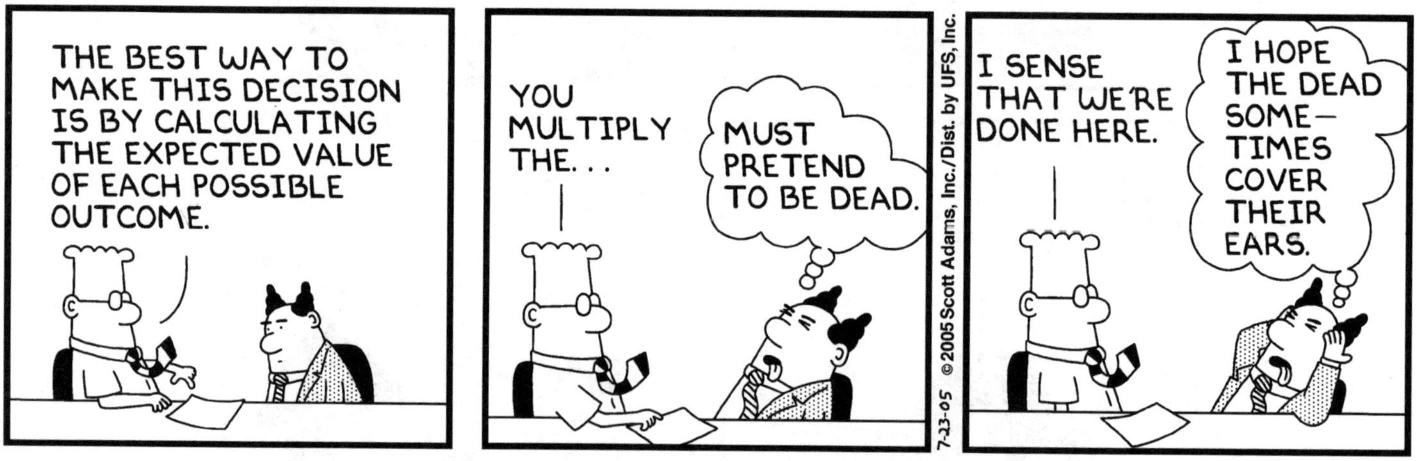
THE BEST WAY TO MAKE THIS DECISION IS BY CALCULATING THE EXPECTED VALUE OF EACH POSSIBLE OUTCOME.
YOU MULTIPLY THE. . .
MUST PRETEND TO BE DEAD.
7-23-05 © 2005 Scott Adams, Inc./Dist. by UFS, Inc.
I SENSE THAT WE'RE DONE HERE.
I HOPE THE DEAD SOME– TIMES COVER THEIR EARS.

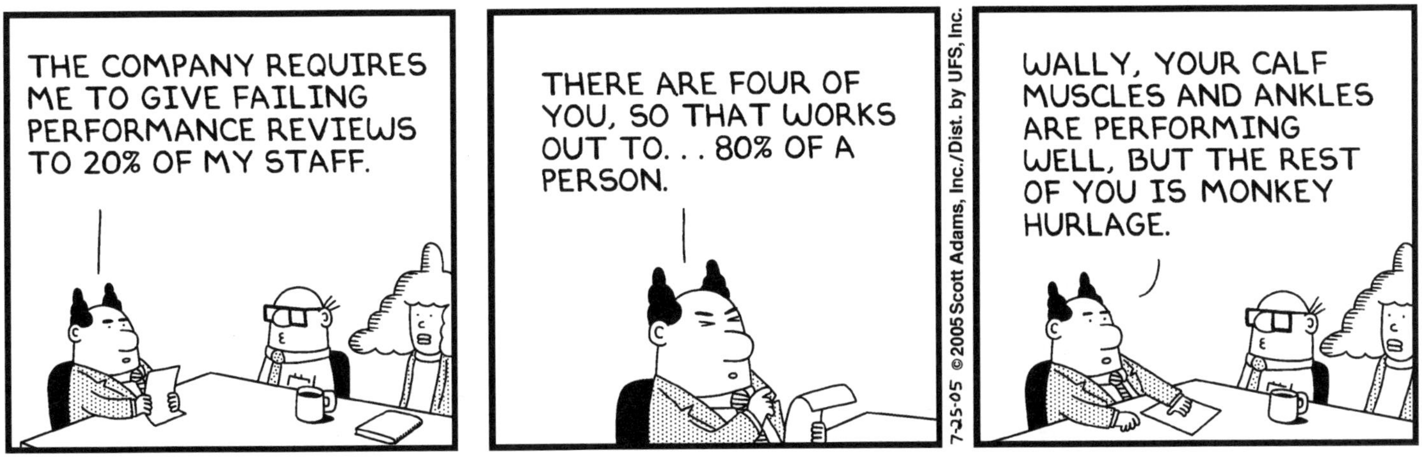
THE COMPANY REQUIRES ME TO GIVE FAILING PERFORMANCE REVIEWS TO 20% OF MY STAFF.
THERE ARE FOUR OF YOU, SO THAT WORKS OUT TO. . . 80% OF A PERSON.
7-25-05 © 2005 Scott Adams, Inc./Dist. by UFS, Inc.
WALLY, YOUR CALF MUSCLES AND ANKLES ARE PERFORMING WELL, BUT THE REST OF YOU IS MONKEY HURLAGE.

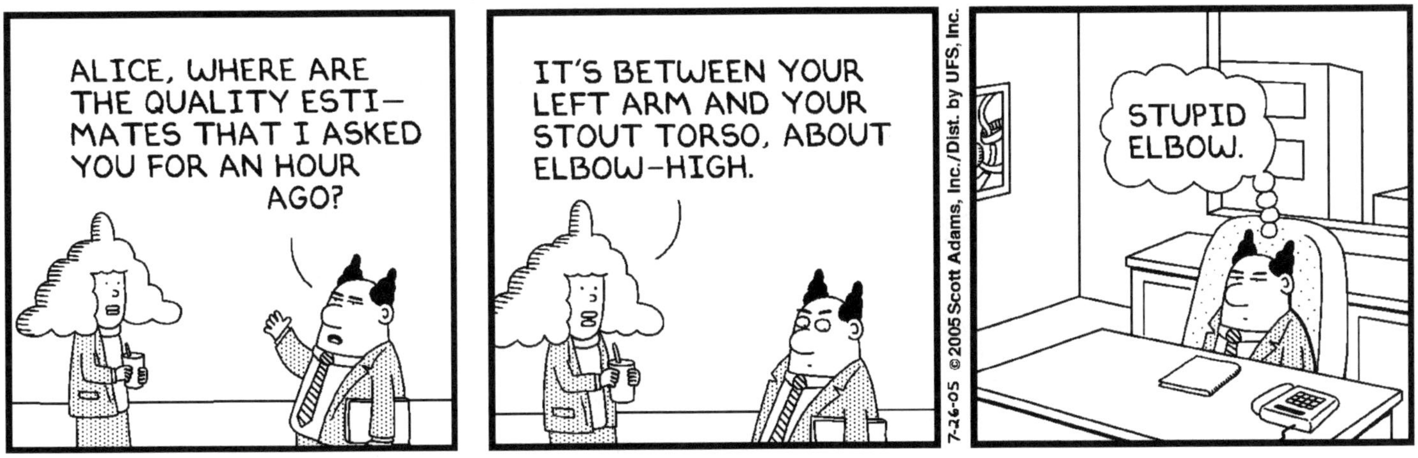
ALICE, WHERE ARE THE QUALITY ESTI-MATES THAT I ASKED YOU FOR AN HOUR AGO?
IT'S BETWEEN YOUR LEFT ARM AND YOUR STOUT TORSO, ABOUT ELBOW-HIGH.
7-26-05 © 2005 Scott Adams, Inc./Dist. by UFS, Inc.
STUPID ELBOW.

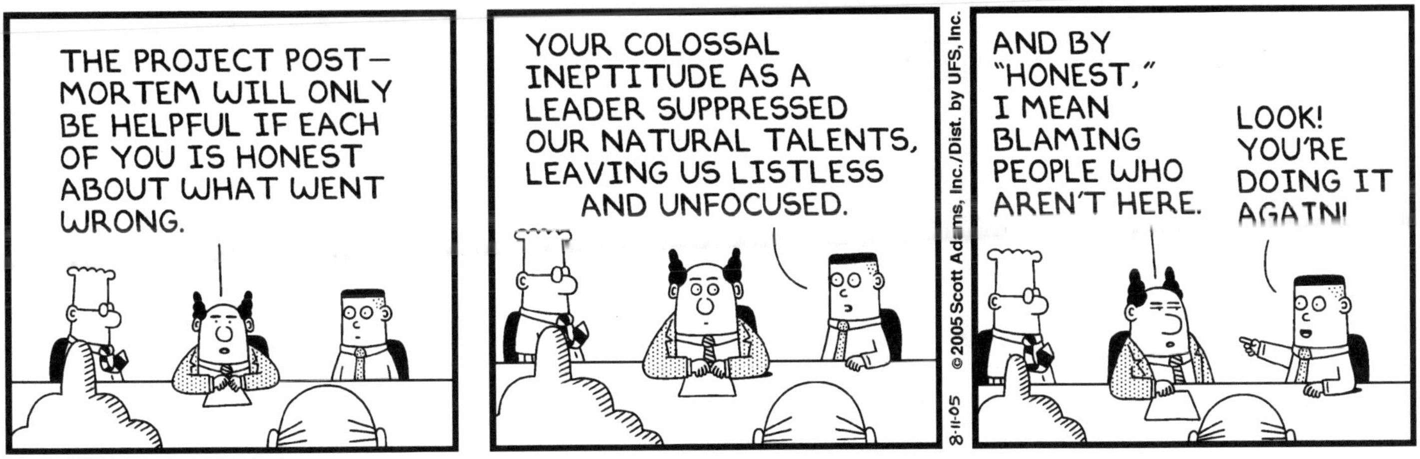
THE PROJECT POST-MORTEM WILL ONLY BE HELPFUL IF EACH OF YOU IS HONEST ABOUT WHAT WENT WRONG.
YOUR COLOSSAL INEPTITUDE AS A LEADER SUPPRESSED OUR NATURAL TALENTS, LEAVING US LISTLESS AND UNFOCUSED.
8-11-05 © 2005 Scott Adams, Inc./Dist. by UFS, Inc.
AND BY "HONEST," I MEAN BLAMING PEOPLE WHO AREN'T HERE.
LOOK! YOU'RE DOING IT AGAIN!

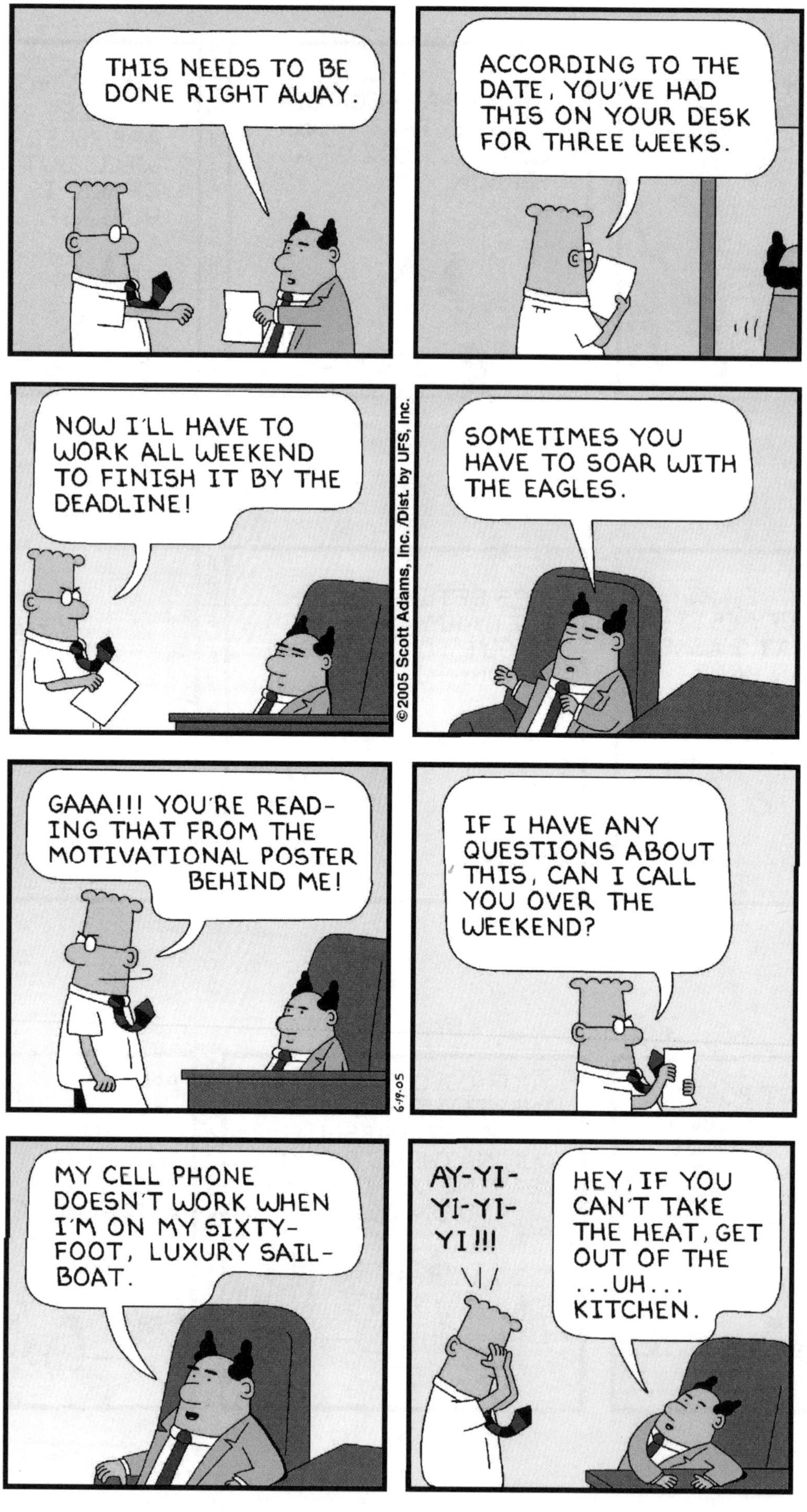

THIS NEEDS TO BE DONE RIGHT AWAY.
ACCORDING TO THE DATE, YOU'VE HAD THIS ON YOUR DESK FOR THREE WEEKS.
NOW I'LL HAVE TO WORK ALL WEEKEND TO FINISH IT BY THE DEADLINE!
SOMETIMES YOU HAVE TO SOAR WITH THE EAGLES.
©2005 Scott Adams, Inc. /Dist. by UFS, Inc.
GAAA!!! YOU'RE READ-ING THAT FROM THE MOTIVATIONAL POSTER BEHIND ME!
6-19-05
IF I HAVE ANY QUESTIONS ABOUT THIS, CAN I CALL YOU OVER THE WEEKEND?
MY CELL PHONE DOESN'T WORK WHEN I'M ON MY SIXTY-FOOT, LUXURY SAIL-BOAT.
AY-YI-YI-YI-YI!!!
HEY, IF YOU CAN'T TAKE THE HEAT, GET OUT OF THE ...UH... KITCHEN.

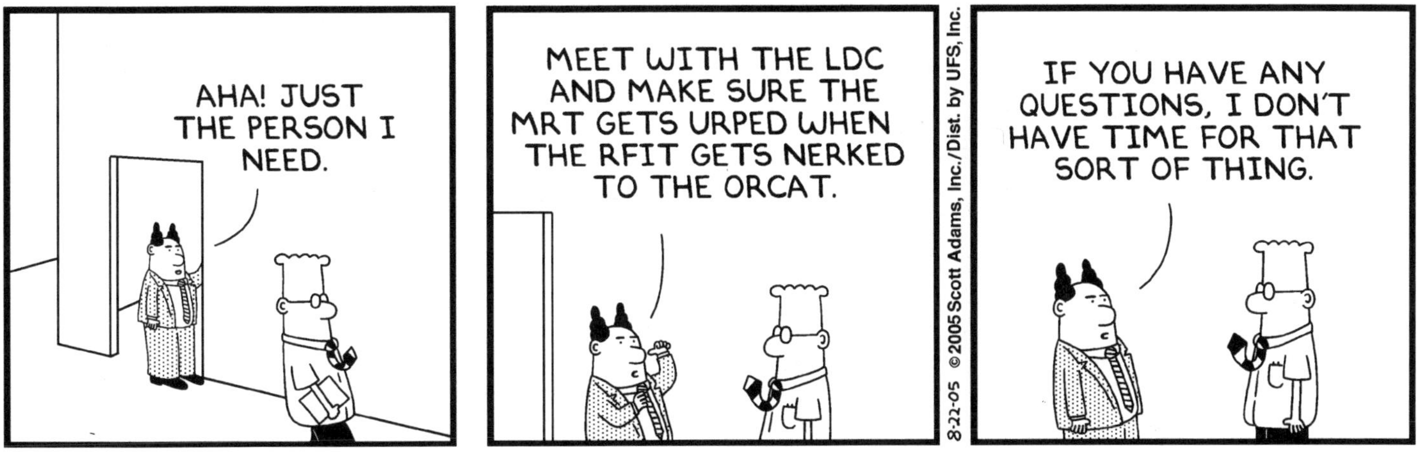
AHA! JUST THE PERSON I NEED.
MEET WITH THE LDC AND MAKE SURE THE MRT GETS URPED WHEN THE RFIT GETS NERKED TO THE ORCAT.
8-22-05 © 2005 Scott Adams, Inc./Dist. by UFS, Inc.
IF YOU HAVE ANY QUESTIONS, I DON'T HAVE TIME FOR THAT SORT OF THING.

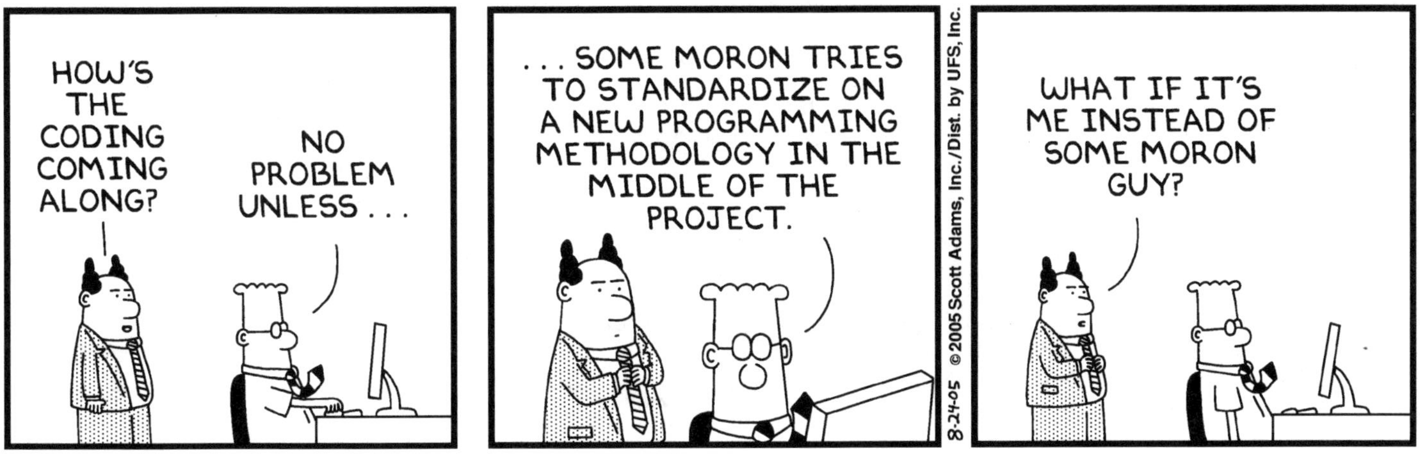
HOW'S THE CODING COMING ALONG?
NO PROBLEM UNLESS . . .
. . . SOME MORON TRIES TO STANDARDIZE ON A NEW PROGRAMMING METHODOLOGY IN THE MIDDLE OF THE PROJECT.
8-24-05 © 2005 Scott Adams, Inc./Dist. by UFS, Inc.
WHAT IF IT'S ME INSTEAD OF SOME MORON GUY?

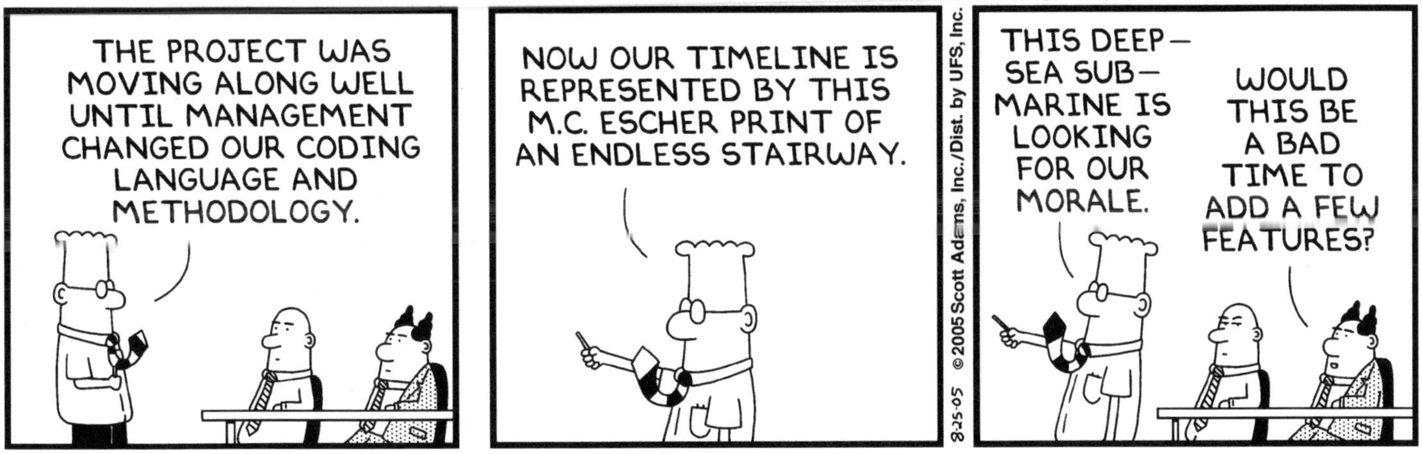
THE PROJECT WAS MOVING ALONG WELL UNTIL MANAGEMENT CHANGED OUR CODING LANGUAGE AND METHODOLOGY.
NOW OUR TIMELINE IS REPRESENTED BY THIS M.C. ESCHER PRINT OF AN ENDLESS STAIRWAY.
8-25-05 © 2005 Scott Adams, Inc./Dist. by UFS, Inc.
THIS DEEP-SEA SUB-MARINE IS LOOKING FOR OUR MORALE.
WOULD THIS BE A BAD TIME TO ADD A FEW FEATURES?

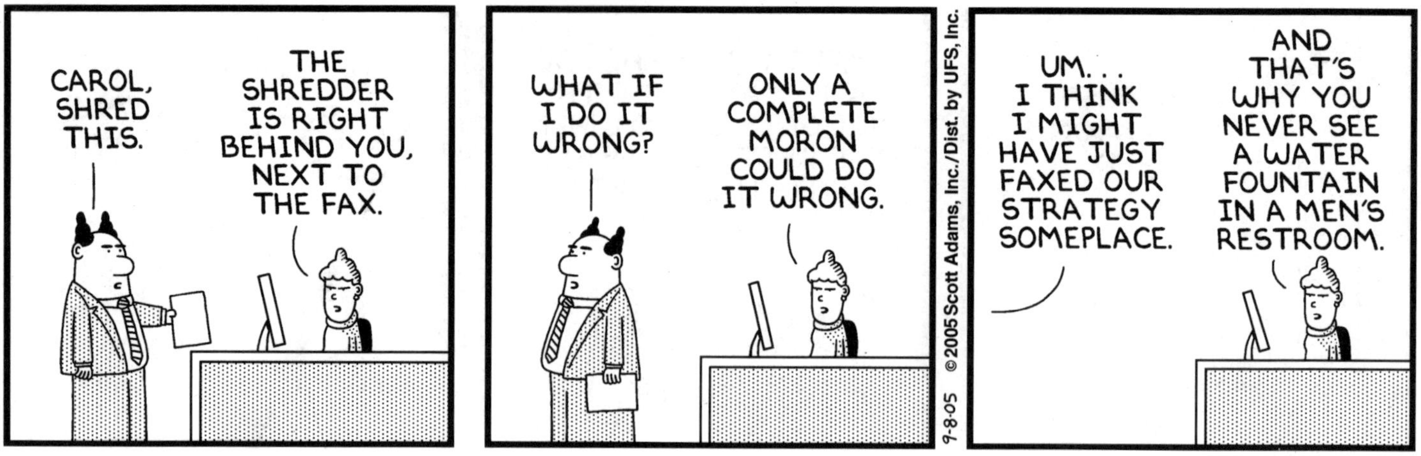
CAROL, SHRED THIS.
THE SHREDDER IS RIGHT BEHIND YOU, NEXT TO THE FAX.
WHAT IF I DO IT WRONG?
ONLY A COMPLETE MORON COULD DO IT WRONG.
9-8-05 © 2005 Scott Adams, Inc./Dist. by UFS, Inc.
UM. . . I THINK I MIGHT HAVE JUST FAXED OUR STRATEGY SOMEPLACE.
AND THAT'S WHY YOU NEVER SEE A WATER FOUNTAIN IN A MEN'S RESTROOM.

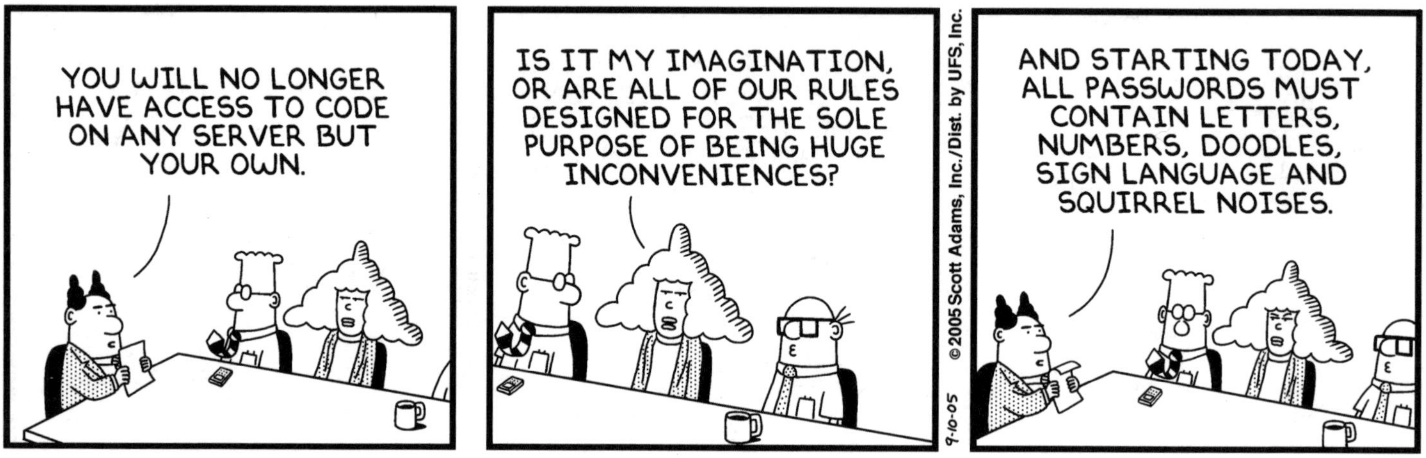
YOU WILL NO LONGER HAVE ACCESS TO CODE ON ANY SERVER BUT YOUR OWN.
IS IT MY IMAGINATION, OR ARE ALL OF OUR RULES DESIGNED FOR THE SOLE PURPOSE OF BEING HUGE INCONVENIENCES?
9-10-05 © 2005 Scott Adams, Inc./Dist. by UFS, Inc.
AND STARTING TODAY, ALL PASSWORDS MUST CONTAIN LETTERS, NUMBERS, DOODLES, SIGN LANGUAGE AND SQUIRREL NOISES.

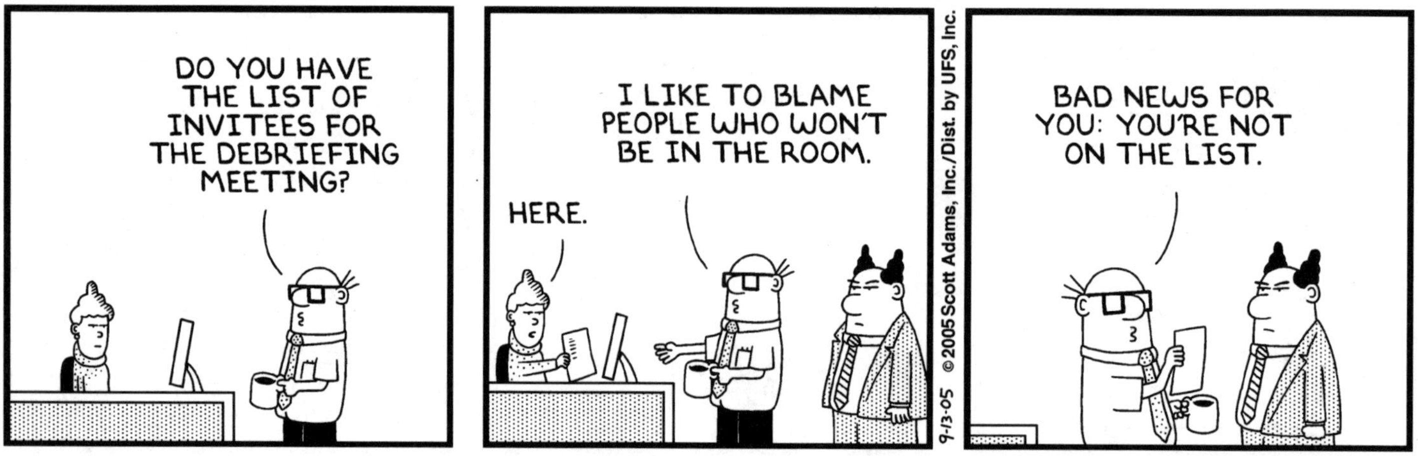
DO YOU HAVE THE LIST OF INVITEES FOR THE DEBRIEFING MEETING?
HERE.
I LIKE TO BLAME PEOPLE WHO WON'T BE IN THE ROOM.
9-13-05 © 2005 Scott Adams, Inc./Dist. by UFS, Inc.
BAD NEWS FOR YOU: YOU'RE NOT ON THE LIST.